Lecture Notes in Artificial Intelligence   12848

Subseries of Lecture Notes in Computer Science

More information about this subseries at http://www.springer.com/series/1244

Kamil Ekštein · František Pártl ·
Miloslav Konopík (Eds.)

Text, Speech, and Dialogue

24th International Conference, TSD 2021
Olomouc, Czech Republic, September 6–9, 2021
Proceedings

 Springer

Editors
Kamil Ekštein
University of West Bohemia
Pilsen, Czech Republic

František Pártl
University of West Bohemia
Pilsen, Czech Republic

Miloslav Konopík
University of West Bohemia
Pilsen, Czech Republic

ISSN 0302-9743   ISSN 1611-3349   (electronic)
Lecture Notes in Artificial Intelligence
ISBN 978-3-030-83526-2   ISBN 978-3-030-83527-9   (eBook)
https://doi.org/10.1007/978-3-030-83527-9

LNCS Sublibrary: SL7 – Artificial Intelligence

This Springer imprint is published by the registered company Springer Nature Switzerland AG
The registered company address is: Gewerbestrasse 11, 6330 Cham, Switzerland

Preface

The annual International Conference on Text, Speech and Dialogue (TSD), which emerged in 1998, constitutes a recognized platform for presenting and discussing state-of-the-art technology and recent achievements in computer processing of natural language. It has become a broad interdisciplinary forum, interweaving the topics of speech technology and language processing. The conference attracts researchers not only from Central and Eastern Europe but also from other parts of the world. Indeed, one of its goals has always been bringing together NLP researchers with various interests from different parts of the world and promoting their mutual cooperation. One of the ambitions of the conference is, as its name suggests, not only to deal with dialogue systems but also to improve dialogue among researchers in areas of NLP, i.e., among the "text" and the "speech" and the "dialogue" people.

TSD 2021 (like the previous conference) was unfortunately substantially affected – even though the organizers did their best to reduce the unwanted impacts – by the COVID-19 pandemic. Luckily, in the late summer of 2021, the pandemic was getting under control and life was returning slowly to normal. However, organizing a conference with an expected turnout of some hundred participants was not an easy task when little was known about how the pandemic and the issued counter-pandemic and prevention measures would evolve. Therefore, the conference was prepared in the so-called "hybrid" mode: some participants actually arrived and took part at the venue while some took part remotely, using the video-conferencing software. Needless to say, such a modus operandi required more advanced organization procedures, planning, strategic decision-making, and logistics than usual.

We chose the beautiful ancient Moravian city of Olomouc as the TSD 2021 venue. It is a charming and peaceful historical place – once also the capital of Moravia – with the seat of the Roman Catholic Archdiocese of Olomouc and the second-oldest university in the Czech Republic (after the Charles University in Prague) established in 1573.

Therefore, the TSD 2021 conference took place on the campus of the co-organizing institution, the Faculty of Arts of Palacký University, Olomouc, during September 6–9, 2021. The conference schedule and the keynote topics were again co-ordinated with the Interspeech conference, and TSD 2021 was listed as an Interspeech 2021 satellite event. Like its predecessors, TSD 2021 highlighted the importance of language and speech processing to both the academic and scientific world including the most recent breakthroughs in current applications. Both experienced researchers and professionals, and newcomers in the field, found in the TSD conference a forum to communicate with people sharing similar interests.

This volume contains a collection of submitted papers presented at the conference. Each of them was thoroughly reviewed by three members of the conference reviewing team consisting of more than 60 top specialists in the conference topic areas. A total of 46 papers out of 101 submitted, altogether contributed by 177 authors and co-authors, were selected by the Program Committee for presentation at the conference and publication in this book. Theoretical and more general contributions were presented in common (plenary) sessions. Problem-oriented sessions, as well as panel discussions, then brought together specialists in narrower problem areas with the aim of exchanging knowledge and skills resulting from research projects of all kinds.

Last but not least, we would like to express our gratitude to the authors for providing their papers on time, to the members of the conference reviewing team and the Program Committee for their careful reviews and paper selection, and to the editors for their hard work preparing this volume. Special thanks go to the members of both the Organizing Committee and the local organizing crew in Olomouc for their tireless effort and enthusiasm during the course of preparation of the conference.

We hope that everyone enjoyed this year's TSD and has benefitted from the event and relished the social program prepared by organizers. And you, dear reader, please, enjoy this book of proceedings.

September 2021

Kamil Ekštein
František Pártl
Miloslav Konopík

Organization

The 24th International Conference on Text, Speech and Dialogue – TSD 2021 – was organized by the Department of Computer Science and Engineering and the NTIS (New Technologies for the Information Society) P2 Research Centre of the Faculty of Applied Sciences, University of West Bohemia, Plzeň (Pilsen), Czech Republic, in co-operation with the the Department of General Linguistics of the Faculty of Arts, Palacký University, Olomouc, Czech Republic, and co-organized by the Faculty of Informatics, Masaryk University, Brno, Czech Republic.

The conference website is located at https://www.kiv.zcu.cz/tsd2021/ or https://www.tsdconference.org/.

Program Committee

Elmar Nöth (Chair)	University of Erlangen-Nuremberg, Germany
Rodrigo Agerri	University of the Basque Country, Spain
Eneko Agirre	University of the Basque Country, Spain
Vladimír Benko	Slovak Academy of Sciences, Slovakia
Archna Bhatia	Institute for Human and Machine Cognition, USA
Jan Černocký	Brno University of Technology, Czechia
Simon Dobrišek	University of Ljubljana, Slovenia
Kamil Ekštein	University of West Bohemia, Czechia
Karina Evgrafova	Saint Petersburg State University, Russia
Yevhen Fedorov	Dnipro National University of Railway Transport, Ukraine
Carlos Ferrer	Central University "Marta Abreu" of Las Villas, Cuba
Volker Fischer	EML European Media Laboratory GmbH, Germany
Darja Fišer	University of Ljubljana, Slovenia
Eleni Galiotou	University of West Attica, Greece
Björn Gambäck	Norwegian University of Science and Technology, Norway
Radovan Garabík	Slovak Academy of Sciences, Slovakia
Alexander Gelbukh	National Polytechnic Institute, Mexico
Louise Guthrie	Institute for Human and Machine Cognition, USA
Tino Haderlein	University of Erlangen-Nuremberg, Germany
Jan Hajič	Charles University, Czechia
Eva Hajičová	Charles University, Czechia
Yannis Haralambous	IMT Atlantique, France
Hynek Hermansky	Johns Hopkins University, USA
Jaroslava Hlaváčová	Charles University, Czechia
Aleš Horák	Masaryk University, Czechia
Eduard Hovy	Carnegie Mellon University, USA

Tamas Varadi	Hungarian Research Institute for Linguistics, Hungary
Zygmunt Vetulani	Adam Mickiewicz University, Poland
Aleksander Wawer	Polish Academy of Science, Poland
Pascal Wiggers	Amsterdam University of Applied Sciences, The Netherlands
Marcin Wolinski	Polish Academy of Sciences, Poland
Alina Wróblewska	Polish Academy of Sciences, Poland
Victor Zakharov	Saint Petersburg State University, Russia
Jerneja Žganec Gros	Alpineon d.o.o., Slovenia

Organizing Committee (University of West Bohemia, Plzeň)

Miloslav Konopík (Chair)
Václav Matoušek (Chair Emeritus)
Lucie Tauchenová (Secretary)
Kamil Ekštein (PR and Communications Manager, Webmaster, Proceedings Editor-in-Chief)
Roman Mouček (Chief Accountant and Financial Manager)
František Pártl (Technical Assistant, Proceedings Assistant Editor)
Ondřej Pražák (Technical Assistant)
Jakub Sido (Technical Assistant, Social Events Manager)

Local Organizing Crew (Palacký University, Olomouc)

Lukáš Zámečník (Chair)
Jana Buzková (Secretary)
Dan Faltýnek
Ľudmila Lacková
Vladimír Matlach
Hana Owsianková (Accommodation Manager)

Keynote Speakers

The organizers would like to thank the following respected scientists and researchers for delivering their keynote talks:

Lucie Flek	Philipps-Universität Marburg, Germany
Kate Knill	University of Cambridge, UK
Olga Vechtomova	University of Waterloo, Canada
Ivan Vulić	University of Cambridge, UK

Acknowledgements

The organizers would like to give special thanks to the following scientists and researchers who substantially contributed to the successful completion of the TSD 2021 review process by voluntarily agreeing to deliver extra reviews:

David Beneš
Martin Bulín
Adam Chýlek
Pavel Ircing
Marie Kunešová
Jan Lehečka
Natalija Loukachevitch
František Pártl

Ondřej Pražák
Pavel Přibáň
Markéta Řezáčková
Michal Seják
Jakub Sido
Jana Straková
Luboš Šmídl
Jan Švec

Supporting Institution

The organizers would like to express their gratitude to the following institution for its continuous support and helpful attitude to the TSD conference:

International Speech Communication Association

https://www.isca-speech.org/iscaweb/

About the Venue

Olomouc, Czechia – More Than Thousand Years of History

Olomouc is a beautiful place on the Morava river with more than a thousand-year-long history. Once a capital of Moravia – one of the three historical Lands of the Bohemian Crown – nowadays it still somehow waits to be rediscovered. The world-renowned tourist guide Lonely Planet highlighted this fact by putting Olomouc onto the list of the top 10 tourist destinations not to be missed during a visit to Europe. It even claimed Olomouc is one of the most unappreciated destinations in the Czech Republic.

By its beauty, Olomouc can, however, easily compete with not only Prague but any of the other most sought-after spots around Europe. It certainly deserves our attention.

One can find the second most important urban conservation zone in the Czech Republic, surrounded by splendorous parks, an incredible concentration of ecclesiastical structures, UNESCO-protected monuments, and even an astronomical clock with a history, perhaps, more interesting than the Prague one. All together safe from the neverending bustle of large cities.

Olomouc has always been the spiritual capital of Moravia. In the Middle Ages, it was the third-largest city in the Lands of the Bohemian Crown (after Prague and Wroclaw) and competed with Brno to hold the status of the Moravian administrative center. From 1642 till 1650, the city was occupied by the Swedish Empire's army led by Field Marshal Lennart Torstenson. Later on, in the half of the 18th century, Olomouc was rebuilt into a mighty stronghold, becoming an important strategic defence center and the seat of a powerful military garrison. During the following years, many barracks, training grounds, depots, and other military facilities were erected in and around the city. These were used by the army even after the stronghold was closed down in 1884, during the years of the Czechoslovak (First) Republic, and after World War II too.

From 1968 until 1991 an enormous garrison of the occupying Soviet Army was seated in Olomouc, and from 2003 until 2013 the Joint Forces Headquarters of the Czech Army resided in the city, thus making it the Czech state defence capital.

The first historically documented settlement in the present-day Olomouc area dates back to the end of the 7th century. It was the oldest fortified Slavic settlement in the Czech Republic and was located some 1.5 km (1 mile) south of the current historic center of the city. At the beginning of the 9th century, the old fortress was conquered, and a new one, the Great Moravian fortress, was erected on Peter's hillock (today, the Archbishop's Palace stands on same site).

In the 10th century, during the reign of prince Boleslav I, Olomouc became one of the militarya dministrative centers of the Přemyslid dynasty on the line of the trans-European trade route from Regensburg through to Kiev.

A highlight of the otherwise dull 11th century was the brave monkey business of prince Břetislav, who in 1021 kidnapped Judith, the daughter of a Bavarian margrave, from the monastery of Schweinfurt, married her immediately, and moved to Olomouc castle to live there.

Another highlight was the founding of the bishopric of Olomouc in 1063. Centuries later, in 1777, it was raised to the rank of an archbishopric. The bishopric was moved from the church of St. Peter (after having been ruined) to the church of St. Wenceslas in 1141 under the episcopacy of bishop Jindřich Zdík. The new bishop's palace was built in the Romanesque style. The bishopric acquired large tracts of land, especially in northern Moravia, and was one of the richest in the area.

A century, Olomouc became one of the most important settlements in Moravia and a seat of the Přemyslid government and one of the appanage princes. In 1306, King Wenceslas III stopped here on his way to Poland, to fight Władysław I the Elbow-high to claim his rights to the Polish crown, and was assassinated. With his death, the whole Přemyslid dynasty, stretching back to the mythical first Czech prince Přemysl the Ploughman, died out.

The foundation of the city at the location of the original settlement is historically documented in the mid 13th century. It soon became one of the most important trade and power centers in the region. Through the Middle Ages, it was the largest city in Moravia and rivalled Brno in holding the position of the regional capital. Olomouc finally surrendered this title after the Swedish Empire's army took the city and held it for eight years (1642–1650).

In 1235, the Mongols launched an invasion of Europe. After the Battle of Legnica in Poland, the Mongols carried their raids into Moravia but were defensively defeated at the mighty stronghold of Olomouc. The upset Mongols moved south-eastwards and soon invaded and defeated Hungary.

In modern history, Olomouc participated in the Protestant Reformation. During the Thirty Years' War, it was occupied by the Swedes and they devastated it almost entirely. In the 1740s, Olomouc was held by the Prussians for a short period. The wars between the Habsburg Empress Maria Theresa and the Prussian King Frederick the Great brought Olomouc strong new fortifications, and Frederick was not successful in trying to besiege the city in 1758.

In 1746 the first learned society in the lands under the control of the Austrian Habsburgs, the Societas eruditorum incognitorum in terris Austriacis, was founded in Olomouc to spread Enlightenment ideas. Its monthly Monatliche Auszüge was the first scientific journal published in the Habsburg empire.

In the revolution year of 1848, Olomouc set the scene for the abdication of the Austro-Hungarian Emperor Ferdinand. Two years later, the Austrian and the Prussian leaders met here at the event called the Punctation of Olmütz. This conference brought them together to plan the restoration of the German Confederation and Prussia accepted leadership by the Austrians.

After the foundation of the Czechoslovak Republic (1918), the importance of the city as an administrative center dimmed slightly in favour of Brno. However, it brought more peacefulness and serenity to the locality, making it a very pleasant place to stay.

Abstracts of Keynotes

Towards User-Centric Text-to-Text Generation: A Survey

Diyi Yang[1] and Lucie Flek[2]

[1] School of Interactive Computing, Georgia Institute of Technology,
Atlanta, USA
diyi.yang@cc.gatech.edu
[2] Conversational AI and Social Analytics (CAISA) Lab,
Department of Mathematics and Computer Science,
University of Marburg, Marburg, Germany
lucie.flek@uni-marburg.de

Abstract. Natural Language Generation (NLG) has received much attention with rapidly developing models and ever-more available data. As a result, a growing amount of work attempts to personalize these systems for better human interaction experience. Still, diverse sets of research across multiple dimensions and numerous levels of depth exist and are scattered across various communities. In this work, we survey the ongoing research efforts and introduce a categorization of these under the umbrella user-centric natural language generation. We further discuss some of the challenges and opportunities in NLG personalization.

Keywords: User modeling · Personalization · NLG

Wasserstein Autoencoders with Mixture of Gaussian Priors for Stylized Text Generation

Amirpasha Ghabussi[1], Lili Mou[2], and Olga Vechtomova[1]

[1] University of Waterloo, Waterloo ON, N2L 3G1, Canada
{aghabussi,ovechtom}@uwaterloo.ca
[2] Alberta Machine Intelligence Institute (Amii),
University of Alberta, Edmonton, AB T6G 2R3, Canada
lmou@ualberta.ca

Abstract. Probabilistic autoencoders are effective for text generation. However, they are unable to control the style of generated text, despite the training samples explicitly labeled with different styles. We present a Wasserstein autoencoder with a Gaussian mixture prior for style-aware sentence generation. Our model is trained on a multi-class dataset and generates sentences in the style of the desired class. It is also capable of interpolating multiple classes. Moreover, we can train our model on relatively small datasets. While a regular WAE or VAE cannot generate diverse sentences with few training samples, our approach generates diverse sentences and preserves the style of the desired classes.

Keywords: Wasserstein autoencoder · Stylized text generation · Natural language processing

Use of Deep Learning in Free Speaking Non-native English Assessment

Kate Knill

Machine Intelligence Laboratory, Department of Engineering, University of
Cambridge, Trumpington Street, Cambridge, CB2 1PZ, UK
http://mi.eng.cam.ac.uk/kmk/
kate.knill@eng.cam.ac.uk

Abstract. More than 1.5 billion people worldwide use English as an additional language which has created a large demand for teaching and assessment. To help meet this need automatic assessment systems can provide support, and an alternative, to human examiners. The ability to provide remote assessment has become even more important with the COVID-19 pandemic. Learners and teachers can benefit from online systems available 24/7 to monitor their progress whenever and wherever the learners like. Free speaking tests where open responses are given to prompted questions allow a learner to demonstrate their proficiency at speaking English. This presents a number of challenges with their spontaneous speech not known in advance. An auto-marker must be able to accurately assess this free speech independent of the speaker's first language (L1) and the audio recording quality which can vary considerably. This talk will look at how deep learning can be applied to help solve free speaking spoken non-native English assessment.

Cross-Lingual Knowledge Transfer and Adaptation in Low-Data Regimes: Achievements, Trends, and Challenges

Ivan Vulić

Language Technology Lab, Department of Theoretical and Applied Linguistics, Faculty of English, University of Cambridge, 9 West Road, Cambridge CB3 9DP, UK
https://sites.google.com/site/ivanvulic/
iv250@cam.ac.uk

Abstract. A key challenge in cross-lingual NLP is developing general language-independent architectures that will be equally applicable to any language. However, this ambition is hindered by the large variation in 1) structural and semantic properties of the world's languages, as well as 2) raw and task data scarcity for many different languages, tasks, and domains. As a consequence, existing language technology is still largely limited to a handful of resource-rich languages. In this talk, we introduce and discuss a range of recent techniques and breakthroughs that aim to deal with such large cross-language variations and low-data regimes efficiently. We cover a range of cutting-edge approaches including adapter-based models for cross-lingual transfer, contextual parameter generation and hypernetworks, learning in few-shot and zero-shot scenarios, and typologically driven learning and source selection. Finally, this talk demonstrates that low-resource languages, despite very positive research trends and results achieved in recent years, still lag behind major languages, and outline several key challenges for future research in this area.

Contents

Speech

Dialogue

Keynote Talks

Towards User-Centric Text-to-Text Generation: A Survey

Diyi Yang[1] and Lucie Flek[2(✉)]

[1] School of Interactive Computing, Georgia Institute of Technology, Atlanta, USA
diyi.yang@cc.gatech.edu
[2] Conversational AI and Social Analytics (CAISA) Lab, Department of Mathematics
and Computer Science, University of Marburg, Marburg, Germany
lucie.flek@uni-marburg.de

Abstract. Natural Language Generation (NLG) has received much attention with rapidly developing models and ever-more available data. As a result, a growing amount of work attempts to personalize these systems for better human interaction experience. Still, diverse sets of research across multiple dimensions and numerous levels of depth exist and are scattered across various communities. In this work, we survey the ongoing research efforts and introduce a categorization of these under the umbrella user-centric natural language generation. We further discuss some of the challenges and opportunities in NLG personalization.

Keywords: User modeling · Personalization · NLG

1 Motivation

With an increasing output quality of text-to-text NLG models, the attention of the field is turning towards the ultimate goal, to enable human-like natural language interactions. Even outside of the dialog-system area, the generated language is produced to fulfill specific communication goals [113], hence should be tailored to the specific audience [43,100]. Human speakers naturally use a conceptual model of the recipient in order to achieve their communication goal more efficiently, for example adjust the style or level of complexity [60,101,126,150]. It is therefore reasonable to assume that such user models improve the quality of NLG systems through better adaptivity and robustness [36,82], and to personalize the system outcomes based on the available relevant information about the user. Research in this area is driven by insights from numerous disciplines, from psychology across linguistics to human-computer interaction, while the industry focus on customer-driven solutions powers the personalization of conversational assistants [8,13,14,22]. As a result, research contributions are scattered across diverse venues. Our aim is to help to limit duplicate research activities, and to organize user-centric efforts within the NLG community. The possibilities of personalizing generated text towards the user range across multiple dimensions and numerous

© Springer Nature Switzerland AG 2021
K. Ekštein et al. (Eds.): TSD 2021, LNAI 12848, pp. 3–22, 2021.
https://doi.org/10.1007/978-3-030-83527-9_1

levels of depth, from factual knowledge over preferences and opinions to stylistic discourse adjustments. We use for all these user adjustment variations an umbrella term *user-centric natural language generation*. We provide a comprehensive overview of recent approaches and propose a categorization of ongoing research directions.

2 Related Surveys

Related to our work, [118] conduct a survey of datasets for dialogue systems, yet noting that "personalization of dialogue systems as an important task, which so far has not received much attention". [32] surveys user profiling datasets, however, without an NLG focus. Given various input types in NLG (e.g., tables [99], RDF triple [44], meaning representation [31]), we narrow our focus to user-centric text-to-text generation when referring to user-centric NLG in this work.

3 User-Centric NLG

Generally, NLG[1] is a process that produces textual content (a sequence of consecutive words) based on a chosen structured or unstructured input. In the ideal case, such textual content shall be syntactically and semantically plausible, resembling human-written text [45,46]. NLG encompasses a wide range of application tasks [43], such as neural machine translation, text summarization, text simplification, paraphrasing with style transfer, human-machine dialog systems, video captioning, narrative generation, or creative writing [43].

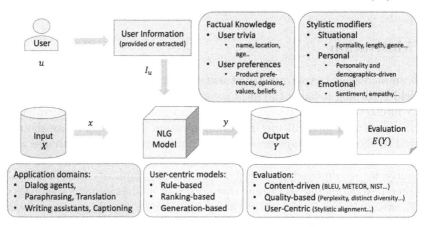

Fig. 1. User-centric natural language generation

3.1 When Is NLG User-Centric?

Given a text generation problem transforming an input x to an output y, we refer to it as **user-centric natural language generation** system when the

---

[1] In this work, NLG mainly refers to text-to-text generation.

output y of the NLG model is conditioned by information I_u available about the user u. In other words, the information I_u is leveraged to alter the projection of an input x to the output space. As illustrated in Fig. 1, this available user information can be of various kinds depending on specific application domains, which we categorize as follows.

3.2   User and Application Domain

In this paper we interpret the **user** in the term "user-centric" as the recipient of the generated text. Note that the previous work on personalized NLG, which we review here, sometimes takes an author-centric rather than recipient-centric view, for example dialog system works often refer to personalization as modeling of the chatbot persona [63]. The specific role of a user is dependent on a particular **application domain**, which also typically characterizes the type of the input. Below are some common application domains and the user and input examples.

- Conversational agents [69]: User is the human participant of the conversation. Input are typically the preceding utterances.
- Personalized machine translation [92,94,107,130]: User is the requester of the translation. Input is the text to be translated. Prior work mainly studied how particular personal trait of the author such as gender gets manifested in the original texts and in translations. [94] introduced a personalized machine translation system where users' preferred translation is predicted first based on similar other users.
- Writing Assistants: User is the final editor of the generated text, typically also the author of the input. Most current automated response generations such as Smart Reply in emails [65] are conducted in a generic way, not an user-specific manner.
- Personalized text simplification [9,72,89]: User is the reader, input is the text to be simplified.

Depending on whether a user is the recipient or the actor of a text, user-centric systems adapt themselves accordingly in terms of how to incorporate personalized or user-specific information into the modeling process.

Diverse Understanding of Personalization. As shown in Table 1, the interpretation of what personalized NLG means varies largely. Many systems optimize for speaker persona consistency or traits, while others operate with recipient's preferences. However, only a few studies considered recipients in their models [28]. We therefore argue, that in order to "solve" user-centric NLG, we must state more explicitly who our users are, what user needs we assume from them, and more importantly, how these user needs are reflected in our system design.

3.3   User Information

As shown in Fig. 1, we categorize user information into the following categories: (1) factual knowledge, which includes (1a) user trivia and (1b) preferences, and

(2) stylistic modifiers, which encompass (2a) situational, (2b) personal, and (2c) emotional choices.

(1) Factual Knowledge. Incorporating factual knowledge specific to a given user is essential in increasing user engagement. Information concerning **user trivia (1a)** can include personal data such as user's name or location, or user attributes such as occupation. For instance, [141] include user facts such as *"i have four kids"*, although factual knowledge is not introduced in a structured way. [19] utilized product user categories to generate personalized product descriptions. [91] uses reinforcement learning to reward chatbot persona consistency using fact lists with information like *"my dad is a priest"*. User facts

Table 1. Overview table of example previous user-centric NLG works that fall into each user information type. Note that the majority of works focuses on modeling the speaker persona rather than personalizing towards a representation of a recipient.

Research work	NLG task	Input X	User u	User info. I_u	I_u example	NLG model
[141]	ConvAgent (chitchat)	Utterances (PERSONA-CHAT)	Person being talked to	Factual - trivia, - preferences	Family, job, hobbies	Memory network
[19]	Product description	Product title (E-commerce)	Target customer	Factual - preferences	Category, aspect focus	Transformer
[101]	Device description	Device patents	Knowledge seeker	Factual - trivia	Background knowledge	Rule-based
[114]	ConvAgent (chitchat)	Argumentative interaction (Kialo Dataset)	Speaker persona	Factual -preferences	Stances, beliefs	Seq2seq
[63]	ConvAgent (goal-oriented)	bAbI dialog	Speaker persona	Style - personal	Age, gender	Memory network
[84]	ConvAgent (goal-oriented)	bAbI dialog	Speaker persona	Factual - preferences	Pref. over KB (embeddings)	Embedding Memory network
[75]	Chitchat	OpenSubtitles	Speaker persona	Style - situational	Specificity	Seq2seq, RL Data distillation
[86]	ConvAgent (chitchat)	PERSONAGE	Speaker persona	Style - personal	Big 5 Personality traits	Rule-based
[50]	ConvAgent (chitchat)	PERSONAGE	Speaker persona	Style - personal	Big 5 personality traits	Seq2seq
[97]	ConvAgent (chitchat)	Restaurant utterances	Speaker persona	Style - personal	Personality traits	Seq2seq
[74]	ConvAgent (chitchat)	Twitter, TV	Speaker, Recipient	Factual, Style (all)	Embeddings	Speaker model
[28]	ConvAgent (healthcare)	PTDS healthcare	Speaker, Recipient	Style - situational	Verbal, Non-verbal	Rule-based
[41]	ConvAgent (chitchat)	Share emotions	Speaker, Recipient	Style - emotional	Empathy	Rule-based
[59]	ConvAgent (chitchat)	Prior utterances	Speaker persona	Style - personal	Personality	N-gram LM
[148]	ConvAgent (chitchat)	Weibo	Speaker persona	Style - emotional	Emotion	Seq2seq
[42]	Reader-aware summarization	Weibo	Speaker, Recipient	Factual - preferences	Opinion	Seq2seq

for personalization include also expertise level in tutoring systems [53,101]. In addition to user trivia, including **user preferences (1b)** (*"i hate Mexican food"* or *"i like to ski"* [141]), such as opinions, values, and beliefs [114] has been of importance for dialog systems, as it leads to producing more coherent and interesting conversations.

(2) Stylistic Modifiers. Stylistic variation can be characterized as a variation in phonological, lexical, syntactic, or discourse realisation of a particular semantic content, due to user's characteristics [15,45]. To date, most of the style adaptation work in the NLG area focused on the **situational stylistic modifiers (2a)**, perceiving language use as a function of intended audience, genre, or situation. For example, professional/colloquial [35], personal/impersonal, formal/informal [18,96,102,103,110,136,143] or polite/impolite [25,38,85,95, 116]. Recently, unsupervised style transfer has gained popularity [70].

Comparably less research has been conducted in the emotional and personal modifiers, such as empathy or demographics. **Personal stylistic modifiers (2b)** in our scheme include user attributes, i.e. both conscious and unconscious traits intrinsic to the text author's individual identity [59]. A common property of these traits is that while their description is typically clear, such as *teenager*, *Scottish*, or *extrovert*, their surface realization is less well-defined [7]. Note that this is different from employing these attributes as user trivia in a factual way. The two main subgroups of personal modifiers are **sociodemographic traits** and **personality**. NLG words explore mostly gendered paraphrasing and gender-conditioned generation [104,105,112,127]. Personality has been employed mostly in the dialog area, mainly on the agent side [50,95,97]. In an early work on personality-driven NLG, the system of [87] estimates generation parameters for stylistic features based on the input of big five personality traits [24]. For example, an introverted style may include more hedging and be less verbose. While the big five model is the most widely accepted in terms of validity, its assessments are challenging to obtain [123]. Some works thus resort to other personality labels [41,132], or combinations of sociodemographic traits and personal interests [146]. Modeling personality of the recipient of the generated text is rare in recent NLG systems, although it has been shown to affect e.g. argument persuasiveness [33,83] and capability of learning from a dialog [26]. For example [53] proposed to use a multi-dimensional user model including hearer's emotional state and interest in the discussion, [26] represented users' stylistic preference for verboseness and their discourse understanding ability, and [11] inferred user's psychological states from their actions to update the model of a user's beliefs and goals. [55] uses LIWC keywords to infer both instructor's and recipient's personality traits to study dialog adaptation.

Emotional stylistic modifiers (2c) encompass the broad range of research in the area of affective NLG [26]. In the early works, manually prepared rules are applied to deliberately select the desired emotional responses [124], and pattern-based models are used to generate text to express emotions [66]. There is a broad range of features beyond affective adjectives that can have emotional impact, such as an increased use of redundancy, first-person pronouns, and adverbs [27]. [47]

introduce neural language models which allows to customize the degree of emotional content in generated sentences through an additional design parameter (happy, angry, sad, anxious, neutral). They note that it is difficult to produce emotions in a natural and coherent way due to the required balance of grammatically and emotional expressiveness. [4] show three novel ways to incorporate emotional aspects into encoder-decoder neural conversation models: word embeddings augmented with affective dictionaries, affect-based loss functions, and affectively diverse beam search for decoding. In their work on emotional chatting machines, [148] demonstrates that simply embedding emotion information in existing neural models cannot produce desirable emotional responses but just ambiguous general expressions with common words. They proposes a mechanism, which, after embedding emotion categories, captures the change of implicit internal emotion states, and boosts the probability of explicit emotion expressions with an external vocabulary. [125] observe, in line with [27], that one doesn't need to explicitly use strong emotional words to express emotional states, but one can implicitly combine neutral words in distinct ways to increase the intensity of the emotional experiences. They develop two NLG models for emotionally-charged text, explicit and implicit. The ability to produce language controlled for emotions is closely tied to the goal of building empathetic social chatbots [28,40,41, 111,121]. To date, these mainly leverage emotional embeddings similar to those described above to generate responses expected by the learned dialog policies. [78] point out the responses themselves don't need to be emotional, but mainly understanding, and propose a model based on empathetic listeners.

Implicit User Modeling. With the rise of deep learning models and the accompanying learned latent representations, boundaries between the user information categories sometimes get blurred, as the knowledge extracted about the user often isn't explicitly interpreted. This line of work uses high-dimensional vectors to refer to different aspects associated with users, implicitly grouping users with similar features (whether factual or stylistic) into similar areas of the vector space. Neural user embeddings in the context of dialog modeling have been introduced by [74], which capture latent speaker persona vectors based on speaker ID. This approach has been further probed and enhances by many others [63], e.g. by pretraining speaker embeddings on larger datasets [69,137,146,147], incorporating user traits into the decoding stage [145], or via mutual attention [88].

4 Data for User-Centric NLG

We identify five main types of datasets that can be leveraged for user-centric NLG, and provide their overview in Table 2. These types include: (1) Attribute-annotated datasets for user profiling, such as in [109], (2) style transfer and attribute transfer paraphrasing datasets such as [110], (3) attribute-annotated machine translation datasets such as [130], (4) persona-annotated dialog datasets such as [141], and (5) large conversational or other human-generated datasets with speaker ID, which allow for unsupervised speaker representation training.

Table 2. Available datasets usable for user-centric NLG

Task	Data and size	User info
[6] Dialog modeling	Movie dialogs, 132K conv.	Speaker ID
[69] Dialog modeling	Movie dialogs, 4.4K conv.	Speaker ID
[3] Character modeling	Movie subtitles, 5.5M turn pairs	Speaker ID
[141] Persona modeling	Chit-chat, 1K pers	Persona traits
[2] User modeling	Reddit, 133M conv 2.1B posts	User data
[74] Persona modeling	Twitter, 74K users (24M conv.)	User data
[146] Persona modeling	Weibo, 8.47M users, 21M conv.	Gender, age, loc.
[134] Attribute transfer	Reddit, Facebook, $\geq$100K posts	Political Slant
[112] Attribute transfer	Twitter, Yelp, $\geq$1M users	Gender
[105] Attribute transfer	Words, phrases	Gender
[110] Style transfer	Yahoo Answers, 110K pairs	Formality
[85] Style transfer	Enron e-mails, 1.39M texts	Politeness
[140] Style transfer	Twitter, 14K Tweets	Offensiveness
[10] Attribute transfer	Product QA $\geq$9K quest	Subjectivity
[76] Attribute transfer	$\geq$1M reviews	Sentiment
[92] Machine translation	TED talks, 2.3K Talks (271K sent.)	Speaker
[107] Machine translation	EuroParl, $\geq$100K sent. pairs (de, fr)	Gender
[130] Machine translation	EuroParl, $\geq$100K pairs (20 lang.)	Gender, age

In addition, as [12] point out, the challenge in the big data era is not to find human generated dialogues, but to employ them appropriately for social dialogue generation. Any existing social media dialogues can be combined with a suite of tools for sentiment analysis, topic identification, summarization, paraphrase, and rephrasing, to bootstrap a socially-apt NLG system.

5 User-Centric Generation Models

Already [150] discuss how natural language systems consult user models in order to improve their understanding of users' requirement and to generate appropriate and relevant responses. Generally, current user-centric generation models can be divided into rule-based, ranking-based and generation-based models.

Rule-based user models often utilize a pre-defined mapping between user types and topics [34], or hand-crafted user and context features [1]. The recent Alexa Prize social-bots also utilized a pre-defined mapping between personality types and topics [34], or hand-crafted user and context features [1].

Ranking-based models [2,90,141] focus on the task of response selection from a pool of candidates. Such response selection relies heavily on learning the matching between the given user post and any response from the pool, such as the deep structured similarity models [56] or the deep attention matching network [149]. [80] proposed to address the personalized response ranking task by incorporating user profiles into the conversation model. Generation-based models attempt to generate response directly from any given input questions. Most widely used models are built upon sequence-to-sequence models, and the recent transformer-based language models pretrained with large corpora [144].

With the development of large scale social media data [69,117,119,128,145], several personalized response generation models have been proposed. [21] introduced a neural model to learn a dynamically updated speaker embedding in a conversational context. They initialized speaker embedding in an unsupervised way by using context-sensitive language generation as an objective, and fine-tuned it at each turn in a dialog to capture changes over time and improve the speaker representation with added data. [74] introduced the Speaker Model that encoded user-id information into an additional vector and fed it into the decoder to capture the identity of the speakers. In addition to using user id to capture personal information, [141] proposed a profile memory network for encoding persona sentences. Recently, there are a few works using meta-learning and reinforcement learning to enhance mutual persona perception [68,79,88]. Generative models can produce novel responses, but they might suffer from grammar errors, repetitive, hallucination, and even uncontrollable outputs, all of which might degrade the performance of user-centric generation. For instance, under personalized dialog settings, [141] claimed that ranking-based models performed better than generative models, suggesting that building user-centric generative models is more challenging.

Hybrid models attempt to combine the strengths of the generative and rank paradigms [138] in a two-stage fashion, i.e., retrieving similar or template responses first, and then using these to help generate new responses. Hybrid models shed light on how to build user-centric NLG models as the first stage can be used to retrieve relevant knowledge/responses and the second stage can fine-tune the retrieved ones to be user-specific.

6   Evaluations

Current automatic evaluation metrics for response generation can be broadly categorized into three classes: content-driven, quality-based and user-centric. **Content** relatedness measures capture the distance of the generated response from its corresponding ground-truth, with representative metrics such as BLEU [98], NIST [30], and METEOR [71]. Speaker sensitive responses evaluation model [5] enhances the relatedness score with a context-response classifier. From a **quality** perspective, the fluency and diversity matter, assessed via perplexity [20] and distinct diversity [73]. From a **user-centric** perspective, we need to evaluate the style matching or fact adherence that compare the generated responses' language to the user's own language. Existing example metrics include the stylistic alignment [93,129] at the surface, lexical and syntactic level, model-driven metrics such as Hits@1/N, calculating how accurate the generated response can be automatically classified to its corresponding user or user group [29,93], and the average negative log-likelihood of generated text to user-specific language model, e.g. for poet's lyrics [131].

Evaluation towards open-ended conversations [64,106] also use Grice's Maxims of Conversation [49], i.e., evaluating whether the generated content violates *Quantity* that gives more or less information than requires, *Quality* that shares false information or things we do not have evidence, *Relation* that stays on the relevant topic, and *Manner* that requires communicating clearly without much disfluency. [67] further introduced a new diagnostic measure called relative utterance quantity (RUQ) to see if the model favors a generic response (e.g., '*I don't know*'). over the reference it was trained on.

Despite various measures in automatically assessing the quality of responses generated, human evaluation still plays a key role in assessing user-centric NLG systems, as the correlation between automated and human quality judgments is very limited [81,93]. Automatic metrics for evaluating user-centric NLG systems could then come in the form of an evaluation model learned from human data, e.g. collected from surveys, in order to provide human-like scores to proposed responses like BLEURT [115]. Recently, [54] argued that although human assessment remains the most trusted form of evaluation, the NLG community takes highly diverse approaches and different quality criteria, making it difficult to compare results and draw conclusions, with adverse implications for meta-evaluation and reproducibility. Their analyses on top of 165 NLG papers call for standard methods and terminology for NLG evaluation.

Human judgement for user-centric NLG requires significant efforts. User information such as styles, opinions or personalized knowledge is often scattered throughout the entire participation history in various formats such as posts, comments, likes or log-ins. It is impossible for annotators to go through these hundreds of activity records to infer whether the generated response fits the user well; furthermore, personalization is hardly reflected in a single message, but mostly inferred from a large collection of users' activities. [123]. Moreover, users' preferences and interests change over time either slowly or rapidly [48,77], making it even harder to third-parties to judge and evaluate. As a result, direct and self-evaluation from users of the user-centric NLG systems deserves more attention.

7   Challenges and Opportunities

User-Centric Data Collection and Evaluation. Collecting large-scale personalized conversations or data for NLG systems is challenging, expensive and cumbersome. First, most datasets suffer from pre-defined or collected user profiles expressed in a limited number of statements. Second, crowdsourcing personalized datasets is likely to result in very artificial content, as the workers need to intentionally inject the received personalization instructions into every utterance, which does not align well with human daily conversations. Correspondingly, state-of-the-art models tend to perform the attribute transfer merely at the lexical level (e.g. inserting negative words for *rude* or "please" for *polite*), while the subtle understanding and modification of higher-level compositionality is still a challenge [39,62,148]. Even more problematic assumption of most user-centric generation systems is that users exhibit their traits, moods and beliefs uniformly in a conversation. However, humans do not always express personalized information everywhere, thus real world data is persona-sparse [147]. This calls for a nuanced modeling of when, where and to what extent personalization needs to be included for NLG systems [17,37,122].

Personalized Pretraining and Safeguards. Getting data is a key challenge when it comes to personalized pre-training [147], which requires extensive data even for each single user. The proliferation of personalization also brings in trust and privacy issues [23,120]. How does user-centric generation relate to ethics and privacy as the personalization always involve using user specific data [51]? One key issue associated with personalized pretraining is that the extensive personal data needed by pretrained language models might include all sorts of dimensions about users, including sensitive and private information which should not be used by user-centric NLG systems [52,108]. For instance, [16] demonstrated that an adversary can perform an extraction attack to recover individual training examples from pretrained language models. These extracted examples include names, phone numbers, email addresses, and even deleted content. Such privacy concerns might become more salient and severe when it comes to user-centric pretraining, as models can easily remember details and leak training data for potential malicious attacks.

Biases and Generalization. The creation of corpora for user-centric NLG might suffer from *self-selection bias* as people who decides to use certain platforms like Twitter or Reddit might be very different. The *reporting bias* further adds complexity to this space as people do not necessarily talk about things in the world in proportion to their persona or personality. Thus, NLG systems built upon available data might be skewed towards certain population (e.g., educational background, access to Internet, specific language uses). The *crowdsourcing bias* [57], i.e., the potential inherent bias of crowd workers who contribute to the tasks might introduce biased ground-truth data.

Gaps Between Users and Systems. We argue that the evaluation process should look into what dimension users expect to see and identify what users want from these generated texts. For example [135] points out the expectations from human and artificial participants of the conversation are not the same, and shall be modeled differently. We need metrics to capture any failures, and mechanisms to explain the decision-making process behind these user-centric NLG models, since the data-driven systems tend to imitate utterances from their training data [61,133,139]. This process is not directly controllable, which may lead to offensive responses [58]. Another challenge is how to disentangle personalization from the generic representation [39], such as using domain adaptation techniques to transfer generic models to specific user groups [142].

8   Conclusion

This work presents a comprehensive overview of recent user-centric text generation across diverse sets of research capturing multiple dimensions of personalizing systems. We categorize these previous research directions, and present the representative tasks and evaluation approaches, as well as challenges and opportunities to facilitate future work on user-centric NLG.

References

1. Ahmadvand, A., et al.: Emory irisbot: an open-domain conversational bot for personalized information access. In: Alexa Prize Proceedings (2018)
2. Al-Rfou, R., Pickett, M., Snaider, J., Sung, Y., Strope, B., Kurzweil, R.: Conversational contextual cues: the case of personalization and history for response ranking. arXiv preprint arXiv:1606.00372 (2016)
3. Ameixa, D., Coheur, L., Fialho, P., Quaresma, P.: Luke, i am your father: dealing with out-of-domain requests by using movies subtitles. In: Bickmore, T., Marsella, S., Sidner, C. (eds.) IVA 2014. LNCS (LNAI), vol. 8637, pp. 13–21. Springer, Cham (2014). https://doi.org/10.1007/978-3-319-09767-1_2
4. Asghar, N., Poupart, P., Hoey, J., Jiang, X., Mou, L.: Affective neural response generation. In: Pasi, G., Piwowarski, B., Azzopardi, L., Hanbury, A. (eds.) ECIR 2018. LNCS, vol. 10772, pp. 154–166. Springer, Cham (2018). https://doi.org/10.1007/978-3-319-76941-7_12
5. Bak, J., Oh, A.: Speaker sensitive response evaluation model. In: Proceedings of the 58th Annual Meeting of the Association for Computational Linguistics, pp. 6376–6385. Association for Computational Linguistics, July 2020. https://doi.org/10.18653/v1/2020.acl-main.568. https://www.aclweb.org/anthology/2020.acl-main.568
6. Banchs, R.E.: Movie-DiC: a movie dialogue corpus for research and development. In: Proceedings of the 50th Annual Meeting of the Association for Computational Linguistics (Volume 2: Short Papers), pp. 203–207 (2012)
7. Belz, A.: ITRI-03-21 and now with feeling: developments in emotional language generation (2003)
8. Biller, M., Konya-Baumbach, E., Kuester, S., von Janda, S.: Chatbot anthropomorphism: a way to trigger perceptions of social presence? In: Blanchard, S. (ed.) 2020 AMA Summer Academic Conference: Bridging Gaps: Marketing in an Age of Disruption, vol. 31, pp. 34–37. American Marketing Association, Chicago (2020). https://madoc.bib.uni-mannheim.de/56482/
9. Bingel, J., Paetzold, G., Søgaard, A.: Lexi: a tool for adaptive, personalized text simplification. In: Proceedings of the 27th International Conference on Computational Linguistics, pp. 245–258 (2018)
10. Bjerva, J., Bhutani, N., Golshan, B., Tan, W.C., Augenstein, I.: SubjQA: a dataset for subjectivity and review comprehension. In: Proceedings of the 2020 Conference on Empirical Methods in Natural Language Processing (EMNLP), pp. 5480–5494 (2020)
11. Bonarini, A.: Modeling issues in multimedia car-driver interaction. In: Proceedings of the 1991 International Conference on Intelligent Multimedia Interfaces, pp. 353–371 (1991)

12. Bowden, K.K., Oraby, S., Misra, A., Wu, J., Lukin, S., Walker, M.: Data-driven dialogue systems for social agents. In: Eskenazi, M., Devillers, L., Mariani, J. (eds.) Advanced Social Interaction with Agents. LNEE, vol. 510, pp. 53–56. Springer, Cham (2019). https://doi.org/10.1007/978-3-319-92108-2_6

13. Bowden, K.K., et al.: Entertaining and opinionated but too controlling: a large-scale user study of an open domain Alexa prize system. In: Proceedings of the 1st International Conference on Conversational User Interfaces, pp. 1–10 (2019)

14. Braun, M., Mainz, A., Chadowitz, R., Pfleging, B., Alt, F.: At your service: designing voice assistant personalities to improve automotive user interfaces. In: Proceedings of the 2019 CHI Conference on Human Factors in Computing Systems, pp. 1–11 (2019)

15. Brooke, J., Flekova, L., Koppel, M., Solorio, T.: Proceedings of the Second Workshop on Stylistic Variation (2018)

16. Carlini, N., et al.: Extracting training data from large language models. arXiv preprint arXiv:2012.07805 (2020)

17. Chaves, A.P., Gerosa, M.A.: How should my chatbot interact? A survey on human-chatbot interaction design. arXiv preprint arXiv:1904.02743 (2019)

18. Chawla, K., Srinivasan, B.V., Chhaya, N.: Generating formality-tuned summaries using input-dependent rewards. In: Proceedings of the 23rd Conference on Computational Natural Language Learning (CoNLL), pp. 833–842. Association for Computational Linguistics, Hong Kong, November 2019. https://doi.org/10.18653/v1/K19-1078. https://www.aclweb.org/anthology/K19-1078

19. Chen, Q., Lin, J., Zhang, Y., Yang, H., Zhou, J., Tang, J.: Towards knowledge-based personalized product description generation in e-commerce. In: Proceedings of the 25th ACM SIGKDD International Conference on Knowledge Discovery & Data Mining, pp. 3040–3050 (2019)

20. Chen, S.F., Beeferman, D., Rosenfeld, R.: Evaluation metrics for language models (1998)

21. Cheng, H., Fang, H., Ostendorf, M.: A dynamic speaker model for conversational interactions. In: Proceedings of the 2019 Conference of the North American Chapter of the Association for Computational Linguistics: Human Language Technologies, Volume 1 (Long and Short Papers), pp. 2772–2785 (2019)

22. Churamani, N., et al.: The impact of personalisation on human-robot interaction in learning scenarios. In: Proceedings of the 5th International Conference on Human Agent Interaction, pp. 171–180 (2017)

23. Coavoux, M., Narayan, S., Cohen, S.B.: Privacy-preserving neural representations of text. In: Proceedings of the 2018 Conference on Empirical Methods in Natural Language Processing, pp. 1–10. Association for Computational Linguistics, Brussels, October–November 2018. https://doi.org/10.18653/v1/D18-1001. https://www.aclweb.org/anthology/D18-1001

24. Costa, P.T., Jr., McCrae, R.R.: Personality disorders and the five-factor model of personality. J. Pers. Disord. 4(4), 362–371 (1990)

25. Danescu-Niculescu-Mizil, C., Sudhof, M., Jurafsky, D., Leskovec, J., Potts, C.: A computational approach to politeness with application to social factors. In: Proceedings of the 51st Annual Meeting of the Association for Computational Linguistics (Volume 1: Long Papers), pp. 250–259. Association for Computational Linguistics, Sofia, August 2013. https://www.aclweb.org/anthology/P13-1025

26. de Rosis, F., Grasso, F.: Affective natural language generation. In: Paiva, A. (ed.) IWAI 1999. LNCS (LNAI), vol. 1814, pp. 204–218. Springer, Heidelberg (2000). https://doi.org/10.1007/10720296_15

27. De Rosis, F., Grasso, F., Castelfranchi, C., Poggi, I.: Modelling conflict-resolution dialogues. In: Müller, H.J., Dieng, R. (eds.) Computational Conflicts, pp. 41–62. Springer, Heidelberg (2000). https://doi.org/10.1007/978-3-642-56980-7_3

28. DeVault, D., et al.: SimSensei Kiosk: a virtual human interviewer for healthcare decision support. In: Proceedings of the 2014 International Conference on Autonomous Agents and Multi-Agent Systems, pp. 1061–1068 (2014)

29. Dinan, E., et al.: The second conversational intelligence challenge (ConvAI2). arXiv preprint arXiv:1902.00098 (2019)

30. Doddington, G.: Automatic evaluation of machine translation quality using n-gram co-occurrence statistics. In: Proceedings of the Second International Conference on Human Language Technology Research, pp. 138–145 (2002)

31. Dušek, O., Howcroft, D.M., Rieser, V.: Semantic noise matters for neural natural language generation. In: Proceedings of the 12th International Conference on Natural Language Generation, pp. 421–426 (2019)

32. Eke, C.I., Norman, A.A., Shuib, L., Nweke, H.F.: A survey of user profiling: state-of-the-art, challenges, and solutions. IEEE Access **7**, 144907–144924 (2019)

33. El Baff, R., Al Khatib, K., Stein, B., Wachsmuth, H.: Persuasiveness of news editorials depending on ideology and personality. In: Proceedings of the Third Workshop on Computational Modeling of People's Opinions, Personality, and Emotion's in Social Media, pp. 29–40 (2020)

34. Fang, H., et al.: Sounding board-university of Washington's Alexa prize submission. In: Alexa Prize Proceedings (2017)

35. Ficler, J., Goldberg, Y.: Controlling linguistic style aspects in neural language generation. In: Proceedings of the Workshop on Stylistic Variation, pp. 94–104. Association for Computational Linguistics, Copenhagen, September 2017. https://doi.org/10.18653/v1/W17-4912. https://www.aclweb.org/anthology/W17-4912

36. Finin, T.W.: GUMS-a general user modeling shell. In: Kobsa, A., Wahlster, W. (eds.) User Models in Dialog Systems. SYMBOLIC, pp. 411–430. Springer, Heidelberg (1989). https://doi.org/10.1007/978-3-642-83230-7_15

37. Flek, L.: Returning the N to NLP: towards contextually personalized classification models. In: Proceedings of the 58th Annual Meeting of the Association for Computational Linguistics, pp. 7828–7838 (2020)

38. Fu, L., Fussell, S., Danescu-Niculescu-Mizil, C.: Facilitating the communication of politeness through fine-grained paraphrasing. In: Proceedings of the 2020 Conference on Empirical Methods in Natural Language Processing (EMNLP), pp. 5127–5140. Association for Computational Linguistics, November 2020. https://doi.org/10.18653/v1/2020.emnlp-main.416. https://www.aclweb.org/anthology/2020.emnlp-main.416

39. Fu, Y., Zhou, H., Chen, J., Li, L.: Rethinking text attribute transfer: a lexical analysis. In: Proceedings of the 12th International Conference on Natural Language Generation, pp. 24–33 (2019)

40. Fung, P., Bertero, D., Xu, P., Park, J.H., Wu, C.S., Madotto, A.: Empathetic dialog systems. In: LREC 2018 (2018)

41. Fung, P., et al.: Zara the supergirl: an empathetic personality recognition system. In: Proceedings of the 2016 Conference of the North American Chapter of the Association for Computational Linguistics: Demonstrations, pp. 87–91 (2016)

42. Gao, S., et al.: Abstractive text summarization by incorporating reader comments. In: Proceedings of the AAAI Conference on Artificial Intelligence, vol. 33, pp. 6399–6406 (2019)

43. Garbacea, C., Mei, Q.: Neural language generation: formulation, methods, and evaluation. arXiv preprint arXiv:2007.15780 (2020)

44. Gardent, C., Shimorina, A., Narayan, S., Perez-Beltrachini, L.: The WebNLG challenge: generating text from RDF data. In: Proceedings of the 10th International Conference on Natural Language Generation, pp. 124–133 (2017)
45. Gatt, A., Krahmer, E.: Survey of the state of the art in natural language generation: core tasks, applications and evaluation. J. Artif. Intell. Res. **61**, 65–170 (2018)
46. Gehrmann, S., et al.: The gem benchmark: natural language generation, its evaluation and metrics. arXiv preprint arXiv:2102.01672 (2021)
47. Ghosh, S., Chollet, M., Laksana, E., Morency, L.P., Scherer, S.: Affect-LM: a neural language model for customizable affective text generation. In: Proceedings of the 55th Annual Meeting of the Association for Computational Linguistics (Volume 1: Long Papers), pp. 634–642 (2017)
48. Golder, S.A., Macy, M.W.: Diurnal and seasonal mood vary with work, sleep, and daylength across diverse cultures. Science **333**(6051), 1878–1881 (2011)
49. Grice, H.P.: Logic and conversation. In: Speech Acts, pp. 41–58. Brill (1975)
50. Harrison, V., Reed, L., Oraby, S., Walker, M.: Maximizing stylistic control and semantic accuracy in NLG: personality variation and discourse contrast. In: Proceedings of the 1st Workshop on Discourse Structure in Neural NLG, pp. 1–12 (2019)
51. Henderson, P., et al.: Ethical challenges in data-driven dialogue systems. In: Proceedings of the 2018 AAAI/ACM Conference on AI, Ethics, and Society, pp. 123–129 (2018)
52. Hitaj, B., Ateniese, G., Perez-Cruz, F.: Deep models under the GAN: information leakage from collaborative deep learning. In: Proceedings of the 2017 ACM SIGSAC Conference on Computer and Communications Security, pp. 603–618 (2017)
53. Hovy, E.: Generating natural language under pragmatic constraints. J. Pragmat. **11**(6), 689–719 (1987)
54. Howcroft, D.M., et al.: Twenty years of confusion in human evaluation: NLG needs evaluation sheets and standardised definitions. In: Proceedings of the 13th International Conference on Natural Language Generation, pp. 169–182 (2020)
55. Hu, Z., Tree, J.E.F., Walker, M.: Modeling linguistic and personality adaptation for natural language generation. In: Proceedings of the 19th annual SIGdial Meeting on Discourse and Dialogue, pp. 20–31 (2018)
56. Huang, P.S., He, X., Gao, J., Deng, L., Acero, A., Heck, L.: Learning deep structured semantic models for web search using clickthrough data. In: Proceedings of the 22nd ACM International Conference on Information & Knowledge Management, pp. 2333–2338 (2013)
57. Hube, C., Fetahu, B., Gadiraju, U.: Understanding and mitigating worker biases in the crowdsourced collection of subjective judgments. In: Proceedings of the 2019 CHI Conference on Human Factors in Computing Systems, pp. 1–12 (2019)
58. Hunt, E.: Tay, Microsoft's AI chatbot, gets a crash course in racism from Twitter. The Guardian, 24 March 2016. http://www.theguardian.com/technology/2016/mar/24/tay-microsofts-ai-chatbot-gets-a-crash-course-in-racism-from-twitter
59. Isard, A., Brockmann, C., Oberlander, J.: Individuality and alignment in generated dialogues. In: Proceedings of the Fourth International Natural Language Generation Conference, pp. 25–32 (2006)
60. Jameson, A.: But what will the listener think? Belief ascription and image maintenance in dialog. In: Kobsa, A., Wahlster, W. (eds.) User Models in Dialog Systems. SYMBOLIC, pp. 255–312. Springer, Heidelberg (1989). https://doi.org/10.1007/978-3-642-83230-7_10

61. Ji, Z., Lu, Z., Li, H.: An information retrieval approach to short text conversation. arXiv:1408.6988 [cs], August 2014. http://arxiv.org/abs/1408.6988
62. Jin, D., Jin, Z., Hu, Z., Vechtomova, O., Mihalcea, R.: Deep learning for text style transfer: a survey (2020)
63. Joshi, C.K., Mi, F., Faltings, B.: Personalization in goal-oriented dialog. arXiv preprint arXiv:1706.07503 (2017)
64. Jwalapuram, P.: Evaluating dialogs based on Grice's maxims. In: Proceedings of the Student Research Workshop Associated with RANLP, pp. 17–24 (2017)
65. Kannan, A., et al.: Smart reply: automated response suggestion for email. In: Proceedings of the 22nd ACM SIGKDD International Conference on Knowledge Discovery and Data Mining, pp. 955–964 (2016)
66. Keshtkar, F., Inkpen, D.: A pattern-based model for generating text to express emotion. In: D'Mello, S., Graesser, A., Schuller, B., Martin, J.-C. (eds.) ACII 2011. LNCS, vol. 6975, pp. 11–21. Springer, Heidelberg (2011). https://doi.org/10.1007/978-3-642-24571-8_2
67. Khayrallah, H., Sedoc, J.: Measuring the 'i don't know' problem through the lens of Gricean quantity. arXiv preprint arXiv:2010.12786 (2020)
68. Kim, H., Kim, B., Kim, G.: Will i sound like me? Improving persona consistency in dialogues through pragmatic self-consciousness (2020)
69. Kottur, S., Wang, X., Carvalho, V.: Exploring personalized neural conversational models. In: IJCAI, pp. 3728–3734 (2017)
70. Krishna, K., Wieting, J., Iyyer, M.: Reformulating unsupervised style transfer as paraphrase generation. In: Proceedings of the 2020 Conference on Empirical Methods in Natural Language Processing (EMNLP), pp. 737–762 (2020)
71. Lavie, A., Agarwal, A.: METEOR: an automatic metric for MT evaluation with high levels of correlation with human judgments. In: Proceedings of the Second Workshop on Statistical Machine Translation, pp. 228–231 (2007)
72. Lee, J.S., Yeung, C.Y.: Personalizing lexical simplification. In: Proceedings of the 27th International Conference on Computational Linguistics, pp. 224–232 (2018)
73. Li, J., Galley, M., Brockett, C., Gao, J., Dolan, B.: A diversity-promoting objective function for neural conversation models. arXiv preprint arXiv:1510.03055 (2015)
74. Li, J., Galley, M., Brockett, C., Spithourakis, G., Gao, J., Dolan, B.: A persona-based neural conversation model. In: Proceedings of the 54th Annual Meeting of the Association for Computational Linguistics (Volume 1: Long Papers), pp. 994–1003 (2016)
75. Li, J., Monroe, W., Jurafsky, D.: Data distillation for controlling specificity in dialogue generation. arXiv preprint arXiv:1702.06703 (2017)
76. Li, J., Jia, R., He, H., Liang, P.: Delete, retrieve, generate: a simple approach to sentiment and style transfer. In: Proceedings of the 2018 Conference of the North American Chapter of the Association for Computational Linguistics: Human Language Technologies, Volume 1 (Long Papers), pp. 1865–1874 (2018)
77. Li, L., Zheng, L., Yang, F., Li, T.: Modeling and broadening temporal user interest in personalized news recommendation. Expert Syst. Appl. 41(7), 3168–3177 (2014)
78. Lin, Z., Madotto, A., Shin, J., Xu, P., Fung, P.: MoEL: mixture of empathetic listeners. In: Proceedings of the 2019 Conference on Empirical Methods in Natural Language Processing and the 9th International Joint Conference on Natural Language Processing (EMNLP-IJCNLP), pp. 121–132 (2019)
79. Lin, Z., Madotto, A., Wu, C.S., Fung, P.: Personalizing dialogue agents via meta-learning (2019)

80. Liu, B., et al.: Content-oriented user modeling for personalized response ranking in chatbots. IEEE/ACM Trans. Audio Speech Lang. Process. **26**(1), 122–133 (2017)
81. Liu, C.W., Lowe, R., Serban, I.V., Noseworthy, M., Charlin, L., Pineau, J.: How not to evaluate your dialogue system: an empirical study of unsupervised evaluation metrics for dialogue response generation. arXiv preprint arXiv:1603.08023 (2016)
82. Lucas, J., Fernández, F., Salazar, J., Ferreiros, J., San Segundo, R.: Managing speaker identity and user profiles in a spoken dialogue system. Procesamiento del lenguaje natural (43), 77–84 (2009)
83. Lukin, S., Anand, P., Walker, M., Whittaker, S.: Argument strength is in the eye of the beholder: audience effects in persuasion. In: Proceedings of the 15th Conference of the European Chapter of the Association for Computational Linguistics: Volume 1, Long Papers, pp. 742–753 (2017)
84. Luo, L., Huang, W., Zeng, Q., Nie, Z., Sun, X.: Learning personalized end-to-end goal-oriented dialog. In: Proceedings of the AAAI Conference on Artificial Intelligence, vol. 33, pp. 6794–6801 (2019)
85. Madaan, A., et al.: Politeness transfer: a tag and generate approach. In: Proceedings of the 58th Annual Meeting of the Association for Computational Linguistics, pp. 1869–1881 (2020)
86. Mairesse, F., Walker, M.: PERSONAGE: personality generation for dialogue. In: Proceedings of the 45th Annual Meeting of the Association of Computational Linguistics, pp. 496–503 (2007)
87. Mairesse, F., Walker, M.: Trainable generation of big-five personality styles through data-driven parameter estimation. In: Proceedings of ACL-2008: HLT, pp. 165–173 (2008)
88. Majumder, B.P., Jhamtani, H., Berg-Kirkpatrick, T., McAuley, J.: Like hiking? You probably enjoy nature: persona-grounded dialog with commonsense expansions (2020)
89. Mallinson, J., Lapata, M.: Controllable sentence simplification: employing syntactic and lexical constraints. arXiv preprint arXiv:1910.04387 (2019)
90. Mazare, P.E., Humeau, S., Raison, M., Bordes, A.: Training millions of personalized dialogue agents. In: Proceedings of the 2018 Conference on Empirical Methods in Natural Language Processing, pp. 2775–2779 (2018)
91. Mesgar, M., Simpson, E., Wang, Y., Gurevych, I.: Generating persona-consistent dialogue responses using deep reinforcement learning. arXiv-2005 (2020)
92. Michel, P., Neubig, G.: Extreme adaptation for personalized neural machine translation. In: Proceedings of the 56th Annual Meeting of the Association for Computational Linguistics (Volume 2: Short Papers), pp. 312–318 (2018)
93. Mir, R., Felbo, B., Obradovich, N., Rahwan, I.: Evaluating style transfer for text. In: Proceedings of the 2019 Conference of the North American Chapter of the Association for Computational Linguistics: Human Language Technologies, Volume 1 (Long and Short Papers), pp. 495–504. Association for Computational Linguistics, Minneapolis, June 2019. https://doi.org/10.18653/v1/N19-1049. https://www.aclweb.org/anthology/N19-1049
94. Mirkin, S., Meunier, J.L.: Personalized machine translation: predicting translational preferences. In: Proceedings of the 2015 Conference on Empirical Methods in Natural Language Processing, pp. 2019–2025 (2015)
95. Niu, T., Bansal, M.: Polite dialogue generation without parallel data. Trans. Assoc. Comput. Linguist. **6**, 373–389 (2018). https://www.aclweb.org/anthology/Q18-1027

96. Niu, X., Martindale, M., Carpuat, M.: A study of style in machine transla-
    tion: controlling the formality of machine translation output. In: Proceedings
    of the 2017 Conference on Empirical Methods in Natural Language Process-
    ing, pp. 2814–2819. Association for Computational Linguistics, Copenhagen,
    September 2017. https://doi.org/10.18653/v1/D17-1299. https://www.aclweb.
    org/anthology/D17-1299

97. Oraby, S., Reed, L., Tandon, S., Sharath, T., Lukin, S., Walker, M.: Controlling
    personality-based stylistic variation with neural natural language generators. In:
    Proceedings of the 19th Annual SIGdial Meeting on Discourse and Dialogue, pp.
    180–190 (2018)

98. Papineni, K., Roukos, S., Ward, T., Zhu, W.J.: BLEU: a method for automatic
    evaluation of machine translation. In: Proceedings of the 40th Annual Meeting of
    the Association for Computational Linguistics, pp. 311–318 (2002)

99. Parikh, A., et al.: ToTTo: a controlled table-to-text generation dataset. In: Pro-
    ceedings of the 2020 Conference on Empirical Methods in Natural Language Pro-
    cessing (EMNLP), pp. 1173–1186 (2020)

100. Paris, C.: User Modelling in Text Generation. Bloomsbury Publishing, London
    (2015)

101. Paris, C.L.: The use of explicit user models in a generation system for tailoring
    answers to the user's level of expertise. In: Kobsa, A., Wahlster, W. (eds.) User
    Models in Dialog Systems. SYMBOLIC, pp. 200–232. Springer, Heidelberg (1989).
    https://doi.org/10.1007/978-3-642-83230-7_8

102. Pavlick, E., Tetreault, J.: An empirical analysis of formality in online commu-
    nication. Trans. Assoc. Comput. Linguist. **4**, 61–74 (2016). https://www.aclweb.
    org/anthology/Q16-1005

103. Peterson, K., Hohensee, M., Xia, F.: Email formality in the workplace: a case
    study on the Enron corpus. In: Proceedings of the Workshop on Language in
    Social Media (LSM 2011), pp. 86–95. Association for Computational Linguistics,
    Portland, June 2011. https://www.aclweb.org/anthology/W11-0711

104. Prabhumoye, S., Tsvetkov, Y., Salakhutdinov, R., Black, A.W.: Style transfer
    through back-translation. arXiv preprint arXiv:1804.09000 (2018)

105. Preotiuc-Pietro, D., Xu, W., Ungar, L.: Discovering user attribute stylistic dif-
    ferences via paraphrasing. In: Proceedings of the AAAI Conference on Artificial
    Intelligence, vol. 30 (2016)

106. Qwaider, M.R., Freihat, A.A., Giunchiglia, F.: TrentoTeam at SemEval-2017
    task 3: an application of Grice maxims in ranking community question answers.
    In: Proceedings of the 11th International Workshop on Semantic Evaluation
    (SemEval-2017), pp. 271–274 (2017)

107. Rabinovich, E., Mirkin, S., Patel, R.N., Specia, L., Wintner, S.: Person-
    alized machine translation: preserving original author traits. arXiv preprint
    arXiv:1610.05461 (2016)

108. Ramaswamy, S., Thakkar, O., Mathews, R., Andrew, G., McMahan, H.B., Bea-
    ufays, F.: Training production language models without memorizing user data.
    arXiv preprint arXiv:2009.10031 (2020)

109. Rangel, F., Rosso, P., Koppel, M., Stamatatos, E., Inches, G.: Overview of the
    author profiling task at PAN 2013. In: CLEF Conference on Multilingual and
    Multimodal Information Access Evaluation, pp. 352–365. CELCT (2013)

110. Rao, S., Tetreault, J.: Dear sir or madam, may i introduce the GYAFC dataset: corpus, benchmarks and metrics for formality style transfer. In: Proceedings of the 2018 Conference of the North American Chapter of the Association for Computational Linguistics: Human Language Technologies, Volume 1 (Long Papers), pp. 129–140. Association for Computational Linguistics, New Orleans, June 2018. https://doi.org/10.18653/v1/N18-1012. https://www.aclweb.org/anthology/N18-1012

111. Rashkin, H., Smith, E.M., Li, M., Boureau, Y.L.: Towards empathetic open-domain conversation models: a new benchmark and dataset. In: Proceedings of the 57th Annual Meeting of the Association for Computational Linguistics, pp. 5370–5381 (2019)

112. Reddy, S., Knight, K.: Obfuscating gender in social media writing. In: Proceedings of the First Workshop on NLP and Computational Social Science, pp. 17–26 (2016)

113. Reiter, E.: Natural language generation challenges for explainable AI. In: Proceedings of the 1st Workshop on Interactive Natural Language Technology for Explainable Artificial Intelligence (NL4XAI 2019), pp. 3–7 (2019)

114. Scialom, T., Tekiroğlu, S.S., Staiano, J., Guerini, M.: Toward stance-based personas for opinionated dialogues. In: Proceedings of the 2020 Conference on Empirical Methods in Natural Language Processing: Findings, pp. 2625–2635 (2020)

115. Sellam, T., Das, D., Parikh, A.: BLEURT: learning robust metrics for text generation. In: Proceedings of the 58th Annual Meeting of the Association for Computational Linguistics, pp. 7881–7892 (2020)

116. Sennrich, R., Haddow, B., Birch, A.: Controlling politeness in neural machine translation via side constraints. In: Proceedings of the 2016 Conference of the North American Chapter of the Association for Computational Linguistics: Human Language Technologies, pp. 35–40 (2016)

117. Serban, I.V., Sordoni, A., Bengio, Y., Courville, A., Pineau, J.: Building end-to-end dialogue systems using generative hierarchical neural network models. In: Thirtieth AAAI Conference on Artificial Intelligence (2016)

118. Serban, I.V., Lowe, R., Henderson, P., Charlin, L., Pineau, J.: A survey of available corpora for building data-driven dialogue systems. arXiv preprint arXiv:1512.05742 (2015)

119. Shang, L., Lu, Z., Li, H.: Neural responding machine for short-text conversation (2015)

120. Shokri, R., Stronati, M., Song, C., Shmatikov, V.: Membership inference attacks against machine learning models. In: 2017 IEEE Symposium on Security and Privacy (SP), pp. 3–18. IEEE (2017)

121. Shum, H.Y., He, X., Li, D.: From Eliza to Xiaoice: challenges and opportunities with social chatbots. Front. Inf. Technol. Electron. Eng. **19**(1), 10–26 (2018)

122. Shumanov, M., Johnson, L.: Making conversations with chatbots more personalized. Comput. Hum. Behav. **117**, 106627 (2020)

123. Shuster, K., Humeau, S., Hu, H., Bordes, A., Weston, J.: Engaging image captioning via personality. In: Proceedings of the IEEE/CVF Conference on Computer Vision and Pattern Recognition, pp. 12516–12526 (2019)

124. Skowron, M.: Affect listeners: acquisition of affective states by means of conversational systems. In: Esposito, A., Campbell, N., Vogel, C., Hussain, A., Nijholt, A. (eds.) Development of Multimodal Interfaces: Active Listening and Synchrony. LNCS, vol. 5967, pp. 169–181. Springer, Heidelberg (2010). https://doi.org/10.1007/978-3-642-12397-9_14

125. Song, Z., Zheng, X., Liu, L., Xu, M., Huang, X.J.: Generating responses with a specific emotion in dialog. In: Proceedings of the 57th Annual Meeting of the Association for Computational Linguistics, pp. 3685–3695 (2019)
126. Su, P., Wang, Y.B., Yu, T., Lee, L.: A dialogue game framework with personalized training using reinforcement learning for computer-assisted language learning. In: 2013 IEEE International Conference on Acoustics, Speech and Signal Processing, pp. 8213–8217. IEEE (2013)
127. Subramanian, S., Lample, G., Smith, E.M., Denoyer, L., Ranzato, M., Boureau, Y.L.: Multiple-attribute text style transfer. arXiv preprint arXiv:1811.00552 (2018)
128. Sutskever, I., Vinyals, O., Le, Q.: Sequence to sequence learning with neural networks. In: Advances in NIPS (2014)
129. Syed, B., Verma, G., Srinivasan, B.V., Natarajan, A., Varma, V.: Adapting language models for non-parallel author-stylized rewriting. In: AAAI, pp. 9008–9015 (2020)
130. Vanmassenhove, E., Hardmeier, C., Way, A.: Getting gender right in neural machine translation. In: Proceedings of the 2018 Conference on Empirical Methods in Natural Language Processing, pp. 3003–3008 (2018)
131. Vechtomova, O., Bahuleyan, H., Ghabussi, A., John, V.: Generating lyrics with variational autoencoder and multi-modal artist embeddings. arXiv preprint arXiv:1812.08318 (2018)
132. Verhoeven, B., Daelemans, W., Plank, B.: TwiSty: a multilingual Twitter stylometry corpus for gender and personality profiling. In: Proceedings of the Tenth International Conference on Language Resources and Evaluation (LREC 2016), pp. 1632–1637. European Language Resources Association (ELRA), Portorož, May 2016. https://www.aclweb.org/anthology/L16-1258
133. Vinyals, O., Le, Q.: A neural conversational model. In: Proceedings of the 31st International Conference on Machine Learning, Lille, France, June 2015. arXiv: 1506.05869
134. Voigt, R., Jurgens, D., Prabhakaran, V., Jurafsky, D., Tsvetkov, Y.: RtGender: a corpus for studying differential responses to gender. In: Proceedings of the Eleventh International Conference on Language Resources and Evaluation (LREC 2018) (2018)
135. Völkel, S.T., et al.: Developing a personality model for speech-based conversational agents using the psycholexical approach. In: Proceedings of the 2020 CHI Conference on Human Factors in Computing Systems, pp. 1–14 (2020)
136. Wang, Y., Wu, Y., Mou, L., Li, Z., Chao, W.: Harnessing pre-trained neural networks with rules for formality style transfer. In: Proceedings of the 2019 Conference on Empirical Methods in Natural Language Processing and the 9th International Joint Conference on Natural Language Processing (EMNLP-IJCNLP), pp. 3573–3578. Association for Computational Linguistics, Hong Kong, November 2019. https://doi.org/10.18653/v1/D19-1365. https://www.aclweb.org/anthology/D19-1365
137. Wolf, T., Sanh, V., Chaumond, J., Delangue, C.: TransferTransfo: a transfer learning approach for neural network based conversational agents. arXiv preprint arXiv:1901.08149 (2019)
138. Wu, Y., Wei, F., Huang, S., Wang, Y., Li, Z., Zhou, M.: Response generation by context-aware prototype editing. In: Proceedings of the AAAI Conference on Artificial Intelligence, vol. 33, pp. 7281–7288 (2019)

139. Yu, Z., Papangelis, A., Rudnicky, A.: TickTock: a non-goal-oriented multimodal dialog system with engagement awareness. In: Turn-Taking and Coordination in Human-Machine Interaction: Papers from the 2015 AAAI Spring Symposium, Palo Alto, CA, USA, pp. 108–111 (2015). https://www.aaai.org/ocs/index.php/SSS/SSS15/paper/viewFile/10315/10119
140. Zampieri, M., Malmasi, S., Nakov, P., Rosenthal, S., Farra, N., Kumar, R.: SemEval-2019 task 6: identifying and categorizing offensive language in social media (offenseval). arXiv preprint arXiv:1903.08983 (2019)
141. Zhang, S., Dinan, E., Urbanek, J., Szlam, A., Kiela, D., Weston, J.: Personalizing dialogue agents: i have a dog, do you have pets too? In: Proceedings of the 56th Annual Meeting of the Association for Computational Linguistics (Volume 1: Long Papers), pp. 2204–2213. Association for Computational Linguistics, Melbourne, July 2018. https://doi.org/10.18653/v1/P18-1205. https://www.aclweb.org/anthology/P18-1205
142. Zhang, W.N., Zhu, Q., Wang, Y., Zhao, Y., Liu, T.: Neural personalized response generation as domain adaptation. World Wide Web **22**(4), 1427–1446 (2019). https://doi.org/10.1007/s11280-018-0598-6
143. Zhang, Y., Ge, T., Sun, X.: Parallel data augmentation for formality style transfer. In: Proceedings of the 58th Annual Meeting of the Association for Computational Linguistics, pp. 3221–3228. Association for Computational Linguistics, July 2020. https://doi.org/10.18653/v1/2020.acl-main.294. https://www.aclweb.org/anthology/2020.acl-main.294
144. Zhang, Y., et al.: DialoGPT: large-scale generative pre-training for conversational response generation. In: Proceedings of the 58th Annual Meeting of the Association for Computational Linguistics: System Demonstrations, pp. 270–278 (2020)
145. Zheng, Y., Chen, G., Huang, M., Liu, S., Zhu, X.: Personalized dialogue generation with diversified traits. arXiv preprint arXiv:1901.09672 (2019)
146. Zheng, Y., Chen, G., Huang, M., Liu, S., Zhu, X.: Personalized dialogue generation with diversified traits (2020)
147. Zheng, Y., Zhang, R., Huang, M., Mao, X.: A pre-training based personalized dialogue generation model with persona-sparse data. In: Proceedings of the AAAI Conference on Artificial Intelligence, vol. 34, pp. 9693–9700 (2020)
148. Zhou, H., Huang, M., Zhang, T., Zhu, X., Liu, B.: Emotional chatting machine: emotional conversation generation with internal and external memory. In: Proceedings of the AAAI Conference on Artificial Intelligence, vol. 32 (2018)
149. Zhou, X., et al.: Multi-turn response selection for chatbots with deep attention matching network. In: Proceedings of the 56th Annual Meeting of the Association for Computational Linguistics (Volume 1: Long Papers), pp. 1118–1127 (2018)
150. Zukerman, I., Litman, D.: Natural language processing and user modeling: synergies and limitations. User Model. User-Adap. Interact. **11**(1), 129–158 (2001). https://doi.org/10.1023/A:1011174108613

Wasserstein Autoencoders with Mixture of Gaussian Priors for Stylized Text Generation

Amirpasha Ghabussi[1], Lili Mou[2], and Olga Vechtomova[1(✉)]

[1] University of Waterloo, Waterloo, ON N2L 3G1, Canada
{aghabussi,ovechtom}@uwaterloo.ca
[2] Alberta Machine Intelligence Institute (Amii), University of Alberta,
Edmonton, AB T6G 2R3, Canada
lmou@ualberta.ca

Abstract. Probabilistic autoencoders are effective for text generation. However, they are unable to control the style of generated text, despite the training samples explicitly labeled with different styles. We present a Wasserstein autoencoder with a Gaussian mixture prior for style-aware sentence generation. Our model is trained on a multi-class dataset and generates sentences in the style of the desired class. It is also capable of interpolating multiple classes. Moreover, we can train our model on relatively small datasets. While a regular WAE or VAE cannot generate diverse sentences with few training samples, our approach generates diverse sentences and preserves the style of the desired classes.

Keywords: Wasserstein autoencoder · Stylized text generation · Natural language processing

1 Introduction

Probabilistic text generation is an important research area in Natural Language Processing. The variational autoencoder (VAE) [11] and the Wasserstein autoencoder (WAE) [18] are two common generative models used for sentence generation. They generate a sentence by learning a latent distribution. At the inference time, they can generate sentences by sampling from the latent distribution. Typically, VAE and WAE impose a normal distribution as the prior. Therefore, they may over-regularize the latent space. This is especially undesired when a training sample has a specific style, as the normal distribution cannot adequately capture text style. Additionally, the latent space cannot be conditioned to generate sentences from each class.

To address the above challenges, we propose a WAE with a Gaussian Mixture Model prior (GMM-WAE)[1], where each of the mixtures captures a specific style. This allows us to generate text in a desired style by sampling from its corresponding distribution. Our approach also makes it possible to generate sentences with a mixture of styles, which is not feasible with a traditional VAE or WAE.

Moreover, our GMM-WAE is able to pool data of different styles together, alleviating the data-hungry issue of neural networks. Our experiments show that GMM-WAE produces high-quality results with both large and small datasets.

---

[1] The source code is available at https://github.com/alwevks/GMM-WAE.

© Springer Nature Switzerland AG 2021
K. Ekštein et al. (Eds.): TSD 2021, LNAI 12848, pp. 23–31, 2021.
https://doi.org/10.1007/978-3-030-83527-9_2

2   Related Work

Stylized text generation [14] has been investigated in previous work for sentiment [4, 8, 9, 15], formality [22], genre [4], and authorship [19] as styles. In this work, we consider a broader view of the style as some distinguishable property of text, and our experiments mainly take the domain as the text style.

There are many approaches for stylized text generation. One approach is using style-specific embeddings for sentence generation [4, 19]. Others focus on learning separate latent representations of style and content. Gao et al. [5] use a structured latent space with an autoencoder and a shared decoder to generate stylized dialogue responses. John et al. [9] apply adversarial and multitask losses to separate style from content.

Mixture of Gaussian prior was previously used for image clustering [3] and image generation [6]. In NLP, Gaussian mixture model (GMM) priors have been used for several tasks. Shen et al. [16] use Gaussian mixtures for machine translation. Gu et al. [7] use an autoencoder network with a GMM prior to learn the latent representation of sentence-level data points, and jointly train a GAN to generate and discriminate in the same space. They use the Wasserstein distance to model dialogue responses. However, they only use GMM as a multi-modal representation of the latent space and do not add conditions to mixture distributions. Wang et al. [20] propose an unsupervised approach using a VAE with a GMM prior for topic modeling. They use bag-of-words for document representation, so their approach cannot be used for sentence generation. Moreover, their unsupervised approach prevents them from having any control over the styles learned by their model.

Our work presents three improvements over the WAE. First, we extend the single Gaussian prior to a Gaussian mixture prior for style-conditioned and style-interpolated sentence generation. Style-conditioned sentences are generated from a chosen class of the dataset. Second, GMM-WAE can generate style-interpolated sentences by mixing two or more classes. No other work has used a GMM-WAE for this purpose. Last, our approach can pool the information from multiple classes into a single model, so GMM-WAE is less prone to the data sparsity problem. While most generative models rely on large datasets, our GMM-WAE achieves high scores on most measures for both large and small datasets.

3   Approach

In this section, we introduce our approach in detail. We use a stochastic WAE [2] with Maximum Mean Discrepancy (MMD) penalty based on a sequence-to-sequence neural network [17]. Using a Gaussian mixture distribution prior, we are able to generate style-conditioned and style-interpolated sentences at the inference time. Our training requires a style-labeled dataset, but does not need parallel data for training.

3.1   Wasserstein Autoencoder

A Wasserstein autoencoder (WAE) [18] imposes a probabilistic modeling on the latent space of an autoencoder h with a prior $p(h)$. For each input sentence x, the encoder predicts a posterior distribution $q(\boldsymbol{h}|\mathbf{x})$. WAE would like the aggregated posterior $q(\boldsymbol{h}) = \sum_{\mathbf{x}} q(\boldsymbol{h}|\mathbf{x}) p_{\text{data}}(\mathbf{x})$ to be similar to the prior $p(\boldsymbol{h})$, where $p_{\text{data}}(\mathbf{x})$ is the input sentence distribution. This constraint can be relaxed by penalizing the Wasserstein distance between $q(\boldsymbol{h})$ and $p(\boldsymbol{h})$, given by the maximum mean discrepancy (MMD) of the two distributions:

$$\text{MMD} = \left\| \int k(\boldsymbol{h}, \cdot) \mathrm{d}P(\boldsymbol{h}) - \int k(\boldsymbol{h}, \cdot) \mathrm{d}Q(\boldsymbol{h}) \right\|_{H_k} \tag{1}$$

where H_k is the reproducing kernel Hilbert space defined by a kernel k. $P(\cdot)$ and $Q(\cdot)$ are cumulative density functions. The commonly used inverse multi-quadratic kernel $k(x, y) = \frac{C}{C + \|x - y\|_2^2}$ is implemented for our experiments.

The MMD penalty can be estimated by empirical samples as:

$$\widehat{\text{MMD}} = \frac{1}{N(N-1)} \left(\sum_{n \neq m} k(\boldsymbol{h}^{(n)}, \boldsymbol{h}^{(m)}) + \sum_{n \neq m} k(\widetilde{\boldsymbol{h}}^{(n)}, \widetilde{\boldsymbol{h}}^{(m)}) \right)$$
$$- \frac{1}{N^2} \sum_{n,m} k(\boldsymbol{h}^{(n)}, \widetilde{\boldsymbol{h}}^{(m)}) \tag{2}$$

where $\widetilde{\boldsymbol{h}}^{(n)}$ is a sample from prior $p(\boldsymbol{h})$, and $\boldsymbol{h}^{(n)}$ is a sample from the aggregated posterior $q(\boldsymbol{h})$.

3.2 WAE with Gaussian Mixture Model Prior (GMM-WAE)

We use a Gaussian mixture model (GMM) as the prior for our WAE. This enables us to model text of different styles in the latent space of an autoencoder. The GMM prior is given by

$$p(\boldsymbol{h}) = \sum_{i=1}^{N} w_i \cdot \mathcal{N}(\boldsymbol{h}; \boldsymbol{\mu}_i, \text{diag}\,\boldsymbol{\sigma}_i^2) \tag{3}$$

where N is the pre-defined number of mixtures, w_i is the mixture probability satisfying $\sum_{i=1}^{N} w_i = 1$, and $w_i \geq 0$, and $\boldsymbol{\mu}_i$ and $\boldsymbol{\sigma}_i$ are Gaussian parameters.

There are multiple benefits from the GMM prior. First, many datasets are a combination of different styles or categories in a broader sense. Therefore, a machine learning model should account for this to learn a good representation of the data. Moreover, compared with training a separate model for each style, training a WAE with the GMM prior allows us to pool the knowledge of different styles together, alleviating the data sparsity problem of deep neural networks.

3.3 Training

The training of GMM-WAE involves three types of losses: reconstruction loss, the MMD loss, and a KL loss to prevent the stochasticity collapse.

For a data instance $\mathrm{x}^{(m)}$, the reconstruction objective aims to decode the same data instance x from a sampled latent code:

$$J_{\text{rec}} = \sum_m \mathbb{E}_{\boldsymbol{h} \sim q(\boldsymbol{h}|\mathrm{x}^{(m)})}[-\log p(\mathrm{x}^{(m)}|\boldsymbol{h})] \tag{4}$$

As shown in [2], a stochastic encoder tends to collapse to a deterministic one, i.e., $\sigma_i \rightarrow \mathbf{0}$. To address this, a Kullback–Leibler (KL) term is added to prevent the encoded Gaussian from collapsing to a Dirac delta function, given by

$$J_{\text{KL}} = \sum_m \text{KL}\left(\mathcal{N}(\boldsymbol{\mu}_{\text{post}}^{(m)}, \text{diag}(\boldsymbol{\sigma}_{\text{post}}^{(m)})^2) \| \mathcal{N}(\boldsymbol{\mu}_{\text{post}}^{(m)}, \mathbf{I})\right) \tag{5}$$

where we model the posterior as a Gaussian and $\boldsymbol{\mu}_{\text{post}}^{(m)}$ and $\boldsymbol{\sigma}_{\text{post}}^{(m)}$ are the predicted parameters. $\mathbf{I}$ is an identity matrix. Notice that the KL term differs from that in a variational autoencoder, as our KL does not pull the mean $\boldsymbol{\mu}_{\text{post}}^{(m)}$, but instead encourages $\boldsymbol{\sigma}_{\text{post}}^{(m)}$ to stretch so as to avoid stochasticity collapse.

Finally, an MMD-based Wasserstein loss is applied to each of the style categories, and the overall training objective is

$$J_{\text{GMM-WAE}} = J_{\text{AE}} + \lambda_{\text{KL}} \cdot J_{\text{KL}} + \lambda_{\text{MMD}} \cdot \sum_{j=1}^{N} \widehat{\text{MMD}}_j \tag{6}$$

where λ_{KL} and λ_{MMD} are hyperparameters weighing these terms.

In the training set, we assume each sample is labeled with its style, and the third term $\widehat{\text{MMD}}_j$ in (6) is the MMD loss applied to a specific style category. During training, we not only perform back-propagation to the encoder and decoder parameters, but also train the mixture of Gaussian parameters ($\boldsymbol{\mu}_i$ and $\boldsymbol{\sigma}_i$). In this way, we can learn a latent structure that explicitly models different styles of data, and in the meantime, data samples of all styles facilitate the training of the WAE model.

Figure 1a demonstrates the training process of our GMM-WAE.

3.4 Sentence Generation with GMM-WAE

Our GMM-WAE can be used in different ways for text generation. In this paper, we consider two settings: style-conditioned generation and style-iterpolated generation.

Style-Conditioned Sentence Generation. In this setup, we generate sentences conditioned on a specific style class. This can be done by setting $w_i = 1$ for the desired ith style and $w_j = 0$ for $j \neq i$. In other words, the latent vector is sampled from $\mathcal{N}(\boldsymbol{\mu}_i, \boldsymbol{\sigma}_i)$, and thus, the generated text will be of the desired style.

Style-Interpolated Sentence Generation. In this setup, generated sentences are conditioned on an interpolation between two latent vector samples. If we would like to generate a mixture of ith and jth styles with equal weights, we sample $\boldsymbol{h}_i \sim \mathcal{N}(\boldsymbol{\mu}_i, \boldsymbol{\sigma}_i)$ and $\boldsymbol{h}_j \sim \mathcal{N}(\boldsymbol{\mu}_j, \boldsymbol{\sigma}_j)$. Then, we mix these latent codes together by $\boldsymbol{h} = \frac{1}{2}\boldsymbol{h}_i + \frac{1}{2}\boldsymbol{h}_j$ for style-interpolated generation.

Figure 1b shows an overview of the inference process.

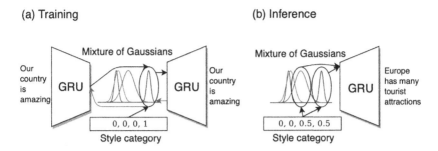

Fig. 1. Training and inference phases. The blue arrows represent backpropagation. During training, we are aware of the style category of each training sample. For inference, we may specify the target style (distribution) for stylized text generation. (Color figure online)

Table 1. Results of style-conditioned text generation.

	D-1↑	D-2↑	Entropy↑	(PPL)↓	Acc↑
Disentangled VAE	0.027	0.117	4.853	**73.81**	77.8
Separate WAE models	0.052	0.214	5.416	95.2	97.9
WAE	0.026	0.154	4.391	85.3	74.2
VAE	0.044	0.158	5.043	92.8	57.5
VAE + Multi	0.040	0.169	5.281	97.7	42.2
VAE + embedding	0.034	0.070	4.153	112.3	85.2
GMM-VAE	0.52	0.201	5.342	94.3	85.5
GMM-WAE (ours)	**0.067**	**0.465**	**5.883**	97.3	**85.8**

Table 2. Results of style-interpolated text generation.

	D-1↑	D-2↑	Entropy↑	(PPL)↓	JSD↓
WAE	0.035	0.207	4.829	91.9	**0.153**
VAE	0.041	0.167	5.001	92.0	0.239
VAE + Multi	0.039	0.169	5.250	98.2	0.178
VAE + embedding	0.038	0.172	5.102	**85.4**	0.160
GMM-VAE	0.044	0.197	5.330	88.4	0.148
GMM-WAE (ours)	**0.075**	**0.490**	**5.975**	99.6	0.161

4 Experiments

We evaluate our approaches with the sentences in the MNLI dataset [21], containing 433k sentences from five domains: Slate, Telephone, Government, Fiction, and Travel. Slate is removed due to its overlap with the other classes. Evaluations are conducted in two settings: (a) using all MNLI data points; (b) using smaller subsets of MNLI to simulate smaller datasets as illustrated in Fig. 2.

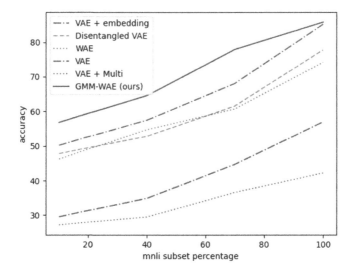

Fig. 2. Comparison of GMM-WAE with other baselines when trained on datasets of different sizes.

We compare our style-conditioned experiments with the following approaches:

- **Separate WAE models.** Four separate WAEs, each trained on an individual domain of MNLI.
- **VAE+embedding.** VAE with randomly initialized trainable class embeddings fed to the decoder [19].
- **Disentangled VAE.** VAE with auxiliary multi-task and adversarial objectives to disentangle latent representations of style and content [9].
- **VAE.** A vanilla VAE trained on the entire dataset. For style-conditioned generation, we sample from the distribution defined by the empirical mean and variance of training data points for each class.
- **GMM-VAE.** We also train a VAE with Gaussian mixture model prior. In GMM-VAE, we also assume the style (i.e., the GMM component) is known, so the KL divergence in GMM-VAE is directly applied to the corresponding Gaussian component.
- **WAE.** A vanilla WAE trained on the entire dataset. The same method was used for stylized generation as in VAE.
- **VAE+Multi.** A single VAE with a multi-task loss to classify the latent representation of each training sample based on their style.

4.1 Results

Style-Conditioned Results. We first analyze style-conditioned text generation, where we specify each domain as the target style and calculate the overall statistics in Table 1. As seen, GMM-WAE generates the most diverse sentences by a high margin. This is measured by entropy and D-1 + D-2 which are the percentage of distinct unigrams and bigrams following the work of [12] and [1]. This is because the decoder learns on a more diverse set of sentences when it is shared across all classes. Another important evaluation metric is the style accuracy. To calculate it we separately train a classifier to predict the style of the generated sentence. Following [4,9] we train a convolutional neural network (CNN) [10] for evaluating the style accuracy. The classifier achieves 98% classification accuracy on the original MNLI dataset. Results show that GMM-WAE outperforms all the single models in terms of the style accuracy. From the table, we also see that training separate WAEs yields the highest style accuracy. This, however, is not a single model and does not constitute a fair comparison.

Style-Interpolated Results. In this experiment, we select all possible two styles for interpolation with equal weights. To evaluate the success of style interpolation, we compute Jensen–Shannon Divergence (JSD) [13] of the unigram distribution against the sentences of the target two styles. Our model comes third. However, our model again outperforms all other approaches in sentence diversity.

Small-Data Training Results. Figure 2 provides the comparison of all approaches on datasets with different sizes. As shown, our model outperforms all the other models when the number of training samples is limited. The trend is consistent, showing that GMM-WAE is able to pool the knowledge of different classes together, which is beneficial to small-data training.

5   Conclusion

In this work, we present a Wasserstein autoencoder with Gaussian mixture model prior (GMM-WAE). We explicitly model the style of text by a component in the GMM prior. Compared with training separate models, our GMM-WAE is able to pool knowledge of different styles together, which is especially good for small-data training. Our GMM-WAE can be used for both style-conditioned generation and style-interpolated generation.

Acknowledgments. The research was supported in part by the Natural Sciences and Engineering Research Council of Canada (NSERC) under Grants RGPIN-2019-04897 and RGPIN-2020-04465. Lili Mou is supported by the Alberta Machine Intelligence Institute (Amii) Fellow Program and the Canada CIFAR AI (CCAI) Chair Program. This research was also enabled in part by the support of Compute Canada (www.computecanada.ca).

References

1. Bahuleyan, H., Mou, L., Vechtomova, O., Poupart, P.: Variational attention for sequence-to-sequence models. In: Proceedings of the 27th International Conference on Computational Linguistics, pp. 1672–1682. Association for Computational Linguistics (2018). https://www.aclweb.org/anthology/C18-1142
2. Bahuleyan, H., Mou, L., Zhou, H., Vechtomova, O.: Stochastic Wasserstein autoencoder for probabilistic sentence generation. In: Proceedings of the 2019 Conference of the North American Chapter of the Association for Computational Linguistics: Human Language Technologies, pp. 4068–4076 (2019). https://www.aclweb.org/anthology/N19-1411

3. Ben-Yosef, M., Weinshall, D.: Gaussian mixture generative adversarial networks for diverse datasets, and the unsupervised clustering of images. arXiv preprint arXiv:1808.10356 (2018). https://arxiv.org/abs/1808.10356

4. Fu, Z., Tan, X., Peng, N., Zhao, D., Yan, R.: Style transfer in text: exploration and evaluation. In: Proceedings of the Thirty-Second AAAI Conference on Artificial Intelligence, pp. 663–670 (2018). https://ojs.aaai.org/index.php/AAAI/article/view/11330

5. Gao, X., et al.: Structuring latent spaces for stylized response generation. In: Proceedings of the 2019 Conference on Empirical Methods in Natural Language Processing and the 9th International Joint Conference on Natural Language Processing, pp. 1814–1823 (2019). https://www.aclweb.org/anthology/D19-1190

6. Gaujac, B., Feige, I., Barber, D.: Gaussian mixture models with Wasserstein distance. arXiv preprint arXiv:1806.04465 (2018). https://arxiv.org/abs/1806.04465

7. Gu, X., Cho, K., Ha, J.W., Kim, S.: DialogWAE: multimodal response generation with conditional Wasserstein auto-encoder. In: International Conference on Learning Representations (2019). https://openreview.net/forum?id=BkgBvsC9FQ

8. Hu, Z., Yang, Z., Liang, X., Salakhutdinov, R., Xing, E.P.: Toward controlled generation of text. In: Proceedings of the 34th International Conference on Machine Learning-Volume 70, pp. 1587–1596. JMLR. org (2017)

9. John, V., Mou, L., Bahuleyan, H., Vechtomova, O.: Disentangled representation learning for non-parallel text style transfer. In: Proceedings of the 57th Annual Meeting of the Association for Computational Linguistics, pp. 424–434 (2019). https://www.aclweb.org/anthology/P19-1041

10. Kim, Y.: Convolutional neural networks for sentence classification. In: Proceedings of the 2014 Conference on Empirical Methods in Natural Language Processing, pp. 1746–1751 (2014). https://www.aclweb.org/anthology/D14-1181

11. Kingma, D.P., Welling, M.: Auto-encoding variational bayes. In: International Conference on Learning Representations (2014). https://openreview.net/forum?id=33X9fd2-9FyZd

12. Li, J., Galley, M., Brockett, C., Gao, J., Dolan, B.: A diversity-promoting objective function for neural conversation models. In: Proceedings of the 2016 Conference of the North American Chapter of the Association for Computational Linguistics: Human Language Technologies, pp. 110–119 (2016). https://www.aclweb.org/anthology/N16-1014/

13. Lin, J.: Divergence measures based on the Shannon entropy. IEEE Trans. Inf. Theory $37(1)$, 145–151 (1991). https://ieeexplore.ieee.org/abstract/document/61115/

14. Mou, L., Vechtomova, O.: Stylized text generation: approaches and applications. In: Proceedings of the 58th Annual Meeting of the Association for Computational Linguistics: Tutorial Abstracts, pp. 19–22 (2020). https://www.aclweb.org/anthology/2020.acl-tutorials.5

15. Shen, T., Lei, T., Barzilay, R., Jaakkola, T.: Style transfer from non-parallel text by cross-alignment. In: Advances in Neural Information Processing Systems, pp. 6830–6841 (2017). https://proceedings.neurips.cc/paper/2017/file/2d2c8394e31101a261abf1784302bf75-Paper.pdf

16. Shen, T., Ott, M., Auli, M., Ranzato, M.: Mixture models for diverse machine translation: tricks of the trade. In: Proceedings of the 36th International Conference on Machine Learning, pp. 5719–5728 (2019). http://proceedings.mlr.press/v97/shen19c.html

17. Sutskever, I., Vinyals, O., Le, Q.V.: Sequence to sequence learning with neural networks. In: Advances in Neural Information Processing Systems, pp. 3104–3112 (2014). https://papers.nips.cc/paper/2014/file/a14ac55a4f27472c5d894ec1c3c743d2-Paper.pdf

18. Tolstikhin, I., Bousquet, O., Gelly, S., Schoelkopf, B.: Wasserstein auto-encoders. In: International Conference on Learning Representations (2018). https://openreview.net/forum?id=HkL7n1-0b

19. Vechtomova, O., Bahuleyan, H., Ghabussi, A., John, V.: Generating lyrics with variational autoencoder and multi-modal artist embeddings. arXiv preprint arXiv:1812.08318 (2018). https://arxiv.org/abs/1812.08318
20. Wang, W., et al.: Topic-guided variational autoencoders for text generation. In: Proceedings of the 2019 Conference of the North American Chapter of the Association for Computational Linguistics: Human Language Technologies, pp. 166–177 (2019). https://www.aclweb.org/anthology/N19-1015
21. Williams, A., Nangia, N., Bowman, S.: A broad-coverage challenge corpus for sentence understanding through inference. In: Proceedings of the 2018 Conference of the North American Chapter of the Association for Computational Linguistics: Human Language Technologies, pp. 1112–1122 (2018). http://aclweb.org/anthology/N18-1101
22. Xu, R., Ge, T., Wei, F.: Formality style transfer with hybrid textual annotations. arXiv preprint arXiv:1903.06353 (2019). https://arxiv.org/abs/1903.06353

Text

Evaluating Semantic Similarity Methods to Build Semantic Predictability Norms of Reading Data

Sidney Leal[1(✉)], Edresson Casanova[1], Gustavo Paetzold[2], and Sandra Aluísio[1]

[1] Instituto de Ciências Matemáticas e de Computação, Universidade de São Paulo (USP),
São Carlos, Brazil
{sidleal,edresson}@usp.br, sandra@icmc.usp.br
[2] Universidade Tecnológica Federal do Paraná (UTFPR) - Campus Toledo, Toledo, Brazil
ghpaetzold@utfpr.edu.br

Abstract. Predictability corpora built via Cloze task generally accompany eye-tracking data for the study of processing costs of linguistic structures in tasks of reading for comprehension. Two semantic measures are commonly calculated to evaluate expectations about forthcoming words: (i) the semantic fit of the target word with the previous context of a sentence, and (ii) semantic similarity scores that represent the semantic similarity between the target word and Cloze task responses for it. For Brazilian Portuguese (BP), there was no large eye-tracking corpora with predictability norms. The goal of this paper is to present a method to calculate the two semantic measures used in the first BP corpus of eye movements during silent reading of short paragraphs by undergraduate students. The method was informed by a large evaluation of both static and contextualized word embeddings, trained on large corpora of texts. Here, we make publicly available: (i) a BP corpus for a sentence-completion task to evaluate semantic similarity, (ii) a new methodology to build this corpus based on the scores of Cloze data taken from our project, and (iii) a hybrid method to compute the two semantic measures in order to build predictability corpora in BP.

Keywords: Semantic predictability · Cloze test · Language models

1 Introduction

Predictability is defined as how much a word can be predicted based on its previous context, i.e., as the probability of knowing a word before reading it. According to Bianchi et al. [1] the task of predictability of a given word is fundamental to analyse the behaviour that humans process information during reading. Predictability corpora are commonly built via Cloze task and generally accompany eye-tracking data for the study of processing costs of linguistic structures in tasks of reading for comprehension [4]. However, only few resources exist, for a small number of languages, for example, English [16], English and French [12], and German [13]. For Brazilian Portuguese, there was no large eye-tracking corpus with predictability norms such as those cited above. In order to fulfill this gap, a large corpus with eye movements during silent reading by undergraduate students was built. The RastrOS corpus is composed of short paragraphs of authentic

© Springer Nature Switzerland AG 2021
K. Ekštein et al. (Eds.): TSD 2021, LNAI 12848, pp. 35–47, 2021.
https://doi.org/10.1007/978-3-030-83527-9_3

texts in Brazilian Portuguese (BP) taken from different textual genres. Thus, it allows an assessment of the combined influence of a set of linguistic-textual factors that can affect linguistic processing during reading, in less artificial conditions for carrying out the task.

In the Provo project [15], using Cloze probabilities as predictors of reading via eye movement patterns, Luke and Christianson (2016) found that for the English language, highly predictable words were quite rare (5% of content words and 20% of function words), and most words had a more-expected candidate consistently available from context even when word identity was not. A highly predictable word is the one which has a high Cloze probability. In Provo, words with .67 or higher probability of being completed by a specific single word were considered highly predictable. In addition, they found that predictability of partial semantic and syntactic information influenced reading times above and beyond Cloze scores, suggesting that predictions generated from context are most often graded rather than full lexical prediction.

The RastrOS corpus was inspired by the Provo project methodology and, therefore, it has three types of Cloze scores: full-orthographic form, PoS and inflectional proper-ties, and semantic predictability scores for all 2494 words in the 50 text paragraphs. In this study, we deal with the semantic predictability, which is divided in two measures: (i) the semantic predictability between the target word of a sentence and the participant's responses, to inform predictability studies that evaluate the role of knowledge of the paradigmatic structure of language and (ii) the semantic fit of the target word with the previous context of a sentence, used in eye-tracking analyses on the knowledge of the language's syntagmatic structure. Although the Provo project has chosen to use Latent Semantic Analysis (LSA) [14] to provide both semantic scores, for BP we have decided to evaluate word embeddings models from two families of methods: (i) those that work with a co-occurrence word matrix, such as LSA, and (ii) predictive methods such as Word2Vec [17] and FastText [2]. We also evaluate one contextualized word representa-tion model—BERT [6], recently trained for BP [23]. Moreover, in the Provo project, the implementation of the semantic predictability between the target word and the partici-pant's responses is made by using the cosine of the angle between the vectors of responses and targets which is a very used distance measure to quantify semantic similarity between words in distributional semantics models. However, it is important to evaluate different distributional semantics models than those that combine single word vectors into a sen-tence context vector using the sum or average of the words' individual embeddings (see [8]) to implement the other semantic measure—semantic fit of the target word with the previous context of a sentence. This decision is important and was pursued to inform Psycholinguistic studies in BP and to allow a great diversity of uses for the RastrOS cor-pus. To the best of our knowledge, there are no publicly available sentence completion task corpora for BP. Therefore, we propose to evaluate semantic similarity using a new dataset for sentence completion task [30,31], which was created in this study. As the dataset of the RastrOS project[1] is composed of sentences from three different genres, we decided to use the same dataset to evaluate several similarity methods.

The remainder of this paper is organized as follows. Section 2 reviews approaches to sentence completion task. Section 3 describes an initial version of the RastrOS corpus

---

[1] http://www.nilc.icmc.usp.br/nilc/index.php/rastros.

used in the evaluations of semantic similarity methods for building the semantic predictability scores of our final corpus. Section 4 presents the process of building our Sentence Completion dataset using Cloze data. Section 5 presents the evaluation of static and contextualized word embeddings using the new dataset created, human benchmark performance, and also the hybrid method to calculate semantic scores proposed for the RastrOS project.

2   Review on Sentence Completion Task and Datasets

The Sentence Completion task was defined in 2011 [30] and consists in, given a sentence with a gap, guessing what word or phrase would best fit the gap.

Early approaches to Sentence Completion employ classic language modelling techniques, such as n-gram language models [29], backoff and class-based models [3,31]. There are also examples of strategies that rely on hand-crafted metrics [27] and word similarity metrics that measure the similarity between each possible answer and the words in the sentence to be completed [31]. More recently, different variants of Recurrent Neural Networks (RNN) models have been used as an alternative to hand-crafted metrics and features. [24] addresses the task using Recurrent Memory Networks, of which the structure is more easily interpretable than regular RNNs. Mirowski and Vlachos [18] also finds that incorporating dependency relations throughout the training process also improves on the performance of regular RNNs for the task. Current state-of-the-art approaches rely on BERT models. Devlin et al. (2019) achieved impressive results in a large Sentence Completion dataset with 113,000 instances [6]. Using another BERT variant that operates at word-level, Park and Park (2020) achieves even more impressive results in two separate Sentence Completion datasets [20].

Because they are relatively easy to obtain, Sentence Completion datasets are abundant for the English language. Some of them are the Microsoft Research Sentence Completion (MRSC) dataset [30], composed of questions from Project Gutenberg novels, and the SAT dataset [27], composed of questions from practice SAT exams. One can also find datasets with questions taken from children's books [11], online newspaper articles [10], summaries [5], mundane everyday stories [19], and college/high-school entrance exams [28]. Nevertheless, datasets for languages other than English are much scarce. The TOPIK dataset [20] for Korean is the only example we could find.

3   The Initial Version of the RastrOS Corpus

The RastrOS project is multicentric and has two phases of data collection with participants. First, cloze scores were collected via an online survey for each word, except the first one, in our 50-paragraph corpus. Each participant read 5 paragraphs from the pool of 50 ones. Second, these same paragraphs were presented to a different set of participants, who read them while their eye movements were being tracked. In the RastrOS project, a high-accuracy eye-tracker was used—the EyeLink 1000 Desktop Mount.

Cloze. For this study we are using project's initial data, without applying exclusion criteria, to inform the implementation of semantic measures of the final project. In total, data from 314 people (172 females) were included. Participants' ages ranged from 17 to 73 years (Average: 22; SD: 7.4); 309 participants filled in the age field. Participants were university undergraduate students and approximately 5.71% were graduated or initiating postgraduate education. Participants completed an online survey administered through a web-based software developed in the RastrOS project. Participants first answered a few demographic questions (gender, age, education level, language history), then proceeded to complete the main body of the survey. For the first question of a paragraph, only the first word in the text was visible. For each question of the survey, participants were instructed to fill each gap that, in their assessment, allows them to follow the linguistic material previously read. As soon as they typed a word, the text with the word expected in the gap was displayed and a new gap appeared. For each new sentence in the paragraph the initial word was displayed. This same procedure was repeated until the paragraph was completed. Each participant was assigned to complete five random paragraphs, giving responses for an average of 245 different words. For each word in each text, an average of 26 participants provided a response (range: 20–33). Responses were edited for spelling. When a response contained multiple words, the first word was coded.

Data. Fifty short passages were taken from a variety of sources, including online news articles, popular science magazines, and literary texts. These 50 different text paragraphs are composed of 120 sentences and their 257 segmented clauses (see Table 1). We also annotated clauses formed by non-finite verbs or small non-finite verb clauses together with finite clauses of our corpus, in order to indicate the number of non-finite verb clauses in the corpus. Moreover, we segmented appositives and parenthetical expressions, adding them to the total of different clause types. It is important to note that several small clauses of several types were kept together with others in the process of segmentation, although their types were annotated. The paragraphs were an average of 49 words long (range: 36–70) and contained 2 sentences on average (range: 1–5). Sentences were on average 20 words long (range: 3–60). Across all texts, there were 2494

Table 1. Statistics of the RastrOS Corpus.

Number of paragraphs	50
Number of sentences	120
Number of clauses	257
Independent clauses (simple clauses)	27
Main clauses (in complex or compound-complex sentences)	72
Coordinate clauses	55
Subordinate nominal and adverbial clauses (dependent clauses)	73
Nonrestrictive and restrictive relative causes (dependent clauses)	40
Non-finite clauses	26
Appositives and parenthetical expressions	17
Number of words	2494
Number of types	1237

words total (2831 tokens including punctuation), including 1237 unique word forms. Table 1 summarizes some statistics of our corpus.

The words were tagged for part of speech (PoS) using the nlpnet tagger [7]. In total, the 50 passages contained 1438 content words (186 adjectives, 119 adverbs, 756 nouns, and 377 verbs) and 992 function words (143 conjunctions, 234 determiners, 445 prepositions, 170 pronouns), and 67 other words and symbols. In addition, inflectional information was also coded for the words within each class where appropriate, using the Unitex-PB Dictionary [25]. Nouns and adjectives were coded for gender and number and verbs were coded for person. Target words ranged from 1 to 18 letters (or hyphen) long (M:4). The frequency of each target word was obtained from the brWaC corpus [26], a large web corpus for Brazilian Portuguese. Word frequencies ranged from 0 to 120 (M:17) words per million. Transitional probabilities, which have been implicated as a possible source of contextual information in reading, were computed from the brWaC corpus by dividing the frequency of the collocation of the target word and the previous word (e.g., the frequency of "I agree") by the frequency of the previous word alone (e.g., the frequency of "I" in all contexts). This provides an estimate of the predictability of the upcoming word, given that the reader has just encountered the previous word.

4   Building the Sentence Completion Dataset via Cloze Data

In this work, the list of alternatives for the target words of a given sentence was obtained from the responses of the students who participated in the Cloze test of the RastrOS project. The Cloze test guarantees a left-context to fill each new gap in a given sentence, using the student's language model. In paragraphs with more than one sentence, Cloze's final sentences gain an even greater context than is provided by the preceding sentences, but it is still a local context; only the last gap in the last sentence of a paragraph provides the overall context for the student to fill in the missing word. The number of sentences in the corpus used by the Cloze test of the RastrOS project is smaller than the one of MRSC dataset which has 1040 sentences, and although small it is a challenging dataset of 113 sentences. Seven sentences were discarded as their contexts were too restrictive for presenting several good distractors. The automatic procedure presented in Sect. 4.1 generates a report to help the human judgement about the four distractors, which is described in Sect. 4.2.

4.1   Automatically Generating Alternates

For each sentence in the dataset, the answers of the cloze test were used as candidate words, following the rules below.

1. Only content target words were selected, from the middle of the sentence to its end, as this interval provides a better decision context for the participants of Cloze. For example, Sentence 1 in Table 2 has 15 words, therefore starting from the word "foi", the content words were presented with their frequency in the brWaC. In addition, two metrics that help to analyze the scenario of participant's choice are also presented: (i) Orthographic Match (Match), which is the total human hits divided by total human responses; and (ii) Certainty (Cert), the amount of modal response divided by total human responses (humans may have been wrong, but they agreed with the error);

2. The responses of the participants were grouped and ordered from the most frequent to the least frequent;
3. Application of a filter to remove responses with grammatical classes (PoS tag) other than the one of the target word;
4. In the second filter, all synonyms of the target word were removed, using a BP thesaurus (sinonimos.com.br) as a resource;
5. Then, the candidate words and their answers were ranked by frequency (from the rarest to the most frequent);
6. The generated report shows the sentence paragraphs to facilitate the initial human assessment;
7. The report also shows synonyms from the chosen thesaurus sinonimos.com.br of each alternative. The synonyms are ranked by frequency in brWaC to facilitate the choice of the less frequent ones.

Table 2. Excerpt of the report generated by the rules in Sect. 4.1. It shows a sentence of the dataset and 5 target words for human evaluation, ordered by frequency in brWaC. Next to each target word there is its PoS, and the values of the Freq, Match and Cert metrics, followed by the list of responses from the Cloze test, already filtered by PoS and synonyms. The target "ciência" is presented in bold as it was chosen by the rules presented in Sect. 4.2.

Sentence 1: *A invenção do zero pelos humanos foi crucial para a matemática e a ciência modernas.* (The invention of zero by humans was crucial to modern mathematics and science.)				
crucial (ADJ)	F:28041	M:0	C:0.4	[responsável]
modernas (ADJ)	F:38839	M:0	C:0.09	[moderna, exata, comum]
matemática (N)	F:66257	M:0.25	C:0.25	[evolução, humanidade, compreensão, ciência, história]
ciência (N)	F:234713	M:0.03	C:0.28	[física, invenção, geometria, abstração, sociedade, calculadora]
foi (N)	F:8232437	M:0.68	C:0.68	[é, trouxe, contribuiu]

4.2 Human Judgment

The initial human choice is related to the triplet: **target word (PoS) // Metrics of the target word (Freq, Match, Cert) // list of alternatives**, which must meet the following 8 rules, which are based on the rules used in the MRSC dataset.

1. Give preference to the rarest target word, with a long list of alternatives.
2. Use the metrics Match and Cert to generate a more challenging dataset.
3. The list of alternatives must contain options that are grammatically correct.
4. Choose alternatives that require some analysis to arrive at the answer.
5. Alternatives that require understanding properties of entities that are mentioned in the sentence are desirable.
6. Dictionary use is encouraged, if necessary.

7. The correct answer should always be a significantly better fit for that sentence than each of the four distractors; it should be possible to write down an explanation as to why the correct answer is the correct answer, that would persuade most reasonable people.
8. The partial list of candidates for a given sentence may include synonyms (taken from sinonimos.com.br) of the candidates if it is necessary to complete the list when the number of alternates is less than four.

Following the Rule 1 for the sentence in Table 2, the words "matemática/Maths" and "ciência/Science" are strong candidates, as they have 8 and 9 alternatives, respectively. With Rule 2, we can see that "matemática" is a relatively predictable word (Match 0.25) and many students agreed on the prediction (Cert 0.25), so for a challenging dataset it would be better not to use it. "ciência" is a better choice, since few students got it right (0.03) and many chose it wrong, but they agreed on the choice that the answer was "física/Physics" (0.28). Checking Rule 3: In the list of alternatives of the word "ciência", all alternatives generate a grammatically correct sentence. Rule 4 helps to exclude the alternatives "física" and "computação/Computer Science", as they are large areas of "ciência"; it also helps to exclude"abstração/abstraction" and "calculadora/calculator", as they are words closely related to the target word "ciência", although not synonyms. Words related to the target word via semantic similarity that are correct in the global context of the sentence must be eliminated. Applying Rule 5, we understand that the alternatives "geometria/Geometry" and "álgebra/Algebra" require analysis of the part-whole relation, since they are subjects of "matemática", so they are chosen; "sociedade/society" remains a viable alternative. Applying Rule 7, the alternative "sociedade" is eliminated, as it fits the sentence very well. It is also noted that "geometria" and "álgebra" are not correct answers, as they are disciplines of "matemática", a word that appears previously in the sentence. Following the seven rules above, the alternatives chosen for "ciência" were: [geometria, língua, álgebra]. Applying Rule 8, another synonym of "língua/language" was chosen. Thus, for the sentence in Table 2, the final list is: [geometria, álgebra, língua, fala]/[geometry, algebra, language, speech] and the final question is presented in Fig. 1.

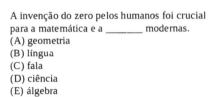

Fig. 1. An example question included in the sentence completion dataset via Cloze data.

5   Evaluation Results and the Hybrid Method Proposed

Corpora and Models Evaluated. As the sentence completion task involves training a method on a large corpus of plain text to then try to predict the missing words in the test set, in this work we are using pretrained static word embeddings available in two large word embeddings repository for BP, described below.

1. NILC Embeddings repository[2] contains models trained on a large corpus composed of 17 Portuguese subcorpora, including literary works in public domain and a collection of classic fiction books, totalizing 1.3 billion tokens. The models were generated using Word2Vec, FastText, Wang2Vec (all three available in both Skip-gram and CBOW versions) and Glove. The models are available in 50, 100, 300, 600 and 1000 dimensions [9].
2. PUCRS BBP Embeddings repository[3] uses a corpus of 4.9 billion tokens, composed of three publicly available resources: brWaC [26], a large multi-domain web corpus for Brazilian Portuguese, with 2.7 billion tokens, BlogSet-BR [21], a Brazilian Portuguese corpus containing 2.1 billions words extracted from 7.4 millions posts over 808 thousand different Brazilian blogs, and a dump of Wikipedia articles in Brazilian Portuguese from 2019-03-01. There are four models available: 300-d Skip-gram and CBOW trained with Word2Vec and 300-d Skip-gram and CBOW trained with FastText [22].

$BERT_{Base}$ and $BERT_{Large}$ and LSA models were trained on part of BBP Embeddings corpus—the brWaC corpus, cited above. LSA model was trained in this work with 300 dimensions. For static word representation vectors, the Word2Vec [17] and FastText [2] models were used, both with 300 dimensions and trained with the CBOW architecture, that predicts a word given a context, on both BBP and NILC corpora.

Following Zweig et al. (2012), we used Total Word Similarity method to evaluate the static word embeddings models presented in Table 3. First the embeddings of the candidate answers (four distractors) and the correct answer for the sentence were calculated, then the embeddings of the rest of the words in the sentence were obtained. For each candidate answer, the total similarity between it and the words of the rest of the sentence was calculated using the cosine distance (using the sum of word vectors). The candidate answer with the shortest distance was chosen.

Table 3. Evaluation results (accuracy) on the sentence completion dataset of the RastrOS project.

Method	Corpus	Hits	Accuracy
LSA	brWaC	26/113	23.01%
Word2Vec	BBP	36/113	31.86%
Word2Vec	NILC	32/113	28.32%
FastText	BBP	39/113	34.51%
FastText	NILC	26/113	23,01%
$BERT_{Base}$	brWaC	65/113	57.52%
$BERT_{Large}$	brWaC	66/113	**58.41%**

[2] http://www.nilc.icmc.usp.br/embeddings.
[3] https://www.inf.pucrs.br/linatural/wordpress/pucrs-bbp-embeddings/.

To use BERT trained in Portuguese by Souza et al. (2020), we chose the model in the Masked Language Model task, where the objective is to predict the masked word. We proposed the following method. First we pass the sentence over to BERT and mask the word that we must complete. Then, we activate the model to obtain the predicted list of tokens from the BERT's trained model vocabulary, ordered by probability. Finally, we choose the highest probability among the five alternatives of the sentence completion dataset of the RastrOS project.

The BERT Large model achieved the best results with **58.41%** accuracy. Although the NILC embeddings corpus contains a wide variety of textual genres, including the literary genre, the models trained on it performed below the same models trained on the BBP corpus. Finally, although the BERT models were trained on a smaller corpus than the largest corpus we used (BBP), they stood out for the task, in the dataset created.

Human Performance. To provide human benchmark performance, we asked six Brazilian native speaking graduate researchers to answer the questions on a small subset with 20 questions. The average accuracy was 76% (range: 60%–85%) and Kappa Fleiss value of 0.59. Zweig and Burges (2011) cite a human performance of 91% (an unaffiliated human answer) on the MRSC dataset in a random subset of 100 questions and Zweig et al. (2012) cite a human performance for high-scholar's (six of them) of 87% accuracy and for graduate students (five students) of 95%, on a dev-test with 95 questions.

Hybrid Method to Calculate Semantic Scores. In the RastrOS project, we calculated the semantic similarity scores—the semantic fit of the target word with the previous context of a sentence, and semantic similarity scores that represent the semantic similarity between the target word and Cloze task responses—differently than Provo project. We calculated both semantic measures taking the previous context in consideration in order to take advantage of BERT results in our sentence completion dataset. We used BERT models trained in Portuguese by Souza et al. (2020) in the task of Masked Language Model, where the objective is to predict the masked word. We proposed the following method to calculate the similarity between two words (target and response predicted) given a context:

1. We pass a sentence to BERT and mask the target word. For example, for the Sentence 1 of our dataset: *A invenção do zero pelos humanos foi crucial para a matemática e a ciência modernas.*, in the task semantic fit we use the context, the target word and the highest probability response predicted by BERT (Task 1). To calculate the semantic similarity between the target word and Cloze task responses we use the context, the target word and a student' response, each time (Task 2) (see Table 4).
2. Then, we activate the model obtaining the probability **p** of the prediction for each vocabulary token of the BERT model.
3. Using these probabilities, for each task shown above we calculate the distance between two possible candidates using the following equation: $dist(p1, p2) = \|p1 - p2\|$, considering $p1$ and $p2$ the probabilities of predicted model for candidate 1 and 2, respectively.
4. After calculating these values for each of the instances of our corpus, we normalize the values using the following equation:

$s(p1, p2, max\_dist) = 1 - (dist(p1, p2)/max\_dist)$, considering max_dist as the largest of the distances obtained for the given task. Thus, obtaining a value between 0 and 1 that shows how similar two words are given a previous context; we consider 1 the most similar.

Table 4. Example using BERT model to predict the values for the two tasks addressed in this study. P1 is the first word, P2 is the second word, O is the Model output before normalization and N after normalization.

Context: [**A invenção do zero pelos humanos foi crucial para a**]	
Task 1: Semantic Fit	P1: **ciência** (Target Word)
	P2: **física** (BERT Prediction)
	O: 0.53 N: **0.97**
Task 2: Semantic Similarity	P1: **ciência** (Target Word)
	P2: **geometria** (Student response)
	O: 3.37 N: **0.83**

However, BERT has a limited vocabulary since low frequency words (rare words) of the training corpus are grouped in the token *UNK* during the training phase. Therefore, the token *UNK* brings the inflated probability of a group of words. The results of this fact are that our proposed method does not provide good results for about 29% of words in the dataset of sentence completion when using the model BERT$_{Large}$, for example. To solve this limitation, we proposed a hybrid method. For those words that are not present in the dictionary of the trained BERT model, the similarity is calculated using the cosine distance of our best static embedding model, evaluated in the dataset of the Sentence Completion task (see Table 3): the FastText trained on the BBP corpus.

6   Conclusions

In this paper, we presented the Cloze Task in the RastrOS project, which has Cloze scores for the full-orthographic form, PoS and inflectional properties and semantic scores for all 2494 words in the 50 text paragraphs. Here, we contributed with: (i) the sentence completion task for BP making available a new **test set** with 113 questions[4]; (ii) a new methodology to build the test set for the sentence completion task, using the scores of Cloze data; and (iii) a hybrid method to calculate the semantic scores based on an evaluation of static and contextualized word embeddings. Although there are several approaches to create a sentence completion dataset (see Sect. 2) we took advantage of Cloze results, using the most difficult answers for students. While our test dataset is small compared with others for English, it is very challenging, given that average human accuracy was 76% in comparison to MRSC's 91%. The procedure created to produce this new test set can be applied in other eye-tracking projects in BP which provide Cloze

---

[4] Dataset and evaluation sources are available at: https://github.com/sidleal/TSD2021.

scores for all the words of a sentence. As far we know, there is no other study evaluating the proposed approach here to build semantic predictability norms, using contextualized word representations like BERT, ELMo, GPT-2. Our work is the most similar to Bianchi et al. (2020) that evaluate different word embeddings models (LSA, Word2Vec, Fast-Text) and N-gram-based language models to estimate how humans predict words in a Cloze test in order to understand eye movements in long Spanish texts. In contrast to Bianchi et al. (2020), we gave a step further regarding the choice of pretrained models as we evaluated a contextualized word representation (BERT) which was important to implement the semantic fit in our work. We understand that BERT is a better fit as this measure requires the calculation of the distance between the embedding of the target word and its entire previous context. We hope that our study opens a bridge between Psycholinguistics and Natural Language Processing to inform new projects in BP.

At the end of the RastrOS project, in July 2021, both sets of data (predictability norms and eye-tracking data) will be publicly available in the OSF platform as part of the RastrOS Corpus.

References

1. Bianchi, B., Monzón, G.B., Ferrer, L., Slezak, D.F., Shalom, D.E., Kamienkowski, J.E.: Human and computer estimations of predictability of words in written language. Sci. Rep. **10**(4396), 1–11 (2020)
2. Bojanowski, P., Grave, E., Joulin, A., Mikolov, T.: Enriching word vectors with subword information. Trans. Assoc. Comput. Linguisti. **5**, 135–146 (2017)
3. Correia, R., Baptista, J., Eskenazi, M., Mamede, N.: Automatic generation of *Cloze* question stems. In: Caseli, H., Villavicencio, A., Teixeira, A., Perdigão, F. (eds.) PROPOR 2012. LNCS (LNAI), vol. 7243, pp. 168–178. Springer, Heidelberg (2012). https://doi.org/10.1007/978-3-642-28885-2_19
4. Demberg, V., Keller, F.: Data from eye-tracking corpora as evidence for theories of syntactic processing complexity. Cognition **109**(2), 192–210 (2008)
5. Deutsch, D., Roth, D.: Summary cloze: a new task for content selection in topic-focused summarization. In: Proceedings of the 2019 Conference on Empirical Methods in Natural Language Processing and the 9th International Joint Conference on Natural Language Processing (EMNLP-IJCNLP). pp. 3711–3720 (2019)
6. Devlin, J., Chang, M.W., Lee, K., Toutanova, K.: BERT: Pre-training of deep bidirectional transformers for language understanding. In: Proceedings of the 2019 Conference of the North American Chapter of the Association for Computational Linguistics: Human Language Technologies, Vol. 1 (Long and Short Papers). pp. 4171–4186. Association for Computational Linguistics, Minneapolis (2019). https://doi.org/10.18653/v1/N19-1423
7. Fonseca, E.F., Garcia Rosa, J.L., Aluísio, Maria, S.: Evaluating word embeddings and a revised corpus for part-of-speech tagging in portuguese. J. Braz. Comput. Soc, Open Access **21**(2), 1340 (2015)
8. Frank, S.: Word embedding distance does not predict word reading time. In: Proceedings of the 39th Annual Conference of the Cognitive Science Society (CogSci). pp. 385–390. Cognitive Science Society, Austin (2017)
9. Hartmann, N.S., Fonseca, E.R., Shulby, C.D., Treviso, M.V., Rodrigues, J.S., Aluísio, S.M.: Portuguese word embeddings: evaluating on word analogies and natural language tasks. In: Anais do XI Simpósio Brasileiro de Tecnologia da Informação e da Linguagem Humana, pp. 122–131. SBC, Porto Alegre(2017)

10. Hermann, K.M. et al .: Teaching machines to read and comprehend. In: Advances in Neural Information Processing Systems pp. 1693–1701 (2015)
11. Hill, F., Bordes, A., Chopra, S., Weston, J.: The goldilocks principle: reading children's books with explicit memory representations. arXiv preprint arXiv:1511.02301 (2015)
12. Kennedy, A., Pynte, J., Murray, W.S., Paul, S.A.: Frequency and predictability effects in the dundee corpus: an eye movement analysis. Q. J. Exp. Psychol. **66**(3), 601–618 (2013). https://doi.org/10.1080/17470218.2012.676054
13. Kliegl, R., Grabner, E., Rolfs, M., Engbert, R.: Length, frequency, and predictability effects of words on eye movements in reading. Eur. J. Cogn. Psychol. **16**(1/2), 262–284 (2004)
14. Landauer, T.K., Laham, D., Rehder, B., Schreiner, M.E.: How well can passage meaning be derived without using word order? A comparison of latent semantic analysis and humans. In: Shafto, M.G., Langley, P. (eds.) Proceedings of the 19th Annual Meeting of the Cognitive Science Society. pp. 412–417 (1997)
15. Luke, S.G., Christianson, K.: Limits on lexical prediction during reading. Cogn. Psychol. **88**, 22–60 (2016). https://doi.org/10.1016/j.cogpsych.2016.06.002
16. Luke, S.G., Christianson, K.: The provo corpus: a large eye-tracking corpus with predictability norms. Behav. Res. Methods **50**, 826–833 (2018)
17. Mikolov, T., Chen, K., Corrado, G., Dean, J.: Efficient estimation of word representations in vector space. In: Bengio, Y., LeCun, Y. (eds.) 1st International Conference on Learning Representations (ICLR 2013), Scottsdale, Arizona, USA, May 2–4, 2013, Workshop Track Proceedings (2013)
18. Mirowski, P., Vlachos, A.: Dependency recurrent neural language models for sentence completion. In: Proceedings of the 53rd Annual Meeting of the Association for Computational Linguistics and the 7th International Joint Conference on Natural Language Processing (Vol. 2: Short Papers). pp. 511–517 (2015)
19. Mostafazadeh, N., Roth, M., Louis, A., Chambers, N., Allen, J.: Lsdsem 2017 shared task: the story cloze test. In: Proceedings of the 2nd Workshop on Linking Models of Lexical, Sentential and Discourse-level Semantics, pp. 46–51 (2017)
20. Park, H., Park, J.: Assessment of word-level neural language models for sentence completion. Appl. Sci. **10**(4), 1340 (2020)
21. Santos, H., Woloszyn, V., Vieira, R.: BlogSet-BR: a Brazilian Portuguese blog corpus. In: Proceedings of the Eleventh International Conference on Language Resources and Evaluation (LREC). pp. 661–664 (2018)
22. Santos, J., Consoli, B., dos Santos, C., Terra, J., Collonini, S., Vieira, R.: Assessing the impact of contextual embeddings for Portuguese named entity recognition. In: 2019 8th Brazilian Conference on Intelligent Systems (BRACIS). pp. 437–442 (2019)
23. Souza, F., Nogueira, R., Lotufo, R.: BERTimbau: pretrained BERT models for Brazilian Portuguese. In: Cerri, R., Prati, R.C. (eds.) BRACIS 2020. LNCS (LNAI), vol. 12319, pp. 403–417. Springer, Cham (2020). https://doi.org/10.1007/978-3-030-61377-8_28
24. Tran, K., Bisazza, A., Monz, C.: Recurrent memory networks for language modeling. In: Proceedings of the 2016 Conference of the North American Chapter of the Association for Computational Linguistics: Human Language Technologies, pp. 321–331. Association for Computational Linguistics, San Diego, June 2016
25. Vale, O.A., Baptista, J.: Novo dicionário de formas flexionadas do unitex-pb avaliação da flexão verbal. In: Anais do X Simpósio Brasileiro de Tecnologia da Informação e da Linguagem Humana, pp. 171–180. Brazilian Computer Society, Porto Alegre (2015)
26. Wagner Filho, J.A., Wilkens, R., Idiart, M., Villavicencio, A.: The brWaC corpus: a new open resource for Brazilian Portuguese. In: Proceedings of the Eleventh International Conference on Language Resources and Evaluation (LREC), pp. 4339–4344 (2018)

27. Woods, A.: Exploiting linguistic features for sentence completion. In: Proceedings of the 54th Annual Meeting of the Association for Computational Linguistics (Vol. 2: Short Papers), pp. 438–442 (2016)
28. Xie, Q., Lai, G., Dai, Z., Hovy, E.: Large-scale cloze test dataset created by teachers. In: Proceedings of the 2018 Conference on Empirical Methods in Natural Language Processing, pp. 2344–2356. Association for Computational Linguistics (2018)
29. Yuret, D.: Ku: Word sense disambiguation by substitution. In: Proceedings of the 4th International Workshop on Semantic Evaluations, pp. 207–213. Association for Computational Linguistics (2007)
30. Zweig, G., Burges, C.J.C.: The microsoft research sentence completion challenge. Tech. Rep., Microsoft Research, Technical Report MSR-TR-2011-129 (2011)
31. Zweig, G., Platt, J.C., Meek, C., Burges, C.J., Yessenalina, A., Liu, Q.: Computational approaches to sentence completion. In: Proceedings of the 50th Annual Meeting of the Association for Computational Linguistics (vol. 1: Long Papers), pp. 601–610. Association for Computational Linguistics, Jeju Island, July 2012

SYN2020: A New Corpus of Czech
with an Innovated Annotation

Tomáš Jelínek[✉], Jan Křivan, Vladimír Petkevič, Hana Skoumalová,
and Jana Šindlerová

Faculty of Arts, Charles University, Prague, Czech Republic
{tomas.jelinek,jan.krivan,vladimir.petkevic,hana.skoumalova,
jana.sindlerova}@ff.cuni.cz

Abstract. The paper introduces the SYN2020 corpus, a newly released representative corpus of written Czech following the tradition of the Czech National Corpus SYN series. The design of SYN2020 incorporates several substantial new features in the area of segmentation, lemmatization and morphological tagging, such as a new treatment of lemma variants, a new system for identifying morphological categories of verbs or a new treatment of multiword tokens. The annotation process, including data and tools used, is described, and the tools and accuracy of the annotation are discussed as well.

Keywords: SYN2020 corpus · Lemmatization · Part-of-speech and morphological annotation · Lemmas and sublemmas · Treatment of multiword tokens · Morphological categories of verbal participles

1 Introduction

The Czech National Corpus Institute has been publishing synchronous written corpora of the Czech language (SYN series corpora) since 2000.[1] With almost 500,000 queries a year, it is currently one of the most widely used language corpora resources in the Czech Republic. The latest SYN2020 corpus is characterized by an innovated concept of linguistic markup and by several new features that will make it easier for the user to work with the corpus and provide him with more detailed information. The corpus will thus become the new standard for most Czech corpora issued by the Czech National Corpus. The KonText search environment offers some new features, too.

Among the new features, the most important one for less advanced users is a new **sublemma** attribute, which makes it possible to search for specific spelling or style variants of a word, such as *okýnko* ('small window'), as opposed to **lemma**, which includes all variants (e.g. *okénko*, *okýnko* and *vokýnko*) under one lemma *okénko*. This attribute is used by a new feature of the KonText environment, which helps users to search for words and their variants. In addition, more advanced users can use sublemmas to study spelling changes and variations in Czech, as well as morphologically complex paradigms.

---

[1] https://www.korpus.cz.

© Springer Nature Switzerland AG 2021
K. Ekštein et al. (Eds.): TSD 2021, LNAI 12848, pp. 48–59, 2021.
https://doi.org/10.1007/978-3-030-83527-9_4

Advanced users can also use the new **verbtag** attribute, which provides access to grammatical categories of verb forms (both synthetic and analytic). In addition, the corpus SYN2020 features a better processing of **"multiword" tokens** that are written as one text word in Czech, but behave syntactically as two words, e.g. *ses*: reflexive *se* and a clitic form of the 2nd person singular indicative of the auxiliary verb *být* ('to be').

Moreover, there are some changes in the morphology and tagset (these modifications are not discussed here in detail): new POSs have been added (B for abbreviations, S for segments and F for foreign words),[2] the word-type classification has been re-evaluated for some words, and the division into various SubPOSs has been comprehensively adjusted for numerals. More advanced users will also appreciate the significantly higher success of lemmatization and morphological and syntactic tagging.

The structure of the paper is as follows: In Sect. 2, the new features of the SYN2020 corpus are described. Section 3 presents the whole annotation process, data and tools we used. Section 4 shows the accuracy rates of the tagging. In Sect. 5, the paper is concluded in brief.

2 New Features

2.1 Sublemma

Many Czech words attested in corpora exist in multiple graphemic forms. Major part concerns variants based on historical sound change processes, currently bearing specific stylistic differences (Czech situation is sometimes referred to as diglossia), e.g. the word *okénko* ('small window') has a stylistically almost equivalent variant *okýnko* and a substandard colloquial variant *vokýnko*. Processes of loanword adaptation form a second numerous group of variants, e.g. variability of vowel quantity *milion/milión* ('million') or of graphemic voicedness *filozof/filosof* ('philosopher'). Loanword variability in Czech has been considerably enhanced by a phoneticizing spelling reform in 1993. The previous editions of the SYN corpora treated such variants inconsistently. Either they were grouped under a common lemma, or they were treated as independent lemmas, based on their (not always systematic) treatment in the morphological dictionary used for the automatic annotation of the corpora. The dictionary MorfFlex [15] was developed outside the Czech National Corpus and independently of its tools and corpora. Its primary purpose is to serve as a resource for PDT-style[3] corpora. Recently, it has been transformed, so that the form of a lemma would remain as close to the actual word form as possible; the original, "broad" lemma is now represented in the lemma specification as a part of the so-called lemma's tail: "filosof_,s_^(^DD**filozof)".

For SYN2020, it was necessary to adopt a more user-friendly lemma representation. Therefore, the lemma information from the dictionary was divided into two attributes: lemma (containing the "broad lemma" in the way SYN users are already used to) and sublemma (lemma variant). For the SYN2020 purposes, the dictionary was manually checked and tested on real data. Consequently, thousands of new lemmas have been added and thousands of sublemmas singled out.

---

[2] Herein we basically follow a list of categories recently introduced for the morphological dictionary MorfFlex (see [7,15]) which was used within our annotation process, see Sect. 3.1.

[3] Prague Dependency Treebank.

The lemma/sublemma difference applies mostly to graphemic variability presented above, such as *okénko/okýnko/vokýnko*, *mýdlo/mejdlo* ('soap'), *milion/milión*, *filozof/filosof*, *teolog/theolog* ('theologist'). However, we extended its scope to other phenomena, morphological in nature, such as suppletion, e.g. the adjectival lemma *špatný* ('bad') is connected to the comparative sublemma *horší*, or negation of adjectives, e.g. the positive lemma *milý* ('kind') is connected to the negative sublemma *nemilý*. The following list shows the sublemma variants for the adjective lemma *dobrý* ('good'):

- *dobrý* (positive);
- *nedobrý* (negation);
- *lepší* (comparative);
- *sebelepší* (alternative gradation);
- *lepčí* (substandard comparative);
- *lepčejší* (substandard comparative).

The SYN2020 includes 12,658 lemmas with two or more sublemmas. These lemmas correspond to 28.79% of all tokens, but only 1.93% of all tokens have a sublemma different from the main lemma. Most often (11,595 lemmas), the number of sublemmas for a particular lemma is 2. The richest sublemma list has been found for the word *odsud* ('from here'), which covers as many as 11 sublemmas, mostly substandard variants.

Variant Selection Tool. The sublemma attribute is used to make the query formulation easier for non-expert users. Until recently, the basic corpus query searched only for lemmas or word forms typed into the search bar (an equivalent for the CQL query [word="xxx" | lemma="xxx"]). When a user typed an alternative graphemic variant of a lemma, the system evaluated the query as a query for the corresponding word form and did not produce the rest of the paradigm in the output. It may have happened then that the users misinterpreted the output as a general result for the whole lemma and thus spoiled their analysis. From now on, the basic query includes the default possibility of searching for a sublemma (an equivalent for the CQL query [word="xxx" | lemma="xxx" | sublemma="xxx"]), and thus the whole paradigm is included in the search results.

Moreover, a new "variant selection tool" is incorporated in the query bar. After typing in a word with multiple sublemmas, the users are offered the whole range of lemma and sublemma possibilities, so that they could either extend or narrow the query according to their intentions.

If the user chooses any of the suggested possibilities, the "query interpretation" is activated, i.e. the user is informed about what exactly is going to be searched for and he/she can further choose to adjust the query (or use the CQL query, which is rather improbable in case of non-expert users).

2.2   Verbtag

In the SYN2020 corpus, a new **verbtag** attribute is assigned to the tokens (primarily verb tokens), which makes available the morphological categories both of synthetic and of analytic verb forms.

For example, the future indicative can be expressed in three ways:

- with a present form of perfective verbs, e.g.
  připravím (prepare(PFV):1SG.IND.PRS[4] 'I will prepare'), or
- with the prefix *po-* with some verbs of movement, e.g.
  poběžím (*po-běžím* FUT-run:1SG.IND.PRS 'I will run'), or
- with an analytic form consisting of the future form of an auxiliary *být* ('be') and an infinitive of the imperfective verb, e.g.
  budu pracovat (be:1SG.IND.FUT work(IPFV):INF 'I will work').

A past participle form (e.g. *pracoval*, work:PTCP.PST.SG.M) can be a member of different analytic forms, e.g.

- present conditional,
  pracoval bych (work:PTCP.PST.SG.M be:1SG.COND.PRS 'I would work'), or
- past indicative,
  pracoval jsem (work:PTCP.PST.SG.M be:1SG.IND.PRS 'I worked').

In analytic verb forms, part of the morphological categories are expressed only

- on the auxiliary verb, e.g.
  pracoval jsi (work:PTCP.PST.SG.M be:2SG.IND.PRS 'you worked'), or
- on an implicit (covert) auxiliary, e.g.
  pracoval (work:PTCP.PST.SG.M [AUX.3SG] 'he worked').

So far, the only way to find out grammatical categories of analytic verb forms has been to specify quite complex expert queries. Now, the complex information about important verbal grammatical categories is available right at hand in a 6-positional tag. The first position indicates whether the tagged verb is lexical or auxiliary (while no more grammatical categories are specified with auxiliaries). The second position identifies the mood, the third one identifies the voice, the fourth one includes information about person, the fifth one about number and the sixth one about tense. E.g., within the analytic verb form in (1) the participle *překvapena* would be assigned the VCP2SP verbtag (V = lexical verb, C = conditional, P = passive, 2 = 2nd person, S = singular, P = present form) and the auxiliary *byla* and *bys* would be assigned the A----- verbtag.

(1)   *byla*   *bys*   *překvapena*
      be:PTCP.PST.SG.F be:2SG.COND surprise:PTCP.PASS.SG.F
      'you would be surprised'

The verbtag also allows the user to search for the categories mismatch within an analytic verb form. For example, the polite form of address "vykání" is now expressed in the following way: all individual parts of the analytic verb form have their real grammatical number (singular or plural) captured in the tag, while the number position in the verbtag is occupied by a special value "v", e.g. within the analytic form in (2) the participle *překvapena* would be assigned the VCP2vP verbtag. Another example of a

---

[4] The system of notation for the glosses and abbreviations used adheres to The Leipzig Glossing Rules [4] http://www.eva.mpg.de/lingua/resources/glossing-rules.php.

category mismatch between the values in tag and in verbtag is 3rd person imperative. In this case, the tag always says 2nd person, while the verbtag says 3rd person.

(2)   *byla*   *byste*   *překvapena*
      be:PTCP.PST.SG.F be:2PL.COND surprise:PTCP.PASS.SG.F
      'you (polite) would be surprised'

Both the data used for training and testing the tools and the annotation process had to be adjusted for the sake of the added verbtag attribute.

2.3 Multiword Tokens

In Czech, as well as in many other languages, sometimes a single graphic word amalgamates two (or more) syntactic words, e.g. the word *ses* is composed of a reflexive *se* and a clitic *s* standing for the 2nd person singular of the present form of the verb *být* ('be'). The annotation standard of the Universal Dependencies [12] name this phenomenon "multiword tokens": "We refer to such cases as multiword tokens because a single orthographic token corresponds to multiple (syntactic) words". Split interpretation of words canonically written as a single unit is by no means new in Slavic languages treatment, e.g., the Polish National Corpus has treated words like *abyśmy* (in_order_to:be:1PL.COND; an equivalent to the Czech *abychom* or *abysme*) as two individual tokens for a long time (see [1], p. 66). Nevertheless, the Polish corpus does not make it possible to search for the amalgamated forms as single tokens.

There are basically three main types of multiword tokens in Czech:

(i) Most frequent are amalgamated subordinating conjuctions *aby* ('(in order) to') and *kdyby* ('if'), sometimes also the uncanonical form of *jakoby* ('like'). These conjunctions appear in various forms, e.g. *abych, kdyby, jakobyste*. These forms comprise a subordinating conjunction (*aby, kdyby, jako*) and a conditional form of the verb *být*: *bych* (be:1SG.COND), *by* (be:COND), *byste* (be:2PL.COND).

(ii) The second type of mutiword tokens arises if *-s*, a short, clitic form of the 2nd person singular indicative of the verb *být*, is attached to a Czech word, most often to the reflexives *se, si* (*ses, sis*), also to past participles, e.g. *přišel* ('came', *přišels*), rarely to particles and adverbs, e.g. *už* ('already', *užs*), *pěkně* ('nicely', *pěkněs*), or passive participles, e.g. *zakleta* ('enchanted', *zakletas*).

(iii) The third type of multiword tokens are prepositions amalgamated with the short, clitic form of pronouns *on* ('he'), *co* ('what'), *copak* ('what'), *což* ('which'), such as *za něj > zaň* (*za-ň* for-he:ACC.SG), *o co > oč* (*o-č* for-what:ACC.SG), *na copak > načpak* (*na-čpak*, on-what:ACC.SG), *za což > začež* (*za-čež* for-which:ACC.SG), etc.

For the purposes of SYN2020, we have decided to use a solution similar to UD, nevertheless, priority has been given to the original forms, rather than to the separated syntactic words. The lemmatization process, as well as the morphological and syntactic annotation treats the individual parts of multiword tokens as separate words. Each of them is thus assigned a separate lemma, tag and syntactic function. Nevertheless, in the final corpus, they are again united as a single token which then has multiple lemmas, tags etc. The values of the corresponding attributes are displayed as "multivalues", e.g., the lemma for a *ses* token is *se|být* and its morphological tag is P7--4----------|VB-S---2P-AAI-1. The data also include the information about word form separation, so that each syntactic word is connected to a separate form. This discrepancy between a word form and its multivalue representation may affect statistical results concerning the number of tokens vs. the number of lemmas, tags or verbtags.

Figure 1 shows the syntactic representation of the sentence in (3) containing two multiword tokens, *aby* and *ses*. Note that in both cases, the individual subparts of the multiword token are dependent on different tokens (the conjunction *aby* is formally a parent token for the whole sentence), the auxiliaries *by* and *s* form together with the past participle *mohl* an analytic verb form.

(3) *Aby   ses   před ním mohl   schovat?*
      to:be:COND REFL:be:2SG.IND.PRS from him can:PTCP.PST.SG.M hide:INF
      'So you could hide from him?'

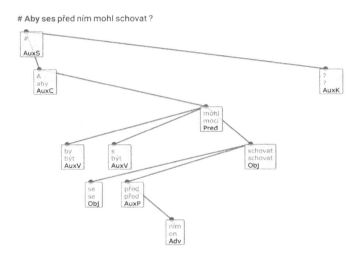

Fig. 1. Syntactic representation of multiword tokens

3   Annotation

In this section, we briefly introduce the process of annotation starting with the input text and ending with fully annotated data. We will also describe the data and tools used for the annotation of the SYN2020 corpus.

3.1   Segmentation, Tokenization and Morphological Analysis

The basic tokenization and segmentation was carried out using the MorphoDiTa tool [17]. MorphoDiTa also served for enhancing the morphological analysis of words, i.e., enhancing the set of possible morphological interpretations of a word (lemma + tag), according to the so-called "Prague" morphological analysis (see [6]). Partly, new changes in the design of the tagset have been incorporated (see [7]). The analysis provided by MorphoDiTa has been then adjusted to better comply with the design concept of SYN2020 and to minimize the number of unrecognized word forms; this applied to ca. 300,000 word forms, most of which finally did not appear in the actual data. The "close-to-the-form" lemmas from the analysis based on the MorfFlex [15] morphological dictionary were nested as sublemmas under new SYN2020 lemmas (e.g., MorfFlex lemmas *filosof* and *filozof* were nested as two sublemmas of the common lemma *filozof*). Also, a number of neologisms have been added, both from the corpus data and from the Czech neologism database Neomat [5].

3.2 Segmentation Adjustment

The automatic segmentation process produced some typical and frequent errors that had to be corrected automatically using simple rule-based algorithms. Typically, the presence of a potential abbreviation in a clause often caused errors in clause splitting or merging. Abbreviations in Czech are canonically followed by a period. If the following word then begins with a capital letter, there may or needn't be a sentence boundary, depending on the type of abbreviation and its context. The segmenter places the sentence boundary by default between the period and the following capital letter, but it can recognize some of the abbreviations and reassess the task. Nevertheless, it fails with other types of abbreviations, e.g., it systematically (and mistakenly) places a sentence boundary between *př.* and *Kr.* (abbreviation meaning before Christ), see (4) (the symbols ⟨/s⟩ ⟨s⟩ label the sentence boundary).

(4)   *Pochází z doby kolem roku 450 př.* ⟨/s⟩ ⟨s⟩ *Kr. a byla nalezena v moři u Sicílie.*
      'It dates from around 450 BC and was found in the sea near Sicily.'

Typical and frequent errors are thus corrected (the sentences are split or merged) automatically, the rules take into account the word forms and their morphological annotation and lemmatization (the potential, still ambiguous morphological analysis).

3.3 Tokenization Adjustment

Other specific algorithms have been used for adjusting the tokenization to comply with SYN2020 standards, i.e., the tokens previously formally separated due to the MorfFlex standards, such as *e-mail, S'-čchuan, 24hodinový, H2O* etc. have been merged into single tokens; on the other hand, multiword tokens have been split to make individual treatment possible during the annotation process. The newly-emerged tokens have been assigned lemma and a set of potential morphological interpretations.

3.4 Applying the Verbtags

Verb forms have been assigned potential verbtags, according to their morphological analysis. As a consequence, the number of tag positions temporarily increased to 21

(15 for the original morphological tag, 6 for the verbtag). The average number of tag-lemma pairs has thus increased from 4.06 to 5.67 per token; considering only verb forms, it has increased from 2.49 to 11.83 tag-lemma combinations per token. Most potential combinations emerge with passive participles concerning gender ambiguity, e.g., the word form *připraveny* offers as many as 75 tag and verbtag combinations for a single lemma.

3.5 Rule-Based Disambiguation

After the adjustment of the MorphoDiTa output to the standards of SYN2020, disambiguation was carried out. First, the LanGr system was employed. LanGr is based on linguistically motivated "rules" that eliminate nonsense interpretations of a token in a given context (see [9, 13] or [14]). For example, the word form *již* cannot be interpreted as a relative pronoun when following a preposition, or the word form *se* cannot be interpreted as a preposition when preceding a verb, etc.

The disambiguation rules reduce the original average of 5.67 lemma-tag-verbtag combinations per token to 1.76 combinations per token, i.e., the set of potential interpretations is reduced by 69%, though they cannot provide complete disambiguation. Therefore, it is necessary to employ also a stochastic tagger.

3.6 Completing the Disambiguation with a Tagger

For coping with the rest of the disambiguation process, we use a new version of the MorphoDiTa tool (MorphoDiTa Research) based on deep learning/neural networks (see [16]). The accuracy of MorphoDiTa as a whole, i.e. 97.32% correct assignment of lemma, tag and verbtag, is substantially better than the accuracy of taggers used for the final disambiguation phases before. Cf. the accuracy of the Featurama or Morče taggers ranging between 95.5 and 96.0% [18].

MorphoDiTa Research makes use of embeddings created by FastText [3], trained on the non-annotated data from the SYNv7 corpus (ca. 5 bil. tokens) and data from the Czech Wikipedia.[5] For the actual tagger training, the data from the Etalon corpus adapted to the SYN2020 standards (including verbtags) has been used. The Etalon corpus contains 2.26 mil. tokens with lemmas, tags and verbtags assigned manually, always by two annotators. It is composed of journalistic texts, non-fiction and fiction. Etalon has been published in the LINDAT repository.[6]

3.7 Parsing

Syntactic annotation has been performed using a parser tool from the NeuroNLP2 group. This parser is also based on neural networks, see [19]. The parser was trained on the data coming from the analytical layer of the PDT (see [2]) and FicTree, the syntactically annotated corpus of fiction (see [8]). The stackpointer parser algorithm has been employed. The parser used skip-gram embeddings created by Wang2vec [10] and trained also on the SYNv7 corpus and the Czech Wikipedia data.

---

[5] https://dumps.wikimedia.org/cswiki.
[6] http://hdl.handle.net/11234/1-3698.

3.8 Sublemmas and Multiword Tokens

After finalizing the disambiguation and syntactic annotation, the sublemmas were added and multiword tokens were merged into single tokens (each part of a multiword token preserving its own lemma and tags, the components are separated with a vertical bar as shown in Sect. 2.3).

4 Annotation Accuracy

The annotation accuracy was primarily tested automatically on the data of the Etalon corpus using the 10-fold cross-validation method. The tagger was gradually trained on 90% of the data and both the tagger and the hybrid disambiguation incorporating the tagger were tested on the remaining 10% of the data. The result is counted as an average of all 10 iterations. The parser was trained on the PDT test data (and on an assigned portion of the FicTree data). Moreover, differences between using MorphoDiTa only and using hybrid disambiguation (LanGr + MorphoDiTa) were manually analyzed, and differences between the syntactic annotation and the verbtag information were partly examined.

4.1 Results of the Automatic Testing: Etalon Data

Table 1 shows the annotation accuracy measured by various parameters (lemmas, morphological tags, verbtags, or individual tag positions). The attribute "verbtag" shows the accuracy of verbtag values for verbs; "case" shows the accuracy of case assignment for the parts of speech expressing case.

Table 1. Accuracy of annotation measured on the Etalon data

Attribute	Accuracy
Lemma+tag+verbtag	97.36%
Tag	97.60%
Lemma	99.67%
Verbtag	98.57%
POS	99.56%
Case	97.76%

The overall accuracy of annotation is 97.36%. Considering the individual morphological features, the case assignment appears as the most problematic one (97.76% of all words expressing case).[7]

---

[7] For amalgamated forms, see Sect. 2.3, the values were calculated on their multiword representations, i.e. before their reamalgamation.

The comparison of the results of the hybrid disambiguation to results of MorphoDiTa only (i.e. without the rule-based LanGr tool) did not show substantial differences. The accuracy of both methods is comparable; using a combination of both tools is slightly better (but statistically insignificant: the overall accuracy of lemma+tag+verbtag is 97.36%, whereas for MorphoDiTa only it is 97.32%).

4.2 Manual Comparison of the Hybrid Disambiguation and the Tagger only Method

The slight advantage of the hybrid method was also confirmed by a manual evaluation of differences between the results of both methods performed on new data (70,000 tokens). In cases where both methods disagreed (1627 tokens), both methods were often wrong (66.6%), if at least one method was correct, it was more often the hybrid method (64.5%).

Although the rule-based disambiguation is laborious, we still want to utilize it in future since (i) the hybrid method performs slightly better than the MorphoDita tagger, (ii) the errors made by the disambiguation rules can be easily identified and corrected and thus the rule-base system is well under control, (iii) the Morphodita tagger sometimes makes mistakes in disambiguating relatively simple syntactic structures, such as preposition case government or attribute-noun concord, which can almost never be the case with the rule-based approach.

4.3 Parsing Accuracy

The parsing accuracy was measured on the test data of the PDT analytical layer and a portion of FicTree data assigned for testing. The accuracy, measured as UAS (unlabeled attachment score, i.e., the percentage of correctly located parent tokens) and as LAS (labeled attachment score, a percentage of correctly located parent tokens with a correctly assigned syntactic function), is shown in Table 2. In the table, both the accuracy of the methods used for annotating the SYN2020 corpus and the previous SYN2015 corpus (annotated by the TurboParser tool [11]) are presented.

Table 2. The parsing accuracy measured on PDT and FicTree data

Corpus	UAS	LAS
SYN2015	88.48%	82.46%
SYN2020	92.39%	88.73%

Comparing the data presented in Table 2, it is clear that using the neural network parser significantly improved the syntactic annotation. The results in LAS show 36% less errors than before.

4.4   Auxiliaries: Verbtag and Parsing

The accuracy of the verbtag assignment with verbs is 98.57% in SYN2020 (see Sect. 4.1). SYN2020 includes syntactic annotation, for which a neural network stack-pointer parser of the NeuroNLP 2 group was used [19]. The parser was trained on an automatically morphologically annotated text; the training without the verbtag annotation produced better results than the training including it, therefore, the syntactic annotation is based on combining information from the word form, lemma and morphological tag, disregarding the verbtag information. In this respect, it appeared interesting to compare the accuracy of syntactic annotation and verbtag annotation for words annotated as auxiliaries (afun AuxV.*, verbtag A-----).

Considering the verbs *být* and *bývat*, the parser and the tagging method differ in 3,45%. In case the parser labels the word *být/bývat* as auxiliary and the tagging method as lexical or copular (0.93% of all *být/bývat* tokens in the corpus), usually, the verbtag is erroneous (79%, counted manually on a 200 cases sample). If the hybrid tagging method labels the word as an auxiliary, but the parser as lexical, it is mostly the case that the syntactic function is assigned erroneously (92% in the sample of 200 cases). That means that in most cases where the parser and the morphological disambiguation differ, the correct interpretation of the verb is an auxiliary, even though the overall percentage of auxiliary verbs among all *být/bývat* occurrences in the corpus is 45.90%.

5   Conclusions

In this article, we described a new corpus from the SYN series, which differs in many respects from the previous corpora of this series. The differences compared to previous corpora occur at all levels of processing—in segmentation, tokenization, and in morphological and syntactic analysis. These differences were motivated by the need to bring linguistic annotation closer to the annotation of PDT and also to provide users with additional information and tools for easier work with the corpus.

The most important changes in morphological and syntactic analysis include the processing of multiword tokens and the addition of verbtags describing both analytic and synthetic verb forms. In addition to lemmas, it is also possible to search by sublemmas, which will make possible a more accurate research of lexical and morphological variants of single lexemes. The user interface has become clearer and now it gives users the possibility to more accurately specify what is actually searched for in the corpus. The tools used for morphological and syntactic tagging have also changed, which has increased the accuracy of the entire annotation.

In the future, the annotation innovations and standards used for the creation of SYN2020 will become a unifying standard for the annotation of newly created corpora, as well as for the adjustment of other existing corpora administered within the Czech National Corpus infrastructure.

Acknowledgements. This paper and the creation of the corpus SYN2020 have been supported by the Ministry of Education of the Czech Republic, through the project Czech National Corpus, no. LM2018137.

References

1. Bański, P., Przepiórkowski, A.: Stand-off TEI annotation: the case of the National Corpus of Polish. In: Proceedings of the Third Linguistic Annotation Workshop (LAW III), pp. 64–67 (2009)
2. Bejček, E., Panevová, J., Popelka, J., Straňák, P., Ševčíková, M., Štěpánek, J., Žabokrtský, Z.: Prague Dependency Treebank 2.5–a revisited version of PDT 2.0. In: Proceedings of COLING 2012, pp. 231–246 (2012)
3. Bojanowski, P., Grave, E., Joulin, A., Mikolov, T.: Enriching word vectors with subword information. arXiv preprint arXiv:1607.04606 (2016)
4. Comrie, B., Haspelmath, M., Bickel, B.: The Leipzig Glossing Rules: Conventions for Interlinear Morpheme-by-morphene Glosses. Max Planck Institute for Evolutionary Anthropology (2008)
5. Goláňová, H., et al.: Novočeský lexikální archiv a excerpce v průběhu let 1911–2011. Slovo a slovesnost **72**(4), 287–300 (2011)
6. Hajič, J.: Disambiguation of rich inflection: computational morphology of Czech. Karolinum (2004)
7. Hajič, J., et al.: Prague dependency treebank-consolidated 1.0. In: Proceedings of the 12th International Conference on Language Resources and Evaluation (LREC 2020), pp. 5208–5218. ELRA, Marseille, France (2020)
8. Jelínek, T.: FicTree: a manually annotated treebank of Czech fiction. In: Hlaváčová, J. (ed.) ITAT 2017 Proceedings, pp. 181–185 (2017)
9. Jelínek, T., Petkevič, V.: Systém jazykového značkování současné psané češtiny. Korpusová lingvistika Praha 2011, sv. 3: Gramatika a značkování korpusů, pp. 154–170 (2011)
10. Ling, W., Dyer, C., Black, A., Trancoso, I.: Two/too simple adaptations of word2vec for syntax problems. In: Proceedings of the 2015 Conference of the North American Chapter of ACL: Human Language Technologies. ACL (2015)
11. Martins, A., Almeida, M., Smith, N.A.: Turning on the turbo: fast third-order non-projective turbo parsers. In: Annual Meeting of the ACL, pp. 617–622, August 2013
12. Nivre, J., et al.: Universal dependencies v2: an evergrowing multilingual treebank collection (2020)
13. Petkevič, V.: Reliable morphological disambiguation of Czech: rule-based approach is necessary. Insight into the Slovak and Czech corpus linguistics, pp. 26–44 (2006)
14. Petkevič, V., et al.: Problémy automatické morfologické disambiguace češtiny. Naše řeč **4–5**, 194–207 (2014)
15. Štěpánková, B., Mikulová, M., Hajič, J.: The MorfFlex Dictionary of Czech as a Source of Linguistic Data. In: Euralex XIX Proceedings Book: Lexicography for inclusion. pp. 387–391 (2020)
16. Straka, M., Straková, J., Hajič, J.: Czech text processing with contextual embeddings: POS tagging, lemmatization, parsing and NER. In: Ekštein, K. (ed.) TSD 2019. LNCS (LNAI), vol. 11697, pp. 137–150. Springer, Cham (2019). https://doi.org/10.1007/978-3-030-27947-9_12
17. Straková, J., Straka, M., Hajič, J.: Open-source tools for morphology, lemmatization, POS tagging and named entity recognition. In: Proceedings of 52nd Annual Meeting of ACL: System Demonstrations, pp. 13–18 (2014)
18. Votrubec, J.: Morphological tagging based on averaged perceptron. In: WDS 2006 Proceedings of Contributed Papers, pp. 191–195. Matfyzpress, Charles University, Praha, Czechia (2006)
19. Xuezhe, M., Zecong, H., Jingzhou, L., Nanyun, P., Neubig, G., Hovy, E.H.: Stack-pointer networks for dependency parsing. In: Proceedings of the 56th Annual Meeting of the Association for Computational Linguistics, pp. 1403–1414. ACL, Melbourne, Australia (2018)

Deep Bag-of-Sub-Emotions for Depression Detection in Social Media

Juan S. Lara[1(⊠)], Mario Ezra Aragón[2], Fabio A. González[1],
and Manuel Montes-y-Gómez[2]

[1] Universidad Nacional de Colombia, Bogotá, Colombia
{julara,fagonzalezo}@unal.edu.co
[2] Instituto Nacional de Astrofísica, Óptica y Electrónica (INAOE),
San Andrés Cholula, Mexico
{mearagon,mmontesg}@inaoep.mx

Abstract. This paper presents DeepBoSE, a novel deep learning model for depression detection in social media. The model is formulated such that it internally computes a differentiable Bag-of-Features (BoF) representation that incorporates emotional information. This is achieved by a reinterpretation of classical weighting schemes like tf-idf into probabilistic deep learning operations. An advantage of the proposed method is that it can be trained under the transfer learning paradigm, which is useful to enhance conventional BoF models that cannot be directly integrated into deep learning architectures. Experiments on the eRisk17 and eRisk18 datasets for the depression detection task show that DeepBoSE outperforms conventional BoF representations and is competitive with the state of the art methods.

1 Introduction

Nowadays, millions of people around the world are affected by different mental disorders that interfere in their thinking and behavior, damaging their quality of life [2]. For example, depression is one of the most common mental disorders and a leading cause of risk for suicide [2]. It is a medical condition associated with loss of interest, a significant change in weight or appetite, and insomnia. Currently, only around 20% of the affected people receive treatment, and most of the spending on mental health is used to maintain psychiatric hospitals instead of detection, prevention, and rehabilitation [17]. Based on these facts, it is imperative to create effective methods to detect depression before it causes irreparable damage to people affected by this disease.

In another order of ideas, it is a fact that for many people the majority of their social life does not take place in their immediate environment, but in a virtual world created by social media platforms like Facebook, Twitter, Reddit, Instagram, among others. This presents a great opportunity to understand depression through the analysis of social media documents, increasing the chances to detect people that present signs of depression, and providing professional assistance as soon as possible [9]. In this matter, several natural language processing (NLP)

© Springer Nature Switzerland AG 2021
K. Ekštein et al. (Eds.): TSD 2021, LNAI 12848, pp. 60–72, 2021.
https://doi.org/10.1007/978-3-030-83527-9_5

methods have been used for depression detection [21], especially, linguistic and sentiment analysis are applied to determine the posts' polarity and to represent the users by histograms of the ratios of their positive, negative and neutral posts.

Although conventional NLP approaches provide a good measure of the emotions in the text data, recent works in depression detection have demonstrated that a better performance is achieved using fine-grained representations. For example, the Bag-of-Sub-Emotions (BoSE) [1] is a representation that creates a dictionary of fine-grained emotions using a clustering strategy and a lexical resource of emotions. Each word in the users' posts is replaced with a label of its closest fine-grained emotion and a histogram of them is computed as the final representation. An important advantage of BoSE is that it achieves a very good performance while preserving interpretability, which differs from most of the state-of-the-art methods that use deep learning for improved performance but cannot be easily interpreted. The main disadvantage of BoSE is that it relies on feature engineering, i.e., it separates the representation and the prediction phases, because, a Bag-of-Features (BoF) must be offline learned and a classifier must be separately trained. In this concern, an end-to-end neural network model has the potential advantage of combining the representation and the classification phases in a fully trainable model that integrates the expressive power of the BoF representation while making it possible to fine-tune it to get higher performance.

Based on the above ideas, we present a novel deep learning model that internally computes an interpretable BoSE representation while taking advantage of deep representation learning. This is achieved using a differentiable reformulation of a BoF representation that is incorporated into an end-to-end model. The main contributions of this work are:

- The Deep Bag of Sub-Emotions (DeepBoSE) model for depression detection that extends the BoSE representation using probabilistic deep learning components.
- A training strategy that combines unsupervised and supervised learning. On the one hand, unsupervised information is used to enhance the clustering strategy that defines the fine-grained emotions; on the other hand, supervised information is incorporated to enhance the representation.

2   Related Work

The study of public mental health through social media has considerably increased in the previous years [9]. In particular, several text-processing strategies have been explored for the automatic detection of depression, which can be divided into two main approaches:

Feature engineering-based approaches: the fundamental component of these kinds of methods is the design of a meaningful representation that captures the general topics and sentiments that users express in their posts. More precisely, a descriptor of a document is computed and classification models like support vector machines, logistic regression, or random forests are used to predict a depression label [9]. Examples of the most relevant used features include word and character

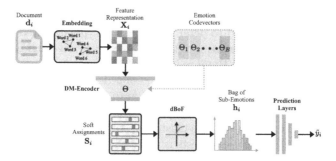

Fig. 1. Conceptual diagram of the DeepBoSE architecture.

n-grams with TF-IDF weighting [4], topic probabilities estimated through latent Dirichlet allocation [22], statistical features, part-of-speech labels [18], linguistic structure measures, and interpersonal awareness and interaction [6].

Although these general NLP descriptors provide a good overall representation of the documents, there are domain-specific features that better describe the emotional and specialized content in the posts, and therefore that are more appropriate for the depression detection task. For example, there is evidence that hypo-maniac states, levels of guilt or shame, and the presence of emotions like anger or sadness in posts of depressed users are correlated with suicide attempts [4]. In order to capture this, a common strategy is to design descriptors that, for example, measure the emotional valence or polarity in the posts [5,16]. Similarly, detailed descriptors like Bag-of-Emotions (BoE) or specialized Bag-of-Features are used to represent the ratios of terms associated with certain emotions or categories like pronouns, cognitive processes, health, among others [7]. In this matter, a common approach is to use the Linguistic Inquiry and Word Count (LIWC) [19], which determines the most psychologically meaningful words according to categories like social relationships, thinking styles or individual differences. LIWC also includes additional lexicons that are typically used to compute these detailed representations [5,7,16,18]. More recently, it was proposed an interesting alternative that consists of using a fine-grained representation of the emotions, referred to as Bag of Sub-Emotions [1]. This idea extends the BoE representations, specifically, the terms are not only assigned to a specific broad emotion, but they are assigned to sub-groups that provide a better approximation of the distribution of the emotions in the texts.

Deep learning-based approaches: recently, deep learning has been used as an alternative to classical feature engineering approaches. Neural networks can automatically learn a representation through several non-linear transformations, which is useful considering that it does not require the effort and the domain knowledge for the manual design of the features. An important advantage of deep representation learning is that it can incorporate supervised information to enhance the descriptors, obtaining specialized representations for depression detection. The most remarkable examples of deep learning applied to depression detection include convolutional neural networks [15], recurrent neural networks [8,15], and approaches that use special components like attention mechanisms [3].

There is a trade-off between feature engineering and deep learning approaches. On the one hand, feature engineering provides methods that are interpretable, and, therefore, that are useful to discover patterns in the data that may help humans to distinguish between depressed and healthy users. However, these methods require an offline computation of the representation, which restricts them to be static during the training of the classification model and to achieve non-outstanding performances. On the other hand, the deep learning approaches automatically learn an appropriate descriptor and combines the representation and classification in a single model, allowing to adapt the representations to achieve higher performances. However, the main disadvantage is that the learned representations in a neural network cannot be easily interpreted. We formulate the DeepBoSE model such that it takes advantage of the interpretability of BoSE as well as from the representation learning capabilities of neural networks. As will be detailed in the next section, the proposed method extends BoSE using probabilistic notions that are embedded in a deep neural network that allows transfer learning.

3   Deep Bag-of-Sub-Emotions

To introduce the Deep Bag of Sub-Emotions (DeepBose), we firstly summarize the BoSE approach, which consists of three main steps: first, a set of fine-grained emotions are unsupervisedly learned from a lexical resource that contains words associated with different emotions and sentiments, this is achieved using a clustering technique that discretizes the distribution of each emotion e in K_e subgroups (named as sub-emotions). Second, the fine-grained emotions are used to represent the documents, specifically, each word is masked or substitute by its closer sub-emotion, and each document is represented by a frequency histogram of their sub-emotions. Third, the histogram representation is used to train a classification model that predicts the depression label.

DeepBoSE uses a similar procedure and combines the second and third steps, i.e., the representation or construction of the histograms and the classification phase are integrated into a single deep learning model, allowing to tune the sub-emotions to the specific task of depression detection through transfer learning. The model architecture is depicted in Fig. 1 and contains four main components: (1) *embedding*, a word embedding strategy is used to compute a vector representation from all the terms in a document; (2) *DM-encoder*, it is a deep learning layer that assigns each embedded term to a specific sub-emotion; (3) *dbof*, it is composed of some deep learning components that permit the intermediate calculation of the BoSE representation from the assignments; (4) *prediction layers*, several fully-connected layers are used to obtain the depression grade from the BoSE representation. Each component and its intermediate representation will be described in the following subsections.

3.1   Model Description

As depicted in Fig. 1, the main purpose of the DeepBoSE architecture is to compute a prediction $\tilde{y}_i$ from a document $\mathbf{d}_i = \{t_1, t_2, \ldots, t_{N_w}\}$ of N_w terms. To achieve this, let us present the mathematical details of the four components in DeepBose:

Embedding: a text embedding $f(\cdot)$ is used to compute a vector representation $\mathbf{x}_j \in \mathbb{R}^{1 \times m}$ of each term t_j as shown in Eq. 1, more precisely, document $\mathbf{d}_i$ is represented as a matrix $\mathbf{X}_i \in \mathbb{R}^{N_w \times m}$ using f. An important property of this embedding is that it preserves semantic relations as numerical similarities, this will allow to numerically assign each embedded term $\mathbf{x}_j$ to its most similar sub-emotion.

$$\mathbf{x}_j = f(t_j) \qquad \mathbf{X}_i = f(\mathbf{d}_i) \tag{1}$$

Dissimilarity mixture encoder (DM-Encoder): we exploit the properties of the Dissimilarity Mixture Autoencoder (DMAE) [10], which is an autoencoder architecture for deep clustering that can be easily incorporated into deep neural networks. DeepBoSE incorporates a DM-Encoder to compute a matrix of soft-assignments $\mathbf{S}_i \in \mathbb{R}^{N_w \times K}$ from the embedded representations $\mathbf{X}_i$. Each entry $s_{j,k} \in \mathbf{S}_i$ represents a soft assignment of the j-th term in document $\mathbf{d}_i$ to the k-th sub-emotion. Sub-emotions are obtained by clustering sets of words associated with different emotions (this is discussed in detail in Subsect. 3.3). There are a total of E emotions and each emotion e is further divided into K_e sub-emotions, so the total number of sub-emotions is $K = \sum_{i=1}^{E} K_e$. The DM-Encoder calculates the soft-assignments $\mathbf{S}_i$ through Eq. 2, where $\sigma(\cdot)$ is the softmax activation function, α is a parameter that controls the sparsity of the assignments, $\mathcal{V}_p$ is a pairwise dissimilarity measure that compares the embedding of each term with a matrix of code vectors $\Theta \in \mathbb{R}^{K \times m}$ and $\mathbf{b} \in \mathbb{R}^{1 \times K}$ are the biases or mixing coefficients. In this case, a specific sub-emotion is represented by a code vector $\theta_k \in \Theta$ and each emotion is represented by its K_e code vectors which are codified in sub-matrices $\Theta_e \in \mathbb{R}^{K_e \times m}$, such that $\Theta = [\Theta_1, \Theta_2, \ldots, \Theta_E]$.

$$\mathbf{S}_i = \sigma(-\alpha \mathcal{V}_p(\mathbf{X}_i, \Theta) + \mathbf{b}) \tag{2}$$

Differentiable Bag-of-Features (dBoF): DeepBoSE uses the dBoF to transform the soft-assignments $\mathbf{S}_i$ into an overall descriptor $\mathbf{h}_i \in \mathbb{R}^{1 \times K}$ using a weights vector $\mathbf{w}_{idf} \in \mathbb{R}^{1 \times K}$. Further, as it will be demonstrated in the Subsect. 3.2, this representation is equivalent to a bag-of-features when the code vectors are not constrained or a bag of sub-emotions when the code vectors contain emotional information as it will be described in the Subsect. 3.3.

$$\mathbf{h}_i = \mathrm{dBoF}(\mathbf{S}_i, \mathbf{w}_{idf}) \tag{3}$$

Prediction layers: a number of d fully-connected layers that describe a function g are used to obtain a prediction $\tilde{y}_i$ from $\mathbf{h}_i$, using a set of weights $W = \{\mathbf{W}_1, \mathbf{W}_2, \ldots, \mathbf{W}_d\}$:

$$\tilde{y}_i = \mathrm{g}(\mathbf{h}_i, W) \tag{4}$$

To summarize, DeepBoSE learns the Θ, $\mathbf{b}$, $\mathbf{w}_{idf}$ and W parameters. It can be trained as any other deep learning model for classification, for instance, if the depression label y_i is binary, then, the output can be a sigmoid activation and the learning process would correspond to the optimization of the binary crossentropy presented in Eq. 5. The model is optimized using N samples from a training set $\mathcal{D} = \{(\mathbf{d_1}, y_1), (\mathbf{d_2}, y_2), \ldots, (\mathbf{d_N}, y_N)\} \; \forall \; y_i \in \{0, 1\})$ and the loss function measures how similar are the predictions $\tilde{y}_i$ and the ground truth y_i.

$$\mathcal{L} = -\frac{1}{N} \sum_{i=1}^{N} (y_i \log \tilde{y}_i + (1 - y_i) \log (1 - \tilde{y}_i)) \tag{5}$$

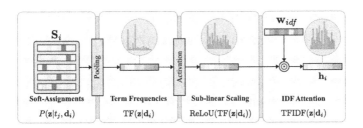

Fig. 2. Deep learning components that define the differentiable Bag-of-Features (dBoF).

3.2   Probabilistic Intepretation of the Differentiable Bag-of-Features

A bag-of-features (BoF) is a probabilistic representation that extends a Bag-of-Words (BoW) and is widely used in NLP and computer vision. A conventional BoF uses a word embedding with a quantization technique to determine the distribution of a vector of discrete latent variables or codebook $\mathbf{z} \in \mathbb{R}^{1 \times K}$, the idea is that a feature representation $\mathbf{h}'_i$ of a document $\mathbf{d}_i$ is computed using this distribution as shown in Eq. 6.

$$\mathbf{h}'_i = P(\mathbf{z}|\mathbf{d}_i) \tag{6}$$

The BoSE representation naturally appears if we constrain the codebook with emotional information, i.e., the codebook $\mathbf{z}$ is divided into a set of E emotions, such that each emotion is a sub-codebook $\mathbf{z}_e \in \mathbb{R}^{1 \times K_e}$ with K_e associated code vectors as shown in Eq. 7.

$$\mathbf{h}'_i = P(\mathbf{z}_1, \mathbf{z}_2, \ldots, \mathbf{z}_E|\mathbf{d}_i) \tag{7}$$

We exploit a property of DMAE that allows reinterpreting the soft-assignments as probabilities, to this end, let $\mathbf{z}$ be a vector of binary latent variables $\mathbf{z} = [z_1, z_2, \ldots, z_K]$ where $z_k = 1$ if a code vector θ_k is representative for the term t_j and $z_k = 0$ otherwise. Then, each value $s_{jk} \in \mathbf{S}_i$ corresponds to the probability

$P(z_k = 1|t_j, \mathbf{d}_i)$ of a code vector $\theta_k \in \Theta$ to be representative for a term t_j in a given document $\mathbf{d}_i$.

A conceptual diagram of the differentiable Bag-of-Features (dBOF) is presented in Fig. 2, it exploits the reinterpretation of the soft-assignments as a probability distribution to calculate a BoF representation of a document. Likewise, it includes a special activation function and an attention mechanism that are equivalent to the TF-IDF weighting schema that is typically used to improve BoF representations. The main purpose of dBoF is to compute the probability distribution $P(\mathbf{z}|\mathbf{d_i})$ that is shown in Eq. 6 from the soft-assignments $\mathbf{S}_i$ through the marginalization of the conditional distribution $P(\mathbf{z}, t_j|\mathbf{d_i})$:

$$
\begin{aligned}
P(\mathbf{z}, t_j, \mathbf{d}_i) &= P(\mathbf{d}_i)P(t_j|\mathbf{d}_i)P(\mathbf{z}|\mathbf{d}_i, t_j) \\
P(\mathbf{z}, t_j|\mathbf{d}_i) &= \frac{P(\mathbf{z}, t_j, \mathbf{d}_i)}{P(\mathbf{d}_i)} \\
P(\mathbf{z}|\mathbf{d}_i) &= \sum_{t_j} P(t_j|\mathbf{d}_i)P(\mathbf{z}|\mathbf{d}_i, t_j)
\end{aligned}
\tag{8}
$$

The distribution $P(t_j|\mathbf{d}_i)$ corresponds to the term frequencies that are typically used in BoW representations. In fact, it can be estimated as $\frac{N_t}{N_w}$, where N_t is the number of times that a term t_j appears in a document d_i of N_w terms. Moreover, since the representation $\mathbf{X}_i$ contains repeated words, each row has a single contribution of $\frac{1}{N_w}$, thus, the distribution of the codebook can be estimated as shown in Eq. 9. It is equivalent to a one-dimensional global average pooling (GlobalAveragePool1D) over the rows of $\mathbf{S}_i$.

$$
P(\mathbf{z}|\mathbf{d_i}) = \frac{1}{N_w} \sum_{j=1}^{N_w} P(\mathbf{z}|t_j, \mathbf{d_i})
\tag{9}
$$

$$
\mathbf{h}'_i = \text{GlobalAveragePool1D}(\mathbf{S_i})
$$

In a like manner, an approximation of the term frequency $\text{TF}(\mathbf{z}|\mathbf{d_i})$ is obtained when the constant $\frac{1}{N_w}$ is not considered and it is equivalent to a one-dimensional global sum pooling (GlobalSumPool1D):

$$
\text{TF}(\mathbf{z}|\mathbf{d_i}) = \sum_{j=1}^{N_w} P(\mathbf{z}|t_j, \mathbf{d_i})
\tag{10}
$$

$$
\mathbf{h}'_i = \text{GlobalSumPool1D}(\mathbf{S_i})
$$

These $\mathbf{h}'_i$ representations are a first approximation of a BoF, nevertheless, weighting and scaling schemes are needed to mitigate the effect of common terms as it is usually done in classical histogram representations. To this end, dBoF also includes deep learning operations that reformulate the term frequency - inverse document frequency (TF-IDF) statistic. First, a sub-linear scaling of the term frequency is calculated through the Rectifier Logarithmic Unit (ReLoU) activation that is presented in Eq. 11.

$$\text{ReLoU}(x) = \begin{cases} \log(x) + 1 & \text{if } x > 1 \\ 0 & \text{otherwise} \end{cases} \tag{11}$$

Second, the Inverse Document Frequency Attention mechanism (IDF-Attention) is proposed as an alternative to the inverse document frequency (IDF) weighting. Specifically, the Hadamard product between a weights vector $\mathbf{w}_{idf} \in \mathbb{R}^{1 \times N_k}$ and the sub-linear representation $\text{ReLoU}(\text{TF}(\mathbf{z}|\mathbf{d_i}))$ is used as the descriptor $\mathbf{h}_i$ and is a final approximation of TF-IDF as shown in Eq. 12. An important advantage of this approach is that it allows initializing these weights using the classical IDF that is computed through counting techniques, nonetheless, $\mathbf{w}_{idf}$ can be modified during the model training and adjusted for the depression detection task.

$$\mathbf{h}_i = \text{TFIDF}(\mathbf{z}|\mathbf{d_i}) = \mathbf{w}_{idf} \odot \text{ReLoU}(\text{TF}(\mathbf{z}|\mathbf{d_i})) \tag{12}$$

As it is shown, the dBoF can compute a TF-IDF approximation using the soft-assignments from DMAE and common deep learning operations. This is important considering that it allows differentiation and gradient-based optimization through backpropagation.

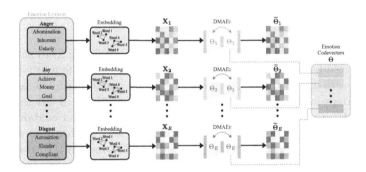

Fig. 3. Construction of the sub-codebooks using DMAE on an emotion lexicon.

3.3   Learning Sub-Groups of Emotions

To include additional emotional information from lexicons in the codebook, we explore a property of DMAE that allows the initialization with other clustering strategies and its enhancement using transfer learning. Specifically, the DM-Encoder is initialized using a set of sub-codebooks Θ as shown in Fig. 1.

To extract relevant information from a specific e emotion in a lexicon, a set K_e of code vectors $\Theta_e \in \mathbb{R}^{K_e \times m}$ is estimated as the parameters of the cluster distributions that are learned in a DMAE model. The complete process to determine these code vectors $\Theta = [\Theta_1, \Theta_2, \ldots, \Theta_E]$ is depicted in Fig. 3, which requires representing each of the N_e words from the e vocabulary as an embedding matrix $\mathbf{X}_e \in \mathbb{R}^{N_e \times m}$. Although the code vectors can be computed using any clustering technique, we use DMAE considering that it allows similarity-based clustering, which is important since a certain dissimilarity function would be more suitable for a given embedded space. Specifically, we use the cosine dissimilarity as in Eq. 13, it is a standard similarity for text embeddings and is the same metric originally used in the BoSE representation [1]. This dissimilarity function is a measure of the alignment or the angle between the embedding $\mathbf{x}_j \in \mathbf{X}_e$ of a term t_j and a code vector $\theta_k \in \Theta$, lower values represent a complete alignment while higher values represent a maximum degree between the vectors.

$$\mathcal{V}(\mathbf{x}_j, \theta_k) = 1 - \frac{\mathbf{x}_j \cdot \theta_k}{||\mathbf{x}_j||\ ||\theta_k||} \tag{13}$$

Finally, all the DMAE instances are optimized using the loss function presented in Eq. 14. Each model is independently trained and the resultant parameters Θ_e are concatenated into a single matrix Θ which is used to initialize the DeepBoSE model.

$$\mathcal{L}_e = \frac{1}{N_e} \sum_{\mathbf{x}_j \in \mathbf{X}_e,\ \tilde{\theta}_j \in \tilde{\Theta}_e} \mathcal{V}\left(\mathbf{x}_j, \tilde{\theta}_j\right) \tag{14}$$

4   Experimental Settings

4.1   Datasets Description

In our evaluation we used the data from the eRisk 2017 and 2018 shared task, it contains Reddit posts with binary labels that indicate if the user is depressed or not. The *eRisk2017* dataset contains a training partition of 486 samples (83 users with depression and 403 healthy) and a test partition of 401 samples (52 users with depression and 349 healthy); the *eRisk2018* dataset contains a training partition of 887 samples (135 with depression and 752 healthy) and a test partition of 820 samples (79 with depression and 741 healthy). In these shared tasks, the F1-score over the positive class (depression) has been used as the main evaluation measure, however, to assess the overall performance of the proposed model we also report the accuracy, macro-average precision, and recall.

4.2   Learning Approaches

The experiments carried out aim to evaluate the effects of unsupervised and supervised learning phases of DeepBoSE. To this end, the following three cases are assessed:

Ofline learning (BoSE): it uses the original BoSE representation [1], where the code vectors Θ are estimated using $\mathcal{E}$ instances of affinity propagation (AP) with cosine similarity, then, counts of unigram and n-gram sequences of hard-assignments are used to build a BoF that is weighted using sub-linear term frequency and TF-IDF.

Unsupervised transfer learning (BoSE+UTL): this case evaluates the performance of a BoSE representation that is computed using DMAE. The same procedure of the first case is used, but the AP models are replaced with E instances of DMAE (initialized with AP). This allows us to evaluate the effects of the unsupervised transfer learning that has shown promising results in deep clustering tasks.

Supervised transfer learning (DeepBose): this corresponds to the training of the proposed model, where the code vectors Θ are initialized using the results of step 2 as depicted in Fig. 1, and a classical TF-IDF representation is computed to determine an appropriate initial value for the IDF weights $\mathbf{w}_{idf}$.

4.3 Hyperparameter Selection

To determine an appropriate combination of hyperparameters we extracted a stratified validation split of 20% from the training set. The models were trained using the remaining 80% and the best hyperparameters were selected by a grid search using the F1-score as criteria. The model's weights were estimated using the Adam optimization algorithm with different learning rates (lr) that were chosen in an exploratory analysis to avoid over and underfitting: UTL $lr = 1e^{-5}$, STL $lr = 1e^{-6}$. We used FastText embeddings that were pretrained on WikiNews to represent the words. For the unsupervised phase, we used the EmoLex lexicon [14], which is composed of eight different emotions (anger, anticipation, disgust, fear, joy, sadness, surprise, and trust) and two sentiments (negative and positive). Considering that DMAE and DeepBoSE are initialized with AP, we used the number of code vectors K_e that AP automatically identifies for BoSE [20]. The softmax inverse temperature α parameter was explored in the range $[10, 10^3]$. For the fully connected layers, we used two intermediate dense layers with a ReLU activation and 64 units per layer, a dropout probability of 0.2 was added to the weights for regularization. Finally, the binary cross-entropy loss was modified using class weights to deal with the class imbalance problem.

5 Results and Analysis

Table 1 presents the results of the proposed method in the depression detection task. It also shows the results from the BoSE representation as well as the best results in both shared tasks [12,13]. The second approach (BoSE+UTL) shows the advantages of using DMAE. More precisely, the unsupervised fine-tuning allowed enriching the original BoSE representation that consisted of AP; this is important since we are using a shallow version of DMAE and the results must be similar to other shallow approaches like AP. Moreover, one of the major disadvantages of AP is that clusters are constrained to points in the original dataset, while DMAE only uses these points as initialization and it is able to determine a new set of improved and unconstrained clusters.

Table 1. Experimental results of the three best teams at eRisk and the three different BoSE-based approaches in the two datasets.

Case	eRisk2017				eRisk2018			
	F1	ACC	PREC	RECALL	F1	ACC	PREC	RECALL
First place	0.64	-	0.60	0.61	0.64	-	0.64	0.65
Second place	0.59	-	0.48	0.79	0.60	-	0.53	0.70
Third place	0.53	-	0.48	0.60	0.58	-	0.60	0.56
BoSE - Unigram	0.6079	0.6176	0.6088	0.6071	0.6065	0.6175	0.6054	0.6076
BoSE - Bigram	0.6359	0.6202	0.6551	0.6178	0.6316	0.6075	**0.6486**	0.6154
BoSE+UTL	0.6206	**0.9177**	**0.7714**	0.5192	0.6171	0.9182	0.5625	0.6835
DeepBoSE	**0.6415**	0.9052	0.6296	**0.6538**	**0.6545**	**0.9304**	0.6279	**0.6835**

All of my other stations work just fine. I was wondering if this is affecting anyone else? The latter seems to happen quite often. I used to put people on a pedestal constantly, but I've cut down on it a lot in the past year or so. It's made my current friendships a lot stronger, but hasn't helped me meet new people at all. I'm a computer science major, so the majority of my gen eds are math/science/cs, usually like 8 guys to every one girl. Not saying it's impossible but it seems a bit unlikely. I'm an introvert (by definition), and I probably have a pretty good sprinkling of social anxiety to go along with it. I'm 20, and stuck at community college so I don't see it happening anytime soon.

a.

bipolar disorder is harder to diagnose, if she is under 18 she cannot be legally diagnosed as bipolar. It can be suspected, but the DM-IV says it shouldn't be diagnosed at that time. Because of that, most teens showing bipolar tendencies are just written off as depressed. Bipolar is different from depression because the subject displays periods of depression, and manic episodes. If she is unusually sad for some time, and the next week she is unusually happy, it's safe to assume she is bipolar. That being said, it doesn't really matter what the diagnosis is. Self harm is dangerous and if she is not getting help then she should do so. She will not appreciate it, but that's because she is sick.

b.

Fig. 4. Saliency map for two sample texts: a. text in which the depression content is implicit; b. text in which the depression content is explicit.

The best results in both datasets were achieved using the DeepBoSE model under the supervised transfer learning approach. This model is formulated in such a way that it approximates the unigram case of BoSE, moreover, the results show that an enhanced unigram model outperforms the n-gram representation of the original BoSE. In addition, these results also show that supervised information has an important role in the depression detection task, specifically, it allows to learn a set of more representative code vectors. This is the expected performance of most neural networks that are used for transfer learning, in fact, general information from an emotion lexicon is first introduced in the model, and then, it is fine-tuned to obtain a specialized model for the specific task.

To highlight the interpretability of DeepBose, we computed the saliency $\mathcal{S}_j = \sum_{x_l \in \mathbf{x}_j} \left\| \frac{\partial \tilde{y}_i}{\partial x_l} \right\|$ of two sample texts that were extracted from users with depression; the saliency maps are shown in Fig. 4. We define the saliency $\mathcal{S}_j$ of a specific term $t_j \in \mathbf{d}_i$ as the sum of the magnitude of the gradient [11] of each component x_l in the embedded representation $\mathbf{x}_j$ of t_j. In the first text, the user does not directly talk about depression, but DeepBoSE was able to focus on some specific terms that are associated with this disorder. In the second text, the user explicitly talks about depression, and DeepBoSE determined the most representative terms including some specific words like "DM-IV", which is a publication for the classification of different mental disorders.

6   Conclusions and Future Work

We presented the DeepBoSE model, which incorporates information from lexical emotion resources, preserves interpretability, and leverages the properties of a deep neural network. This model demonstrated competitive performance with respect to state-of-the-art methods and improved the results from the original BoSE representation. For future work, we plan to exploit the deep representation learning capabilities of the deep clustering methods, and also to consider the incorporation of novel embedding techniques like transformers, which have shown to outperform other text embeddings in several similar tasks.

Acknowledgments. This research was supported by CONACyT-Mexico (Scholarship 654803 and Projects: A1-S-26314 and CB-2015-01-257383).

References

1. Aragón, M.E., López-Monroy, A.P., González-Gurrola, L.C., Gómez, M.M.: Detecting depression in social media using fine-grained emotions. In: Proceedings of the 2019 Conference of the North American Chapter of the Association for Computational Linguistics: Human Language Technologies, Volume 1 (Long and Short Papers) (2019)
2. Bromet, R.K.E., Jonge, P., Shahly, V., Wilcox, M.: The burden of depressive illness. In: Public Health Perspectives on Depressive Disorders (2017)
3. Cong, Q., Feng, Z., Li, F., Xiang, Y., Rao, G., Tao, C.: XA-BiLSTM: a deep learning approach for depression detection in imbalanced data. In: 2018 IEEE International Conference on Bioinformatics and Biomedicine (BIBM), pp. 1624–1627. IEEE (2018)
4. Coppersmith, G., Ngo, K., Leary, R., Wood, A.: Exploratory analysis of social media prior to a suicide attempt. In: Proceedings of the Third Workshop on Computational Linguistics and Clinical Psychology, pp. 106–117 (2016)
5. De Choudhury, M., Counts, S., Horvitz, E.J., Hoff, A.: Characterizing and predicting postpartum depression from shared Facebook data. In: Proceedings of the 17th ACM Conference on Computer Supported Cooperative Work and Social Computing, pp. 626–638 (2014)
6. De Choudhury, M., Kiciman, E., Dredze, M., Coppersmith, G., Kumar, M.: Discovering shifts to suicidal ideation from mental health content in social media. In: Proceedings of the 2016 CHI Conference on Human Factors in Computing Systems, pp. 2098–2110 (2016)
7. Eichstaedt, J.C., et al.: Facebook language predicts depression in medical records. Proc. Nat. Acad. Sci. **115**(44), 11203–11208 (2018)
8. Gkotsis, G., et al.: Characterisation of mental health conditions in social media using informed deep learning. Sci. Rep. **7**, 45141 (2017)
9. Guntuku, S.C., Yaden, D.B., Kern, M.L., Ungar, L.H., Eichstaedt, J.C.: Detecting depression and mental illness on social media: an integrative review. Curr. Opinion Behav. Sci. **18**, 43–49 (2017)
10. Lara, J.S., González, F.A.: Dissimilarity mixture autoencoder for deep clustering. arXiv:2006.08177 (2020)
11. Li, J., Chen, X., Hovy, E.H., Jurafsky, D.: Visualizing and understanding neural models in NLP. In: HLT-NAACL (2016)

12. Losada, D.E., Crestani, F., Parapar, J.: eRISK 2017: CLEF lab on early risk prediction on the internet: experimental foundations. In: Jones, G.J.F., et al. (eds.) CLEF 2017. LNCS, vol. 10456, pp. 346–360. Springer, Cham (2017). https://doi.org/10.1007/978-3-319-65813-1_30

13. Losada, D.E., Crestani, F., Parapar, J.: Overview of eRisk 2018: early risk prediction on the internet (extended lab overview). In: Proceedings of the 9th International Conference of the CLEF Association. CLEF 2018, Avignon, France (2018)

14. Mohammad, S.M., Turney, P.D.: Crowdsourcing a word-emotion association lexicon. Comput. Intell. **29**(3), 436–465 (2012)

15. Orabi, A.H., Buddhitha, P., Orabi, M.H., Inkpen, D.: Deep learning for depression detection of twitter users. In: Proceedings of the Fifth Workshop on Computational Linguistics and Clinical Psychology: From Keyboard to Clinic, pp. 88–97 (2018)

16. Reece, A.G., Reagan, A.J., Lix, K.L., Dodds, P.S., Danforth, C.M., Langer, E.J.: Forecasting the onset and course of mental illness with twitter data. Sci. Rep. **7**(1), 1–11 (2017)

17. Renteria-Rodriguez, M.E.: Salud mental en mexico. NOTA-INCyTU NÚMERO 007 (2018)

18. Sawhney, R., Manchanda, P., Singh, R., Aggarwal, S.: A computational approach to feature extraction for identification of suicidal ideation in tweets. In: Proceedings of ACL 2018, Student Research Workshop, pp. 91–98 (2018)

19. Tausczik, Y.R., Pennebaker, J.W.: The psychological meaning of words: LIWC and computerized text analysis methods. J. Lang. Soc. Psychol. **29**(1), 24–54 (2010)

20. Thavikulwat, P.: Affinity propagation: a clustering algorithm for computer-assisted business simulation and experimental exercises. In: Developments in Business Simulation and Experiential Learning (2008)

21. Xue, Y., Li, Q., Jin, L., Feng, L., Clifton, D.A., Clifford, G.D.: Detecting adolescent psychological pressures from micro-blog. In: Zhang, Y., Yao, G., He, J., Wang, L., Smalheiser, N.R., Yin, X. (eds.) HIS 2014. LNCS, vol. 8423, pp. 83–94. Springer, Cham (2014). https://doi.org/10.1007/978-3-319-06269-3_10

22. Yazdavar, A.H., et al.: Semi-supervised approach to monitoring clinical depressive symptoms in social media. In: Proceedings of the 2017 IEEE/ACM International Conference on Advances in Social Networks Analysis and Mining 2017, pp. 1191–1198 (2017)

Rewriting Fictional Texts Using Pivot Paraphrase Generation and Character Modification

Dou Liu[1]([✉]), Tingting Zhu[1], Jörg Schlötterer[2][iD], Christin Seifert[1,2][iD], and Shenghui Wang[1][iD]

[1] University of Twente, Enschede, The Netherlands
{d.liu-2,t.zhu}@student.utwente.nl, shenghui.wang@utwente.nl
[2] University of Duisburg-Essen, Essen, Germany
{christin.seifert,joerg.schloetterer}@uni-due.de

Abstract. Gender bias in natural language is pervasive, but easily overlooked. Current research mostly focuses on using statistical methods to uncover patterns of gender bias in textual corpora. In order to study gender bias in a more controlled manner, we propose to build a parallel corpus in which gender and other characteristics of the characters in the same story switch between their opposite alternatives. In this paper, we present a two-step fiction rewriting model to automatically construct such a parallel corpus at scale. In the first step, we paraphrase the original text, i.e., the same storyline is expressed differently, in order to ensure linguistic diversity in the corpus. In the second step, we replace the gender of the characters with their opposites and modify their characteristics by either using synonyms or antonyms. We evaluate our fiction rewriting model by checking the readability of the rewritten texts and measuring readers' acceptance in a user study. Results show that rewriting with antonyms and synonyms barely changes the original readability level; and human readers perceive synonymously rewritten texts mostly reasonable. Antonymously rewritten texts were perceived less reasonable in the user study and a post-hoc evaluation indicates that this might be mostly due to grammar and spelling issues introduced by the rewriting. Hence, our proposed approach allows the automated generation of a synonymous parallel corpus to study bias in a controlled way, but needs improvement for antonymous rewritten texts.

Keywords: Text rewriting · Gender parallel corpus · Paraphrase generation · Character modification

1 Introduction

A fictional text contains a compelling plot and a series of characters. The description and narration of these characters play a crucial role in the readers' acceptance of the story. If we rewrite a fictional text in which the characters change

---

C. Seifert and S. Wang—Contributed equally.

K. Ekštein et al. (Eds.): TSD 2021, LNAI 12848, pp. 73–85, 2021.
https://doi.org/10.1007/978-3-030-83527-9_6

their gender[1] or other characteristics, for example, if the Little Red Riding Hood is not a girl but a boy, or Peter Pan is actually disciplined instead of being mischievous, do readers still think that the story is acceptable and fun to read?

Measuring readers' reactions to a gender-parallel story with the same storyline as the original but whose characters have a different gender or opposite characteristics brings an interesting perspective and a controlled way to study gender bias. In order to conduct this type of studies at scale, an automated process that produces such a parallel corpus at a large scale is desirable.

In this paper, we propose a two-step approach for rewriting fictional texts and constructing a parallel corpus. First, a fictional text is paraphrased by a pivot-based paraphrase generation model, to keep the storyline but vary its expression. We apply this step in order to increase the textual diversity in the corpus. In a second step, we modify the gender and other characteristics of the characters using a combination of Named Entity Recognition, Part-of-Speech Tagging, and Character Recognition. We compare four different methods to identify the synonyms or antonyms to describe person characteristics, and perform a technical evaluation as well as a user study to assess the readability of the rewritten texts and readers' acceptance. A web demo, source code and evaluation examples are made available[2].

2   Related Work

Gender bias for characters in literary works is pervasive, but easily neglected or overlooked [6]. Current research on gender bias focuses on statistical semantics of gender-sensitive words or patterns in large scale corpora [3,10,27]. For gender stereotype detection, Cryan et al. [5] demonstrated end-to-end classification approaches to outperform lexicon-based approaches in terms of robustness and accuracy, even on moderately sized corpora. Field and Tsvetkov [9] use propensity matching and adversarial learning to reduce the influence of confounding factors in identifying gender bias in comments. Rudinger et al. [24] rely on a high-quality corpus containing contrast text to detect gender bias in co-reference resolution models. Habash et al. [11] manually created a gender parallel corpus and proposed an approach to de-bias the output of a gender-blind machine translation with gender-specific alternative re-inflections. While the aforementioned methods study or address gender-bias, they typically rely on large-scale (parallel) corpora. Our goal is not to study gender bias itself, but to develop an automatic process for the creation of a gender parallel corpus, which can then be used to study gender bias in a controlled way. That is, we seek a method to rewrite the original text, switching gender and other characteristics.

Most previous work of **text rewriting** (e.g. [12,15,25,28]) has focused on style transfer, e.g., transferring modern English to Shakespearean English [12]. Santos et al. [25] presented an encoder-decoder network to transfer offensive

---

[1] In this paper, we simplify the notion of gender to the binary concept of male and female.

[2] https://doi.org/10.5281/zenodo.4904849.

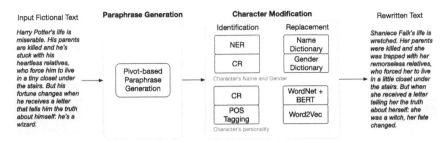

Fig. 1. Overview of the fictional texts rewriting model. First, the input text [23] is paraphrased using a pivot language. Second, we detect characters using NER and CR and modify their gender and other characteristics using dictionaries and language models.

language. Woodsend et al. [28] used automatically extracted rewriting rules to increase the amount of labeled data for semantic role labeling. Changing style in texts can be seen as a **Paraphrase Generation (PG)** problem, which in turn can be considered a monolingual machine translation problem. Bannard et al. [1] introduced a pivot-based method for PG based on the assumption that two English phrases that translate to the same phrase in a pivot language are potential paraphrases. Moreover, Zhao et al. [29] leveraged multiple MT engines for paraphrase generation and showed that this approach is useful for obtaining valuable candidate paraphrases.

Approaches for **Named Entity Recognition (NER)** have transformed from rule-based methods (e.g., [19]) to machine-learning based methods (e.g., [14]) to deep learning methods with automatic feature generation (e.g., [16]). Qi et al. [22] introduced a toolkit for NLP with the state-of-art performance in NER tasks. Similarly, the CoreNLP toolkit [17] encompasses methods for **Coreference Resolution (CR)** with the state-of-the-art performance. The replacement process in our rewriting model requires a notion of **semantic similarity**. Mikolov et al. [20] proposed Word2Vec to obtain a feature space capturing the semantic similarity between words. Faruqui et al. [8] introduced retrofitting word vectors to incorporate knowledge from semantic lexicons and showed that these word vectors perform better on semantic tasks than those word vectors trained without it. As a sub-task of BERT [7], mask-filling can also be used to select the most similar word when several alternative words are given for a sentence.

3   Approach

Figure 1 provides an overview of our approach. The input is a fictional text, e.g., the summary of a published book or a short story written by a human author. Rewriting is then performed in two steps: i) paraphrase generation to express the original text differently and ensure variance in the corpus and ii) character modification, to detect characters and modify their characteristics. Applied to a corpus of fictional texts with controlled modifications, the original texts and

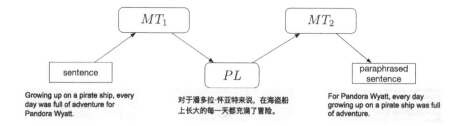

Fig. 2. A single-pivot paraphrase generation system first translates the input sentence [18] to the pivot language (*PL*) and then back to the original language.

the rewritten ones form a parallel corpus to which readers' preferences can be measured.

3.1 Paraphrase Generation

The paraphrase generation step is applied to increase the textual diversity in the corpus. Conducting a gender bias user study with only changing the fictional characters' gender may easily reveal the study purpose to users and influence their behavior. Further, the original author's writing style could be a confounding factor when studying gender bias. If the parallel corpus is composed of only paraphrased texts, i.e., in a text pair one text that is paraphrased and one that is paraphrased and modified, instead of the original text and a paraphrased and modified version, this factor can be eliminated.

We use a single-pivot paraphrasing system as proposed by Bannard [1]. The basic assumption for pivot-based paraphrase generation (PG) is that two English phrases translated to the same phrase in a pivot language, are potential paraphrases. A single-pivot PG system (cf. Fig. 2), is defined as the triple (MT_1, PL, MT_2), with MT_1 being a machine translation engine which translates a source sentence into the pivot language, PL is the pivot language, and MT_2 a machine translation engine which translates the intermediate sentence in the pivot language back to the source language. The final translation result is the paraphrase of the original sentence. We choose Chinese as the pivot language because Chinese is the mother tongue of the two first authors and therefore the intermediate translations can be manually checked, and Chinese is a gender-neutral language, which prevents introducing additional gender bias during the paraphrasing step. Chinese has gendered pronouns just like English, but does not have grammatical gender in the sense of noun class distinctions.

We use the LingoCloud API [2] for translating the texts from English to Chinese and back, i.e., as MT_1 and MT_2. Figure 2 shows an example for the orginal English sentence, it's paraphrased version and the intermediate Chinese translation.

Fig. 3. A rewriting example. The original text [18] is paraphrased before the characteristics of the main character are detected and modified.

3.2 Character Modification

After the original text is paraphrased, we modify the characters in the text, by first detecting the characters and subsequently modifying their name, gender and characteristics (cf. Fig. 1). Figure 3 presents the rewriting steps using an example.

To **detect characters** and their mentions, we use Named Entity Recognition (NER) and Coreference Resolution (CR) from CoreNLP [17] and Stanza [22]. An initial comparison on CoreNLP and Stanza's NER performance shows that Stanza provides more accurate results[3], and therefore, we use Stanza to detect the PERSON entities. The CR from CoreNLP is used to detect all mentions of the characters.

To **modify characters**, we use a POS tagger to detect adjectives in the near proximity (at most two tokens away) to the detected characters, assuming that those adjectives describe their characteristics. Once the characteristics are identified, we rewrite the text by switching the character to the opposite gender and rewrite attributes by either using synonyms or antonyms. To change the *gender* of a fictional character, we first determine its gender using dictionaries. For our model, we simplify the notion of gender to a binary attribute[4]. We use a gender-name dictionary[5] and a dictionary with pairs of gender-specific words (e.g. *prince* vs *princess*)[6]. When the gender of the character is determined, we randomly select a common first name with the opposite gender and a common surname from the Surname list[7] or choose the opposite gender-specific to replace the original name: For example, *Princess Diana* is replaced by *Prince Philippe*, or *Harry Potter* with *Shaniece Falk* (cf. Fig. 1). One rewriting option is to replace the identified characteristics (i.e., the adjectives in the near proximity) with their *synonyms*. In other words, similar characteristics are now associated with the opposite gender. We compare the following four methods to replace adjectives:

---

[3] CoreNLP treats the first name and the last name as two different name entities while Stanza combines them into one.

[4] We will address this limitation in future work.

[5] https://data.world/alexandra/baby-names.

[6] www.fit.vutbr.cz/imikolov/rnnlm/word-test.v1.txt.

[7] https://data.world/uscensusbureau/frequently-occurring-surnames-from-the-census-2000.

- **WordNet:** We select a synonym from WordNet [21].
- **Self-trained Word2Vec (W2V_own):** We train a Word2Vec model using our own corpus of book summaries that is additionally retrofitted with a semantic lexicon as described in [8]. We select the most similar adjective based on semantic similarity.
- **Google News Word2Vec (W2V_google):** We use the Word2Vec model pre-trained on Google News corpus[8] to select the most similar adjective.
- **BERT Mask Filling (BERT):** We consider the adjective as a masked token, and use the prediction of a pre-trained BERT model [7] as replacement.

Another rewriting option is to replace the characteristics with their antonyms, in order to support possible study in gender bias or other fields which need to change the characteristics to the opposite. To replace characteristics with their *antonyms* we follow nearly the same methodology as above except for the following adaptions:

- **W2V_own and W2V_google:** In order to find the opposite adjectives in the vector space, we subtract the adjectives' sentimental polarity (i.e., positive or negative) and add the opposite polarity. For instance, for the positive word *optimistic*, we select the word whose embedding is closest to the vector representing *optimistic - positive + negative*. We use SenticNet [4] to obtain the sentimental polarity of the adjective.
- **BERT:** We combine WordNet with the pre-trained BERT model to select appropriate alternatives to replace the adjectives. First, a set of antonyms of the target adjective is selected from WordNet. With the target adjective masked out, each candidate antonym is ranked by the pre-trained BERT model. The antonym with the highest score, i.e., the one that fits the pre-trained language model best, is chosen as the replacement.

4 Evaluation

We evaluate our approach on a corpus of English fictional texts. To assess the quality of our rewriting model, we evaluate NER and CR separately, assess the readability of the rewritten texts, and conduct a user study to measure the performance of different rewriting methods and the overall acceptance of the rewritten texts.

4.1 Dataset

Our corpus consists of the summaries of 72,487 English books that are catalogued as fictional juvenile works in the WorldCat library catalogue[9]. The average length of the summaries is 216 words, and the vocabulary size is 26,768 words. This dataset is used to train our own Word2Vec embeddings for the character replacement, as mentioned in Sect. 3.2. This corpus also serves as the original fictional texts based on which the parallel corpus is built.

---

[8] https://github.com/mmihaltz/word2vec-GoogleNews-vectors.
[9] https://www.worldcat.org/.

Table 1. Example errors for NER and CR

Method	Sentence	Error
NER	*...who were the three people she spoke of when **Death** carried her away' Casey must...*	The person name 'Death' is not identified correctly
CR	*...As **she** explores the wreckage of **her** own marriage, **Plump** offers a beautifully told ..*	Plump, the pronouns 'she' and 'her' refer to the same person 'Plump'. The pronouns are annotated, but 'Plump' is not annotated

4.2 Performance of NER and CR

To evaluate NER and CR, the first two authors independently annotated 20 randomly chosen texts and agreed on a final annotation in case of differences. We obtained F_1 scores for NER on Stanza of 0.953 and CR with CoreNLP of 0.868. The results show that Stanza and CoreNLP perform well on our dataset. Stanza is able to identify persons with high accuracy, while CoreNLP can identify referential relationships between the fictional characters and personal pronouns with reasonable accuracy. However, we observe some errors, as shown in Table 1. Such errors may prevent readers from accepting the rewritten texts, while this is not necessarily related to any implicit biases.

4.3 Text Readability

Ideally, apart from changing the gender and characteristics of the character, the original texts should remain consistent in its story. This also applies to readability; that is, the rewritten text should be at the same or similar readability level as the original one. Therefore, we assess the impact of our model on the readability of the rewritten texts. As readability measures, we use the Flesch-Kincaid Grade Level [13] and the Automated Readability Index [26]. The former score is a linear combination of average sentence length and the average number of syllables of a word, while the latter calculates readability as a linear combination of characters per word and sentence length.

We calculate the readability in terms of school grade level for both, the original and the rewritten texts. Both measures of readability are then averaged for each text. The readability difference is then calculated by subtracting the original text's grade level from that of the rewritten one. We assess how different stages in our model, i.e., the paraphrase generation and different character modification methods, affect the readability. Text readability evaluation is performed on 100 randomly selected texts. The results are shown in Table 2. The metrics are defined as follows:

Diff$_{absolute}$. Averaging each method's absolute differences shows the absolute difference on the readability without considering if the rewritten text is easier or harder for the reader to read.

Table 2. Result of readability evaluation. The *Original–Rewritten* results are between original and rewritten text (either directly after paraphrasing or the final rewritten text generated by different replacement methods). The *PG-CM* results are between the paraphrased text and the final rewritten one.

Indicator	Method	Character modification (CM)								Mean
	Paraphrase generation (PG)	Synonymous rewriting				Antonymous rewriting				
		WordNet	W2V_own	W2V_google	BERT	WordNet	W2V_own	W2V_google	BERT	
Diff_absolute (Original-Rewritten)	1.94	2.01	2.07	1.96	2.27	2.00	2.10	1.98	2.27	2.08
Diff_simplify (Original-Rewritten)	1.61*	1.08*	1.48*	1.20*	1.84*	1.18*	1.53*	1.33*	1.85*	1.43
Diff_complicate (Original-Rewritten)	0.98	2.77	1.78	2.27	1.27	2.48	1.72	1.94	1.27	1.94
Diff_absolute (PG-CM)	-	1.22	0.72	0.96	0.74	1.06	0.69	0.75	0.75	0.86
Diff_simplify (PG-CM)	-	0.05	0.16	0.06	0.44*	0.06	0.18	0.07	0.45*	0.18
Diff_complicate (PG-CM)	-	3.50*	1.70*	2.70*	0.90	2.98*	1.52*	2.04*	0.92	2.03

*This indicates that the majority (more than half) of rewritten texts are easier (or more difficult) to read.

Diff_simplify. This only takes into account the rewritten texts that have lower grade level on readability and show the average difference.

Diff_complicate. This indicator calculates the average difference only if the rewriting text has a higher readability level.

Overall, the readability level of the rewritten texts differs from that of the original by two grades, as indicated by the mean Diff_absolute (Original–Method). Most rewritten texts are easier to read, as the symbol * is mostly attached to the indicator Diff_simplify (Original–Method). It also shows that the paraphrase generation step has a more significant influence on readability than character modification. The difference between paraphrased text and character modified text (*PG-CM*) shows that, except for the BERT Mask Filling method, other three replacement methods tend to make the texts more complicated to read. A closer inspection also indicates that the first three methods tend to provide more obscure adjectives as the replacement.

In conclusion, the paraphrasing in our model impacts readability by mostly simplifying the original texts. Synonymous Rewriting and Antonymous Rewriting have no significant difference in terms of the impact on readability. The BERT Mask filling method tends to simplify the texts, while the other three replacement methods do the opposite.

4.4   User Study

A two-stage user study was conducted to evaluate our rewriting methods and the rewritten texts' overall acceptance. We collected human readers' assessments on different rewriting methods applied on individual sentences in the first stage. In the second stage, we investigated human readers' overall attitude towards the synonymously or antonymously rewritten texts. In total, 23 students in the English speaking Master program of the University participated in the user study.

Rewriting Method Evaluation. As described in Sect. 3.2, we implemented four different methods to modify the character's characteristics by replacing corresponding adjectives with their synonyms or antonyms. In the first stage of the user study, we collect human readers' judgments to determine which method produces the most naturally rewritten sentences. We randomly selected two groups of sentences, each containing two individual sentences. For the first group, each sentence was synonymously rewritten while the sentences in the second were antonymously rewritten. During the user study, participants were asked to judge for each of the four rewritten sentences the appropriateness of replacements on a 5-point Likert scale (1: completely disagree, 5: completely agree) and the question is phrased as "Please rate the above sentences based on whether their substitutions(the bold words) are appropriate". In order to avoid bias, the original sentences were not shown to the participants.

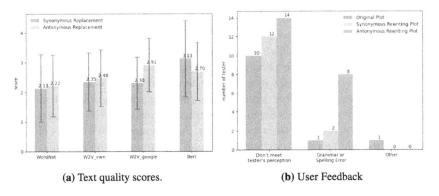

(a) Text quality scores.   (b) User Feedback

Fig. 4. User study results. (a) shows the approval scores of the sentences rewritten by different methods (a higher score is better). (b) shows the frequencies of the reasons chosen by the participants when judging a plot is unreasonable.

The user study results are shown in Fig. 4a. For the synonymously rewritten sentences, the BERT method had the highest score. WordNet, W2V_own, W2V_google showed better results for rewriting with antonyms than with synonyms. W2V_google was perceived best for antonymously rewritten sentences. The inferior performance for antonyms vs. synonyms using BERT can be explained as follows: the method first gets candidate antonyms from WordNet before calculating their probability scores; however, some antonyms do not exist in the pre-trained BERT model. This may lead to a less appropriate candidate being chosen as the replacement. The result suggests to use BERT for rewriting using synonyms and W2V_google to rewrite the texts antonymously.

Overall Acceptance. In the second stage, participants were asked to evaluate six fictional texts (two original, two synonymously rewritten and two antonymously rewritten ones). These six texts depict six different storylines. Based on our preliminary manual inspection and the readability evaluation results, we chose the BERT method to modify characters' characteristics for Synonymous Rewriting and Antonymous Rewriting. The six fictional texts were presented to the participants in a randomized order. In detail, the participants were asked "How do you feel after reading?" first and needed to select one level from *reasonable, almost reasonable* or *unreasonable* for each text. Additionally, the participants were asked "Why do you think the plot is reasonable or unreasonable?" and needed to select the major reason for their choices or provide their own reasons.

From the feedback collected during this study stage, 73.91% of the participants judged the original fictional texts reasonable or almost reasonable, and 69.57% judged the synonymously rewritten texts reasonable or almost reasonable. This is interesting because it suggests that switching gender barely makes the whole story less reasonable. At the same time, only 52.17% had the same judgments towards the antonymously rewritten texts. The reasons for judging a text not reasonable are provided in Fig. 4b. An almost equal amount of users did not think the texts meet their perception, no matter they were original or rewritten. We do not know the exact reasons for the mismatch between the texts and human reader's perception, but synonymous rewriting does not seem to have an influence. Slightly more users deemed the antonymously rewritten texts unreasonable due to not meeting their perception. Antonymous rewriting is clearly a more difficult task, as many participants found grammar or spelling mistakes in the antonymously rewritten texts. However, these grammar issues are a potential reason why less users deem antonymously rewritten texts reasonable.

4.5   Detecting Spelling and Grammar Issues

The user study reveals a high percentage of antonymously rewritten texts not deemed reasonable, due to grammar issues. Here, we investigate, whether grammar issues can be identified programmatically as a pre-requisite to potentially resolve them and improve antonymous rewriting in future work. We use the open source software LanguageTool[10] containing over 4,800 rules to detect potential spelling mistakes and grammar errors. For a description of the categories please refer to the LanguageTool community[11].

We randomly selected 100 fictional plots from our corpus on which we perform the paraphrase generation and character modification with all eight characteris-

---

[10] https://pypi.org/project/language-tool-python/, python wrapper for https://languagetool.org.
[11] https://community.languagetool.org/rule/list?lang=en.

Table 3. Spelling and grammar errors of 100 fictional texts at different stages. The first column indicates the stage of the rewriting model and the remaining columns represent categories of spelling or grammar errors defined by **LanguageTool**.

Stage	Misspelling	Typographical	Whitespace	Grammar	Style	Uncategorized	Duplication
Original	401	193	46	22	7	2	0
PG	421	53	44	20	9	0	3
Synonymous rewriting							
W2V_own	769	110	101	68	9	1	20
W2V_google	996	45	102	50	8	0	6
WordNet	933	133	102	48	11	1	1
BERT	650	109	93	10	11	1	2
Antonymous rewriting							
W2V_own	768	111	101	50	10	1	9
W2V_google	833	39	102	54	8	0	1
WordNet	767	130	101	39	9	1	1
BERT	833	107	91	24	9	1	1

tic replacement methods. The results of the spelling and grammar check for each stage (from the original text over paraphrasing to the final rewritten text produced by a particular method) are shown in Table 3. The rather high amount of misspellings (401) in the original text can be explained by the made-up names for the character and locations in the fictional plots. Since many rare names exist in our name dictionary, the number of misspelling errors increases after we replace the character's name during the character modification. The paraphrasing step barely changes the amount of errors, except for the typographical issues, which decrease from 193 to 53. We found many incorrectly opening and closing quotation marks in the original text, an issue the paraphrasing step mitigates.

The character modification part is also found to introduce additional whitespace errors. These are due to tokenization, i.e., treating a single word wrongly as two tokens when splitting a sentence into individual tokens. The increase of duplication errors for W2V_own may be explained by the limited vocabulary of our corpus.

While the text quality evaluation (cf. Sect. 4.4) suggests the use of W2V_google for antonymous rewriting, the spelling and grammar check results confirm our choice of BERT. BERT outperforms the other methods in particular in terms of grammar issues, both for synonymous and antonymous rewriting. Still, the amount of grammar issues in antonymous rewriting (24) is more than twice as high as in synonymous rewriting (10), confirming the results from the user study. Yet, these results suggest that grammar issues can be identified programmatically, providing an opportunity to also resolve them programmatically in the future.

5   Conclusion

In this paper, we proposed a fiction rewriting model to build a parallel corpus for future studies of gender bias. Our model combines paraphrase generation with character detection and characteristic replacement. The evaluation shows that, compared to the original fiction, the user acceptance of synonymously rewritten texts is roughly on par with the original, while antonymously rewritten texts perform worse. An analysis shows that rewriting with antonyms tends to generate unnatural texts or introduce grammatical mistakes. In conclusion, synonymously rewritten fictional texts produced by our approach can be deemed suitable for building a gender parallel corpus, while antonymous rewriting needs some future improvements, e.g., an automatic grammar correction. Future work could investigate the alteration of further aspects of the stories (e.g., location, events) and investigate their influence, as well as improve the naturalness of the rewriting method, especially for the antonymous rewriting.

References

1. Bannard, C., Callison-Burch, C.: Paraphrasing with bilingual parallel corpora. In: Proceedings of the 43rd Annual Meeting of the Association for Computational Linguistics (ACL 2005), pp. 597–604 (2005)
2. CaiyunWiki: LingoCloud API in 5 minutes (2020). https://open.caiyunapp.com/LingoCloud_API_in_5_minutes. Accessed 01 June 2020
3. Caliskan, A., Bryson, J.J., Narayanan, A.: Semantics derived automatically from language corpora contain human-like biases. Science **356**(6334), 183–186 (2017)
4. Cambria, E., Li, Y., Xing, F.Z., Poria, S., Kwok, K.: Senticnet 6: ensemble application of symbolic and subsymbolic AI for sentiment analysis. In: Proceedings of the 29th ACM International Conference on Information and Knowledge Management, pp. 105–114 (2020)
5. Cryan, J., Tang, S., Zhang, X., Metzger, M., Zheng, H., Zhao, B.Y.: Detecting gender stereotypes: lexicon vs. supervised learning methods. In: Proceedings of the 2020 CHI Conference on Human Factors in Computing Systems, pp. 1–11 (2020)
6. Davis, E.: The physical traints that define men and women in literature. https://pudding.cool/2020/07/gendered-descriptions/
7. Devlin, J., Chang, M.W., Lee, K., Toutanova, K.: BERT: Pre-training of deep bidirectional transformers for language understanding. arXiv preprint arXiv:1810.04805 (2018)
8. Faruqui, M., Dodge, J., Jauhar, S.K., Dyer, C., Hovy, E., Smith, N.A.: Retrofitting word vectors to semantic lexicons. In: Proceedings of NAACL (2015)
9. Field, A., Tsvetkov, Y.: Unsupervised discovery of implicit gender bias. arXiv preprint arXiv:2004.08361 (2020)
10. Garg, N., Schiebinger, L., Jurafsky, D., Zou, J.: Word embeddings quantify 100 years of gender and ethnic stereotypes. Proc. Nat. Acad. Sci. **115**(16), E3635–E3644 (2018)
11. Habash, N., Bouamor, H., Chung, C.: Automatic gender identification and reinflection in Arabic. In: Proceedings of the First Workshop on Gender Bias in Natural Language Processing, pp. 155–165 (2019)
12. Jhamtani, H., Gangal, V., Hovy, E., Nyberg, E.: Shakespearizing modern language using copy-enriched sequence-to-sequence models. arXiv preprint arXiv:1707.01161 (2017)

13. Kincaid, J.P., Fishburne, R.P., Jr., Rogers, R.L., Chissom, B.S.: Derivation of new readability formulas (automated readability index, fog count and flesch reading ease formula) for navy enlisted personnel. Technical Report, Naval Technical Training Command Millington TN Research Branch (1975)
14. Klein, D., Smarr, J., Nguyen, H., Manning, C.D.: Named entity recognition with character-level models. In: Proceedings of the Seventh Conference on Natural Language Learning at HLT-NAACL 2003-Volume 4, pp. 180–183. Association for Computational Linguistics (2003)
15. Lample, G., Subramanian, S., Smith, E., Denoyer, L., Ranzato, M., Boureau, Y.L.: Multiple-attribute text rewriting. In: International Conference on Learning Representations (2019). https://openreview.net/forum?id=H1g2NhC5KQ
16. Li, J., Sun, A., Han, J., Li, C.: A survey on deep learning for named entity recognition. IEEE Trans. Knowl. Data Eng., 1 (2020). https://doi.org/10.1109/TKDE. 2020.2981314
17. Manning, C.D., Surdeanu, M., Bauer, J., Finkel, J.R., Bethard, S., McClosky, D.: The stanford CORENLP natural language processing toolkit. In: Proceedings of 52nd Annual Meeting of the Association for Computational Linguistics: System Demonstrations, pp. 55–60 (2014)
18. McCollum, H.: Tangled Hearts. Highland Hearts, Entangled Publishing, LLC (2014). https://books.google.nl/books?id=XcRRAQAAQBAJ
19. Mikheev, A.: Automatic rule induction for unknown-word guessing. Computat. Linguist. **23**(3), 405–423 (1997)
20. Mikolov, T., Chen, K., Corrado, G., Dean, J.: Efficient estimation of word representations in vector space. arXiv preprint arXiv:1301.3781 (2013)
21. Miller, G.A.: Wordnet: a lexical database for English. Commun. ACM **38**(11), 39–41 (1995)
22. Qi, P., Zhang, Y., Zhang, Y., Bolton, J., Manning, C.D.: Stanza: A python natural language processing toolkit for many human languages. arXiv preprint arXiv:2003.07082 (2020)
23. Rowling, J., GrandPré, M.: Harry Potter and the Sorcerer's Stone. Grades 7–9, A.A.L. Books Inc., Series. A.A. Levine Books, Hoboken (1998). https://books. google.nl/books?id=dmouxgEACAAJ
24. Rudinger, R., Naradowsky, J., Leonard, B., Durme, B.V.: Gender bias in coreference resolution (2018)
25. Santos, C.N.D., Melnyk, I., Padhi, I.: Fighting offensive language on social media with unsupervised text style transfer. arXiv preprint arXiv:1805.07685 (2018)
26. Senter, R., Smith, E.A.: Automated readability index. CINCINNATI UNIV OH, Technical Report (1967)
27. Sun, T., et al.: Mitigating gender bias in natural language processing: Literature review. In: Proceedings of the 57th Annual Meeting of the Association for Computational Linguistics, pp. 1630–1640. Association for Computational Linguistics, Florence, Italy, July 2019. https://doi.org/10.18653/v1/P19-1159, https://www. aclweb.org/anthology/P19-1159
28. Woodsend, K., Lapata, M.: Text rewriting improves semantic role labeling. J. Artif. Intell. Res. **51**, 133–164 (2014)
29. Zhao, S., Wang, H., Lan, X., Liu, T.: Leveraging multiple MT engines for paraphrase generation. In: Proceedings of the 23rd International Conference on Computational Linguistics (Coling 2010), pp. 1326–1334 (2010)

Transformer-Based Automatic Punctuation Prediction and Word Casing Reconstruction of the ASR Output

Jan Švec[1]([⊠])[iD], Jan Lehečka[1][iD], Luboš Šmídl[2][iD], and Pavel Ircing[2][iD]

[1] NTIS, University of West Bohemia, Pilsen, Czech Republic
{honzas,jlehecka}@ntis.zcu.cz
[2] Department of Cybernetics, University of West Bohemia, Pilsen, Czech Republic
{smidl,ircing}@kky.zcu.cz

Abstract. The paper proposes a module for automatic punctuation prediction and casing reconstruction based on transformers architectures (BERT/T5) that constitutes the current state-of-the-art in many similar NLP tasks. The main motivation for our work was to increase the readability of the ASR output. The ASR output is usually in the form of a continuous stream of text, without punctuation marks and with all words in lowercase. The resulting punctuation and casing reconstruction module is evaluated on both the written text and the actual ASR output in three languages (English, Czech and Slovak).

Keywords: ASR · BERT · T5 · Punctuation predictor · Word casing reconstruction

1 Introduction

Various automatic methods for adding correct punctuation marks into the output of the automatic speech recognition (ASR) system were being proposed ever since the ASR systems started to be widely used for speech transcription in practical tasks. Most ASR systems are not designed to insert punctuation marks in their output nor to handle word casing; yet the correct placement of those linguistic features greatly improves the readability of the ASR output and could also result in the better performance of "downstream" NLP modules in the case when the text output is further processed.

The modules developed for punctuation prediction have always employed the best NLP techniques available. As the current state-of-the-art for sequence-to-sequence NLP tasks – and this is how the punctuation restoration is usually handled – are the various types of recurrent neural networks or networks with multi-headed self-attention mechanism, those networks are most frequently used and also achieve the best results [3,5,21,22]. Other approaches also combine linguistic information such as syntactic trees or n-gram language models [1,23] or prosodic information [8,20].

Recent techniques use the transfer-learning approach, where a generic sequence processing model is trained in an unsupervised manner from the huge text corpus and subsequently fine-tuned on the target task. In this paper we will deal with the Bidirectional Encoder Representations from Transformers (BERT) [2] and the Text-to-Text

© Springer Nature Switzerland AG 2021
K. Ekštein et al. (Eds.): TSD 2021, LNAI 12848, pp. 86–94, 2021.
https://doi.org/10.1007/978-3-030-83527-9_7

Transfer Transformer (T5) [16]. While the BERT model was successfully applied to the punctuation prediction task [12], the T5 model has not been (to our knowledge) used in this context.

The approach of [12] is to use the pre-trained BERT model and stack a bidirectional LSTM layer and a Conditional Random Field (CRF) layer on top of it to obtain the punctuation predictions. We think that this approach is against the motto of the transformers *attention is all you need* [24], because it uses *three* different mechanisms to capture the time-dependency of the input tokens: self-attention, bidirectional LSTM and CRF with Viterbi decoding.

In this paper, we present two different ways of extending a basic BERT encoder to predict the punctuation and the word casing in an input text. The first approach consists of a stack of dense layers atop of the pre-trained BERT together with the simple pooling method. The second approach employs the recent T5 model and treats the punctuation detection and word casing restoration as the text-to-text translation. The T5 model virtually consists of an encoder with the same structure as the BERT model and an attention-based decoder which allows sequence generation of output texts. In both cases, we use only the lexical information from an ASR output since this approach simplifies the processing pipeline. At the same time, the method could be used as a post-processing step independently on the ASR in use.

2 Proposed Models

BERT-Based Model. The model consists of BERT model followed by additional classification layers predicting both the punctuation marks and word casing at the same time. For multi-task classification, we use a time-distributed dense layer with 256 ReLU units which is shared by both classification tasks to model dependency between punctuation and word casing. For each classification task we use two additional time-distributed dense layers with 128 and 64 ReLU units and the final classification softmax layer. The overall scheme of the neural network architecture is depicted in Fig. 1.

As punctuation labels, we use four labels related to the three most common punctuation marks (full stop, comma, question mark) and no punctuation. For word casing reconstruction, we use three classes: lowercase, uppercase and titlecase (only the first letter of the word is in uppercase). We use the sum of categorical cross-entropy losses of both softmax outputs with equal weights as the training criterion. The implementation of multi-task training allows to integrate even more groups of target usable for grammar correction or detection of errors in textual data [14, 19].

To tokenize input texts, we use SentencePiece model (see Sect. 2.1). Because the BERT's output is related to input tokens (not words), we assign the target label to each SentencePiece of the word, i.e. if there is a full stop after the word, all SentencePieces of the word are labelled with the full stop label and similarly for the casing restoration problem.

In the prediction phase, it is necessary to combine the predictions for the partial SentencePieces into a word-level predictions using a per-word pooling. We use a simple average pooling algorithm to obtain the word-level predictions. We also hardcoded a rule which sets the titlecase class to the word immediately following a full stop or

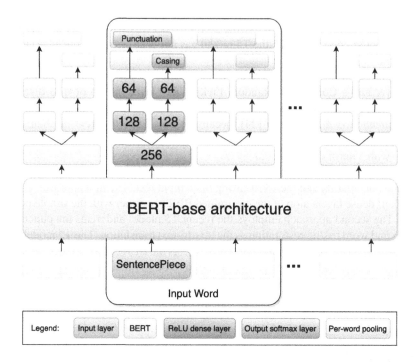

Fig. 1. The architecture of the BERT-based neural network.

a question mark. This titlecase label could be overwritten with the prediction of the uppercase class. The same heuristic is used for the T5 model.

During fine-tuning, we updated the parameters of the following encoder layers: self-attention normalization layers, feed forward normalization layers, multi-headed self-attention of the last layer and the adapter layers [6]. The classification layers are initialized and fully trained.

T5-Based Model. In the T5 experiments, we used the models which were pre-trained on general texts in an unsupervised manner and subsequently fine-tuned to the punctuation and casing restoration tasks. During the fine-tuning we trained only the weights of the decoder, keeping the weights of an encoder and the shared SentencePiece embeddings fixed. The model was trained to map from the input sequence of lower-case tokens (i.e. in the same form as output of an ASR) to the sequence of correctly cased tokens including punctuation. This could be illustrated using Fig. 2, where *ASR result* is used as an input and *Reference text* as an output of the T5 model.

Baseline Models. To compare the performance of the evaluated models, we also trained a simple baseline RNN model. This model has a similar structure to our BERT model on Fig. 1, but the pre-trained BERT is replaced with two layers of bidirectional LSTM (bidiLSTM) with the same dimensionality. For this baseline model we don't use any pre-training. The second baseline method is the BERT with the bidirectional LSTM and CRF layers on top of it (in tables denoted as BERT+CRF) [12].

Table 1. Statistics of experimental data (k – thousands, M – millions, # – number of).

Statistics	English	Czech	Slovak
# SentencePieces	31k	100k	50k
# fine-tuning words	128M	128M	128M
Size of ASR lexicon	206k	1.4M	754k
ASR WER [%]	19.7	7.9	11.0
# Test words excl. punct.	373k	478k	403k
# Full stops	17k	32k	27k
# Commas	19k	39k	31k
# Question marks	494	926	628
# Titlecase words	54k	61k	54k
# Uppercase words	3k	2k	4k

2.1 SentencePiece Model

The SentencePiece method [9] provides a *lossless tokenization*, i.e. the tokenized text could be transformed into a sequence of tokens and back without any loss of characters or punctuation and spacing. This is important for the T5 model, where the Sentence-Piece model is used to construct the lexical representation of output token indices.

The only parameter needed to train the SentencePiece model is the size of the vocabulary. A great advantage of SentencePiece models is the production of self-contained models, which are easily usable in subsequent tasks and provide reproducible results. The SentencePiece tokenization was used for all models, except the English BERT model where the original WordPiece tokenization provided as part of the Google's BERT-base model was used.[1] The sizes of SentencePiece vocabularies are shown in Table 1.

2.2 BERT Pre-training

For experiments with English data, we used Google's pre-trained BERT-base English uncased model (version from March 11th, 2020)[2]. For Czech and Slovak, we pre-trained our own models from a collection of web data processed in our web mining tool [18]. The web text data are suitable not for classical NLP tasks such as topic identification [10, 11] but also supports many ASR-specific models [17]. Our motivation was to train an ASR-friendly BERT, so we removed all punctuation marks and word casing information from the training data. We kept the architecture of the Czech and Slovak models the same as for Google's BERT-base model. More detail about the pre-training of our models could be found in [19].

---

[1] To simplify the text, we will further denote the WordPieces as SentencePieces as well.
[2] https://github.com/google-research/bert.

```
Reference text: Seeking to paint Mr Trump as a modern-day Nixon, Mr
Crow asked as he wrapped up his portion of the closing presentation:
"How many falsehoods can we take? When will it be one too many?"

ASR result: seeking to paint mister tramp as a modern day nixon mister
crow asked as he wrapped up his portion of the closing  presentation
how many falsehoods can we take when will it be one too many

Processed: Seeking to paint Mister Tramp as a modern day Nixon. Mister
Crow asked as he wrapped up his portion of the closing presentation
How many falsehoods can we take? When will it be one too many?
```

Fig. 2. An example output of the proposed BERT model. The reference text is an excerpt from the Independent's article *"Democrats link Trump to Nixon as they lay impeachment case to rest"* (Feb 3, 2020, https://tinyurl.com/y8mfk44n).

2.3 T5 Pre-training

In addition to the pre-trained BERT models we also experimented with the Text-to-Text Transfer Transformer (T5) model [16]. Generally, the T5 model is trained as the full encoder-decoder transformer. We use the T5-base architecture, whose encoder is in structure equivalent to the BERT-base model. The structure of the decoder is similar, only with additional input-to-output attention layers. The training criterion for the T5 model is similar to the BERT – the model tries to recover missing token spans in the output. The general advantage of the T5 model is the ability to perform many text-to-text tasks like text summarization, topic detection or sentiment analysis.

For experiments with English data, we used the Google's T5-base English model (version from October 21th, 2019)[3] trained from Common Crawl data[4]. We replicated the same pre-processing procedure to obtain the Czech and Slovak data and we pre-trained our own T5 models for these languages.

3   Experimental Evaluation

Since we focus on the processing of the ASR output, we wanted to evaluate also the influence of ASR errors on the prediction performance for both the punctuation prediction and the casing restoration.

To evaluate a sufficiently large corpus including punctuation, we decided to use the synthesized speech data. Using such setup we are able to carefully select large chunks of text while having the corresponding speech representation in all three languages at the same time. By synthesizing the data we are sure that the evaluation data are not part of the pre-training nor the fine-tuning data.

For this evaluation we used the ARTIC text-to-speech system [4,7] to synthesize the audio data and subsequently the UWebASR speech recognizer service provided as part of the CLARIN infrastructure [25]. For English, we used the models trained

---

[3] https://github.com/google-research/text-to-text-transfer-transformer.

[4] https://commoncrawl.org/.

from LibriSpeech [15]. For Czech and Slovak, the recognition models are trained using the mixture of data ranging from read speech to spontaneous speech and similarly the language model contains both the transcripts of spontaneous speech and the web-mined text data. There is no overlap with the test data for any of the evaluated languages. The ASR performances and statistics of test sets are shown in Table 1.

To evaluate the models, we selected the test set containing 10k textual paragraphs from February 2020 collected in our web mining tool [18]. The paragraphs were selected to be longer than 20 words and not to contain numbers written using digits to avoid ambiguities in TTS and ASR cycle. The statistics of the test data are shown in Table reftab:statistics. No portion of the test data was used in BERT/T5 pre-training nor in ASR training. We trained three models for three languages: English, Czech and Slovak. The models were trained using ADAM optimizer for 100 epochs. Each epoch contained 10k sequences of SentencePieces with a maximum length of 128. The learning rate decayed from 10^{-3} to 10^{-4}.

For each language we evaluated the classification performance of the punctuation marks on the clean textual data. We evaluated the F1 metric as a harmonic mean of precision and recall for each punctuation mark and then we computed a weighted average F1 with weights corresponding to the support of the given label. We also used the Slot Error Rate (SER) metric defined as SER $= \frac{I+D+S}{C+D+S}$ where C is the number of correctly classified punctuation marks and I, D and S are the numbers of wrongly inserted, deleted and substituted punctuation marks in the hypothesis [13]. The denominator $C + D + S$ is equal to the number of punctuation marks in the reference. The slot error rate metric has a similar meaning and interpretation as the word error rate (WER) used to evaluate the speech recognition systems.

To evaluate the word casing reconstruction, we computed F1 for the titlecase and uppercase classes. To align predictions with reference texts, we used Levenshtein distance treating the punctuation as other tokens.

To avoid the bias caused by the fact that almost every paragraph ends with a full stop, we joined all the sentences into a single stream of tokens. This way no punctuation marks could be predicted only based on the position in the input sequence.

4 Results

First, we evaluated the F1 and SER metrics for punctuation detection (top part of Table 2) and F1 for casing restoration (top part of Table 3) on the ground-truth textual data, i.e. no TTS nor ASR were involved.

In the subsequent experiment we used the TTS/ASR chain to produce the recognized data with ASR errors (for WER on the test data see Table 1). The overall SER deteriorates with the introduction of ASR errors (bottom part of Table 2). For casing restoration, the prediction of the uppercase class is much worse in the data with ASR errors than in the textual data. This is caused by the fact that the TTS actually spells out the abbreviations – which constitute the vast majority of uppercase words – and subsequently the ASR recognizes the sequence of spelled out letters, not the original abbreviation.

The results of the baseline BidiLSTM are outperformed by all the attention-based methods (BERT and T5) in both considered tasks by a large margin. The differences

Table 2. *Punctuation prediction results.* We are showing results for three languages (English, Czech and Slovak), and models evaluated on two types of data: *ground-truth* textual data without ASR errors and *ASR output*. All values in the table are in percents.

	Model	English		Czech		Slovak	
		F1	SER	F1	SER	F1	SER
Ground-truth	BidiLSTM	74.7	39.7	82.8	25.1	83.7	24.7
	BERT+CRF	79.9	32.3	86.7	18.7	88.6	17.0
	BERT	80.0	32.0	86.4	18.9	88.4	17.1
	T5	81.2	30.4	86.4	19.4	87.0	19.5
ASR output	BidiLSTM	59.3	67.4	79.1	32.0	77.3	36.8
	BERT+CRF	63.1	62.6	83.2	25.1	82.6	28.4
	BERT	64.0	59.8	83.1	25.2	82.5	28.4
	T5	64.9	59.6	82.6	26.2	80.9	31.1

Table 3. *Casing restoration results.* We are showing F1 scores for three languages (English, Czech and Slovak), two casing classes (Title-/Upper-case) and models evaluated on two types of data: *ground-truth* textual data without ASR errors and *ASR output*. F1 values in percents.

	Model	English		Czech		Slovak	
		Title	Upper	Title	Upper	Title	Upper
Ground-truth	BidiLSTM	91.5	93.6	88.4	93.8	89.9	93.9
	BERT+CRF	93.4	94.5	91.6	94.5	93.5	94.7
	BERT	93.6	94.5	91.3	93.4	93.4	94.5
	T5	94.1	93.1	91.3	93.5	92.6	94.5
ASR output	BidiLSTM	70.6	8.5	80.1	43.2	74.2	39.6
	BERT+CRF	72.4	11.4	83.7	44.0	78.7	42.5
	BERT	72.9	11.0	83.3	43.1	78.6	41.8
	T5	73.1	12.0	83.0	45.6	77.0	41.0

between BERT+CRF and the proposed (much simpler) BERT model are negligible and we can conclude that the use of the dense layers with word-level pooling is sufficient to robustly recover the punctuation and word casing. The results of the T5 model are also comparable with the encoder-only BERT architecture and the encoder-decoder architecture of T5 could be easily adapted to more general tasks than the baseline BERT+CRF.

5 Conclusions

The paper presented a simple classification model for punctuation detection and casing restoration based on a pre-trained transformer-based models: BERT and T5. The models are easily trainable as it requires only tokenized texts with punctuation and pre-trained BERT/T5 models for a given language. We trained models for three languages and we experimentally evaluated the behavior of such models under the presence of ASR errors.

We proposed two different approaches for employing the pre-trained models (BERT/T5) in the punctuation prediction and word casing reconstruction tasks. We compared the models with the state-of-the-art method combining BERT+LSTM+CRF and we can state that the same results could be achieved by a much simpler (BERT) or a more general (T5) models.

The motivation for future work could be illustrated by an example output of the model. Figure 2 shows the reference text, a lowercase ASR output and finally the output of the proposed method with predicted punctuation and restored casing. Therefore in future work, we would like to target some sub-problems: (1) the suitability of the BERT model to real-time speech processing. We can use a causal attention mask for the computation of BERT encoder self-attentions and perform an incremental ASR post-processing; (2) the extension to other punctuation marks such as quotes and colons. This could be more suitable for the T5 model because multiple punctuation marks such as colons and quotes could be inserted after a single token; (3) to train the models from ASR data to better model recognition errors.

Acknowledgment. This research was supported by the Technology Agency of the Czech Republic, project No. TN01000024. Computational resources were supplied by the project "e-Infrastruktura CZ" (e-INFRA LM2018140).

References

1. Batista, F., Caseiro, D., Mamede, N.J., Trancoso, I.: Recovering punctuation marks for automatic speech recognition. In: Proceedings of Interspeech, vol. 2007, pp. 2153–2156 (2007)
2. Devlin, J., Chang, M.W., Lee, K., Toutanova, K.: BERT: pre-training of deep bidirectional transformers for language understanding. In: Proceedings of the 2019 Conference of the NAACL: HLT, vol. 1, pp. 4171–4186. ACL, Minneapolis, Minnesota (2019)
3. Żelasko, P., Szymański, P., Mizgajski, J., Szymczak, A., Carmiel, Y., Dehak, N.: Punctuation prediction model for conversational speech. In: Proceedings of Interspeech 2018, pp. 2633–2637 (2018). https://doi.org/10.21437/Interspeech
4. Hanzlíček, Z., Matoušek, J., Tihelka, D.: Experiments on reducing footprint of unit selection TTS system. In: Habernal, I., Matoušek, V. (eds.) TSD 2013. LNCS (LNAI), vol. 8082, pp. 249–256. Springer, Heidelberg (2013). https://doi.org/10.1007/978-3-642-40585-3_32
5. Sojka, P., Kopeček, I., Pala, K., Horák, A. (eds.): TSD 2020. LNCS (LNAI), vol. 12284. Springer, Cham (2020). https://doi.org/10.1007/978-3-030-58323-1
6. Houlsby, N., et al.: Parameter-efficient transfer learning for NLP. In: Proceedings of the 36th International Conference on Machine Learning, vol. 97, pp. 2790–2799. PMLR, Long Beach, California, USA (2019)
7. Kala, J., Matoušek, J.: Very fast unit selection using viterbi search with zero-concatenation-cost chains. In: Proceedings of IEEE ICASSP, pp. 2569–2573 (2014)
8. Kolár, J., Lamel, L.: Development and evaluation of automatic punctuation for French and English speech-to-text. In: Proceedings of Interspeech, vol. 2012, pp. 1376–1379 (2012)
9. Kudo, T., Richardson, J.: Sentencepiece: a simple and language independent subword tokenizer and detokenizer for neural text processing. arXiv preprint arXiv:1808.06226 (2018)
10. Lehečka, J., Švec, J.: Improving multi-label document classification of Czech news articles. In: Král, P., Matoušek, V. (eds.) TSD 2015. LNCS (LNAI), vol. 9302, pp. 307–315. Springer, Cham (2015). https://doi.org/10.1007/978-3-319-24033-6_35

11. Lehečka, J., Švec, J., Ircing, P., Šmídl, L.: Adjusting BERT's pooling layer for large-scale multi-label text classification. In: Sojka, P., Kopeček, I., Pala, K., Horák, A. (eds.) TSD 2020. LNCS (LNAI), vol. 12284, pp. 214–221. Springer, Cham (2020). https://doi.org/10. 1007/978-3-030-58323-1_23
12. Makhija, K., Ho, T.N., Chng, E.S.: Transfer learning for punctuation prediction. In: Asia-Pacific Signal and Information Processing Association Annual Conference, pp. 268–273. IEEE (2019)
13. Makhoul, J., Kubala, F., Schwartz, R., Weischedel, R.: Performance measures for information extraction. In: Proceedings of DARPA Broadcast News Workshop (08 2000)
14. Matoušek, J., Tihelka, D.: Annotation errors detection in TTS corpora. In: INTERSPEECH, Lyon, France, pp. 1511–1515 (2013)
15. Panayotov, V., Chen, G., Povey, D., Khudanpur, S.: Librispeech: an ASR corpus based on public domain audio books. In: Proceedings of IEEE ICASSP, pp. 5206–5210 (2015)
16. Raffel, C., et al.: Exploring the limits of transfer learning with a unified text-to-text transformer. J. Mach. Learn. Res. **21**(140), 1–67 (2020)
17. Švec, J., Hoidekr, J., Soutner, D., Vavruška, J.: Web Text data mining for building large scale language modelling corpus. In: Habernal, I., Matoušek, V. (eds.) TSD 2011. LNCS (LNAI), vol. 6836, pp. 356–363. Springer, Heidelberg (2011). https://doi.org/10.1007/978-3-642-23538-2_45
18. Švec, J., et al.: General framework for mining, processing and storing large amounts of electronic texts for language modeling purposes. Lang. Resour. Eval. **48**(2), 227–248 (2013). https://doi.org/10.1007/s10579-013-9246-z
19. Švec, J., Lehečka, J., Šmídl, L., Ircing, P.: Automatic correction of i/y spelling in Czech ASR output. In: Sojka, P., Kopeček, I., Pala, K., Horák, A. (eds.) TSD 2020. LNCS (LNAI), vol. 12284, pp. 321–330. Springer, Cham (2020). https://doi.org/10.1007/978-3-030-58323-1_35
20. Szaszák, G., Ákos Tündik, M.: Leveraging a character, word and prosody triplet for an asr error robust and agglutination friendly punctuation approach. In: Proceedings of Interspeech 2019, pp. 2988–2992 (2019). https://doi.org/10.21437/Interspeech. 2019-2132
21. Tilk, O., Alumäe, T.: LSTM for punctuation restoration in speech transcripts. In: Proceedings of Interspeech, vol. 2015, pp. 683–687 (2015)
22. Tilk, O., Alumäe, T.: Bidirectional recurrent neural network with attention mechanism for punctuation restoration. In: Proceedings of Interspeech 2016, pp. 3047–3051 (2016). https://doi.org/10.21437/Interspeech. 2016-1517
23. Ueffing, N., Bisani, M., Vozila, P.: Improved models for automatic punctuation prediction for spoken and written text. In: Proceedings of Interspeech, vol. 2013, pp. 3097–3101 (2013)
24. Vaswani, A., et al.: Attention is all you need. In: Advances in Neural Information Processing Systems 2017-Decem(Nips), pp. 5999–6009 (2017)
25. Švec, J., Bulín, M., Pražák, A., Ircing, P.: UWebASR - Web-based ASR engine for Czech and Slovak. In: CLARIN Annual Conference 2018 Proceedings (2018)

A Database and Visualization of the Similarity of Contemporary Lexicons

Gábor Bella[1(✉)] , Khuyagbaatar Batsuren[2] , and Fausto Giunchiglia[1]

[1] University of Trento, via Sommarive, 5, 38123 Trento, Italy
{gabor.bella,fausto.giunchiglia}@unitn.it
[2] National University of Mongolia, Ulanbaatar, Mongolia
khuyagbaatar@num.edu.mn

Abstract. Lexical similarity data, quantifying the "proximity" of languages based on the similarity of their lexicons, has been increasingly used to estimate the cross-lingual reusability of language resources, for tasks such as bilingual lexicon induction or cross-lingual transfer. Existing similarity data, however, originates from the field of comparative linguistics, computed from very small expert-curated vocabularies that are not supposed to be representative of modern lexicons. We explore a different, fully automated approach to lexical similarity computation, based on an existing 8-million-entry cognate database created from online lexicons orders of magnitude larger than the word lists typically used in linguistics. We compare our results to earlier efforts, and automatically produce intuitive visualizations that have traditionally been hand-crafted. With a new, freely available database of over 27 thousand language pairs over 331 languages, we hope to provide more relevant data to cross-lingual NLP applications, as well as material for the synchronic study of contemporary lexicons.

Keywords: Lexical similarity · Cognate · Language diversity · Lexicostatistics · Visualization

1 Introduction

The notion of *lexical similarity*, also known as *lexical distance*, refers to a quantified comparison of the proportion of words shared across languages. It is defined by *The Ethnologue* as *"the percentage of lexical similarity between two linguistic varieties is determined by comparing a set of standardized wordlists and counting those forms that show similarity in both form and meaning."*[1] Computaton methods are typically based on the amount of *cognates*—words of common origin with (more or less) similar pronunciation and meaning—found for a given language pair. The resulting similarity data is used in comparative linguistics to infer or back up hypotheses of phylogeny among languages. In computational linguistics, lexical similarity has also been used in bilingual lexicon induction and, more generally, in the context of the cross-lingual transfer

---

[1] https://www.ethnologue.com/about/language-info.

© Springer Nature Switzerland AG 2021
K. Ekštein et al. (Eds.): TSD 2021, LNAI 12848, pp. 95–104, 2021.
https://doi.org/10.1007/978-3-030-83527-9_8

of language processing tools and resources, in order to estimate the differing performance of specific language pairs or directly as input features [7, 11, 13]. Graphical visualizations of lexical similarity—beyond their popularity among the general public—are useful for a quick qualitative interpretation of the similarity data.

The typical approach in comparative linguistics has been to use a small number (typically less than 100) of carefully selected words with equivalent meanings in each language studied. The word meanings are deliberately chosen from the core vocabularies, and comparisons are made strictly on phonetic representations, also taking sound changes into account in historical studies.

Because these methods have been carefully tuned to the needs of language genealogy, they are less adapted to studies characterizing contemporary vocabularies. For the purposes of computational linguistics or the synchronic study of language diversity [8], similarity information computed on "everyday" written lexicons is more representative than data deliberately tuned for historical studies. English, for instance, borrowed a significant portion of its vocabulary from (the otherwise only distantly related) French. Due to the relative lexical homogeneity of the Romance family, these French borrowings bring the English lexicon closer to Spanish, Portuguese, or Romanian as well. While such evidence of lexical proximity can be useful for computational applications, similarity data from comparative linguistics does not provide this type of insight as they consider borrowings as "noise" over phylogenetic evidence and exclude them by design.

We investigate a different approach based on the the free online *CogNet* database[2] of 8.1-million cognate pairs covering 338 languages, itself computed from large-scale online lexicons. CogNet can be considered reliable (with a precision evaluated to 96%) and is based on a permissive interpretation of the notion of cognacy that includes loanwords, and as such it is well suited to practical cross-lingual applications. From CogNet we compute pairwise similarities among 331 languages, that we make freely downloadable for downstream uses in computational linguistics, e.g. cross-lingual NLP applications. We also provide visualizations of our results that provide an immediate qualitative interpretation of the similarity data and that, contrary to prior work, are computed fully automatically.

The rest of the paper is organized as follows. Section 2 presents the state of the art with respect to known lexical similarity databases and computation methods, as well as existing visualization techniques. Section 3 describes our lexical similarity computation method. Section 4 compares our results quantitatively against existing lexicostatistical similarity data. Section 5 presents our visualization method and results, as well as providing a qualitative visual interpretation of historic versus contemporary lexical similarity. Section 6, finally, provides conclusions.

2   State of the Art

The comparison of lexicons has a methodology established in the framework of *lexicostatistics*, with the underlying idea of inferring the phylogeny of languages from their

---

[2] http://cognet.ukc.disi.unitn.it.

lexicons considered in diachrony [14, 17]. Studies typically span a large number (hundreds or even thousands) of languages, using a small but fully meaning-aligned vocabulary selected from each language. To be able to consider phonetic evolution spanning millennia, very basic words are used—such as *water*, *sun*, or *hand*—and only in phonetic representations, such as from the well-known *Swadesh list* [16]. While such data are of the highest possible quality, they are scarce and only reflect a tiny fraction of the lexicon. Thus, while well-suited for diachronic studies, by design they provide less information about the present state of lexicons and the more recent linguistic and cultural influences to which they were subjected.

There are many examples of popular graph-based visualizations of such data.[3] While informative to non-experts, they are typically human-drawn based on only a handful of language pairs, and therefore are prone to subjective and potentially biased emphasis on certain languages or relationships. For example, for Estonian, the second graph listed in the footnote highlights its two distant European phylogenetic relatives (Hungarian and Finnish), as well as Latvian from the neighboring country, while it does not say anything about its significant Germanic and Slavic loans.

The most similar project we know of is *EZ Glot*.[4] They used a total of roughly 1.5 million contemporary dictionary words taken from overall 93 languages, mined from resources such as *Wiktionary*, *OmegaWiki*, *FreeDict*, or *Apertium*. The precision of their input evidence was self-evaluated to be about 80%.

While our work is also based on comparing online lexicons, we took as our starting point a high-quality cognate database, CogNet [1, 2], evaluated through multiple methods to a precision of 96% and covering 338 languages. CogNet employs etymologic and phonetic evidence, as well as transliteration across 40 scripts, expanding the language pairs covered. In terms of visualization, in contrast to hand-produced graphs, our approach is entirely automatic and free from the bias of manual cherry-picking, favoring a global optimum as it is computed over the entire similarity graph.

3   Automated Similarity Computation

Our input data, v2 of the CogNet database, consists of over 8 million sense-tagged cognate pairs. CogNet was computed from the *Universal Knowledge Core* resource [9], itself built from wordnets, Wiktionary, and other high-quality lexical resources [3, 4, 6, 12].

The identification of cognate pairs having already been done by CogNet, we compute the cognate-content-based similarity between the lexicons of languages A and B as follows:

$$S_{AB} = \frac{\sum_{\forall <c_i^A, c_i^B>} \alpha + (1-\alpha)\mathrm{sim}(c_i^A, c_i^B)}{\frac{2|L_A||L_B|}{|L_A|+|L_B|}}$$

---

[3] To cite a few: https://en.wikipedia.org/wiki/Romance_languages,
https://elms.wpcomstaging.com/2008/03/04/lexical-distance-among-languages-of-europe/,
https://alternativetransport.wordpress.com/2015/05/05/34/.

[4] http://www.ezglot.com.

Table 1. Evaluation results with respect to ASJP data (root mean square error, standard deviation, and correlation), for three robustness levels (full dataset including all language pairs, pairs with medium or high robustness, and pairs with high robustness). We also provide comparisons to EZ Glot over the 27 language pairs it supports.

Dataset	Size	Difference w.r.t. ASJP		
		RMSE	σ	R
CogNet full data	6,420	9.61	8.26	**0.61**
CogNet high+medium robustness	3,975	8.83	7.61	**0.65**
CogNet high robustness	1,399	10.72	8.94	**0.69**
CogNet over EZ Glot language pairs	27	23.01	16.01	**0.69**
EZ Glot	27	30.07	17.27	**0.48**

where $<c_i^A, c_i^B>$ is the ith cognate word pair retrieved from CogNet for the languages A and B and $\text{sim}(c_i^A, c_i^B)$ is a string similarity value:

$$\text{sim}(w_1, w_2) = \frac{\max(l_{w_1}, l_{w_2}) - \text{LD}(w_1, w_2)}{\max(l_{w_1}, l_{w_2})}$$

where LD is the Levenshtein distance and l_w is the length of word w, our hypothesis being that the more similar the cognate words between two languages, the closer the languages themselves to each other. In case w_1 and w_2 use different writing systems, we compare their Latin transliterations, also provided by CogNet. The smoothing factor $0 < \alpha < 1$ lets us avoid penalizing dissimilar cognates excessively, while $\alpha = 1$ cancels word similarity and simplifies the numerator to cognate counting.

The denominator of S_{AB} normalizes the sum by the harmonic mean of the lexicon sizes $|L_A|$ and $|L_B|$: these can range from tens to more than a hundred thousand word senses. Normalization addresses lexicon incompleteness, in order to avoid bias towards larger lexicons that obviously provide more cognates. The harmonic mean we use is lower than the arithmetic and geometric means but higher than the minimum value (i.e. the size of the smaller lexicon). This choice is intuitively explained by the fact that the amount of cognates found between two lexicons depends on the sizes of both, but is more strongly determined by the smaller lexicon.

Another source of bias is the presence of specialized vocabulary inside lexicons. Even though CogNet was built solely from general lexicons, some of them still contain a significant amount of domain terms (such as binomial nomenclature or medical terms), as the boundary between the general and the specialized vocabulary is never clear-cut. Domain terms such as *myocardiopathy* or *interferometer* tend to be shared across a large number of languages. Due to the tendency of domain terminology to be universal and potentially to grow orders of magnitude larger than the general lexicon, their presence in our input lexicons would have resulted in the uniformization of the similarities computed.

In order to exclude domain terms, we filtered our input to include only a subset of about 2,500 concepts that correspond to *basic-level categories*, i.e. that are neither too abstract nor too specialised and that are the most frequently used in general language.

Note that the core vocabulary words used in comparative linguistics are also taken from basic-level categories, representing everyday objects and phenomena. Thus, in our case, *dog* or *heart* would remain in our input while the too specific—and from our perspective irrelevant—*Staffordshire bullterrier* or *myocardial infarction* would be filtered out. As an existing list of basic-level categories, we used the *BLC* resource developed as part of the development of the Basque wordnet [15]. From this resource we used the broadest, frequency-based category list, as it also takes corpus-based frequencies into account and is therefore more representative of general language.

Finally, we annotated our similarity scores in terms of the robustness of supporting evidence as *low*, *medium*, or *high*, depending on the lexicon sizes used to compute cognates: robustness is considered low below a harmonic mean of 1,000 senses, and high above 10,000.

Our final result is a database of 27,196 language pairs, containing language names, ISO 639-3 language tags, similarity values, and a robustness annotation for each similarity value. 11.4% of all similarities are highly robust while 34.9% have medium robustness).

4   Comparison to Results from Lexicostatistics

In lexicostatistics, the standard benchmark is the ability of similarity data to predict well-established phylogenetic classifications. As we have different goals and work with different input data (e.g. we do not restrict our study to the core historical vocabularies), we cannot consider phylogeny as a gold standard against which to evaluate our results. Instead, we have quantified the difference between our similarity data and recent results from lexicostatistics, as produced by the state-of-the-art *ASJP* tool (based on the latest v19 of the ASJP Database)[5]. We have also compared the (more scarce) symmetric similarity data that was available from EZ Glot to ASJP data.

The intersection of our output with ASJP contained 6,420 language pairs, and 27 European language pairs with EZ Glot. After linearly scaling similarities to fall between 0 and 100, We computed the Pearson correlation coefficient R, the standard deviation σ, as well as the root mean square error RMSE with respect to ASJP, for both CogNet and EZ Glot. Among these three measures, we consider correlation to be the most robust, being invariant to linear transformations such as how data is scaled. We generated three test sets: one restricted to high-robustness result (consisting of 1,399 pairs), one containing both high and medium results (3,975 pairs), and finally the full dataset (6,420 pairs).

The results are shown in Table 1 and in the scatterplot in Fig. 1. From both we see significant variance with respect to ASJP results. Yet, correlation with ASJP remains generally strong and is clearly increasing with robustness (from 0.61 up to 0.69). This result suggests that our robustness annotations are meaningful. EZ Glot results are more distant from ASJP and are more weakly correlated ($R = 0.48$, while for CogNet $R = 0.69$ over the same 27-language-pair subset). We experimentally set $\alpha = 0.5$, although its effect was minor, for instance over the full dataset $R(\alpha = 0) = 0.590$, $R(\alpha = 0.5) = 0.610$, while for simple cognate counting $R(\alpha = 1) = 0.597$.

---

[5] https://asjp.clld.org.

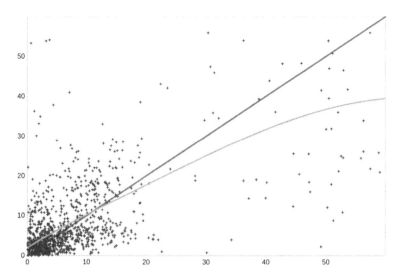

Fig. 1. Comparison of our similarity results from the high-robustness dataset (y axis) with the corresponding language pairs from ASJP (x axis). With respect to the core historical vocabularies covered by ASJP, the green trendline shows a generally higher similarity among genetically unrelated languages and a lower similarity among strongly related ones. (Color figure online)

The green trendline on the scatterplot shows that, on the whole, we compute higher similarities than ASJP for genetically unrelated languages (bottom left, $S < 10$) and lower similarities for genetically strongly related ones (top right). We attribute these non-negligible differences in part to borrowings across contemporary globalized lexicons and, in particular, to *universal words* (e.g. *"tennis"*, *"sumo"*, or *"internet"*) that increase the similarity of otherwise unrelated languages. On the other hand, *language change*—well known to affect the lexicon to a greater extent than it affects grammar—explains why the vocabularies of historically related languages generally show a higher dissimilarity today. This is our interpretation of the slope of the green trendline that always stays below unity.

5 Automated Visualization

Our aim was to reproduce the popular graph-based visualization of lexical similarities in a fully automated manner and based on the entire similarity graph, as opposed to human-produced illustrations based on cherry-picked data. We used the well-known *Sigma* graph visualization library,[6] combined with the JavaScript implementation of the *ForceAtlas2* algorithm [10]. The latter applies a physical model that considers graph edges to be springs, with tensions being proportional to the edge weights. We modeled languages as nodes and their lexical similarities as weighted edges, resulting in more similar languages displayed closer together. Because of the nature of the solution based

---

[6] http://sigmajs.org.

Fig. 2. Detail from the automatically-computed lexical similarity visualization, with colors corresponding to language families (top) and to the geographic location of speakers (bottom).

Fig. 3. Detail from the visualization of ASJP similarity data.

on a physical tension-based model that dynamically evolves towards a global equilibrium, our visualizations favor a global optimum as opposed to locally precise distances. Thus, the visualizations produced give a realistic view of the "big picture", but distances of specific language pairs should be interpreted qualitatively rather than quantitatively.

Figure 2 shows a small portion of the graph computed.[7] In order to keep the graph compact, we restricted it to high-robustness similarities, covering about a hundred languages. In order to get an intuitive idea of the effect of both phylogeny and geography on the similarity of contemporary lexicons, we created two versions of the graph: in the first one (top), nodes are colored according to language families, as it is usually done in comparative linguistics that focuses on phylogenetic relationships. In the second version (bottom), we colored the nodes according to the approximate geographic position of language speakers, taking into account latitude–longitude coordinates as well as continents. Simply put, speakers of similar-colored languages live closer together. Both phylogenetic and geographic metadata were retrieved from the *World Atlas of Language Structures* [5].[8]

The visualization tool can also be used to display similarity data from different sources (provided that it is converted to the input format expected by the Sigma library). In particular, we used the tool to obtain a visual impression of the difference between our contemporary similarity data and those produced by the phylogeny-oriented ASJP tool. The result on ASJP data can be seen in Fig. 3.

The visualizations in Figs. 2 and 3 provide remarkable insight into language change and the state of modern lexicons. In both the contemporary and the ASJP datasets, language families are clearly identifiable as their respective nodes tend to aggregate together. The clusters are, however, much more salient in the ASJP data (Fig. 3), where subfamilies within the Indo-European phylum form separate groups, all the while remaining within an Indo-European "macro-cluster". Dravidian languages from the

---

[7] The full graphs are visible on the page http://ukc.datascientia.eu/lexdist.

[8] http://wals.info.

Indian subcontinent (right-hand-side, in yellow) are far removed from the culturally and geographically close Indic group. Such a result was expected, as ASJP lexicons are optimized to highlight phylogenetic relationships. Due to borrowings, modern lexicons are less clearly distinguished from each other. This is evident, in Fig. 2, from the proximity of the Germanic, Romance, and Slavic families, or from unrelated languages such as Japanese or Tagalog "approaching" the Indo-European families due to borrowings. Likewise, the fact that English is detached from the Germanic cluster to move closer to the Romance family reflects its massive French loanword content.

Further insights are gained on the effect of geography on contemporary lexicons. The bottom image in Fig. 2 shows that even-colored (geographically close) nodes tend to group together (with self-evident exceptions such as Afrikaans). Remarkably, the languages of India aggregate into a single cluster far apart, despite the internal linguistic heterogeneity of the Indian subcontinent that is home to three fully distinct language families—Indic, Dravidian, and Sino-Tibetan—and despite the Indo-European relatedness of the Indic family. In this case, the effect of geography and culture seems stronger than phylogeny or English borrowings.

6   Conclusions and Future Work

We have found significant correlation between the similarity data obtained from large contemporary lexicons and from lexicostatistical databases geared towards language phylogeny research. At the same time, we have also found that, on the whole, large contemporary lexicons tend to resemble each other more. We believe that the uniformizing effect of globalized culture on languages plays a role in this observation.

Due to these differences, we consider our data to be more relevant to cross-lingual uses applied to contemporary language, such as machine translation, cross-lingual transfer, or bilingual lexicon induction, where—other things being equal—lexical similarities may predict efficiency over language pairs. On the other hand, our data is not suitable for use in historical linguistics that is based on a more strict definition of cognacy and on a more controlled concept set.

Our full lexical similarity data, as well as the dynamic visualizations, are made freely available online.[9]

Acknowledgments. This paper was partly supported by the *InteropEHRate* project, co-funded by the European Union (EU) Horizon 2020 programme under grant number 826106.

References

1. Batsuren, K., Bella, G., Giunchiglia, F.: Cognet: a large-scale cognate database. In: Proceedings of the 57th Annual Meeting of the Association for Computational Linguistics, pp. 3136–3145 (2019)
2. Batsuren, K., Bella, G., Giunchiglia, F.: A large and evolving cognate database. Lang. Resour. Eval. 1–25 (2021). https://doi.org/10.1007/s10579-021-09544-6

---

[9] http://ukc.datascientia.eu/.

3. Batsuren, K., Ganbold, A., Chagnaa, A., Giunchiglia, F.: Building the Mongolian wordnet. In: Proceedings of the 10th Global Wordnet Conference, pp. 238–244 (2019)
4. Bella, G., et al.: A major wordnet for a minority language: Scottish Gaelic. In: Proceedings of The 12th Language Resources and Evaluation Conference, pp. 2812–2818 (2020)
5. Comrie, B.: The World Atlas of Language Structures. Oxford University Press, Oxford (2005)
6. Dellert, J., et al.: Northeuralex: a wide-coverage lexical database of Northern Eurasia. Lang. Resour. Eval. **54**(1), 273–301 (2020)
7. Garcia, M., Gómez-Rodríguez, C., Alonso, M.A.: New treebank or repurposed? on the feasibility of cross-lingual parsing of romance languages with universal dependencies. Nat. Lang. Eng. **24**(1), 91–122 (2018)
8. Giunchiglia, F., Batsuren, K., Bella, G.: Understanding and exploiting language diversity. In: Proceedings of the Twenty-Sixth International Joint Conference on Artificial Intelligence (IJCAI 2017), pp. 4009–4017 (2017)
9. Giunchiglia, F., Batsuren, K., Freihat, A.A.: One world–seven thousand languages. In: Proceedings 19th International Conference on Computational Linguistics and Intelligent Text Processing (CiCling 2018), 18–24 March 2018 (2018)
10. Jacomy, M., Venturini, T., Heymann, S., Bastian, M.: Forceatlas2, a continuous graph layout algorithm for handy network visualization designed for the gephi software. PLoS ONE **9**(6), e98679 (2014)
11. Lin, Y.H., et al.: Choosing transfer languages for cross-lingual learning. arXiv preprint arXiv:1905.12688 (2019)
12. Nair, N.C., Velayuthan, R.S., Batsuren, K.: Aligning the indowordnet with the Princeton wordnet. In: Proceedings of the 3rd International Conference on Natural Language and Speech Processing, pp. 9–16 (2019)
13. Nasution, A.H., Murakami, Y., Ishida, T.: Constraint-based bilingual lexicon induction for closely related languages. In: Proceedings of the Tenth International Conference on Language Resources and Evaluation (LREC 2016), pp. 3291–3298 (2016)
14. Petroni, F., Serva, M.: Measures of lexical distance between languages. Phys. Stat. Mech. Appl. **389**(11), 2280–2283 (2010)
15. Pociello, E., Agirre, E., Aldezabal, I.: Methodology and construction of the basque wordnet. Lang. Resour. Eval. **45**(2), 121–142 (2011)
16. Swadesh, M.: Towards greater accuracy in lexicostatistic dating. Int. J. Am. linguist. **21**(2), 121–137 (1955)
17. Wichmann, S., et al.: The ASIP database (version 13). http://email.eva.mpg.de/~wichmann/ASJPHomePage.htm 3 (2010)

The Detection of Actors for German

Manfred Klenner[⊠] and Anne Göhring

Department of Computational Linguistics, University of Zurich, Zurich, Switzerland
{klenner,goehring}@cl.uzh.ch
https://www.cl.uzh.ch/

Abstract. In this short paper, we discuss a straight-forward approach for the identification of noun phrases denoting actors (agents). We use a multilayer perceptron applied to the word embeddings of the head nouns in order to learn a model. A list of 9,000 actors together with 11,000 non-actors generated from a newspaper corpus are used as a silver standard. An evaluation of the results seems to indicate that the model generalises well on unseen data.

Keywords: Animacy detection · Actor detection · German language

1 Introduction

An *actor* according to our definition is a person or a group of persons. Actor denoting noun phrases comprise named-entities, e.g. person and company names, but also profession names ('the doctor said . . . ') and institution referring expressions ('The administration decided . . . ') and noun phrases that metonymically refer to humans, e.g. capital cities in order to refer to a government ('Washington has announced . . . '). That is, actor phrase recognition is not just named-entity recognition. It strives to identify any type of noun phrases that could be used to refer to humans[1].

We are aware of the fact that metonymy detection is a challenging task and it should take the context of a word (the whole sentence) into account. However, our approach does not claim to recognise actual metonymic usage of a noun phrase but rather whether it *could* be used metonymically (e.g. as a logical metonymy in the sense of [7]).

We trained a binary classifier on the basis of FastText word embeddings [1] to tell actor denoting words from non-actor denoting words. As a silver standard, we used a list of 9,000 generic nouns that can be used to denote actors (incl. professions, organisations and institutions, countries, names for groups etc.) and 11,250 nouns that are randomly chosen from a big newspaper corpus[2] (e.g. 'tree', 'border', 'solution', 'time', . . .). A word is a non-actor if it is not a member of the actor list. This introduces some noise, since the actor list is incomplete.

---

[1] At some point we might also have to take artificial agents into account.

[2] The corpus comprises about 1,000,000 articles, we used the parsed version.

© Springer Nature Switzerland AG 2021
K. Ekštein et al. (Eds.): TSD 2021, LNAI 12848, pp. 105–110, 2021.
https://doi.org/10.1007/978-3-030-83527-9_9

The list of generic actor nouns was compiled from various resources (e.g. a country name list) from the Internet and by exploiting the German wordnet GermaNet [4]. Here we extracted the words under various nodes, e.g. 'human', 'institution' and 'profession'.

2 Actor Noun Identification

The data set contains 20,250 words. We used sklearn's multilayer perceptron (MLP) implementation with a hidden layer size of 100 and the maximum iteration set to 300. The random and shuffled train/test split was 75/25%. The accuracy of the test set run in this binary classification task (actor versus non-actor) was 91.17%. This seems to be an impressive result, given that training set and test set are exclusive. The MLP model must have learned to generalise well to have such a performance on unseen data.

Since our list of actor denoting nouns is (certainly) incomplete and - as we found out from a small sample we took - contains false entries, we generated two lists from the 8.83% erroneous classifications of the test set: the list of false positives - nouns classified by the model as actor denoting nouns but which are not on the actor list. And we generated the list of false negatives - i.e. nouns that the model classified as non-actor denoting nouns but which according to the actor list were actor nouns.

Table 1. False actors (positives) and non-actors (negatives)

	Actor list	Model is right
False positives	255	161 (73.1%)
False negatives	197	135 (68.52%)

We manually evaluated these two lists: the false positives and the false negatives. A noun from false positives that actually is an actor confirms the model and is noise on the actor list, a noun that is not an actor is a false positive of the model list and confirms the actor list. Conversely, a noun from false negatives that actually is an actor confirms the actor list and a noun that is not an actor again identifies noise.

As we can see in Table 1, the incompleteness of the lexicon is high: only 26.9% of the model suggested actors are really false actors (not only "not in our actor list"). That is our model is able to generalise well. It is able to detect new actors with a precision of 73.1%. From the nouns that - according to the actor list - are falsely classified by the model as non-actors, actually 68.52% are actors and thus really falsely classified. The remaining 31.48% of the nouns in false negatives actually are non-actors and should be removed from the actor list, they are wrong entries. The correctly classified data, 91% accuracy, thus is not really a reliable result - these *correctly* classified data must contain cases of false positives as well. The actor list at this stage seemed to be a bit noisy.

3   Improving the Actor List

Instead of manually inspecting over 9,000 words, we decided to automatically try to clean the list. The very idea here was to use verbs of saying (verba dicendi). We generated this list from GermaNet, it comprises 395 verbs (e.g. to communicate, say, comment, answer, complain, etc.). The subjects of these verbs normally are actors[3]. We searched in our newspaper corpus for nouns that on the one hand were subjects of these verbs and on the other hand were on the actor list. We found 5,900 actors that way and this is our reduced actor list. We repeated the experiment from the last section with the new actor list (and the same number of non-actors). First of all, the overall accuracy slightly increased: from 91.17% to 92.14%. This is the accuracy measured on the basis of the reduced actor list. The list still is incomplete (now, maybe, even more). The evaluation of the false positives resulted in an accuracy of 75% (compared to 73.1%, see Table 2).

Table 2. False actors (positive) and false non-actors (negatives)

	Actor list	Model is right	Reduced actor list	Model is right
False positives	255	161 (73.1%)	164	123 (75%)
False negatives	197	135 (68.52%)	173	139 (80.34%)

This is even a bit better than before. The evaluation of the false negatives showed that our attempt to improve the quality of the actor list was successful although there are still entries in it that we manually classified as non-actors. The accuracy now is 80.34% (compared to 68.52%).

4   Polar Actor Noun Phrases

As we have seen in the last section, our actor noun identification performs well (>92%), but suffers from the noise of the actor lexicon (which is used for training and testing). The question thus is: how well does the actor classifier perform given a real task (not just the reproduction of the test split of the actor and non-actor lexicons). Our ultimate goal is to quantify (actor) noun phrases with respect to their (negative) polarity strength in the context of hate speech (e.g. 'the stupid German chancellor'). Actor classification (as described in this paper) is just the first step. But errors propagate, thus, an evaluation is needed that adapts to the final scenario: given a noun phrase with one or more polar adjectives, how good is the actor detection in this setting?

The corpus for this little experiment comprises about 300,000 Facebook posts of a German right-wing party (called AfD). Our interest here is to find the targets (we might say, victims) towards whom the members of the AfD address their anger and rage. That is, we are looking for noun phrases that are intended

---

[3] But note that some verbs are ambiguous, e.g. 'anfahren' could mean 'to start' (a car) or 'to bump into' or (the intended reading) 'to shout at'.

to denote negative actors. In order to do so, we extracted from the Facebook posts noun phrases that comprise one or more negative adjectives from a German polarity lexicon[4] [3] and which have an actor noun as head according to our learned actor classifier (but which are not in the actor lexicon, so we are interested in new examples). The goal was to find out how accurate the actor detection works in the envisaged end scenario. Is it good enough?

The procedure was as follows: we parsed all sentences from the AfD corpus with the ParZu parser [8]. Then we searched for noun phrases that contained at least one negative adjective and whose head noun was classified by the learned MLP model as an actor. We took a sample of 160 noun phrases from the result and manually evaluated whether a phrase really comprises an actor noun or not. It turned out that in 44 out of 160 cases a non-actor was classified as an actor. The accuracy, thus, is 76.5%. This clearly gives a better empirical evaluation as the 91% we found in the train/test split directly using the (non-)actor lists. We might cautiously claim that a system trained on a somewhat noisy actor data still produces useful results.

5   Related Work

Our task of actor identification is strongly related to animacy detection. The only difference is that we do not care for non human animate beings (e.g. animals). We have not found literature for German animacy detection, but only for other languages, mainly for English. The main difference to our work is that we use only the word embeddings of actor and non-actor nouns and no other features. Thus, our classifier is generic - it does not take into account the context of the word. This was a deliberate decision, since there is no gold standard for the German language available that could deliver context information for training.

Previous models make use of different morpho-syntactic features, other approaches rely on lexical and semantic resources like WordNet, and sometimes named entity recognition systems support the animacy classification. [2] build a discriminative classifier on three types of features to annotate noun phrases of parsed spoken English sentences with fine-grained, hierarchical animacy tags. Their 10-class model achieves an overall accuracy of 84.9% for all labeled NPs. Projecting the automatically assigned tags to the binary decision animate/inanimate, the accuracy reaches 93.5%. The data-driven system in [6] aims to catch the context-dependent, thus dynamic animacy aspect of entities, especially in stories. They train a "linguistically uninformed" animacy classification model using n-grams and word embeddings to extract a list of characters in Dutch folktales. Their best model additionally uses part-of-speech tags and achieves $0.92 F_1$ score for animacy. [5] combine a supervised machine learning approach with five hand-written rules to classify the animacy of co-reference chains instead of individual words. Both rules and SVM depend on various linguistic features, available in WordNet and obtained by pre-processing the English

---

[4] The lexicon is freely available from the IGGSA website: https://sites.google.com/site/iggsahome/downloads.

texts with e.g. dependency parser, semantic role labeler, named entity recognition, as well as using word embeddings. This hybrid system reaches $0.90\,F_1$ score on referring expressions' animacy.

6   Conclusions

In this paper we discussed an approach for actor identification. Since there is no gold standard available for German from which the context of an actor mention could be extracted (and learned), our model relies on the generative capacity of tuning word embedding based classification. Our overall goal is to detect and quantify negative actors in texts. The current paper describes our attempts to realise and evaluate the first step: a neural model that is able to distinguish words that might be used to denote actors and non-actors. The model is based on silver standard of an actor and a non-actor lists. The evaluation showed that the model generalise sufficiently - although the silver standard is noisy. After an automatic cleaning of the silver standard the new model was better. A further evaluation in the spirit of our envisioned application showed a performance of 75% accuracy which is good for a model that just uses word embeddings.

Acknowledgements. Our work is supported by the Swiss National Foundation under the project number 105215_179302.

References

1. Bojanowski, P., Grave, E., Joulin, A., Mikolov, T.: Enriching word vectors with subword information. arXiv preprint arXiv:1607.04606 (2016)
2. Bowman, S.R., Chopra, H.: Automatic animacy classification. In: Proceedings of the NAACL HLT 2012 Student Research Workshop, pp. 7–10. Association for Computational Linguistics, Montréal, Canada, June 2012. https://www.aclweb.org/anthology/N12-2002
3. Clematide, S., Klenner, M.: Evaluation and extension of a polarity lexicon for German. In: Proceedings of the First Workshop on Computational Approaches to Subjectivity and Sentiment Analysis (WASSA), pp. 7–13 (2010)
4. Hamp, B., Feldweg, H.: GermaNet - a lexical-semantic net for German. In: Automatic Information Extraction and Building of Lexical Semantic Resources for NLP Applications (1997).https://www.aclweb.org/anthology/W97-0802
5. Jahan, L., Chauhan, G., Finlayson, M.: A new approach to animacy detection. In: Proceedings of the 27th International Conference on Computational Linguistics, pp. 1–12. Association for Computational Linguistics, Santa Fe, New Mexico, USA, August 2018. https://www.aclweb.org/anthology/C18-1001
6. Karsdorp, F., van der Meulen, M., Meder, T., van den Bosch, A.: Animacy Detection in Stories. In: Finlayson, M.A., Miller, B., Lieto, A., Ronfard, R. (eds.) 6th Workshop on Computational Models of Narrative (CMN 2015). OpenAccess Series in Informatics (OASIcs), vol. 45, pp. 82–97. Schloss Dagstuhl-Leibniz-Zentrum fuer Informatik, Dagstuhl, Germany (2015). https://doi.org/10.4230/OASIcs.CMN.2015.82, http://drops.dagstuhl.de/opus/volltexte/2015/5284

7. Pustejovsky, J.: The Generative Lexicon. MIT Press, Cambridge (1998). http://mitpress.mit.edu/books/generative-lexicon

8. Sennrich, R., Volk, M., Schneider, G.: Exploiting synergies between open resources for German dependency parsing, POS-tagging, and morphological analysis. In: Recent Advances in Natural Language Processing (RANLP 2013), pp. 601–609, September 2013

Verbal Autopsy: First Steps Towards Questionnaire Reduction

Ander Cejudo[1]([✉]), Owen Trigueros[1], Alicia Pérez[1], Arantza Casillas[1], and Daniel Cobos[2,3]

[1] HiTZ: Basque Center for Language Technology, IXA, UPV/EHU, Basque Country, Spain
acejudo001@ikasle.ehu.eus,
{owen.trigueros,alicia.perez,arantza.casillas}@ehu.eus
https://www.ixa.eus
[2] Swiss Tropical and Public Health Institute, Basel, Switzerland
daniel.cobos@swisstph.ch
https://www.swisstph.ch
[3] University of Basel, Basel, Switzerland

Abstract. Verbal Autopsy (VA) is the instrument used to collect Causes of Death (CoD) in places in which the access to health services is out of reach. It consists of a questionnaire addressed to the caregiver of the deceased and involves closed questions (CQ) about signs and symptoms prior to the decease. There is a global effort to reduce the number of questions in the questionnaire to the minimum essential information to ascertain a CoD. To this end we took two courses of action. On the one hand, the relation of the responses with respect to the CoD was considered by means of the entropy in a supervised feature subset selection (FSS) approach. On the other hand, we inspected the questions themselves by means of semantic similarity leading to an unsupervised approach based on semantic similarity (SFSS). In an attempt to assess, quantitatively, the impact of reducing the questionnaire, we assessed the use of these FSS approaches on the CoD predictive capability of a classifier. Experimental results showed that unsupervised semantic similarity feature subset selection (SFSS) approach was competitive to identify similar questions. Nevertheless, naturally, supervised FSS based on the entropy of the responses performed better for CoD prediction. To sum up, the necessity of reviewing the VA questionnaire was accompanied with quantitative evidence.

1 Introduction

Vital Statistics are the key to understand the disease burden in a country and to respond as the foundation of socioeconomic development policies [3,16,30]. The main source of mortality statistics are medical certificates of cause of death filled by trained physicians. However, many areas in the world do not have access to a trained clinician or to the health care system overall. These areas remain in the dark when it comes to mortality statistics and thus their health priorities are not considered in decision making processes [15].

K. Ekštein et al. (Eds.): TSD 2021, LNAI 12848, pp. 111–123, 2021.
https://doi.org/10.1007/978-3-030-83527-9_10

In order to have information on the number of deaths and their causes in areas where a physician is not available, the WHO proposed the Verbal Autopsy (VA) as the second best option in the absence of medical certification [29]. A VA consists of an interview to the family or caregivers of the deceased. The interviewer should be familiar with the language of the interviewee and does not necessarily hold medical expertise [10,26]. The VA includes a narrative or open response describing the events prior to death and a set of closed questions (CQs) about signs and symptoms of the deceased. The responses to the VA questionnaire are then analyzed either by clinical experts with or without the support of algorithms to ascertain the Cause of Death (CoD) and to produce mortality statistics. Previous efforts to predict the CoD [11,14,25] have focused on analyzing, statistically, the responses of the CQs. Currently there is a global effort to analyze response patterns in data collected using different VA questionnaires and to identify problematic questions that could be removed or rephrased in order to improve the performance of VA interview. Nevertheless, no quantitative evidence to support the decision have been provided yet.

The **motivation** of this work is to reduce the questionnaire, to save time, first, to the family of the deceased, and also to the interviewer and the doctors in charge of reviewing the responses to decide on the CoD. There are hundreds of questions which must be translated and reviewed reducing the number of questions would save resources and accelerate the whole process. For that reason, our **goal** is to select a subset of questions based on quantitative evidence for the experts to explore and either remove or reformulate. It is out of the scope of this work to offer a method to get the questions rephrased, this is left to the judgment of the experts.

We want to point out that the main goal is the item reduction and not the CoD prediction task. For that reason, in this work we use simple classifiers which are suitable due to the data amount and we do not try to improve the results attained by previous related works. We hypothesized that semantically related questions would be good candidates to be either removed or rephrased. On the other hand, the rationale is to focus on the responses given to the CQs (rather than on the formulation of the questions) as predictive features to ascertain the CoD, hence, we turned to feature subset selection. In this approach, as the objective function we employed the entropy of the responses with respect to the CoD. Entropy is a method used to measure the disorder of a dataset with respect to a variable, in this case, the CoD. Finally, the impact of these two feature ablation approaches was assessed in a down-stream application, that is, CoD prediction.

2   Materials: Verbal Autopsy GS

Our approach rests on inference from data. Antecedents made use of different sized collections of VA from several countries: India with million reports [1], Malaysia [12], or Vietnam [27], Angola [23] among others. These data, as well as other electronic health records, might convey sensitive information and they are confidential [8,9]. Possibly due to these issues, to the best of our knowledge, none of the aforementioned datasets are publicly available.

By contrast, the Population Health Metrics Research Consortium (PHMRC) made available the Gold Standard Validation Database [19], denoted as VA-GS from now onward. It comprises three questionnaires, one per age-rank (neonate, child, adult), in their turn with 105, 82 and 138 questions in the VA-GS corpus, with a vocabulary size of 257, 203 and 272 words and a word average of 9.16, 8.03 and 6.31 per each question, respectively. Table 1 summarizes details of the VA-GS corpus that are relevant to our study.

Table 1. Quantitative description of verbal autopsy gold standard: number of autopsies (VA: instances), closed questions (CQ: attributes), causes of death (CoD: classes).

	Neonate	Child	Adult
VA	1252	1341	4849
CQ	105	82	138
CoD	6	21	34

Naturally, the set of CoD is unevenly distributed by age-rank, as shown in Fig. 1. The set of instances was split into training and test sets by means of stratified random sampling 70% for training and the rest for assessment (the total amount is made explicit in Table 1). Given that the focus of this work rests on the closed questions, we provided some examples in Table 2.

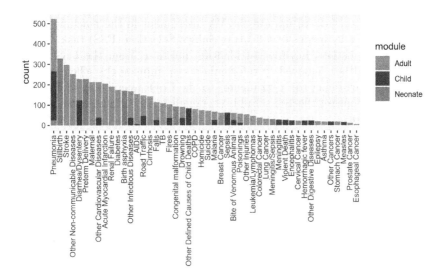

Fig. 1. CoD distribution per age-rank in the VA-GS (denoted as "module" in the legend)

Even though VA-GS corpus is smaller than the aforementioned corpora, we found that it can be of much help to address the main goal i.e. create a more efficient VA questionnaire. Needless to say, current trends in NLP, mainly deep neural approaches, incorporate big data. In this task, for the volume of data, classical machine learning approaches can be more appropiate. Moreover, the size of the questionnaire is not as large as it would be expected to tackle this task.

Table 2. Example of some CQs.

Id	Closed questions
q_1	Decedent suffered drowning
q_2	Number of years of education completed
q_3	Did [name] have fast breathing?
q_4	Did [name] have difficulty breathing?
q_5	Decedent suffered road traffic injury

Finally, through this paper we would like to claim the release of collections of clinical texts in order to promote and benefit from the advances that clinical text mining can bring.

3 Methods

The item reduction task to update the VA instrument in the machine learning area is carried out by means of a Feature Subset Selection (FSS) task. The idea is to propose a method in order to identify questions from the questionnaire that should be either removed or reformulated to improve the efficiency of the interview, without being too detrimental to the CoD ascertainment capability. That is, the responses collected should be enough for the clinician to be able to determine the CoD.

In this work, we turn to simple natural language processing and machine learning approaches. Section 3.1 shows the use of dense spaces to gather semantically related CQs. Section 3.2 delves into preliminary approaches explored for FSS in the context of questionnaire reduction. Section 3.3 presents the classifier used to assess the impact of alternative feature ablation techniques as a secondary assessment of the FSS.

3.1 Semantic Similarity

A shallow manual inspection of the formulation of the CQs revealed remarkable similarities. With this appreciation, the formulation of each question (the string $q_i \in \Sigma^*$) was represented as an embedding, i.e. in an n-dimensional dense space ($e : \Sigma^* \longrightarrow \mathbb{R}^n$). The pair-wise distance between questions i and j was computed through cosine similarity of their corresponding embedded representation: $d(q_i, q_j) = cos(e(q_i), e(q_j))$.

Having represented the formulation of the questions in a dense space and, in an attempt to get a graphic visualization T-SNE [17] was applied to reduce the dimension to $\mathbb{R}^3$. The CQs were inspected through TensorBoard Projector [24]. An example is given in Fig. 2, where the question "Did the frequent loose or liquid stools continue until death?" is closely related to "How many days before death did the frequent loose or liquid stools start?" and also to "How many days before death did the loose or liquid stools stop?".

This representation seemed to meet the hypothesis that close questions would be located closely. Moreover, this simple NLP-based approach provides quantitative evidence to group related questions for the experts to consider and make the differences as explicit as possible to avoid redundancies.

This approach opens a door, not only to the removal of CQs but also to the inclusion of new CQs in the questionnaire as this prototype enables the graphical exploration of related questions before incorporating a question.

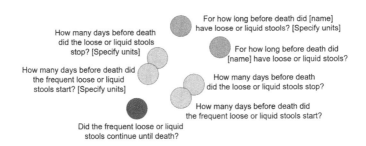

Fig. 2. Representation of the formulation for the questions projected through Tensor-Board

3.2 Automatic Selection of Closed Questions

Previous section served us as a first approach to represent the formulation of the questions embedded and get them depicted in an intuitive framework for experts to make their decisions based on a graph and a metric. Intuitively, the semantic distance matrix conveyed valuable information to find similar questions. With this results, we propose a method for feature ablation based, merely, on the formulation of the question and not on the answer.

This first approach, from now on referred to as Semantic Feature Subset Selection abbreviated as **SFSS**, consists of identifying the most similar m pairs of questions. Assuming that if similar questions are potentially redundant an element of the pair was discarded. We have removed the question that is longer, in terms of number of words, from each pair as we want to make the interview and the reviewing process as short as possible assuming that short wording is easier to translate and clearer to understand.

SFSS is an unsupervised feature selection method (i.e. the CoD is not involved in the feature selection process). Needless to say, given that the goal is to optimize the CoD prediction ability, the intuition is to make use of classical supervised feature subset selection approaches (denoted as **FSS**) based on mutual information. Supervised methods make use of the CoD to determine the least relevant questions. There is another relevant difference between SFSS and FSS, the fact that SFSS focuses on the wording of the question, while FSS focuses on the responses given to the CQs.

To be precise, as the objective function, we opted for minimizing the **entropy** as it is one of the most common item reduction strategies. Finally, as a baseline, we compared both methods with a random feature ablation approach. A random selection of features is unsupervised. We find it important to assess the sensitivity of informed methods (SFSS and FSS) with respect to uninformed ones. The aim was to assess the information provided by informed methods that is not simply attained by chance. Furthermore, for the random method, each process was run 8 times and the mean of the results attained are provided in the experimental framework.

3.3   Cause of Death Extraction Approach

The main use of the VA is to ascertain the CoD given the set of responses with respect to the CQ. The most widespread tools and front-ends[1] (Tariff [13], Insilico [18] and InterVA [4]) convey algorithms dealing with the responses of the CQ from standard VAs and are bound to the complete set of CQs. Our goal, however, is to assess the impact of CQ reduction in the CoD prediction accuracy and thus, found the need to re-train versatile models with different sets of features each time instead of bounding to rigid front-ends.

Even if there are several works that have tackled the inference of models to predict the CoD from verbal autopsies, direct comparisons are hardly feasible since none of them used freely available data-sets and, what is more important, the same features. For instance [31] involved the One Million Death Study (MDS) dataset [28]. MDS has 12,045 records of adults compared to 4,849 in VA-GS (used in this work) and 18 causes of death compared to 34 in VA-GS as shown in Table 1. [20] turned to PHMRC dataset along with MDS and other two datasets and [7] employed the same dataset but different metrics and the results are segmented by sites.

In our work we are assessing the impact of automatic CQ ablation approaches (addressed in Sect. 3.2) on inferred classifiers. We have tested a wide range of simple classifiers like K-Nearest Neighbors, Naive Bayes, Logistic Regression and Neural Networks. Preliminary experiments were carried out with the full set of features. These results showed that combining them into an ensemble classifier attained the best results. Considered all the classifiers explored, preliminary results in terms of weighted F-measure varied between 0.180 and 0.381 for the adult segment, between 0.288 and 0.5282 for the child segment and between 0.604 and 0.715 for the neonate. The approach that emerged as the best performing

---

[1] Tariff, Insilico and InterVA are available through: https://www.who.int/healthinfo/ statistics/verbalautopsystandards/en/.

one in all the segments was an ensemble that combines a Random Forest [2], a Naive Bayes, an XGBoost [6] and a Logistic Regression [32]. From this ensemble, to decide the resulting CoD, a soft voting method was employed [5]. Both XGB and RF use 50 estimators and a max depth of 20. Having decided on the classifier and the set-up, this decision was maintained in all the experimental layout. To implement this we made use of scikit-learn library [21].

While current trends in machine learning are experiencing a remarkable success by means of deep neural networks, the size of the data is not sufficient for these techniques to have good results.

4   Experimental Results

4.1   Identification of Candidate Questions

In order to choose the candidate questions proposed to be either be removed or rephrased, we turned to semantic similarity, representing each question as an embedding in $\mathbb{R}^n$. The embedded-space was built by means of Glove [22] leading to a vocabulary of size 400×10^3 with 6 billion words for training setup. We explored semantic spaces of different dimensions (varying n) and we found that spaces of dimension lower than $n = 300$ (e.g. $\mathbb{R}^{50}$) provided smaller ability to ascertain the CoD.

Let us exemplify the results related to semantic similarity with the example shown in Table 2. After having represented the questions in the embedded space, pair-wise similarity was computed in Table 3. As it could be expected, q_3 and q_4 are the most similar questions, by contrast, q_1 and q_2 are the least similar.

Table 3. Example: heatmap of distance from q_j to q_i for the questions given in Table 2.

	q_1	q_2	q_3	q_4	q_5
q_1	1.00	0.37	0.42	0.48	0.70
q_2	0.37	1.00	0.78	0.79	0.64
q_3	0.42	0.78	1.00	0.97	0.68
q_4	0.48	0.79	0.97	1.00	0.69
q_5	0.70	0.64	0.68	0.69	1.00

It is arguable, however, that q_3 (*fast breathing*) and q_4 (*difficulty breathing*) are redundant. This is why we consider this approach as a means to aid experts to make decisions on the questionnaire reduction, reformulation or inclusion but not as a fully automatic device.

In brief, the main goal of this approach is not to provide a foolproof automated method, but to offer an intuitive method to help the experts to review and develop the next version of the questionnaire.

4.2   CoD Prediction Reducing CQs

In this section the impact of reducing the questionnaire is assessed. A quantitative analysis and discussion is provided first, followed by a qualitative analysis focused on errors. Last, in an attempt to enable the research community to reproduce these findings, we released several resources.

Feature Ablation. Figure 3 shows, for each age-rank, the performance in terms of weighted F-measure of the classifier (described in Sect. 3.3) to predict the CoD as the CQs are removed by each of the methods employed (described in Sect. 4.2): the unsupervised FSS based on semantic similarity (denoted as SFSS) and the supervised entropy-based FSS (denoted as entropy). As a baseline, we analyzed a random FSS approach that serves as the lowest threshold for any admissible non-random approach. The classifier was trained on the training set and assessed on the test set.

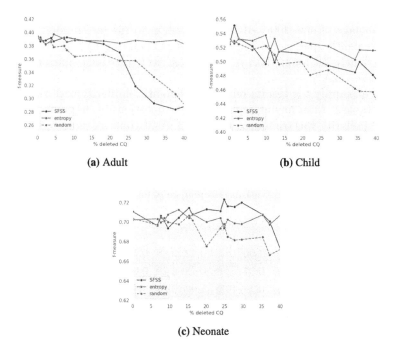

(a) Adult

(b) Child

(c) Neonate

Fig. 3. CoD prediction F-measure (ordinate) removing a percentage of CQs (abscissa) by means of different FSS approaches: semantic (SFSS), entropy based (entropy) and randomly.

Figure 3 shows that employing all the CQs, i.e. removing 0% (abscissa) of the CQs, the ensemble attains an F-measure of 39.3, 53.1 and 71.08 respectively for adult, child and neonate age-ranks. Naturally, deleting 0% of CQs the three representations attain the same F-measure but small variations can appear due to inner random processes (as it is the case of the initialization of the Logistic Regression). With a set of indispensable (i.e. relevant and not-redundant) predictive features, feature ablation would yield a significant drop in prediction ability. This behavior was not observed in any of the modules or at least not until a high percentage of CQs was deleted, beyond the 40%. From 0% to 40%, entropy-based FSS approach just decreases 0.01% for the adult segment and 2.8% for the child segment. Interestingly, for the neonate segment attribute removal led to an increment of 1.55%. This fact suggests that the number of questions in this questionnaire is excessive for the number of possible causes of death in this age segment.

For the adult segment, it is not until the removal of 22.4% of the CQs that the CoD prediction performance drops with a loss of 5.78%. Next, the decay gets below the performance of a random FSS, indicating that using SFSS beyond the 20% is not advisable. Note that the supervised approach (entropy) keeps stable until the removal of 38% CQs.

While entropy shows the best behavior for both adult and child segments, for the neonate, SFSS attains the best results removing CQs in a rank between 15% and 38%. Overall, both SFSS and entropy are above the random approach and the former gets the highest F-measure having removed 24.7% of CQs with an increment of 1.77% compared to the initial performance.

Error Analysis. Note that this is a multi-class classification task and per-class (CoD) F-measures were averaged to get the Fig. 3. The confusion matrix shows, explicitly, expected and predicted CoD and opens room for an error analysis. For readability, due to the high number of classes involved for adult and child segments (see Table 1), in Fig. 4 we just show the matrices associated with the segment Neonate. "Stillbirth" tends to be correctly predicted with or without feature ablation. Predicting "Preterm Delivery" (focus on column) often causes confusion with "Birth asphyxia" (row). Indeed VAs that should have been labeled as "Preterm Delivery" are often confounded with other labels using all the CQs (i.e. applying 0% reduction) and the same applies to using 30% of the CQs selected by the entropy method but this type of confusion diminishes using the subset of CQs selected by the SFSS method. In brief, with different set of CQs, not only the number but also the type of errors assumed by the classifiers change. Weighting the type and cost of each error is an aspect that should be addressed by experts.

In addition, "Pneumonia" is never predicted which indicates that there is an absence of breathing issues related questions and regarding the Fig. 3 even the random method has a low loss. These results suggest that there are redundant or similar questions that should be either deleted or reformulated. It is important to note that we have not taken into account that some questions on the PHMRC questionnaire depend on the answers of others in order to be asked. This means that some questions are not always asked. As future work, this methods can be

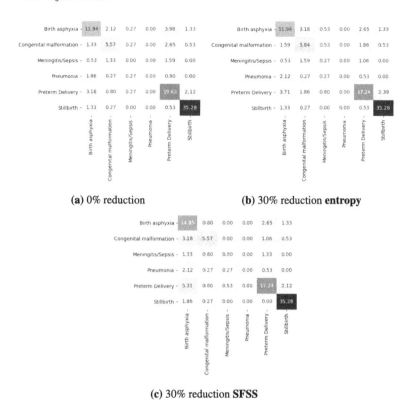

(a) 0% reduction   (b) 30% reduction **entropy**

(c) 30% reduction **SFSS**

Fig. 4. Confusion matrix for CoD prediction in the Neonate segment without feature ablation (0% reduction) or with 30% reduction employing entropy. Gold CoD is given by rows and predicted CoD by columns.

improved by taking into account the hierarchy between the CQs, as well as the missing ones.

4.3 Promoting Reproducible Research: Software Release

In an attempt to promote reproducibility, through this paper we made available several resources: the software implemented to carry out these experiments, the indices employed to get the corpus split into train/test and the formulation of the CQ projected in TensorBoard for visual inspection. The use of these resources are subject to the citation of this work. This all is available in: https://github.com/anderct105/va-questionnaire-3d

5   Conclusions

This work applied simple though valuable techniques to contribute to the global discussion around improving the efficiency of implementing VA as part of the routine mortality surveillance systems in countries. We explored a semantic similarity approach to seek questions with similar formulation. In addition, we turned to well-known supervised feature subset selection approaches applied to the responses of the questions with the objective function being the optimization of the entropy of the responses with respect to the CoD. We assessed the impact of CQ ablation over automatic prediction of CoD. As it could be expected, the supervised FSS has a better performance. The key issue is that all the methods presented offer quantitative means to aid experts on the discussion of the re-formulation of the questionnaire.

The work contributed to the goal of detecting and reducing questions using the semantic and revealed that a considerable amount of features can be removed without being detrimental to an automatic classifier. As a secondary contribution, we released the software to promote reproducibility and also the CQ ranked according to the methods employed.

We carried out the first steps that try to extrapolate NLP techniques to overcome the problem of improving the performance of VA instrument. We are aware of the fact that there is substantial room for improvement. First, we believe that working with larger corpora can be beneficial to detect the subset of necessary CQs to conduct the interview. Furthermore, other semantic similarity distances could be explored and combined with alternative feature ablation methods. Moreover, it should be noted that it is very important to take into account the order in which the questions are formulated and it has to be reflected in the automatic question reduction process.

Lastly, through this article we tried to give visibility to the development of Verbal Autopsy instrument. Our impression is that this field can be benefited from the research in the field of Natural Language Processing and Understanding and we would like to ask the aid of the community to get involved in this task. In fact, the most widely used approaches to ascertain the CoD just involve the CQs as predictive features, nevertheless, rarely take the narrative into account. Our impression is that the development of the VA can be benefited from both sides: the re-formulation of the CQs and the incorporation of the narrative in the process.

Acknowledgements. This work was partially funded by the Spanish Ministry of Science and Innovation (DOTT-HEALTH/PAT-MED PID2019-106942RB-C31), European Commission (FEDER) and the Basque Government (IXA IT-1343-19).

References

1. Aleksandrowicz, L., et al.: Performance criteria for verbal autopsy-based systems to estimate national causes of death: development and application to the Indian million death study. BMC Med. **12**(1), 21 (2014)
2. Breiman, L.: Random forests. Mach. Learn. **45**(1), 5–32 (2001)
3. Byass, P.: Uncounted causes of death. Lancet **387**(10013), 26–27 (2016)
4. Byass, P., et al.: Strengthening standardised interpretation of verbal autopsy data: the new interva-4 tool. Glob. Health Action **5**(1), 19281 (2012)

5. Cao, J., Kwong, S., Wang, R., Li, X., Li, K., Kong, X.: Class-specific soft voting based multiple extreme learning machines ensemble. Neurocomputing **149**, 275–284 (2015)
6. Chen, T., Guestrin, C.: Xgboost: a scalable tree boosting system. In: Proceedings of the 22nd ACM SIGKDD International Conference on Knowledge Discovery and Data Mining, pp. 785–794 (2016)
7. Clark, S.J., Li, Z., McCormick, T.H.: Quantifying the contributions of training data and algorithm logic to the performance of automated cause-assignment algorithms for verbal autopsy (2018)
8. Cohen, K.B., Demner-Fushman, D.: Biomedical natural language processing, vol. 11. John Benjamins Publishing Company (2014)
9. Dalianis, H.: Clinical Text Mining: Secondary Use of Electronic Patient Records. Springer Nature (2018). https://doi.org/10.1007/978-3-319-78503-5
10. D'Ambruoso, L., et al.: The case for verbal autopsy in health systems strengthening. Lancet Glob. Health **5**(1), e20–e21 (2017)
11. Flaxman, A.D., Joseph, J.C., Murray, C.J., Riley, I.D., Lopez, A.D.: Performance of InSilicoVA for assigning causes of death to verbal autopsies: multisite validation study using clinical diagnostic gold standards. BMC Med. **16**(1), 56 (2018)
12. Ganapathy, S., Yi, K., Omar, M., Anuar, M., Jeevananthan, C., Rao, C.: Validation of verbal autopsy: determination of cause of deaths in Malaysia 2013. BMC Public Health **17**(1), 653 (2017)
13. James, S.L., Flaxman, A.D., Murray, C.J.: Performance of the tariff method: validation of a simple additive algorithm for analysis of verbal autopsies. Popul. Health Metrics **9**(1), 31 (2011)
14. Li, Z., McCormick, T., Clark, S.: Replicate Tariff Method for Verbal Autopsy Version. R Foundation for Statistical Computing, Vienna (2016)
15. Lo, S., Horton, R.: Everyone counts-so count everyone. Lancet **386**(10001), 1313–1314 (2015)
16. Lopez, A.D., AbouZahr, C., Shibuya, K., Gollogly, L.: Keeping count: births, deaths, and causes of death. Lancet **370**(9601), 1744–1746 (2007)
17. Maaten, L.V.D., Hinton, G.: Visualizing data using t-SNE. J. Mach. Learn. Res. **9**(Nov), 2579–2605 (2008)
18. McCormick, T.H., Li, Z.R., Calvert, C., Crampin, A.C., Kahn, K., Clark, S.J.: Probabilistic cause-of-death assignment using verbal autopsies. J. Am. Stat. Assoc. **111**(515), 1036–1049 (2016)
19. Murray, C.J., et al.: Population health metrics research consortium gold standard verbal autopsy validation study: design, implementation, and development of analysis datasets. Popul. Health Metrics **9**(1), 27 (2011)
20. Murtaza, S.S., Kolpak, P., Bener, A., Jha, P.: Automated verbal autopsy classification: using one-against-all ensemble method and Naïve Bayes classifier. Gates Open Res. **2**, 63 (2018)
21. Pedregosa, F., et al.: Scikit-learn: machine learning in Python. J. Mach. Learn. Res. **12**, 2825–2830 (2011)
22. Pennington, J., Socher, R., Manning, C.D.: Glove: global vectors for word representation. In: Empirical Methods in Natural Language Processing (EMNLP), pp. 1532–1543 (2014)
23. Rosário, E.V.N., et al.: Main causes of death in Dande, Angola: results from verbal autopsies of deaths occurring during 2009–2012. BMC Public Health **16**(1), 719 (2016)
24. TensorFlow: Visualizing data using the embedding projector in tensorboard (2021)

25. Thomas, J., Li, Z., McCortsnemick, T., Clark, S., Byass, P.: Package interVA5. R foundation for statistical computing, Vienna, Austria (2018). https://CRAN.R-project.org/package=InterVA5

26. Thomas, L.M., D'Ambruoso, L., Balabanova, D.: Verbal autopsy in health policy and systems: a literature review. BMJ Glob. Health **3**(2), e000639 (2018)

27. Tran, H.T., Nguyen, H.P., Walker, S.M., Hill, P.S., Rao, C.: Validation of verbal autopsy methods using hospital medical records: a case study in Vietnam. BMC Med. Res. Methodol. **18**(1), 43 (2018)

28. Westly, E.: One million deaths. Nature **504**(7478), 22 (2013)

29. World Health Organization: The 2016 WHO verbal autopsy instrument. https://www.who.int/healthinfo/statistics/verbalautopsystandards/en/. (2016)

30. World Health Organization, et al.: The World Health report: 2005: make every mother and child count. Technical report, Geneva: World Health Organization (2005)

31. Yan, Z., Jeblee, S., Hirst, G.: Can character embeddings improve cause-of-death classification for verbal autopsy narratives? In: Proceedings of the 18th BioNLP Workshop and Shared Task, pp. 234–239. Association for Computational Linguistics, Florence (2019). https://doi.org/10.18653/v1/W19-5025. https://www.aclweb.org/anthology/W19-5025

32. Yu, H.F., Huang, F.L., Lin, C.J.: Dual coordinate descent methods for logistic regression and maximum entropy models. Mach. Learn. **85**(1–2), 41–75 (2011)

Effective FAQ Retrieval and Question Matching Tasks with Unsupervised Knowledge Injection

Wen-Ting Tseng[1](✉), Yung-Chang Hsu[2](✉), and Berlin Chen[1](✉)

[1] National Taiwan Normal University, Taipei, Taiwan
`60847014s@gapps.ntnu.edu.tw`, `berlin@csie.ntnu.edu.tw`
[2] EZAI, Taipei, Taiwan
`mic@ez-ai.com.tw`

Abstract. Frequently asked question (FAQ) retrieval, with the purpose of providing information on frequent questions or concerns, has far-reaching applications in many areas like e-commerce services, online forums and many others, where a collection of question-answer (Q-A) pairs compiled a priori can be employed to retrieve an appropriate answer in response to a user's query that is likely to reoccur frequently. To this end, predominant approaches to FAQ retrieval typically rank question-answer pairs by considering either the similarity between the query and a question (q-Q), the relevance between the query and the associated answer of a question (q-A), or combining the clues gathered from the q-Q similarity measure and the q-A relevance measure. In this paper, we extend this line of research by combining the clues gathered from the q-Q similarity measure and the q-A relevance measure, and meanwhile injecting extra word interaction information, distilled from a generic (open-domain) knowledge base, into a contextual language model for inferring the q-A relevance. Furthermore, we also explore to capitalize on domain-specific topically-relevant relations between words in an unsupervised manner, acting as a surrogate to the supervised domain-specific knowledge base information. As such, it enables the model to equip sentence representations with the knowledge about domain-specific and topically-relevant relations among words, thereby providing a better q-A relevance measure. We evaluate variants of our approach on a publicly-available Chinese FAQ dataset (viz. TaipeiQA), and further apply and contextualize it to a large-scale question-matching task (viz. LCQMC), which aims to search questions from a QA dataset that have a similar intent as an input query. Extensive experimental results on these two datasets confirm the promising performance of the proposed approach in relation to some state-of-the-art ones.

Keywords: Frequently asked question · Knowledge graph · Language model

© Springer Nature Switzerland AG 2021
K. Ekštein et al. (Eds.): TSD 2021, LNAI 12848, pp. 124–134, 2021.
https://doi.org/10.1007/978-3-030-83527-9_11

1   Introduction

With the explosive growth of text (and multimedia) information repositories and services on the Internet, developments of effective frequently asked question (FAQ) retrieval [1] techniques have become a pressing need for a wide variety of application areas, like e-commerce services, online forums and so forth. FAQ retrieval has the goal of providing information on frequent questions or concerns, which is fulfilled by leveraging a collection of question-answer (denoted by Q-A) pairs compiled ahead of time to search an appropriate answer in response to a user's query (denoted by q for short) that is supposed to reoccur frequently. Recently, a common thread in various approaches to FAQ retrieval has been to rank question-answer pairs by considering either the similarity between the query and a question (viz. the q-Q similarity measure), or the relevance between the query and the associated answer of a question (viz. the q-A relevance measure). For example, the q-Q similarity measure can be computed with unsupervised information retrieval (IR) models, such as the Okapi BM25 method [2] and the vector space method [3], to name a few. Meanwhile, the q-A relevance can be determined with a simple supervised neural model stacked on top of a pre-trained contextual language model, which takes a query as the input and predicts the likelihoods of all answers given the query. Prevailing contextual language models, such as the bidirectional encoder representations from transformers (BERT) [4], embeddings from language models (ELMo) [5], generative pre-trained transformer (GPT), and the generalized autoregressive pretraining method (XLNet) [6], can serve this purpose to obtain context-aware query embeddings. Among them, BERT has recently aroused much attention due to its excellent performance on capturing semantic interactions between two or more text units.

The supervised neural model usually is trained (and the contextual language model is fine-tuned) on the Q-A pairs collected a priori for a given FAQ retrieval task [7]. Although such pre-trained contextual language models can learn general language representations from large-scale corpora, they may fail to capture the important open-domain or domain-specific knowledge about deeper semantic and pragmatic interactions of entities (or words) involved in a given knowledge-driven FAQ retrieval task. As such, there is good reason to explore extra open-domain or domain-specific knowledge clues for use in FAQ retrieval. However, manually building a domain-specific knowledge base could be tedious and expensive in terms of time and personnel.

Building on these insights, we propose an effective approach to FAQ retrieval, which has at least three distinctive characteristics. First, both the q-Q similarity measure obtained by the Okapi BM25 method and the q-A relevance measure obtained by a BERT-based supervised method are linearly combined to rank Q-A pairs for better retrieval performance. On one hand, Okapi BM25 performs bag-of-word term matching between the query and a question, it can facilitate high-precision retrieval. On the other hand, since the BERT- based supervised method determines the relevance between the query and an answer based on context-aware semantic embeddings, which can model long-range dependency and get around the term-mismatch problem to some extent. In addition, an effective voting mechanism to rerank answer hypotheses for better performance is proposed. Second, inspired by the notion of knowledge-enabled BERT (K-BERT) modeling [8], we investigate to inject triplets of entity relations distilled from an open-domain knowledge base into BERT to expand and refine the representations of an input query for more accurate relevance estimation. Third, since a domain-specific knowledge base is not always readily available, we leverage an unsupervised topic modeling method, viz. probabilistic latent topic analysis (PLSA) [9], to extract triplets of topically-relevant words from the collection of Q-A pairs, which can enrich the query representations for the FAQ retrieval task at hand. To further confirm the utility of our approach, we further apply and contextualize it to question-matching, which is highly relevant to FAQ retrieval and has drawn increasing attention recently.

2   Approach to FAQ Retrieval and Question Matching

This section first sheds light on the instantiations of the two disparate measures that we employ to rank the collection of Q-A pairs given that a user's query is posed for FAQ retrieval: 1) the q-Q similarity measure and 2) the q-A relevance measure. An effective voting mechanism is proposed to leverage the clues gathered from the q-Q similarity measure and the q-A relevance measure for selecting a more accurate answer. After that, we introduce the ways that the triplets of entity-level or word-level semantic and pragmatic relations extracted from an open-domain knowledge base and in-domain topical clusters are incorporated into the BERT-based method to increase the accuracy of the q-A relevance measure.

2.1   The q-Q Similarity Measure

The task of FAQ retrieval is to rank a collection of question-answer $(Q\text{-}A)$ pairs,

$$\{(Q_1, A_1), \ldots, (Q_n, A_n), \ldots, (Q_N, A_N),$$

with respect to a user's query, and then return the answer of the topmost ranked one as the desired answer. Note here that a distinct answer may be associated with different questions, which means that the number of distinct answers may be smaller than or equal to N. Furthermore, due to the fact that a query may not have been seen before, a common first thought is to calculate the q-Q similarity measure by resorting to an unsupervised method developed by the IR community, such as the Okapi BM25 method:

$$\text{BM25}\,(q, Q_n) = \sum_{l=1}^{L} \frac{(K_1 + 1)\, f\,(w_l, Q_n)}{K_1 \left[(1 - b) + b \frac{len(Q_n)}{avg_{Qlen}}\right] + f\,(w_l, Q_n)} IQF\,(w_l) \qquad (1)$$

where the query q can be expressed by $q = w_1, \ldots, w_L$, $f(w_l, Q_n)$ is the frequency of word w_l within the question Q_n, $len\,(Q_n)$ is the length of Q_n, avg_{Qlen} denotes the average question length for the collection, and $IQF(w_l)$ is the inverse question frequency of w_l. In addition, K_1 and b are tunable parameters.

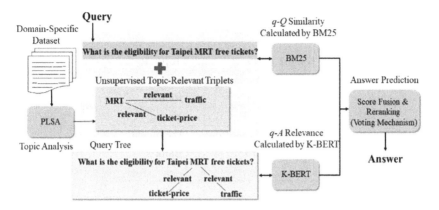

Fig. 1. A schematic depiction of our proposed modelling approach to unsupervised knowledge injection.

2.2 The q-A Relevance Measure

Apart from calculating the q-Q similarity measure, we can also estimate the q-A relevance measure for ranking the collection of Q-A pairs. Instead of using the unsupervised Okapi BM25 method, we in this paper employ a supervised neural method for this purpose, which encompasses a single layer neural network stacked on top of a pre-trained BERT-based neural network. In the test phase, the whole model will accept an arbitrary query q as the input and its output layer will predict the posterior probability $P(A_n|q)$, $n = 1, \ldots, N$, of any answer A_n (denoted also by $BERT(q, A_n)$). The answer A_n that has the highest $P(A_n|q)$ value will be regarded as the desired answer that is anticipated to be the most relevant to q. On the other side, in the training phase, since the test queries are not given in advance, we can instead capitalize on the corresponding relations of existing Q-A pairs for model training. More specifically, the one-layer neural network is trained (and meanwhile the parameters of BERT are fine-tuned) by maximizing the $P(A_n, Q_n)$ for all the Q-A pairs in the collection. Following a similar vein, other supervised methods based on contextual language models, such as BiLSTM, CNN, ELMO, BiMPM, ELMo, and many others, can also be used to calculate $P(A_n|q)$ [5,7,10].

To bring together the modeling advantages of the q-Q similarity measure and the q-A relevance measure, the ultimate ranking score $RS\,(Q_n, A_n, q)$ for a Q-A pair with respect to a query q can be obtained through the following linear combination:

$$\text{RS}\,(Q_n, A_n, q) = \alpha \frac{BM25(q, Q_n)}{\sum_{n'=1}^{N} BM25(q, Q_{n'})} + (1 - \alpha)BERT(q, A_n) \qquad (2)$$

where α is tunable parameter used to control the relative contributions of the two measures.

Table 1. An illustration of the words that have the largest probability values of $P(w|T_k)$ for some topics of the TaipeiQA task.

Topic 1	Topic 2	...	Topic 10
Taipei	Library	.	Loan
City	Book	.	Pioneer
MRT	Read	.	Young
Taiwan	Information	.	Financing
Capital	Data	.	Bank
.	.		.
.	.		.
.	.		.

2.3   Voting Mechanism

Apart from simply selecting the answer that corresponds to Q-A pair that has the highest $RS(Q_n, A_n, q)$ score, we can instead leverage a voting mechanism to pick up the answer that has the majority occurrence count in the top-M ranked results in terms of the $RS(Q_n, A_n, q)$ scores for all the Q-A pairs (in our experiments, we set M to 5). Namely, if there is an answer that has an occurrence count greater or equal to $\lceil M/2 \rceil$ in the top-M ranked results, it will be selected as the target answer of the input query q. Otherwise, the answer corresponding to the highest $RS(Q_n, A_n, q)$ score will be selected in response to q.

2.4   Supervised and Unsupervised Knowledge Injections for the q-A Relevance Measure

The aforementioned BERT-based method for estimating the q-A relevance measure employs a pre-trained Transformer [11] architecture, equipped with multi-head attention mechanisms, which has been proven effective for capturing semantic interactions between text units [4]. However, it might not perform well on knowledge-driven tasks like FAQ retrieval or question-matching, due to the incapability of modelling open-domain or/and domain-specific knowledge about deeper semantic and pragmatic interactions of words (entities). To ameliorate this problem, a new wave of research has emerged recently to incorporate information gleaned from an open-domain knowledge base [12], such as WordNet [13], HowNet [14], YAGO [15], or a domain-specific knowledge base, such as MedicalKG, into the BERT-based model structure. Representative methods include, but is not limited to, the THU-ERNE [16] method and the Knowledge-enabled BERT (K-BERT) method. On the practical side, K-BERT seems more attractive than THU-ERNE, because it can easily inject a given open-domain or domain-specific knowledge base, in the form of a set of triplets $(w_i, \text{relation}_r, w_j)$ that describe disparate relations between words or entities, into a pretrained BERT-based model structure through the so-called soft-position and visible-matrix operations [8]. As such, in this paper, we make a further attempt to exploit K-BERT to incorporate both open-domain and domain-specific knowledge clues for use in the q-A relevance measure [17–21].

2.5 Unsupervised Knowledge Injections for the q-A Relevance Measure

Since hand-crafting a domain-specific knowledge base for an FAQ retrieval task (or a question-matching task) would be extremely laborious and time-consuming, in this paper we alternatively employ probabilistic latent topic analysis (PLSA), a celebrated unsupervised topic modelling method, to extract the domain-specific word-level topical relations, incapsulated in the collection of Q-A pairs for the FAQ retrieval task of interest. Given the collection of question-answer (Q-A) pairs,

$$\{(Q_1, A_1), \ldots, (Q_n, A_n), \ldots, (Q_N, A_N),$$

the PLSA formulation decomposes the word-usage distribution of a Q-A pair by

$$P(w|Q_n, A_n) = \sum_{k=1}^{K} P(w, T_k) P(T_k|Q_n, A_n), \tag{3}$$

where w denotes an arbitrary word, T_k marks an automatically generated topic and K is the total number of topics (in our experiments, we set K to 10 by default). More specifically, we assume the top significant words of a given PLSA-generated topic T_k have a domain-specific topically-relevant relation, which can also be represented in triplets as well to be digested by K-BERT. As such, for each topic T_k, we can select those top-L words, 10 words for example, which have the largest probability values of $P(w|T_k)$ and establish symmetric topically-relevant relations among them, namely $(w_i, \text{relevance}_{T_k}, w_j)$ and $(w_j, \text{relevance}_{T_k}, w_i)$ for any pair of words (w_i, w_j) involved in the Top-L words. To our knowledge, this is the first attempt to harness the synergistic power of unsupervised domain-specific, topically-relevant word relations and K-BERT for use in the q-A relevance measure for FAQ retrieval. Along this same vein, use can capitalize on PLSA to generate domain-specific topically-relevant relations of words for the question-matching task as well. Figure 1 shows a schematic depiction of our proposed modelling approach to unsupervised knowledge injection, while Table 1 is an illustration of the words that have the largest probability values of $P(w|T_k)$ for some topics of the TaipeiQA task.

Table 2. Evaluations of various modelling approaches on the TaipeiQA task.

	Precision	Recall	F1	Accuracy	MRR
BM25	0.743	0.700	0.720	0.743	0.775
BERT	0.688	0.675	0.681	0.697	0.771
ELMO	0.738	0.570	0.643	0.466	0.528
BILSTM	0.798	0.577	0.669	0.439	0.501
BM25+BERT	0.763	0.747	0.754	0.785	0.798
K-BERT (HowNet)	0.705	0.685	0.694	0.706	0.774
K-BERT (TaipeiQA)	0.757	0.724	0.740	0.731	0.791
K-BERT (HowNet+TaipeiQA)	0.754	0.722	0.737	0.726	0.788
BM25+K-BERT (TaipeiQA)	0.812	0.792	0.801	0.811	0.802
BM25+KBERT (TaiperQA) [VOTE]	**0.813**	**0.793**	**0.802**	**0.812**	**0.807**

Table 3. Evaluations of various modelling approaches on the LCQMC task.

	Precision	Recall	F1	Accuracy
BM25	0.659	0.659	0.659	0.659
BERT	0.855	0.842	0.848	0.842
BiLSTM	0.706	0.893	0.788	0.761
CNN	0.671	0.856	0.752	0.718
BiMPM	0.776	0.939	0.849	0.834
BM25+BERT	0.856	0.842	0.848	0.845
K-BERT(HowNet)	0.859	0.872	0.865	0.859
K-BERT(LCQMC)	0.877	0.870	0.873	0.870
K-BERT (HowNet+LCQMC)	0.873	0.862	0.867	0.862
BM25+K-BERT (LCQMC)	0.877	0.870	0.871	0.870
BM25+K-BERT (LCQMC) [VOTE]	**0.877**	**0.870**	**0.873**	**0.871**

3   Experimental Datasets and Setup

We assess the effectiveness of our proposed approach on two publicly-available Chinese datasets: TaipeiQA and LCQMC [10]. TaipeiQA is an FAQ dataset crawled from the official website of the Taipei City Government, which consists of 8,521 Q-A pairs and is further divided into three parts: the training set (68%), the validation set (20%) and the test set (12%). Note here that the questions in the validation and test sets are taken as unseen queries, which are used to tune the model parameters and evaluate the performance of FAQ retrieval, respectively. On the other hand, LCQMC is a publicly-available large-scale Chinese question-matching corpus, which consists of 260,068 question pairs and is further divided into three parts: the training set (60%), the validation set (20%)

and the test set (20%). The task of LCQMC is to determine the similarity of a pair of questions in terms of their intents, which is more general than paraphrasing. In implementation for the LCQMC task, the input of Okapi BM25 is a pair of questions and the output is the corresponding similarity measure. As for the BERT-based supervised method, its input to BERT (and K-BERT) is changed to be a pair of questions, while the output of the upper-stacked one-layer neural network is a real value between 0 and 1 that quantifies the similarity between the two (the larger the value, the higher the similarity). In addition, for both the TaipeiQA and LCQMC tasks, HowNet will be taken as the open-domain knowledge base.

4   Evaluation Metrics

In this paper, we adopt five evaluation methods to evaluate the performance for our task, including precision, recall, F1 score, accuracy and mean reciprocal rank (MRR). We can use confusion matrix to calculate precision, recall, accuracy F1 score such as Eq. 4.

$$F1 = \frac{2 \cdot \text{Precision} \cdot \text{Recall}}{\text{Precision} + \text{Recall}} \qquad (4)$$

On the other hand, MRR is a measure of the quality of response answers. For a single query, the reciprocal rank is $\frac{1}{\text{rank}}$ where rank is the position of the highest ranked answer. For multiple queries Q, the MRR is the mean of the Q reciprocal ranks.

$$MRR = \frac{1}{Q} \sum_{i=1}^{|Q|} \frac{1}{\text{rank}_i} \qquad (5)$$

5   Experimental Results

In the first set of experiments, we assess the performance of our baseline approach (denoted by BM25+BERT) on the TaipeiQA task with different evaluation metric [22,23], in relation to those approaches either using unsupervised method (BM25) or supervised methods (BiLSTM and ELMO) in isolation. As can be seen from the first five rows of Table 2, BM25+BERT performs better than the other approaches for most evaluation metrics, which reveals the complementarity between Okapi BM25 and BERT for the FQA retrieval task studied here.

In the second set of experiments, we evaluate the effectiveness of the enhanced BERT modelling (viz. K-BERT), which has been injected with knowledge clues either from the open domain (viz. K-BERT(HowNet)) [24,25], from the unsupervised domain-specific topical clusters (viz. K-BERT(TaipeiQA)), or from their combination (viz. K-BERT(HowNet+TaipeiQA)). It is evident from Table 2, K-BERT(TaipeiQA) offers considerable improvements over BERT and K-BERT(HowNet). This indeed confirms the utility of our unsupervised topical knowledge distilling method (cf. Sects. 2.4 and 2.5). The last row of Table 3 depicts the results of the combination of Okapi BM25 and K-BERT(TaipeiQA), which yields the best results for the TaipeiQA task.

In the third set of experiments, we report on the results of our baseline and enhanced approaches on the LCQMC question-matching task, in comparison to some unsupervised and supervised approaches, where the results of the three supervised approaches (viz. BiLSTM, CNN and BiMPM) are adopted from [10]. Similar trends can be observed from Table 3 BM25+K-BERT(LCQMC) performs remarkably well for the LCQMC task.

As a final point in this section, we evaluate the FAQ performance levels of K-BERT(TaipeiQA) with respect to different numbers of PLSA topics used for extracting the domain-specific knowledge clues, as shown in Fig. 2. Consulting Fig. 2 we notice that the performance of K-BERT(TaipeiQA) is steadily improved when the number of PLSA being used becomes larger; the improvement, however, seems to reach a peak elevation when the number is set to 10, and then to degrade when the number exceeds 10. However, how to automatically determine the number of topics, as well as the number of significant words for each topic to establish domain-specific topically-relevant relations, still awaits further studies.

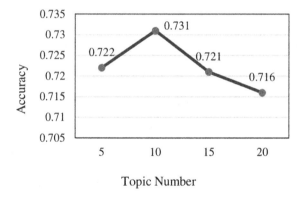

Fig. 2. The FAQ performance levels of K-BERT (TaipeiQA) with respect to different numbers of the PLSA topics.

6   Conclusion and Future Work

In this paper, we have presented an effective, hybrid approach for FAQ retrieval, exploring the synergistic effect of combing unsupervised IR method (Okapi BM25) and supervised contextual language models (BERT and K-BERT). In addition, a novel knowledge injection mechanism leveraging clues drawn from unsupervised domain-specific topical clusters has been proposed. As to future work, we plan to investigate more sophisticated unsupervised knowledge injection mechanisms and learning algorithms, as well as their applications to document summarization, readability assessment and among others.

Acknowledgment. This research is supported in part by ASUS AICS and the Ministry of Science and Technology (MOST), Taiwan, under Grant Number MOST 109-2634-F-008-006- through Pervasive Artificial Intelligence Research (PAIR) Labs, Taiwan, and Grant Numbers MOST 108-2221-E-003-005-MY3 and MOST 109-2221-E-003-020-MY3. Any findings and implications in the paper do not necessarily reflect those of the sponsors.

References

1. Karan, M., Šnajder, J.: Paraphrase-focused learning to rank for domain-specific frequently asked questions retrieval. Expert Syst. Appl. **91**, 418–433 (2018)
2. Robertson, S., Zaragoza, H.: The probabilistic relevance framework: BM25 and beyond. Found. Trends Inf. Retrieval **3**(4), 333–389 (2009)
3. Salton, G., Wong, A., Yang, C.: A vector space model for automatic indexing. Commun. ACM **18**(11), 613–620 (1975)
4. Devlin, J., Chang, M.-W., et al.: BERT: pre-training of deep bidirectional transformers for language understanding. In: Proceedings of the Conference of the North American Chapter of the Association for Computational Linguistics: Human Language Technologies. pp. 4171–4186 (2019)
5. Peters, M., Neumann, M., et al.: Deep contextualized word representations. In: Proceedings of the Conference of the North American Chapter of the Association for Computational Linguistics: Human Language Technologies, pp. 2227–2237 (2018)
6. Yang, Z., Dai, Z., et al.: XLNet: generalized autoregressive pretraining for language understanding. In: Proceedings of Conference on Neural Information Processing Systems, pp. 5753–5763 (2019)
7. Sakata, W., Shibata, T., et al.: FAQ retrieval using query-question similarity and BERT-based query-answer relevance. In: Proceedings of the International ACM SIGIR Conference on Research and Development in Information Retrieval, pp. 1113–1116 (2019)
8. Liu, W., Zhou, P., et al.: K-BERT: enabling language representation with knowledge graph. In: Proceedings of the AAAI Conference on Artificial Intelligence AAAI, pp. 2901–2908 (2020)
9. Hofmann, T.: Probabilistic latent semantic analysis. In: Proceedings of the Conference on Uncertainty in Artificial Intelligence, pp. 289–296 (1999)
10. Liu, X., Chen, Q., et al.: LCQMC: a large-scale Chinese question matching corpus. In: Proceedings of the International Conference on Computational Linguistics, pp. 1952–1962 (2018)
11. Vaswani, A., Shazeer, N., et al.: Attention is all you need. In: Proceedings of Conference on Neural Information Processing Systems, pp. 5998–6008 (2017)
12. Cui, W., Xiao, Y., et al.: KBQA: learning question answering over QA corpora and knowledge bases. Proc. VLDB Endowment **10**(5), 656–676 (2017)
13. Miller, G.A.: WordNet: a lexical database for English. Commun. ACM **38**(11), 39–41 (1995)
14. Dong, Z., Dong, Q., Hao, C.: HowNet and its computation of meaning. In: Proceedings of the International Conference on Computational Linguistics, pp. 53–56 (2010)
15. Suchanek, F.M., Kasneci, G., Weikum, G.: YAGO: a core of semantic knowledge. In: Proceedings of the International Conference on World Wide Web, pp. 697–706 (2007)

16. Zhang, Z., Xu, H., et al.: ERNIE: enhanced language representation with informative entities. In: Proceedings of the Annual Meeting of the Association for Computational Linguistics, pp. 1441–1451 (2019)
17. Yao, L., Mao, C., Luo, Y.: KG-BERT: BERT for knowledge graph completion (2019). arXiv preprint arXiv:1909.03193
18. Ji, S., Pan,S., et al.: A survey on knowledge graphs: representation, acquisition and applications (2020). arXiv preprint arXiv:2002.00388
19. Wang, Q., Mao, Z., et al.: Knowledge graph embedding: a survey of approaches and applications. IEEE Trans. Knowl. Data Eng. **29**(12), 2724–2743 (2017)
20. Ji, G., He,S., et al.: Knowledge graph embedding via dynamic mapping matrix. In: Proceedings of the 53rd Annual Meeting of the Association for Computational Linguistics and the 7th International Joint Conference on Natural Language Processing (volume 1: Long papers), pp. 687–696 (2015)
21. Ji, G., Liu, K., et al.: Knowledge graph completion with adaptive sparse transfer matrix. In: Thirtieth AAAI Conference on Artificial Intelligence (2016)
22. Sokolova, M., Lapalme, G.: A systematic analysis of performance measures for classification tasks. Inf. Process. Manage. **45**(4), 427–437 (2009)
23. Kiritchenko, S., Matwin, S., Nock, R., Famili, A.F.: Learning and evaluation in the presence of class hierarchies: application to text categorization. In: Lamontagne, L., Marchand, M. (eds.) AI 2006. LNCS (LNAI), vol. 4013, pp. 395–406. Springer, Heidelberg (2006). https://doi.org/10.1007/11766247_34
24. Wang, Z., Zhang, J., et al.: Knowledge graph and text jointly embedding. In: Proceedings of the 2014 Conference on Empirical Methods in Natural Language Processing (EMNLP), pp. 1591–1601 (2014)
25. Peters, M.E., Mark, N., et al.: Deep contextualized word representations (2018). arXiv preprint arXiv:1802.05365

Exploring Conditional Language Model Based Data Augmentation Approaches for Hate Speech Classification

Ashwin Geet D'Sa[1]([✉]), Irina Illina[1], Dominique Fohr[1], Dietrich Klakow[2], and Dana Ruiter[2]

[1] Université de Lorraine, CNRS, Inria, LORIA, Nancy, France
{ashwin-geet.dsa,irina.illina,dominique.fohr}@loria.fr
[2] Spoken Language System Group, Saarland University, Saarbrücken, Germany
{dietrich.klakow,druiter}@lsv.uni-saarland.de

Abstract. Deep Neural Network (DNN) based classifiers have gained increased attention in hate speech classification. However, the performance of DNN classifiers increases with quantity of available training data and in reality, hate speech datasets consist of only a small amount of labeled data. To counter this, Data Augmentation (DA) techniques are often used to increase the number of labeled samples and therefore, improve the classifier's performance. In this article, we explore augmentation of training samples using a conditional language model. Our approach uses a single class conditioned Generative Pre-Trained Transformer-2 (GPT-2) language model for DA, avoiding the need for multiple class specific GPT-2 models. We study the effect of increasing the quantity of the augmented data and show that adding a few hundred samples significantly improves the classifier's performance. Furthermore, we evaluate the effect of filtering the generated data used for DA. Our approach demonstrates up to 7.3% and up to 25.0% of relative improvements in macro-averaged F1 on two widely used hate speech corpora.

Keywords: Natural language processing · Hate speech classification · Data augmentation

1 Introduction

Increased usage of social media has led to a rise in online hate speech. Hate speech is an anti-social behavior, against a social group based on ethnicity, nationality, religion, gender, etc. [7]. It induces a feeling of threat, violence, and fear to the targeted group or individual. Manual tagging of such comments on social media is time-consuming and

This work was funded by the M-PHASIS project supported by the French National Research Agency (ANR) and German National Research Agency (DFG) under contract ANR-18-FRAL-0005. Experiments presented in this article were carried out using the Grid'5000 testbed, supported by a scientific interest group hosted by Inria and including CNRS, RENATER, several Universities, and other organizations. We thank Hayakawa Akira for his valuable comments and feedback and on this article.

© Springer Nature Switzerland AG 2021
K. Ekštein et al. (Eds.): TSD 2021, LNAI 12848, pp. 135–146, 2021.
https://doi.org/10.1007/978-3-030-83527-9_12

very expensive. Hence, Natural Language Processing (NLP) and classification techniques can help moderators identify hate speech.

The research interest towards hate speech classification has increased [3,5,14,17]. The performance of the commonly used neural network classifiers depends on the amount of training data that is available, and unfortunately most of the hate speech datasets have only a small amount of labeled data to train the classifier.

Various Data Augmentation (DA) approaches have been explored in literature to train better performing text classification or representation models. One group of approaches includes replication of samples by performing minor modifications such as addition, deletion, swapping of words, and synonym replacement [24]. Some approaches in this group replicate samples through word replacements based on embeddings of the word and its surrounding context [16,23,26]. Other group of approaches have explored translation and back-translation [20,22], auto-regressive language models [1], and auto-encoders [13].

Similar DA techniques have been explored in the domain of hate speech classification. One group of approaches replicate samples by replacing similar words, based on pre-trained embeddings and cosine distance [19]. Word replacement based on features from ConceptNet and Wikidata knowledge graphs were explored in [21]. Approaches based on text transformation using back-translation are explored in [2]. Approaches based on sample generation using Long short-term memory (LSTM) and GPT-2 [18] are explored in [19,27].

Given the significant improvements in the classification performance using the language generation based DA methods, we follow the approach by Wullach et al. [27]. The goal of this article is the experimental study of behavior of data augmentation approach in [27]. However, the contributions of this article comes with two key differences. (a) We fine-tune a single class conditioned GPT-2 language model [15], as opposed to class specific fine-tuned GPT-2 models in [27]. (b) We attempt three class classification of hate, abuse, and normal speech, which is known to be a relatively complex task due to overlap between hate speech and abusive speech [6,10]. Additionally, we also explore the effect of the quantity and the quality of the generated data required to improve the classification performance.

To summarize, the contributions of this article are:

– Generation of training samples using conditional language model for DA in multi-class classification of hate speech.
– Analysis of how classification performance varies depending on the quantity of the additional samples.
– Study on how filtering the generated samples affects the performance.

2   Data Augmentation

In this section, we describe our approach for DA using the GPT-2 model to generate new training samples.

2.1   Conditional Language Modeling

A typical language modeling task involves learning the joint probability distribution of a sequence [4]. Given the vocabulary V containing a fixed set of distinct tokens, a sequence of n tokens $z = (z_1, z_2, ..., z_n)$ where $z_i \in V$, the joint probability distribution of the sequence is given as:

$$p(z) = \prod_{i=1}^{n} p(z_i | z_{<i}) \tag{1}$$

Given a dataset containing m samples $D = \{z^1, z^2, ..., z^m\}$, a neural language model learns the parameter set θ such that it reduces the negative log-likelihood:

$$L(D) = - \sum_{j=1}^{|D|} \log p(z_i^j | z_{<i}^j; \theta) \tag{2}$$

The language model can be trained with a conditional context c, extending equation (1) to:

$$p(z|c) = \prod_{i=1}^{n} p(z_i | c, z_{<i}) \tag{3}$$

Likewise, Eq. (2) extends to:

$$L(D) = - \sum_{j=1}^{|D|} \log p(z_i^j | c^j, z_{<i}^j; \theta) \tag{4}$$

Given a conditional context c, the learned parameter set θ can be used to sample l tokens and generate a new sequence $\hat{z}$ using $p(\hat{z}_t | c, \hat{z}_{<t}; \theta)$, where $t = \{1, 2, .., l\}$.

2.2   Proposed Methodology

Figure 1 shows the block diagram of our approach. We fine-tune a single pre-trained GPT-2 model for the given datasets (see Sect. 3.1) using conditional language modeling objective. We then use the fine-tuned GPT-2 model to generate a large number of samples for each class. We filter the samples using a Bidirectional Encoder Representations from Transformers (BERT) [8] model that has been fine-tuned on the original training set. Top-N samples sorted by the BERT model are augmented to the original training set to train a Convolutional-Gated Recurrent Unit (C-GRU) based classifier.

GPT-2 Fine-Tuning and Data Generation: We fine-tune a GPT-2 model on the original training set by conditioning it on the class labels. To achieve this, we prepend the class label of the sample as a conditional context. For example, a 'normal' class sentence such as *"a cat is sitting on the mat"* is transformed to *"**normal** a cat is sitting on the mat"* before using it as input to fine-tune GPT-2 model.

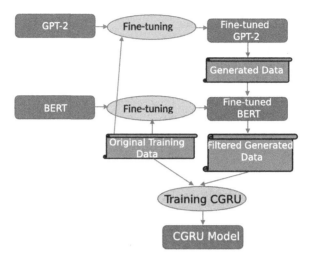

Fig. 1. Block diagram for training an improved classifier with DA.

Filtering the Generated Sequences: Sometimes, the generated content does not match the target class. Thus, we adopt a technique similar in [27] to filter the generated samples by fine-tuning the BERT model for the multi-class classification. In order to avoid a bias induced by imbalanced class sample size in the BERT classifier, we downsample the classes to have an equal amount of samples in each class. The samples generated by the fine-tuned GPT-2 model are then passed through the fine-tuned BERT model in order to sort them according to the score given by the BERT model, finally retaining only the top-N for DA.

Hate Speech Classifier: As presented in [28], the C-GRU based architecture is a powerful hate speech classifier. This model is faster to train and requires smaller computational power since it has fewer model parameters in comparison to the transformer based BERT model. Thus, as adopted in [27] we choose a similar architecture for our hate speech classification. With the C-GRU based architecture, the input sequence is first passed through convolutional layers followed by the GRU layer.

3 Experimental Setup

This section describes the datasets, text pre-processing, and the choice of hyper-parameters for the models.

3.1 Data Description

For the multi-class classification of hate speech, we chose two widely used hate speech datasets containing tweets sampled from Twitter, one by Founta et al. [12] and the other

Table 1. Statistics of Founta and Davidson datasets.

Dataset	#Samples	Normal	Abusive	Hateful
Founta	86.9K	63%	31%	6%
Davidson	24.7K	17%	77%	6%

by Davidson et al. [6]. Here onwards, referred to as 'Founta' and 'Davidson'. Each dataset is randomly split into three sets, 'training', 'validation', and 'test', containing 60%, 20%, and 20% respectively.

Founta dataset is collected by boosted random sampling of data from Twitter. The dataset is annotated into four classes, named, 'normal', 'abusive', 'hateful', and 'spam'. In our study, we do not use the samples from the 'spam' class and this reduces the number of samples in the dataset from 100K to 86.9K.

Davidson dataset is collected by sampling the tweets based on keywords from the hatebase lexicon. The dataset is annotated into three classes 'hate speech', 'offensive language', and 'neither'. Since the definition of the class labels used by Founta et al. [12] was similar to Davidson et al. [6], in this article, we have referred to these classes as 'hateful', 'abusive', and 'normal' respectively.

A summary of the two corpora is available in Table 1. As indicated, 'hateful' tweets are the minority in both datasets.

3.2 Data Preprocessing

We removed all numbers and special characters except '.', ',', '!', '?', and *apostrophe*, and repeated occurrences of the same special character are changed to a single one. Twitter user handles are changed to '@USER'. The '#' symbol in the hashtag is removed, and the multi-word hashtags are split based on the presence of uppercase characters in the hashtags. For example, '#leaveThisPlace' is changed to 'leave This Place'. Finally, the data is converted to lowercase.

3.3 Model Parameters

Our model parameters are adopted from [27]. We use the implementation of huggingface's transformers API [25] to fine-tune the 'GPT-2 large' model.[1] The final generative model is chosen based on the lowest loss computed on validation set after each epoch. The class label is used as a prompt text to the fine-tuned GPT-2 model to generate samples for each specific class. Overall, we generate 600K samples for each class label.

To fine-tune the BERT model, we used the pre-trained 'BERT-base-uncased' model trained on the English corpus. We fine-tuned two BERT models, one on the training set of Founta, another on the training set of Davidson. The generated data is sorted according to the softmax score obtained by the fine-tuned BERT model.

---

[1] https://huggingface.co/gpt2-large.

For the C-GRU classifier, words occurring less than three times are considered as out-of-vocabulary words, and are replaced with a '⟨UNK⟩' token. For both BERT models and the C-GRU models, at the end of each epoch, the macro-averaged F1 measure is evaluated on the validation set to choose the best models. The best models are then used to sort the generated samples or for the classification.

4   Results and Discussion

We report mean and standard deviation of test set in percentage macro-averaged F1 evaluated over five separate runs. Each run uses a C-GRU classifier with a different random weight initialisation. The 95% confidence interval on macro-averaged F1 obtained using paired bootstrap [9, 11] is ±1.6 and ±2.8 for the Founta and Davidson test sets, respectively.

4.1   Improvements with Data Augmentation

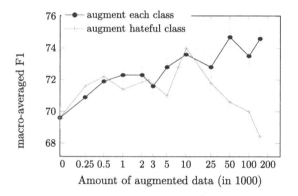

Fig. 2. Macro-averaged F1 on Founta test set using DA. The classifier is trained using DA with increasing amounts of generated data (X-Axis).

Figure 2 and Fig. 3 show the macro-average F1 by varying the amount of augmented data for the Founta and Davidson datasets respectively. In these experiments, the generated data is combined with the original training data to train the classifier. We have explored two strategies, (a) augmenting each class with an equal amount of data; (b) augmenting data only in the 'hateful' class, because the number of samples in 'hateful' class is very small. Baseline macro-averaged F1 obtained using the C-GRU classifier without DA is 69.6 ± 0.7 for the Founta dataset and 56.5 ± 0.3 for the Davidson dataset.

Figure 2 and Fig. 3 show that DA improves the classifier performance for the 'augment each class' and gives up to 7.3% of relative improvement for the Founta test set and up to 25.0% for the Davidson test set. We observe performance gains even with few hundred samples augmented with the original training set, however, the performance gain reduces as the amount of additional augmented data increases. We would

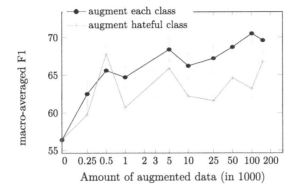

Fig. 3. Macro-averaged F1 on Davidson test set using DA. The classifier is trained using DA with increasing amounts of generated data (X-Axis).

like to highlight that our implementation of the non class conditional GPT-2 model based augmentation [27] resulted in similar results. Thus, we have achieved comparable performance by using three times lesser parameters to augment training data by using a class conditioned GPT-2 model.

In the 'augment hateful class' case, we observe a relative improvement to the classification performance by up to 6.2% for the Founta test set and up to 20.2% for the Davidson test set. After adding data we initially observed improvements in macro-average F1, however, as the amount of augmenting data increased, the macro-average F1 declined. An analysis of the confusion matrices revealed that the reduction in the performance is due to the classifier getting biased and predicting the 'normal' class samples incorrectly as 'hateful'. As we increase the data added only to the 'hateful' class, the model's prior probability of predicting the data as the 'hateful' class also increases.

4.2 Quality of Augmented Data

Table 2 shows the classification performance of the C-GRU that was trained with only the generated data. For both datasets, we observe an increase in the classifier's performance as the amount of generated data used to train the classifier is increased. For the Davidson dataset, we note that the performance is higher than the baseline when more than 50K generated samples are used for training. These results show that the generated data can be efficiently used for DA since it characterises the original training data and its classes.

Furthermore, we analysed the quality of generated samples by using it as test samples for the model trained using only the original training set. We trained the C-GRU model on Founta training set and compared confusion matrices obtained from the Founta test set and the top 50K samples generated from each class. The confusion matrices are shown in Fig. 4. We observe that the classification performance on the generated set is much better than classification on the test set, implying that generated data

Table 2. Macro-averaged F1 for classifier trained using only the generated data.

Amount of generated data used for each class	Founta test set	Davidson test set
Baseline (no DA)	69.6 ± 0.7	56.5 ± 0.2
5K	60.2 ± 1.2	48.4 ± 1.8
10K	60.5 ± 1.6	56.0 ± 2.0
25K	64.1 ± 1.1	56.2 ± 3.7
50K	**64.6 ± 0.8**	62.6 ± 1.1
100K	64.0 ± 0.8	**67.2 ± 1.0**
150K	63.0 ± 0.2	**67.2 ± 0.8**

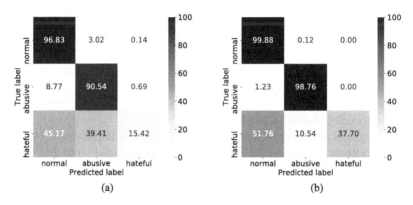

(a)   (b)

Fig. 4. (a) Confusion matrix obtained on Founta test set. (b) Confusion matrix obtained on generated samples.

is similar to the original training set. Further, we tried to improve the filtering technique by fine-tuning the BERT model using the data from both the original training set and generated set. Our preliminary experiments did not show any improvement in the final classification results.

4.3   Influence of Filtering the Samples

Table 3 shows the effect of using a fine-tuned BERT model for filtering the samples generated by GPT-2 for DA on the Founta dataset and the Davidson dataset. Here, we randomly choose N generated samples and compared them against the top-N samples sorted by the fine-tuned BERT model. Choosing the samples filtered by the fine-tuned BERT model gave a relative improvement of up to 5.2% for the Founta dataset and up to 7.7% for the Davidson dataset over the randomly chosen samples for augmentation.

Table 3. Comparison of classification performance on Founta and Davidson test sets by augmenting N randomly sampled data versus top-N filtered by BERT.

	Founta test set		Davidson test set	
Amount of generated data used for each class	Random Sampling	Top-N scored by BERT	Random Sampling	Top-N scored by BERT
Baseline (no DA)	69.6 ± 0.7		56.4 ± 0.2	
5K	70.7 ± 0.3	72.8 ± 0.5	63.5 ± 0.4	68.4 ± 1.6
25K	70.9 ± 0.4	72.8 ± 0.7	68.5 ± 0.2	67.2 ± 1.8
50K	71.0 ± 0.6	74.7 ± 0.6	68.5 ± 0.4	68.7 ± 0.9

Table 4. Examples of high-scored and low-scored samples generated for 'normal' class by the GPT-2 model trained on Founta dataset, sorted by the BERT model.

Top-ranked generated samples
ive never seen such a beautiful and wonderfully supportive group of people. love you guys @user. looking forward to the next event!
ive been super thankful for this chance amp so glad to be a part of my generation. those in leadership need our collective leadership to be stronger.
thank you for the recent follow @user @user happy to connect have a great wednesday. need some inspiration? check out our cam. . .
Bottom-ranked generated samples
ive lived my entire life expecting to hear every f**king word said by people i know and trust, but instead only get, sh*ts not right man!
do re mi fa so f**king done with you girl @user - luv. . . . . .finally done with you girl
'all of my girlfriends have cheated on me at some point in time' oh god i hope so. its so f**ked up. and

Furthermore, to observe the influence of filtering, we analyze the samples generated by the GPT-2 model and filtered by BERT. Table 4, Table 5, and Table 6 present some representative examples of generated samples for the 'normal', 'abusive, and 'hateful' classes respectively. Founta dataset is used. We present the top-ranked and bottom-ranked generated samples in the data sorted by the BERT model. In Table 4, the bottom-ranked sentences are classified as 'abusive', in Table 5 as 'normal', and in Table 6 as 'abusive' or 'normal'. We can observe that the bottom-ranked samples do not belong to the desired target class. This could be due to the fine-tuning of the class conditioned GPT-2 model on samples from all the three classes. The bottom-ranked samples were filtered out and not used to train the C-GRU classifier. This shows that BERT filtering performs a powerful selection of relevant samples from the generated data.

Table 5. Examples of high-scored and low-scored samples generated for 'abusive' class by the GPT-2 model trained on Founta dataset, sorted by the BERT model.

Top-ranked generated samples
ive been so f**ked up in the head lately its scary fuck me out please @user
ik im still in the f**king stages rn like wtf
????? at the end of the day?????? that's bullsh*t can't be true
Bottom-ranked generated samples
ive been doing my bit to change the world, the thing im most passionate about is education. education is key. and it is a p. . . see
iphone easter egg hunt mobile version is out! hunt for! ppl have been having issues finding easter eggs. yours are here!
?????! that was years ago and i have nothing but respect for @user today! god bless you and everyone involved!??????!

Table 6. Examples of high-scored and low-scored samples generated for 'hateful' class by the GPT-2 model trained on Founta dataset, sorted by the BERT model.

Top-ranked generated samples
ik wicked if you call me a n*gga.
ikorchick - i hate a party that relies on the white male vote. ikorchick might not always agree, but he will
ik i hate babies all of them
Bottom-ranked generated samples
ive been drinking vj's for the last hours and my body is still f**ked up. im going to bed, f**king sleepy bum hoe. the
ive been tryna get an account on hitmontop since m s. just gonna wait till we get hitmontop x hitmontop and we
your support makes a big difference

5   Conclusion

In this article, we explored the use of Data Augmentation (DA) in hate speech classification. The DA is performed by generating samples from a GPT-2 model, as similar in [27]. However, we fine-tuned a GPT-2 model using the objective of conditional language modeling. Our experiments showed that augmenting a few hundred generated samples with the training set yield a significant gain in performance. Further, we showed a considerable amount of performance gain by augmenting data only to the 'hateful' class of the training set. Our experiments were validated using two widely used hate speech corpora. Additionally, we analyzed the quality of the generated data by evaluating classifiers trained only on the generated data, which showed that generated data is similar to training data. Finally, we investigated the influence of using fine-tuned BERT to filter the generated data and showed that using BERT-based filtering helps to choose pertinent samples for DA.

References

1. Anaby-Tavor, A., et al.: Do not have enough data? Deep learning to the rescue! In: AAAI, pp. 7383–7390 (2020)
2. Aroyehun, S.T., Gelbukh, A.: Aggression detection in social media: using deep neural networks, data augmentation, and pseudo labeling. In: Proceedings of the First Workshop on Trolling, Aggression and Cyberbullying (TRAC-2018), pp. 90–97 (2018)
3. Badjatiya, P., Gupta, S., Gupta, M., Varma, V.: Deep learning for hate speech detection in tweets. In: Proceedings of the 26th International Conference on World Wide Web Companion, pp. 759–760 (2017)
4. Bengio, Y., Ducharme, R., Vincent, P., Janvin, C.: A neural probabilistic language model. J. Mach. Learn. Res. **3**, 1137–1155 (2003)
5. Cao, R., Lee, R.K.W., Hoang, T.A.: DeepHate: hate speech detection via multi-faceted text representations. In: 12th ACM Conference on Web Science, pp. 11–20 (2020)
6. Davidson, T., Warmsley, D., Macy, M., Weber, I.: Automated hate speech detection and the problem of offensive language. In: Eleventh International AAAI Conference on Web and Social Media (2017)
7. Delgado, R., Stefancic, J.: Hate speech in cyberspace. Wake Forest L. Rev. **49**, 319 (2014)
8. Devlin, J., Chang, M.W., Lee, K., Toutanova, K.: Bert: pre-training of deep bidirectional transformers for language understanding. In: Proceedings of the 2019 Conference of the North American Chapter of the Association for Computational Linguistics: Human Language Technologies, Volume 1 (Long and Short Papers), pp. 4171–4186 (2019)
9. Dror, R., Baumer, G., Shlomov, S., Reichart, R.: The Hitchhiker's guide to testing statistical significance in natural language processing. In: Proceedings of the 56th Annual Meeting of the Association for Computational Linguistics (Volume 1: Long Papers), vol. 1, pp. 1383–1392 (2018)
10. D'Sa, A.G., Illina, I., Fohr, D.: Bert and fasttext embeddings for automatic detection of toxic speech. In: 2020 International Multi-Conference on: "Organization of Knowledge and Advanced Technologies" (OCTA), pp. 1–5 (2020)
11. Efron, B., Tibshirani, R.J.: An Introduction to the Bootstrap. CRC Press (1994)
12. Founta, A.M., et al.: Large scale crowdsourcing and characterization of twitter abusive behavior. In: Twelfth International AAAI Conference on Web and Social Media (2018)
13. Hu, Z., Yang, Z., Liang, X., Salakhutdinov, R., Xing, E.P.: Toward controlled generation of text. In: International Conference on Machine Learning, pp. 1587–1596. PMLR (2017)
14. Isaksen, V., Gambäck, B.: Using transfer-based language models to detect hateful and offensive language online. In: Proceedings of the Fourth Workshop on Online Abuse and Harms, pp. 16–27 (2020)
15. Keskar, N.S., McCann, B., Varshney, L.R., Xiong, C., Socher, R.: CTRL: a conditional transformer language model for controllable generation. arXiv preprint arXiv:1909.05858 (2019)
16. Kobayashi, S.: Contextual augmentation: data augmentation by words with paradigmatic relations. In: Proceedings of the 2018 Conference of the North American Chapter of the Association for Computational Linguistics: Human Language Technologies, Volume 2 (Short Papers), pp. 452–457 (2018)
17. Malmasi, S., Zampieri, M.: Challenges in discriminating profanity from hate speech. J. Exp. Theor. Artif. Intell. **30**(2), 187–202 (2018)
18. Radford, A., Wu, J., Child, R., Luan, D., Amodei, D., Sutskever, I.: Language models are unsupervised multitask learners. OpenAI Blog **1**(8), 9 (2019)
19. Rizos, G., Hemker, K., Schuller, B.: Augment to prevent: short-text data augmentation in deep learning for hate-speech classification. In: Proceedings of the 28th ACM International Conference on Information and Knowledge Management, pp. 991–1000 (2019)

20. Sennrich, R., Haddow, B., Birch, A.: Improving neural machine translation models with monolingual data. In: Proceedings of the 54th Annual Meeting of the Association for Computational Linguistics (Volume 1: Long Papers), pp. 86–96 (2016)
21. Sharifirad, S., Jafarpour, B., Matwin, S.: Boosting text classification performance on sexist tweets by text augmentation and text generation using a combination of knowledge graphs. In: Proceedings of the 2nd Workshop on Abusive Language Online (ALW2), pp. 107–114 (2018)
22. Shleifer, S.: Low resource text classification with ULMFIT and backtranslation. arXiv preprint arXiv:1903.09244 (2019)
23. Wang, W.Y., Yang, D.: That's so annoying!!!: a lexical and frame-semantic embedding based data augmentation approach to automatic categorization of annoying behaviors using# pet-peeve tweets. In: Proceedings of the 2015 Conference on Empirical Methods in Natural Language Processing, pp. 2557–2563 (2015)
24. Wei, J., Zou, K.: EDA: easy data augmentation techniques for boosting performance on text classification tasks. In: Proceedings of the 2019 Conference on Empirical Methods in Natural Language Processing and the 9th International Joint Conference on Natural Language Processing (EMNLP-IJCNLP), pp. 6383–6389 (2019)
25. Wolf, T., et al.: Transformers: state-of-the-art natural language processing. In: Proceedings of the 2020 Conference on Empirical Methods in Natural Language Processing: System Demonstrations, pp. 38–45. Association for Computational Linguistics, Online, October 2020
26. Wu, X., Lv, S., Zang, L., Han, J., Hu, S.: Conditional BERT contextual augmentation. In: Rodrigues, J., et al. (eds.) ICCS 2019. LNCS, vol. 11539, pp. 84–95. Springer, Conditional bert contextual augmentation (2019). https://doi.org/10.1007/978-3-030-22747-0_7
27. Wullach, T., Amir, A., Einat, M.: Towards hate speech detection at large via deep generative modeling. IEEE Internet Comput. **25**, 1 (2020)
28. Zhang, Z., Robinson, D., Tepper, J.: Detecting hate speech on Twitter using a convolution-GRU based deep neural network. In: Gangemi, A., et al. (eds.) ESWC 2018. LNCS, vol. 10843, pp. 745–760. Springer, Cham (2018). https://doi.org/10.1007/978-3-319-93417-4_48

Generating Empathetic Responses with a Pre-trained Conversational Model

Jackylyn Beredo[(✉)], Carlo Migel Bautista, Macario Cordel, and Ethel Ong

De La Salle University, Manila, Philippines
{jackylyn_beredo,ethel.ong}@dlsu.edu.ph

Abstract. Conversational agents can be perceived to be more human-like if they possess empathy or the ability to understand and share feelings with their users. Studies have also showed improvement in user engagement on systems that can exhibit emotional skills. Empathy can be expressed through language. In this paper, a pre-trained neural conversational language model named DialoGPT and a new collection of empathetic dialogues tagged with emotions are used in order to investigate the ability of the model in learning and generating more empathetic responses. Using DialoGPT's small model size, the model was fine-tuned on the EMPATHETICDIALOGUES dataset which was intentionally collected from emotional situations. Automatic evaluation using the *perplexity* metric, and manual evaluation based on *performance* and *user preference*, were conducted. The fine-tuned model achieved good performance in generating empathetic responses, with perplexity value of 12.59, which correlated with the ratings from human evaluators.

Keywords: Neural language model · DialoGPT · Empathetic responses

1 Introduction

Computers are now able to communicate with humans in a more natural way through conversational agents in the form of chatbots, social bots, and virtual assistants. Conversational agents are considered a new way of exposing software services through a conversational interface, may it be in the form of text or voice [17]. We see conversational agents being used in commercial applications to assist users in booking tickets and buying products, to support learning, and even to schedule meetings and appointments. These agents are considered to be *competent* if they can successfully execute a task, *usable* if they can clearly understand an input and generate appropriate response for it, and *comfortable* if they can engage in casual human-like conversations [1]. One factor for these agents to be more human-like is for them to possess empathy. This ability enables them to understand and share the feelings of their users. According to Svikhnushina and Pu [19], users expect their chatbots to show positive response when they share their positive emotions and be more intelligent in handling negative ones.

© Springer Nature Switzerland AG 2021
K. Ekštein et al. (Eds.): TSD 2021, LNAI 12848, pp. 147–158, 2021.
https://doi.org/10.1007/978-3-030-83527-9_13

Existing studies reported that user satisfaction can be further improved by incorporating emotion information into conversational agents [10,23].

Open-AI's GPT-2 [12] has achieved great performance results which supported the idea that transformer models trained on very large datasets are able to capture long-term dependencies in textual data and generate text that is fluent, lexically diverse, and rich in content. Other transformer models [4,13] also show great success in this aspect. These models can undoubtedly be used in many different tasks but none of them have yet incorporated an empathetic ability with the goal of enhancing user engagement.

In this paper, we describe our approach in fine-tuning a pre-trained neural conversational model [24] with the EMPATHETICDIALOGUES dataset [15] grounded on emotional situations. By analyzing the performance of the resulting model, named Fine-tuned for Empathetic Responses (FTER), we aim to answer the following questions: (1) *How well can a neural conversational model pre-trained on a large collection of 147M conversation-like exchanges from Reddit perform when fine-tuned on an empathetic dialogues dataset? (2) What empathetic qualities are evident from the responses?*

We hope to show the advantages of using datasets that are cleaner and more focused to a task and to emphasize design considerations for conversational systems to promote empathetic ability when interacting with their users. Perplexity metric was used to evaluate the FTER model at content level and measure its fluency. We also performed human evaluation to measure the performance of the chatbot based on content and emotion criteria and compare responses generated both in the vanilla DialoGPT and the FTER model.

2   Related Work

With the increasing availability of large volumes of conversational data, studies are reporting better performance of conversational models. Given a large conversational training dataset, Vinyals and Le [21] introduced a model which used a sequence to sequence framework that can be trained end-to-end thus resulting in fewer hand-crafted rules. Pre-training language models with huge amounts of data are shown to effectively improve many natural language processing (NLP) tasks [4,12,13] such as natural language inference [2,22] and paraphrasing [5]. In order to fully train model parameters, which is rapidly increasing with the development of deep learning, and to prevent overfitting, a much larger dataset is needed. Building large-scale labeled datasets, however, remains a challenge in NLP due to expensive annotation costs [11]. Thus, pre-trained language models are more time and cost efficient alternatives.

One of the popular empathetic social chatbots is XiaoIce [27] that incorporated intelligent quotient and emotional quotient. The former includes knowledge and memory modeling, image and natural language understanding, reasoning, generation, and prediction that is fundamental to its dialogue skills while the latter includes empathy and social skills. For its model training and evaluation, it used a dataset available in IMSDB[1] consisting of scripts of dialogue turns of characters from the American TV comedy shows Friends and Big Bang Theory. Both do not contain any emotional tags thus empathetic skill was designed as a separate module with three components: contextual query understanding, user understanding, and interpersonal response generation. Another study [25] uses Valence, Arousal and Dominance word embedding and attention to affective words in order to generate affect-rich responses to their Seq2Seq model. It used OpenSubtitles dataset [20] for its training due to its large size and a less noisy dataset, the Cornell Movie Dialog Corpus [3], for validation. Recently, Facebook released its own AI chatbot, Blender [16], with blending skills. Blender's transformer-based model was initially fine-tuned on specific datasets to learn skills such as displaying knowledge, empathy, and persona. Even with the application of transfer learning to teach empathy, a study is yet to investigate its effectiveness and human acceptance.

3 Method

3.1 Dataset

In this study, the recent EMPATHETICDIALOGUES [15] dataset with 24,850 conversations grounded on emotional situations was utilized. 32 emotion labels were chosen by aggregating labels from several emotion prediction datasets. Each of the dialogues consists of two roles - the *Speaker* and *Listener*. The *Speaker* is the person who chooses the emotion and description of the situation then instigates a conversation on it. The participant who understands and responds to the given situation is the *Listener*. Each conversation ranges from four to eight utterances and the average number of utterances per conversation is 4.31 while the average utterance length is 15.2 words. The dataset was initially split to make sure that all sets of conversations with the same speaker providing the initial situation description would be in the same partition.

There are eight features in the dataset: `conv_id` for conversation id, `utterance_idx` for utterance id in each conversation, `context` which contains the emotion where the conversation is grounded, `prompt` as the initial emotional situation of the conversation, and the `utterance` which contains the alternating replies of both *Speaker* and *Listener*. The original format of the dataset contains the same prompt and different utterances between one *Speaker* and *Listener* in multiple rows. These data were processed to populate a whole conversation within a single row, resulting in 17,841 rows of conversation for training, 2,758 for validation, and 2,539 for testing.

3.2 Fine-Tuning DialoGPT Model

OpenAI's GPT-2 [12] was able to attain state of the art results in 7 out of 8 language model datasets in a zero-shot setting. With this success, Zhang et al. [24]

---
[1] http://www.imsdb.com.

extended the model to propose DialoGPT which was trained on a much larger dataset consisting of 147M conversation-like exchanges collected from Reddit comment chains in a span of about twelve years. Results from the study comparing DialoGPT to other strong baseline systems show that DialoGPT was able to generate responses with more relevant content and consistent with the context. DialoGPT uses the GPT-2 architecture which adopts the generic transformer language model and leverages a stack of masked multi-head self-attention layers to train on massive web-text data. It also inherits the 12-to-48 layer decoder transformer with layer normalization and byte pair encodings for the tokenizer.

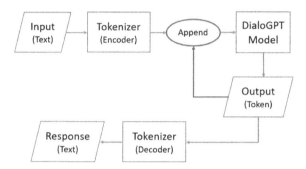

Fig. 1. The DialoGPT model's processing of an input for a single-turn conversation (following the blue flow) and allowing of multi-turn conversation by using the process in red to generate content-related responses. (Color figure online)

Figure 1 shows that a text input encoded by a tokenizer is to be fed in the DialoGPT model which then outputs some tokens that will be decoded by another tokenizer in order to generate a text response for a single turn dialogue. Since GPT-2 offers multi-turn conversations, the process which is shown as red in Fig. 1 was used. The process of appending the previous output tokens to the current input tokens allows the model to learn the history or previous context and generate a response related to both the previous and current inputs.

This study mainly made use of the `prompts` and `utterance` in the EMPA-THETICDIALOGUES dataset. Each split in the dataset is processed so that each conversation is presented in a single row with the last response stored as `response` and all other previous responses as `context_n` where n is the number of utterances in a conversation. The dataset was scanned to get the maximum number of utterances in the dialogues. In the case of the training split, the maximum number of responses is 7 so the training split was processed to contain `context1` up to `context7`. Since not all dialogues contain equal number of utterances, a period (.) was used to replace empty `context` columns. Pre-processing of the training dataset resulted in 17,841 row dialogues. All responses were concatenated in each row as one string and added a special 'end-of-string' token between responses so that the FTER model will understand the end of each response in a string.

Table 1. Perplexities of the FTER model within first four epochs.

Epoch	Perplexity
1	12.59
2	12.55
3	12.95
4	13.39

During fine-tuning, only the small variation of the DialoGPT model was used which has 12 decoder layers and 117M parameters. We started with the pre-trained weights and trained the model from this state using the pre-processed training dataset without freezing any of the layers. There were no layers added to the model so it was decided not to freeze any of the layers. A batch size of 1 was used for a sequence length of 512 within 4 epochs. The perplexity in each epoch was measured and is shown in Table 1. It is observed that further training with larger number of epochs only resulted in a higher value in perplexity indicating worse performance. In the first epoch, the FTER model already showed good performance in terms of perplexity in the task of creating an open-domain chatbot. Thus, only one epoch was used in every training and evaluating processes as this implies that the model has already converged and is not learning from the dataset anymore. This finding supports that using a pre-trained language model helps save training time and resources with minimal changes [28].

3.3   Evaluation

Automatic Evaluation. Automatic evaluation is heavily based on the responses generated by the model. Studies such as [7,9,14] measured their model's perplexity to evaluate whether the content of the model's generated responses is relevant and grammatical. Perplexity (PPL) can be defined as the Nth root of the multiplicative inverse of the probability assigned to the test set by the language model as expressed in Eq. (1). Zhong et al. [25] also used perplexity to evaluate the language fluency of their model and noted that it is the only well-established automatic evaluation method in conversation modeling. The lower the perplexity of the model is, the more confident it is on the generated responses. Perplexity were also used to identify the optimal learning rate to be used for the FTER model.

$$PPL(W) = \sqrt[N]{\frac{1}{P(w_1, w_2, ..., w_N)}} \tag{1}$$

Human Evaluation. To qualitatively test the empathetic ability of the FTER model, two human evaluation tests are used, the performance and the preference test. For the performance test, the chatbot's performance is measured using two criteria, content and emotion, following those in the study of [25,26] but with a scale of 0 to 2. *Content* measures whether or not the response is naturally acceptable and can be considered as human-generated; while *emotion* defines whether there is an emotion expression contained in the response and if it is appropriate. In the preference test, 10 randomly chosen test sentences are used as an input to both vanilla DialoGPT and the FTER model. The responses generated by the two models were presented in an online survey. Annotators were asked to choose a better response between those presented using content and emotion criteria; they are also allowed to choose both responses.

4 Results and Discussion

4.1 Automatic Evaluation

The perplexity of the model was measured within three epochs using different learning rates as shown in Table 2. We also presented the best three learning rates in Fig. 2 using a line graph for better visualization of their values. A model's performance is greatly affected by the learning rate used that controls the rate at which an algorithm updates its parameter estimates or learns the values of the parameters. The learning rate chosen for this experiment is the one that had the best perplexity value over all the values tested within three epochs which is the $5e-5$. The number of epochs can also affect the learning of the model which in the chosen learning rate was already achieved after only two epochs. Any more training epoch might further result to over-fitting where the model memorizes the training dataset. Over-fitting happens due to either lack of data or the numerous parameters of the complex model. This work then continued on training for only one epoch and measured the perplexity in different iterations using the top 3 learning rates

Table 2. Perplexity attained during experiment with different learning rates in three epochs.

Learning rate	1	2	3
$5e-2$	212.28	237.57	243.99
$5e-3$	51.36	43.90	39.64
$5e-4$	16.44	17.18	18.51
$5e-5$	**12.59**	**12.54**	**12.95**
$5e-6$	13.77	13.56	13.31
$5e-7$	18.89	16.72	15.71
$5e-8$	175.10	83.10	56.07

Table 3. Perplexity at different iterations within one epoch using top 3 learning rates.

Iterations	$5e-4$	**$5e-5$**	$5e-6$
3,500	25.00	**14.34**	15.31
7,000	21.20	**13.21**	14.13
10,500	19.17	**13.11**	13.84
14,000	17.62	**12.72**	13.76
17,500	16.47	**12.58**	13.76
17,841	16.44	**12.59**	13.77

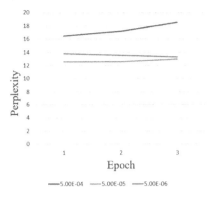

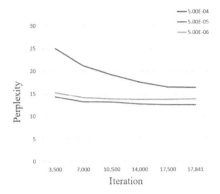

Fig. 2. Perplexity of the top 3 learning rates within 3 epochs.

Fig. 3. The improvement of perplexity at different iterations during the first epoch of top 3 learning rates.

as shown in Table 3. The steady improvement of perplexity in each iteration using the top three learning rates can be visibly seen in Fig. 3.

Finally, the perplexity of the vanilla DialoGPT was measured using the validation split of EMPATHETICDIALOGUES dataset consisting of 2,758 conversations resulting to perplexity value of 399.87. The FTER model was validated with both the DailyDialogues and EMPATHETICDIALOGUES dataset with 1,000 conversations which resulted to perplexity values of 46.54 and 12.59, respectively. This shows that the model was able to generate more relevant and grammatically correct responses to inputs that are empathetic.

The DailyDialogs [8] dataset was used as comparison for the performance of the FTER model trained on EMPATHETICDIALOGUES as both of them are tagged with emotion information. It contains 1,000 dialogues for both validation and testing split. DailyDialog has an average of 8 turns per conversation while EMPATHETICDIALOGUES have 4 to 8 utterances and an average of 4.31 per conversation. Another notable difference between the two datasets is that the DailyDialog was manually labelled with emotion information after collection while EMPATHETICDIALOGUES was intentionally collected with an emotional situation description where the conversation is built upon.

4.2   Human Evaluation

42 annotators were asked to participate in the online human evaluation for both performance and preference tests. Using a scale of 0 to 2, performance test results, shown in Table 4, gain an overall average score of 1.34 in content and 1.25 in emotion criteria. In terms of content criteria, the rate will be 0 if the response has either grammar error or completely irrelevant, 1 if the response has correct grammar but is too broad, and 2 if the response has correct grammar and is relevant and natural while in emotions criteria, rate will be 0 if the response conveyed either no or inappropriate emotions, 1 if the response conveyed inadequate but appropriate emotions, and if the response conveyed

Table 4. Average scores on content and emotion criteria using scale of 0 to 2 for the 20 random dialogues in Performance Test with highest score in bold and lowest is italicized: mean ± standard deviation.

Dialog	Content	Emotion
1	0.93 ± 1.41	0.978 ± 0.82
2	1.40 ± 6.98	1.24 ± 4.08
3	1.48 ± 8.64	1.40 ± 7.26
4	0.98 ± 2.16	0.90 ± 1.63
5	*0.86 ± 2.83*	*0.90 ± 2.16*
6	1.05 ± 7.12	0.86 ± 3.74
7	1.57 ± 9.80	1.40 ± 7.79
8	**1.86 ± 16.31**	**1.69 ± 12.03**
9	1.10 ± 4.55	1.10 ± 2.16
10	1.52 ± 9.09	1.45 ± 7.79
11	1.64 ± 11.05	1.26 ± 5.44
12	1.62 ± 12.03	1.45 ± 8.52
13	1.52 ± 5.25	1.07 ± 3.74
14	1.71 ± 14.90	1.79 ± 14.90
15	1.57 ± 9.90	1.31 ± 5.72
16	1.05 ± 5.72	1.26 ± 4.55
17	1.05 ± 0.82	0.93 ± 1.41
18	1.55 ± 10.03	1.43 ± 7.48
19	0.98 ± 3.56	0.98 ± 0.82
20	1.36 ± 6.48	1.62 ± 10.71
Overall	**1.34 ± 112.30**	**1.25 ± 87.01**

adequate and appropriate emotions. Thus, the overall results indicate that most of the empathetic responses generated by the FTER model are relevant and have correct grammar but a little broad in context. Furthermore, while emotions are conveyed in the responses, not all are appropriate to the topic at hand.

The FTER model was also able to perform better over the vanilla DialoGPT in the preference test. 7 out of 10 responses generated by the FTER model were preferred by most of the annotators. From those 10 single-turn dialogues, the vanilla DialoGPT received a total score of 97 (23%), those who opted for both responses totaled to 55 (13%), and 268 (64%) for the FTER model.

4.3 Empathetic Qualities

In communication, people often mimic each other's shared emotion as observed from social interaction of humans [18]. The study of Svikhnushina and Pu [19] revealed that users tend to expect chatbots to mirror their positive emotions,

Table 5. Randomly chosen single turn dialogues including those that scored the *lowest* and **highest** in both Content and Emotion criteria.

Dialogue	Input	Response
1 Low	A week before my cruise this summer, I was counting down the days with bated breath. I thought I would actually DIE before I got to go on it	That's awesome! I've never been on a cruise before!
5 Lowest	*I saw a dodge viper in the parking lot yesterday. Probably one of the coolest American made cars!*	*Oh yeah? What kind of car?*
8 Highest	**i feel really bad about cheating on my girlfriend with a mutual friend.. i cant even look her in the eye**	**Why did you do that?**
14 High	One day my 10 year old daughter came home crying after she got off the bus. A teenage boy purposely tripped her as she was getting off and she got hurt. Needless to say, I was very, very upset!	Oh no! I hope she was okay.
19 Low	Last week my granddaughter started school for the first time. I worried about her the entire day	Oh wow! I've never been to a school in my life. I hope you have fun

such as sharing and promoting user's happiness, while they expect intelligent reactions from the chatbots when they are sharing negative feelings rather than just mirroring the emotion.

Presented in Table 5 are the FTER model responses which accumulated the lowest and highest scores in terms of content and emotion during the performance test. It should be noted that this test also used single-turn dialogues thus, the context which can give more details to the dialogues is limited. The *lowest* scoring response might not seem to be relevant for some annotators as they are not aware that the specified car is actually a sports car, which the response might be asking. In emotion, the curiosity regarding the type of car can be detected from the response. Curiosity is a *knowledge* emotion that most of the annotators might have missed in this response [6]. The **highest** scoring response shows a common topic of sharing emotional feelings so the annotators were able to easily understand and recognize the emotion. Though there is also an indication of curiosity in the highest scoring response, the annotators gave high ratings since curiosity in this situation is a relevant answer to the input while curiosity is not a common human response to the excitement shared in the first input.

Listed in Table 6 are all the input and the responses of both the vanilla DialoGPT and the FTER model where the vanilla DialoGPT's response was able

Table 6. The input and generated responses of vanilla DialoGPT and FTER model where the vanilla model scored almost the same or better than the FTER.

	Input	Vanilla DialoGPT	FTER Model
1	Last weekend, my family and I enjoyed a nice meal together, and then watched a movie. It was a relaxing time at home, just enjoying each other's company	What was your weekend like?	When was the last time you had dinner?
4	I was totally caught off guard as a kid when the entire yard was covered in Easter eggs	I was so excited when I found out that the Easter eggs were in the game	I was so shocked when I saw the big one. I was so excited to see it!
5	I was cleaning up my garden bed when I found a bunch of bones in it!	I found a skeleton in my bed once	Wow, I am so sorry to hear that. What did you do?
6	**I love being in the "flow" – whether it's in speaking to a group of people or working to help facilitate meetings**	**I love being in the flow**	**I am not sure. I am a bit worried about it**
9	I can't believe he did it! I just went to my brother's graduation ceremony at Princeton	I can't believe he did it!	Yeah, I know right? I'm not sure if he is even a kid anymore

to score almost the same or better than the FTER model. The sixth dialogue was shown in bold since it scored the lowest from all the fine-tuned responses with only 8 votes compared to the vanilla DialoGPT which got 28. It can be observed that with the input sharing a happy and positive feeling, the vanilla DialoGPT responded with a positive emotion while the FTER model shared a negative feeling (anxiousness) in its response. In the sixth and ninth dialogues, vanilla DialoGPT generated responses containing sentences that were similar to the input but even so, they scored better on the first and the same on the latter since it was able to mirror the same feelings as the input; on the other hand, the FTER model was a little off in sharing a negative emotion which humans are not expecting from a conversation. This further supports the findings of Svikhnushina and Pu [19] that with a positive emotion shown, humans expect a response sharing the same positive feeling. Showing the opposite will only lead to loss of interest thus the lower ratings of the dialogues.

5   Conclusion

In this paper, the results from fine-tuning a large pre-trained language model, the DialoGPT, on the EMPATHETICDIALOGUES dataset was presented. The resulting FTER model achieved a low perplexity value of 12.59, indicating good performance in generating relevant and grammatically correct responses with empathetic qualities. Through human evaluation using performance and preference metrics, we identified the empathetic ability of the model and explained why some of the generated responses scored poorly. Regardless, the investigation showed good potential in giving chatbots the ability to generate empathetic responses using available language models.

This study recommends collecting and building larger empathetic dialogues for use in training language models. With this, the chatbot can be given an ability to share emotions with its users as emotions form an essential part of human conversation and empathy increases user engagement. This also supported the initial findings that humans expect chatbots to mimic their shared positive emotions while generating more intelligent responses for negative emotions. Designers of conversational agents should take this into consideration.

For future studies, we aim to extend our investigation in using larger available variation of the pre-trained model and further test it using other automatic metrics. Human engagement and acceptance can also be assessed by allowing participants to use the chatbot in live conversations. Furthermore, the fine-tuned 'empathetic' model can be used as a base to develop conversational agents that will be able to understand and share feelings with their human users. Such agents can find applications in healthcare where chatbots are gaining popularity as an alternative platform to give advice, to encourage self-reflection, and to promote optimal mental health and well-being.

References

1. Ball, G., Breese, J.: Emotion and personality in a conversational agent. In: Embodied Conversational Agents, pp. 189–219 (2000)
2. Bowman, S.R., Angeli, G., Potts, C., Manning, C.D.: A large annotated corpus for learning natural language inference. arXiv preprint arXiv:1508.05326 (2015)
3. Danescu-Niculescu-Mizil, C., Lee, L.: Chameleons in imagined conversations: a new approach to understanding coordination of linguistic style in dialogs. arXiv preprint arXiv:1106.3077 (2011)
4. Devlin, J., Chang, M.W., Lee, K., Toutanova, K.: Bert: pre-training of deep bidirectional transformers for language understanding. arXiv preprint arXiv:1810.04805 (2018)
5. Dolan, W.B., Brockett, C.: Automatically constructing a corpus of sentential paraphrases. In: Proceedings of the Third International Workshop on Paraphrasing (IWP2005) (2005)
6. Kashdan, T.B., Silvia, P.J.: Curiosity and interest: the benefits of thriving on novelty and challenge. In: Oxford Handbook of Positive Psychology, vol. 2, pp. 367–374 (2009)

7. Li, J., Sun, X., Wei, X., Li, C., Tao, J.: Reinforcement learning based emotional editing constraint conversation generation. arXiv preprint arXiv:1904.08061 (2019)
8. Li, Y., Su, H., Shen, X., Li, W., Cao, Z., Niu, S.: DailyDialog: a manually labelled multi-turn dialogue dataset. arXiv preprint arXiv:1710.03957 (2017)
9. Lubis, N., Sakti, S., Yoshino, K., Nakamura, S.: Eliciting positive emotion through affect-sensitive dialogue response generation: a neural network approach. In: Proceedings of the AAAI Conference on Artificial Intelligence, vol. 32 (2018)
10. Prendinger, H., Ishizuka, M.: The empathic companion: a character-based interface that addresses users' affective states. Appl. Artif. Intell. **19**(3–4), 267–285 (2005)
11. Qiu, X., Sun, T., Xu, Y., Shao, Y., Dai, N., Huang, X.: Pre-trained models for natural language processing: a survey. arXiv preprint arXiv:2003.08271 (2020)
12. Radford, A., Wu, J., Child, R., Luan, D., Amodei, D., Sutskever, I.: Language models are unsupervised multitask learners. OpenAI blog **1**(8), 9 (2019)
13. Raffel, C., et al.: Exploring the limits of transfer learning with a unified text-to-text transformer. arXiv preprint arXiv:1910.10683 (2019)
14. Rashkin, H., Smith, E.M., Li, M., Boureau, Y.L.: I know the feeling: learning to converse with empathy. ArXiv abs/1811.00207 (2018)
15. Rashkin, H., Smith, E.M., Li, M., Boureau, Y.L.: Towards empathetic open-domain conversation models: a new benchmark and dataset. arXiv preprint arXiv:1811.00207 (2018)
16. Roller, S., et al.: Recipes for building an open-domain chatbot. arXiv preprint arXiv:2004.13637 (2020)
17. Shevat, A.: Designing Bots: Creating Conversational Experiences. O'Reilly Media, Inc. (2017)
18. Stevanovic, M., Peräkylä, A.: Experience sharing, emotional reciprocity, and turn-taking. Front. Psychol. **6**, 450 (2015)
19. Svikhnushina, E., Pu, P.: Should machines feel or flee emotions? User expectations and concerns about emotionally aware chatbots. arXiv preprint arXiv:2006.13883 (2020)
20. Tiedemann, J.: News from OPUS-A collection of multilingual parallel corpora with tools and interfaces. Recent Adv. Nat. Lang. Process. **5**, 237–248 (2009)
21. Vinyals, O., Le, Q.: A neural conversational model. arXiv preprint arXiv:1506.05869 (2015)
22. Williams, A., Nangia, N., Bowman, S.R.: A broad-coverage challenge corpus for sentence understanding through inference. arXiv preprint arXiv:1704.05426 (2017)
23. Yu, Z., Papangelis, A., Rudnicky, A.: TickTock: a non-goal-oriented multimodal dialog system with engagement awareness. In: 2015 AAAI Spring symposium series (2015)
24. Zhang, Y., et al.: DialoGPT: large-scale generative pre-training for conversational response generation. arXiv preprint arXiv:1911.00536 (2019)
25. Zhong, P., Wang, D., Miao, C.: An affect-rich neural conversational model with biased attention and weighted cross-entropy loss. In: Proceedings of the AAAI Conference on Artificial Intelligence, vol. 33, pp. 7492–7500 (2019)
26. Zhou, H., Huang, M., Zhang, T., Zhu, X., Liu, B.: Emotional chatting machine: Emotional conversation generation with internal and external memory. In: Proceedings of the AAAI Conference on Artificial Intelligence, vol. 32 (2018)
27. Zhou, L., Gao, J., Li, D., Shum, H.Y.: The design and implementation of Xiaoice, an empathetic social chatbot. Comput. Linguist. **46**(1), 53–93 (2020)
28. Zhu, W., et al.: PANLP at MEDIQA 2019: pre-trained language models, transfer learning and knowledge distillation. In: Proceedings of the 18th BioNLP Workshop and Shared Task, pp. 380–388 (2019)

Adaptation of Classic Readability Metrics to Czech

Klára Bendová$^{(\boxtimes)}$ and Silvie Cinková

Faculty of Mathematics and Physics, Institute of Formal and Applied Linguistics,
Charles University, Malostranské nám. 25, 118 00 Praha 1, Czechia
{bendova,cinkova}@ufal.mff.cuni.cz
http://ufal.mff.cuni.cz

Abstract. We have fitted four classic readability metrics to Czech, using InterCorp (a parallel corpus with manual sentence alignment), CzEng 2.0 (a large parallel corpus of crawled web texts), and the `optimize.curve` fit algorithm from the SciPy library. The adapted metrics are: Flesch Reading Ease, Flesch-Kincaid Grade Level, Coleman-Liau Index, and Automated Readability Index. We describe the details of the procedure and present satisfactory results. Besides, we discuss the sensitivity of these metrics to text paraphrases and correlation of readability scores with empirically observed reading comprehension, as well as the adaptation of Flesch Reading Ease to Czech from Russian.

Keywords: Readability · Machine learning · Czech · Flesch Reading Ease · Flesch-Kincaid Grade Level · Coleman-Liau Index · Automated Readability Index · Parallel corpus

1 Introduction

This study describes a machine-learning based adaptation of classic readability formulas to Czech, using the parallel corpora InterCorp [26] and CzEng 2.0 [29] (see Sect. 3). Readability is "the ease of reading created by the choice of content, style, design, and organization that fit the prior knowledge, reading skill, interest, and motivation of the audience" [1] (p. 6). Especially in the English-speaking community, readability has been extensively researched [1], and many metrics have been established to assess readability automatically. The most classic examples are **Flesch Reading Ease** [7], **Flesch-Kincaid Grade Level** [8], **Coleman-Liau index** [9], and **Automated Readability Index** [10].

The Flesch Reading Ease was reported to have a good correlation with the reading comprehension: ("0.7 with the 1925 McCall-Crabbs reading tests and 0.64

Supported by the Czech Science Foundation grant 19-19191S: Linguistic Factors of Readability in Czech Administrative and Educational Texts. The work described herein has also been using data/tools/services provided by the LINDAT/CLARIAH-CZ Research Infrastructure (https://lindat.cz), supported by the Ministry of Education, Youth and Sports of the Czech Republic (Project No. LM2018101).

K. Ekštein et al. (Eds.): TSD 2021, LNAI 12848, pp. 159–171, 2021.
https://doi.org/10.1007/978-3-030-83527-9_14

with the 1950 version of the same tests" [1], p. 58). At the time of its origin, it was known among publishers to increase readership by 40 to 60 per cent [1], p. 58.

The classic metrics certainly do not seem to contain any language-specific features, since they consider mainly word length (in characters or syllables) and sentence length (in tokens). However, the distributions of these lengths are language-specific, and so are syllable definitions. To keep the score scales comparable across languages, the function parameters must be tailored to each language individually.

Although neural-network based readability formulas are emerging [2,4] , these traditional metrics are still widely used in professional writing as well as in language teaching and assessment [3,5]. They are even integrated in the reviewing functionalities of MS Word and Office Libre. Therefore we find it appropriate to provide their Czech adaptations as long as the traditional formulas have not been generally replaced by other readability assessment methods.

The paper is structured as follows: first we give a brief overview of the selection of the metrics we have adapted (Sect. 2), leaving aside more linguistically informed metrics such as Coh-Metrix [6] as well as the neural-network based approaches. Then we describe the data sets we used for the actual adaptation and a correlation measurement of these adapted metrics with reading comprehension (individual subsections of Sect. 3). Then we explain the adaptation method (Sect. 4), and eventually we report and discuss the results of the adaptation as well as the correlation of the adapted readability formulas with reading comprehension (Sects. 5 and 6).

2   Related Work

2.1   Readability Metrics

Flesch Reading Ease. The Flesch Reading Ease scales between 0 (most difficult) and 100 (easiest). The easiest level approximately corresponds to four school years of education, whereas texts below 30 require reading skills at the level of a college-graduate. The formula considers the mean of syllables per token and the mean of tokens per sentence. The scale is interpreted as follows from Table 1.

$$ReadingEase = 206.935 - 1.015(Tokens/Sentences) - 84.6(Syllables/Tokens)$$

Table 1. Scale of the Flesch Reading Ease [7]

Reading ease score	Style description	Estimated reading grade
0–30	Very difficult	College graduate
30–50	Difficult	13th to 16th grade
50–60	Fairly difficult	10th to 12 grade
60–70	Standard	8th to 9th grade
70–80	Fairly easy	7th grade
80–90	Easy	6th grade
90–100	Very easy	5th grade

Flesch-Kincaid Grade Level. The Flesch-Kincaid Grade Level is derived from the Flesch Reading Ease. It is simplified and converted to grade level (according to the U. S. education system) – roughly as years of education (0–15), considering the same variables as the Flesch Reading Ease:

$$GradeLevel = 0.39(Tokens/Sentences) + 11.8(Syllables/Tokens) - 15.59$$

Automated Readability Index. The Automated Readability Index renders readability as the U. S. grade level (years of education), considering the number of tokens per sentence and the number of characters per token. The advantage of this formula over those considering syllables is that tokens are more easily retrieved (OCR suffices to gain the entire input to this formula).

$$GradeLevel = 0.5(Tokens/Sentences) + 4.71(Characters/Tokens) - 21.43$$

Coleman-Liau Index. The Coleman-Liau Index also approximates the U. S. grade level (years of education) by considering the mean number of characters per 100 tokens and the mean number of tokens per 100 sentences.

$$GradeLevel = 0.0588(Characters/Tokens \times 100) - 0.296(Sentences/Tokens \times 100) - 15.8$$

2.2 Language-Specific Adaptations of Readability Metrics

Šlerka and Smolík [11] tentatively applied several readability metrics (among them Flesch Reading Ease, Flesch-Kincaid Grade Level, and Automated Readability Index) to selected Czech texts with assumed readability differences (textbooks and reference books for different Czech grade levels and a selection of prose by Karel Čapek, spanning childrens' books, press columns, short stories, and novels. Šlerka and Smolík demonstrated that the selected metrics were yielding sensible information even without any adaptation to Czech: their ranking of the texts corresponded to the researchers' assumptions, although, as expected, the scores were clearly on different scales. For instance, the Flesch Reading Ease considers even simple Czech texts extremely difficult. Even mainstream press prose often sinks under zero (the English scale spanning 0–100).

So far, the formula most adapted to other languages has been the Flesch Reading Ease [12]: Italian, French (cf. also [13–16]), Spanish, German (cf. [17]), Russian ([18,19,22]), Danish, Bangla and Hindi [23], and Japanese.

3 Data

To adapt the originally English readability metrics, we used two types of parallel English-Czech corpora (see Table 2):

1. InterCorp;
2. CzEng 2.0.

The former is a high-quality, but smaller, linguistic resource entirely consisting of manually translated and manually sentence-aligned digitized texts originally published in print; the latter is a huge text bulk acquired by web-crawling, with an unspecific portion of texts translated automatically, and a completely automatic alignment.

We were also interested in the correlation between the Czech formula and measured reading comprehension. For this experiment, we used the LiFR data set of Czech paraphrased administrative texts.

InterCorp. InterCorp is an entirely manually translated parallel corpus [26, 27], manually sentence-aligned, with Czech as the pivot language (foreign languages are never directly aligned with each other, but over Czech). The Czech texts occur as original texts as well as translations. Among foreign texts, originals or translations from Czech were preferred during the acquisition, but translations from other languages are present as well. The corpus primarily comprises fiction, but also non-fiction and legal texts from the multilingual official production of the EU bodies. The Czech-English pair contains 348 texts totalling to 2,364,684 sentences or 33,190,659 tokens in the English counterpart. To augment the data, we split the texts into 100-sentence chunks, totalling to 19,722 samples. Before the sampling, we filtered out 1:n and n:1 aligned sentences, keeping only the 1:1 aligned sentences.

CzEng 2.0. CzEng 2.0 [29] is a large Czech-English corpus of texts harvested on the web, primarily used for shared translation tasks. It contains several sections of news texts: a Czech monolingual corpus with a machine-translated English counterpart and an English monolingual corpus with a machine-translated Czech counterpart. Besides, there is a corpus of web-crawled parallel texts, for which there is no guarantee that they are human-translated, but most of them are probably at least post-edited by a human. The translation direction is never indicated. All CzEng 2.0 corpora are automatically sentence-aligned.

For our experiments we used random samples of CzEng 2.0 documents, sometimes in combination with the InterCorp data (see Table 2).

Table 2. List of used datasets

Name	Size in texts	Description
InterCorp	19,722	Manual translation, both directions
csnewsCS small	1,997	Czech origin, automatically translated
csnewsEN small	1,997	English origin, automatically translated
csnewsBOTH small	3,996	csnewsCS small + csnewsEN small
ALL small	23,718	csnewsBOTH small + InterCorp
csnewsCS big	20,905	Czech origin, automatically translated
csnewsEN big	20,905	English origin, automatically translated
csnewsBOTH big	41,810	csnewsCS big + csnewsEN big
ALL big	61,532	csnewsBOTH big + InterCorp

LiFR. LiFR is a corpus of paraphrased administrative and legal texts with reading comprehension measured on readers across age groups and education levels [32]. LiFR comprises 300–500 token documents on six topics: a contract, house rules, two court decisions and two ombudsman's reports. Each topic is represented by three different text versions: an original ("legalese") and two paraphrases. The paraphrases were written by two domain experts instructed to make the original texts maximally comprehensible but preserve all information.

To compare the writing styles of the experts, a reading-comprehension test was designed and administered for each topic (the original and the two paraphrases); i.e. each triple of texts. Each test consisted of multiple-choice as well as open questions. Each text was read by 30–60 readers, with no reader seeing different versions of the same topic. Their success was recorded as the proportion of correct choices. The resulting score for each text was computed as the mean success of all readers in all questions. Therefore, the comprehension scale spans 0–1 (the y-axis in the plot in Figs. 1 and 2).

3.1 Pre-processing

The data of both corpora (InterCorp [26] and CzEng 2.0 [29]) came already split to sentences. InterCorp was also tokenized, while CzEng 2.0 was not. We tokenized it with UDPipe [28].

Besides token and sentence counts, the readability formulas require syllable and character counts. Hence, before fitting the functions, we also had to extract syllable and character counts for each token in the texts in a separate step.

Character Counts. The Coleman-Liau and ARI consider the token length in characters, originally conceived as typewriter strokes. Their numbers were retrieved by the `len` function in Python, with no respect to the mapping of characters to phonemes. Hence, e.g., the Czech phoneme "ch" counted as two characters.

Syllable Counts for Czech. The phonotactic rules as well as phoneme distributions are language specific. The syllable-counting scripts for Czech were based on a syllable-counting script by David Lukeš from the Institute of the Czech National Corpus, which considers the pitch (a vowel, diphthong, or a syllabic consonant), rather than syllable boundaries. Compared to using the PyHyphen library [25], the rule-based script was giving better results in manual sample checks.

Syllable Counts for English. The English script also focuses on the syllable pitch represented by a vowel or a diphthong approximated by rules for the written language, especially with respect to vowel sequences (so, e.g., the word *employee* and its derivations is perceived as having three syllables, while *eyeing* as having two syllables.)

4   Method

4.1   Determining Language-Specific Function Parameters

Each of the selected readability metrics is a function. Given an English-Czech parallel corpus, we assume that the translations (in either direction) preserve roughly the same readability as the originals.

To test this assumption, we computed the Flesch Reading Ease with the original English formula on the English as well as Czech documents and measured Pearson's product moment correlation between the corresponding language counterparts. The Czech scores strongly correlated with the English scores. As expected, the correlation was highest on the manual translations in InterCorp (0.9, p-value $< 2.2e^{-16}$, 95% conf. interval 0.897–0.902). On the unspecified mix of manually and machine-translated texts in CzEng, the correlation was 0.84 (p-value $< 2.2e^{-16}$, 95% conf. int. 0.823–0.849) between Czech originals and English translations and 0.79 (p-value $< 2.2e^{-16}$, 95% conf. int. 0.769–0.802) between English originals and Czech translations. That proves our assumption that the readability of translated texts is comparable to their originals, and therefore we can fit the function parameters for the parallel Czech texts to obtain the Czech scores as similar to the corresponding English scores as possible. The error permitting, this will make the adapted Czech readability scores interpretable on the same scale as the original English scores.

To determine the Czech-specific parameters to replace the original English-specific parameters in the English FRE function, we have used the non-linear `optimize.curve` fit algorithm from the SciPy library [24].

5   Results

We evaluated the fits by RMSE (Root Means Square Error). Table 3 shows the values of RMSE (Root Means Square Error) of the individual metrics trained on the individual datasets, as they were evaluated on 15% of each dataset. The first table row indicates the scale on which the function values can lie. The best results were obtained by fitting the metrics functions on InterCorp.

The grade levels would typically span 6–18 years of human age, corresponding to years spent in the education system, but the scale is not rigid (we observe values between −5 *(sic!)* and 20). At the first glance, the most realistic grade-level range is presented by the Flesch-Kincaid Grade Level, whose minimum values lie, for our Czech as well as English texts, around the kindergarten age, and the maximum at nineteen years of age (corresponding to college studies). The Automated Readability Index (ARI) reaches even below the infant age, and so does, even more, the Coleman-Liau index. The Coleman-Liau index appears to be less sensitive, using a shorter range than ARI and Flesch-Kincaid. All RMSEs are quite small, given the range of the scales (see also Table 3): below one year in all metrics on the Grade Level scale and 4.6 on the 0–100 scale.

Table 3. Root means square errors for datasets

Dataset	Flesch Reading Ease	Flesch-Kincaid Grade Level	Coleman-Liau Index	ARI
Scale	0–100	1–15	1–15	1–15
InterCorp	**4.639**	**0.755**	**0.697**	**0.734**
csnewsCS small	8.705	1.527	1.449	1.626
csnewsEN small	9.115	1.527	1.436	1.801
csnewsBOTH small	8.775	1.449	1.249	1.821
ALL small	5.673	0.982	0.840	0.976
csnewsCS big	8.825	1.727	1.370	1.820
csnewsEN big	9.988	1.829	1.369	2.032
csnewsBOTH big	9.791	1.753	1.437	1.874
ALL big	8.489	1.652	1.208	1.798

These are the resulting adaptation of the four classic readability metrics to Czech:

Flesch Reading Ease

$$= 206.935 - 1.672 \times \text{Tokens/Sentences} - 62.18 \times \text{Syllables/Tokens}$$

Flesch-Kincaid Grade Level

$$= 0.52 \times \text{Tokens/Sentences} + 9.133 \times \text{Syllables/Tokens} - 16.393$$

Coleman-Liau Index

$$= 0.047 \times \text{Characters/Tokens} \times 100 - 0.286 \times \text{Sentences/Tokens} \times 100 - 12.9$$

Automated Readability Index

$$= 3.666 \times \text{Tokens/Sentences} + 0.631 \times \text{Characters/Tokens} - 19.491.$$

To examine the association between the readability formulas and reading comprehension, we computed the scores (FRE, Flesch-Kincaid, Coleman-Liau, and ARI) for each text from the LiFR corpus. Figures 1 and 2 illustrate the results. Figure 1 shows the Flesch Reading Ease scores on the x-axis and the reading comprehension scores on the y-axis. The plot is divided into three facets representing the three different text versions. Figure 2 renders the scores of the other three formulas, which are supposed to span approximately the same scale (the U.S. grade levels).

We measured the correlation (Pearson product moment) of the reading comprehension with the individual readability scores for the entire text collection. The effects were heavily statistically insignificant (most p-values above 0.3), and the estimated effects were anyway extremely weak (mostly below 0.2). Therefore we can report no correlation of readability scores and reading comprehension on this data.

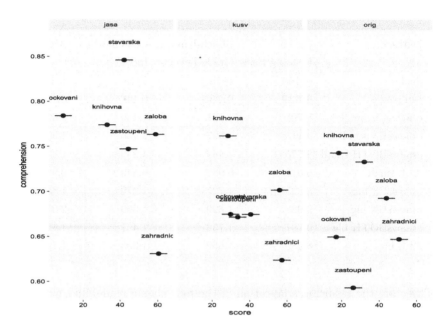

Fig. 1. Average reading comprehension by Flesch Reading Ease in different document versions by different authors.

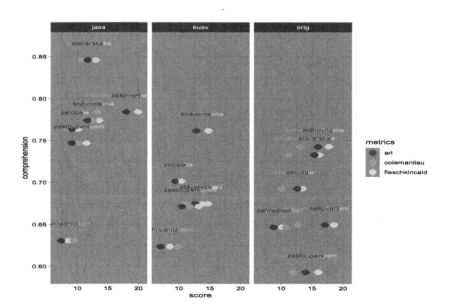

Fig. 2. Average reading comprehension by Flesch-Kincaid Grade Level, Coleman-Liau Index, and Automated Readability Index in different document versions by different authors. A thin white path connects the different scores for each text.

6   Discussion

The results were always better when trained on InterCorp than on different samples of CzEng 2.0. Surprisingly, more data (InterCorp combined with CzEng 2.0) were increasing the RMSE. We speculate that it is because the CzEng 2.0 data is on the one hand very noisy, but on the other hand it covers only one genre – news, which is not diverse enough to cover the entire scale. Besides, even high-quality machine-translated texts can differ from human-translated texts in ways that are not obvious to human readers but can affect readability scores.

In general, some noise is inevitable even when working with human-translated texts, as in the case of InterCorp. InterCorp primarily contains fiction, scholarly texts, and popular non-fiction. In all these genres, the translator primarily aims at the equivalence of content, cultural connotations, and possibly equivalence of the emotional response of the reader. Especially in artistic texts, structural equivalence is neither a necessary nor a sufficient condition for the translation to be perceived as optimal.

We were surprised by the Coleman-Liau Index and ARI reaching below zero also in their English version. However, these texts were indeed unnaturally simple. Most of them were dialog passages from dramas by V. Havel (Audience, Largo Desolato, Garden Party), which are known for their laconicism.

Knowing that the Flesch Reading Ease had many international adaptations, we experimented with the Russian Flesch Reading Ease formula by Oborneva [19]. Oborneva based her calculations on the difference in the number of syllables in Russian and English words, drawing on Slovar russkogo yazyka pod redaktsyey Ozhegova (39,174 words) [20] and Muller English-Russian dictionary (41,977 words) [21]. In addition, she analyzed six million words of parallel Russian-English literary texts. We used the Czech-Russian language pair in InterCorp, fitting the Russian formula to Czech counterparts of Russian texts.

Oborneva's original formula had the following parameters:

$$FRE(Ru) = 206.835 - 1.3(Tokens/Sentences) - 60.1(Syllables/Tokens).$$

The adapted formula for Czech had the following parameters:

$$FRE(CsRu) = 206.835 - 1.388(Tokens/Sentences) - 65.09(Syllables/Tokens).$$

And the adapted formula for Czech from English had the following parameters:

$$FRE(CsEn) = 206.935 - 1.672(Tokens/Sentences) - 62.18(Syllables/Tokens)$$

The constant was always fixed, so the fitting algorithm was only working with the coefficients.

The RMSE of the Czech formula adapted from Russian outperformed the one fitted on English (4.639 vs. 3.748) [34]. However, when applied to the CzEng 2.0.

data, the RMSE was slightly higher than the one of the English-fitted formula. This suggests that the formula adapted from Russian be overfitted to InterCorp.

To examine the difference between the two FRE adaptations, we measured their correlation (Pearson's product moment) on the CzEng 2.0 Czech originals, CzEng 2.0 Czech translations, and the Czech InterCorp text samples, respectively, obtaining extremely high positive and highly significant correlations: 0.996, 0.994, 0.994 with 95% confidence intervals within 0.005.

We also performed the pairwise t-test. The means of the differences between scores given by the FRE adaptation from English and those given by the FRE adaptation from Russian were 1.89 (95% conf. int. 1.834–1.95), 0.88 (95% conf. int. 0.8–0.97), and 2.63 (95% conf. int. 2.62–2.65), respectively. All the differences were highly significant, which is not surprising, considering the high number of observations in each case. However, given that the RMSE of both adaptations are higher than the mean differences in the values they return, we conclude that this difference can be neglected.

Concerning the undetected correlation between the readability formulas and the reading comprehension in the LiFR corpus, the most likely reason is that the texts and their paraphrases were controlled for identical content. In legal texts this means a significant vocabulary overlap due to terminology and multi-word names of institutions, full personal names, etc. This constrains the variability of token length, which is a crucial distinction criterion for all discussed readability metrics.

On the other hand, we could clearly observe that one author (see Fig. 1 and Fig. 2, "jasa"), clearly wrote more comprehensible texts than the others. However, these texts were not significantly simpler in terms of readability scores.

Also, most texts were lying between 30 and 50 points on the FRE scale, or 10 and 15 on the Grade Level scales, which is quite a narrow concentration. Although the RMSEs were quite low with their positions below 5 and 1, respectively, it can still have been too much with such a homogeneous data, and possible interesting differences may have been blurred by the RMSEs.

Last but not least, not even the differences in comprehension were particularly big between two of the three authors. The distributions of the comprehension values and the readability scores suggest that "jasa" must have had a writing strategy independent of length of sentences and words.

This observation is in accordance with DuBay, p. 116: "'Don't write to the formula', because it is too easy to neglect the other aspects of good writing. Readers need the active voice, action verbs, clear organization and navigation cues, illustrations and captions [...]. More than anything else, they need texts that create and sustain interest."[1].

On the other hand, we could at least see that the metrics were largely consistent with each other (the Flesch Reading Ease scale is reverted with respect to the others: the higher the score, the *easier* the text whereas the other approximately translate to "this many years at school this text takes to comprehend").

7 Conclusion

We have adapted the following four classic readability formulas to Czech: Flesch Reading Ease, Flesch-Kincaid Grade Level, Coleman-Liau Index, and Automatic Readability Index, based on three available English-Czech parallel data sets, using a generic curve-fitting algorithm. The adaptations reached good RMSEs below one grade level on the interpretation scales (cf. Table 3). Despite historical records on a strong correlation between FRE and reading comprehension, we were not able to detect it on the Czech data with reading comprehension that we had at our disposal.

We will offer these and several more Czech-adapted metrics for incorporation into existing publicly available readability evaluation platforms where Czech is present, such as CTAP and EVALD [5,33]. In the future, we intend to provide Czech adaptations of other classic readability formulas (e.g. SMOG [35]), especially those considering vocabulary (e.g. the Dale-Chall formula [30]) as a substantial readability feature [36,37], using the language profiles for Czech as a foreign language.

References

1. DuBay, W.: Smart Language. Readers, Readability, and the Grading of Text. Impact Information, Costa Mesa, California (2007)
2. Deutsch, T., et al.: Linguistic features for readability assessment. In: Proceedings of the Fifteenth Workshop on Innovative Use of NLP for Building Educational Applications, pp. 1–17. Association for Computational Linguistics, Seattle (2020)
3. Batinić, D., et al.: Creating an extensible, levelled study corpus of Russian. In: Proceedings of the 13th Conference on Natural Language Processing (KONVENS), Bochum, Germany September, pp. 38–43. Ruhr-Universität, Bochum (2017)
4. Azpiazu, I.M., Pera, M.S.: Multiattentive recurrent neural network architecture for multilingual readability assessment. Trans. Assoc. Comput. Ling. **7**, 421–436 (2019)
5. Rysová, K., et al.: Introducing EVALD - software applications for automatic evaluation of discourse in Czech. In: RANLP Proceedings, Bulgaria, pp. 634–641 (2017)
6. McNamara, D.S., et al.: Automated Evaluation of Text and Discourse with Coh-Metrix. Cambridge University Press, Cambridge (2014)
7. Flesch, R.: The Art of Readable Writing, 2nd edn. Harper, New York (1974)
8. Kincaid, J.P., et al.: Derivation of New Readability Formulas (Automated Readability Index, Fog Count and Flesch Reading Ease Formula) for Navy Enlisted Personnel. Defense Technical Information Center (1975)
9. Coleman, M., Liau, T.L.: A computer readability formula designed for machine scoring. J. Appl. Psychol. **60**, 283–284 (1975)
10. Senter, R.J., Smith, E.A.: Automated Readability Index. AMRL-TR. Aerospace Medical Research Laboratories (US), Wright-Patterson Air Force Base (1967)
11. Šlerka, J., Smolík, F.: Automatická měřítka čitelnosti pro česky psané texty. Studie z aplikované lingvistiky **1**(1), 33–44 (2010)
12. Garais, E.-G.: Web applications readability. Romanian Econ. Bus. Rev. **5**, 117–121 (2011)

13. Kandel, L., Moles, A.: Application de l'indice de flesch à la langue française. Cahiers Etudes de Radio-Télévision **19**, 253–274 (1958)
14. De Landsheere, G.: Pour une application des tests de lisibilité de Flesch à la langue française. Le Travail Humain, pp. 141–154 (1963)
15. Henry, G.: Comment mesurer la lisibilité. Labor, Brussels (1975)
16. François, T., Fairon, C.: An AI readability formula for French as a foreign language, p. 477 (2012)
17. Amstad, T.: Wie verständlich sind unsere Zeitungen? Studenten-Schreib-Service (1978)
18. Guryanov, I., et al.: Text complexity: periods of study in Russian linguistics. Revista Publicando **4**, 616–25 (2017)
19. Oborneva, I.V.: Mathematical model for evaluation of didactic texts. Proc. Moscow State Pedag Univ. **4**, 141–147 (2006)
20. Ozhegov, S.I.: Slovar russkogo yazyka. Russkij jazik, Moskva (2010)
21. Muller, V.K.: Anglo-russkij slovar. Russkij Jazyk, Moscow (1985)
22. Solnyshkina, M., Ivanov, V., Solovyev, V.: Readability formula for Russian texts: a modified version. In: Batyrshin, I., Martínez-Villaseñor, M.L., Ponce Espinosa, H.E. (eds.) MICAI 2018, Part II. LNCS (LNAI), vol. 11289, pp. 132–145. Springer, Cham (2018). https://doi.org/10.1007/978-3-030-04497-8_11
23. Sinha, M., et al.: New readability measures for Bangla and Hindi texts. In: Proceedings of COLING 2012: Posters, pp. 1141–1150. The COLING 2012 Organizing Committee, Mumbai (2012)
24. SciPy 1.0 Contributors, Virtanen, P., Gommers, R., Oliphant, T.E., Haberland, M., Reddy, T., et al.: SciPy 1.0: fundamental algorithms for scientific computing in Python. Nature Meth. **17**, pp. 261–272 (2020)
25. Leo, Dr., Behmo, R.: Pyhyphen. The hyphenation library of LibreOffice and FireFox wrapped for Python. Version 4.0.0, 15 February 2021. https://pypi.org/project/PyHyphen/. Accessed 2 Apr 2021
26. Rosen, A.: InterCorp - a look behind the façade of a parallel corpus. In: Gruszczyńska, E., Leńko-Szymańska, A. (eds.) Polskojęzyczne korpusy równoległe. Polish-language Parallel Corpora, pp. 21–40. Instytut Lingwistyki Stosowanej, Warszawa (2016)
27. Čermák, F., Rosen, A.: The case of InterCorp, a multilingual parallel corpus. Int. J. Corpus Ling. **13**, 411–427 (2012)
28. Straková, J., et al.: Open-source tools for morphology, lemmatization, POS tagging and named entity recognition. In: Proceedings of 52nd Annual Meeting of the Association for Computational Linguistics: System Demonstrations, pp. 13–18. ACL, Stroudsburg (2014)
29. Kocmi, T., et al.: Announcing CzEng 2.0 Parallel Corpus with over 2 Gigawords (2020)
30. DuBay, W.H.: The Classic Readability Studies (2007)
31. Wickham, H.: ggplot2: Elegant Graphics for Data Analysis. Verlag, New York (2016). https://doi.org/10.1007/978-0-387-98141-3
32. Chromý, J., Cinková, S., Šamánková, J.: Srozumitelnost českého odborného a úředního textu - proč se jí zabývat a jak ji měřit. Stud. Appl. Ling. **12**(1) (2021)
33. Chen, X., Meurers, D.: CTAP: a web-based tool supporting automatic complexity analysis. In: Proceedings of the Workshop on Computational Linguistics for Linguistic Complexity (CL4LC), pp. 113–119. The COLING 2016 Organizing Committee, Osaka (2016)
34. Bendová, K.: Using a parallel Corpus to adapt the Flesch Reading Ease Formula to Czech. To appear in Jazykovedný časopis

35. Mclaughlin, G.: SMOG grading - a new readability formula. J. Read. **12**, 639–646 (1969)
36. Falkenjack, J., Mühlenbock, K., Jönsson, A.: Features indicating readability in Swedish text. Presented at the (2013)
37. Gonzalez-Dios, I., Aranzabe, M.J., Díaz de Ilarraza, A., Salaberri, H.: Simple or Complex? Assessing the readability of Basque Texts. In: Proceedings of COLING 2014, the 25th International Conference on Computational Linguistics: Technical Papers, pp. 334–344. Dublin City University and Association for Computational Linguistics, Dublin (2014)

New Parallel Corpora of Baltic and Slavic Languages — Assumptions of Corpus Construction

Maksim Duszkin[1], Danuta Roszko[2], and Roman Roszko[1]([✉])

[1] Institute of Slavic Studies PAS, Warsaw, Poland
{maksim.duszkin,roman.roszko}@ispan.waw.pl
[2] University of Warsaw, Warsaw, Poland
d.roszko@uw.edu.pl
https://ispan.waw.pl/default/en/
https://en.uw.edu.pl/

Abstract. In this article, we describe the design principles of the ten newly published CLARIN-PL corpora of Slavic and Baltic languages. In relation to other non-commercial online corpora, we highlight the distinctive features of these CLARIN-PL corpora: resource selection, preprocessing, manual segmentation at the sentence level, lemmatisation, annotation and metadata. We also present current and planned work on the development of the CLARIN-PL Balto–Slavic corpora.

Keywords: CLARIN ERIC · CLARIN-PL parallel corpora · Parallel corpora of Baltic and Slavic languages · Parallel corpora modelling

1 Introduction

Since the 1980s, the Semantics Group (hereinafter referred to as the Group) of the Institute of Slavic Studies of the Polish Academy of Sciences (ISS-PAS) has been conducting contrastive studies of Slavic and Baltic languages. To this end, it developed a theoretical contrastive research method that employs a semantic interlanguage and proceeded to construct experimental corpora, e.g. the *Bulgarian–Polish–Lithuanian Corpus* [12] in cooperation with the Institute of Mathematics and Computer Science of the Bulgarian Academy of Sciences. Over time, as part of the development of the Polish CLARIN ERIC infrastructure, the Group proceeded to develop two corpora: a trilingual *Polish–Bulgarian–Russian Corpus* [15] and a bilingual *Polish–Lithuanian Corpus* [23]. They served as the basis for creating new corpora which are described in this article.

2 State of the Art

The corpora developed by the Group compete with a number other non-commercial corpora of Slavic and Baltic languages available on the Internet,

© Springer Nature Switzerland AG 2021
K. Ekštein et al. (Eds.): TSD 2021, LNAI 12848, pp. 172–183, 2021.
https://doi.org/10.1007/978-3-030-83527-9_15

including *ParaSol* corpus, *InterCorp*, *Russian National Corpus* (in the *Parallel corpora* section) and several others. Due to the fact that the corpora presented in this article form a network consisting of Bulgarian, Lithuanian, Polish, Russian and Ukrainian languages, our comments regarding other corpora are limited to these languages.

In the *ParaSol* corpus [29], all these language pairs are available. The corpus size for specific language pairs is not explicitly given. If necessary, a user can determine it on the basis of data indicating the size of texts in each of the languages. The corpus is lemmatised and morphosyntactically annotated. The alignment of the texts in this corpus was carried out automatically. Unfortunately, the results of this alignment are not always satisfactory. For example, in response to the query `[lemma="делать"]` [to do] some incorrect results appear:

RU: *Делаем вывод:*	**PL**: *powodu, żeby podejrzewać Malachiasza, że wiedział, iż Wenancjusz dostał się do biblioteki i coś z niej zabrał.*	**UK**: *Тепер ми знаємо, що цього він не робив.*
[We conclude:]	[reason to suspect Malachi knew that Venantius had got into the library and taken something from it.]	[We now know that he didn't do that.]

A project that includes many different corpora, from which one can select those that support the language pairs of interest, is *OPUS* [28]. The project is still under development (last known update: February 2021). Unfortunately, this corpus has a search engine that is not convenient to its potential users. It is not possible to search simultaneously in all corpora; instead, one has to select one particular corpus using a drop-down list containing dozens of options. The names of the corpora (for example *TEP*, *Tanzil*, *ELRA-W0279*) do not tell anything to the average user and neither does the corpus indicate the available languages. It should be added that some corpora within this project may contain partially annotated morphosyntactic texts, e.g. in the *Books* corpus, Russian is annotated, but Polish is not. Based on the official information, the materials contained in the corpus are not subject to any manual correction. Hence, the texts contain a fair number of errors of various kinds, including alignment issues. For example, as a result of the query `"да"` [yes] (ru–lt corpus) we get, among other things, a pair of misattributed sentences:

RU: *Очень и очень, да.*	**LT**: *Didžiuojiesi savim Frenkai?*
[Very much so, yes.]	[Are you proud of yourself, Frank?]

InterCorp project's parallel corpora [11], resemble the corpora we are preparing the most and are currently available on the website of the *Czech National Corpus* [3]. It is worth noting that the advanced search engine *KonText*, developed for the *Czech National Corpus*, is also used to support the CLARIN-PL corpora. *InterCorp* is under active development, with its latest (13th) version published in 2020, and incorporates 40 languages, including bg, ru, pl, uk, lt, and all their pairs. 27 languages have been tagged, while 25 have been lemmatised (i.e. all these languages except for Lithuanian). Texts in pairs with bg, ru, pl, uk, lt have mostly been aligned automatically (apart from the 'Core' part, which has been manually aligned). *InterCorp* is a huge project: the Polish sub-corpus contains about 88 million words, while the Lithuanian sub-corpus contains about 30 million words.

As the project is mainly based on automatic language processing tools, the corpus collections are not free of errors in both alignment and morphosyntactic annotation. Numerous errors appearing in the automatically aligned part can make it difficult for the user to properly access the tool. For example, the Polish sentence "*Co robicie?*" [What are you doing?] is shown as parallel to the Ukrainian sentence "*А Павло відповів:*" [And Paul replied:]. It is one of the incorrect sentence alignments displayed on the first page of the search results of the query [lemma="robić"] [to do] limited to all subcorpora except the 'Core'). In practice, in order to obtain better results, the user has to take additional steps by limiting the search to the manually aligned 'Core' part in the 'Restrict search' options. Annotation errors are, in our opinion, relatively less frequent, but they do happen. For instance, the results of a query concerning the Russian cardinal numeral of the feminine gender in the instrumentalis: [tag Mcf-i] contained incorrect answers, e.g. RU "*проскочить между двумя легионерами*" [slip between two legionnaires].

Besides the three corpora mentioned above, other smaller projects exist. They focus on a smaller number of languages, e.g. they involve bilingual corpora with one base language or two bilingual corpora for two languages (e.g. corpus ru–pl and corpus pl–ru).

A few words should also be said about the parallel corpus module within the *Russian National Corpus* project, which supports all the language pairs for Russian (bg–ru, ru–bg, lt–ru, ru–lt, uk–ru, ru–uk). Morphosyntactic annotation and lemmatisation in these corpora were carried out automatically. It should be added that the annotation of most of these languages did not involve disambiguation (all possible interpretations are displayed in the information about the wordforms). Polish is an exception here as disambiguation has been carried out wherever possible.

Unfortunately, the description of the content and structure of the project [6] contains no up-to-date official information on the currently available parallel corpora. The article cited by the authors here [13] refers to the state as of 16 years ago. If one was to judge it by the information provided in this article, the alignment of corpora within the project was done automatically, using the *Parteks* program [13, p. 265]. Among the results of several search queries, we were unable to find significant errors.

Polish and Ukrainian languages are supported by the aligned, morphosyntactically annotated *PolUKR* corpus [17]. However, it appears that the search engine software does not always work properly. As attempts were made to test the corpus using some of the queries given on the 'How to search' page, it was not possible to obtain any results using tag searches. For example, the query [tag = "V.*"] returned 0 results, similarly to the queries [tag = "V..n.*"] and [tag = "N-f--sn"].

The query [lemma = "dzień|noc|ranek|wieczór"] [day|night|morning |evening] produced 261 sentences, none of which contained the correct output; instead, the results only contained the letter strings *noc* being the fragments of various unrelated wordforms, e.g. *zjed**noc**zonej* [united], *pół**noc**nych* [northern].

The *Polish-Russian Parallel Corpus* project [5] is also worth mentioning. It contains parallel corpora for the pairs pl–ru, ru–pl; according to the website, the corpus consists of 30 million wordforms. The downside of this project is the limited functionality of the search engine. In fact, it is only possible to search for letter strings, i.e. whole words, parts of words, several words, several whole words and a part of a word etc. (the search is also mislabelled as 'Word form search') or for single words that meet certain morphosyntactic criteria. The possibilities of this search option are rather limited, as the query can only concern one word (one form), i.e. it is not possible to create queries that combine specific forms such as "lemma śpiewać [to sing] + any adverb". The project was launched in 2013 and most likely has not been updated since then.

The *Corpus of Parallel Russian and Bulgarian Texts* [1] is another notable resource. It consists of two independent parts — the Bulgarian–Russian corpus and the Russian–Bulgarian corpus — and was last updated in 2014. The search engine of this project has some drawbacks. For example, it does not support searching for forms containing less than four letters. Both corpora also lack lemmatisation and morphosyntactic annotation.

Two corpus resources of the *PELCRA* group should also be mentioned. These encompass the manually aligned corpus with the basic Polish language *Multilingual (Polish–*) Parallel Corpus* and *PELCRA Polish–Russian Parallel Corpus* [19]. In each case, one of the pairing languages in these corpora is Polish. They do not have their own search engine and are made available to the users as downloadable files and, to our best knowledge, they lack lemmatisation and are not tagged morphosyntactically.

Brief Summary. Most multilingual corpora are automatically aligned, so errors happen at this level quite frequently. Not all of the texts have undergone linguistic and technical verification before being added to the corpora (they contain spelling mistakes etc.) Almost all corpora were created many years ago and are likely to be outdated. In our opinion, there are problems at the software level in the *PolUKR* corpus, while the capabilities of the search engines used in the *Polish-Russian Parallel Corpus* and *The Corpus of Parallel Russian and Bulgarian Texts* are very limited (in comparison to e.g. *InterCorp*), see Table 1.

3   Methodology

At each stage of the works, the construction of the corpora described here was linked to the linguistic research conducted by the Group, allowing us to refine the principles of corpus construction, which are described in Subsects. 3.1–3.7.

Table 1. Comparison of multilingual non-commercial corpora containing Bulgarian, Lithuanian, Polish, Russian and Ukrainian languages.

Corpus	Language pairs	Size	Availability	Alignment	Tagging & Lemmatisation	Last update
ParaSol [29]	All	Tiny	Online	Auto	Auto	2014
OPUS [28]	All (Only in certain subcorpora)	HUGE	Online/ download	Auto	Auto/none	2021
InterCorp [11]	All	LARGE	Online	Auto/manual	Auto/none	2020
RNC [13]	ru↔bg, ru↔pl, ru↔lt, ru↔uk, ru↔bg↔pl↔uk	Large	Online	Auto	Auto	n/a
PolUKR [17]	pl↔uk	Tiny	Online	Manual	Auto	2011
Pol-Ros [5]	pl↔ru	Large	Online	Auto	Auto	2013
RBCorpus [1]	bg↔ru	Small	Online	Manual	None	2014
Polish–* [19]	pl↔ru, pl↔lt, pl↔bg, pl↔uk	Large	Download	Auto	None	2013
Pl–Ru [19]	pl↔ru	Small	Download	Manual	None	2013

3.1 Selection of Texts

The selection of texts for individual corpora reconciles the expectations of individual users and the quality requirements, which means that the balance of individual corpora may be far from the standards used for the reference corpora. For example, in the Polish–Ukrainian corpus, film dialogues and journalistic texts constitute a significant part of the resources. On the other hand, in the Polish–Lithuanian corpus, legal and specialist language is widely represented. Moreover, only in the Lithuanian–Polish corpus, the majority of the texts are mutual translations (i.e. from Polish into Lithuanian or Lithuanian into Polish). In the Polish–Bulgarian corpus, fiction works are represented the most in comparison to the other corpora. In the Polish–Russian corpus, film dialogues and works of fiction constitute an important part of the resources.

In our understanding, quality requirements are a preliminary criterion for assessing the correctness and representativeness of a text. We reject works with a low editorial level and those whose language deviates from the norm specific to the language variety. Therefore, machine translations and texts containing numerous grammatical errors are rejected. Legal, juridical and other specialised texts are subjected to preliminary lemmatisation in order to include, on the basis of statistical data obtained, those texts whose vocabulary is the most diverse (characterised by a large number of lemmas and terminological diversity).

3.2 Pre-processing of Texts

Each work accepted to the corpus resources undergoes preprocessing. At this stage, spelling errors (including the frequent lack of diacritics, e.g. PL *sąd* [court] written as *sad* [orchard]), typos, case-sensitivity and dictionary forms are corrected and punctuation is completed. Segmentation is carried out, with the result that the smallest units, i.e. tokens, are distinguished. In the non-fiction resources, the notations of currency, time and geographical expressions are normalised. In language preprocessing for Polish, CLARIN-PL tools are used, e.g. *Punctuator* [31], *TxtClean* [9], *Speller* [7], *Tokenizer* [8]. The sentences below are the examples of sentence preprocessing in Polish:

On entry	*Ide na górke po jabka, są po 2.50zł.*
Segmentation result	*Ide na górke po jabka , są po 2 . 50 . zł .*
Normalisation result	*Idę na górkę po jabłka , tam są po 2,50 zł.*

During preprocessing, the spelling of some Ukrainian texts (mainly film dialogues) is aligned to the spelling standard adopted for the language in 2019. Much attention is paid to the thorough proofreading of film dialogues, where translators' and editors' comments and technical descriptions are removed. In addition, professional proofreaders and translators check the consistency of the translations in the individual language pairs. Discrepancies are reconciled during the segmentation process at the sentence level. What is more, the spelling of proper names (first names, surnames, town names, institutions, etc.) is standardised throughout the dialogue. Linguistic intervention in the spelling of legal texts is the lowest.

3.3 Segmentation

In the CLARIN-PL multilingual corpora, two levels of segmentation were introduced. The first level is based on the sentence unit. It ensures the proper mutual correspondence of sentences between languages. The second level of segmentation is based on the unit of the wordform, which is taken as a token ('position' in *KonText*). In some cases, a token may be a part of a wordform. For example, in Polish the past tense form *czytałem* [I read] is a compound of the two tokens *czytał* and *em*:

```
<tok> <orth>czytał</orth> <lex disamb="1"><base>czytać</base><ctag>praet:
sg:m1:imperf</ctag></lex> </tok>
<ns/>
<tok> <orth>em</orth> <lex disamb="1"><base>być</base><ctag>aglt:sg:pri:
imperf:wok</ctag></lex> </tok>
```

At this stage of our work on the corpora, we have chosen not to bind tokens between languages and to group tokens into compound expressions.

Parallel Segmentation at the Sentence Level. The simultaneous segmentation of two parallel texts into sentences meets the condition of communicative completeness. Due to the genetic and typological proximity of the languages juxtaposed, it was not necessary to decide on the nature of the sentence as a structural, semantic or structural-semantic unit. It was assumed that both the beginning and the end of a sentence have their exponents in the notation. These are respectively: a capital letter (as the beginning of a sentence) and a full stop, or an exclamation mark, or a question mark, or an ellipsis (as a sign ending a sentence). An alphanumeric string beginning with a capital letter and ending with one of the above mentioned terminating characters is defined as a sentence, which is thus assigned communicative completeness. Sentence segmentation for one language is not problematic. However, sentence segmentation in parallel texts already requires the segmentation rules to be clarified since sentence segmentation rules across different languages may differ from one another. Therefore, in the absence of a simple (sentence to sentence) correspondence, an algorithm was used to associate the same content with the sentence structure of each language so that simultaneously in the distinguished aligned segments, the beginning of each segment was a capital letter and the end — any character ending the sentence. As a result, the number of sentences forming a sentence segment in the two languages may differ.

Sentence segmentation of multilingual resources required the rules to be clarified. The sentence-ending character can also be a comma, a colon and a semicolon. This is particularly evident in the specific language pairs in which the author uses a typical sentence-ending symbol mark in one language, while in the other language one of the above-mentioned substitutes is used instead. This phenomenon is common in works of fiction as well as legal and juridical texts. It was therefore decided to introduce segments with an ending mark different from proper sentence ending marks while maintaining the condition of communicative completeness. This modification of the assumptions about distinguishing sentence segments is applied in fiction in which no sentence division is introduced. For example, the short story *Miesto laikrodis* [Town Clock] by the Lithuanian writer Algis Kuklys is a single long sentence containing almost 1500 wordforms.

In legal and juridical texts, sentences may also end in another variant, i.e. a paragraph changes without the use of any end-of-sentence mark. This variant of sentence segmentation is also included in the corpora described here.

In order to provide the user with complete information about the text, two conventional marks [—] and [. . .] were introduced into the corpus. The first one ([—]) informs the corpus user that there is no equivalent sentence segment in one language, e.g.

PL: *Zdejmij medalik ze Św. Krzysztofem.* [Remove the medal with St Christopher.]	**UK**: *Знімай медаль святого Христофора.* [Remove the medal with St Christopher.]
[—]	*Зараз же.* [In a moment.]
Silny smród. [It stinks a lot.]	*Сморід страшенний.* [It stinks a lot.]

The second one ([. . .]) indicates that a piece of text has been omitted. In the case of legal texts, this mark serves primarily the purpose of anonymisation, e.g. to omit the name of the company. In other cases, this mark [. . .] informs about the omission of fragments, which are longer foreign-language inclusions, lists of references or enumerations and other similar entities presenting no value for the corpus user. To identify foreign language inclusions, we use the *Inkluz* tool [2].

Segmentation at the Level of the Smallest Distinguishable Units. The segmentation process of distinguishing tokens is carried out for each language independently. The first segmentation step already takes place at the language preprocessing stage. After the introduction of linguistic changes offered by professional translators and correctors during proofreading and the segmentation at the sentence level the final segmentation of the texts is performed.

3.4 Automatic Lemmatisation and Tagging the Inflectional Layer of Tokens

In our corpora, we used a variant of the automatic lemmatisation and morphosyntactic tagging process. We tried to choose the best tagger for each language. The choice of a particular tool was preceded by an analysis of both the effectiveness of the tool and the quality of the tagset. Considering effectiveness, we wanted the number of correctly recognised and described forms to be as high as possible. In the case of tagsets, we analysed the values assigned to particular classes of lexemes and flexemes. Flexeme is a new concept introduced into Polish grammar by Janusz Bień [10], later described in more detail by Adam Przepiórkowski [21] and used in the tagset of the *National Corpus of Polish*. For example, the class of verb lexemes in Polish contains 12 flexemes: the non-finite form, the agglutinant of the verb *być* [to be], etc.

Polish resources were tagged with one of three tools: *MorphoDiTa-PL* [20], *Concraft2* [32], and the *CMC tagger* [30], which is currently being adapted to the tagset of the *Grammatical Dictionary of the Polish Language* [24].

To tag Russian-language resources, we used the morphological parser *MyStem* developed by Ilya Segalovich and Vitaly Titov [25] at Yandex. The choice of this tagger was determined by both the effectiveness confirmed in our tests and the compatibility of the tags with the *Russian National Corpus*.

For Lithuanian, we initially used the tagger *MorfoLema* [18], then *Morfologinis anotatorius* [22], and finally, all resources were tagged in *KLC Morfologijos servisas*.[1]

Initially, we tagged Bulgarian resources with *BgTagger* [16], but we decided to change it to *CL@RK System* [26] in the last year of developing the corpus. The decision to make this change was driven by the ability of *CL@RK System* to tag a text on the syntactic level, as well as the effectiveness and availability of the tool.

Ukrainian resources were tagged with the *UDPipe* tool [27].

3.5 Manual Lemmatisation and Tagging of the Forms Not Detected by the Automatic Lemmatisation and Tagging Process

Some of the resources misidentified or undescribed in the automatic lemmatisation and tagging process were given hand-written descriptions. Most often these were proper names and wordforms which were intentionally unfinished by the author of the text or distorted, e.g. PL *Idzieeeesz?* instead of *Idziesz?* [Are you coming?].

---

[1] While preparing the corpora, we gained access to *KLC Morfologijos servisas*, a newly developed tool by the Centre of Computational Linguistics team at the Vytautas Magnus University, the tool had not yet been published at the time this article was written.

3.6 Metadata

In order to provide users with more information about the texts included in the corpora and to enable searching through resources narrowed down to selected parameters, we introduced an extensive metadata annotation of the texts. We have taken into account such parameters as: `text.group`, `text.txtype`, `text.srclang`, `text.original`, `text.translator`, `text.author`, `text.srcauthor`, `text.title`, `text.srctitle`, `text.year`, `text.decade` and others. The *KonText* search engine allows the user to freely select texts using metadata. For example, the user can limit the search to the texts whose source language is French and narrow down the query to the works published between 2001 and 2010 by selecting `text.srclang: fr French` and `text.decade: 2001-2010` respectively. Based on the metadata, the user can create any number of his/her own subcorpora.

3.7 Converting Resources into a Format Compatible with the *KonText* and Publishing Corpora

The final stage of the work on the corpora is to prepare the resources for publication in the *KonText* search engine on the CLARIN-PL website [4]. At the moment of writing this article, the corpora are undergoing testing. The publication of the Polish–Bulgarian, Polish–Lithuanian, Polish–Russian, Polish–Ukrainian, Russian–Bulgarian, Russian–Lithuanian, Russian–Ukrainian, Lithuanian–Bulgarian, Lithuanian–Ukrainian and Bulgarian–Ukrainian corpora is planned for June–July 2021.

4 Parallel Corpora of Baltic and Slavic Languages on the CLARIN-PL Website (2021 Version)

4.1 Corpora Including the Polish Language

The basic corpus resource consists of four Polish language corpora: Polish–Bulgarian, Polish–Lithuanian, Polish–Russian, Polish–Ukrainian. They are significantly developed versions of the corpora that were made available on the CLARIN-PL website in 2018. The main differences between the 2018 and 2021 versions of the corpora are presented in Table 2.

The balance of the individual corpora is in line with the demand of the research teams who use them. For example, the Polish–Lithuanian corpus contains the largest number of mutual translations (from Polish into Lithuanian and vice versa) and is dominated by fiction, legal, specialist and training texts. The Polish–Bulgarian corpus, on the other hand, contains mostly legal texts and fiction. The Polish–Russian corpus has a rich representation of legal texts, fiction and film dialogues. The Polish–Ukrainian corpus contains mainly journalistic texts, film dialogues and scientific texts.

Table 2. Balto–Slavic CLARIN-PL corpora. Comparison of the 2018 and 2021 versions.

	Corpora 2018	Corpora 2021
Volume	36,278,988 wordforms	54,820,106 wordforms
Pre-processing of text	Yes	Yes, advanced
Segmentation	Yes	Yes, improved
Lemmatisation	Automatic, only Polish and Lithuanian resources	Automatic with manual correction of 'difficult' forms, all resources
Tagging	Automatic, only Polish and Lithuanian resources (inflectional layer)	Automatic with manual correction of 'difficult' forms, all resources
Metadata	Basic (file name, author, translator, title)	Extended

4.2   New Corpus Resources for Slavic and Baltic Languages Without Polish

We paired Bulgarian, Lithuanian, Russian and Ukrainian resources that were prepared for the corpora described in Subsect. 4.1. Thus, we created and published new corpora: ru–bg, ru–lt, ru–uk, lt–bg, lt–uk and bg–uk. The particular interest of linguists after the publishing of the initial working versions has led us to expand the resources of the individual corpora. Similarly to corpora presented in Sect. 4.1, these corpora were also subjected to text preprocessing, manual segmentation at sentence and wordform levels, lemmatisation, tagging and extensive meta-annotation. The size of these corpora exceeds 26 million wordforms. The largest of them, the Lithuanian–Bulgarian corpus contains mainly legal texts (160 works). The Russian–Bulgarian corpus includes legal texts (60), fiction texts (22), juridical texts (4), scientific texts (4) and journalistic texts (2). The Russian–Lithuanian corpus includes legal texts (30), scientific texts (4) and juridical texts (2). The Russian–Ukrainian corpus includes legal texts (60), scientific texts (6) and fiction texts (4). The Bulgarian–Ukrainian corpus includes 60 legal texts and 2 fiction texts. The Lithuanian–Ukrainian corpus, the smallest of them all, contains 30 legal texts and 10 juridical works.

5   Conclusions and Future Work

The CLARIN-PL multilingual corpora are a response of the Group of ISS-PAS to the specific needs of researchers. The first pl–lt and pl–bg resources met mainly the needs of linguists at ISS-PAS. On the other hand, the proposal to create further corpora (pl–ru, pl–uk, ru–bg, ru–lt, ru–uk, lt–bg and bg–uk) has come from the users of the Polish CLARIN-PL infrastructure. The volume and internal balance of the corpus resources presented here were determined by the needs of specific research teams (mainly from Bulgaria, Lithuania, Poland and Ukraine).

All the described corpora have been preprocessed, manually aligned at the sentence level, automatically annotated, and tagged and described with extensive metadata. Some resources that were misrecognised or not recognised in the automatic lemmatisation and tagging process have been manually annotated. All corpora are available after free registration and login via *KonText* interface [4]. Every user of these corpora will receive support at every stage of their own research.

Ongoing Tasks. At the end of 2020, the Group started working on quasi-reference multilingual corpora: Polish–Bulgarian, Polish–Lithuanian, Polish–Russian and Polish–Slovenian. In this task, the overarching goal is to create corpora that are fully manually aligned, lemmatized, annotated and perfectly balanced for the purpose of training new monolingual and multilingual tools.

The corpus resources described in this article are being continually improved, expanded and adapted to the changing standards.

Planned Tasks. In the near future, it is planned to create a plug-in for *KonText — Query Builder*, which will allow the user to efficiently formulate queries without previous CQL syntax knowledge. In addition, disambiguation of the inflectional layer annotation for the Russian language is planned. The construction of further corpora is also planned, which will include the following new languages: Belarussian, Croatian, Czech, Latvian, Macedonian, Serbian and Slovak. All corpora with Polish will be synchronised with *plWordNet* [14].

Acknowledgements. This work was partially supported by (1) the Polish Ministry of Education and Science, CLARIN-PL Project; (2) CLARIN — Common Language Resources and Technology Infrastructure, project no. POIR.04.02.00-00C002/19.

References

1. Corpus of Parallel Russian and Bulgarian Texts. http://rbcorpus.com
2. Inkluz. https://ws.clarin-pl.eu/inkluz.shtml
3. InterCorp. https://intercorp.korpus.cz
4. KonText. https://kontext.clarin-pl.eu
5. Polish-Russian Parallel Corpus. http://www.pol-ros.polon.uw.edu.pl
6. Russian National Corpus: Corpora structure. https://ruscorpora.ru/new/corpora-structure.html
7. Speller. http://ws.clarin-pl.eu/speller.shtml
8. Tokenizer. http://ws.clarin-pl.eu/tokenizer.shtml
9. TxtClean. http://ws.clarin-pl.eu/txtclean.shtml
10. Bień, J.: Rozprawy Uniwersytetu Warszawskiego / Dissertationes Univesitatis Varsoviensis, chap. Koncepcja słownikowej informacji morfologicznej i jej komputerowej weryfikacji, Wydawnictwa Uniwersytetu Warszawskiego (1991)
11. Čermák, F., Rosen, A.: The case of InterCorp, a multilingual parallel corpus. Int. J. Corpus Ling. 17, 411-427 (2012)
12. Dimitrova, L., Koseska, V., Roszko, D., Roszko, R.: Trilingual aligned corpus — current state and new applications. Cogn. Stud. Études Cogn. **14**, 13–20 (2014)
13. Dobrovol'sky, D., Kretov, A., Sharoff, S.: Natsional'nyy korpus russkogo yazyka: 2003–2005, chap. Korpus parallel'nykh tekstov: Arkhitektura i vozmozhnosti ispol'zovaniya. Indrik (2005)
14. Janz, A., Kocoń, J., Piasecki, M., Zaśko-Zielińska, M.: PlWordNet as a basis for large emotive lexicons of Polish. In: LTC 2017 8th Language & Technology Conference, pp. 189–193 (2017)

15. Kisiel, A., Koseska-Toszewa, V., Kotsyba, N., Staśkowiak-Satoła, J., Sosnowski, W.: Polish-Bulgarian-Russian Parallel Corpus (2016). http://hdl.handle.net/ 11321/308. CLARIN-PL Digital Repository
16. Koeva, S., Genov, A.: Bulgarian language processing chain. In: Proceeding of the Workshop on the Integration of Multilingual Resources and Tools in Web Applications, 26 September 2011 (2011)
17. Kotsyba, N.: Polskojęzyczne korpusy równoległe. Polish-language Parallel Corpora, chap. Polsko-Ukraiński Korpus Równoległy PolUKR i jego następca PolUKR-2. Instytut Lingwistyki Stosowanej (2016)
18. Marcinkevičienė, R.: Vytauto Didžiojo universiteto mokslo klasteriai, chap. Teksto ir balso skaitmeniniai tyrimai, išteklių ir technologiju kūrimas bei taikymas (2012)
19. Pęzik, P., Ogrodniczuk, M., Przepiórkowski, A.: Parallel and spoken corpora in an open repository of Polish language resources. In: Proceedings of the 5th Language & Technology Conference: Human Language Technologies as a Challenge for Computer Science and Linguistics (2011)
20. Piasecki, M., Walentynowicz, W.: Morphodita-based tagger adapted to the Polish language technology. In: Proceedings of Human Language Technologies as a Challenge for Computer Science and Linguistics (2017)
21. Przepiórkowski, A.: Korpus IPI PAN. Wersja wstępna, Instytut Podstaw Informatyki PAN (2004)
22. Rimkutė, E., Valskys, V., Vaskelienė, J.: Lietuvių kalbos leksemų morfologinis anotavimas: ypatumai ir sunkumai. Kalbų studijos 15, 63–70 (2009)
23. Roszko, D., Roszko, R.: Polish-Lithuanian Parallel Corpus (2016). https://clarin-pl.eu/dspace/handle/11321/309. CLARIN-PL Digital Repository
24. Saloni, Z.: Podstawy teoretyczne "Słownika gramatycznego języka polskiego" (2012/2020). http://sgjp.pl/static/pdf/Podstawy_teoretyczne_SGJP.pdf
25. Segalovich, I.: A fast morphological algorithm with unknown word guessing induced by a dictionary for a web search engine. In: Proceedings of the International Conference on Machine Learning; Models, Technologies and Applications, MLMTA 2003, Las Vegas, Nevada, USA, 23–26 June 2003 (2003)
26. Simov, K., Simov, A., Osenova, P.: An XML architecture for shallow and deep processing. In: The Proceedings of the ESSLLI 2004 Workshop on Combining Shallow and Deep Processing for NLP (2004)
27. Straka, M., Straková, J.: UDPipe (2016). http://hdl.handle.net/11234/1-1702. LINDAT/CLARIAH-CZ Digital Library at the Institute of Formal and Applied Linguistics (ÚFAL), Faculty of Mathematics and Physics, Charles University
28. Tiedemann, J.: OPUS — parallel corpora for everyone. In: Proceedings of the 19th Annual Conference of the European Association for Machine Translation (EAMT) (2016). Baltic Journal of Modern Computing
29. von Waldenfels, R., Meyer, R.: ParaSol: A Parallel Corpus of Slavic and Other Languages (2006)
30. Walentynowicz, W., Piasecki, M., Oleksy, M.: Tagger for Polish computer mediated communication texts. In: Proceedings of the International Conference on Recent Advances in Natural Language Processing (RANLP 2019) (2019)
31. Walkowiak, T.: Language processing modelling notation — orchestration of NLP microservices. In: Advances in Dependability Engineering of Complex Systems: Proceedings of the Twelfth International Conference on Dependability and Complex Systems DepCoS-RELCOMEX (2017)
32. Waszczuk, J.: Harnessing the CRF complexity with domain-specific constraints. The case of morphosyntactic tagging of a highly inflected language. In: Proceedings of COLING 2012 (2012)

Use of Augmentation and Distant Supervision for Sentiment Analysis in Russian

Anton Golubev[1]($\boxtimes$) and Natalia Loukachevitch[2]($\boxtimes$)

[1] Bauman Moscow State Technical University, Moscow, Russia
[2] Lomonosov Moscow State University, Moscow, Russia

Abstract. In this study, we test several augmentation and distant supervision techniques to increase sentiment datasets in Russian. We use transfer learning approach pre-trained on created additional data to improve the performance. We compare our proposed approach based on distant supervision with existing augmentation methods. The best results were achieved using three-step approach of sequential training on general, thematic and original train samples. The results were improved by more than 3% to the current state-of-the-art methods for most of the benchmarks using data automatically annotated with distant supervision technique.

Keywords: Targeted sentiment analysis · Distant supervision · Augmentation · Transfer learning

1 Introduction

The best results in various natural language processing applications are obtained with machine learning approaches, which requires the creation of training sets. Manual creation of datasets requires a lot of efforts and time. Therefore various automated techniques for increasing training datasets are suggested. Among most popular methods is augmentation, when additional variants of dataset examples are created [7, 26, 27]. Another approach for increasing training datasets is distant supervision, when additional data are automatically annotated using some auxiliary resources. [8, 20]. Current transfer learning approaches [28] allow using more effective techniques of exploiting automatically annotated data. Transfer learning includes a pre-training step based on auxiliary data and applying previously gained knowledge to a target task.

Both approaches for increasing training datasets are widely used in sentiment analysis tasks. In this paper we study augmentation and distant supervision techniques in sentiment analysis task for Russian [8, 20]. Sentiment analysis or opinion mining is an important natural language processing task used to determine sentiment attitude of the text. Nowadays most state-of-the-art results are obtained using deep learning models, which require training on specialized labeled datasets. To improve the model performance, transfer learning approach

© Springer Nature Switzerland AG 2021
K. Ekštein et al. (Eds.): TSD 2021, LNAI 12848, pp. 184–196, 2021.
https://doi.org/10.1007/978-3-030-83527-9_16

can be used. This approach includes a pre-training step of learning general representations from a source task and an adaptation step of applying previously gained knowledge to a target task.

The most known Russian sentiment analysis datasets include ROMIP-2013 and SentiRuEval2015-2016 [5,14,15] consisting of annotated data on banks and telecom operators reviews from Twitter posts and news quotes. Current best results on these datasets were obtained using pre-trained RuBERT [9,24] and conversational BERT model [4,6] fine-tuned as architectures treating a sentiment classification task as a natural language inference (NLI) or question answering (QA) problem [9].

In this study, we introduce a method for automatic generation of annotated samples from a Russian news corpus using distant supervision technique. We compare different variants of combining additional data with original train samples and several augmentation techniques. We test the transfer learning approach based on BERT models. For most datasets, the results were improved by more than 3% to the current state-of-the-art performance. On SentiRuEval-2015 Telecom Operators Dataset, the BERT-NLI model treating a sentiment classification problem as a natural language inference task, reached human level according to one of the metrics.

2   Related Work

Russian sentiment analysis datasets are based on different data sources [24], including reviews [5,23], news stories [5], posts from social networks [14,19,20]. The best results on most available datasets are obtained using transfer learning approaches based on the BERT model [6], more specifically on RuBERT [4] and Russian variant of BERT [2,9,18,24]. In [9], the authors tested several variants of RuBERT and different settings of its applications, and found that the best results on sentiment analysis tasks on several datasets were achieved using Conversational RuBERT trained on Russian social networks posts and comments. Among several architectures, the BERT-NLI model treating the sentiment classification problem as a natural language inference task usually has the highest results.

For automatic generation of annotated data for classification tasks [7,26,27], researchers may use augmentation approach, when more data are generated using the initial training dataset, and the distant supervision approach, which exploits additional resources (users' tags, manual lexicons, etc.) for automatic additional annotation of unlabeled data [8,20].

The simplest augmentation method is to replace source words with their synonyms from manual thesauri (for example, WordNet [15,16]) or with words that are close to the source words according to a distributional model trained on a large text collection [26]. Synonyms may not fit into the context, therefore the replacement of words can be based on word predictions from a language model [11]. The authors of [27] used four simple augmentation techniques for the classification tasks: replacing words with their synonyms (WordNet), occasional word insertion, occasional word deletion and occasional word order changing. The average improvement of 0.8% for F-score was achieved. The study showed that all four operations contributed to the obtained improvement [27]. Back-translation is also often considered as a technique for augmenting training data [7].

In distant supervision for Twitter sentiment analysis, users' positive or negative emoticons or hashtags can be used [17,20,22]. Authors of [21] use the RuSentiFrames lexicon for creating a large automatically annotated dataset for recognition of sentiment relations between mentioned entities.

In this study we automatically create a dataset for targeted sentiment analysis, which extracts a sentiment attitude towards a specific entity. The use of an automatic dataset together with manually annotated data allows us to improve the state-of-the-art results.

3   Russian Sentiment Benchmark Datasets

In our study, we consider the following Russian datasets (benchmarks): news quotes from the ROMIP-2013 evaluation [5] and Twitter datasets from SentiRuEval 2015–2016 evaluations [14,15]. The collection of the news quotes contains opinions in direct or indirect speech extracted from news articles [5]. Twitter datasets from SentiRuEval-2015-2016 evaluations were annotated for the task of reputation monitoring [1,14], which means searching sentiment-oriented opinions about banks and telecom companies.

Table 1. Benchmark sample sizes and sentiment class distributions (%)

Dataset	Train sample				Test sample			
	Volume	Posit.	Negat.	Neutral	Volume	Posit.	Negat.	Neutral
ROMIP-2013[a]	4260	26	44	30	5500	32	41	27
SRE-2015 Banks[b]	6232	7	36	57	4612	8	14	78
SRE-2015 Telecom[b]	5241	19	34	47	4173	10	23	67
SRE-2016 Banks[c]	10725	7	26	67	3418	9	23	68
SRE-2016 Telecom[c]	9209	15	28	57	2460	10	47	43

[a] http://romip.ru/en/collections/sentiment-news-collection-2012.html
[b] https://drive.google.com/drive/folders/1bAxIDjVz_0UQn-iJwhnUwngjivS2kfM3
[c] https://drive.google.com/drive/folders/0BxlA8wH3PTUfV1F1UTBwVTJPd3c

Table 1 presents the main characteristics of datasets including train and test sample sizes and sentiment classes distributions. It can be seen in Table 1 that the neutral class is prevailing in all Twitter datasets, while ROMIP-2013 data is rather balanced. For this reason, along with the standard metrics of F_1 *macro* and accuracy, $F_1^{+-} macro$ and $F_1^{+-} micro$ ignoring the neutral class were also calculated. Insignificant part of samples contains two or more sentiment analysis objects, so these tweets are duplicated with corresponding attitude labels [15].

4   Automatic Generation of Annotated Data

For many deep learning models an increase in the amount of training data leads to an improvement in results. This way, we decided to expand benchmark training sets by producing synthetic data, which is known as augmentation technique. In this study, we compare existing augmentation methods based on word embedding substitution and back translation with our proposed distant supervision approach consisting of selection of sentences containing sentiment words.

4.1   Augmentation

The purpose of augmentation is to modify existing dataset to produce more data similar to the original one. It is widely used in computer vision and sound processing, where it was proven to be effective in many researches. However, applying such approach to NLP domain is harder and less studied since the complexity of the different languages and tasks. For the sentiment analysis task, the disadvantage is that augmentation does not add new sentiment objects to the sentences, but only includes additional noise in the original examples. In our study, we use four augmentation techniques [7,27]. They will be described together with the examples based on the following sentence:

"Megaphone is the best mobile operator in Russia with the fastest Internet."

Synonym Replacement. Replacing n random words with their synonyms. This method was implemented using FastText[1] embeddings. The value of n is calculated based on the length of the sentence l with the following formula: $n = \alpha \cdot l$, where α was experimentally set equal to 0.2. The most similar word for each of selected n candidates was replaced by the closest synonym in terms of cosine similarity between word embeddings. It was important not to replace sentiment objects, so we created a list of entities with DeepPavlov's NER to keep them in augmented sentences.

*"Megaphone is the best **telecom** operator in Russia with the **flashing** Internet."*

*"Megaphone is the **leading** mobile **controller** in Russia with the fastest Internet."*

Random Swap. Swapping the positions of two random words in the sentence. Not necessarily neighboring words can be swapped, but also words that are at some distance from each other. We set the word spacing threshold equal to 4. The first word in the sentence was found using the uniform distribution with the exception of a sentiment object. Further, a non-zero integer number was randomly selected from the interval $[-4, 4]$ and the shift was performed. A negative value means movement along the text to the left. If the word selected

---

[1] http://docs.deeppavlov.ai/en/master/features/pretrained_vectors.html.

for the permutation was too close to the border, the boundaries of the interval were revised.

"Megaphone is the best **operator mobile** *in Russia with the fastest internet."*

"Megaphone is the best mobile operator in Russia with **Internet** *fastest* **the***."*

Random Deletion. Removing n random words from sentence. The value of n is calculated based on the length of the sentence l with the following formula: $n = \alpha \cdot l$, where α was experimentally set equal to 0.3. As in the case of synonym replacement, we used a list of entities not to delete them from the augmented sentence. The deleted words are highlighted in red below.

"Megaphone is the best mobile operator in Russia with the fastest Internet."

"Megaphone is the best mobile operator in Russia with the fastest Internet."

Back-Translation. Translating a sentence to another language and back. This technique is based on back-translation to paraphrase a text while retaining the initial meaning. This technique mostly preserves the same semantics of the sentences but generates different syntax. The French language was used for the back-translation method because of the high content of speech turns, which contributed to the formation of quality examples without distorting the meaning.

"Megaphone is the best **Russian mobile operator** *with the fastest Internet."*

" **The best Russian mobile operator with the fastest Internet** *is Megaphone."*

4.2   Distant Supervision Approach

The main idea of an automatic annotation of dataset is based on the use of a sentiment lexicon comprising negative and positive words and phrases with their sentiment scores. We utilize Russian sentiment lexicon RuSentiLex [13], which includes general sentiment words of Russian language, slang words from Twitter and words with positive or negative associations (connotations) from the news corpus. For ambigous words, having several senses with different sentiment orientations, RuSentiLex describes senses with references to the concepts of RuThes thesaurus [12]. The current version of RuSentiLex contains 16445 senses.

As a source for automatic dataset generation, we use 4 Gb Russian news corpus, collected from various sources and representing different topics, which is important in fact that the benchmarks under analysis cover several topics.

The automatically annotated dataset includes general and thematic parts. For creation of the general part, we select monosemous positive and negative nouns from the RuSentiLex lexicon, which can be used as references to people or companies, which are sentiment targets in the benchmarks. We construct positive and negative word lists and suppose that if a word from the list occurs in a sentence, it has a context of the same sentiment. The list of positive and negative references to people or companies (seed words) includes 822 negative references and 108 positive ones. Examples of such words are presented below (translated from Russian):

- positive: *"champion, hero, good-looker"*, etc.;
- negative: *"outsider, swindler, liar, defrauder, deserter"*, etc.

Sentences may contain several seed words with different sentiments. In such cases, we duplicate sentences with labels in accordance with their attitudes. The examples of extracted sentences are as follows (all further examples are translated from Russian):

- positive: *"A MASK is one who, on a gratuitous basis, helps the development of science and art, provides them with material assistance from their own funds"*;
- negative: *"Such irresponsibility—non-payments—hits not only the MASK himself, but also throughout the house in which he lives"*.

To generate the thematic part of the automatic sample, we search for sentences that mention relevant named entities depending on a task (banks or operators) using the named entity recognition model (NER) from DeepPavlov [4] co-occurred with sentiment words in the same sentences. To ensure that a sentiment word refers to an entity, we restrict the distance between two words to be not more than four words.

We remove examples containing a particle *"not"* near sentiment word because it could change attitude of text in relation to target. Sentences with sentiment word located in quotation marks were also removed because they could distort the meaning of the sentence being a proper name. Examples of extracted thematic sentiment sentences are as follows:

- for banks (positive): *"MASK increased its net profit in November by 10.7%"*
- for mobile operators (negative): *"FAS suspects MASK of imposing paid services on subscribers."*

Since the benchmarks contain also the neutral sentiment class, we need to extract sentences without sentiments. For this task, we choose among examples selected by NER those that do not contain any sentiment words from the lexicon. Examples of extracted neutral sentences for both general and thematic parts are presented below:

- for persons: *"MASK is already starting training with its new team."*
- for banks: *"On March 14, MASK announced that it was starting rebranding."*
- for mobile operators: *"MASK has offered its subscribers a new service."*

Let us summarize difference between general and thematic additional samples. The general dataset consists of sentences that include general positive or negative nouns (hero, liar), which usually denote persons or organizations. The thematic dataset consists of sentences that have a named entity from a specific domain (bank, mobile operators) co-occurred with negative or positive sentiment words. Neutral sentences can be only thematic.

While creating an additional dataset, we take into account the distribution of sentiment words in the resulting sample, trying to bring it as close as possible to uniform. A source corpus contains enough examples with a negative sentiment to form a balanced dataset, which can not be said about words with the positive sentiment. We made automatically generated dataset and source code publicly available[2].

5   Text Preprocessing

To create an additional sample from the Russian news corpus, it was necessary to divide raw articles into separate sentences. For this task, we used rule-based sentence splitter from spaCy library [10], which is able to determine sentence boundaries automatically. This solution showed better quality in preliminary studies in comparison with NLTK variant [3] and simple splitter based on regular expressions.

In addition to conceptual steps of creating an automatic dataset described in previous section, a few cleaning measures were performed. In accordance with calculated quantiles of sentences from test samples, too short and long examples were removed from additional data. To remove duplicate sentences from different sources, we use the metrics of cosine similarity between pairs of tf-idf representations of the examples. When the value of the specified boundary value was exceeded, one of the sentences was randomly removed. Conducting experiments with different thresholds and exploring resulting samples, we set value equal to 0.8.

After bringing the additional sample to the desired format, standard preprocessing track, including replacing similar text elements with appropriate tokens and removing special symbols was carried out for all datasets [9].

6   BERT Architectures

In our study, we consider three variants of fine-tuning BERT models [6] for sentiment analysis. These architectures can be subdivided into the single-sentence approach using only initial text as an input and the two-sentence approach [9,25], which converts the sentiment analysis task into a sentence-pair classification task by appending an additional sentence to the initial text.

The sentence-single model represents a vanilla BERT with an additional single linear layer on the top. The unique token *[CLS]* is added for the classification task at the beginning of the sentence. The sentence-pair architecture adds an auxiliary sentence to the original input, inserting the *[SEP]* token between two

---

[2] https://github.com/antongolubev5/Auto-Dataset-For-Transfer-Learning.

sentences. The difference between two models is in addition of a linear layer: for the sentence-pair model it is added over the final hidden state of *[CLS]* token, while for the sentence-single variant it is added on the top of the entire last layer.

For the targeted sentiment analysis task, there are labels for each object of attitude so they can be replaced by a special token *[MASK]*. Since general sentiment analysis problem has no certain attitude objects, token is assigned to the whole sentence and located at the beginning.

The sentence-pair model has two kind of architecture based on question answering (QA) and natural language inference (NLI) problems. The auxiliary sentences for each model are as follows:

- pair-NLI: *"The sentiment polarity of MASK is"*
- pair-QA: *"What do you think about MASK?"*

As a pre-trained model, we use Conversational RuBERT[3] from DeepPavlov framework [4] trained on Russian social networks posts and comments which showed better results in preliminary study.

7   Experiments and Results

In this study, we propose a multistage transfer learning approach consisting in independent sequential training on several samples with intermediate freezing of the model weights. We compare both approaches with the current state-of-the-art results obtained on these datasets [9,24].

7.1   Use of Augmentation

In case of augmentation, we automatically generate a sample based on the initial train data. We use this sample for the first step of proposed multistage approach and continue training on the train data from the benchmark. During the experiment, we studied the dependence of the results on the additional sample size and the distribution of augmented sentences by methods. It was found that with increasing sample size, the results improve too. The boundary between extension of additional data and increasing the results was set at a sample size of 16000 examples with an uniform distribution of sentences between four methods described in Sect. 4. Such distribution showed significantly better results in comparison with augmentation by each method separately.

The results and comparison with state-of-the-art level are presented in Table 2. The use of the augmented sample allowed us to slightly improve the current best results by some metrics.

---

[3] http://docs.deeppavlov.ai/en/master/features/models/bert.html.

Table 2. Results based on use of augmentation

Dataset	Model	Accuracy	F_1 macro	F_1^{+-} macro	F_1^{+-} micro
ROMIP-2013	BERT-single	78.51	69.68	84.19	84.62
	BERT-pair-QA	79.62	70.04	84.57	84.81
	BERT-pair-NLI	**80.87**	**71.04**	85.39	85.54
	Current SOTA	80.28	70.62	**85.52**	**85.68**
SRE-2015 Banks	BERT-single	84.51	77.92	66.55	68.71
	BERT-pair-QA	85.78	78.62	67.11	69.52
	BERT-pair-NLI	86.47	**79.65**	**67.52**	**70.43**
	Current SOTA	**86.88**	79.51	67.44	70.09
SRE-2015 Telecom	BERT-single	75.72	66.71	62.06	66.11
	BERT-pair-QA	76.31	67.53	62.79	66.69
	BERT-pair-NLI	**77.07**	68.28	**63.94**	**67.81**
	Current SOTA	76.63	**68.54**	63.47	67.51
SRE-2016 Banks	BERT-single	80.78	72.46	68.52	70.36
	BERT-pair-QA	81.79	73.04	69.11	71.54
	BERT-pair-NLI	**82.68**	73.87	**69.78**	**72.08**
	Current SOTA	82.28	**74.06**	69.53	71.76
SRE-2016 Telecom	BERT-single	67.28	68.76	64.62	75.67
	BERT-pair-QA	66.87	69.51	65.79	76.12
	BERT-pair-NLI	68.15	**70.89**	66.35	**77.15**
	Current SOTA	–	70.68	**66.40**	76.71

7.2 Use of Distant Supervision

For distant supervision approach, we train models in three steps. At first, the models are trained on the general data, then the weights are frozen and the training continues on the thematic examples retrieved with the list of organizations and NER from DeepPavlov. After the second weights freezing, the last stage of learning on the benchmark train samples begins. This sequence represents the three-step transfer learning approach.

During the second experiment, we also studied the dependence between the results and size of additional sample. The optimal dataset size was set at a number of 27000: the first step sample contains 18000 general examples and the second sample consists of 9000 thematic examples (both are equally balanced across sentiment classes).

The use of three-step approach combined with addition of sentiment thematic contexts to the sample, improved the results by a few more points. New state-of-the-art results as well as comparison with manual labelling for SentiRuEval-2015 Telecom dataset are presented in Table 3. According to the organizers of evaluation, one participant sent the results of manual annotation of the test sample [15]. As it can be seen, BERT-pair-NLI model reaches human sentiment analysis level by F_1^{+-} micro metric.

Table 3. Results based on distant supervision

Dataset	Model	Accuracy	F_1 macro	F_1^{+-} macro	F_1^{+-} micro
ROMIP-2013	BERT-single	80.27	71.78	85.82	86.07
	BERT-pair-QA	80.78	72.09	86.14	86.42
	BERT-pair-NLI	**82.33**	**72.69**	**86.77**	**87.04**
	Current SOTA	80.28	70.62	85.52	85.68
SRE-2015 Banks	BERT-single	87.65	80.79	65.74	67.46
	BERT-pair-QA	87.92	81.12	66.47	68.55
	BERT-pair-NLI	**88.14**	**81.63**	**68.76**	**72.28**
	Current SOTA	86.88	79.51	67.44	70.09
SRE-2015 Telecom	BERT-single	77.85	70.42	62.29	67.38
	BERT-pair-QA	**79.21**	70.94	65.68	69.11
	BERT-pair-NLI	79.12	**71.16**	**65.71**	**70.65**
	Current SOTA	76.63	68.54	63.47	67.51
	Manual	–	–	70.30	70.90
SRE-2016 Banks	BERT-single	83.21	75.31	68.45	71.69
	BERT-pair-QA	**85.59**	**78.93**	**74.05**	**75.12**
	BERT-pair-NLI	85.43	76.85	70.23	72.07
	Current SOTA	82.28	74.06	69.53	71.76
SRE-2016 Telecom	BERT-single	76.79	70.64	66.16	75.27
	BERT-pair-QA	78.42	70.54	**68.65**	**77.45**
	BERT-pair-NLI	**78.62**	**71.18**	69.36	76.85
	Current SOTA	–	70.68	66.40	76.71

7.3 Difficult Examples

Some examples are still difficult for the improved models. For example, the following negative sarcastic examples were erroneously classified by all models as neutral:

– *Sberbank of Russia – 170 years on the queue market!*;
– *While we are waiting for a Sberbank employee, I could have gone to lunch 3 times.*

In the following example with different sentiments towards two mobile operators, the models could not detect the positive attitude towards the Beeline operator:

– *MTS does not work! Forever out of reach. The connection is constantly interrupted. We transfer the whole family to Beeline.*

As an experiment, we decided to study how models trained on additional samples created separately by each augmentation method cope with these examples. The only augmentation approach that correctly processed some of difficult examples was the synonym replacement technique, which successfully solved the first two examples from the list above. This can be possibly explained by the fact that during the augmentation, words with a sarcastic connotation are replaced by more transparent ones for the model, which makes it possible to classify difficult examples correctly.

8   Conclusion

In this study, we presented a method for automatic generation of an annotated sample from a news corpus using the distant supervision technique and compared it to existing augmentation techniques. We tested different options of combining the additional data with several Russian sentiment analysis benchmarks and improved current state-of-the-art results by more than 3% using BERT models together with the transfer learning approach of sequential training on general, thematic and benchmark train samples with intermediate freezing of the model weights. On one of the benchmarks, the BERT-NLI model treating a sentiment classification problem as a natural language inference task, reached human level according to one of the metrics.

Acknowledgments. The reported study was funded by RFBR according to the research project № 20-07-01059.

References

1. Amigó, E., et al.: Overview of RepLab 2013: evaluating online reputation monitoring systems. In: Forner, P., Müller, H., Paredes, R., Rosso, P., Stein, B. (eds.) CLEF 2013. LNCS, vol. 8138, pp. 333–352. Springer, Heidelberg (2013). https://doi.org/10.1007/978-3-642-40802-1_31

2. Baymurzina, D., Kuznetsov, D., Burtsev, M.: Language model embeddings improve sentiment analysis in Russian. In: Komp'juternaja Lingvistika i Intellektual'nye Tehnologii, pp. 53–62 (2019)

3. Bird, S., Klein, E., Loper, E.: Natural Language Processing with Python. O'reilly Media Inc., Sebastopol (2009)

4. Burtsev, M.: DeepPavlov: open-source library for dialogue systems. In: Proceedings of ACL 2018, System Demonstrations, pp. 122–127 (2018)

5. Chetviorkin, I., Loukachevitch, N.: Evaluating sentiment analysis systems in Russian. In: Proceedings of the 4th Biennial International Workshop on Balto-Slavic Natural Language Processing, pp. 12–17 (2013)

6. Devlin, J., Chang, M.W., Lee, K., Toutanova, K.: BERT: pre-training of deep bidirectional transformers for language understanding. arXiv preprint arXiv:1810.04805 (2018)

7. Duong, H.-T., Nguyen-Thi, T.-A.: A review: preprocessing techniques and data augmentation for sentiment analysis. Comput. Soc. Netw. 8(1), 1–16 (2020). https://doi.org/10.1186/s40649-020-00080-x

8. Go, A., Bhayani, R., Huang, L.: Twitter sentiment classification using distant supervision. CS224N project report, Stanford 1(12), 2009 (2009)

9. Golubev, A., Loukachevitch, N.: Improving results on Russian sentiment datasets. In: Filchenkov, A., Kauttonen, J., Pivovarova, L. (eds.) AINL 2020. CCIS, vol. 1292, pp. 109–121. Springer, Cham (2020). https://doi.org/10.1007/978-3-030-59082-6_8

10. Honnibal, M., Montani, I., Van Landeghem, S., Boyd, A.: SpaCy: industrial-strength natural language processing in python. Zenodo (2020). https://doi.org/10.5281/zenodo.1212303
11. Kobayashi, S.: Contextual augmentation: data augmentation by words with paradigmatic relations. In: Proceedings of the 2018 Conference of the North American Chapter of the Association for Computational Linguistics: Human Language Technologies (Short Papers), vol. 2, pp. 452–457 (2018)
12. Loukachevitch, N., Dobrov, B.V.: RuTHes linguistic ontology vs. Russian wordnets. In: Proceedings of the Seventh Global Wordnet Conference, pp. 154–162 (2014)
13. Loukachevitch, N., Levchik, A.: Creating a general Russian sentiment lexicon. In: Proceedings of the Tenth International Conference on Language Resources and Evaluation (LREC 2016), pp. 1171–1176 (2016)
14. Loukachevitch, N., Rubtsova, Y.: Entity-oriented sentiment analysis of tweets: results and problems. In: Král, P., Matoušek, V. (eds.) TSD 2015. LNCS (LNAI), vol. 9302, pp. 551–559. Springer, Cham (2015). https://doi.org/10.1007/978-3-319-24033-6_62
15. Loukachevitch, N., Rubtsova, Y.: SentiRuEval-2016: overcoming time gap and data sparsity in tweet sentiment analysis. In: Proceedings of International Conference Dialog-2016 (2016)
16. Miller, G.A.: Wordnet: a lexical database for English. Commun. ACM 38(11), 39–41 (1995)
17. Mohammad, S., Salameh, M., Kiritchenko, S.: Sentiment lexicons for Arabic social media. In: Proceedings of the Tenth International Conference on Language Resources and Evaluation (LREC 2016), pp. 33–37 (2016)
18. Moshkin, V., Konstantinov, A., Yarushkina, N.: Application of the BERT language model for sentiment analysis of social network posts. In: Kuznetsov, S.O., Panov, A.I., Yakovlev, K.S. (eds.) RCAI 2020. LNCS (LNAI), vol. 12412, pp. 274–283. Springer, Cham (2020). https://doi.org/10.1007/978-3-030-59535-7_20
19. Rogers, A., Romanov, A., Rumshisky, A., Volkova, S., Gronas, M., Gribov, A.: RuSentiment: an enriched sentiment analysis dataset for social media in Russian. In: Proceedings of the 27th International Conference on Computational Linguistics, pp. 755–763 (2018)
20. Rubtsova, Y.: Constructing a corpus for sentiment classification training. Softw. Syst. 109, 72–78 (2015)
21. Rusnachenko, N., Loukachevitch, N., Tutubalina, E.: Distant supervision for sentiment attitude extraction. In: Proceedings of the International Conference on Recent Advances in Natural Language Processing (RANLP 2019), pp. 1022–1030 (2019)
22. Sahni, T., Chandak, C., Chedeti, N.R., Singh, M.: Efficient twitter sentiment classification using subjective distant supervision. In: 2017 9th International Conference on Communication Systems and Networks (COMSNETS), pp. 548–553. IEEE (2017)
23. Smetanin, S., Komarov, M.: Sentiment analysis of product reviews in Russian using convolutional neural networks. In: 2019 IEEE 21st Conference on Business Informatics (CBI), vol. 1, pp. 482–486. IEEE (2019)
24. Smetanin, S., Komarov, M.: Deep transfer learning baselines for sentiment analysis in Russian. Inf. Process. Manage. 58(3), 102484 (2021)
25. Sun, C., Huang, L., Qiu, X.: Utilizing BERT for aspect-based sentiment analysis via constructing auxiliary sentence. In: Proceedings of the 2019 Conference of the North American Chapter of the Association for Computational Linguistics: Human Language Technologies, vol. 1, pp. 380–385 (2019)

26. Wang, W.Y., Yang, D.: That's so annoying!!!: A lexical and frame-semantic embedding based data augmentation approach to automatic categorization of annoying behaviors using# petpeeve tweets. In: Proceedings of the 2015 Conference on Empirical Methods in Natural Language Processing, pp. 2557–2563 (2015)
27. Wei, J., Zou, K.: EDA: easy data augmentation techniques for boosting performance on text classification tasks. In: Proceedings of the 2019 Conference on Empirical Methods in Natural Language Processing and the 9th International Joint Conference on Natural Language Processing (EMNLP-IJCNLP), pp. 6383–6389 (2019)
28. Zhuang, F., et al.: A comprehensive survey on transfer learning. Proc. IEEE **109**(1), 43–76 (2020)

RobeCzech: Czech RoBERTa, a Monolingual Contextualized Language Representation Model

Milan Straka(✉)⬭, Jakub Náplava⬭, Jana Straková⬭, and David Samuel⬭

Faculty of Mathematics and Physics, Institute of Formal and Applied Linguistics, Charles University, Malostranské nám. 25, Prague 118 00, Czech Republic
{straka,naplava,strakova,samuel}@ufal.mff.cuni.cz

Abstract. We present RobeCzech, a monolingual RoBERTa language representation model trained on Czech data. RoBERTa is a robustly optimized Transformer-based pretraining approach. We show that RobeCzech considerably outperforms equally-sized multilingual and Czech-trained contextualized language representation models, surpasses current state of the art in all five evaluated NLP tasks and reaches state-of-the-art results in four of them. The RobeCzech model is released publicly at https://hdl.handle.net/11234/1-3691 and https://huggingface.co/ufal/robeczech-base.

Keywords: RobeCzech · Czech RoBERTa · RoBERTa

1 Introduction

We introduce RobeCzech: Czech RoBERTa, a Czech contextualized language representation model based on the Transformer architecture and trained solely on Czech data. RobeCzech is a monolingual version of RoBERTa [23], a robustly optimized BERT [8] pretraining approach.

In this paper, we describe the RobeCzech training process and we evaluate RobeCzech in comparison with current multilingual and Czech-trained contextualized language representation models: multilingual BERT [8], multilingual XLM-RoBERTa [6] (base and large), Slavic BERT [1] tuned on 4 Slavic languages, including Czech; and Czert [36], another monolingual, Czech BERT model.

We show that RobeCzech considerably outperforms all models of similar size, and at the same time, it reaches new state-of-the-art results in four NLP tasks: morphological tagging and lemmatization, dependency parsing, named entity recognition and semantic parsing. In the last evaluated task, the sentiment analysis, RobeCzech also improves over state of the art and delivers the best results of all models of similar size, only being surpassed by XLM-RoBERTa large [6], a model 4 times the size of all the other evaluated models (Table 1).

We release the RobeCzech model for public use.

ⓒ Springer Nature Switzerland AG 2021
K. Ekštein et al. (Eds.): TSD 2021, LNAI 12848, pp. 197–209, 2021.
https://doi.org/10.1007/978-3-030-83527-9_17

2   Related Work

Contextualized language representation models have recently accelerated progress in NLP. Significant advances have been reached particularly with Bidirectional Encoder Representations from Transformers, widely known as BERT [8], inspiring interest in Transformer-like architectures. We especially highlight RoBERTa [23] and its derivation XLM-RoBERTa [6].

The above mentioned language representation models were trained either only on English or as multilingual, though with an (implicit) strength in the most represented languages (i.e., English). Therefore, research has recently been focusing on monolingual BERT models, giving birth to national BERT mutations, e.g. French [26], Finnish [43], Romanian [27] and Czech [36].

Our model is similar to the above mentioned Czert [36] in the sense that it is also a Czech contextualized language representation model, but unlike Czert, which is based on BERT, we trained a Czech version of RoBERTa. According to both the original Czert results [36] and the hereby presented evaluation on five NLP tasks, RobeCzech is better than Czert in all experiments by a considerable margin.

3   Training the Czech RoBERTa

We trained RobeCzech on a collection of the following publicly available texts:

- SYN v4 [21], a large corpus of contemporary written Czech, 4,188M tokens;
- Czes [7], a collection of Czech newspaper and magazine articles, 432M tokens;
- documents with at least 400 tokens from the Czech part of the web corpus W2C [24,25], tokenized with MorphoDiTa [42], 16M tokens;
- plain texts extracted from Czech Wikipedia dump 20201020 using WikiExtractor,[1] tokenized with MorphoDiTa [42], 123M tokens.

All these corpora contain whole documents, even if the SYN v4 is block-shuffled (blocks with at most 100 words respecting sentence boundaries are permuted in a document) and in total contain 4,917M tokens.

The texts are tokenized into subwords with a byte-level BPE (BBPE) tokenizer [33]. The tokenizer is trained on the entire corpus and we limit its vocabulary size to 52,000 items.

The RobeCzech model is trained using the official code released in the Fairseq library.[2] The training batch size is 8,192 and each training batch consists of sentences sampled contiguously, even across document boundaries, such that the total length of each sample is at most 512 tokens (*FULL-SENTENCES* setting [23]). We use Adam optimizer [16] with $\beta_1 = 0.9$ and $\beta_2 = 0.98$ to minimize the masked language-modeling objective. The learning rate is adapted using the polynomial decay schema with 10,000 warmup updates and the peak learning rate set to $7 \cdot 10^{-4}$. A total amount of 91,075 optimization steps were performed, which took approximately 3 months on 8 QUADRO P5000 GPU cards.

---

[1] https://github.com/attardi/wikiextractor.
[2] https://github.com/pytorch/fairseq/blob/master/examples/roberta/.

4   Evaluation Tasks

We evaluate our Czech RoBERTa model on five NLP tasks in comparison with a variety of recently proposed mono- and multi-lingual contextualized language representation models (to our best knowledge, these are all publicly available models trained at least partially on Czech):

Table 1. Number of parameters.

Model	Embedding	Transformer	Total parameters
mBERT uncased	82M	85M	167M
Czert	24M	85M	109M
Slavic BERT	92M	85M	177M
XLM-R base	192M	85M	277M
XLM-R large	257M	302M	559M
RobeCzech	40M	85M	125M

- **mBERT** [8]: well-known multilingual BERT language representation model.
- **Czert** [36]: the first Czech monolingual model based on BERT.
- **Slavic BERT** [1]: multilingual BERT tuned specifically for NER on 4 Slavic languages data (Russian, Bulgarian, Czech and Polish).
- **XLM-RoBERTa** [6], **base and large:** multilingual contextualized representations trained at large scale.

Except for XLM-RoBERTa large, which is 4 times larger than others, all models are of *base* size [8], see Table 1.

We evaluate RobeCzech in five NLP tasks, three of them leveraging frozen contextualized word embeddings, two approached with fine-tuning:

- **morphological analysis and lemmatization:** frozen contextualized word embeddings,
- **dependency parsing**: frozen contextualized word embeddings,
- **named entity recognition:** frozen contextualized word embeddings,
- **semantic parsing:** fine-tuned,
- **sentiment analysis:** fine-tuned.

4.1   Morphological Tagging and Lemmatization on PDT 3.5

Dataset. We evaluate the morphological POS tagging and lemmatization on the morphological layer of the *Prague Dependency Treebank 3.5* [14].

Metric. The morphological POS tagging and lemmatization is evaluated using accuracy.

Architecture. We adopt the *UDPipe 2* architecture [38], reproducing the methodology of [39]. After embedding input words, three bidirectional LSTM layers [15] are applied, followed by a softmax classification layer for POS and lemmas. In case of lemmas, the network predicts a simple edit script from input form to desired lemma. Since edit patterns are shared between lemmas due to regularities in morphology, the output categorization layer is reduced from the full vocabulary to only 1568 classes (in PDT 3.5 [14]). In all our experiments, we use the same word embeddings as [39]: pretrained `word2vec` embeddings [28], end-to-end word embeddings and character-level word embeddings [5,11,22]. The contextualized word embeddings are used frozen-style as additional inputs to the neural network.

4.2 Dependency Parsing on PDT 3.5

Dataset. We evaluate the dependency parsing on the analytical layer of the *Prague Dependency Treebank 3.5* [14].

Metric. In evaluation, we compute both the unlabeled attachment score (UAS) and labeled attachment score (LAS).

Architecture. We perform dependency parsing jointly with POS tagging and lemmatization, following the experiments of [39] showing that this approach is superior to using predicted POS tags and lemmas on input. We utilize the *UDPipe 2* architecture [39]: after embeddings input words and three bidirectional LSTM layers [15], a biaffine attention layer [10] produces labeled dependency trees. The input word embeddings are the same as in the previous Sect. 4.1 and the contextualized word embeddings are additionally concatenated to the baseline input.

4.3 Morphosyntactic Analysis on Universal Dependencies

Dataset. We further evaluate the joint morphosyntactic analysis on the *UD Czech PDT* treebank of the *Universal Dependencies 2.3* [30].

Metric. We use the standard evaluation script from *CoNLL 2018 Shared Task: Multilingual Parsing from Raw Text to Universal Dependencies* [45], which produces the following metrics:

- **UPOS** – universal POS tags accuracy,
- **XPOS** – language-specific POS tags accuracy,
- **UFeats** – universal subset of morphological features accuracy,
- **Lemmas** – lemmatization accuracy,
- **UAS** – unlabeled attachment score, **LAS** – labeled attachment score,
- **MLAS** – morphology-aware LAS, **BLEX** – bi-lexical dependency score.

Architecture. Following Sect. 4.2, we employ the *UDPipe 2* [39] architecture with frozen contextualized word embeddings.

4.4 Named Entity Recognition

Dataset. We evaluate the Czech NER on all versions of the *Czech Named Entity Corpus*, both the original [35] with nested entities and the CoNLL version [19] with reduction to flat entities only.

Metric. The standard evaluation metric for NER is F1 score computed over detected named entities spans.

Architecture. We reproduce the current NER SoTA architecture [40], using the *LSTM-CRF* and *seq2seq* variants for flat and nested NER, respectively. All experiments include the Czech FastText word embeddings [4] of dimension 300, end-to-end trained word embeddings and character-level word embeddings [5,11,22] as inputs to the network. The contextualized word embeddings are used as frozen, additional inputs to the network.

4.5 Semantic Parsing on Prague Tectogrammatical Graphs

Dataset. We use the *Prague Tectogrammatical Graphs* (PTG) provided for the CoNLL 2020 shared task, *Cross-Framework Meaning Representation Parsing* (MRP 2020) [31]. The original annotation comes from the tectogrammatical layer of the *Prague Dependency Treebank* [14]; the graphs for the shared task were obtained by relaxing its original limitation to trees – for example by explicitly modeling co-reference by additional edges instead of special node attributes [44].

Metric. We employ the official metric from MRP 2020, which first finds the maximum common edge subgraph to align the evaluated and the target graph. Then, it computes the micro-averaged F1 score over different features of the semantic graphs – top nodes, node labels, node properties, anchors, edges between nodes and edge attributes.

Architecture. We reimplement the current SoTA architecture for PTG parsing called *PERIN* [34]. This model does not assume any hard-coded ordering of the graph nodes, but instead dynamically finds the best matching between the predicted and the target ones.

Following *UDify* [17], we compute the contextualized subword embedding by taking the weighted sum of all hidden layers in a language representation model. The scalar weight for each layer is a learnable parameter. To obtain a single embedding for every token, we sum the embeddings of all its subwords. Finally, the summed embeddings are normalized with layer normalization [3] to stabilize the training.

The pretrained encoder is finetuned with a lower learning rate than the rest of the model. The learning rate follows the inverse square root schedule with warmup and is frozen for the first 2000 steps before the warmup starts. The warmup phase takes 6000 steps and the learning rate peak is $6 \cdot 10^{-5}$.

4.6   Sentiment Analysis

Dataset. We evaluate sentiment analysis on Czech Facebook dataset (CFD) [12, 13]. This dataset contains 2,587 positive, 5,174 neutral and 1,991 negative posts (the 248 bipolar posts are ignored, following [13,36]).

Metric. The performance is evaluated using macro-averaged F1 score. Because the dataset has no designed test set, we follow the approach of the dataset authors [13] and perform 10-fold cross-validation, reporting mean and standard deviation of the folds' F1 scores.

Architecture. We employ the standard text classification architecture consisting of a BERT encoder, followed by a softmax-activated classification layer processing the computed embedding of the given document text obtained from the CLS token embedding from the last layer [8,23].

We train the models using a lazy variant of the Adam optimizer [16] with a batch size of 64. During the first epoch, the BERT encoder is frozen and only the classifier is trained with the default learning rate of 10^{-3}. From the second epoch, the whole model is updated, starting by 4 epochs of cosine warm-up from zero to a specified peak learning rate, followed by 10 epochs of cosine decay back to zero.

Table 2. Overall results.

	Morphosynt.		Morphosynt.		NER		Semant.	Sentim.
	PDT3.5		UD2.3		CNEC1.1		PTG	CFD
	POS	LAS	XPOS	LAS	Nested	Flat	Avg.	F1
mBERT	98.00	89.74	97.61	92.34	86.71	86.45	90.62	75.43
Czert	98.43	90.68	98.07	93.13	85.38	84.69	90.66	78.52
Slavic BERT	97.70	88.50	97.29	91.49	85.85	85.12	91.27	74.85
XLM-R base	97.62	88.14	97.29	91.30	83.25	82.76	91.55	79.40
XLM-R large	98.41	91.27	98.15	93.49	87.41	86.86	92.11	**82.29**
RobeCzech	**98.50**	**91.42**	**98.31**	**93.77**	**87.82**	**87.47**	**92.36**	80.13
Previous SoTA	98.05	89.89	97.71	93.38	86.88	86.57	92.24	76.55

We consider peak learning rates $10^{-5}, 2 \cdot 10^{-5}, 3 \cdot 10^{-5}$ and $5 \cdot 10^{-5}$. In order to choose the peak learning rate, we put aside random 10% of the train data for each fold as a development set and evaluate each trained model on its corresponding development set. Finally, we choose a single peak learning rate for every model according to the 10-fold means of the development macro-averaged F1 scores. The selected peak learning rates are reported for each evaluated model.

Table 3. Morphological tagging and lemmatization on PDT3.5.

Model	Without dictionary			With dictionary		
	POS	Lemmas	Both	POS	Lemmas	Both
mBERT	97.86	98.69	97.21	98.00	98.96	97.59
Czert	98.30	98.73	97.65	98.43	98.98	98.02
Slavic BERT	97.51	98.58	96.81	97.70	98.89	97.27
XLM-R base	97.43	98.56	96.76	97.62	98.85	97.20
XLM-R large	98.30	98.76	97.69	98.41	98.98	98.01
RobeCzech	**98.43**	**98.79**	**97.83**	**98.50**	**99.00**	**98.11**
Morče (2009) [37]	–	–	–	95.67	–	–
MorphoDiTa (2016) [42]	–	–	–	95.55	97.85	95.06
LemmaTag (2018) [18]	96.90	98.37	–	–	–	–
UDPipe 2+mBERT+Flair [39]	97.94	98.75	97.31	98.05	98.98	97.65

Table 4. Dependency parsing on PDT3.5.

Model	UAS	LAS	Joint POS	Joint Lemmas
mBERT	93.01	89.74	*97.62*	*98.49*
Czert	93.57	90.68	*98.10*	*98.53*
Slavic BERT	92.14	88.50	*97.20*	*98.29*
XLM-R base	91.80	88.14	*97.22*	*98.34*
XLM-R large	94.07	91.27	*98.12*	*98.54*
RobeCzech	**94.14**	**91.42**	*98.28*	*98.62*
UDPipe 2+mBERT+Flair [39]	93.07	89.89	*97.72*	*98.51*

5 Results

Table 2 summarizes the overall results of all considered language representation models in all evaluated tasks. RobeCzech improves over current state of the art in all five evaluated NLP tasks, and at the same time, clearly outperforms

Table 5. Morphosyntactic analysis on UD 2.3. Models marked^f are fine-tuned, otherwise with frozen embeddings.

Model	UPOS	XPOS	UFeats	Lemmas	UAS	LAS	MLAS	BLEX
mBERT	99.31	97.61	97.55	99.06	94.27	92.34	87.75	89.91
Czert	99.32	98.07	98.05	99.09	94.75	93.13	89.19	90.92
Slavic BERT	99.22	97.29	97.22	98.99	93.53	91.49	86.37	88.79
XLM-R base	99.18	97.29	97.24	99.02	93.32	91.30	86.18	88.62
XLM-R large	99.36	98.15	98.10	99.17	95.15	93.49	89.64	91.40
RobeCzech	**99.36**	**98.31**	**98.28**	**99.18**	**95.36**	**93.77**	**90.18**	**91.82**
UDPipe 2 +mBERT+Flair [39]	99.34	97.71	97.67	99.12	94.43	92.56	88.09	90.22
UDify^f [17]	99.24	–	94.77	98.93	95.07	93.38	–	–
Czert^f [36]	99.30	–	–	–	–	–	–	–

Table 6. Named entity recognition F1 scores (3 runs average) in comparison with previous reports. Models marked^f are fine-tuned, otherwise with frozen embeddings.

Model	CNEC1.1	CNEC2.0	CoNLL CNEC1.1	CoNLL CNEC2.0
mBERT	86.71	84.21	86.45	87.04
Czert	85.38	82.84	84.69	85.33
Slavic BERT	85.85	82.71	85.12	85.28
XLM-R base	83.25	80.33	82.76	82.85
XLM-R large	87.41	84.46	86.86	87.06
RobeCzech	**87.82**	**85.51**	**87.47**	**87.49**
seq2seq+mBERT [39,40]	86.73	84.66	–	–
seq2seq+mBERT+Flair [39,40]	86.88	84.27	–	–
LSTM-CRF, LDA [20]	–	–	81.77	–
LSTM-CRF [41]	83.15	–	83.27	84.22
LSTM-CRF+BERT [29]	–	–	–	86.39
Czert^f [36]	–	–	86.27	–
mBERT^f [8], by [36]	–	–	86.23	–
Slavic BERT^f [1], by [36]	–	–	86.57	–

Table 7. Semantic parsing F1 scores on prague tectogrammatical graphs.

Model	Labels	Properties	Anchors	Edges	Attributes	Average
mBERT	95.72	92.60	97.20	80.77	72.83	90.62
Czert	95.72	92.69	97.23	80.91	72.37	90.66
Slavic BERT	95.92	92.91	97.51	82.48	75.08	91.27
XLM-R base	96.09	93.12	97.60	83.03	76.16	91.55
XLM-R large	96.42	93.31	97.92	84.46	77.89	92.11
RobeCzech frozen	95.85	92.76	97.41	82.60	74.95	91.23
RobeCzech	**96.57**	**93.58**	**97.97**	**84.92**	**78.29**	**92.36**
HUJI-KU+mBERT [2]	–	72.44	72.10	44.91	–	58.49
HIT-SCIR+mBERT [9]	84.14	79.01	92.34	64.96	47.68	77.93
Hitachi+mBERT [32]	87.69	91.48	93.99	76.90	66.07	87.35
ÚFAL+XLM-R large [34]	96.23	93.56	97.86	84.61	78.62	92.24

Table 8. Sentiment analysis 10-fold macro F1 scores on Czech Facebook dataset.

Model	10-fold Macro F1	10-fold Std	Chosen LR
mBERT	75.43	±1.38	$5 \cdot 10^{-5}$
Czert	78.52	±1.16	$2 \cdot 10^{-5}$
Slavic BERT	74.85	±1.27	$5 \cdot 10^{-5}$
XLM-R base	79.40	±1.07	$1 \cdot 10^{-5}$
XLM-R large	**82.29**	±1.19	$1 \cdot 10^{-5}$
RobeCzech	80.13	±1.21	$3 \cdot 10^{-5}$
Czert [36]	76.55	–	$3 \cdot 10^{-6}$
MaxEnt [13]	69.4	–	–

current multilingual and Czech-trained contextualized language representation models, being surpassed only in one of the five tasks by a model 4 times its size (XLM-RoBERTa large [6], Table 2). Notably, RobeCzech reaches 25% error reduction in POS tagging both on PDT 3.5 and UD 2.3, and 15% error reduction in dependency parsing on PDT 3.5, significantly improving performance of Czech morphosyntactic analysis.

Furthermore, for each of the evaluated tasks, we show the detailed results in Tables 3, 4, 5, 6, 7 and 8.

The results demonstrate that the large variant of XLM-RoBERTa reaches considerably better results compared to base size of other multilingual models. Yet, RobeCzech still surpasses it on four tasks, most notably in the frozen scenario. We hypothesize that in the frozen scenario the larger model cannot capitalize on its superior capacity, compared to for example sentiment analysis, where its capacity proves determining.

6   Conclusion

We introduced RobeCzech, a Czech contextualized language representation model based on RoBERTa. We described the training process and we evaluated RobeCzech in comparison with, to our best knowledge, currently known multilingual and Czech-trained contextualized language representation models. We show that RobeCzech considerably improves over state of the art in all five evaluated NLP tasks. Notably, it yields 25% error reduction in POS tagging both on PDT 3.5 and UD 2.3 and 15% error reduction in dependency parsing on PDT 3.5. We publish RobeCzech publicly at https://hdl.handle.net/11234/1-3691 and https://huggingface.co/ufal/robeczech-base.

Acknowledgements. The research described herein has been supported by the Czech Science Foundation grant No. GX20-16819X, Mellon Foundation Award No. G-1901-06505 and by the Grant Agency of Charles University 578218. The resources used have been provided by the LINDAT/CLARIAH-CZ Research Infrastructure, project No. LM2018101 of the Ministry of Education, Youth and Sports of the Czech Republic.

References

1. Arkhipov, M., Trofimova, M., Kuratov, Y., Sorokin, A.: Tuning multilingual trans-formers for language-specific named entity recognition. In: Proceedings of the 7th Workshop on Balto-Slavic Natural Language Processing, pp. 89–93. Association for Computational Linguistics, Florence, August 2019
2. Arviv, O., Cui, R., Hershcovich, D.: HUJI-KU at MRP 2020: two transition-based neural parsers. In: Proceedings of the CoNLL 2020 Shared Task: Cross-Framework Meaning Representation Parsing, pp. 73–82. Association for Computational Linguistics, November 2020. https://doi.org/10.18653/v1/2020.conll-shared.7
3. Ba, J.L., Kiros, J.R., Hinton, G.E.: Layer normalization. arXiv preprint arXiv:1607.06450 (2016)
4. Bojanowski, P., Grave, E., Joulin, A., Mikolov, T.: Enriching word vectors with subword information. Trans. Assoc. Comput. Linguist. **5**, 135–146 (2017)
5. Cho, K., van Merrienboer, B., Bahdanau, D., Bengio, Y.: On the properties of neural machine translation: encoder-decoder approaches. CoRR (2014)
6. Conneau, A., et al.: Unsupervised cross-lingual representation learning at scale. In: Proceedings of the 58th Annual Meeting of the Association for Computational Linguistics, pp. 8440–8451. Association for Computational Linguistics, July 2020
7. Czes (2011). http://hdl.handle.net/11858/00-097C-0000-0001-CCCF-C. LINDAT/CLARIAH-CZ digital library at the Institute of Formal and Applied Linguistics (ÚFAL), Faculty of Mathematics and Physics, Charles University
8. Devlin, J., Chang, M.W., Lee, K., Toutanova, K.: BERT: pre-training of deep bidirectional transformers for language understanding. In: Proceedings of the 2019 Conference of the North American Chapter of the Association for Computational Linguistics: Human Language Technologies, Volume 1 (Long and Short Papers), pp. 4171–4186 (2019)
9. Dou, L., Feng, Y., Ji, Y., Che, W., Liu, T.: HIT-SCIR at MRP 2020: transition-based parser and iterative inference parser. In: Proceedings of the CoNLL 2020 Shared Task: Cross-framework Meaning Representation Parsing, pp. 65–72. Association for Computational Linguistics, November 2020. https://doi.org/10.18653/v1/2020.conll-shared.6
10. Dozat, T., Manning, C.D.: Deep biaffine attention for neural dependency parsing. CoRR abs/1611.01734 (2016)
11. Graves, A., Schmidhuber, J.: Framewise phoneme classification with bidirectional LSTM and other neural network architectures. Neural Netw. **18**, 602–610 (2005)
12. Habernal, I., Ptáček, T., Steinberger, J.: Facebook data for sentiment analysis (2013). http://hdl.handle.net/11858/00-097C-0000-0022-FE82-7. LINDAT/CLARIAH-CZ digital library at the Institute of Formal and Applied Linguistics (ÚFAL), Faculty of Mathematics and Physics, Charles University
13. Habernal, I., Ptáček, T., Steinberger, J.: Sentiment analysis in Czech social media using supervised machine learning. In: Proceedings of the 4th Workshop on Computational Approaches to Subjectivity, Sentiment and Social Media Analysis, Atlanta, Georgia, pp. 65–74. Association for Computational Linguistics, June 2013
14. Hajič, J., et al.: Prague Dependency Treebank 3.5 (2018). http://hdl.handle.net/11234/1-2621. LINDAT/CLARIN digital library at the Institute of Formal and Applied Linguistics (ÚFAL), Faculty of Mathematics and Physics, Charles University
15. Hochreiter, S., Schmidhuber, J.: Long short-term memory. Neural Comput. **9**(8), 1735–1780 (1997)

16. Kingma, D., Ba, J.: Adam: a method for stochastic optimization. In: International Conference on Learning Representations, December 2014
17. Kondratyuk, D., Straka, M.: 75 languages, 1 model: parsing universal dependencies universally. In: Proceedings of the 2019 Conference on Empirical Methods in Natural Language Processing and the 9th International Joint Conference on Natural Language Processing (EMNLP-IJCNLP), Hong Kong, China, pp. 2779–2795. Association for Computational Linguistics, November 2019. https://doi.org/10.18653/v1/D19-1279
18. Kondratyuk, D., Gavenčiak, T., Straka, M., Hajič, J.: LemmaTag: jointly tagging and lemmatizing for morphologically rich languages with BRNNs. In: Proceedings of the 2018 Conference on Empirical Methods in Natural Language Processing, pp. 4921–4928. Association for Computational Linguistics (2018)
19. Konkol, M., Konopík, M.: CRF-based Czech named entity recognizer and consolidation of Czech NER research. In: Habernal, I., Matoušek, V. (eds.) TSD 2013. LNCS (LNAI), vol. 8082, pp. 153–160. Springer, Heidelberg (2013). https://doi.org/10.1007/978-3-642-40585-3_20
20. Konopík, M., Pražák, O.: LDA in character-LSTM-CRF named entity recognition. In: Sojka, P., Horák, A., Kopeček, I., Pala, K. (eds.) TSD 2018. LNCS (LNAI), vol. 11107, pp. 58–66. Springer, Cham (2018). https://doi.org/10.1007/978-3-030-00794-2_6
21. Křen, M., et al.: SYN v4: large corpus of written Czech (2016). http://hdl.handle.net/11234/1-1846. LINDAT/CLARIAH-CZ digital library at the Institute of Formal and Applied Linguistics (ÚFAL), Faculty of Mathematics and Physics, Charles University
22. Ling, W., et al.: Finding function in form: compositional character models for open vocabulary word representation. CoRR (2015)
23. Liu, Y., et al.: RoBERTa: a robustly optimized BERT pretraining approach. CoRR abs/1907.11692 (2019)
24. Majliš, M.: W2C - Web to Corpus - Corpora (2011). http://hdl.handle.net/11858/00-097C-0000-0022-6133-9. LINDAT/CLARIAH-CZ digital library at the Institute of Formal and Applied Linguistics (ÚFAL), Faculty of Mathematics and Physics, Charles University
25. Majliš, M., Žabokrtský, Z.: Language richness of the web. In: Proceedings of the Eighth International Conference on Language Resources and Evaluation (LREC 2012), Istanbul, Turkey, pp. 2927–2934. European Language Resources Association (ELRA), May 2012
26. Martin, L., et al.: CamemBERT: a tasty French language model. In: Proceedings of the 58th Annual Meeting of the Association for Computational Linguistics, pp. 7203–7219. Association for Computational Linguistics, July 2020
27. Masala, M., Ruseti, S., Dascalu, M.: RoBERT - a Romanian BERT model. In: Proceedings of the 28th International Conference on Computational Linguistics, Barcelona, Spain, pp. 6626–6637. International Committee on Computational Linguistics, December 2020
28. Mikolov, T., Sutskever, I., Chen, K., Corrado, G., Dean, J.: Distributed representations of words and phrases and their compositionality. In: Advances in Neural Information Processing Systems 26, pp. 3111–3119. Curran Associates, Inc. (2013)
29. Müller, Š.: Text summarization using named entity recognition. Master's thesis, Czech Technical University in Prague (2020)
30. Nivre, J., et al.: Universal Dependencies 2.3 (2018). http://hdl.handle.net/11234/1-2895. LINDAT/CLARIN digital library at the Institute of Formal and Applied Linguistics (ÚFAL), Faculty of Mathematics and Physics, Charles University

31. Oepen, S., et al.: MRP 2020: the second shared task on cross-framework and cross-lingual meaning representation parsing. In: Proceedings of the CoNLL 2020 Shared Task: Cross-framework Meaning Representation Parsing, pp. 1–22. Association for Computational Linguistics, November 2020. https://doi.org/10.18653/v1/2020.conll-shared.1

32. Ozaki, H., Morio, G., Koreeda, Y., Morishita, T., Miyoshi, T.: Hitachi at MRP 2020: text-to-graph-notation transducer. In: Proceedings of the CoNLL 2020 Shared Task: Cross-framework Meaning Representation Parsing, pp. 40–52. Association for Computational Linguistics, November 2020. https://doi.org/10.18653/v1/2020.conll-shared.4

33. Radford, A., Wu, J., Child, R., Luan, D., Amodei, D., Sutskever, I.: Language models are unsupervised multitask learners. OpenAI Blog **1**(8), 9 (2019)

34. Samuel, D., Straka, M.: ÚFAL at MRP 2020: permutation-invariant semantic parsing in PERIN. In: Proceedings of the CoNLL 2020 Shared Task: Cross-Framework Meaning Representation Parsing, pp. 53–64. Association for Computational Linguistics, November 2020

35. Ševčíková, M., Žabokrtský, Z., Krůza, O.: Named entities in Czech: annotating data and developing NE tagger. In: Matoušek, V., Mautner, P. (eds.) TSD 2007. LNCS (LNAI), vol. 4629, pp. 188–195. Springer, Heidelberg (2007). https://doi.org/10.1007/978-3-540-74628-7_26

36. Sido, J., Pražák, O., Přibáň, P., Pašek, J., Seják, M., Konopík, M.: Czert - Czech BERT-like Model for Language Representation (2021). https://arxiv.org/abs/2103.13031

37. Spoustová, D.J., Hajič, J., Raab, J., Spousta, M.: Semi-supervised training for the averaged perceptron POS tagger. In: Proceedings of the 12th Conference of the European Chapter of the ACL (EACL 2009), pp. 763–771. Association for Computational Linguistics, March 2009

38. Straka, M.: UDPipe 2.0 prototype at CoNLL 2018 UD shared task. In: Proceedings of CoNLL 2018: The SIGNLL Conference on Computational Natural Language Learning, Stroudsburg, PA, USA, pp. 197–207. Association for Computational Linguistics (2018)

39. Straka, M., Straková, J., Hajič, J.: Czech text processing with contextual embeddings: POS tagging, lemmatization, parsing and NER. In: Ekštein, K. (ed.) TSD 2019. LNCS (LNAI), vol. 11697, pp. 137–150. Springer, Cham (2019). https://doi.org/10.1007/978-3-030-27947-9_12

40. Straková, J., Straka, M., Hajič, J.: Neural architectures for nested NER through linearization. In: Proceedings of the 57th Annual Meeting of the Association for Computational Linguistics, Stroudsburg, PA, USA, pp. 5326–5331. Association for Computational Linguistics (2019)

41. Straková, J., Straka, M., Hajič, J., Popel, M.: Hluboké učenív automatické analýze českého textu. Slovo a slovesnost **80**(4), 306–327 (2019)

42. Straková, J., Straka, M., Hajič, J.: Open-source tools for morphology, lemmatization, POS tagging and named entity recognition. In: Proceedings of 52nd Annual Meeting of the Association for Computational Linguistics: System Demonstrations, Johns Hopkins University, Baltimore, MD, USA, pp. 13–18. Association for Computational Linguistics (2014)

43. Virtanen, A., et al.: Multilingual is not enough: BERT for Finnish. CoRR abs/1912.07076 (2019)

44. Zeman, D., Hajic, J.: FGD at MRP 2020: prague tectogrammatical graphs. In: Proceedings of the CoNLL 2020 Shared Task: Cross-Framework Meaning Representation Parsing, pp. 33–39. Association for Computational Linguistics, November 2020. https://doi.org/10.18653/v1/2020.conll-shared.3
45. Zeman, D., et al.: CoNLL 2018 shared task: multilingual parsing from raw text to universal dependencies. In: Proceedings of the CoNLL 2018 Shared Task: Multilingual Parsing from Raw Text to Universal Dependencies, Brussels, Belgium, pp. 1–21. Association for Computational Linguistics, October 2018

Labelled EPIE: A Dataset for Idiom Sense Disambiguation

Prateek Saxena$^{(\boxtimes)}$ [iD] and Soma Paul [iD]

International Institute of Information Technology, Hyderabad, India
prateek.saxena@research.iiit.ac.in, soma@iiit.ac.in

Abstract. Natural Language Understanding has made recent advancements where context-aware token representation and word disambiguation have become possible to a large extent. In this scenario, comprehension of phrasal semantics particularly in the context of multi word expressions (MWE) and idioms, is the subsequent task to be addressed. Word level metaphor detection is unable to handle phrases or MWE(s) which occur in both literal and idiomatic context. State of the art transformer architectures can be useful in this context, but the absence of a large comprehensive dataset is a bottleneck. In this paper, we present a labelled EPIE dataset containing 3136 occurrences for 358 formal idioms. To prove the efficacy of our dataset, we also train a sequence classification model effectively and perform cross-dataset evaluation on three independent datasets. Our method achieves good results on all datasets with F1 score of 96% on our test data, and 82%, 74% and 76% F1 score on SemEval All Words, SemEval Lex Sample, and PIE Corpus datasets respectively.

Keywords: Idioms · Idiomatic expressions · Multi-word expressions · Idiomaticity classification

1 Introduction

Idiomatic Expressions have garnered a lot of interest over the years in the NLP community. Idiomatic Expressions are well known phrases, fixed or flexible, the semantics of which is non compositional in nature. They are also sometimes referred to as multi word expressions(MWEs). These expressions occur in a variety of linguistic contexts and therefore, a linguistically precise handling of such expressions has a lot of challenges, some of them highlighted by [17]. [14] and [5] talk about the different complexities associated with handling idiomatic expressions and a lack of clear determinable patterns in different instances of the same idiomatic expressions in data. Their inherent syntactic complexities and high frequency in data has made it unavoidable to handle them in a special manner in order to have better machine comprehension in NLP. Machine Translation systems achieve only half of the BLEU scores on sentences containing idiomatic expressions than the ones that do not according to [15]. Additionally, [14] also

© Springer Nature Switzerland AG 2021
K. Ekštein et al. (Eds.): TSD 2021, LNAI 12848, pp. 210–221, 2021.
https://doi.org/10.1007/978-3-030-83527-9_18

makes a distinction among idiomatic expressions, namely static idioms and formal idioms. Static Idioms are syntactically fixed idiomatic expressions i.e. they occur in the same surface form in all the contexts whereas formal idioms are syntactically flexible. Formal idioms can occur with multiple qualitative modifiers and can occur in different surface forms and different pronominal attachments. This linguistic freedom that formal idiomatic expressions exhibit, makes them more difficult to handle than static idioms. In addition to the syntactic flexibility, a lot of formal idiomatic expressions also occur in literal contexts as well. For example, *drag one's feet* is a very common formal idiomatic expression, the meaning of which corresponds to *being slow to act*. However, in multiple instances, *drag one's feet* is used in a literal context, like in the sentence 'Children tend to *drag their feet* while walking'. These occurrences of formal idiomatic expressions in literal context makes any kind of automatic handling based on syntactic behaviour impossible. Therefore, it becomes important to have models trained on disambiguating such instances necessary for any meaningful resolution to the problem. This problem can be modelled as a classification task, with the idiomatic expression sequence getting assigned a label, thus, disambiguating the idiomaticity of the phrase in the given context. However, classification models are like any other machine learning NLP models i.e. they are dependent on good training data which in this context would be data which contains literal and idiomatic usages for a wide variety of idiomatic expressions. [11] also identifies this as step 2 of the predefined steps of handling idiomatic expressions, the first being detection of such lexical occurrences.

It is with this motivation that we identify our task of creating a labelled dataset, labelling both idiomatic and literal instances of multiple formal idiomatic expressions. We annotate the formal idiom instances of the EPIE dataset [16]. The EPIE dataset contains 25,207 instances of 717 idiomatic expressions. We label a subset of this dataset, containing instances of only the formal idiomatic expressions. We label a total of 3,136 instances, denoting idiomatic or literal usage of 358 formal idiomatic expressions. We also use the labelled dataset to train a sequence classification model inspired from the work of [8] on metaphorical word detection. We adapt a transformer based classification model for our task, with training resulting in high accuracy, precision and recall scores. We also test our trained model on three independent labelled datasets to check the coverage of our model. These datasets are, "all word" and "lex sample" datasets of SemEval-2013 Task 5b Dataset [10], and the PIE Corpus [9]. For all these datasets we have used the whole corpus i.e. training, dev and test datasets together for testing.

The major contributions for our work can be summarized as follows:

- We publicly release a labelled EPIE formal idioms dataset containing 3136 instances of 358 formal idioms. Each instance is labelled with 1 or 0, with 1 denoting an idiomatic usage and 0 denoting a literal usage. These instances have been manually annotated by two annotators with perfect inter annotator agreement.[1]

---

[1] Dataset available at: https://github.com/prateeksaxena2809/EPIE_Corpus.

– We extend the work of [16] by classifying the multi-word expression extracted with [16] and disambiguating whether it is in idiomatic usage or literal usage in a sequence.
– We present a transformer based architecture tweaked for our task which is simpler that recent state-of-the-art models such as [13] without compromising performance. We present the efficacy of our dataset and trained model by performing cross-dataset evaluation on three independent datasets.

2   Related Work

The distinction by [14] defines formal idioms as idiomatic expressions which undergo linguistic changes and can have qualitative modifiers in their constructions. In addition to this, the contexts in which these formal idiomatic expressions occur also have a wider coverage in both literal and idiomatic usages. As formal idiomatic expressions are harder to handle automatically, our work, therefore, focuses on labelling a wide range of examples for formal idiomatic expressions.

BERT [7] has been used extensively to capture context aware linguistic information into the neural network model. BERT uses multiple embeddings to capture word level, position level and segment level information, and exploits multi headed attention layers to capture semantic relationship between tokens. Also, BERT enables building and augmenting neural network layers on top of existing models with ease. For our task, we have used BERT tokenizer and augmented the data for our purpose to then initialize and fine tune a BERT for Sequence Classification model for labelling idiomaticity.

[8] provides a model for metaphor word detection in context. They use an idiomaticity label which defines the usage of a particular word as metaphorical or literal in the given context. [8] presents two tasks, namely sequence labelling and word classification. For sequence labelling task, each word of the input sequence is labelled with an idiomaticity label whereas for the classification task, one word from the whole input sequence is labelled with the idiomaticity label. For our task, we have chosen to extend the classification task to assign idiomaticity label to an idiomatic expression. We have used the insights provided in the paper as well as a comparative baseline to compare our model. However, the paper detects metaphor words in a given context whereas we classify whole idiomatic phrases usage as idiomatic or literal within the sentence using a single label. [13] presents a recent work on "MWE-aware" metaphor identification systems. They use BERT, Graph Convolution Network (GCN) and multi-headed self attention for metaphor identification. This work provides a good starting point for metaphor identification systems focusing on verbal MWEs. Our work aims to provide a simpler system for idiomaticity detection which works for a wider range of idiomatic expressions than verbal MWEs including other idiomatic expressions like compound nominals and verb particle constructions.

There are many datasets for idiomatic expressions containing both idiomatic and literal usages labelled into the dataset. The PIE Corpus [9] containing around 1100 labelled instances of 200 candidate idioms and the SemEval-2013

Task 5 Dataset [10] contains around 3000 labelled instances of 53 to 65 candidate idioms. These datasets are thorough but do not provide a wide coverage of idiomatic expressions. The EPIE Dataset [16] containing 3136 labelled instances for 358 idiomatic expressions, provides a large dataset with a wider coverage, which is why we labelled the EPIE Dataset [16] for our task.

3   Data

We have used the EPIE dataset [16] for our task. The EPIE dataset consists of 25, 207 samples where the sentences are extracted from the British National corpus (BNC) [6] with lexical occurrences of idioms extracted from the IMIL dataset [1]. However, the EPIE dataset does not disambiguate between idiomatic usage versus literal usage of the potential idiomatic phrase within each sample.

For our task, we have manually annotated the EPIE formal idioms samples, which is a subset of EPIE dataset containing 3136 samples. Formal idioms may undergo lexical modifications in their usage in a sentence. This makes detection and disambiguation of such expression difficult for automatic systems. For example, the formal idiom, *cry over spilled milk*, can be used with lexical modifications in idiomatic usage in 'There is no use *crying over spilled milk*' and 'He *cried over spilled milk* for a whole month' and in literal usage in 'The baby dropped her bottle and started *crying over the spilled milk*'. We label each instance of the formal idioms with 1 for idiomatic usage in the sample and 0 for literal usage. We have used two annotators to label all instances and have seen unanimous cross annotator agreement scores for all instances. This is due to the instruction posed to each annotator for annotating each instance - *Label 1(idiomatic) if it is possible to have an idiomatic usage of the given phrase in the given context and 0(literal) otherwise.* Some examples are:

- All that we earn goes into *keeping the wolf from the door* - labelled 1(idiomatic)
- It is hard to *keep your head above water* - labelled 1(idiomatic)
- Try to *keep your head above water* when learning to swim. - labelled 0(literal)
- He is the *black sheep* of the family. - labelled 1(idiomatic)

Due to the instruction above, the ambiguous instances i.e. the instances which can have both idiomatic and literal sense in a given context have also been labelled as idiomatic by the annotators as our first criteria in the instruction, which is having an idiomatic usage possible, is fulfilled. In example 2 above, since it is possible to have an idiomatic usage, it has been labelled as idiomatic. We did this in order to have more idiomatic instances in the dataset to offset the high frequency of literal usages in a general dataset.

Each entry in the dataset contains the candidate idiom, the sentence, the start and end offsets for the idiomatic expressions in the sentence and the idiomaticity label. We label a total of 3136 instances of 358 formal idioms. Our labelled dataset has a total of 2761 idiomatic usage instances and 375 literal usage instances. We publicly release our dataset.

4   Model

The Ge Gao model [8] for metaphor detection detects the target metaphor word by comparing it to the context in which it occurs. The intuition is that when a word is used metaphorically in a context, it is less similar to the words of the context than when the same word is used literally. In the following example,

– The heat *ignited* the matchstick.

the word *ignited* is used literally as there is a close relation between the word *ignite* and *matchstick*. However, in this example,

– His speech *ignited* a revolution.

the same word *ignited* is used metaphorically as there is not a close relation between *ignite* and any of the constituent words in the context. Ge Gao's study is limited for single word metaphors. A more recent work on idiomatic expressions as observed in [13] uses Graph Convolution Network (GCN) to identify verbal multi-word expressions. They train a BERT model augmented with a GCN and a multi-headed self-attention layer. The study focuses only on idiomatic phrases which begin with a verb, such as *keep an eye on* and does not handle idiomatic expressions such as *behind his back* which is a prepositional phrase or *black sheep* which is a compound nominal.

To identify idiomatic usage of any multi-word expression, we propose the following two patterns are required to be learnt by our system (details in Fig. 2):

– the constituent tokens of the idiomatic expression have high similarity with each other.
– the constituent tokens of the idiomatic expression have low similarity to the words in the outer context in which they occur.

Our model uses a BERT-based architecture which captures this relationship between a multi word expression in metaphorical usage and its context. Using only a BERT model makes our system simpler than BERT+GCN+self-attention yet taking advantage of self-attention mechanism of transformers. To achieve this, we take inspiration from sentence pair modelling using BERT [2,3,12] which studies the semantic relationship between 2 sequences such as textual entailment, paraphrasing and sentence-pair similarity. For our task, however, the input sequence is not 2 consecutive sentences, but a phrase(the idiomatic expression) embedded in a larger context(sentence). To enforce this constraint, we use the token type identifiers of BERT tokenizer. The potential idiomatic expression tokens are annotated with 1 and the context words are annotated by 0. In order to preserve the context information, the idiomatic expression cannot be encoded separately as an independent sequence because then it would appear as an incomplete phrase. Consequently, the context cannot be encoded separately from the idiomatic expression as an independent sequence because then the context would appear as two separate sequences i.e. left context and right context with nothing in the middle. As observed in Fig. 1, the input sequence is

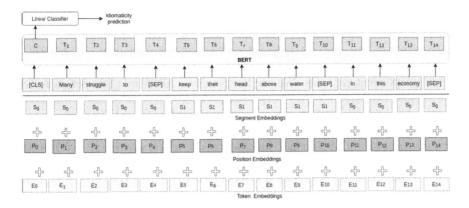

Fig. 1. Idiom sense disambiguation using Bert for sequence classification. The target idiomatic expression has segment embeddings for id 1 and the context has segment embeddings for id 0

encoded into BERT embeddings for each token which encodes the word embedding, whether the token is idiomatic represented by the token type identifier and the position of each token within the sequence and is transformed by BERT into a sequence of hidden states. The hidden state of the *[CLS]* token is used with a linear classifier to identify the idiomacity of the multi-word expression within the input sequence.

5   Experiments

We use the 80%:10%:10% training, dev and test split on our dataset for the experiments. For our baseline, we have used the classification model of [8], as that seems closest to our task at hand. We have kept the same hyperparameters for our task with 300 dimensional glove embeddings, 1024 dimensional elmo embeddings and 50 dimensional index embeddings. The only difference is that instead of a single token, we have used the index embedding indicator to identify all constituent tokens of the phrase to be classified. We have used the same pretrained options settings and weights for ELMO as [8].

We train a transformer based model for our task. We modify the 'token type ids' output from the BERT tokenizer to identify the idiom expression tokens within the sequence with id 1 and the context tokens with id 0. This in addition to the 'input ids' and 'attention mask' is fed into the transformer based BERT for sequence classification model. We name this model as BERTModified as we send a modified sequence into the model. We also train a model without explicitly encoding the idiom phrase span information in the 'token type ids'. However, we insert 2 *[SEP]* tokens demarking the idiom span boundary in the context. This is done to test whether BERT is able to disambiguate the idiom phrase span implicitly from just the tokenization. We name this model as BERTBaseline. We use the 'bert-base-uncased' model from huggingface [18] for our input sequence tokenization and the initialization of weights of our architecture. The hyperparameter values for both our models can be seen in Table 1.

For our experiments, we train all settings of our model on our annotated data (Formal Idioms Test Dataset) and evaluate it on our annotated test data and 3 independent datasets. We use the SemEval All Words Dataset, SemEval Lex Sample Dataset and PIE Corpus dataset for the cross-dataset evaluation. The SemEval All Words Dataset and the SemEval Lex Sample Dataset are part of the SemEval2013-Task 5 named 'Evaluating Phrasal Semantics' [10]. These datasets are part of the second task in Task 5 which addressed deciding the compositionality of a phrase in a given context. Each line of these dataset has a sentence containing a phrase and a label of 0 or 1 denoting the compositionality of the phrase within the sentence. The dataset has been created using idioms from English Wiktionary using the JWKTL Wiktionary API [19] and usage contexts from the ukWAC corpus [4]. The PIE corpus is an evaluation corpus for the automatic detection of potential idiomatic expressions(PIEs) with usages from 23 documents of the British National Corpus [6]. Each entry of the PIE corpus is a 5 sentence window, with the idiomatic expression possibly present in the middle sentence. Each entry of the PIE corpus is labelled with the PIE label which denotes whether the middle sentence contains the PIE in question, and a sense label which denotes whether the expressions has been used literally or idiomatically. We merge the train, dev and test sets of individual datasets and use all the samples from the respective datasets for evaluating our models.

Table 1. Hyperparameter values used for our model.

Hyperparameter	Value
Sentence max length	110
Number of epochs	10
Batch size	8
GPU size	4 GB
Weight decay	0.01
Warmup steps	50

6   Results

The results comparison with the baseline can be seen in Table 2. As it is clear from the Table, modified bert based transformer architecture outperforms the baseline as well as the unmodified transformer architecture.

Table 2. Test results comparison with the baseline model. Train, Dev and Test set were split by 80%, 10% and 10% respectively.

Model	Accuracy	Precision	Recall	F1
Gao et al. (2018) [8]	0.91	0.91	0.98	0.93
BERTBaseline	0.85	0.85	0.99	0.92
BERTModified	**0.95**	**0.96**	**0.98**	**0.97**

Table 3. Test Results from the model trained on Formal Idioms Training Dataset. Formal Idioms Test Dataset is 20% split from the Formal Idioms Dataset. The model has been tested on the whole (train, test and dev) dataset combined for all the other datasets i.e. *SemEval All Words Dataset, SemEval Lex Sample Dataset* and *PIE Corpus*.

Test dataset	Accuracy	Precision	Recall	F1
Formal Idioms Test Dataset	**0.94**	**0.95**	**0.97**	**0.96**
SemEval All Words Dataset	0.74	0.70	0.98	0.82
SemEval Lex Sample Dataset	0.66	0.60	0.96	0.74
PIE Corpus	0.66	0.63	0.97	0.76

Table 4. Correctly labelled sentences from the independent test datasets. The second column denotes the correct label for the idiomatic phrase. The first 2 sentences belong to the PIE corpus, the second 2 belong to the SemEval all words corpus and the last two sentences belong to the SemEval lex sample corpus.

Sentences	Usage
All along, as I reported at the time, Sarah wanted to take the baby with her	Idiomatic
The chilean black dolphin is caught in surface nets *all along* the chilean coast	Literal
Choosing plans for the whole group inevitably means making some compromises somewhere *along the line*	Idiomatic
The third brigade was running into counter attacks all *along the line* and was a risk	Literal
At the end of the day, the board looks at the person as a whole	Idiomatic
The restaurant is very inexpensive and worth the car trip *at the end of the day*	Literal

The results for tests on the SemEval and PIE corpus can be seen in Table 3. Clearly, the formal idioms test dataset gives the best results as it is split from the training data and thus, is the most related to the training data. However, the model also gives good results with the SemEval and the PIE corpus. The high

Table 5. Wrongly labelled sentences from the independent test datasets. The second column denotes the correct label for the idiomatic phrase. The first 2 sentences belong to the PIE corpus, the second 2 belong to the SemEval all words corpus and the last two sentences belong to the SemEval lex sample corpus.

Sentences	Usage
They played some great stuff and ran us *all over the place*	Idiomatic
He was laughing as I was still to *get off the ground*	Literal
It is *cutting it close* at this time and someone must be responsible for the intake of the ER	Idiomatic
If you visit Darlington or other stations *along the line*, you will find things to see and do	Literal
At the end of the day, I had retrieved most of the file	Idiomatic
Those who carried the banner for Winwick were proud to see it fluttering aloft *at the end of the day*	Literal

recall and low precision test values across the board suggests that, although the model is trained to identify idiomatic usage, it also sometimes identifies literal usages as idiomatic.

Table 4 shows some correctly labelled sentences from the independent test datasets. We show one idiomatic and one literal instance from each of the three datasets. As is observed, the model is able to identify correlations like *along* and *coast* in the second example and *trip* and *day* in the sixth example to identify a literal context and a lack of correlations to identify an idiomatic context.

Table 5 shows some wrongly labelled sentences from the independents test datasets. For these too, we show one idiomatic and one literal instance from each of the three datasets. As observed in these instances, the model is not able to find correlations between *stations* and *along* or *line* in the fourth example and identify a literal context. It also wrongly associates a correlation between *played* and *place* in the first example to label the instance as literal. In addition to this, some instances in datasets of idiomatic expressions are ambiguous in general and a label assigned to it by the model, idiomatic or literal, is erroneous or correct only in comparison to the label assigned in the dataset, but not in general.

Figure 2 shows the correlation between self attention weights for attention head 10 for layer 0 of the trained BERTModified model among words from the idiomatic expression and words in the context for one idiomatic usage example and one literal usage example for the idiomatic expression *keep one's head above water*. The higher the correlation, the brighter the colour of the block. The two sentences used for the correlation are,

- It is clear that *keeping your head above water* is half the trick in swimming. - Literal usage
- Many struggle to *keep their head above water* in this economy. - Idiomatic usage

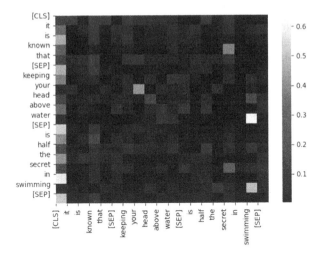

(a) Attention Weights for literal usage in 'it is known that keeping your head above water is half the secret in swimming'.

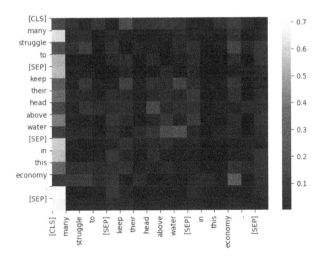

(b) Attention Weights for idiomatic usage 'many struggle to keep their head above water in this economy'.

Fig. 2. Attention Weights for layer 0, attention-head 10. As observed, in the literal usage in sub-figure (a), there is a high correlation between 'water' and context token 'swimming', whereas there are no such correlations between the tokens of the idiomatic expression and context in the idiomatic usage in sub-figure (b).

As observed from the brightest spot in Fig. 2a, we see that there is high correlation between the constituent word *water* present in the idiomatic expression and *swimming* present in the outer context of the expression, which results in the model identifying the usage as literal. Compared to this, we see very sparse correlations in Fig. 2b, which results in the model identifying the usage as idiomatic.

7   Future Work

Our work, with other previous works helps identify idiomatic usages of known multi word expressions in a given context. A possible downstream task to our work can be in machine comprehension of sentences containing these idiomatic usages. This can be done either by surface realization and phrasal replacement of these phrases into literal translations, or convert the sentences into semantic frames to aid NLP tasks like machine translation, summarization and comprehension.

8   Conclusion

In this paper, we address the task of idiomaticity classification of potential idiomatic expressions in a given context to aid natural language understanding for downstream tasks like machine comprehension, text summarization and machine translation. To achieve this, we present an annotated EPIE Dataset labelled with idiomatic/literal usage of potential idiomatic phrases. Our dataset contains 3136 labelled occurrences of 358 formal idiomatic expressions. To evaluate the efficacy of our data, we also present a transformer based classification model to label usages of idiomatic expressions in the sentences as idiomatic or literal. We train this model using our labelled EPIE dataset and show that it performs better than the baseline and gives good results on three independent datasets.

References

1. Agrawal, R., Kumar, V.C., Muralidaran, V., Sharma, D.: No more beating about the bush: a step towards idiom handling for Indian language NLP. In: Proceedings of the Eleventh International Conference on Language Resources and Evaluation (LREC 2018) (2018)
2. Ahmed, M., Mercer, R.E.: Efficient transformer-based sentence encoding for sentence pair modelling. In: Meurs, M.-J., Rudzicz, F. (eds.) Canadian AI 2019. LNCS (LNAI), vol. 11489, pp. 146–159. Springer, Cham (2019). https://doi.org/10.1007/978-3-030-18305-9_12
3. Arase, Y., Tsujii, J.: Transfer fine-tuning of BERT with phrasal paraphrases. Comput. Speech Lang. **66**, 101164 (2021). https://doi.org/10.1016/j.csl.2020.101164. https://www.sciencedirect.com/science/article/pii/S0885230820300978
4. Baroni, M., Bernardini, S., Ferraresi, A., Zanchetta, E.: The WaCky wide web: a collection of very large linguistically processed web-crawled corpora. Lang. Resour. Eval. **43**(3), 209–226 (2009)

5. Cap, F., Nirmal, M., Weller, M., Im Walde, S.S.: How to account for idiomatic German support verb constructions in statistical machine translation. In: Proceedings of the 11th Workshop on Multiword Expressions, pp. 19–28 (2015)
6. Consortium, B., et al.: British National Corpus. Oxford Text Archive Core Collection (2007)
7. Devlin, J., Chang, M.W., Lee, K., Toutanova, K.: BERT: pre-training of deep bidirectional transformers for language understanding. arXiv preprint arXiv:1810.04805 (2018)
8. Gao, G., Choi, E., Choi, Y., Zettlemoyer, L.: Neural metaphor detection in context. arXiv preprint arXiv:1808.09653 (2018)
9. Haagsma, H., Nissim, M., Bos, J.: Casting a wide net: robust extraction of potentially idiomatic expressions. arXiv preprint arXiv:1911.08829 (2019)
10. Korkontzelos, I., Zesch, T., Zanzotto, F.M., Biemann, C.: SemEval-2013 task 5: evaluating phrasal semantics. In: Second Joint Conference on Lexical and Computational Semantics (* SEM), Volume 2: Proceedings of the Seventh International Workshop on Semantic Evaluation (SemEval 2013), pp. 39–47 (2013)
11. Liu, C., Hwa, R.: Phrasal substitution of idiomatic expressions. In: Proceedings of the 2016 Conference of the North American Chapter of the Association for Computational Linguistics: Human Language Technologies, pp. 363–373 (2016)
12. Reimers, N., Gurevych, I.: Sentence-BERT: sentence embeddings using Siamese BERT-networks. CoRR abs/1908.10084 (2019). http://arxiv.org/abs/1908.10084
13. Rohanian, O., Rei, M., Taslimipoor, S., Ha, L.A.: Verbal multiword expressions for identification of metaphor. In: Proceedings of the 58th Annual Meeting of the Association for Computational Linguistics, pp. 2890–2895. Association for Computational Linguistics, July 2020. https://doi.org/10.18653/v1/2020.acl-main.259. https://www.aclweb.org/anthology/2020.acl-main.259
14. Sag, I.A., Baldwin, T., Bond, F., Copestake, A., Flickinger, D.: Multiword expressions: a pain in the neck for NLP. In: Gelbukh, A. (ed.) CICLing 2002. LNCS, vol. 2276, pp. 1–15. Springer, Heidelberg (2002). https://doi.org/10.1007/3-540-45715-1_1
15. Salton, G., Ross, R., Kelleher, J.: An empirical study of the impact of idioms on phrase based statistical machine translation of English to Brazilian-Portuguese (2014)
16. Saxena, P., Paul, S.: EPIE dataset: a corpus for possible idiomatic expressions. In: Sojka, P., Kopeček, I., Pala, K., Horák, A. (eds.) TSD 2020. LNCS (LNAI), vol. 12284, pp. 87–94. Springer, Cham (2020). https://doi.org/10.1007/978-3-030-58323-1_9
17. Volk, M., Weber, N.: The automatic translation of idioms. Machine translation vs. translation memory systems. Sprachwissenschaft, Computerlinguistik und neue Medien (1), 167–192 (1998)
18. Wolf, T., et al.: Huggingface's transformers: state-of-the-art natural language processing. arXiv preprint arXiv:1910.03771 (2019)
19. Zesch, T., Müller, C., Gurevych, I.: Extracting lexical semantic knowledge from Wikipedia and Wiktionary. LREC **8**, 1646–1652 (2008)

Introducing NYTK-NerKor, A Gold Standard Hungarian Named Entity Annotated Corpus

Eszter Simon and Noémi Vadász[✉]

Hungarian Research Centre for Linguistics, Budapest, Hungary
vadasz.noemi@nytud.hu

Abstract. Here we present NYTK-NerKor, a gold standard Hungarian named entity annotated corpus containing 1 million tokens. This is the largest corpus ever in its kind. It contains balanced text selection from five genres: fiction, legal, news, web, and Wikipedia. A ca. 200,000 tokens subcorpus contains gold standard morphological annotation besides NE labels. We provide official train, development and test datasets in a proportion of 80%-10%-10%. All sets provide a balanced selection from all genres and sources, while the morphologically annotated subcorpus is also represented in all sets in a balanced way. The format of data files are CoNLL-U Plus, in which the NE annotation follows the CoNLL2002 labelling standard, while morphological information is encoded using the well-known Universal Dependencies POS tags and morphosyntactic features. The novelty of NYTK-NerKor as opposed to similar existing corpora is that it is: by an order of magnitude larger, freely available for any purposes, containing text material from different genres and sources, and following international standards in its format and tagset. The corpus is available under the license CC-BY-SA 4.0 from its GitHub repository: https://github.com/nytud/NYTK-NerKor.

Keywords: Named Entity Recognition · Text corpus · Hungarian

1 Introduction

Information Extraction (IE) is one of the main subtasks of computational linguistics, aiming at automatically extracting structured information from unstructured or semi-structured machine-readable documents. It covers a wide range of subtasks from finding all the company names in a text to finding all the actors of an event. Such capabilities are increasingly important for sifting through the enormous volumes of online text to find pieces of relevant information the user wants. Named Entity Recognition (NER), the task of automatic identification of selected types of Named Entities (NEs), is one of the most intensively studied tasks of IE. Most texts include lots of names, thus NER is of key importance in many Natural Language Processing (NLP) tasks.

© Springer Nature Switzerland AG 2021
K. Ekštein et al. (Eds.): TSD 2021, LNAI 12848, pp. 222–234, 2021.
https://doi.org/10.1007/978-3-030-83527-9_19

The NER task has two substeps: first, locating the NEs in unstructured texts, and second, classifying them into pre-defined categories. For building a supervised NER system, first we need a manually annotated gold standard corpus. Typically, the algorithm itself learns its parameters from the corpus, and the evaluation of the system is through comparing its output to an other part of the corpus. That is why large manually annotated corpora are needed, and that was the motivation behind building NYTK-NerKor, a Hungarian gold standard NE annotated corpus consisting of 1 million tokens. Hereinafter, for simplicity, the resource will be referred to as NerKor.

2   Related Work

Supervised statistical and neural approaches require a large amount of gold standard datasets to boost performance quality. To be a gold standard corpus, a dataset has to meet several requirements, for example to be exhaustive or aiming for representativeness; to be large enough for training and testing supervised systems on it; and to contain accurate linguistic annotation added by hand.

However, building gold standard corpora is a time-consuming, highly skilled and delicate job, therefore large gold standard datasets are rare and valuable. This is the situation even in the case of Hungarian NE annotated corpora. The gold standard corpora in the field of NER are highly domain-specific, containing mostly newswire, and are restricted in size and availability.

The most well-known gold standard NE tagged corpus for Hungarian is the Szeged NER corpus [13]. It is a subcorpus of the Szeged Treebank [3], annotated with NE class labels in line with the annotation scheme of the CoNLL2003 NER shared task [15]. The corpus consists of short business news articles, containing altogether ca. 225,000 tokens. The license of the Szeged Treebank has been passed down for Szeged NER corpus, thus it can only be used for research purposes.

Since the Szeged NER corpus is highly domain-specific, the need emerged for a large, heterogeneous, manually tagged NE corpus for Hungarian, which could serve as a reference corpus for training and testing NER systems. That was the aim of the HunNER [7] project in the 2000s. Unfortunately, the corpus itself stayed unfinished, but the annotation guidelines have proven to be remarkably durable.

Some parts of the annotation guidelines were used by building the Criminal NE corpus[1], which contains texts related to the topic of criminally liable financial offences. Articles were selected from the Hungarian National Corpus [18], inheriting its license, which means that it is restricted in use. The corpus contains altogether ca. 560,000 tokens. The range of annotated NE categories was also based on the CoNLL2003 annotation scheme. The corpus has two annotated versions: one follows the Tag for Meaning rule, while the other one is annotated according to the standard Tag for Tagging approach. (Some NEs may have metonymic readings in certain contexts, which raises certain questions even at the level of annotation. There are two approaches to follow. First, one can always tag a NE according to its contextual reference. In this case, the 'White

---

[1] https://rgai.inf.u-szeged.hu/node/130

House' in the example sentence *The White House announced that the President will welcome Prime Minister* would be tagged as an organization name. This rule is called Tag for Meaning. The second approach is called Tag for Tagging, when NEs are always tagged according to their primary reference, regardless of the context. Following this rule, the 'White House' in the above example would be tagged as a location name.)

Besides gold standard corpora described above, there is also a silver standard corpus for Hungarian. The hunNERwiki [10] corpus has been automatically generated from the Hungarian Wikipedia, using the same annotation scheme as the Szeged NER corpus, and containing more than 19 million tokens. In accordance with the Wikipedia copyright policy, the hunNERwiki corpus is available under the CC-BY-SA 3.0 license.

The Hungarian language is categorized as one of the mid-resourced European languages by the META-NET White Paper series [8], therefore the landscape of NE annotated corpora for Hungarian is quite similar to that of other European languages. There are several websites listing available corpora for NLP tasks, such as one in the CLARIN Knowledge base[2]. Skimming through this site, one can find manually annotated NE corpora for several languages ranging in size from 46,000 to 1 million tokens. For English, the internationally most well known and widely used NE corpus is the OntoNotes 5.0[3], the English part of which contains ca. 1.5 million tokens.

To conclude, the NerKor corpus is the largest manually NE annotated corpus for Hungarian: it is by an order of magnitude larger than its ancestors. Moreover, it is comparable in size to the similar corpora built for other languages, even the English language, which is the best resourced language in the world. As opposed to existing Hungarian corpora, it is freely available for any purposes, not only for research purposes.

3   The Size of the Corpus

The corpus contains text material from five different genres: fiction, legal texts, news, web, and Wikipedia (for details on genres and sources, see Sect. 4). The amount of one million tokens is divided between the genres in a balanced way, thus each genre subcorpus comprises ca. 200,000 tokens.

We wanted to create a reference corpus which can be used for training and evaluating classic machine learning systems as well as neural systems. Since morphological features play an important role in NER systems based on classic machine learning techniques, such as maximum entropy, we also provide a subcorpus with manual morphological annotation (for details on morphological annotation, see Sect. 7). The Szeged NER corpus, the most widely used Hungarian NE corpus, contains altogether 225,000 tokens, whose 90% has been generally used as a training data, and with this, over 96% F-measure could be reached [9].

[2] https://www.clarin.eu/resource-families/manually-annotated-corpora#Named20Entity20recognition
[3] https://catalog.ldc.upenn.edu/LDC2013T19

Based on that, we supposed that such an amount of labelled data containing morphological information should be enough, therefore a 200,000 tokens subcorpus supplied with manually corrected morphosyntactic annotation has also been created.

Subcorpora by genre and subcorpora by morphological annotation are in intersection, thus the morphological subcorpus also contains various text genres. Table 1 shows the size of subcorpora (number of files, sentences and tokens).

Table 1. The size of subcorpora.

Genre	Morph/no-morph	File	Sentence	Token
Fiction	Morph	0	0	0
	No-morph	122	24,535	203,216
	Total	122	24,535	203,216
Legal	Morph	0	0	0
	No-morph	39	7,632	202,195
	Total	39	7,632	202,195
News	Morph	35	477	9,178
	No-morph	47	9,280	204,478
	Total	82	9,757	213,656
Web	Morph	398	10,886	188,250
	No-morph	0	0	0
	Total	398	10,886	188,250
Wikipedia	Morph	85	1,618	26,764
	No-morph	72	13,096	194,033
	Total	157	14,714	220,797
Altogether	Morph	518	12,981	224,192
	No-morph	280	54,543	803,922
	Total	798	67,524	1,028,114

Table 2 shows the number of NEs in NE classes, the total number of NEs, and the density of NEs by genres. Wikipedia texts are the most crowded with NEs, which is not surprising, as the aim of creating an encyclopedia is to condense all available knowledge of mankind, in which names have an inevitably important role. Location and person names are dominating, maybe because persons and locations traditionally have more importance in history. Newswire texts usually contain quite a large amount of names, mostly organizations – that is the case even in this corpus. Legal texts also contain a high portion of organization names, as unique persons contribute less to legislation than official committees, parties, organizations. On the contrary, fictional stories are usually organized around persons – that may be the reason behind that the portion of person names in fiction is high.

Table 2. The number of NEs in NE classes, the total number of NEs, and the density of NEs by genres.

	PER	LOC	ORG	MISC	NEs	Density (%)
Fiction	5,224	1,042	217	287	6,770	3.33
Legal	255	1,302	6,840	1,871	10,268	5.07
News	4,588	2,329	5,294	3,699	15,910	7.44
Web	2,826	1,343	1,788	2,434	8,391	4.45
Wikipedia	8,892	9,114	5,362	4,253	27,621	12.50
Total	21,785	15,130	19,501	12,544	68,960	6.70

We wanted to create a reference corpus, which can be used for anyone in the NLP community to train, fine-tune and evaluate her own NER system. For having comparable results, standard train, development and test datasets are needed. For this purpose, we created a default train–development–test cut in 80%-10%-10%, respectively. All sets provide a balanced selection from all genres and sources. The morphologically annotated subcorpus is also represented in all sets in a balanced way. For exact numbers, see Table 3.

Table 3. Token numbers of train, development and test sets by subcorpora.

Genre	Morph/no-morph	Train	Devel	Test
Fiction	Morph	0	0	0
	No-morph	161,505	20,884	20,827
	Total	161,505	20,884	20,827
Legal	Morph	0	0	0
	No-morph	157,710	22,552	21,933
	Total	157,710	22,552	21,933
News	Morph	7,314	935	929
	No-morph	163,780	19,848	20,850
	Total	171,094	20,783	21,779
Web	Morph	150,762	18,724	18,764
	No-morph	0	0	0
	Total	150,762	18,724	18,764
Wikipedia	Morph	21,331	2,679	2,754
	No-morph	154,574	20,074	19,385
	Total	175,905	22,753	22,139
Altogether	Morph	179,407	22,338	22,447
	No-morph	637,569	83,358	82,995
	Total	816,976	105,696	105,442

4   Genres and Sources

One of the main aspects of text collection and selection was the license of the source, since the possibility of unrestricted future use was a must-have feature of the corpus. Another aspect was that we wanted to collect as recent text material as possible.

Additionally, the KorKor corpus [16] was incorporated to the NerKor corpus. KorKor is a manually annotated multi-layer Hungarian pilot corpus containing morphosyntactic, dependency, anaphora, and coreference annotation. Since KorKor already contains morphological annotation, texts coming from it had become part of the morphologically annotated subcorpus of NerKor. The genres of KorKor are news and Wikipedia. The rows news–morph (9,178 tokens) and wikipedia–morph (26,764 tokens) of Table 1 come from KorKor.

The **fiction** subcorpus comprises two text types: classic fictional genres such as novels and movie subtitles. The sources of novels were Hungarian Electronic Library[4] and Project Gutenberg[5], from where only older novels (from the first half of the 20th century) were selected for which Hungarian copyright has expired. The source of subtitles was the 2018 subpart of OpenSubtitles[6] downloaded from the Opus corpus website[7].

The **legal** texts come from EU sources: i) parts of the EU Constitution from 2004, downloaded from the Opus corpus website; ii) documents from the European Economic and Social Committee from 2017, also downloaded from the Opus corpus website; iii) selection from JRC-Acquis [12] from the years over 2000; and iv) selection from DGT-Acquis [11] from 2004.

The sources of the **news** subcorpus are: i) selection from the Press Release Database of European Commission from 2016, downloaded from the Opus corpus website; ii) selection from the Hungarian edition of Global Voices from the years 2010–2017, also downloaded from the Opus corpus website (some articles come directly from the KorKor corpus); and iii) selection from the 2019 part of the NewsCrawl dataset [1].

The **web** subcorpus contains a selection from the Hungarian Webcorpus 2.0 [5] from the years 2017–2019.

The **Wikipedia** subcorpus contains texts from the Hungarian Wikipedia, but not directly from a Wikipedia dump. First, some articles are incorporated as parts of the KorKor corpus, while other parts are selected from the hunNER-wiki corpus already containing silver standard NE annotation. Only sentences containing at least one NE were selected for inclusion to NerKor.

---

[4] http://mek.oszk.hu/indexeng.phtml
[5] https://www.gutenberg.org/
[6] https://www.opensubtitles.org
[7] https://opus.nlpl.eu/index.php

5   The Format of the Annotation

Tha format of the corpus is CoNLL-U Plus[8]. This is the extended version of the CoNLL-U format originally applied in the Universal Dependencies (UD)[9] project but recently become an international standard. Each file has six columns and the standard `.conllup` file extension. The first line in each file is:
`# global.columns = FORM LEMMA UPOS XPOS FEATS CONLL:NER`,
where:

FORM the token itself;
LEMMA the lemma of the token;
UPOS UD POS tag;
XPOS full morphological annotation (POS + morphosyntactic features) provided by the `emMorph` morphological analyser (see Sect. 7);
FEATS UD morphosyntactic features;
CONLL:NER NE annotation.

Although only a part of the corpus contains morphological annotation, all files have the same columns to ensure a consistent format in the entire corpus. Incomplete annotations are marked by an underscore sign ('_'), following the CoNLL-U Plus rules.

6   Named Entity Annotation

The main annotation set of the corpus is NEs. The NE annotation follows the labelling standard of the CoNLL2002 shared task [14]. The four NE categories are: person (PER), organization (ORG), location (LOC) and miscellaneous (MISC). The tags are in the IOB2 format: a B- prefix denotes the first item of a NE phrase and an I- prefix any non-initial word. Non-names are marked by an O label (that is a capital letter O, not a zero).

Even though there are several NE labelling standards with more fine-grained annotation, we voted for using CoNLL2002. The reasons behind the decision are: still, this is a widely-known international standard and all existing NE tagged corpora for the Hungarian language follows this (see Sect. 2).

The whole corpus must be covered by the NE annotation, which means that each token must get a NE tag, even punctuation marks. Only the sentence separator line must remain empty.

6.1   Annotation Principles

The principles of annotating NEs are laid down by the annotation guidelines, which is based on the guidelines used in the HunNER project (see Sect. 2). Based on the feedback by the annotators, the guidelines has become more and more detailed and precise during the project. The annotation principles were the following:

---

[8] https://universaldependencies.org/ext-format.html
[9] https://universaldependencies.org/

- Only proper names are to be annotated. Phrases referring to unique entities of the world but not with a proper name are not to be annotated. For example, 'White House' should be annotated as a NE, but 'the white house on the corner' should not.
- Names are not compositional. Since the reference of a name cannot be built up from the reference of its parts, names cannot be segmented into smaller parts. For example, 'Roosevelt Square' should be annotated as a LOC, while 'Roosevelt' inside it should not be annotated as a PER. Always the longest sequence of tokens composing a name is to be annotated.
- There are no overlapping and embedded NE annotations. Thus, each annotation must end before a new one begins.
- We follow the Tag for Meaning annotation approach (see Sect. 2), thus each NE is to be annotated according to its contextual reference.
- Inflected forms of NEs are to be tagged, while derived forms are not.
- If a NE is part of a compound whose head is a common noun, the NE is not to be annotated. (Compounds in Hungarian are written in one token, e.g., *Orbán-kormány* ('Orbán Government').)
- Articles preceding the NE are not to be annotated as a part of the NE. There are however exceptions: if the definite article is officially the part of the name, e.g., *The Hague, The Times*.
- Abbreviated forms of a NE (e.g., acronyms, monograms) are also treated as NEs thus are to be annotated.

7   Morphological Annotation

As mentioned above, one fifth of the corpus contains morphological annotation in two different tagsets. First, we created automatic morphological annotation by emMorph, which was corrected manually, then second, the corrected tags were converted to the tagset of UD v2.

7.1   The **emMorph** Tagset

The emMorph [6] morphological analyser is the most recent morphological analyser for Hungarian producing state-of-the-art performance. It has been integrated to the emtsv Hungarian language processing pipeline [4,19]. It provides full morphosyntactic analysis including the lemma, the POS tag, and all morphosyntactic features. For example, ad [/V][Pst.Def.2Sg] is the output for the wordform *adtad* ('you gave'), where ad is the lemma, [/V] is the POS tag, and [Pst.Def.2Sg] are the morphosyntactic features encoding that the verb is in indicative mode, past tense, second person singular, definite conjugation. The full list of morphological tags are available via the URL http://e-magyar. hu/en/textmodules/emmorph_codelist, while a short description and converters can be found on the GitHub page of panmorph [17]: https://github.com/dlt-rilmta/panmorph.

7.2 The UD Tagset

The UD morphological annotation consists of a POS tag[10], while morphosyntactic information is encoded by universal[11] and language-specific[12] linearized
feature–value pairs, e.g., for the same verb (*'adtad'*) as above:
```
VERB
Definite=Def|Mood=Ind|Number=Sing|Person=2|Tense=Past|
VerbForm=Fin|Voice=Act
```
The output of emMorph was automatically converted to the UD v2 tagset.
The UD tagset is less detailed, therefore lossless mapping is possible and no
manual check is required. The converter has been integrated to emtsv as a new
module under the name emmorph2ud2, and additionally, it is available in its
own GitHub repository: https://github.com/vadno/emmorph2ud2.

8 The Workflow of Annotation

Since the two annotations tasks (NE and morphological tagging) had two different workflows, here we describe them in separate subsections.

8.1 The Workflow of NE Annotation

Pre-processing. Some pre-processing steps were carried out in all texts,
depending on their source.

First, files needed some cleaning. In the case of fiction texts, cover pages and
foreign language parts were removed, then they were converted into plain text.
Texts from almost all sources were deduplicated, except for the novels, to save
the integrity of the literature texts. In the case of legal texts and news, the plain
text were extracted from the XML source files.

The original documents were cut into smaller, manageable files. All files were
processed with emtsv from tokenization to POS tagging. Automatic pre-tagging
of NEs was also done with the NER modules of emtsv, except for the data from
the hunNERwiki corpus, which already had a silver standard NE annotation with
the same tagset. Texts from KorKor and Hungarian Webcorpus 2.0 needed only
NE pre-tagging, since they have been previously analysed by emtsv.

The output of emtsv is the so-called xtsv format [4], which was converted
into CoNLL2002 format[13], because this format is suitable for WebAnno [2],
the annotation tool we used. In files following the format of CoNLL2002, each
word is put on a separate line and there is an empty line after each sentence.
The NE annotation is in IOB2 format and follows the token separated by a
white space character. Since the NER modules of emtsv work with a slightly
modified annotation format, in which beginning, interval, ending, and stand-
alone elements of NEs are also marked by prefixes, conversion between the two
tagsets had to be carried out.

[10] https://universaldependencies.org/u/pos/index.html
[11] https://universaldependencies.org/u/feat/index.html
[12] https://github.com/dlt-rilmta/panmorph
[13] https://www.clips.uantwerpen.be/conll2002/ner/

The Annotation Process. Each text file was annotated by two annotators. The annotators have checked and corrected the automatic pre-tagging using the Correction function of WebAnno. This function allows to approve the tag with a click, to modify or delete the tag, to shift the borders of the sequence, or to add new annotation.

A total of 11 annotators worked in this process, who were selected based on their performance in a test task. We kept in touch with them regularly through virtual meetings and a mailing list. All problems they have faced with were discussed together, and the results of these discussions were incorporated into the guidelines. The files were allocated to the annotators in a mixed way, which means that annotator pairs were evenly distributed to reach even quality. The pace of progress was ca. 6,200 tokens/day.

Curation. After two annotators have checked and corrected NE tags, the two versions of annotation were merged into a final annotation. The Curation function of WebAnno allows to compare the versions of annotation, and the curator can decide of the two results per label. Additionally, the curator can delete, modify or add new annotation as well. Three curators were involved in this task. In the end, the files were exported from WebAnno in the format of CoNLL2002.

Post-processing. Unfortunately, WebAnno does not support modifications of tokenization and sentence segmentation in the same step as the correction of NE annotation. Therefore, tokenization errors or misspellings had to be corrected in a separate step, after the annotators have recorded these errors. Spelling errors were not corrected in two kinds of texts: in novels, to save the integrity of these works; and in web texts, to save one of the main attributes of these texts, namely uneditness and spontaneity. Before conversion to the final format, CoNLL-U Plus, the files were subject to a final sanity check, to make sure all the columns are in the right place and that the labels are in the correct format.

Inter-annotator Agreement. As inter-annotator agreement for the NE task, we calculated F-measure. First, we compared the two annotations of each file. In this case, any of the two annotations can be treated as the gold standard, while the other one as the automatic annotation, since the precision of comparing A with B is the same as the recall of a comparison between B and A. The overall F-measure is 87.7% (LOC: 90.86%, MISC: 71.69%, ORG: 85.24%, PER: 93.16%). Second, we compared every annotator's annotation to the corresponding curated file: the overall F-measure is 92.07% (LOC: 94.2%, MISC: 80.47%, ORG: 90.66%, PER: 95.76%).

8.2   The Workflow of Morphological Annotation

Selection of the Texts and Pre-processing. Files including morphological annotation besides NE tags were collected from two sources. First, since the

KorKor corpus was annotated along similar principles, its fully gold standard part (annotated by two annotators) could be built in without further processing, passed on directly to the NE annotation process. The remaining part of KorKor was annotated by only one annotator, so it needed checking and correction of the morphological annotation by an other annotator. Second, the other source was the Hungarian Webcorpus 2.0, a corpus of Hungarian texts crawled from the web and processed by emtsv.

Thus, the standard processing steps from sentence segmentation to disambiguated morphological annotation were already conducted on the selected text material from the KorKor corpus and Hungarian Webcorpus 2.0. Therefore, no pre-processing was needed except for a format conversion, to make the files ready for the manual phase.

The Annotation Process. Each text file was annotated by two annotators. The wokflow of the annotation was designed to provide the annotators as much information as possible to make the right decision regarding the given token and its morphological properties. For each token, the task was to check the lemma and the full morphosyntactic code with the POS tag provided by the morphological disambiguation module of emtsv. If that was proved to be incorrect, the annotator could select the correct one of all possible lemma–code pairs provided by the morphological analyser module of emtsv. If neither of them was correct, the lemma and the tag had to be entered manually. In addition, tokenization errors had to be corrected as well.

The Google Spreadsheets provided the annotation interface, because of the complexity of the setting. The work was eased by conditional formatting. Tokenization errors could be corrected using pre-defined commands, which were parsed during the automatic processing of the tables resulting the text of the correct tokenization, lemmata and tags.

Six linguists were involved in this task as annotators. Two of them have also worked in the project KorKor on the same task before. The communication and the allocation of the texts went the same way as in the case of the NE annotation (see Sect. 8.1). The pace of progress was ca. 1,070 tokens/hour.

Further Steps. Having the xtsv files with manually corrected morphological annotation, they were fed into emtsv again to get automatic NE tagging. From this point, the process is the same as previously described in Sect. 8.1.

After the NE tags were manually corrected, the files were exported from WebAnno and the files with the corrected morphological tags were merged. As the tokenization did not change during the NE annotation process, the last two columns of the CoNLL2002 files were simply pasted into the xtsv files containing the corrected morphological tags.

Tokenization errors and misspellings reported by the annotators were corrected in the merged xtsv files, then the final format conversion resulted in the corpus files of the format CoNLL-U Plus.

Inter-annotator Agreement. The inter-annotator agreement rate in terms of Cohen's κ for the lemmatization: 97,6%, and for the full morphological analysis (POS + morphosyntactic features): 94,52%. These results express overall agreement as an average rate for all documents and annotators.

References

1. Barrault, L., et al.: Findings of the 2019 conference on machine translation (WMT19). In: Proceedings of the 4th Conference on Machine Translation (Volume 2: Shared Task Papers, Day 1), Florence, Italy, pp. 1–61. Association for Computational Linguistics (2019)
2. Eckart de Castilho, R., Mújdricza-Maydt, É., Yimam, S.M., Hartmann, S., Gurevych, I., Frank, A., Biemann, C.: A web-based tool for the integrated annotation of semantic and syntactic structures. In: Proceedings of the Workshop on Language Technology Resources and Tools for Digital Humanities (LT4DH), Osaka, Japan, pp. 76–84 (2016)
3. Csendes, D., Csirik, J., Gyimóthy, T., Kocsor, A.: The szeged treebank. In: Matoušek, V., Mautner, P., Pavelka, T. (eds.) TSD 2005. LNCS (LNAI), vol. 3658, pp. 123–131. Springer, Heidelberg (2005). https://doi.org/10.1007/11551874_16
4. Indig, B., Sass, B., Simon, E., Mittelholcz, I., Vadász, N., Makrai, M.: One format to rule them all - the emtsv pipeline for Hungarian. In: Proceedings of the 13th Linguistic Annotation Workshop, Florence, Italy, pp. 155–165. Association for Computational Linguistics (2019)
5. Nemeskey, D.M.: Natural Language Processing methods for Language Modeling. Ph.D. thesis, Eötvös Loránd University (2020)
6. Novák, A., Siklósi, B., Oravecz, Cs.: A new integrated open-source morphological analyzer for Hungarian. In: Proceedings of the 10th International Conference on Language Resources and Evaluation, LREC 2016. European Language Resources Association (ELRA) (2016)
7. Simon, E., Farkas, R., Halácsy, P., Sass, B., Szarvas, Gy., Varga, D.: A HunNER korpusz (The HunNER corpus). In: Alexin, Z., Csendes, D. (eds.) IV. Magyar Számítógépes Nyelvészeti Konferencia (4th Conference on Hungarian Computational Linguistics). Szeged (2006)
8. Simon, E., Lendvai, P., Németh, G., Olaszy, G., Vicsi, K.: A magyar nyelv a digitális korban - The Hungarian Language in the Digital Age. In: Rehm, G., Uszkoreit, H. (eds.) META-NET White Paper Series. Springer, Heidelberg (2012). https://doi.org/10.1007/978-3-642-30379-1
9. Simon, E.: Approaches to Hungarian Named Entity Recognition. Ph.D. thesis, Ph.D. School in Cognitive Sciences, Budapest University of Technology and Economics (2013)
10. Simon, E., Nemeskey, D.M.: Automatically generated NE tagged corpora for English and Hungarian. In: Proceedings of the 4th Named Entity Workshop (NEWS) 2012, Jeju, Korea, pp. 38–46. Association for Computational Linguistics (2012)
11. Steinberger, R., et al.: An overview of the European Union's highly multilingual parallel corpora file. Lang. Resour. Eval. **48**, 679–707 (2014)
12. Steinberger, R., et al.: The JRC-Acquis: a multilingual aligned parallel corpus with 20+ languages. In: Proceedings of the 5th International Conference on Language Resources and Evaluation, LREC 2006, Genoa, Italy (2006)

13. Szarvas, Gy., Farkas, R., Felföldi, L., Kocsor, A., Csirik, J.: A highly accurate Named Entity corpus for Hungarian. In: Electronic Proceedings of the 5th International Conference on Language Resources and Evaluation (2006)
14. Tjong Kim Sang, E.F.: Introduction to the CoNLL-2002 shared task: language-independent named entity recognition. In: Roth, D., van den Bosch, A. (eds.) Proceedings of CoNLL-2002, Taipei, Taiwan, pp. 155–158 (2002)
15. Tjong Kim Sang, E.F., De Meulder, F.: Introduction to the CoNLL-2003 shared task: language-independent named entity recognition. In: Daelemans, W., Osborne, M. (eds.) Proceedings of CoNLL-2003, Edmonton, Canada (2003)
16. Vadász, N.: KorKorpusz: kézzel annotált, többrétegű pilotkorpusz építése (The KorKor corpus: building of a manually annotated multi-layer pilot corpus). In: XVI. Magyar Számítógépes Nyelvészeti Konferencia (16th Conference on Hungarian Computational Linguistics), pp. 141–154. Szegedi Tudományegyetem, Szeged (2020)
17. Vadász, N., Simon, E.: Konverterek magyar morfológiai címkekészletek között (Converters between Hungarian morphological tagsets). In: Berend, G., Gosztolya, G., Vincze, V. (eds.) XV. Magyar Számítógépes Nyelvészeti Konferencia (15th Conference on Hungarian Computational Linguistics), pp. 99–111. Szegedi Tudományegyetem Informatikai Intézet, Szeged (2019)
18. Váradi, T.: The Hungarian national corpus. In: Proceedings of the 3rd International Conference on Language Resources and Evaluation, LREC-2002, Las Palmas de Gran Canaria, pp. 385–389. European Language Resources Association (2002)
19. Váradi, T., et al.: E-magyar – a digital language processing system. In: Calzolari, N., et al. (eds.) Proceedings of the 11th International Conference on Language Resources and Evaluation, LREC 2018, Miyazaki, Japan. European Language Resources Association (ELRA) (2018)

Semantic Templates for Generating Long-Form Technical Questions

Samiran Pal, Avinash Singh, Soham Datta, Sangameshwar Patil[✉],
Indrajit Bhattacharya, and Girish Palshikar

TCS Research, Pune, India
{samiran.pal,singh.avinash9,d.soham,sangameshwar.patil,
b.indrajit,gk.palshikar}@tcs.com

Abstract. Question generation (QG) from technical text has multiple important applications such as creation of question-banks for examinations, interviews as well as in intelligent tutoring systems. However, much of the existing work for QG has focused on open-domain and not specifically on technical domain. We propose to generate technical questions using semantic templates. We also focus on ensuring that a large fraction of the generated questions are long-form, i.e., they require longer answers spanning multiple sentences. This is in contrast with existing work which has predominantly focused on generating factoid questions which have a few words or phrases as answers. Using the technical topics selected from undergraduate and graduate-level courses in Computer Science, we show that the proposed approach is able to generate questions with high acceptance rate. Further, we also show that the proposed template-based approach can be effectively leveraged using the distant supervision paradigm to finetune and significantly improve the existing sequence-to-sequence deep learning models for generating long-form, technical questions.

Keywords: Technical question generation · Distant supervision · Long-form questions · Sequence-to-sequence models · Natural language generation

1 Introduction

Asking interesting and probing questions is a crucial human ability in various conversational situations, such as criminal investigations, legal argumentation, interviews and sales, to name a few. With the advent of sophisticated speech and NLP technologies, the same ability is now important in practical applications such as conversational systems (chat-bots), question answering, intelligent tutoring, and online debating. Recognizing this, automatic *question generation (QG)* from given input text has attracted a significant amount of research, most of which employs supervised machine learning techniques [7,10,17,20]. External reward sources have also been used for fine tuning QG models [7,10].

© Springer Nature Switzerland AG 2021
K. Ekštein et al. (Eds.): TSD 2021, LNAI 12848, pp. 235–247, 2021.
https://doi.org/10.1007/978-3-030-83527-9_20

Fan et al. [4] explore visual natural QG as language generation task with content and linguistics as specific attributes. Clarification QG problem was handled in [20] by modelling hypothetical answers as latent variable into GAN architecture. In [17], they consider the challenges when answer length is increased, and provide first use of transformer based model which outperforms LSTM. See [11] for an extensive review of techniques for QG. QG has been defined [16] as the task of generating grammatically correct, semantically sound, comprehensible, interesting, salient and relevant questions from the given input, typically a text document, but possibly a structured database or a knowledge base also. Ideally, the generated questions should also have diverse structure and *cover* as many concepts from the input as possible.

In this paper, we focus on generating questions for a specific *technical* subject, which are also *long-form* questions that are likely to have answers containing around 5 sentences or so. This setting is in contrast to much work in the literature, which focuses on generating *open-domain* questions which are not specific to any particular domain. Further, much existing work also focuses on generating *factoid questions*, which typically have very short phrases as answers (e.g., mentions of named entities such as PERSON, DATE, LOCATION etc.). QG techniques for technical questions are useful in creating question banks, which are used in examinations, intelligent tutoring systems, and interviews.

QG techniques for technical questions bring their own challenges. First, apart from generic comprehensibility, the generated questions should "make sense" in the technical domain, which is hard to ensure. For example, How do you execute foreign keys? is syntactically correct, but meaningless in the subject of Databases. Also, most technical questions need to be interesting and challenging, which is again hard to ensure. Ensuring that the questions cover the subject adequately is also important. It is not obvious how to ensure that the generated questions are long-form i.e., have around 5 sentences as answers.

In this paper, we take an approach to generate technical long-form questions using semantic templates. Using the technical topics selected from undergraduate and graduate-level courses in Computer Science, we show that the proposed approach is able to generate questions which have high acceptability rate when evaluated by human experts. Further, we also show that the proposed template-based approach can be productively leveraged using the distant supervision paradigm to finetune and significantly improve the state-of-the-art BART sequence-to-sequence learning model [12] for the challenging task of technical question generation.

Rest of the paper is organized as follows. We discuss the related work in Sect. 2, followed by the details of semantic templates in Sect. 3. In Sect. 4, we show how distant supervision can be used to improve existing Seq2seq deep learning models using the set of questions generated by the proposed approach. We provide empirical validation of the proposed approach in Sect. 5 and note our conclusions in Sect. 6.

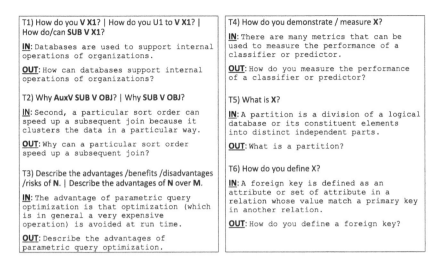

Fig. 1. Examples of questions generated from input text for our different template algorithms

2   Related Work

Early work in QG used manually created rules, templates and pattern matching on input sentences to generate questions. Broadly, we share the slot-based templates approach of these works, but we also use dependency parse (most early work used constituency parse), and incorporate complex semantic constraints, such as those based on semantic roles, named entities and relation extractions. Other unique features of our approach are: our focus on generating long-form questions that have answers containing around 5 sentences, input text of technical subjects, and answer unaware QG. We use the templates as distant supervision to create training data for deep learning systems for QG. The idea of using external resources to augment training data (distant supervision) is well-known; we do not review such work. However, we are not aware of any existing work on distant supervision techniques specifically for question generation.

The authors of [1] used rules to identify situational information (mental state, causality, temporality) in informational sentences and use it to instantiate templates. The paper [2] uses seed questions with sentences containing the factoid answers, and learns simple syntactic patterns for questions, with semantic constraints based on named entities on answers. The papers [8,24] use similar approaches. In [6] they used syntactic rules that transformed declarative sentences into questions, which were then ranked by a logistic regression model.

Newer methods for QG use deep learning, and in contrast to this work, most of them focus on factoid, open-domain questions, and most of them need answers as part of training data. The authors of [22] generate factoid questions from Freebase (subject, relation, object) triplets (where the object is the correct answer), by learning an encoder representation of the triplet and decoding it using a

GRU RNN with an attention-mechanism to generate the associated question. The paper [3] use bidirectional LSTM to encode a sentence and a paragraph and then use a decoder to generate the question from the concatenated sentence and paragraph encodings. In [25] they use a GAN framework along with an observed and a hidden variable to capture question types and variability in questions respectively. The paper [26] uses a maxout pointer mechanism with gated self-attention encoder to generate questions using a paragraph as the context. The authors of [13] proposes a sequence-to-sequence generative model with passage encoding, copying and a GCN-based clue word predictor. In [14] they propose an architecture that makes use of clues and styles (i.e., type of question) to generate questions using a seq2seq encoder-decoder architecture with attention and a copy mechanism, employing clue embedding, passage embedding, and style encoding; they also incorporate a filter to remove low quality questions.

3 Question Templates

We state each template as a *template algorithm* that takes a document (i.e., a sequence of sentences), and analyzes the structure of each sentence, generating a question having a fixed structure, if certain conditions are satisfied. Each input sentence is processed only if it satisfies some basic conditions, such as it contains less than 30 words or does not contain a mathematical formula or symbol etc. The restriction to smaller sentences is because of the empirical observation that dependency parsing tends to make more errors for longer sentences.

Each template has a fixed syntactic structure for the to-be-generated question and contains some *slots* that need to be filled up (*instantiated*) appropriately from the given (input) text document. The template basically imposes some arguably *semantic* constraints that must be satisfied by the *values* (occurring in the input sentence) for each slot. If all these constraints are satisfied, then a question is generated with the instantiated slot values. We use the dependency parse tree, as constructed by SpaCy tool, for analyzing the structure of the input sentence. The semantic constraints are stated as part of the *template algorithm*. The template algorithms could be alternatively stated using tree regular expressions or abstract semantic representation (AMR). We specify the template using an algorithmic form primarily for its simplicity and ability to accommodate constraints which are hard or even impossible to state in other formalisms because of their limited expressive power. Most templates impose a constraint on the possible value for a slot that it should not contain any pronouns or any *coreference marker* words, such as this, that, those, these, previous, which, same, some, every, none, where etc. The reason is that such words (without anaphora or coreference resolution) make the generated question unclear and incomplete i.e., unable to stand on its own. Finally to make the slots values appropriate we impose additional syntactic constraints that ensure generation of syntactically valid constraints by taking into account the tense, case, number etc.

A key feature of the template algorithms is that they attempt to preserve the semantics of the input sentence, so that the generated question *makes sense* in the given technical subject. We cannot, of course, hope to "prove" this statement. Still, to illustrate, the input sentence for the template T4 in Fig. 1 implicitly states that classifiers have a measurable property called performance. The generated question is clearly consistent with this semantics, which would not be the case if the generated question were, for instance, How do you measure the metrics of a classifier or predictor?.

Template 1: A powerful class of technical questions consists of asking *how* some task/activity can be performed. Such questions are almost always reasonably challenging, and the answers are typically long-form. The template algorithm (Fig. 2(a)) applies to only those sentences containing "to V", where V is an *action verb* in simple present tense and V has a direct object phrase X. The template algorithm (Fig. 2(a))uses a simple WordNet-based check to identify action verbs; in addition, it can use a list of domain-specific action verbs. We expand the direct object phrase X to $X1$ by appending to it any prepositional phrases occurring immediately after X. This expansion helps in completion of the question's meaning. If there is no verb U connected to V through DRs like "xcomp" or "advcl", then the algorithm outputs the question "How can you V $X1$?, where the slots $V, X1$ are now instantiated. If such a verb U exists, is not an action verb, and has a "valid" subject phrase SUB then the algorithm outputs the question "How do/can SUB V $X1$?. The third type of question is generated if U is an action verb. As stated, the template does not handle multiple occurrence of strings of type "to W"; however, it is easy to modify the template to accommodate this.

For the sentence One way to classify databases involves the type of their contents, for example: bibliographic, document-text, statistical, or multimedia objects., we get $V =$ classify which is in simple present tense, there is "aux" DR between V and to, V is clearly an action verb, direct object X of V is databases, no PPs occur immediately after X (so $X1 = X$), $X1$ does not contain any pronouns or coreference markers, no verb U is connected to V, and so the generated question is How do you classify databases?.

For the example sentence of T1 in Fig. 1, $V =$ support, $X =$ internal operations , $X1 =$ internal operations of organizations, $U =$ small used, $U1 =$ se, $SUB =$ databases, then assuming use is not an action verb, the generated question is How can databases support internal operations of organizations?.

Template 2: Causality is an important aspect of knowledge and questions on understanding of causal knowledge in a technical subject are interesting and challenging. This template generates such *why* questions from sentences which express causal knowledge. A sentence often mentions a *causal relation*, where a *causal trigger* connects a *cause* phrase with an *effect* phrase within the same sentence. Extraction of mentions of cause-effect relations is a well-known problem in information extraction; see [18] for a survey of ML and NLP techniques for this. Some standard causal triggers are because, due to, therefore, leads to etc. Many verbs can also serve as causal triggers, as in: The heavy rain **delayed** the local trains. We have trained an ML model for cause-effect relation extraction, which is used in the routine *extract_CE_relation(S)*. It returns the cause phrase, effect phrase, and the causal trigger from the given sentence S; returns NULL if no causal relation is mentioned in S.

Figure 2(b) shows the template algorithm for generating this type of questions. Often the effect phrase includes a verb V along with its subject and object, which are used to generate the question. If an auxiliary verb U is associated with V in the

// words which make subject of a verb uninteresting
BL := {way,ways,method,methods,approach,approaches};
for each sentence S in P **do**:
a. **if** S does not contain string "to V" where V is a verb in simple present tense **then continue**; **end if**
b. **if** there is no "aux" DR between "to" and V **then continue**; **endif**
c. **if** V is NOT an "action" verb **then continue**; **endif**
d. Let X := direct object phrase of V // headword of X, V related by dobj or obj DR
e. **if** there is no such X **then continue**; **endif**
f. Let $X1$ be the phrase obtained by adding to X at most 3 consecutive prepositional phrases (PP) occurring after X but without crossing comma or colon, semicolon, a verb (unless it is inside a PP);
g. **if** $X1$ contains any pronoun **or** any co-reference marker word **then continue**; **endif**
h. **if** $X1$ contains any verb which is not inside a PP **then continue**; **endif**
i.   Let U be a verb connected to V using "xcomp" or "advcl" DR;
j. **if** there is no such U **then** print "How can you V $X1$?"; **continue**; **endif**
k.   Let SUB := subject of U; // SUB is connected to U using "nsubj" or "nsubjpass" DRs
l. **if** U does not have any subject **then** S_empty := **true**
        else S_empty := **false**; **endif**
m. **if** !S_empty **and** (SUB contains a pronoun **or** SUB contains a coreference marker word **or** SUB contains a word in BL) **then**
        S_bad := **true else** S_bad := **false**; **endif**
n.   Let $U1$:= root form of U;
o. **if** !S_empty **and** !S_bad **then**
        if $U1$ is **not** an action verb **then** print "How do/can SUB V $X1$?" **else continue**; **endif**
p. **else**
        if $U1$ is an action verb **then** print "How do you $U1$ to V $X1$?";
        else print "How do you V $X1$?" **endif**
q. **endif**
end for

(a) Algorithm for template "How do you V X1?" and its variants

for each sentence S in P **do**:
(CP, EP, TP) := extract_CE_relation(S) // extract causal relation mentioned in S
a. **if** there is no causal relation mention in S **then continue**; **endif**
b. **if** EP contains any pronoun **or** any coreference marker **then continue**; **endif**
c. **if** EP contains words like "example", ex.", "examples", "instance" **then continue**; **endif**
d. Let V := the main verb in EP + particles connected to V with DR "prt" (if present) +   negation words connected to V using DR "neg" (if present) + a verb connected to V using DR "auxpass" + a phrase connected to V using DR "advmod" (if present)
e. **if** there is no main verb in EP **then continue**; **endif**
f. Let AV := the auxiliary verb in EP which is connected to V by DR "aux"; // can, could, may, has, had, have etc.
g. **if** there is no such auxiliary verb in EP **and** V ≠ copula **then continue**; **endif**
h. Let SUB := phrase in EP connected to V by DR "nsubj" or "nsubjpass";
i. **if** there is no such phrase in EP **then continue**; **endif**
j. Let OBJ be the phrase in EP connected to V by DR "dobj";
k. **if** there is no such phrase **then** OBJ := sequence of PPs immediately following V; **endif**
l. **if** there is no such sequence of PPs **and** V is copula **then** OBJ := phrase connected to V using DR "attr" **or** using DR "acomp" **endif**
m. **if** OBJ == NULL **then continue**; **endif**
n. **if** OBJ contains any pronoun **or** any coreference marker **then continue**; **endif**
o. **if** OBJ contains words like "example", ex.", "examples", "instance" **then continue**; **endif**
p. **if** AV ≠ NULL **then** print "Why AV SUB V OBJ?" **else** print "Why SUB V OBJ?" **endif**
end for

(b) Algorithm for template "Why AV SUB V OBJ" and its variants

WL := {advantage, advantages, benefit, benefits, disadvantage, disadvantages, risk, risks};
for each sentence S in P **do**:
a. **if** S does not contain a word from WL **then continue**; **endif**
b.   Let X be the word from WL that occurs in S with POS tag "noun";
c. **if** X is the headword of an entire phrase O connected to a copula verb V by DR "dobj" **and** O is connected by DR "prep" to preposition "over" **and** this "over" is connected to an entire phrase M using DR "pobj" **and** V is connected by DR "nsubj" to an entire phrase Y **the**
        i.   **if** Y contains any pronoun **or** any coreference marker **then continue**; **endif**
        ii. Let N be the above PP headed by "of" // N := "of" + Y
        iii. Let Z be the plural of X; // advantage → advantages, risk → risks etc.
        iv. print "Describe the Z of N over M."
d. **else if** X is connected by DR "prep" to the preposition "of" **and** this "of" is connected to an entire phrase Y using DR "pobj" **then**
        i.   **if** Y contains any pronoun **or** any coreference marker **then continue**; **endif**
        ii. Let N be the above PP headed by "of" // N := "of" + Y
        iii. Let Z be the plural of X; // advantage → advantages, risk → risks etc.
        iv. print "Describe the Z of N."
e. **endif**
end for

(c)Algorithm for template "Describe_the_advantage|disadvantage|.._of_X?" and its variants

// can add more verbs like improve, reduce, optimize
WL := {measure, demonstrate};
for each sentence S in P **do**:
a. **if** S does not contain "to V" where V is some verb from WL **then continue**; **endif**
b.testing
b. Let X be entire phrase connected to V by DR "dobj"
c. **if** there is no such X **then continue**; **endif**
d. **if** X contains a pronoun **or** a coreference marker **then continue**; **endif**
e. **if** X contains words like "example", ex.", "examples", "instance" **then continue**; **endif**
f. **if** X contains a comma **then** remove the comma and all text thereafter **endif**
g. print "How do you V X?"
end for

(d) Algorithm for template "How do you (measure|demonstrate|..) X?"

Fig. 2. Definitions of different template algorithms.

effect phrase, then it is included in the generated question. For the example sentence of T2 in Fig. 1, EP = a particular sort order can speed up a subsequent join, V = speed up, AV = can, SUB = a particular sort order, OBJ = a subsequent join and the generated question is: Why can a particular sort order speed up a subsequent join?.

Template 3: A useful class of technical questions asks about the advantages/benefits/disadvantages/risks of a particular object, concept, technique, process etc. A similar type of question asks about the advantages/disadvantages of one such entity over another, related entity. A typical sentence describing the advantages/disadvantages etc. of something is as follows: a copula verb has a subject that includes, say, advantages, to which a PP headed by of is connected by the dependency relation **dobj**. Figure 2(c) shows the template algorithm for generating this type of questions.

For the example T3 in Fig. 1, X = advantage, Y = parametric query optimization, N = of parametric query optimization, Z = advantages, and the generated question is: Describe the advantages of parametric query optimization.

Template 4: A small but useful class of technical questions asks about ways of measuring something, ways of demonstrating something etc. Figure 2(d) shows the template algorithm for generating this type of questions. Basically, in sentences containing to V where V is some verb like measure, demonstrate etc., it looks for the object of V and generates a question by using it. For the example T4 in Fig. 1, V = measure, X = the performance of a classifier or predictor, and the generated question is: How do you measure the performance of a classifier or predictor?.

Templates 5 and 6: An important class of technical questions consists of asking about the definition or description of some technical concept X within the given subject. The key question is: how to identify suitable values (instantiations) for X? Several algorithms are available for identifying technical terms in a given corpus related to a specific technical subject; see [21] for a recent comparative study of these techniques. They can be used to identify all technical terms X present in a given corpus, and then we can generate the question What is X?. Given our requirement of high precision, we propose a simple alternative.

First, a technical term is often in the form of a *noun compound* i.e., a sequence of nouns/proper nouns, possibly beginning with an article and optionally containing an adjective. Examples: Database virtualization, foreign key, Java Database Connectivity, Database index, Stored procedure etc. Further, we impose a simple χ^2-test based check, adapted from [9], that the headword is indeed a technical term in the corpus. Second, a technical term is sometimes expressed as a noun compound followed by a verb in gerund form; e.g., Database activity monitoring, Database auditing, Two-phase locking etc. The template algorithm simply checks if in the given sentence containing is a, the subject X of is is in either of these forms, with some additional restrictions (to avoid invalid terms) like not containing a number, a pronoun or a coreference marker. If yes, then it generates the question What is X?. For example sentence of T5 in Fig. 1, the subject of is is a partition. Template (6) works in a similar manner, except that it looks for sentences containing is defined as.

Limitations: The questions generated using the templates mainly have two issues. First, sometimes the question is meaningless, because the slot values are incorrect. Example: from If the tree is a complete binary tree, this method wastes no space., template 5 generates the question What is the tree?, which does not make sense. Another issue is about incomplete context in the question, which reduces the acceptability of the question. For example, a question like What is an entity? is not clear without including a context description. For example, we could add the subject name to the generated question, as in In the context of Database: What is an entity?, which clarifies the question.

4   Using Templates for Distant Supervision

The proposed template-based approach can be productively leveraged for the challenging task of technical question generation by using the distant supervision paradigm. Many pretrained sequence-to-sequence (seq2seq) models are available for natural language generation (NLG) tasks such as summarization, question-answering (QA) etc. For instance, BART [12] has been pre-trained for extractive QA task using SQuAD [19]. In this paper, we propose two enhancements to the BART model. First, we adapt BART for question generation task and then finetune it for the technical question generation. Figure 3 gives overview of the pre-training and finetuning steps. Note that the BART paper provides a pre-trained model for the extractive QA task, but not for the QG task.

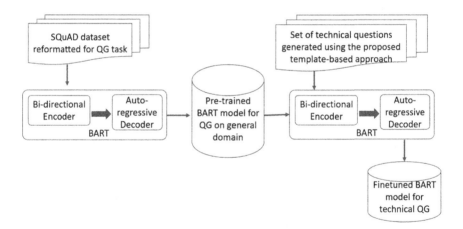

Fig. 3. Deep learning pipeline for training the BART model for QG task and then finetuning it for technical QG

BART [12] is a recently proposed denoising autoencoder for pretraining seq2seq deep learning networks. It has proved to be useful for NLG when it is finetuned for specific tasks. To create a pre-trained BART model for QG, we reformat the SQuAD dataset using the scheme proposed by [15]. The BART encoder is provided a text paragraph from SQuAD as input and the questions generated from the paragraph as the target sequence to be generated. This pre-trained model is then finetuned using sentences selected from Wikipedia pages on technical topics and the questions generated from these sentences by the proposed template-based approach.

We use the pretrained BART model as a baseline to compare against the performance after the finetuning process. We also note that most of the existing DL models for QG (e.g., [14]) require the answer to be provided along with the input sentence and the target question to be generated. However, answer-aware QG is not meaningful for most application scenarios for long-form technical QG. Additionally, there are no large datasets which provide both technical questions as well as answers along with the input text. Hence, we use the answer-agnostic seq2seq model (BART) to assess the effectiveness of finetuning process for question generation.

5 Empirical Evaluation

We evaluate the effectiveness of the proposed method based on two use-cases: (i) ability of the proposed method to generate semantically valid, long-form technical questions, and (ii) utility of the generated set of questions to finetune and improve a pre-trained deep learning (DL) model for the challenging task of technical question generation.

Dataset: We use the CRUMBTRAIL algorithm [23] to select a subset of Wikipedia pages belonging to technical subjects in Computer Science and Signal Processing (such as algorithms, machine learning, database, natural language processing, deep learning etc.). To create the seedset for the CRUMBTRAIL algorithm, we use the 576 Wikipedia pages which are related to the topics mentioned in the syllabi of MIT OCW[1] courses for 17 different technical subjects. Starting from the seed pages, the CRUMBTRAIL algorithm makes use of the underlying graph structure of Wikipedia and DBPedia to select 11870 Wiki articles related to the technical topics. We use the proposed template-based approach to create 16835 questions related to the technical subjects. These questions and the corresponding sentences are used for finetuning the BART model. We use 13468 (i.e., 80%) of these questions as training data and 3367 (i.e., 20%) questions as validation data in the finetuning process.

The textual content of 576 Wikipedia pages, which are selected based on the MIT OCW syllabi, is used as the test data. There are conversion and formatting errors while converting the mediawiki markup to plain text data, especially for the mathematical formulae. To minimize the impact of such noise, the template-based algorithms (Fig. 2) filter out some potentially noisy sentences such as sentences containing mathematical formula or symbols. We use the same filtering criteria to select input sentences from the Wikipedia pages to the BART model. We use S to denote the set of sentences in the input text for a technical subject after filtering noisy sentences.

Evaluation Metrics: A critical measure to evaluate effectiveness of question generation is that they should be acceptable as valid questions to human experts. This is especially important for technical questions as they are intended to be used for assessment of humans (such as students in an examination or candidates in interviews). Further, since there are no gold standard datasets for technical question generation, automated evaluation using the n-gram overlap metrics such as BLEU, METEOR, ROUGE etc. used in [3,10,13] is not feasible. Hence, we randomly sample a subset of questions and seek human expert feedback whether the questions are semantically valid for a given domain and whether they require long-form answers (i.e., answers spanning around 2 to 5 sentences).

An additional aspect for technical questions is the variety of concepts covered by the generated set of questions. This is important to ensure that the question banks created

---

[1] https://ocw.mit.edu.

using the generated questions cover adequate number of concepts from the technical topics. To quantify the concept coverage, we annotate the generated questions using an automated concept annotation tool, TAGME [5]. For each question, this provides us with a set of mentions and concepts (Wikipedia article nodes) from DBPedia as a whole.

Let Q_T be the set of questions generated automatically using the proposed template-based question generation technique. Let $Q_T^v \subseteq Q_T$ denote the set of questions that are deemed semantically valid by a human-expert and $Q_T^l \subseteq Q_T^v$ be the set of semantically valid questions that need long-form answers as deemed by the human expert. For the sets of questions generated using the pre-trained BART model, let $Q_{pre}, Q_{pre}^v, Q_{pre}^l$ be the counterparts of Q_T, Q_T^v, Q_T^l respectively. Similarly, let $Q_{ft}, Q_{ft}^v, Q_{ft}^l$ be the counterparts in the case of the finetuned BART model.

Metrics for Semantic Validity and Long-Form Quality of Questions: We define $\alpha_T^v = \frac{|Q_T^v|}{|Q_T|}$ to measure the fraction of semantically valid questions generated by the question generation process. Similarly, $\alpha_T^l = \frac{|Q_T^l|}{|Q_T|}$ is the fraction of *long-form* questions. Let $\alpha_{pre}^v, \alpha_{pre}^l$ and $\alpha_{ft}^v, \alpha_{ft}^l$ be the corresponding measures in case of pre-trained DL model and fine-tuned DL model respectively.

Metrics for Concept Coverage: Let C_T^v and C_T^l denote the number of concepts covered by the questions in Q_T^v and Q_T^l respectively. Let C_{pre}^v, C_{pre}^l and C_{ft}^v, C_{ft}^l be their counterparts for the pre-trained and the finetuned BART models, respectively.

Table 1. Acceptability and concept-coverage metrics on random samples of questions (T = Template-based, pre = Pre-trained BART, ft = Finetuned BART.)

	Algorithms	Deep Learning	Database	ML	NLP	Signal proc	Average
$|S|$	2422	560	671	2149	897	2092	1465.17
α_T^v	0.60	0.62	0.72	0.72	0.74	0.60	**0.67**
α_T^l	0.58	0.60	0.72	0.70	0.74	0.46	**0.63**
C_T^v	88	70	104	79	103	61	84.2
C_T^l	86	66	104	78	103	45	80.3
$|Q_T|$	228	147	141	226	72	254	178
α_{pre}^v	0.41	0.52	0.59	0.28	0.47	0.42	0.45
α_{pre}^l	0.05	0.14	0.16	0.20	0.37	0.13	0.18
C_{pre}^v	148	178	159	82	146	140	**142.2**
C_{pre}^l	14	39	51	49	110	48	51.8
$|Q_{pre}|$	3074	704	850	2834	1191	2712	**1894.2**
α_{ft}^v	0.45	0.59	0.66	0.42	0.46	0.42	**0.50**
α_{ft}^l	0.35	0.53	0.66	0.42	0.45	0.21	**0.44**
C_{ft}^v	105	175	174	96	112	106	128
C_{ft}^l	82	157	174	96	110	62	**113.5**
$|Q_{ft}|$	2147	496	625	2006	859	1879	1335.3

Experimental Results and Analysis: Table 1 summarizes the acceptability rates and concept-coverage for the different approaches used for question generation. For the template-based approach, 50 questions were randomly sampled from generated questions for each technical subject. For the pre-trained and finetuned BART models, the random sample size chosen for human expert annotation was 100 per technical subject. We observe that the proposed template-based approach has highest acceptability rate for the semantically valid questions (α_T^v) and for long-form questions (α_T^l). This high quality of the template based approach has the flip side of relatively lower quantity in terms of total number of questions generated.

The pre-trained BART model is able to generate larger number of questions ($|Q_{pre}|$). However, we need to note that it has the lowest acceptability rate, especially for the most important category of interest, i.e., the long-form questions (α_{pre}^l). This is because it is trained on the SQuAD dataset which is an open-domain dataset and has predominantly *factoid* questions. It is not focused on technical questions. We observe that finetuning the pre-trained BART model helps us to retain its ability to generate a large number of questions and at the same time, improve the acceptability rate. Note that after finetuning the BART model with technical questions generated using the template-based approach, the acceptability rate shows significant increase. In fact, α_{ft}^l increases by 144% with respect to α_{pre}^l. We also observe that the finetuned model has significantly better concept coverage for long-form questions than both the pre-trained as well as template-based approaches. It implies that the finetuned model retains the ability to generalize the technical question generation process to a larger number of concepts. Thus, we can conclude that the set of questions generated by the proposed template-based approach can be effectively used to finetune and significantly improve an existing seq2seq DL model for generating long-form, technical questions.

6 Conclusion

Question generation from technical text has many applications in the domains of education and recruitment. Existing approaches for question generation have limitations as they are focused on factoid questions with short answers. In this paper, we proposed the use of semantic templates to generate questions from technical text. We empirically verified that the proposed approach is able to generated semantically valid questions that require long-form answers. We also showed that the proposed approach is effective in finetuning and significantly improving a state-of-the-art deep learning based sequence to sequence model for generating technical questions.

References

1. Chen, W., Aist, G., Mostow, J.: Generating questions automatically from informational text. In: 2nd Workshop on Question Generation (2009)
2. Curto, S., Mendes, A.C., Coheur, L.: Exploring linguistically-rich patterns for question generation. In: UCNLG+Eval: Language Generation and Evaluation Workshop (2011)
3. Du, X., Shao, J., Cardie, C.: Learning to ask: neural question generation for reading comprehension. In: 55th Annual Meeting of the Association for Computational Linguistics (Volume 1: Long Papers) (2017)

4. Fan, Z., Wei, Z., Wang, S., Liu, Y., Huang, X.: A reinforcement learning framework for natural question generation using bi-discriminators. In: 27th International Conference on Computational Linguistics (COLING) (2018)
5. Ferragina, P., Scaiella, U.: Fast and accurate annotation of short texts with Wikipedia pages. IEEE Softw. **29**(1), 70–75 (2012)
6. Heilman, M., Smith, N.A.: Good question! statistical ranking for question generation. In: Human Language Technologies: 2010 Annual Conference of the North American Chapter of the Association for Computational Linguistics (2010)
7. Hosking, T., Riedel, S.: Evaluating rewards for question generation models. In: NAACL-HLT (2019)
8. Kalady, S., Elikkottil, A., Das, R.: Natural language question generation using syntax and keywords. In: 3rd Workshop on Question Generation (2010)
9. Kilgarriff, A.: Comparing corpora. Int. J. Corpus Linguist. **6**, 97–133 (2001)
10. Kumar, V., Ramakrishnan, G., Li, Y.F.: Putting the horse before the cart: a generator-evaluator framework for question generation from text. In: 23rd Conference on Computational Natural Language Learning (2019)
11. Kurdi, G., Leo, J., Parsia, B., Sattler, U., Al-Emari, S.: A systematic review of automatic question generation for educational purposes. Int. J. Artif. Intell. Educ. **30**(1), 121–204 (2019). https://doi.org/10.1007/s40593-019-00186-y
12. Lewis, M., et al.: BART: denoising sequence-to-sequence pre-training for natural language generation, translation, and comprehension. In: Proceedings of the 58th Annual Meeting of the ACL (2020)
13. Liu, B., et al.: Learning to generate questions by learning what not to generate. In: WWW (2019)
14. Liu, B., Wei, H., Niu, D., Chen, H., He, Y.: Asking questions the human way: scalable question-answer generation from text corpus. In: WWW (2020)
15. Lopez, L.E., Cruz, D.K., Cruz, J.C.B., Cheng, C.: Transformer-based end-to-end question generation (2021)
16. Mannem, P., Prasad, R., Joshi, A.: Question generation from paragraphs at UPenn: QGSTEC system description. In: 3rd Workshop on Question Generation, QG 2000 (2000)
17. Mishra, S.K., Goel, P., Sharma, A., Jagannatha, A., Jacobs, D., Daume, H.: Towards automatic generation of questions from long answers. arXiv:2004.05109 (2020)
18. Pawar, S., Palshikar, G.K., Bhattacharyya, P.: Relation extraction: a survey. arxiv:1712.05191 (2017)
19. Rajpurkar, P., Zhang, J., Lopyrev, K., Liang, P.: SQuAD: 100,000+ questions for machine comprehension of text. In: EMNLP (2016)
20. Rao, S., Daume, H.: Answer-based adversarial training for generating clarification questions. In: NAACL-HLT (2019)
21. Šajatović, A., Buljan, M., Šnajder, J., Dalbelo Bašić, B.: Evaluating automatic term extraction methods on individual documents. In: Joint Workshop on Multiword Expressions and WordNet, MWE-WN 2019 (2019)
22. Serban, I.V., et al.: Generating factoid questions with recurrent neural networks: the 30M factoid question-answer corpus. In: 54th Annual Meeting of the Association for Computational Linguistics (Volume 1: Long Papers) (2016)
23. Stefano, F., Finocchi, I., Ponzetto, S.P., Paola, V.: Efficient pruning of large knowledge graphs. In: IJCAI (2018)
24. Wyse, B., Piwek, P.: Generating questions from OpenLearn study units. In: 2nd Workshop on Question Generation (2009)

25. Yao, K., Zhang, L., Luo, T., Tao, L., Wu, Y.: Teaching machines to ask questions. In: IJCAI (2018)
26. Zhao, Y., Ni, X., Ding, Y., Ke, Q.: Paragraph-level neural question generation with maxout pointer and gated self-attention networks. In: EMNLP (2018)

Rethinking Adversarial Training for Language Adaptation

Gil Rocha[(✉)] and Henrique Lopes Cardoso

Laboratório de Inteligência Artificial e Ciência de Computadores (LIACC),
Faculdade de Engenharia, Universidade do Porto, Porto, Portugal
{gil.rocha,hlc}@fe.up.pt

Abstract. Recent advances in pre-trained language models revolutionized the field of natural language processing. However, these approaches require large-scale annotated resources, that are only available for some languages. Collecting data in every language is unrealistic, hence the growing interest in cross-lingual methods that can leverage the knowledge acquired in one language to different target languages. To address these challenges, Adversarial Training has been successfully employed in a variety of tasks and languages. Empirical analysis for the task of natural language inference suggests that, with the advent of neural language models, more challenging auxiliary tasks should be formulated to further improve the transfer of knowledge via Adversarial Training. We propose alternative formulations for the adversarial component, which we believe to be promising in different cross-lingual scenarios.

Keywords: Machine learning · Natural language processing · Cross-language learning · Natural Language Inference

1 Introduction

Most existing approaches to address semantic-demanding tasks in natural language processing rely on the availability of manually annotated resources. However, acquiring annotated resources in different languages is a challenging and time-consuming task. Consequently, the study of methods that can leverage the knowledge acquired when trained on a source language to a target language are essential. Recent studies have been proposed to address this task without requiring labeled data on the target language. This is of upmost importance for less-resourced language, in which labeled data is scarce.

For the task of Natural Language Inference (NLI) [4], Adversarial Training [6] has been successfully employed using multilingual word embeddings [6,24]. One key advantage of Adversarial Training over other proposed approaches [24] is that we obtain a single encoder that can be employed across different languages, while other approaches require different encoders for each target language, which can be expensive to acquire in different scenarios.

© Springer Nature Switzerland AG 2021
K. Ekštein et al. (Eds.): TSD 2021, LNAI 12848, pp. 248–260, 2021.
https://doi.org/10.1007/978-3-030-83527-9_21

Recent multilingual language models [10] settled new state-of-the-art results on different downstream tasks, including NLI, and across a wide variety of languages [32]. In this paper, we show that Adversarial Training is unable to improve the cross-lingual ability of deep learning models, compared to the baseline Direct Transfer [20] procedure. We investigate the reasons behind this phenomena and found that the auxiliary task employed in conventional Adversarial Training is unsuited for models employing multilingual language models. Based on these observations, we propose future directions for Adversarial Training in this setting with the goal of improving the transfer of knowledge across different languages.

2   Related Work

Modern deep learning architectures conceived to address natural language processing tasks in cross-lingual settings rely on the existence of multilingual word embeddings (MWEs) [25] and, more recently, on multilingual language models [10]. These resources are obtained via unsupervised learning techniques exploiting large-scale corpora, and are used to initialize the representations of each token in an input sequence. Over the years, different approaches have been proposed to create pre-trained MWEs, such as bilingual word embeddings (BWE) [35], fastText [2,13], and Multilingual Unsupervised and Supervised Embeddings (MUSE) [18]. More recently, pre-trained language models lead to impressive improvements on several downstream tasks [10,19,34]. Devlin *et al.* [10] introduced the Masked Language Model (MLM) task, where a random sample of tokens in the input sequence is replaced with a special token: [MASK]. Employing a Transformer-based neural network to predict the masked tokens from large-scale text resources (in an unsupervised fashion), Devlin *et al.* proposed Bidirectional Encoder Representations from Transformers (BERT). The multilingual counterpart of BERT, mBERT, is obtained following a similar procedure when employed on text resources in different languages. Even if we can obtain multilingual language models with MLM objective (such as mBERT), it only requires monolingual data (in the sense that input sequences in different language are processed separately). To leverage parallel data when it is available, Lample and Conneau [17] introduce the translation language modeling (TLM) objective for improving cross-lingual pre-training. Following a similar procedure to Devlin *et al.* [10], they employ a Transformer-based neural network and explore widely available parallel sentences resources, proposing the pre-trained multilingual language model XLM.

The Natural Language Inference (NLI) task has emerged as one of the main tasks to evaluate NLP systems for sentence understanding. Given two text fragments, "Text" (T) and "Hypothesis" (H), the goal is to determine whether the meaning of H is in an *entailment, contradiction* or neither (*neutral*) relation to the text fragment T. Consequently, this task is framed in a 3-way classification setting [9].

Current state-of-the-art approaches for NLI depart from pre-trained language models (e.g. BERT, XLM) and explore different architectures to capture the relations between T and H: cross-encoder [10] and siamese-encoder [23].

To tackle NLI in a cross-lingual setting, different unsupervised language adaptation techniques have been explored [8,24]. The Cross-Lingual Natural Language Inference corpus (XNLI) [8] is one the largest available resources for this task, with annotated data in 15 languages. It consists of a crowd-sourced collection of 433k sentence pairs in English annotated with one of the 3 labels mentioned above, covering a range of ten genres of spoken and written text. The test set is balanced and composed of 750 examples from each of the ten text genres. Professional translators provided translations of the test set for each of the 14 target languages.

To leverage the knowledge from the source language (English) to different target languages, the most common approaches [24] are Adversarial Training [6], Sentence Encoder Alignment [8], and Shared-Private architectures [3]. The former aims to learn representations that are useful for the task at hand, and at the same time agnostic to the input language. One key advantage of this approach is that it learns a single representation that can be employed in different languages, and does not require the availability of parallel data. The remaining approaches leverage parallel data. The Sentence Encoder Alignment learns to map a target language encoder to the fine-tuned source language encoder. The shared-private encoder learns a language-agnostic representation of the data that is useful for the task at hand (shared encoder) and a language-aware representation (private encoder) that is used to prevent the shared encoder from capturing language-specific information.

3   Adversarial Training for Cross-Lingual NLI

Our goal is to leverage the knowledge learned while performing supervised learning on a source language to a given target language, without requiring annotated data in the target language (unsupervised language adaptation). To this end, we employ the method Adversarial Training, a promising technique for unsupervised language adaptation across different languages and tasks [6,24]. Given the advantages of the architecture (a single encoder for many languages and no requirements of parallel sentences), Adversarial Training can have a high impact in less-resourced languages. We illustrate its use, benefits and limitations through experiments conducted on the XNLI corpus.

As detailed by Chen *et al.* [6], there are three main components in neural network architecture employing this approach: a feature extractor $\mathcal{F}$ that maps an input sequence x to a shared feature space, a task classifier $\mathcal{P}$ that predicts the label for x given the feature representation $\mathcal{F}(x)$, and a language discriminator $\mathcal{Q}$ that given $\mathcal{F}(x)$ predicts whether x is from the source or target language. The goal of Adversarial Training is to minimize both the task classifier and adversarial component losses:

$$\mathcal{L} = \mathcal{L}_{task} + \lambda \mathcal{L}_{adv} \qquad (1)$$

where, $\mathcal{L}_{task}$ is the traditional cross-entropy loss of the predicted labels compared to the ground-truth, $\mathcal{L}_{adv}$ is the Wasserstein distance [1] between the feature

Table 1. XNLI experiments - accuracy scores

Embeddings	Method	EN	AR	DE	ZH
MWE	Direct Transfer	68.62	39.86	40.28	40.68
	Adversarial		**45.59**	**44.77**	**47.29**
mBERT	Direct Transfer	72.73	57.98	**62.73**	**64.93**
	Adversarial		**58.96**	61.18	63.87

distributions of input sequences in the source and target languages, and λ is a hyper-parameter that balances the importance of the adversarial component.

For the scope of this paper, we employ English (EN) as the source language. To study the impact of Adversarial Training on languages spanning different language families, we report scores on the following target languages: Arabic (AR), German (DE), and Chinese (ZH).

3.1 Experimental Setup

To pre-process and encode input sequences, we employ (a) conventional MWEs and (b) a recent state-of-the-art multilingual language model. For approach (a), we employ the fastText pre-trained 300 dimensional MWEs. We use MOSES tokenizer [15] for sentences in Arabic, English and German, and Stanford segmenter [5] for Chinese. In the Feature Extractor component $\mathcal{F}$ we use a BiL-STM [12] with 128 hidden units, concatenating the final hidden states of both right-to-left and left-to-right passes [28]. For optimization, we use Adam [14] with default parameters. For approach (b), the $\mathcal{F}$ component employs mBERT [10], a state-of-the-art multilingual language model. We adopt the implementation details suggested by Devlin *et al.* [10], using the Transformers library [31]. For pre-processing, we use WordPiece tokenization [33] for all languages. To obtain a sentence-level representation from mBERT, we extract the 768 hidden units corresponding to the last Self-Attention layer for the "CLS" (classification) token. For optimization, we also use Adam but using a learning rate of 2e−5 (as suggested by Devlin *et al.* [10]).

In both approaches, the Task Classifier $\mathcal{P}$ and Language Discriminator $\mathcal{Q}$ components are composed of a feed-forward neural network with a 128 units hidden layer, regularized with dropout [27] at a rate of 0.2.

As previously detailed, for the task of NLI we aim to identify the relation between two input sequences: T and H. To encode this relation, two separate $\mathcal{F}$ layers (one to encode T and another to encode H) are employed and merged using an aggregation layer. Typically, the encoders have tied weights, which motivates the denomination for this formulation as Siamese-Encoder [23]. A variety of aggregation functions have been proposed [4,7]. We employ one of the most widely used aggregation functions [7,23] that corresponds to the concatenation of four components: $\langle T, H, |T - H|, T * H \rangle$, where '$T - H$' is the element-wise difference and '$T * H$' is the element-wise product.

3.2   Results

Table 1 summarizes the results obtained for the XNLI experiments. As evaluation metric, we use the accuracy score because the dataset is balanced. In the
"Embeddings" column we divide the results for each of the approaches employed
to pre-process and encode the input sequences in the $\mathcal{F}$ layer: MWE and mBERT.
In the "Method" column, we divide between: (a) "Direct Transfer", corresponds
to the baseline approach, we evaluate the model directly on the target language
after supervised training on the source language, without further adaptation to
the target language, and (b) "Adversarial", corresponds to the Adversarial Training method. Column "EN" corresponds to the scores obtained after supervised
training on the source language. Columns "AR", "DE", and "ZH" correspond
to the scores obtained in the target language.

Regarding the results obtained using MWEs, we observe that Adversarial
Training improves the overall accuracy of the model for all the target languages
compared to the baseline approach Direct Transfer (improving by +5.61% on
average, across the target languages). This is in-line with prior work [24], which
concludes that Adversarial Training is robust technique for unsupervised language adaptation in different scenarios. Compared the results obtained on the
source language, we observe a considerable drop of the scores on the target
languages, meaning that further improvements on unsupervised language adaptation methods can be made in a attempt to close the gap between source and
target languages.

However, employing multilingual language models (mBERT), we observe that
Adversarial Training cannot improve the scores on the target languages compared to the baseline approach Direct Transfer, performing below Direct Transfer
in 2 out of 3 target languages. Regarding the scores obtained on the source language, we notice that mBERT improves by +4.11% compared to MWEs. More
remarkably, the gap between the source and target languages is much smaller
employing mBERT, evidence that multilingual language models provide not only
better representations for the task at hand, but also interesting properties for
cross-lingual transfer.

3.3   Analysis

Regarding the results obtained on the XNLI task, we observe that: (a) Adversarial Training provided substantial improvements on the target languages when
combined with MWEs, but cannot improve over Direct Transfer with mBERT;
and (b) mBERT closes the gap between source and target languages, suggesting
that mBERT provides strong baseline scores from scratch. Motivated by these
observations, we conclude that mBERT provides sentence-level representations
across different languages that are closer in feature space compared to MWEs.

To verify our hypothesis, we sampled 500 sentences (the H input sequence)
from the EN and DE validation sets, corresponding to the same input sequences
in terms of meaning in each language. Similarly to the approach proposed by
Chen et al. [6], we employed t-SNE [30] with Principal Component Analysis

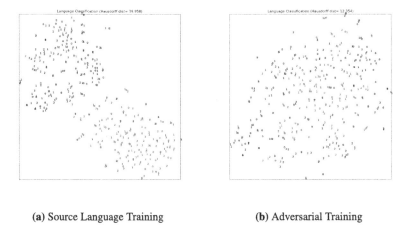

(a) Source Language Training   (b) Adversarial Training

Fig. 1. Multilingual Word Embeddings (MWEs) representations (Color figure online)

(PCA) [29] to reduce the representation into a two dimensional feature space, resulting in a two dimensional representation of the input sequences in both languages, as shown in Figs. 1 and 2. To assess the distance between the set of representations for the source language compared to the set of representations in the target language, we measure the Averaged Hausdorff Distance (AHD) [26]. An AHD distance of zero means that the set of points in both languages coincide, while higher values mean that the distance between the two sets of points increased.

Figure 1 depicts the representations obtained when employing MWEs. On the left side, the representations obtained after supervised training on the source language. On the right side, the representations after Adversarial Training. Blue points correspond to input sequences in EN, while red points to DE. Numbers correspond to predicted labels, with the following mapping: 0 means "neutral", 1 means "entailment", while 2 corresponds to "contradiction". We can observe that on the left side the languages are easy to distinguish, yielding an AHD of 39.96. However, on the right side, after employing Adversarial Training, the languages are difficult to distinguish, yielding an AHD of 12.35. Consequently, we can conclude that Adversarial Training succeeds in the task of making $\mathcal{F}$ agnostic to the input language.

Figure 2 depicts the representations for mBERT. We can observe that the languages are difficult to distinguish in both plots. After supervised training the AHD is 7.95 and after Adversarial Training is 6.59. Thus, we can conclude that the sentence-level representation from mBERT are already close to language-agnostic, from which Adversarial Training provides only marginal improvements.

Given the strong cross-lingual abilities of mBERT, we hypothesize that Adversarial Training cannot provide further improvements on the target languages because the auxiliary task objective is already close to optimal from the outset. In the following section, we propose alternative auxiliary tasks designed to

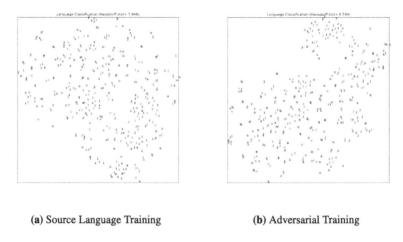

(a) Source Language Training   **(b)** Adversarial Training

Fig. 2. mBERT representations (Color figure online)

improve the transfer of knowledge across languages when employing the Adversarial Training method.

4   Towards Robust Auxiliary Tasks for Language Adaptation

As discussed in Sect. 3, employing conventional Adversarial Training with recent multilingual language models performs on par compared to the baseline approach (Direct Transfer). This can be partially attributed to the state-of-the-art cross-lingual capabilities of recent pre-trained multilingual language models (e.g. mBERT [10]), known to obtain impressive results in a Direct Transfer scenario on several downstream tasks [32]. Based on experiments for the XNLI task, we observed that the adversarial component converges in the first few epochs (i.e. the neural network is unable to distinguish the language of the input sequence). We claim that the inability of adversarial training to provide better scores compared to the direct transfer setting is due to the fact that the auxiliary task is not hard enough to be employed as an adversarial technique.

Following the same motivation to employ adversarial training for unsupervised language adaptation (i.e. obtain an encoder representation useful for the task at hand and transferable across languages), we propose that, instead of discriminating the input language, the $\mathcal{F}$ layer should produce representations on top of which a decoder-based neural network could generate the original input sequence (following the traditional auto-encoder formulation [16]), where the input sequence might be from either the source or target language. Compared to the original language discrimination task, based on which the $\mathcal{F}$ layer might only be capturing salient properties of the input sequence, we believe that this formulation will require the $\mathcal{F}$ layer to capture more information regarding the input sequences (i.e. generating valid content in a language requires more knowledge than language discrimination). Given the requirement that the same $\mathcal{F}$ layer should be able to capture useful representations for both source and target languages, this formulation constrains the model to obtain higher-level representations of the input sequence in relation to the input language. This is a harder task for the adversarial component, which we hypothesize is a promising approach for unsupervised language adaptation.

4.1   Masked Language Modeling

Instead of formulating this problem following the original auto-encoder setting, in which the decoder objective is to predict the complete input sequence, we suggest following recent proposals in language modeling and employing the Masked Language Model (MLM) objective [10]. This is in line with prior work on monolingual settings [21,22], which also found that performing fine-tuning for downstream tasks including language modeling as an auxiliary objective can improve the generalization capability of the supervised model and can accelerate convergence. However, for multilingual settings, we foresee additional challenges. Fine-tuning a pre-trained language model based on labeled data in the source language updates the learning weights of the model specifically for source language inputs. Given that input sequences in the target language are not taken into consideration during fine-tuning, it is reasonable to expect that representations for input sequences in the target language will become outdated and not specifically tuned to address the task at hand. Consequently, starting from a pre-trained model known to obtain close to language-agnostic sentence-level representations (as observed in Sect. 3.3), fine-tuning can indeed interfere in the cross-lingual characteristics of the model via updates that are only performed based on the source language.

We propose to add an auxiliary MLM objective that must be jointly optimized while fine-tuning the model using supervised source language data on the target task (NLI in this case), as suggested by Radford *et al.* [21]. To employ this procedure in a cross-lingual setting, which was not considered in Radford *et al.*'s work, we propose that the auxiliary MLM objective is optimized providing input sequences in both source and target languages. Following this procedure, we aim that the updates made to the model while fine-tuning will be useful to address the task at hand and, at the same time, we encourage the neural network to keep the performance on the unsupervised language modeling objective (MLM in this case). By optimizing MLM using input sequences on both source and target languages, we hypothesize that the task-specific fine-tuning will impact both languages, by encouraging representations for the source and target languages to be jointly updated.

To summarize, the loss that we aim to minimize is:

$$\mathcal{L} \ = \ \mathcal{L}_{task} + \beta \, \mathcal{L}_{mlm} \tag{2}$$

where $\mathcal{L}_{task}$ is the supervised loss function for the task at hand, $\mathcal{L}_{mlm}$ is the unsupervised masked language modeling objective for input sequences in both source and target languages, and β weights the impact of the auxiliary task objective in the overall loss. As proposed in previous work [11], we propose to use a scheduler, where the value of β increases as the number of epochs evolves (which allows the model to focus on learning task-specific representations in the first epochs, adapting these representations to become robust in cross-lingual settings afterwards).

4.2   Translation Language Modeling

Lample and Conneau [17] proposed the Translation Language Modeling (TLM) objective – an extension of the MLM objective – to cross-lingual scenarios. Instead of considering monolingual input sequences, they extract parallel sentences from widely available resources to obtain bilingual input sequences following a S [SEP] T [SEP] template, where S is the sentence in the source and T is the sentence in the target language. To predict a token masked in one of the sentences, the model can either attend to the surrounding tokens in the same sentence or to the parallel sentence, encouraging the model to condition token representations taking into considerations source and target language content. The proposed multilingual language modeling procedure (TLM) improves the capabilities of the pre-trained models in a Direct Transfer scenario compared to MLM when evaluated on different downstream tasks, including XNLI [17].

A drawback for this approach is that it requires the availability of parallel sentences in the source and target language, which can be challenging to obtain for less-resourced languages. Nevertheless, given the impressive results obtained in different cross-lingual scenarios, we propose to use $\mathcal{L}_{tlm}$ as an auxiliary task when parallel sentences are available. As detailed by Lample and Conneau [17], TLM is used in combination with MLM, alternating between these two objectives during the training phase. Similar to the previous formulation, the loss to minimize would be:

$$\mathcal{L} = \mathcal{L}_{task} + \beta \, \mathcal{L}_{mlm+tlm} \qquad (3)$$

4.3   Combining Adversarial Training and Language Modeling

At this point, we cannot ensure that the $\mathcal{F}$ layer obtains language-specific or language-agnostic representations. As a thought experiment and following the previous formulations, if the neural network is large enough, it could be divided into two partitions: one specialized in the source language (tuned for the target task and for the language modeling objective on the source language), the other in the target language (only tuned for the language modeling objective in the target language). If this phenomena occurs, then the representations for input sequences in the target language will not be aligned with the fine-tuned representations obtained for input sequences in the source language.

To counter this, we propose to combine the losses of both adversarial and masked language modeling tasks: L_{adv} and $L_{mlm+tlm}$. If parallel sentences for the source and target language pairs are scarce, we recommend using L_{mlm} instead of $L_{mlm+tlm}$ The intuition is to encourage the $\mathcal{F}$ layer to obtain sentence-level representations that are agnostic to the input language (as in the conventional Adversarial Training approach) but that can nevertheless provide enough information to retain the language modeling capabilities in both languages, which are critical to encode the representations for the target task. This is crucial for the target language, for which no supervision is provided during the training phase.

The final loss would be calculated as follows:

$$\mathcal{L} = \mathcal{L}_{task} + \lambda\,\mathcal{L}_{adv} + \beta\,\mathcal{L}_{mlm+tlm} \tag{4}$$

where λ and β are weights that control the interaction of the loss terms.

Combining these auxiliary tasks, the representations obtained for the feature extractor $\mathcal{F}$ should be general enough to be employed in a variety of languages, taking advantage of the capabilities demonstrated by neural language models.

5   Conclusions

We study the impact of multilingual word embeddings and language models on Adversarial Training in a challenging natural language understanding task. Empirical results show that language models provide impressive improvements for NLI. However, when we employ multilingual language models, Adversarial Training is unable to provide further improvements on a variety of target languages compared to the baseline Direct Transfer approach. Our analysis unveils that the conventional language discrimination task considered in Adversarial Training is trivially solved when we employ recent language models, evidence of the cross-lingual capabilities of these models. On the other hand, our results show that the gap between source and target language scores demands for more robust transfer of knowledge across languages.

To further improve the cross-lingual transfer using Adversarial Training, we propose alternative formulations for the adversarial component, tailored to take advantage of recent advancements in language modeling. We hope that our analysis and proposals can pave the way to more robust cross-lingual models.

Acknowledgments. Gil Rocha is supported by a PhD grant (SFRH/BD/140125/ 2018) from Fundação para a Ciência e a Tecnologia (FCT). This research is supported by LIACC (FCT/UID/CEC/0027/2020) and by project DARGMINTS, funded by FCT (POCI/01/0145/FEDER/031460).

References

1. Arjovsky, M., Chintala, S., Bottou, L.: Wasserstein generative adversarial networks. In: Precup, D., Teh, Y.W. (eds.) Proceedings of the 34th International Conference on Machine Learning. Proceedings of Machine Learning Research, vol. 70, pp. 214–223, 06–11 August 2017. PMLR, International Convention Centre, Sydney (2017)
2. Bojanowski, P., Grave, E., Joulin, A., Mikolov, T.: Enriching word vectors with subword information. Trans. Assoc. Comput. Linguist. **5**, 135–146 (2017)

3. Bousmalis, K., Trigeorgis, G., Silberman, N., Krishnan, D., Erhan, D.: Domain separation networks. In: Proceedings of the 30th International Conference on Neural Information Processing Systems, NIPS 2016, pp. 343–351. Curran Associates Inc. (2016)

4. Bowman, S.R., Angeli, G., Potts, C., Manning, C.D.: A large annotated corpus for learning natural language inference. In: Proceedings of the 2015 Conference on Empirical Methods in Natural Language Processing, pp. 632–642. Association for Computational Linguistics, Lisbon, September 2015. https://doi.org/10.18653/v1/D15-1075

5. Chang, P.C., Galley, M., Manning, C.D.: Optimizing Chinese word segmentation for machine translation performance. In: Proceedings of the Third Workshop on Statistical Machine Translation, StatMT 2008, pp. 224–232. Association for Computational Linguistics, Stroudsburg (2008)

6. Chen, X., Sun, Y., Athiwaratkun, B., Cardie, C., Weinberger, K.Q.: Adversarial deep averaging networks for cross-lingual sentiment classification. TACL **6**, 557–570 (2018)

7. Conneau, A., Kiela, D., Schwenk, H., Barrault, L., Bordes, A.: Supervised learning of universal sentence representations from natural language inference data. In: Proceedings of the 2017 Conference on Empirical Methods in Natural Language Processing, pp. 670–680. Association for Computational Linguistics, Copenhagen, September 2017. https://doi.org/10.18653/v1/D17-1070

8. Conneau, A., et al.: XNLI: evaluating cross-lingual sentence representations. In: Proceedings of the 2018 Conference on Empirical Methods in Natural Language Processing, pp. 2475–2485. Association for Computational Linguistics, Brussels (2018)

9. Dagan, I., Roth, D., Sammons, M., Zanzotto, F.M.: Recognizing Textual Entailment: Models and Applications. Synthesis Lectures on Human Language Technologies. Morgan & Claypool Publishers (2013)

10. Devlin, J., Chang, M.W., Lee, K., Toutanova, K.: BERT: pre-training of deep bidirectional transformers for language understanding. In: Proceedings of the 2019 Conference of the North American Chapter of the Association for Computational Linguistics: Human Language Technologies, Volume 1 (Long and Short Papers), pp. 4171–4186. Association for Computational Linguistics, Minneapolis, June 2019. https://doi.org/10.18653/v1/N19-1423

11. Ganin, Y., Lempitsky, V.: Unsupervised domain adaptation by backpropagation. In: Bach, F., Blei, D. (eds.) Proceedings of the 32nd International Conference on Machine Learning. Proceedings of Machine Learning Research, vol. 37, pp. 1180–1189, 07–09 July 2015. PMLR, Lille (2015)

12. Hochreiter, S., Schmidhuber, J.: Long short-term memory. Neural Comput. **9**(8), 1735–1780 (1997). https://doi.org/10.1162/neco.1997.9.8.1735

13. Joulin, A., Bojanowski, P., Mikolov, T., Jégou, H., Grave, E.: Loss in translation: learning bilingual word mapping with a retrieval criterion. In: Proceedings of the 2018 Conference on Empirical Methods in Natural Language Processing (2018)

14. Kingma, D.P., Ba, J.: Adam: a method for stochastic optimization. CoRR abs/1412.6980 (2014)

15. Koehn, P., et al.: Moses: open source toolkit for statistical machine translation. In: Proceedings of the 45th Annual Meeting of the Association for Computational Linguistics Companion Volume Proceedings of the Demo and Poster Sessions, pp. 177–180. ACL, Prague, June 2007

16. Kramer, M.A.: Nonlinear principal component analysis using autoassociative neural networks. AIChE J. **37**(2), 233–243 (1991). https://doi.org/10.1002/aic. 690370209
17. Lample, G., Conneau, A.: Cross-lingual language model pretraining. CoRR abs/1901.07291 (2019)
18. Lample, G., Conneau, A., Ranzato, M., Denoyer, L., Jégou, H.: Word translation without parallel data. In: 6th International Conference on Learning Representations, ICLR 2018, Vancouver, BC, Canada, 30 April–3 May 2018, Conference Track Proceedings (2018)
19. Liu, Y., et al.: RoBERTa: a robustly optimized BERT pretraining approach. CoRR abs/1907.11692 (2019)
20. McDonald, R., Petrov, S., Hall, K.: Multi-source transfer of delexicalized dependency parsers. In: Proceedings of the 2011 Conference on Empirical Methods in Natural Language Processing, pp. 62–72. Association for Computational Linguistics, Edinburgh, July 2011
21. Radford, A., Narasimhan, K., Salimans, T., Sutskever, I.: Improving language understanding with unsupervised learning. Technical report, OpenAI (2018)
22. Rei, M.: Semi-supervised multitask learning for sequence labeling. In: Proceedings of the 55th Annual Meeting of the Association for Computational Linguistics (Volume 1: Long Papers), pp. 2121–2130. Association for Computational Linguistics, Vancouver, July 2017. https://doi.org/10.18653/v1/P17-1194
23. Reimers, N., Gurevych, I.: Sentence-BERT: sentence embeddings using Siamese BERT-networks. In: Proceedings of the 2019 Conference on Empirical Methods in Natural Language Processing and the 9th International Joint Conference on Natural Language Processing (EMNLP-IJCNLP), pp. 3982–3992. Association for Computational Linguistics, Hong Kong, November 2019. https://doi.org/10.18653/v1/ D19-1410
24. Rocha, G., Lopes Cardoso, H.: A comparative analysis of unsupervised language adaptation methods. In: Proceedings of the 2nd Workshop on Deep Learning Approaches for Low-Resource NLP (DeepLo 2019), pp. 11–21. Association for Computational Linguistics, Hong Kong, November 2019. https://doi.org/10. 18653/v1/D19-6102
25. Ruder, S.: A survey of cross-lingual embedding models. CoRR abs/1706.04902 (2017)
26. Shapiro, M., Blaschko, M.: On hausdorff distance measures. Technical report, Department of Computer Science, University of Massachusetts Amherst, August 2004
27. Srivastava, N., Hinton, G., Krizhevsky, A., Sutskever, I., Salakhutdinov, R.: Dropout: a simple way to prevent neural networks from overfitting. J. Mach. Learn. Res. **15**, 1929–1958 (2014)
28. Sutskever, I., Vinyals, O., Le, Q.V.: Sequence to sequence learning with neural networks. In: Ghahramani, Z., Welling, M., Cortes, C., Lawrence, N.D., Weinberger, K.Q. (eds.) Advances in Neural Information Processing Systems, vol. 27, pp. 3104–3112. Curran Associates, Inc. (2014)
29. Tipping, M.E., Bishop, C.M.: Probabilistic principal component analysis. J. Roy. Stat. Soc. Ser. B **61**(3), 611–622 (1999)
30. van der Maaten, L., Hinton, G.: Visualizing high-dimensional data using t-SNE. J. Mach. Learn. Res. **9**, 2579–2605 (2008). Pagination: 27

31. Wolf, T., et al.: Transformers: state-of-the-art natural language processing. In: Proceedings of the 2020 Conference on Empirical Methods in Natural Language Processing: System Demonstrations, pp. 38–45. Association for Computational Linguistics, October 2020. https://www.aclweb.org/anthology/2020.emnlp-demos.6

32. Wu, S., Dredze, M.: Beto, bentz, becas: the surprising cross-lingual effectiveness of BERT. In: Proceedings of the 2019 Conference on Empirical Methods in Natural Language Processing and the 9th International Joint Conference on Natural Language Processing (EMNLP-IJCNLP), pp. 833–844. Association for Computational Linguistics, Hong Kong, November 2019. https://doi.org/10.18653/v1/D19-1077

33. Wu, Y., et al.: Google's neural machine translation system: bridging the gap between human and machine translation. CoRR abs/1609.08144 (2016)

34. Yang, Z., Dai, Z., Yang, Y., Carbonell, J.G., Salakhutdinov, R., Le, Q.V.: XLNet: generalized autoregressive pretraining for language understanding. CoRR abs/1906.08237 (2019)

35. Zhou, X., Wan, X., Xiao, J.: Cross-lingual sentiment classification with bilingual document representation learning. In: Proceedings of the 54th Annual Meeting of the Association for Computational Linguistics (Volume 1: Long Papers), pp. 1403–1412. Association for Computational Linguistics, Berlin, August 2016. https://doi.org/10.18653/v1/P16-1133

A Corpus with Wavesurfer and TEI: Speech and Video in TEITOK

Maarten Janssen(⊠) (iD)

Institute of Formal and Applied Linguistics, Charles University,
Faculty of Mathematics and Physics, Prague, Czech Republic
maartenjanssen@ufal.mff.cuni.cz

Abstract. In this paper, we demonstrate how TEITOK provides a full online interface for speech and even video corpora, that are fully searchable using the CQL query language, can contain all speech-related annotation such as repetitions, gaps, and mispronunciations, and provides a full interface for time-aligned annotations scrolling below the waveform and showing the video if there is any. Corpora are stored in the TEI/XML standard, with import and output functions for other established standards like ELAN, Praat, or Transcriber. It is even possible to directly annotate corpora in TEITOK.

Keywords: TEI · Spoken corpus · Multimedia corpora

1 Introduction

TEITOK [4] is a online platform for visualizing, searching, and editing corpora in which the corpus texts are kept in the TEI/XML format - a rich and widely used XML standard for digital texts (http://www.tei-c.org). Although TEITOK was originally designed for textual (facsimile based) corpora, it was always intended as a multi-purpose environment, and early on incorporated the spoken corpus functionality from Spock [6]. Over time, more speech-related functions were added, and by now TEITOK provides a full-fledged online platform in which you can view, search, and edit spoken corpora.

This paper will discuss these aspects of TEITOK in turn, with a focus on their use in spoken corpora: first the document visualization, then the search function, and finally the corpus editing options.

2 Visualization

TEITOK has a modular design, in which each module interacts in a different way with the TEI/XML files. For spoken corpora, the most relevant modules are described in this chapter: the standard document view, and the wavesurfer view. But if the spoken corpus is a learner corpus or a dialect corpus, there are many other modules of importance, such as the modules for stand-off error annotation and the module for map-based searches (discussed in Sect. 3.1).

© Springer Nature Switzerland AG 2021
K. Ekštein et al. (Eds.): TSD 2021, LNAI 12848, pp. 261–268, 2021.
https://doi.org/10.1007/978-3-030-83527-9_22

2.1   Document View

A TEITOK corpus consists of a collection of TEI/XML files, which can contain any of the annotations TEI provides, including all the tags designed for spoken data[1]: codes for gaps, repetitions, reformulations, truncations, short and long pauses, etc.

In the standard document view, the raw XML document is used directly in the browser, where it is styled using cascading style sheets (CSS). Each corpus can define it's own styles the rendering of otherwise standardized codes. For spoken corpora, this makes it possible to have the corpus visually follow one of the many traditional annotation styles for spoken corpora, such as having truncations marked by a & after the truncated word. But in the definitions that come standard with TEITOK, only gaps are indicated by a symbol: [...], while all other mark-up codes are displayed using colours to increase readability.

The standard in TEI is to have utterances be marked by a <u> node, with an optional attribute @who indicating the speaker. In the standard TEITOK view, the display of the utterances with their speaker also is handled by CSS, and is by default displayed by having the @who attribute display if front of each line, to get an interview-style display, as seen in Fig. 1.

Fig. 1. Example of a TEITOK document view

For spoken corpora, the audio file corresponding to the transcription is placed in a <media> node, typically in the <recording> in the teiHeader. If there is an audio file, it is shown above the text, as in Fig. 1 (the audio interface just below the view options). The media file can also be a video file, which would be shown as a floating div.

---

[1] https://www.tei-c.org/release/doc/tei-p5-doc/es/html/TS.html.

For time-aligned corpora, TEITOK places a @start and @end tag on the aligned node in the transcription, which indicates the beginning and end of the segment in the corresponding media node in the teiHeader. This is a more direct way of alignment than used in the ISO-TEI standard (ISO 24624:2016), since that format makes the various interaction between the text and the audio in TEITOK almost impossible. The default aligned segment is the utterance, but any node can be aligned with the audio.

If the transcription is time-aligned, there is a audio button in the view options, which will toggle a play button in front of each aligned segment, as shown in Fig. 1, and clicking the button will play the corresponding segment of the audio (or video) file.

The transcriptions in TEITOK are tokenized, and each token can be adorned with a customizable array of annotations. Those can be linguistic annotations, such as POS and lemma, but also speech-related annotations, such as corrections of mispronounced words, IPA transcriptions, or tags indicating pronunciation-related phenomena on the word. When hovering the mouse over a token in the transcription, those token-based annotations will be shown in a pop-up, as can be seen for the word *nacionalidade* in Fig. 1, showing the (deglossed) POS tag and the lemma.

2.2 Wavesurfer View

The document view presents an interface that displays the linguistic annotations, while at the same time allowing to play the corresponding audio file. But it is not really a speech-oriented visualization: stand-alone speech applications are organized not around the text, but around the waveform view of the sound file. TEITOK attempts to provide a similar experience in the wavesurfer view.

In the wavesurfer view, the speech signal is displayed using the wavesurfer Javascript module[2], a popular and powerful web-based interface to sound files. In the TEITOK implementation, you can play the sound file, pause it, jump to parts of the sound using a mini-map (a small version of the waveform), zoom in an out, and slow down and speed up the sound. If the sound is from a video, the video itself will additionally be displayed in a floating div.

Below the waveform, the transcription is shown in much the same way as in the document view - with all XML code displayed using CSS. The resulting interface is shown in Fig. 2. When playing the audio, the waveform will scroll horizontally and the transcription vertically, where the current utterance is highlighted in both parts and kept centralized in the window.

3 Searching

TEITOK uses the Corpus WorkBench (CWB) [3] as a way to index the TEI/XML files and make them searchable. The TEI/XML files are used to create a CWB corpus, along with byte-offsets over XML files. That makes it possible to define queries in the powerful Corpus Query Language (CQL) to search the corpus, and get XML fragments as a result. The XML contains all the annotations, including things that might not have

---

[2] https://wavesurfer-js.org/.

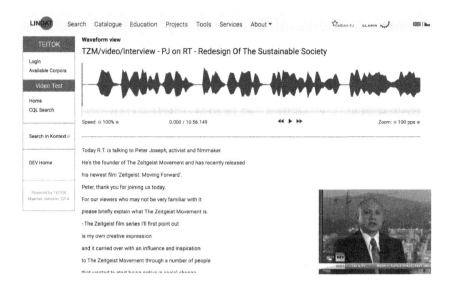

Fig. 2. Example of a TEITOK Wavesurfer view with video

been exported to the CWB corpus, such as pauses or repetitions. With this set-up, a CQL search in TEITOK on spoken corpora renders the full spoken annotation transcript in the keyword-in-context (KWIC) results.

In time-aligned spoken corpora, the sound file is of course of crucial importance, and a pure KWIC result, even when displayed in full XML, does not allow you to listen to the sound directly, although you can of course jump to the text view or the waveform view from the result list. That is why for spoken corpora, TEITOK offers the option to not display KWIC lines, but rather lists of utterance, with a play button in front with which you can directly listen to the utterance.

In this way, TEITOK provides the option to formulate rich transcription-based search queries to search for phenomena in the transcription, and then directly access the audio segment. This option TEITOK inherits from Spock, and this allows you to for instance search for all occurrences of *que* (that) or *com* (with) in Portuguese, which are followed by a determiner, where the pronunciation is said to be socially determined. At current, there are more CQL-based corpora tool that can play sound for search results, for instance KonText[3], but Spock was one of the first systems to provide advanced text-based corpus searches to get access to speech material. The search options in CQL are much richer than the type of search available in more purely speech-driven systems like EXMARaLDA [8], since you can not only search for the transcription itself, but also for instance for the lemma or part-of-speech tag.

It is not always easy to locate interesting phonological phenomena purely on the base of orthography. But TEITOK allows users to define themselves which data are encoded in the corpus. To make it possible to search more directly for phonological

---

[3] https://github.com/czcorpus/kontext.

phenomena, there are typically two types of additional of annotations that are helpful: an IPA transcription, and/or hard-coded tags.

The inclusion of IPA makes it possible to directly search inside the IPA transcription, or even combine the IPA transcription with the orthography. While the inclusion of hard-coded tags makes it possible to mark speech-related phenomena, such as complex syllables, unstressed vowels, elisions, etc. by means of a code on the token. This is done either manually or by computational means, and then use those codes in the search queries to get even richer search options.

3.1 Map Based Searches

For spoken data, the provenance of the speaker is typically much more important than for written data, since in spoken data dialectal variation tends to play a much larger role. If the corpus documents are provided with geographical coordinates, it is possible to display all the documents on the world map and search for documents by their location. This is especially relevant for dialect corpora, such as MADISON[4], allowing users to find documents around a specific location.

With coordinate information, it is also possible to compare different CQL queries, and see the differences between them on the map. An example is given in Fig. 3, taken from the bilingual PostScriptum corpus [2], showing that (unsurprisingly) the form *muger* (an older Spanish orthography for the word *mujer* = woman) is predominantly used in Spain, while *mulher* (the current Portuguese spelling) prevails in Portugal. This way, complex CQL queries can be used to determine dialect borders based on speech-based characteristics.

4   Editing

TEITOK is not only meant as a tool to make corpora visible and searchable, but also to edit and maintain them. This section first explains how to get existing transcription into TEITOK, then how to annotate, edit, and correct data in TEITOK, and finally how transcriptions can be made directly in the system.

4.1   Converting

Most spoken corpora have been transcribed in a relatively small set of transcription tools. In order to get existing corpora into TEITOK, there is a Git project[5] that provides conversion scripts to convert documents from most of those tools, including EXMaR-ALDa .exb files, Praat TextGrid files, CHAT .cha files, subtitle .srt files, and transcriber .trs files. And it is possible to convert the TEITOK/XML files to other formats as well, including the ISO-TEI format mentioned before. More conversion scripts are being added, as well as improvements upon the existing conversion scripts.

---

[4] http://teitok.clul.ul.pt/madison/.
[5] https://github.com/ufal/teitok-tools.

Fig. 3. Example of a comparison of two CQL queries on the world map

For most of these formats, the conversion keeps only the transcription itself and the time alignment, as well as speaker names and metadata where possible. The symbol-based transcriptions, such as a double slash (*//*) for a long pause, will have to be converted manually or by means of a dedicated script, since there typically is no common standard for such transcription symbols. Only for a small number of standards, such as the heritage format of CHAT (CA), codes for pauses, repetitions, and gaps are also converted to TEI/XML.

Once the corpus files have been converted to the TEITOK format, they can be added to the corpus, either using the online interface, or by uploading them directly by means of SFTP.

4.2   Annotating

After the corpus files are added to the corpus, they need to be tokenized, which can be done directly in the TEITOK system. Tokenization will add token nodes around all the words (tokens) in the transcription. Once tokenized, all tokens in the transcription can be adorned with additional information, such as POS tags, lemmas, etc. For many languages, the morphosyntactic annotation, as well as a dependency parse, can be provided automatically using UDPIPE [9] or NeoTag [5], and there are scripts to use a number of other automatic tools as well, which can furthermore be adapted to work with most tagging tools.

TEITOK can have multiple orthographic realizations for the same token. This makes it possible in spoken corpora to transcribe pronunciation errors as they were produced, and provide the (interpreted) correction as an additional annotation layer. Furthermore,

TEITOK uses a set-up in which there can be more grammatical tokens than there are orthographic tokens.

Correcting annotations in TEITOK is very easy - as is shown in Fig. 1, all annotations are shown on mouse-over. And if there is an error in the annotation, the only thing that is needed is to click on the token, which will show a HTML form where the incorrect annotation can be easily corrected. This is especially relevant for smaller corpora (which spoken corpora typically are), since it makes it easy to manually correct any automatic annotation.

4.3 Transcribing

In order to work with files that have not been previously transcribed, it is also possible to directly transcribe files in TEITOK. For this, the same wavesurfer interface as shown in Fig. 2 is used, but in edit mode it allows selecting segments in the waveform view, and provide a transcription for it. When transcribing directly in TEITOK, all annotations like truncations, gaps, and pauses are encoded directly in their TEI/XML equivalent.

The upshot of transcribing directly in TEITOK is that the annotation will be formatted immediately using CSS, hence providing a direct visual feedback for the transcription. And the fact that the transcription is provided directly in the target format means that no information can get lost in the conversion process.

The transcription module is easy to use, as has been proven in the Lithuanian Learner Corpus [7], in which all sound files have been transcribed by students directly in TEITOK.

5   Conclusion

TEITOK provides a rich environment for speech-oriented corpus interaction: you can search for phenomena in the corpus by the CQL language and listen directly to the search results, and get an interface similar to that of dedicated speech software with the waveform above transcriptions. And it does so in a way that is experience as easy to use by the projects using it.

Of course, TEITOK is still fundamentally a text-driven corpus environment. But the various speech-specific additions make it a rich and well-received online interface for (time-aligned) spoken corpora. It does not have any of the truly speech-related analysis functions of a tool like Praat [1], but a web browser tends to be a bad interface for such interactions. TEITOK makes it easy to find relevant spoken segments, after which (if the corpus permissions allows it) it is always possible to download the results for speech analysis using locally installed software. Yet where it comes to online interfaces, TEITOK provides a user friendly, feature rich version of the corpus.

References

1. Boersma, P., Weenink, D.: Praat: doing phonetics by computer (version 6.0.37) (2018). http:// www.praat.org
2. CLUL: P.S. post scriptum. arquivo digital de escrita quotidiana em portugal e espanha na Época moderna. http://ps.clul.ul.pt
3. Evert, S., Hardie, A.: Twenty-first century corpus workbench: Updating a query architecture for the new millennium. In: Corpus Linguistics 2011 (2011)
4. Janssen, M.: TEITOK: text-faithful annotated corpora. In: Proceedings of the 10th International Conference on Language Resources and Evaluation, LREC 2016, pp. 4037–4043 (2016)
5. Janssen, M.: Neotag: a POS tagger for grammatical neologism detection. In: Calzolari, N., et al. (eds.) LREC, pp. 2118–2124. European Language Resources Association (ELRA) (2012)
6. Janssen, M., Freitas, T.: Spock - a spoken corpus client. In: Proceedings of the Sixth International Conference on Language Resources and Evaluation (LREC 2008) (May 2008)
7. Ruzaitė, J.: Learner corpora for lesser taught languages: a workin-progress report on the Lithuanian learner corpus (2019)
8. Schmidt, T.: Exmaralda - ein modellierungs- und visualisierungsverfahren für die computergestützte transkription gesprochener sprache. In: Buchberger, E. (ed.) Proceedings of Konvens 2004, vol. 5 (2004). http://www.exmaralda.org/files/Konvens_Paper.pdf, dE
9. Straka, M., Straková, J.: UDPipe (2016). LINDAT/CLARIAH-CZ digital library at the Institute of Formal and Applied Linguistics (ÚFAL), Faculty of Mathematics and Physics, Charles University. http://hdl.handle.net/11234/1-1702

Exploiting Subjectivity Knowledge Transfer for End-to-End Aspect-Based Sentiment Analysis

Samuel Pecar[1][✉] and Marian Simko[2]

[1] Faculty of Electrical Engineering and Informatics, Technical University of Kosice, Kosice, Slovakia
[2] Kempelen Institute of Intelligent Technologies, Bratislava, Slovakia
`marian.simko@kinit.sk`

Abstract. While classic aspect-based sentiment analysis typically includes three sub-tasks (aspect extraction, opinion extraction, and aspect-level sentiment classification), recent studies focus on exploring possibilities of knowledge sharing from different tasks, such as document-level sentiment analysis or document-level domain classification that are less demanding on dataset resources. Several recent studies managed to propose different frameworks for solving nearly complete end-to-end aspect-based sentiment analysis in a unified manner. However, none of them studied the possibility of transferring knowledge about their subjectivity or opinion typology between sub-tasks. In this work, we propose subjectivity-aware learning as a novel auxiliary task for aspect-based sentiment analysis. Besides, we also propose another novel task defined as opinion type detection. We performed extensive experiments on the state-of-the-art dataset that show improvement of model performance while employing subjectivity learning. All models report improvement in overall F1 score for aspect-based sentiment analysis. In addition, we also set new benchmark results for the separate task of subjectivity detection and opinion type detection for the restaurant domain of SemEval 2015 dataset.

Keywords: Sentiment analysis · Aspect-based sentiment analysis · Subjectivity detection · Multi-task learning

1 Introduction

Aspect-based sentiment analysis (ABSA) is a long standing task in natural language processing and also a fine-grained task of general document-level sentiment analysis. Its aim is to identify opinions towards specific aspects in a particular sequence (e.g. sentence or paragraph). ABSA usually consists of several sub-tasks, such as aspect term extraction (AE), opinion term extraction (OE) and aspect-level sentiment classification (SC). For example, given the sentence *Those rolls were big, but not good and sashimi was n't fresh.*, AE aims to extract aspect terms *rolls* and *sashimi*, and OE aims to extract opinion terms *big*, *good*, and *fresh*. In addition, SC has to assign sentiment polarity *conflict* and *negative* to aspects *rolls* and *sashimi*, respectively.

© Springer Nature Switzerland AG 2021
K. Ekštein et al. (Eds.): TSD 2021, LNAI 12848, pp. 269–280, 2021.
https://doi.org/10.1007/978-3-030-83527-9_23

Despite ABSA being a well-known task, there are still many challenges to address. One of the major challenges is the absence of quality and large-scale datasets. Current state-of-the-art datasets, such as SemEval 2014 [23] and SemEval 2015 [22], are relatively small (2000–4000 samples per domain) and reproducibility is also not satisfied since there is not very high inter-annotator agreement on the annotations. Datasets SemEval 2014 and 2015 come with annotations on aspect terms and their polarities (aspect category and its polarity are not relevant for our purposes), while opinion terms were annotated later and reported in two other works [7,24]. However, those versions are annotated by different standards and do not have a complete match on labels. Nevertheless, those datasets come with certain differences. While SemEval 2014 contains only samples with opinions that are expressed, SemEval 2015 contains the whole reviews and non-opinionated (non-subjective) sentences are included within this dataset. The dataset containing whole reviews appears much more challenging. Current state-of-the-art models achieve better results for dataset SemEval 2014. For example, RACL [3] can identify correct aspect, opinions, and polarities with F1 over 80 (resulting in overall F1 for aspect and sentiment only at 75) for restaurant domain from SemEval 2014 but results for restaurant domain from SemEval 2015 is for aspect, opinion, and sentiment F1 only over 70 (resulting in overall F1 for aspect and sentiment only at 66). A very similar drop in the performance could be observed also for the other state-of-the-art models, such as IMN [9], E2E-TBSA [13], SPAN-BERT [10], or DOER [15].

We argue that annotations from the SemEval dataset are not fully suitable for the complete ABSA task. The key reason is no explicit annotation and knowledge about the subjectivity of particular sentences in the training data. We suppose such knowledge could help improve the overall performance of state-of-the-art methods. For example, in SemEval datasets, aspect within factual sentences are annotated as neutral and knowledge about the subjectivity (factual sentence) could help to improve performance on aspect-level sentiment classification sub-task since there is a dependency between subjectivity and actual sentiment annotation. Furthermore, we analyzed also types of subjective opinions expressed in customer reviews to extend subjective and non-subjective dichotomy to a broader typology of opinions that could be helpful for other downstream tasks, such as review generation [16] or opinion summarization [17] (see Sect. 3.2 for more detailed information). The problem of subjectivity detection was presented also in a work of Chaturvedi et al. [1] where authors discuss how facts can be distinguished from opinions. However, despite the wide substitution of factual sentence and neutral sentiment [1,22], we argue that there is a significant difference between actual neutral sentiment in opinionated sentence and sentiment in the factual sentence. While factual sentence does not carry any sentiment (e.g. *We had only pizza.*), neutral sentiment can be marked as neither positive nor negative (e.g. *Our pizza was ok*).

In this work, we come with several contributions for the area of aspect-based sentiment analysis, namely:

- we investigate new auxiliary tasks of *subjectivity detection* and *opinion type detection* for aspect-based sentiment analysis that help to improve overall performance on different sub-tasks of aspect-based sentiment analysis.
- we release new subjectivity and opinion type annotations on sentence-level for the state-of-the-art dataset for aspect-based sentiment analysis SemEval 2015.

In addition, we propose also a naive method for obtaining subjectivity annotation without the need for human annotators.

2   Related Work

Sentiment analysis as well as its fine-grained form aspect-based sentiment analysis (ABSA) have been widely studied in recent years. ABSA consists of several sub-tasks (AE, OE, and SC) that could be viewed also as separate tasks but recent works [3,9] showed all particular tasks are strongly related and could benefit from each other while learned jointly. While subjectivity detection can be seen as classic text classification with a very similar focus on method development as sentiment analysis, we rather focus on the way how the task of aspect-based sentiment analysis is learned. We further organize recent studies on how the ABSA task is performed: separate and unified methods.

2.1   Separate Methods

Many studies see ABSA as a multi-stage problem with several separate sub-tasks and focus only on particular challenges within a particular sub-task. We can see those stages as aspect term extraction (AE) [4,25,26] and aspect-level sentiment classification (SC) [2,6,8,11,12]. However, some works see opinion term extraction (OE) as an auxiliary task for AE and try to model this relationship and boost performance for AE task [25]. To perform full end-to-end aspect-based sentiment analysis (E2E-ABSA), we still need to perform both stages in a pipeline manner. However, employing such a pipeline approach leads to propagating error from AE to downstream task SC. On the other hand, separate tasks still have their challenges where the lack of quality and large-scale datasets stand out. This problem is often tackled by introducing novel auxiliary task, such as document-level sentiment analysis for aspect-level sentiment classification [8], using specific domain embeddings together with general embedding layer [26], or using mined rules from dependency parsing for better identification of aspect terms [4]. On the other hand, there have been also studies on more effective modeling, such as using capsules [2,6,11], or transformation networks that combine strengths of RNNs and CNNs [12]. While previous works focused only on separate tasks, a recent study [20] introduced a two-staged framework where aspects, opinions, and polarities are identified separately in the first stage and in the second stage triplets of aspects, polarities, and their opinion term expressions are created.

2.2   Unified Methods

Recent studies showed ABSA could be performed also in unified manner where tasks use either *collapsed labels* [13,14,27] or *joint training* [3,9,15]. Collapsed tagging scheme combines aspect and polarity labels into one particular label, such as $Y = B - pos, I - pos, B - neg, ...$ where *B-pos* refer to the beginning of positive aspect term and *I-pos* to inside of positive aspect term, thus all sub-tasks share all features. Joint training keeps those labels separate and shares only specific parts of features while keeping some parts private. Recently, Li et al. exploited the correlation between

AE and SC tasks while using collapsed tagging scheme [13]. Authors later extended their work with the usage of the BERT model for ABSA [14]. A recent study by He et al. proposed novel interactive training where OE task is fused into AE while jointly learned together with SC [9]. Another study models only AE and SC tasks with explicit relationship modeling [15]. The idea of explicit modeling of relationships was followed by the work of Chen and Quian that discussed keeping AE and OE tasks separate while modeling multiple different relationships between the AE, OE, and SC [3].

3 Opinion Typology

In this section, we describe how we defined the tasks for aspect-based sentiment analysis along with auxiliary tasks. We also present more detailed information about the dataset used in our experiments.

3.1 Tasks Definitions

Typically, aspect-based sentiment analysis consists of sub-tasks aspect extraction (AE), opinion extraction (OE), and aspect-level sentiment classification (SC) which could be defined as a classic sequence labeling problem. Given sentence $S_e = w_1, w_2, ..., w_n$, each of tasks AE, OE, and SC aims to predict a a tag sequence $Y = \{y_1, y_2, ..., y_n\}$ where y_n is represented for particular tasks as follows:

- for AE, $y_i^{AE} \in \{B^O, I^O, O\}$ denotes *beginning of aspect term, inside of aspect term*, and *outside of* aspect term
- for OE, $y_i^{OE} \in \{B^A, I^A, O\}$ denotes *beginning of opinion term, inside of opinion term*, and *outside of* opinion term.
- for SC, $y_i^{SC} \in \{pos, neu, neg\}$ denotes *positive, neutral, negative* polarity for particular words. Following the previous works in ABSA [3,9], we ignore conflict labels for this task.

In addition, we define two more auxiliary tasks, subjectivity detection (SD) and opinion type detection (OTD), which could be formulated as sequence classification problem. Given sentence $S_e = w_1, w_2, ..., w_n$, both tasks SD and OTD aims to predict a label Y where:

- for SD, $Y \in \{subj, non\_subj\}$ denotes *subjective sentence* or *non-subjective sentence*, respectively.
- for OTD, $Y \in \{misc, opinionated, sugg\_cust, sugg\_mng, exp, unrelated\}$ denotes categories defined in Sect. 3.2.

3.2 Dataset

In this work, we selected the dataset introduced for SemEval 2015 task 12 [22]. As we already discussed, this dataset contains whole reviews thus also non-subjective or non-opinionated sentences are also included. This dataset became also more challenging than the previous one from 2014 [23]. However, this dataset contains only aspect term annotations for the restaurant domain only. Since the original dataset does not contain any opinion term annotation, we used opinion term annotations introduced by Wang et al. [24] which are used also by several state-of-the-art methods for ABSA [3,9].

In Table 1, we provide more detailed information on restaurant dataset from SemEval 2015 [22] with extension by Wang et al. [24]. This dataset was originally introduced with an explicit split to the training and testing set. Along with the number of reviews present in the dataset, we show the number of sentences, aspects, and opinions. For aspect statistics, we show also the number of aspects with specific polarity.

Table 1. Detailed statistics on aspect, opinions, and polarities for restaurant domain dataset from SemEval 2015.

	Train	Test	Total
Reviews	254	96	350
Sentences	1,315	685	2,000
Aspects	1,199	542	1,741
– positive	902	319	1,221
– negative	252	179	431
– neutral	34	27	61
– conflict	11	17	28
Opinions	1,196	503	1,699

The subjectivity of sentences is closely connected also to aspects, opinions, and polarities. Information that the sentence is non-subjective (factual) could indicate that it does not contain any aspect or, on the other hand, contains only aspects with neutral polarity (in SemEval dataset aspects with no sentiment are labeled as neutral). While the representation of non-subjective sentences is pretty straightforward and only factual sentences should be included, the subjectivity of reviewers could be expressed in much more ways and knowledge that sentence is subjective (opinionated) could not be sufficient for further processing. We identified several opinion types where only the miscellaneous category represents non-subjective (factual) sentences and other typologies represents different types of expressed opinions:

- **Miscellaneous** - represents samples where only factual information without any expressed opinion is included (e.g. *We live nearby BFC.*; *Went to Village last night for my birthday.*).
- **Opinionated Sentence** - contains sentences with expressed opinions, such as explicit or implicit aspect terms (e.g. *The pizza is overpriced and soggy.*; *The staff is incredibly helpful and attentive.*).
- **Suggestion to Customers** - contains sentences with a suggestion or recommendation that could be useful for other customers. It can be related to the entity itself or any aspect of the visit of the service (e.g. *For the price, you cannot eat this well in Manhattan.*; *You cannot go wrong at the Red Eye Grill.*).

- **Suggestion to Management** - contains sentences with suggestions towards the entity itself or entity management (e.g. *I wish they would change back to what it was before.*).
- **Expectation** - contains customer expectation towards the entity. Sometimes it is not even clear from sequence whether the expectation was fulfilled or not (e.g. *I expected quite a bit more from such an expensive menu.*).
- **Unrelated Opinion** - contains samples with expressed opinions towards an unrelated entity (e.g. *I was in love with Pongsri on 48th, but compared to Suan it is slow in service and overpriced.*).

In Table 2, we present the number of sentences with specific opinion types introduced earlier in this section, as well as the number of subjective and non-subjective sentences. For standard subjective sentences, all opinion types except miscellaneous are considered as subjective and only miscellaneous sentences are considered as non-subjective. In addition, we introduce also the naive approach where subjectivity is computed automatically. Subjective annotation is calculated when at least one explicit aspect or opinion is present in the sentence. If neither explicit aspect nor explicit opinion is present in the sentence then the sentence is considered non-subjective.

Table 2. Detailed statistics on subjectivity and opinion types for restaurant domain dataset from SemEval 2015.

	Train	Test	Total
Subjective	1, 151	571	1, 722
Non-subjective	164	114	278
Miscellaneous	164	114	278
Opinionated sentence	874	450	1, 324
Suggestion to customers	237	78	315
Suggestion to management	21	37	58
Expectation	12	5	17
Unrelated opinion	7	1	8
Subjective (Naive)	836	401	1, 237
Non-subjective (Naive)	479	284	763

4   Evaluation Methodology

In this section, we describe what baselines we are using for experiments and changes in baseline architectures that are necessary to perform subjectivity-aware learning.

4.1   Baselines

First, to demonstrate the effectiveness of the new auxiliary task for unified ABSA, we compare the performance of the following baseline with and without these auxiliary tasks. The hyper-parameters for all experiments are set as reported in the original paper.

- **IMN** [9] is a unified method for ABSA with joint training for AE and SC tasks with separate labels while OE task is fused into AE task forming aspect and opinion co-extraction task (AOE). In our experiments, we used a version of $\mathbf{IMN}^{-d}$ that uses only aspect-level tasks and document-level tasks are omitted.

Second, we also would like to compare the performance of auxiliary tasks when they are trained separately. We consider three baselines, two non-BERT and one BERT-based:

- **Simple Att** denotes the same architecture as was used by IMN [9] for document-level task based on attention layer with the usage of standard glove embeddings [21].
- **Simple CNN-Att** denotes the architecture as was used by IMN [9] for document-level task based on attention layer with the usage of multiple stacked CNN layers and standard glove embeddings [21].
- **BERT** denotes using BERT language model [5] followed by linear layer to predict corresponding labels.

4.2 Architecture

Since we proposed novel auxiliary tasks, the new architecture is based on baselines described in the previous subsection. General architecture how the auxiliary tasks are included is showed in Fig. 1.

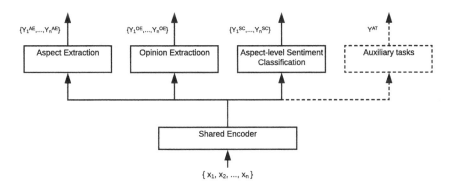

Fig. 1. General architecture of model including auxiliary tasks.

IMN. Subjectivity encoder for IMN is employed in the same way as the original model employs encoders for document-level auxiliary tasks where the shared encoder is followed by attention and linear layers and output probabilities with attention weights are passed together with probabilities for main tasks in the message passing mechanism.

5   Experiments

In this section, we discuss experiments and their setups, including used dataset, evaluation metrics, and finally the results of the experiments for both E2E ABSA and separate auxiliary tasks: subjectivity detection (SD), naive subjectivity detection (SDN), and opinion type detection (OTD).

5.1   Data

We conduct all experiments on the restaurant domain of the dataset introduced in SemEval 2015 with our annotations for the opinion types and subjectivity (see Sect. 3.2 for detailed description). We used the original explicit split for the test set and randomly split 20 % of the train set for the dev set. While described restaurant dataset is relatively small and the number of occurrences for some of the opinion types is too small, we decided to merge some classes and used only *Miscellaneous*, *Opinionated sentence* and *Suggestions* categories. *Suggestion to Management* was merged with *Suggestion to Customers* due to similar opinion expression but towards the different entity. We merged *Expectation* and *Unrelated opinion* to general *Opinionated sentence* category.

5.2   Evaluation Metrics

For evaluation of all experiments, we use four metrics for E2E-ABSA selected also in previous research [3,9] and two additional metrics to assess the quality of auxiliary task predictions. For evaluation of ABSA sub-tasks, we use metrics of F1 for all three subtasks - **F1-a**, **F1-o**, and **F1-s** denotes F1 for task of aspect extraction (AE), opinion extraction (OE) and aspect-level sentiment classification (SC), respectively. Besides, another metric **F1-i** is used for evaluation of overall performance that combines measures of F1-a and F1-s, since a correct prediction is considered only when both aspect and sentiment polarity is predicted correctly. For all three possible auxiliary tasks, we use two metrics **acc** and **F1**.

5.3   Results

In this subsection, we present results on how the auxiliary tasks affected IMN model performance when used as the training tasks. In addition, we present also a performance on the separate classification of auxiliary tasks.

E2E ABSA. In Table 3, we show results of IMN^{-D} model when learned together with newly introduced auxiliary tasks. While the best results were achieved with the usage of naive subjectivity labels, the results show all auxiliary tasks helped improve overall performance on E2E ABSA when learned together. Results also show that improvement in overall performance was achieved mostly by its improvement in aspect-level sentiment classification. Interestingly, performance improvement for SD and OTD tasks was lower than for SDN tasks. We suppose it is caused due to different annotation standards used for particular parts of the dataset. While we created annotation for subjectivity and opinion types, original work [22] introduced only the annotation for aspect and polarities. The original dataset has also a limited scope and some sentences were labeled as out of scope (e.g. sentences comparing different entities; see [22] for more detailed description). In addition, opinion annotation was added later by another work of Wang et al. [24]. Unfortunately, it is unknown how the annotation was created and the annotation guideline is not available. We believe if all parts were created by the common annotation standard, SD and OTD tasks could provide comparable performance as a model with SDN task.

Table 3. IMN^{-D} model comparison for E2E-ABSA with different auxiliary tasks. Note: the reported results are averaged on 5 runs.

	Model	F1-a	F1-o	F1-s	F1-i
IMN^{-D}	Base	69.80	72.11	60.65	57.91
	SD task	69.89	72.03	**67.26**	58.57
	SDN task	**70.18**	**73.35**	61.81	**59.00**
	OTD task	69.10	72.27	61.85	58.43

Auxiliary Tasks. In Table 4, we show results for all baseline models and separate auxiliary tasks. As expected, BERT model produces much better results than the model with standard GloVe embeddings. Despite simplification of classes and its reduction of minor ones, the task of opinion type detection is still the most challenging, and results for all models are significantly worse. While all models achieved better accuracy for standard subjectivity detection than its naive version, the macro F1 measure showed it was achieved mostly by prediction of major class.

Table 4. Model comparison for auxiliary task classification. Note: the reported results are averaged on 5 runs.

	Model	acc	F1
SD task	Simple Att	83.36	45.46
	Simple CNN-Att	82.94	44.83
	BERT	87.29	70.63
SDN task	Simple Att	79.50	78.67
	Simple CNN-Att	77.81	77.37
	BERT	83.06	82.10
OTD task	Simple Att	66.57	26.64
	Simple CNN-Att	64.79	25.83
	BERT	78.68	66.67

6   Conclusion

In this paper, we introduced several opinion types that could appear in customer reviews and investigated the effect of new auxiliary tasks – subjectivity detection, naive subjectivity detection, and opinion type detection – for the performance of aspect-based sentiment analysis models. Our experiments showed all auxiliary tasks help to improve overall performance for end-to-end aspect-based sentiment analysis, especially in overall measure $F1$-i. Our experiments also showed that subjectivity knowledge transfer was particularly helpful for the performance of aspect-level sentiment classification. Besides, we performed also an experiment on separate auxiliary tasks and reported new benchmark results. The BERT model could be considered as the new baseline for this dataset.

Due to the rather small size of the state-of-the-art dataset used, we explored the impact of the auxiliary tasks on ABSA sub-tasks to a basic extent. We assume a new larger dataset created with the same annotation standards could emphasize the effect of newly introduced auxiliary tasks more significantly. We believe that the proposed work poses an important step towards the fine-grained analysis of sentiment typology in review analysis and draws the task of aspect-based sentiment analysis closer to the real-world sentiment analysis scenarios. Another future work area lies in the research of minor languages [18, 19] that lack even small datasets for particular fine-grained tasks.

References

1. Chaturvedi, I., Cambria, E., Welsch, R.E., Herrera, F.: Distinguishing between facts and opinions for sentiment analysis: survey and challenges. Inf. Fusion **44**, 65–77 (2018)
2. Chen, Z., Qian, T.: Transfer capsule network for aspect level sentiment classification. In: Proceedings of the 57th Annual Meeting of the Association for Computational Linguistics, pp. 547–556. Association for Computational Linguistics, Florence, Italy (Jul 2019). https://doi.org/10.18653/v1/P19-1052. https://www.aclweb.org/anthology/P19-1052
3. Chen, Z., Qian, T.: Relation-aware collaborative learning for unified aspect-based sentiment analysis. In: Proceedings of the 58th Annual Meeting of the Association for Computational Linguistics, pp. 3685–3694. Association for Computational Linguistics (Jul 2020). https://doi.org/10.18653/v1/2020.acl-main.340. https://www.aclweb.org/anthology/2020.acl-main.340
4. Dai, H., Song, Y.: Neural aspect and opinion term extraction with mined rules as weak supervision. In: Proceedings of the 57th Annual Meeting of the Association for Computational Linguistics, pp. 5268–5277. Association for Computational Linguistics, Florence, Italy (Jul 2019). https://doi.org/10.18653/v1/P19-1520. https://www.aclweb.org/anthology/P19-1520
5. Devlin, J., Chang, M.W., Lee, K., Toutanova, K.: BERT: pre-training of deep bidirectional transformers for language understanding. In: Proceedings of the 2019 Conference of the North American Chapter of the Association for Computational Linguistics: Human Language Technologies, Volume 1 (Long and Short Papers), pp. 4171–4186. Association for Computational Linguistics, Minneapolis, Minnesota (Jun 2019). https://doi.org/10.18653/v1/N19-1423. https://www.aclweb.org/anthology/N19-1423

6. Du, C., et al.: Capsule network with interactive attention for aspect-level sentiment classification. In: Proceedings of the 2019 Conference on Empirical Methods in Natural Language Processing and the 9th International Joint Conference on Natural Language Processing (EMNLP-IJCNLP), pp. 5489–5498. Association for Computational Linguistics, Hong Kong, China (Nov 2019). https://doi.org/10.18653/v1/D19-1551. https://www.aclweb.org/anthology/D19-1551

7. Fan, Z., Wu, Z., Dai, X.Y., Huang, S., Chen, J.: Target-oriented opinion words extraction with target-fused neural sequence labeling. In: Proceedings of the 2019 Conference of the North American Chapter of the Association for Computational Linguistics: Human Language Technologies, Volume 1 (Long and Short Papers), pp. 2509–2518. Association for Computational Linguistics, Minneapolis, Minnesota (Jun 2019). https://doi.org/10.18653/v1/N19-1259. https://www.aclweb.org/anthology/N19-1259

8. He, R., Lee, W.S., Ng, H.T., Dahlmeier, D.: Exploiting document knowledge for aspect-level sentiment classification. In: Proceedings of the 56th Annual Meeting of the Association for Computational Linguistics (Volume 2: Short Papers), pp. 579–585. Association for Computational Linguistics, Melbourne, Australia (Jul 2018). https://doi.org/10.18653/v1/P18-2092. https://www.aclweb.org/anthology/P18-2092

9. He, R., Lee, W.S., Ng, H.T., Dahlmeier, D.: An interactive multi-task learning network for end-to-end aspect-based sentiment analysis. In: Proceedings of the 57th Annual Meeting of the Association for Computational Linguistics, pp. 504–515. Association for Computational Linguistics, Florence, Italy (Jul 2019). https://doi.org/10.18653/v1/P19-1048. https://www.aclweb.org/anthology/P19-1048

10. Hu, M., Peng, Y., Huang, Z., Li, D., Lv, Y.: Open-domain targeted sentiment analysis via span-based extraction and classification. In: Proceedings of the 57th Annual Meeting of the Association for Computational Linguistics, pp. 537–546. Association for Computational Linguistics, Florence, Italy (Jul 2019). https://doi.org/10.18653/v1/P19-1051. https://www.aclweb.org/anthology/P19-1051

11. Jiang, Q., Chen, L., Xu, R., Ao, X., Yang, M.: A challenge dataset and effective models for aspect-based sentiment analysis. In: Proceedings of the 2019 Conference on Empirical Methods in Natural Language Processing and the 9th International Joint Conference on Natural Language Processing (EMNLP-IJCNLP), pp. 6280–6285. Association for Computational Linguistics, Hong Kong, China (Nov 2019). https://doi.org/10.18653/v1/D19-1654. https://www.aclweb.org/anthology/D19-1654

12. Li, X., Bing, L., Lam, W., Shi, B.: Transformation networks for target-oriented sentiment classification. In: Proceedings of the 56th Annual Meeting of the Association for Computational Linguistics (Volume 1: Long Papers), pp. 946–956. Association for Computational Linguistics, Melbourne, Australia (Jul 2018). https://doi.org/10.18653/v1/P18-1087. https://www.aclweb.org/anthology/P18-1087

13. Li, X., Bing, L., Li, P., Lam, W.: A unified model for opinion target extraction and target sentiment prediction. In: Proceedings of the AAAI Conference on Artificial Intelligence, vol. 33, No. 01, pp. 6714–6721 (2019)

14. Li, X., Bing, L., Zhang, W., Lam, W.: Exploiting BERT for end-to-end aspect-based sentiment analysis. In: Proceedings of the 5th Workshop on Noisy User-Generated Text (W-NUT 2019), pp. 34–41. Association for Computational Linguistics, Hong Kong, China (Nov 2019). https://doi.org/10.18653/v1/D19-5505. https://www.aclweb.org/anthology/D19-5505

15. Luo, H., Li, T., Liu, B., Zhang, J.: DOER: dual cross-shared RNN for aspect term-polarity co-extraction. In: Proceedings of the 57th Annual Meeting of the Association for Computational Linguistics. pp. 591–601. Association for Computational Linguistics, Florence, Italy (Jul 2019). https://doi.org/10.18653/v1/P19-1056. https://www.aclweb.org/anthology/P19-1056

16. Ni, J., McAuley, J.: Personalized review generation by expanding phrases and attending on aspect-aware representations. In: Proceedings of the 56th Annual Meeting of the Association for Computational Linguistics (Volume 2: Short Papers), pp. 706–711. Association for Computational Linguistics, Melbourne, Australia (Jul 2018). https://doi.org/10.18653/v1/P18-2112. https://www.aclweb.org/anthology/P18-2112

17. Pecar, S.: Towards opinion summarization of customer reviews. In: Proceedings of ACL 2018, Student Research Workshop, pp. 1–8. Association for Computational Linguistics, Melbourne, Australia (Jul 2018). https://doi.org/10.18653/v1/P18-3001. https://www.aclweb.org/anthology/P18-3001

18. Pecar, S., Simko, M., Bielikova, M.: Sentiment analysis of customer reviews: impact of text pre-processing. In: 2018 World Symposium on Digital Intelligence for Systems and Machines (DISA), pp. 251–256. IEEE (2018)

19. Pecar, S., Simko, M., Bielikova, M.: Improving sentiment classification in Slovak language. In: Proceedings of the 7th Workshop on Balto-Slavic Natural Language Processing, pp. 114–119. Association for Computational Linguistics, Florence, Italy (Aug 2019). https://doi.org/10.18653/v1/W19-3716. https://www.aclweb.org/anthology/W19-3716

20. Peng, H., Xu, L., Bing, L., Huang, F., Lu, W., Si, L.: Knowing what, how and why: a near complete solution for aspect-based sentiment analysis. In: AAAI, pp. 8600–8607 (2020)

21. Pennington, J., Socher, R., Manning, C.: GloVe: global vectors for word representation. In: Proceedings of the 2014 Conference on Empirical Methods in Natural Language Processing (EMNLP), pp. 1532–1543. Association for Computational Linguistics, Doha, Qatar (Oct 2014). https://doi.org/10.3115/v1/D14-1162. https://www.aclweb.org/anthology/D14-1162

22. Pontiki, M., Galanis, D., Papageorgiou, H., Manandhar, S., Androutsopoulos, I.: SemEval-2015 task 12: apect based sentiment analysis. In: Proceedings of the 9th International Workshop on Semantic Evaluation (SemEval 2015), pp. 486–495. Association for Computational Linguistics, Denver, Colorado (Jun 2015). https://doi.org/10.18653/v1/S15-2082. https://www.aclweb.org/anthology/S15-2082

23. Pontiki, M., Galanis, D., Pavlopoulos, J., Papageorgiou, H., Androutsopoulos, I., Manandhar, S.: SemEval-2014 task 4: aspect based sentiment analysis. In: Proceedings of the 8th International Workshop on Semantic Evaluation (SemEval 2014), pp. 27–35. Association for Computational Linguistics, Dublin, Ireland (Aug 2014). https://doi.org/10.3115/v1/S14-2004. https://www.aclweb.org/anthology/S14-2004

24. Wang, W., Pan, S.J., Dahlmeier, D., Xiao, X.: Recursive neural conditional random fields for aspect-based sentiment analysis. In: Proceedings of the 2016 Conference on Empirical Methods in Natural Language Processing, pp. 616–626. Association for Computational Linguistics, Austin, Texas (Nov 2016). https://doi.org/10.18653/v1/D16-1059. https://www.aclweb.org/anthology/D16-1059

25. Wang, W., Pan, S.J., Dahlmeier, D., Xiao, X.: Coupled multi-layer attentions for co-extraction of aspect and opinion terms. In: Thirty-First AAAI Conference on Artificial Intelligence, pp. 3316–3322 (2017)

26. Xu, H., Liu, B., Shu, L., Yu, P.S.: Double embeddings and CNN-based sequence labeling for aspect extraction. In: Proceedings of the 56th Annual Meeting of the Association for Computational Linguistics (Volume 2: Short Papers), pp. 592–598. Association for Computational Linguistics, Melbourne, Australia (Jul 2018). https://doi.org/10.18653/v1/P18-2094. https://www.aclweb.org/anthology/P18-2094

27. Zhang, M., Zhang, Y., Vo, D.T.: Neural networks for open domain targeted sentiment. In: Proceedings of the 2015 Conference on Empirical Methods in Natural Language Processing, pp. 612–621. Association for Computational Linguistics, Lisbon, Portugal (Sep 2015). https://doi.org/10.18653/v1/D15-1073, https://www.aclweb.org/anthology/D15-1073

Towards Personal Data Anonymization
for Social Messaging

Ondřej Sotolář$^{(\boxtimes)}$, Jaromír Plhák, and David Šmahel (ID)

IRTIS, Faculty of Informatics, Masaryk University, Botanická 68a,
602 00 Brno, Czech Republic
{xsotolar,xplhak}@fi.muni.cz, davs@mail.muni.cz

Abstract. We present a method for building text corpora for the supervised learning of text-to-text anonymization while maintaining a strict privacy policy. In our solution, personal data entities are detected, classified, and anonymized. We use available machine-learning methods, like named-entity recognition, and improve their performance by grouping multiple entities into larger units based on the theory of tabular data anonymization. Experimental results on annotated Czech Facebook Messenger conversations reveal that our solution has recall comparable to human annotators. On the other hand, precision is much lower because of the low efficiency of the named entity recognition in the domain of social messaging conversations. The resulting anonymized text is of high utility because of the replacement methods that produce natural text.

Keywords: Text anonymization · Personal data · Sanitization · De-identification · Privacy protection

1 Introduction

The presence of personal data poses a problem for building text corpora across all research fields. In the European Union, it is required to apply reliable personal data protection according to the General Data Protection Regulation [5]. *Personal data* are defined as any information that can lead to the identification of a living person. While the authors of the data can allow its arbitrary handling via informed consent, that might not be enough to enable sharing, processing, or even the collection itself because of the actual or suspected presence of third-party information. Furthermore, informed consents are usually given to a concrete institution, which complicates sharing data, if another institution would express interest in them later. This makes constructing corpora from texts that contain personal data challenging because reliable anonymization[1] of unstructured text is still an area of ongoing research. Simultaneously, the possibility of building new datasets creates a strong motivation for overcoming the legal and ethical obstacles.

---

[1] Anonymity is property of data and anonymization is the process of altering data so that the protected individuals can no longer be identified directly or indirectly [26].

© Springer Nature Switzerland AG 2021
K. Ekštein et al. (Eds.): TSD 2021, LNAI 12848, pp. 281–292, 2021.
https://doi.org/10.1007/978-3-030-83527-9_24

Although various solutions exist, they are usually not transferable to domains different from those for which they were created. The anonymity of a text document is, in fact, dependent on the domain and locale, and, likewise, the desired privacy guarantee is affected by the confidentiality of the environment of the intended use. For our target domain and locale, there is currently no suitable solution. Therefore, we propose a novel, ethical approach to building anonymous corpora, which we demonstrate by building a corpus for training models for personal data recognition. We designed a method for personal data detection and evaluated its efficiency with standard precision, recall, and F1 metrics. We also improved the masking of such data with regards to the utility of the resulting text and evaluated it on downstream tasks.

The methods presented here have a direct practical application for ongoing social-science research that focuses on information and communication technology usage and its impact on individuals. The latest data collection methods in this field (EMA [13]) focus on recording the subjects' activity on their own electronic devices, such as smartphones, as shown in [14] and combine them with responses in timed questionnaires completed by the users. Thus they solve the reliability problem associated with self-reported studies. However, before collecting, storing, and processing the data, it must be anonymized to comply with GDPR. We focused on the anonymization of Czech text retrieved from instant messenger conversations of youths because it comprises the bulk of the data that will be collected. The textual data will be used for semantical analysis within the confidential environment of the research team.

We demonstrated that the language style in this domain is substantially different from that of other publicly available corpora and text representations, and thus, models trained on texts from a different domain achieve a substantially lower performance. Therefore, it is necessary to build a corpus from data in our domain for training a well-performing model.

2   Related Work

Tabular data privacy models, such as k-anonymity [15], ϵ-differential privacy [3], and all of the derivative models, enable the measurement of the balance between data privacy and utility based on the unambiguous semantics of table-column definitions. This property makes the aforementioned models unusable for unstructured text where the amount and type of sensitive data are unknown beforehand. From this field, we borrowed the definitions for *identifier* (ID) and *quasi-identifier* (QID). An entity is an identifier if it strongly identifies the individual to which the entity refers (e.g., a full name). A quasi-identifier is an entity that leads to identification only in combination with other entities.

When anonymizing unstructured text, the first step is the detection of personal data. One approach is based on named entity recognition (NER), which searches for the entities of identifiers and quasi-identifiers that constitute personal data [6,7,10]. This method reduces the problem to a NER problem, and, thus, the models do not allow measuring either text utility or data privacy.

Another approach detects semantically similar text to a predefined set of sensitive terms [8]. This allows capturing sensitive content beyond named entities, but it fails for previously unknown sensitive terms. Some models from this family, such as C-Sanitized [16], allow for the direct measurement of data utility and privacy because they are based on the information-theoretic concept of information content; thus, they can compare the content of a document before and after anonymization. In our case, the sensitive terms are not known beforehand; therefore, we use the former approach and propose measuring data utility on downstream tasks.

The second step is the handling of found personal data. For text-to-text anonymization, we need to define the masking, generalization, and suppression methods. The simplest systems do not consider this and use constant or numbered masks [12,17], which, at most, keep the entity type [25]. As a result, much of the information that is useful for downstream tasks, such as part-of-speech and any remaining semantics, are lost. A better approach, utilized by the semantic C-Sanitized model, uses ontologies to provide generalizations for the masks. The authors attempt neither to retain the original word forms nor to generalize non-semantic terms, such as names.

Nevertheless, measuring the utility and privacy remains challenging. Measuring the privacy of anonymized text remains an unsolved problem because it is difficult to simulate the deductive skills of individual human readers. An attempt has been made with Bayesian testing [9].

When text itself is not needed, and its numerical representation suffices, it has been shown that it is possible to perturb that representation (with noise) while keeping its usefulness for downstream tasks and simultaneously preventing the reconstruction of the original text [1,11]. These models can optimize the privacy-utility balance by using the dataset itself and providing an ϵ-differential guarantee of privacy. The latter approach is not usable for our goal to build text corpora because the authors have not designed a method to convert the noisy representation back to meaningful text.

3 Dataset

Our target domain is the online conversations realized through the instant messenger Facebook Messenger of youths in Czech. In this domain, the language style is highly informal, composed of short messages that are most often written as simple-structure sentences or fragments. Capital letters are used less or in irregular places. Typos are common. Furthermore, words and phrases from different languages (mostly English and Slovak) are often unexpectedly mixed into the messages. Nicknames, both related to a personal name and not, are often bent into out-of-place forms and used more frequently than regular names.

This is in stark contrast to commonly used corpora, such as the Czech Named Entity Corpus (CNEC) [18], the most comprehensive corpus for NER in Czech, which is composed of texts in journalistic style with well-formed sentences and good grammar. It is also different from other commonly used corpora and representations constructed from web crawl, such as Fasttext [2].

We conducted a preliminary experiment, where we hypothesized that when the language style gets closer to our domain, the performance of models trained on out-of-domain datasets will decrease. For this purpose, we trained a featureless NER recognizer on the supertypes *Personal name* and *Instution*. We compared the model's performance on the CNEC corpus before and after converting it to lowercase, stripping it of diacritics, and introducing a typo. The model was composed of a BiLSTM on top of a LSTM with dropouts, and it utilizes the weights of the pre-trained web-crawl Fasttext embeddings as inputs in the Embedding layer. The results are shown in Table 1 and they support our hypothesis.

Table 1. The importance of case, diacritics, and typos in CNEC for NER.

Solution	Precision	Recall	F1
CNEC	71.36	68.25	69.44
CNEC lowercase, no diacritics	62.35	57.96	59.83
Above + 1 character typo	60.02	54.0	54.38

4   Methods

Our goal was to anonymize personal data. In this section, we describe the methods we designed to annotate, detect, and mask them.

4.1   Annotation Schema

We condensed existing named entity hierarchies (such as [4]) into the simple Schema 1 that captured easily identifying personal data while staying quick to annotate. It differs from other schemata in that it does no instruct to annotate all entities, but rather to label identifiers and the surrounding quasi-identifiers.

- *Name:* any name that contains a surname, or a first name belonging to a surname in close proximity.
- *ID:* birth number, tax identification, bank account, credit card, ID card, passport, driver's license number, etc.
- *Location:* street name with house number, GPS coordinates, IP address.
- *Contact Information:* email, phone number, URL, etc.

Schema 1. Annotation schema

It is important that the annotators labeled only the conversations they authored because we could not share third-party information between annotators. As a significant side effect of this decision, we could not measure the inter-annotator agreement. To overcome this, we added additional synthetic entities

Table 2. Weighted average success rate of annotators on synthetic entities.

Solution	Precision	Recall	F1
Human annotator	99.84	79.17	88.31

into the source conversations, which we designed to be equally difficult to detect across all annotators. This resulted in a control set of 1,226 synthetic entities on which we measured the annotator accuracy as shown in Table 2. The annotation was not iterative, to which we attribute the low recall score. The reason for the non-iterative process was the scarcity of found entities.

Using this schema, we constructed an annotated corpus of unstructured Czech text from the Facebook Messenger conversations of five student volunteers, using the Brat annotation tool [20]. The corpus consisted of 797 conversations in separate text files, which totaled approximately 279K lines of text and 1,5M words. The annotators labeled a total of 1,004 naturally occurring entities (i.e., a gold dataset). The type distribution of natural entities was highly imbalanced, with the majority of 82% cases of the *Name* type, and the minority of 11% *Contact Information*, 4% *Location*, and 3% *ID*.

By labeling the gold entities, the data authors effectively performed the detection step themselves. After we anonymized the gold entities with the methods described in Sect. 4.3 we could ethically use the corpus for other tasks.

4.2   Personal Data Detection

The detection is a three-step process: 1. find named entities with a pre-trained NER model; 2. find other named entities with a custom rule matcher; and, 3. compose the entities into groups. The groups are defined as:

Personal Data Entity. $PDE_t(I \in NE, Q \subseteq NE_1 \times ...NE_n)$ *is a tree of depth 1 defined by the identifying NE I and a set of QIDs Q from the NE set.*

Named Entity Recognition. Due to the small number of entities from the annotation, we decided against using the corpus to develop our own NER architecture; rather we leveraged an existing model that performs well on the CNEC corpus and we design methods to make it fit our annotation schema and domain. We started with a subset of the 42 fine-grained named entity types, which are related to personal data, of the CNEC 2.0 corpus as shown in Fig. 1. For the detection, we use the NameTag [22] model trained on CNEC that, until recently, achieved state-of-the-art performance on the corpus[2]. While it has been surpassed by [21,23], the difference does not have huge impact for our problem and it has the advantage of being a fast and complete software with bindings to major programming languages. We evaluate its performance on our gold dataset in the first row of Table 3.

---

[2] F1 79.23 on fine types.

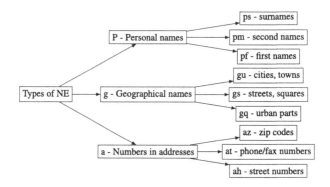

Fig. 1. Relevant part of the CNEC types.

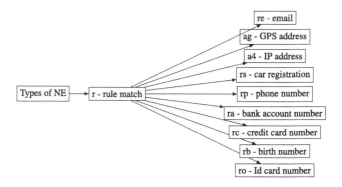

Fig. 2. Complement to the CNEC types.

Improving NER with Rules. The CNEC corpus does not contain nearly enough structured entities typical for Czech, such as phone numbers, card numbers, and other quasi-numerical types. Therefore, models trained on it show a significant miss rate for these types. We added a rule matcher to produce additional entities shown in Fig. 2. The impact is shown in the second row of Table 3. We do not see a point in boosting CNEC with synthetic entities because instead of generating them with rules, we can use the rules directly. Additionally, the gold entities of this type are too few to make a difference in training. We propose a solution to collect enough naturally-occurring entities in Sect. 6.

Composing Named Entities into PDEs. Finally, we convert the named entities to PDEs by deciding which entities are ID or QID candidates that can be linked to each other. The reasoning behind this is to match the decisions of annotators who were instructed not to annotate all named entities, but IDs and QIDs only. Thus, each PDE carries the types of entities of which it is composed but also the new type that corresponds to our annotation schema. The composition is implemented with a rule-based system that searches each identifier's neighborhood window for other entities and then makes the decision based on the entity type combination. The combinations that worked best were: *surname with first names, address with a street number*; and the best windows size was 10 tokens. The impact is shown in the third row of Table 3.

4.3 Anonymization

Anonymization is realized differently for each entity type. We define the property of **repeatability**, which is the ability to replace multiple occurrences of the same entity with a consistent replacing value[3]. Because inflection is essential in Czech, our methods keep the correct form of the replacement value.

Names are suppressed by a replacement value selected from a gazetteer by a hash function, which ensures repeatability. Four gazetteers were used for: first names, surnames, and both grammatical genders. Morphological analysis was performed with MorphoDiTa [24] on the original value to bend the replacement value into the correct form.

IDs deserve robust anonymization without repeatability. They are suppressed by a randomly generated replacement value. However, the replacement value tries to retain the original format through pattern matching to keep the semantics.

Location is generalized and suppressed, and it supports repeatability. For physical address, the solution suppresses the city/town name and street address and randomizes the other address parts, such as the street number and postal code. The replacement value for the street name is another street name selected from a gazetteer.

Contact Information supports repeatability. The selected anonymization method was a hash-value suppression in combination with the retention of the original data format.

5 Results

5.1 Detection Efficiency

We evaluated the detection efficiency by comparing the solution to the gold entities. We tuned the parameters to achieve a recall value comparable to the human annotators in Table 2. The human recall was achieved on synthetic entities with regular structure while the solution metrics were on the natural entity set. Table 3 shows the weighted aggregate results.

---

[3] e.g. "Ondřej Sotolář", "Ondřeji" are replaced with "Jan Novák", "Jane" respectively.

Table 3. Evaluation of PDE recognition on the test corpus: natural entity set.

Solution	Precision	Recall	F1
NER	8.05	71.36	14.46
Above + rules	8.78	**86.5**	15.94
Above + PDE composition	**29.92**	78.7	**43.36**

5.2 Data Utility

We evaluate the data utility of the anonymized text on the downstream tasks of NER and text classification. The results of our methods described below are promising because, for tasks that revolve around named entities, they seem to affect the resulting text much less than the older, simpler methods [12,17,25].

Named Entity Recognition performance change is measured by how much different variations of the anonymized text change the result of entity recognition. We used the Nametag 1 model and the CNEC 2.0 corpus as the dataset. The entities found in the original text serve as the *gold set* and we evaluate the other versions against it. In Table 4 we test the current state of the art of: *suppressing the entities* and *replacing the entities with type tags*. The resulting entities look like *'XXX'* (keeping length) and *'NAME, LOCATION, etc.'* respectively. We compare them against our methods, which use various ways to keep the original word form (described in Sect. 4.3).

Table 4. Comparison of anonymized text utility on the NER task.

Solution	Precision	Recall	F1
Original text	100	100	100
Suppression [17]	80.21	58.19	67.45
Type tags [12, 25]	94.29	68.4	79.28
Our solution	**95.63**	**88.47**	**91.91**

Classification was evaluated on with a simple supervised classification task. We assigned the label *Risky Behavior* to a sample of the anonymized rows. The original corpus was then recreated by swapping the anonymized rows for the originals. We tested with two different models: 1. three-layer feed-forward neural network with an embedding layer on top; and, 2. Deep Open Classification model [19] with FastText embeddings. After training and evaluating the models on all the datasets, **we found no statistically significant difference** (with cross-validation) between the performance of the classifier trained on the original and anonymized data.

5.3   Performance Discussion

Considering detection, when the recall is comparable to human rate, the precision is relatively low. Because of the imbalance between the entity types in the gold set, most errors occur in the *Name* type. After surveying the data, we concluded that the reason is the combination of low grammatical quality of the text and the missing inter-annotator agreement impacting the annotation quality.

As for data utility, our solution keeps the original syntax and semantics significantly better than the previous solutions. This is because of the replacement method's ability to produce natural-looking text. The impact is more significant on tasks that depend heavily on the anonymizer's target parts of the text, the named entities. The imperfect score on the NER task is caused by the implementation. The anonymizer sometimes fails to disambiguate the entities, compose them into PDEs, and also for the numerical types, the entities are sometimes in an unknown format.

6   Limitations and Further Work

The precision of the presented solution is very low, especially compared to human annotators, and many false-positive PDEs were detected. Even though we have shown in our evaluation in the previous section that these drawbacks do not significantly impact the data utility of the resulting text, we believe that a much better model can be built with a larger and higher quality corpus. In our opinion, pair annotation is necessary because a solid inter-annotator agreement is crucial to building a good corpus. In Table 2 we can see that without it the annotation quality is low.

An improved annotation schema should be more detailed to cover the possible quasi-identifiers more broadly. Most importantly, the rule to label identifiers and quasi-identifiers should be removed entirely. Scarcity should be no longer a problem for the majority classes. For the minority classes, it could be overcome by using an active learning approach of scoring the normalized entity frequency (the entities being detected by the methods described here) to annotate the documents with the highest score first.

We also suggest improving the tracking of identifiers across tokens by using co-reference resolution, especially for personal names. In addition to improving repeatability, such tracking can improve the morphological analysis for the replacement values by providing more instances to disambiguate the entity.

We would advise not to give up on developing better rules and combining them with the neural model to improve the recognition. Even the best neural models sometimes miss obvious entities for reasons that are difficult to explain. This might be fine for other applications, but it is unacceptable for our task, where recall is much more important than precision. Furthermore, missing an evident personal data entity undermines the reader's trust in the solution, even though it might be statistically sound. Preliminary results have shown that, in our domain, searching the first three letters of a first name greatly improves the recall of the *First name* type without negatively affecting precision because it manages to capture nicknames well. We believe that it is possible to expand the idea by generating derivations of the names and using them, too. Generating optimal rules automatically should also be considered.

7   Conclusions

We presented an innovative approach for the previously unsolved problem of personal data anonymization for the Czech language. The method uses named-entity recognition, and it was incrementally enhanced with custom-made rules to link multiple named entities based on the theory of tabular data anonymization in order to improve the success rate. Our approach maintains the high utility of the text which we proved by measuring it on downstream tasks. This is achieved by producing natural looking replacement values that retain the forms of the originals, which is an improvement over the existing methods. We evaluated the fully functional anonymizer with a newly created Czech corpus of Facebook Messenger conversations with regards to both detection efficiency and data utility. The results show that the recall rate is comparable with human annotators and the utility stays the same as that of the original text. Furthermore, we solved the ethical problem of building an anonymous corpus.

Acknowledgements. This work has received funding from the Czech Science Foundation, project no. 19-27828X.

References

1. Beigi, G., Shu, K., Guo, R., Wang, S., Liu, H.: Privacy preserving text representation learning. In: Proceedings of the 30th ACM Conference on Hypertext and Social Media, pp. 275–276 (2019). https://doi.org/10.1145/3342220.3344925
2. Bojanowski, P., Grave, E., Joulin, A., Mikolov, T.: Enriching word vectors with subword information. Trans. Assoc. Comput. Linguist. **5**, 135–146 (2017). https://doi.org/10.1162/tacl_a_00051
3. Chawla, S., Dwork, C., McSherry, F., Smith, A., Wee, H.: Toward privacy in public databases. In: Kilian, J. (ed.) TCC 2005. LNCS, vol. 3378, pp. 363–385. Springer, Heidelberg (2005). https://doi.org/10.1007/978-3-540-30576-7_20
4. Dasgupta, R., Ganesan, B., Kannan, A., Reinwald, B., Kumar, A.: Fine grained classification of personal data entities. Preprint at https://arxiv.org/abs/1811.09368 (2018)
5. GDPR: Regulation (EU) 2016/679 of the European parliament and of the council of 27 April 2016 on the protection of natural persons with regard to the processing of personal data and on the free movement of such data, and repealing directive 95/46/EC (general data protection regulation) (2016). https://op.europa.eu/en/publication-detail/-/publication/3e485e15-11bd-11e6-ba9a-01aa75ed71a1/language-en
6. Graliński, F., Jassem, K., Marcińczuk, M., Wawrzyniak, P.: Named entity recognition in machine anonymization. In: Recent Advances in Intelligent Information Systems, pp. 247–260 (2009)

7. Hassan, F., Domingo-Ferrer, J., Soria-Comas, J.: Anonymization of unstructured data via named-entity recognition. In: Torra, V., Narukawa, Y., Aguiló, I., González-Hidalgo, M. (eds.) MDAI 2018. LNCS (LNAI), vol. 11144, pp. 296–305. Springer, Cham (2018). https://doi.org/10.1007/978-3-030-00202-2_24
8. Hassan, F., Sánchez, D., Soria-Comas, J., Domingo-Ferrer, J.: Automatic anonymization of textual documents: detecting sensitive information via word embeddings. In: 2019 18th IEEE International Conference on Trust, Security and Privacy In Computing and Communications/13th IEEE International Conference on Big Data Science and Engineering (TrustCom/BigDataSE), pp. 358–365. IEEE (2019). https://doi.org/10.1109/TrustCom/BigDataSE.2019.00055
9. Kleinberg, B., Mozes, M., van der Toolen, Y., et al.: NETANOS-named entity-based text anonymization for open science. Preprint at https://osf.io/w9nhb (2017)
10. Marimon, M., et al.: Automatic de-identification of medical texts in Spanish: the MEDDOCAN track, corpus, guidelines, methods and evaluation of results. In: Proceedings of the Iberian Languages Evaluation Forum (IberLEF 2019) (2019)
11. Mosallanezhad, A., Beigi, G., Liu, H.: Deep reinforcement learning-based text anonymization against private-attribute inference. In: Proceedings of the 2019 Conference on Empirical Methods in Natural Language Processing and the 9th International Joint Conference on Natural Language Processing (EMNLP-IJCNLP), pp. 2360–2369 (2019). https://doi.org/10.18653/v1/D19-1240
12. Neamatullah, I., et al.: Automated de-identification of free-text medical records. BMC Med. Inform. Decis. Making **8**(1), 1–17 (2008)
13. Porras-Segovia, A., et al.: Smartphone-based ecological momentary assessment (EMA) in psychiatric patients and student controls: a real-world feasibility study. J. Affect. Disord. **274**, 733–741 (2020). https://doi.org/10.1016/j.jad.2020.05.067
14. Reeves, B., et al.: Screenomics: a framework to capture and analyze personal life experiences and the ways that technology shapes them. Hum.-Comput. Interact. **36**(2), 150–201 (2019). https://doi.org/10.1080/07370024.2019.1578652
15. Samarati, P., Sweeney, L.: Protecting privacy when disclosing information: k-anonymity and its enforcement through generalization and suppression. Technical report, SRI International (1998)
16. Sánchez, D., Batet, M.: C-sanitized: a privacy model for document redaction and sanitization. J. Am. Soc. Inf. Sci. **67**(1), 148–163 (2016). https://doi.org/10.1002/asi.23363
17. UK Data Service: Text anonymization helper tool (2016). https://bitbucket.org/ukda/ukds.tools.textanonhelper
18. Ševčíková, M., Žabokrtský, Z., Krůza, O.: Named entities in Czech: annotating data and developing NE tagger. In: Matoušek, V., Mautner, P. (eds.) TSD 2007. LNCS (LNAI), vol. 4629, pp. 188–195. Springer, Heidelberg (2007). https://doi.org/10.1007/978-3-540-74628-7_26
19. Shu, L., Xu, H., Liu, B.: DOC: deep open classification of text documents. Preprint at https://arxiv.org/abs/1709.08716 (2017)
20. Stenetorp, P., Pyysalo, S., Topić, G., Ohta, T., Ananiadou, S., Tsujii, J.: BRAT: a web-based tool for NLP-assisted text annotation. In: Proceedings of the Demonstrations at the 13th Conference of the European Chapter of the Association for Computational Linguistics, pp. 102–107. Association for Computational Linguistics (2012)
21. Straková, J., Straka, M., Hajič, J.: Neural architectures for nested NER through linearization. In: Proceedings of the 57th Annual Meeting of the Association for Computational Linguistics, pp. 5326–5331. Association for Computational Linguistics, Stroudsburg (2019)

22. Straková, J., Straka, M., Hajic, J.: Open-source tools for morphology, lemmatization, POS tagging and named entity recognition. In: Proceedings of 52nd Annual Meeting of the Association for Computational Linguistics: System Demonstrations, pp. 13–18 (2014)

23. Straková, J., Straka, M., Hajič, J.: Neural networks for featureless named entity recognition in Czech. In: Sojka, P., Horák, A., Kopeček, I., Pala, K. (eds.) TSD 2016. LNCS (LNAI), vol. 9924, pp. 173–181. Springer, Cham (2016). https://doi.org/10.1007/978-3-319-45510-5_20

24. Straková, J., Straka, M., Hajič, J.: Open-source tools for morphology, lemmatization, POS tagging and named entity recognition. In: Proceedings of 52nd Annual Meeting of the Association for Computational Linguistics: System Demonstrations, pp. 13–18. Association for Computational Linguistics, Baltimore, June 2014. http://www.aclweb.org/anthology/P/P14/P14-5003.pdf

25. Vico, H., Calegari, D.: Software architecture for document anonymization. Electron. Notes Theor. Comput. Sci. **314**, 83–100 (2015). https://doi.org/10.1016/j.entcs.2015.05.006

26. WIP: Opinion 05/2014 on anonymisation techniques (2016). https://ec.europa.eu/justice/article-29/documentation/opinion-recommendation/files/2014/wp216_en.pdf

ParCzech 3.0: A Large Czech Speech Corpus with Rich Metadata

Matyáš Kopp◉, Vladislav Stankov◉, Jan Oldřich Krůza◉, Pavel Straňák◉, and Ondřej Bojar$^{(\boxtimes)}$◉

Charles University, Faculty of Mathematics and Physics, ÚFAL,
Malostranské nám. 25, Praha 1, 11800 Prague, Czech Republic
{kopp,stankov,kruza,stranak,bojar}@ufal.mff.cuni.cz

Abstract. We present ParCzech 3.0, a speech corpus of the Czech parliamentary speeches from The Czech Chamber of Deputies which took place from 25th November 2013 to 1st April 2021.

Different from previous speech corpora of Czech, we preserve not just orthography but also all the available metadata (speaker identities, gender, web pages links, affiliations committees, political groups, etc.) and complement this with automatic morphological and syntactic annotation, and named entities recognition. The corpus is encoded in the TEI format which allows for a straightforward and versatile exploitation.

The rather rich metadata and annotation make the corpus relevant for a wide audience of researchers ranging from engineers in the speech community to theoretical linguists studying rhetorical patterns at scale.

Keywords: Czech speech corpus · TEI · Speech corpora · Speech recognition · Parliamentary debates · Parliament of the Czech Republic

1 Introduction

Public sessions such as parliamentary hearings have been a great source of data for natural language processing ever since [10] and the interest to use them is still steadily growing, see e.g. the ParlaMint initiative.[1] For the data collection to be readily usable in research, considerable effort has to be spent on its processing – and such processing often differs depending on the intended use.

The aim of this work is to unify the efforts in collecting Czech corpora from The Czech Chamber of Deputies and make the data usable for both training of automatic speech recognition systems (ASR) as well as for corpus studies at various layers of linguistic description. Specifically, we process all the hearings which took place from 25th November 2013 to 1st April 2021, covering the whole 7th and the majority of the 8th term of the chamber.

---

[1] https://www.clarin.eu/event/2020/clarin-cafe-join-our-parliamentary-flavoured-coffee-parlamint.

ⓒ Springer Nature Switzerland AG 2021
K. Ekštein et al. (Eds.): TSD 2021, LNAI 12848, pp. 293–304, 2021.
https://doi.org/10.1007/978-3-030-83527-9_25

Being short of extensive resources for manual annotation, we have to rely on what has been provided by the chamber of deputies, and on our automatic tools. The recorded speeches were published with manually revised transcripts, which however sometimes correct or improve the actual wording in the sound. Occasionally, errors in the collection lead to mismatching audio and transcript files and other processing errors. We have to work with such an input and we at least attempt to automatically identify which recordings are flawless and in which more errors are to be expected.

Section 2 briefly reviews existing corpora derived from Czech parliamentary data. Section 3 details our methodology, including the alignment between the transcripts and the speech. Section 4 presents the corpus in its TEI and speech formats, including corpus statistics. Section 5 concludes the paper.

2   Related Work

Czech parliamentary data is being used in speech recognition since [5] and [9] in 2010. The first unaligned mp3 files were released on the web of the Chamber of Deputies 2006[2]. Some of the derived corpora are motivated exclusively by training of speech recognition systems. They provide as many aligned short text and speech segments as possible, focusing on the verbatim match between the sound and the transcription and dropping segments aligned less reliably. Aspects important to other uses, including letter case and punctuation are often disregarded. General corpora, on the other hand, lack the necessary segmentation of speech and are thus convenient for search or linguistic analyses, but not for training of speech processing systems.

The 7th term of The Czech Chamber of Deputies has been published in ParCzech PS7 1.0 [3] and ParCzech PS7 2.0 [4]. They both cover the period from 25th November 2013 to 16th October 2017.

ParCzech PS7 1.0 is encoded in TEI-based XML format suitable for TEITOK [6] document search and visualisation platform. Annotations on the morphological layer are done with MorphoDiTa and automatic named entity recognition with NameTag [13].

ParCzech PS7 2.0 covers the same data, but it improves the cleaning process, keeps links to the original data and hypertext links in the text. Morphological and syntactic analyses, and named entity recognition are improved by using UDPipe 2 [11] and NameTag 2 [12], resp. Data is additionally distributed in TEI format (Text Encoding Initiative, [14]).

Both corpora provide the original audio data, but no alignment between the sound and text was done at the time.

Recently, a large speech corpus based on Czech parliament plenary sessions was described in [7]. The corpus uses data from November 2017 till November 2019 and consists of approximately 444 h of audio and corresponding transcription and speaker information.

An attempt to use the Czech parliamentary meeting recordings as training data for ASR has been also published at 2019's FedCSIS [8]. The work presents an alignment system that exploits GMM-based speech recognition featuring word-level alignment,

---

[2] https://www.psp.cz/eknih/2002ps/audio/2006/01/17/index.htm.

which is then used to align the original stenographs to the recordings by means of comparing the stenograph with the ASR output with Levenshtein distance. [8] presented primarily a system intended to gather training data for another speech recognition system, hence the ambition is different than in our case. Whereas we attempt to provide the parliament data as a compact, annotated corpus, [8] have no need to align the whole corpus. Significant parts of the data, actually the majority of sentences, are discarded in favour of precise phoneme-grapheme matching which is essential for ASR training data.

3   Methodology

Our work builds upon [2] and improves it by using the more standardized TEI format [1], more detailed speaker metadata, speaker affiliations to different parliamentary groups (political groups, committees, commissions, delegations, etc.) or other institutions, and finally audio alignment.

3.1   Data Gathering

The official web of The Czech Chamber of Deputies contains stenographic texts from the chamber of deputies' sittings that are structured into terms, meetings, sittings, and agenda items.

There are two possible ways to get the texts. The first option is downloading the official zip archives[3] and the second one is scraping directly the web[4]. We have chosen the second option because the first one misses some metadata, e.g. links to audio, voting, and parliamentary prints.

The scraped data are unfortunately not encoded consistently across the whole web. Our downloading procedure is thus based on an ideal structure of the web page that should contain speaker's name and a hypertext link to the profile web page, sitting date, and the link to the corresponding audio recording in the side menu. If some data is missing on a real page, downloading procedure tries to find it on other web pages. The missing audio link can be taken from the list of audio files[5]. If it is not listed there, our downloading script guesses the missing URL from the date and time mentioned on the imperfect web page. In this way, we gain the maximum number of audio files, even those that are not linked.

3.2   Data Processing and Annotation

We use a Perl script to encode stenographic protocols directly to TEI format. Speaker names, personal web links, and hypertext links in texts are preserved. Furthermore, dates and times stored in stenographic notes are decoded. Notes are emphasized and subsequently annotated as phenomena or occurrences. For example *(Ministr*

---

[3] https://psp.cz/eknih/2013ps/stenprot/zip/index.htm.

[4] https://psp.cz/eknih/2013ps/stenprot/index.htm.

[5] e.g. https://psp.cz/eknih/2013ps/audio/index.htm.

Babiš přinesl kopie účtenek k řečnickému pultu. Veselost v sále pokračuje.) is annotated as `<kinesictype="kinesic"><desc>`(Ministr Babiš přinesl kopie
účtenek k řečnickému pultu. Veselost v sále pokračuje.)`</desc>`
`</kinesic>`.

Persons are not identified with a unique identifier in the protocols. Luckily, members of parliament and government usually have assigned hypertext links that can help
person identification. So we draw on two sources of data: the Czech government web
(www.vlada.cz) which contains short bibliography of members of government, and the
database of the Chamber of Deputies[6] which contains personal data of not only members of the lower chamber, but also some senators.

We join these source data based on the first name, surname, and birth date and then
generate a unique ID for each person. We include other personal data if available: sex,
website, Facebook link, profile photo URL, and affiliation to different organizations
with a role: president, minister, member, observer, verifier.

At this point of corpus building procedure, we have text data in the TEI format
segmented to utterances and paragraphs[7].

For ease of use in corpus and other studies, we process all the data with UDPipe 2
to provide tokenization and morphological and syntactic analysis. Furthermore, named
entities are automatically annotated with NameTag 2.

3.3 Sentence- and Word-Level Alignment with Speech

For the purposes of the training of speech recognition systems, a speech corpus needs to
be broken into segments of not more than a few dozens of seconds, each equipped with
the transcription. Such a segmentation can be achieved with relatively simple detection
of silence.

Given the proper segmentation of the text into paragraphs and sentences, we prefer
to cast this segmentation also on the speech signal. We automatically identify time spans
for each word and then follow the segmentation into sentences as given in the transcript
to break the sound.

To extract word timings from the audio, a GMM-based ASR system [8] was used.
This system outputs recognized words with their timestamps, given the original stenographic transcripts. Since spoken language differs from the written, sometimes recordings do not match the transcription exactly. Our procedure is not a 'forced decoding' per
se, which would find the best alignment and strictly adhere to the words in the transcript.
Instead, it proposes a (time-stamped) sequence of words which is close but not necessarily identical to the expected transcript. We find the alignment between the sound and
the transcript by matching the two sequences of words, the transcript and the predicted
ones, taking each word as an atomic unit. If words do not match, a penalty is given,
multiplied by character-level edit distance between these words. One possible choice
of the algorithm for sequence alignment is Needleman–Wunsch algorithm with affine
gap penalties. The reward for match is the length of the matched words; for mismatch,
a multiple of the edit distance of the two words is subtracted. Experiments showed that

---

[6] https://psp.cz/sqw/hp.sqw?k=1300.
[7] Paragraphs are made by stenographers and can be revised by speaker.

the multiple can be set to 3. The algorithm utilizes two parameters: start gap penalty and extend gap penalty. These were set to -5 and -4 based on our experiments with a small subset of the data.

Known issues. For an unknown reason, the ASR system may fail to recognize a small part in the original audio file, but in most cases this can be solved by providing the failed audio segment again with some silence added at the beginning. Using a greedy approach, the best recognition can be selected by maximizing the alignment score. Not more than 7% of the corpus (in terms of duration) was corrupted by the failure and this simple technique can recover more than 70% of the failed part. As observations showed, in most cases the unresolved failed segments are true silences in the recordings.

Another issue is that the ASR system may mishear some words, skip them or output phonetically similar words. Thus, once the alignment is done and visualised, one can notice that some words were recognized as an n-tuple of words which as a whole is phonetically similar to the original word. The fix itself boils down to detecting when the original word is surrounded by empty strings and then gluing up transcribed words together, minimizing the edit distance.

After the post-processing, the original audio file can be split into segments, where each segment will have its corresponding transcription. The segments are usually sentences, but sometimes one segment may contain more than one sentence. This happens when the last word of the sentence and the first word of the next sentence are not recognized. In this situation, the sentences are merged into a larger segment.

4 Corpus Description

Here we describe the final layout of the corpus as released. We distribute the corpus in three variants: (1) the original HTML and audio files, (2) a large collection of individual files, short segments of audio and transcript useful for training of speech systems, and (3) TEI-encoded texts with explicit references to the audio files and the annotation described in Sect. 3.2.

4.1 Source HTML and Audio Files

To allow for a complete revisit of our extraction procedures, we provide all HTML files that our downloading script visited, in the original tree structure. There are two main sub-trees. The first one contains all stenographic protocols with original pages, and the second one contains the directory structure of a list of audio files.

The original audio files are referenced from the TEI version of the corpus and thus should be seen as an inherent part of our corpus. This is important because many older audio files are no longer available for download even if the audio link still exists on the parliamentary website.

4.2 Version for ASR

In the ASR version of the corpus, each original recording is represented by a folder, containing segment folders and a file with global statistics. These statistics are about alignment of the whole stenographic transcription to the recognized words. Each segment folder contains the following files:

- **Audio file.** This is a `.wav` file corresponding to the segment.
- **Pretty transcript.** Stenographic transcription of the audio file with the original letter casing and punctuation.
- **ASR transcript.** Stenographic transcription of the sound file in upper case and with no punctuation.
- **Words information.** Information about words inside the segments in a `.tsv` file. This detailed format provides each word with its starting and ending time (both can be -1 in case if the word was not recognized), normalized Levenshtein distance between the stenographic transcript (which appears in this `.tsv` file) and the recognized word (which is no longer shown but it served as the basis for the estimation of the timestamps), normalized duration that is computed as duration of the word in seconds divided by the number of characters, and also the speaker information. Additionally, there is the ID for each word, so one can find any word in TEI data (see below) and extract additional morphological and syntactic information.
- **Speakers.** This files lists speakers' IDs in the segment. These IDs then can be used to extract additional information about speakers like age or sex.
- **Statistics.** The file contains statistics that describe the segment and can be useful for data analysis, e.g.: the number of words, number of characters, percentage of missed words, or percentage of missed characters. We also report sound coverage, computed as percentage of sound where some word was recognized, divided by the duration of the segment, and "end correctness" which signalizes whether the end of the segment was not recognized; this is only an issue for the last segment. We note that the percentage of missed characters is the sum of the lengths of the missed words normalized by the lengths of all words in the segment, hence missing shorter words will not influence this statistic much.

Sometimes the alignment between the recognized audio file and the stenographic transcript fails. We provide global statistics for each original audio file to help identifying these cases, for example: percentage of missed words (words that are aligned to empty strings), median normalized edit distance and also 80th percentile of the normalized edit distance. Normalized edit distance is 1 if the true word is aligned to the empty string, meaning that original word is not recognized. To avoid overoptimistic edit distance results, words of length less than 3 are ignored in this calculation. To detect transcripts that poorly, if at all, match the audio recordings, we created a statistic that counts each sequence of words missed in the recognized audio as one gap, instead of counting each word separately. The intuition is to ignore the gap size since bad alignment is detected better from gap frequency than from the gap size. We normalize the number of continuous gaps to the interval $[0; 1]$ by dividing it by the number of words in the stenographic transcription plus the number of continuous gaps.

Using the provided file-level and segment-level statistics one can filter the data, trading their size for quality. We make a recommendation and provide a filtered version of the corpus. For the filtered version, 2% of the audio recordings were first removed based on the statistic of normalized continuous gaps. Then we preserved only segments with correct endings, percentage of missed characters lower than 6.5%, sound coverage above 62.5%, 80th percentile of the normalized edit distance below 30% and a small enough standard deviation of the normalized edit distance. Additionally, too short (duration lower than 0.82 s) and too long (duration higher than 54 s) segments were discarded.

Because we release full data, too, one can create custom filtering.

4.3 TEI Encoding

As mentioned above, one of the provided corpus variants is in ParlaCLARIN TEI format [1]. ParlaCLARIN is a set of guidelines that provide recommendations on the encoding of various issues, but there are still many possibilities of how a single issue can be handled. In this section, we describe the encoding choices in our corpus.

Directories and Files. We compiled two versions of TEI data. The first one is a raw text version that contains all persons and organizations' metadata, categorized stenographers' notes, hypertext links from the source text, and links to source data. The second version extends the raw version with linguistic annotations and the alignment to audio.

There is one main file in each corpus version, that glues all related files together. We refer to the file as the "teiCorpus file". The two teiCorpus files are `ParCzech.xml` and `ParCzech.ana.xml` for raw and annotated versions, respectively. The header of the file contains definitions of taxonomies used in particular TEI files and lists of persons and organizations. A sequence of XML `<include>` elements comes after the header. Files are sorted by dates. Included TEI files are structured into directories – each directory represents a meeting in a term, e.g. `ps2013-001` contains data from the first meeting in the term that starts in the year 2013.

Users who want to only work with data from the complete 7th term can use teiCorpus files `ParCzechPS7.xml` or `ParCzechPS7.ana.xml`. These files include only TEI files related to the 7th term.

Every TEI file contains continuous stenographic notes from agenda items or initial sitting speech. Filenames consist of dash-separated parts: the first part contains the starting year of given term (`ps2013`), and then follow meeting number (`001`), sitting number (`02`), order of agenda item within sitting day (`003`), and agenda item (`008`). So the full pathname of the given example is `ps2013-001/ps2013-001-02-003-008.xml` for the raw version of TEI files. The annotated version has the suffix `.ana.xml`. Single agenda items can be discussed multiple times in a sitting day, so the last part of the filename (`008`) shouldn't be unique. If a user of the corpus wants to follow one particular topic, i.e. the 8th agenda item of the 1st meeting in term starting at the year 2013, they can use this pattern `ps2013-001/ps2013-001-??-???-008.xml` to filter all TEI files containing the discussed topic. The disadvantage of this solution is that the chairman's speech is split at the topic change point.

Encoding. Each TEI file contains two parts. The first one stored in `<teiHeader>` element contains metadata about file content and the second one (`<text>`) contains real stenographic protocols and timelines for each audio file, see Fig. 1.

```
<?xml version="1.0" encoding="utf-8"?>
<TEI xmlns="http://www.tei-c.org/ns/1.0" xml:id="ps2013-001-02-003-008.ana" [...] >
  <teiHeader>
    <fileDesc>
      [...] <!-- title, version, measurements, publisher, license and release date -->
      <sourceDesc>
        [.]<bibl> <!-- source description, source url, and date -->
        <recordingStmt>
          <recording type="audio"> <!-- list of media files -->
            <media xml:id="ps2013-001-02-003-008.audio1" mimeType="audio/mp3"
              source="https://www.psp.cz/eknih/2013ps/audio/2013/11/27/2013112711581212.mp3"
              url="2013ps/audio/2013/11/27/2013112711581212.mp3"/>
          </recording>
        </recordingStmt>
      </sourceDesc>
    </fileDesc>
    [...] <!-- description of file, elements statistics, where and when sitting sets -->
  </teiHeader>
  <text>
    <body>
      [.]<div type="debateSection"> <!-- steno -->
      <!-- list of timings for each audio file: -->
      [.]<timeline [...] corresp="#ps2013-001-02-003-008.audio1" cert="0.891">
    </body>
  <text>
<TEI>
```

Fig. 1. TEI file structure example

The part of the TEI file with stenographic protocols is further divided into speeches by individual members of parliament, government and guests. A single speech is represented with the `<u>` element and annotated with attributes that determine the speaker's identity, role (`chair`, `regular`, or `guest`), and speech identification with XML ID. Speeches then contain segments (`<seg>`). Each segment has one or more sentences `<s>` with words `<w>` and punctuation `<pc>`.

TEI does not allow `start` and `end` synchronisation attributes in word elements so we use anchors `<anchor>` to encode word-level timing.

```
<s xml:id="ps2013-001-02-003-008.u1.p1.s2">
  <anchor synch="#ps2013-001-02-003-008.u1.p1.s2.w1.ab"/>
  <w xml:id="ps2013-001-02-003-008.u1.p1.s2.w1" [...] >Informace</w>
  <anchor synch="#ps2013-001-02-003-008.u1.p1.s2.w1.ae"/>
  <anchor synch="#ps2013-001-02-003-008.u1.p1.s2.w2.ab"/>
  <w xml:id="ps2013-001-02-003-008.u1.p1.s2.w2" [...] >mandátového</w>
  <anchor synch="#ps2013-001-02-003-008.u1.p1.s2.w2.ae"/>
  [...]
</s>
```

Fig. 2. TEI words synchronization example

Figure 2 illustrates the synchronization of the first two words of sentence "Informace mandátového a imunitního výboru o ověření platnosti volby poslanců.". The first `<anchor>`, referring to ID ps2013-001-02-003-008.u1.p1.s2.w1.ab, points to the time the word "Informace" starts (the suffix ab stands for "audio begin") and the second anchor (referring to ps2013-001-02-003-008.u1.p1.s2.w1.ae) determines the word's ending time (the suffix ae stands for "audio end"). If the alignment algorithm failed to find a good match, the anchor is missing. Sentence-level timing is determined

```
<timeline unit="ms" origin="#ps2013-001-02-003-008.audio1.origin"
       corresp="#ps2013-001-02-003-008.audio1" cert="0.891">
  <when xml:id="ps2013-001-02-003-008.audio1.origin"
       absolute="2013-11-27T11:58:00"/>
  <when xml:id="ps2013-001-02-003-008.u1.p1.s2.w1.ab" interval="388290.0"
       since="#ps2013-001-02-003-008.audio1.origin"/>
  <when xml:id="ps2013-001-02-003-008.u1.p1.s2.w1.ae" interval="388900.0"
       since="#ps2013-001-02-003-008.audio1.origin"/>

</timeline>
```

Fig. 3. TEI timeline example

from the first and the last anchor in the sentence. An advantage of the representation using anchors instead of tag attributes is the possibility to add data from other speech-text aligners to the same TEI file.

Formally, the interesting times for each audio file are defined an accompanying `<timeline>` (Fig. 3). Here the `origin` attribute refers to the `<when>` element that contains the exact absolute time and date of the recording. Further `<when>` elements define targets for the `ab` and `ae` anchors relative to this origin.

The attribute `cert` with values from interval $[0, 1]$ determines the level of certainty based on the 80th percentile of normalized edit distance subtracted from 1 or `cert` has been set to 0 for timelines corresponding to 2% of statistic of normalized continuous gaps filtered audio files, described in Sect. 4.2.

4.4   Division into Training, Development and Test Sets

For the purposes of ASR training, we extract three pairs of development (dev) and evaluation (test) sets, and one common training (train) set. All these sets were created from segments which passed our filters. Technically, this is realized using a simple filelist which specifies the destination set for each segment. Consequently, all these sets are disjoint.

The dev and test sets were created for three different purposes:

Speakers Dev and Test were extracted from the clean data first, taking all utterances of a few speakers. This dev and test are thus useful in experiments, where you want to assess system performance on unseen speakers. The proportion of men and women in this dev and test set is artificially balanced, oversampling women compared to the corpus average.

Context Dev and Test were formed in a way that preserves partitioning from original audio recordings. Thus, few audio recordings were taken out from the clean data and all their segments put into the context dev or test set. This way, the context of each utterance is available and discourse phenomena can be studied up to the level of the original division info files (and subject to filtering).

Segments Dev and Test were created from the rest of filtered data by sampling random segments.

4.5   Corpus Statistics

Table 1 shows statistics counted on the annotated TEI files. The corpus contains all speakers in the focused period and in addition also the members of parliament of the 7th and 8th term who did not have a speech. The number of source audio files and source web pages do not match, because some of the audio files are not available.

Table 1. ParCzech 3.0 statistics for the TEI format

Number of TEI files	5 409
Number of utterances	154 460
Number of sentences	1 479 990
Number of words	22 546 417
Number of unique persons	486
Number of source audio files	20 674
Number of steno source web pages	20 775
Source audio length (hours incl. overlaps)	4 815.31
Time period	25th Nov 2013 – 1st Apr 2021

Table 2 compares the cleaned corpus for training and testing ASR models with original data. After applying the filtering as described in Sect. 4.2, the correctly aligned audio files amount to 1 332.38 h and 606 540 segments. The average duration of each filtered segment is 7.90 s with the standard deviation of 7.14 s. Each segment consists of 16.72 words on average (with a standard deviation of 13.73 words); punctuation is not included in these word counts. In total, the corpus contains 10 146 591 words. After filtering the percentage of words aligned to the sound increased from 89.6% to 96.3%. We can also see that duration range and segment size range are smaller after filtering.

Table 3 summarizes the sizes of our divisions of the filtered data.

Table 2. ParCzech 3.0 statistics for the ASR format before and after data cleaning

	Original data	Filtered data
Hours	3 071.57	1 332.38
Segments	1 391 785	606 540
Average segment duration in seconds	7.94±11.53	7.90±7.14
Average number of words in a segment	15.91±16.32	16.72±13.73
Words	22 153 778	10 146 591
Aligned words percentage	89.6%	96.3%
Unique Speakers	475	474
Segment size range	[1, 1058]	[2, 138]
Duration range	[0.0, 720.76]	[0.82, 53.99]

Table 3. Statistics for the ASR train, test, dev sets. "Files" shows the number of original mp3 recordings that contributed to the given set; some files have contributed to more than one set. "Segment Duration" in seconds (average and std. dev.).

Set	Total			Segment	Words		Unique
	Segments	Files	Hours	Duration	Per Segment	Total	Speakers
Train	579 169	19 931	1 271	7.9 ± 7.1	16.7 ± 13.7	9 679 268	417
Speakers Dev	4 596	744	10.7	8.4 ± 7.1	17.8 ± 13.4	81 708	30
Speakers Test	4 261	689	10.6	9.0 ± 7.0	18.4 ± 12.9	78 277	30
Context Dev	4 556	149	10.0	7.9 ± 7.0	16.8 ± 13.5	76 512	186
Context Test	4 868	149	10.0	7.4 ± 6.8	16.1 ± 13.5	78 360	186
Segment Dev	4 575	4 020	10.0	7.9 ± 7.3	16.7 ± 14.0	76 243	301
Segment Test	4 515	3 986	10.0	8.0 ± 7.2	16.9 ± 13.8	76 223	291

5 Conclusion

We presented ParCzech 3.0, a sizeable speech corpus of Czech which preserves and formalizes as much metadata as possible (speakers and their gender, structure of the meetings and more) and adds also automatic annotation: morphological tags, syntactic structure and named entities.

The corpus comes in three data formats: the original HTML, TEI XML with rich metadata and annotation, and simple segmented plain texts with sound files directly usable for training of speech recognition systems.

ParCzech 3.0 corpus is available in the LINDAT repository under CC0 Public Domain waiver: http://hdl.handle.net/11234/1-3631.

Acknowledgements. This work has received funding from the European Union's Horizon 2020 Research and Innovation Programme under Grant Agreement No 825460 (ELITR) and the grant 19-26934X (NEUREM3) of the Czech Science Foundation, and Project No. LM2018101 LINDAT/CLARIAH-CZ of the Ministry of Education, Youth and Sports of the Czech Republic.

References

1. Erjavec, T., Pančur, A.: Parla-CLARIN: TEI guidelines for corpora of parliamentary proceedings, September 2019. https://doi.org/10.5281/zenodo.3446164
2. Hladká, B., Kopp, M., Straňák, P.: Compiling Czech parliamentary stenographic protocols into a corpus. In: Proceedings of the LREC 2020 Workshop on Creating, Using and Linking of Parliamentary Corpora with Other Types of Political Discourse (ParlaCLARIN II), pp. 18–22. ELRA, Paris (2020)
3. Hladká, B., Kopp, M., Straňák, P.: ParCzech PS7 1.0 (2020). http://hdl.handle.net/11234/1-3174, LINDAT/CLARIAH-CZ digital library at ÚFAL, Faculty of Mathematics and Physics, Charles University
4. Hladká, B., Kopp, M., Straňák, P.: ParCzech PS7 2.0 (2020), http://hdl.handle.net/11234/1-3436, LINDAT/CLARIAH-CZ digital library at ÚFAL, Faculty of Mathematics and Physics, Charles University

5. Jakubíček, M., Kovář, V.: CzechParl: corpus of stenographic protocols from Czech Parliament. In: RASLAN 2010, pp. 41–46 (2010). http://nlp.fi.muni.cz/raslan/2010/paper11.pdf
6. Janssen, M.: TEITOK: text-faithful annotated corpora. In: Proceeding of LREC 2016, pp. 4037–4043 (2016)
7. Kratochvíl, J., Polak, P., Bojar, O.: Large corpus of Czech parliament plenary hearings. In: Proceedings of LREC 2020, pp. 6363–6367. ELRA (2020). https://www.aclweb.org/anthology/2020.lrec-1.781/
8. Krůza, J.O.: Czech parliament meeting recordings as ASR training data. In: Proceedings of the 2020 FCCSIS. Annals of Computer Science and Information Systems, vol. 21, pp. 185–188. IEEE (2020). https://doi.org/10.15439/2020F119
9. Pražák, A., Šmídl, L.: Czech parliament meetings (2012). http://hdl.handle.net/11858/00-097C-0000-0005-CF9C-4, LINDAT/CLARIAH-CZ digital library at ÚFAL, Faculty of Mathematics and Physics, Charles University
10. Roukos, S., Graff, D., Melamed, D.: Hansard French/English LDC95T20 (1995). https://doi.org/10.35111/jhgn-rv21
11. Straka, M.: UDPipe 2.0 prototype at CoNLL 2018 UD shared task. In: Proceedings of the CoNLL 2018 ST: Multilingual Parsing from Raw Text to Universal Dependencies, pp. 197–207. ACL (2018). https://doi.org/10.18653/v1/K18-2020
12. Straková, J., Straka, M., Hajič, J.: Neural architectures for nested NER through linearization. In: Proceedings of ACL, pp. 5326–5331 (2019)
13. Straková, J., Straka, M., Hajič, J.: Open-source tools for morphology, lemmatization, POS tagging and named entity recognition. In: Proceedings of ACL System Demonstrations, pp. 13–18, June 2014. https://doi.org/10.3115/v1/P14-5003
14. TEI Consortium: TEI P5: Guidelines for Electronic Text Encoding and Interchange. 4.2.1., 1 March 2021. TEI Consortium. http://www.tei-c.org/Guidelines/P5/

Using Zero-Shot Transfer to Initialize azWikiNER, a Gold Standard Named Entity Corpus for the Azerbaijani Language

Kamran Ibiyev[(✉)] and Attila Novak

Faculty of Information Technology and Bionics, Pázmány Péter Catholic University,
50/a Práter street, Budapest 1083, Hungary
ibiyev.kamran@itk.ppke.hu
https://itk.ppke.hu/en

Abstract. Named Entity Recognition (NER) is one of the primary fields of Natural Language Processing, focused on analyzing and determining the entities in a given text. In this paper, we present a gold standard named entity dataset for Azerbaijani created from the Azerbaijani portion of WikiAnn, a 'silver standard' NER dataset generated from Wikipedia. In a zero-shot cross-lingual transfer scenario, we used an M-BERT-based NER model trained on the English Ontonotes corpus to add new entity types to the corpus. The output of the model was then hand-corrected. We evaluate the accuracy of the original WikiAnn corpus, the zero-shot performance of two models trained on the Ontonotes corpus, and two transformer-based NER models trained on the training part of the final corpus: one based on M-BERT and another based XLM-RoBERTa. We release the corpus and the trained models to the public.

Keywords: Named Entity Recognition · M-BERT · XLM-RoBERTa · WikiAnn · Azerbaijani

1   Introduction

Named Entity Recognition is a subfield of Information Extraction that can determine the entities in the given text. It is a fundamental part of many NLP tasks and is used in various applications like information extraction [20], question answering [3], document de-identification [25], machine translation [10], conversational models [9] and et cetera. The task of Named Entity Recognition is to determine and classify the entities in the given text based on the predefined categories like organizations, dates, times, persons, locations, and so on. Neural NER models usually depend upon convolutional or recurrent neural architectures, occasionally adding a CRF (Conditional random fields) classifier at the top [5,14,30]. Recently, deep contextualized representations relying on bidirectional LSTMs [17], transformers [7] or contextual string embeddings [1] have

© Springer Nature Switzerland AG 2021
K. Ekštein et al. (Eds.): TSD 2021, LNAI 12848, pp. 305–317, 2021.
https://doi.org/10.1007/978-3-030-83527-9_26

achieved state-of-the-art performance on NER tasks. These neural structures usually demand sizable training corpora marked up with named entities, like ConLL 2003 [24] or Ontonotes 5 [12].

2   Literature Review

Pre-training of a language model has been demonstrated to efficiently improve the performance of natural language processing tasks [6,17,23]. Above-mentioned tasks contain sentence-level tasks like paraphrase [8] as well as natural language inference [4,27]. The objective of these tasks is to predict the correlation among propositions, by analyzing them as a whole content. The performance of neural models has also been successfully improved in token-level tasks like question answering and named entity recognition. Here the models are expected to make fine-grained distinctions at the token level [21,24].

Feature-based strategies and fine-tuning are used for implementing pre-trained language representations to downstream tasks. There are 2 types of pre-trained representations: context-free and contextual. Contextual representations can be unidirectional or bidirectional. Context-free models (word2vec, GloVe) create only one single embedding representation for each word. For instance, they would create the same context-free representation for the word "right" in sentences "Yes, you are right" and "Please, turn right". Context-free embedding models can be used in the feature-based approach and were, in fact, the first neural representations used in this setting.

In contrast to the context-free representation approach, the contextual method creates a representation of every single word that is depending upon the other words in that sentence. To elaborate it more, we will analyze the sentence"He's standing there right in front of her" a unidirectional contextual approach would constitute "right" based on "He's standing there" but not "in front of her." In contrast to the unidirectional contextual approach, BERT approaches with a deeply bidirectional model and represents "right" handling both its left and right context—"He's standing there ..... in front of her".

ELMo is a good example of a feature-based technique that uses a contextual model and applies a task-specific design that contains the pre-trained representations as constant features. As an example of the fine-turning strategy, Generative Pre-trained Transformer (OpenAI GPT) can be mentioned. It presents basic task-specific parameters and is trained by fine-tuning all pre-trained parameters. Both methods use fine-tuning during pre-training, and for learning general language representations they use unidirectional language models. BERT (Bidirectional Encoder Representations from Transformers) [17], is a language representation model where, in contrast to the previous two language representation models, bidirectional representations are pre-trained from an unlabelled text. Figure 1 indicates BERT's neural network structure and compares it with previous state-of-the-art contextual pre-training methods. The arrows show the information flow from one layer to the next. The green section displays the eventual contextualized representation of the input token.

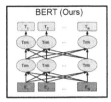 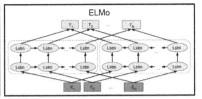

Fig. 1. Comparison of BERT, OpenAI GPT and ELMo. *Source*: Adapted from [7]

As it is shown in Fig. 1 while BERT adopts a bidirectional Transformer, OpenAI GPT adopts only a left-to-right Transformer. Regarding ELMo, it adopts the chain design of autonomously trained left-to-right and right-to-left LSTMs. Between these three approaches, just BERT is collectively conditioned on both left and right context in all layers. Moreover, ELMo is a feature-based technique, whereas BERT and OpenAI GPT are fine-tuning techniques.

In this research, we train a new model based on the gold standard dataset that we created and compare it with the original zero-shot model. Moreover, we trained two models from scratch - one based on m-BERT and another one based on XLM-RoBERTa, and evaluated the outputs.

3   Materials and Methods

Multilingual BERT is a 12-layer transformer as it is in the English BERT model [7], but the main difference between them is, while en-BERT is trained just in the English language, m-BERT is trained with 104 languages of Wikipedia portal.

The FLAIR framework has many advantages in terms of simplicity and unity of different types of document and word embeddings. It provides the possibility of training and distribution of state-of-the-art sequence labeling, text classification, and language models.

For simplification of the interface, this framework does not show any complex embedding-specific engineering tasks, it makes the use of different embeddings possible without a big effort. Another whip hand of this framework is that it provides the opportunity to download publicly available NLP datasets and transforms them into data structures to do experiments and evaluations. It provides a list of pre-trained models giving an opportunity to users to implement already trained models to their document or text. It also provides an extensive variety of embeddings namely BERT embeddings [7], byte pair embeddings [11], ELMo transformer embeddings [18], ELMo embeddings [17] as well as Flair embeddings [2]. In Fig. 2 currently available word and document embeddings, options provided by FLAIR displayed.

If the training data is not large enough, the knowledge obtained from associated tasks can be transferred to the objective domain applying the methods like a simple transfer [22] and discriminative fine-tuning [23]. Gathering and applying data from several languages to train one model can be handled in various forms, like converting a model from a high-resource to low-resource language [29], benefiting from multilingual datasets, and unsupervised representation learning.

4   Existing Solutions

Lately, there has been remarkable enthusiasm in handling human language with synthetic data generation interpreting annotation like hyperlinks in a programmed manner [19], while getting more data by processing annotation in online portals like Wikipedia. Wikipedia is a huge multi-lingual portal with 295 languages, 35 million articles that contain 3 billion words. The handy point of Wikipedia is it includes inherently annotated markup and plenty of information. Anchor links between Wikipedia pages can be interpreted as a name mention function.

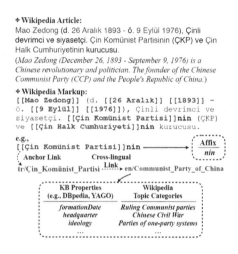

Fig. 2. Examples of Wikipedia Markups and KB Properties. *Source*: Adapted from [15]

In this research, we use the WikiAnn dataset [15], which annotates the entities in the given text based on predefined categories like organizations, persons, and locations and currently supports entities in Wikipedia for 282 languages. WikiAnn was automatically created by extracting and classifying anchor links on Wikipedia. Because of this, the WikiAnn dataset has troubles like biased entity type distributions in languages with less Wikipedia data (see Fig. 4), and incorrect entity types because of the automatic type classification.

Furthermore, since WikiAnn is designed to extract data from Wikipedia automatically, some problems with annotation can be seen. In the example below we can see that although the "Paternal age effect" is not a Named Entity, the system extracted it as the sequence of an organization and a person entity.

```
Paternal none B-ORG
age none I-PER
effect none I-PER
on none O
DNA none O
```

In the examples below, part in parentheses should not be included in the named entity or, in the second example, should be tagged as a location.

```
Richard none B-PER      Abraham none B-ORG
O'Connor none I-PER     Lincoln none I-ORG
( none I-PER            High none I-ORG
politician none I-PER   School none I-ORG
) none I-PER            ( none I-ORG
                        San none I-ORG
                        Jose none I-ORG
                        , none I-ORG
                        California none I-ORG
                        ) none I-ORG
```

Here we can see that in some cases the system recognized the Named Entity, but mistagged it. In the following example, a person is tagged as an organization.

```
William none B-ORG
S. none I-ORG
Burroughs none I-ORG
Jr none I-ORG
. none I-ORG
```

Here we see another kind of mistagging as only *League One* should be tagged as an organization, the complete expression is the name of an award.

```
League none B-ORG
One none I-ORG
Manager none I-ORG
of none I-ORG
the none I-ORG
year none I-ORG
: none I-ORG
2007-08 none I-ORG
```

Although the indicated examples come from the English Wikipedia, the situation is similar in other languages as well.

Overall, regardless of some mistagging and other minor issues, WikiAnn is useful and it is the only existing NER dataset that contains data in many languages.

FLAIR interface provides some datasets such as WNUT_17, WIKINER_ENGLISH, UD_ENGLISH, CONLL_03_SPANISH that makes it possible to load with one line of code. We can train NER over these datasets as well as our own text corpus.

For training NER we have to get large dataset(s), but for this process, the host machine requires a so powerful GPU and many times to train a model. After creating the (multi)corpus we split our dataset into dev, test, and train parts.

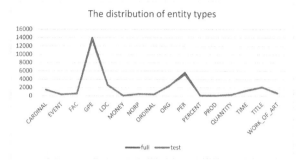

Fig. 3. The distribution of entity types

5   Corpus Annotation Method

Firstly we took the WikiAnn corpus and annotated it using the DeepPavlov Ontonotes model, then we merged the entities. While merging we took the span of the entity from the gold standard annotation output and if the type of the entity suggested by the zero-shot model was compatible with the original data type, then we changed the entity type to the one proposed by the model, for types of the entities which was not in the original corpus, we introduced the entity from the output of DeepPavlov model. Then we manually checked and corrected the whole corpus.

There are numerous text-annotation tools such as GATE Teamware, WebAnno, AlvisAE, Knowtator which have both advantages and disadvantages. As a text-annotation environment, I decided to use the INCEpTION platform [13]. Because it is an open-source web application that provides possibilities to annotate the texts interactively and semantically. One of the considerable advantages of INCEpTION over the mentioned tools is that the recommendations during the annotating since it learns from the end-user actions automatically. For integrating the WikiAnn Azerbaijani dataset to the INCEpTION platform, we converted the CoNLL-2002 format. The involvement of CoNLL-2002 format is language-independent named entity recognition [26].

Three annotators worked on the original WikiAnn annotation correcting errors in the machine-generated silver standard annotation. One of the annotators was a linguist. After new entities were introduced using the Ontonotes based model two annotators reviewed the final annotation.

New NE tags were introduced which were not existing in the machine-generated WikiAnn corpus. The Ontonotes model introduced numerous new entity types into the corpus, and we manually added a new tag called TITLE that we used to annotate profession, roles, military ranks.

Moreover, we trained two models from scratch on the final version of the corpus - one of them based on Multilingual BERT (cased) and another one based on XLM-RoBERTa and evaluated the output. Both models are available in HuggingFace transformers library [28]. Both M-BERT and XLM-RoBERTa models are available in this library.

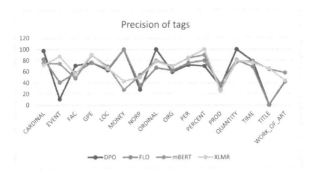

Fig. 4. Precision of tags

6 Evaluation

For tracking the experiments and visualization of the training results, we used the Weights and Biases tool [16] integrated with the HuggingFace transformers library. Corpus size: 155621 tokens with 30257 phrases in the final corpus after filtering repeated segments. Filtered WikiAnn contains 23742 phrases, of which 15362 (64.7%) are tagged as locations (mostly geopolitical entities) (Table 1).

Table 1. Quality of the original WikiAnn annotation for Azerbaijani and the frequency of entity types. Facility and GPE were considered Locations when comparing the WikiAnn annotation to the final corpus

	P	R	F1	Frequency
LOC	88.39	81.77	84.95	15362
ORG	54.64	78.71	64.50	3492
PER	94.27	81.77	87.58	4888

7 Limitations

In the annotated dataset, we have relatively few PRODUCT and EVENT entities; it is dominated by GPE and PER entities (Fig. 3). The reason is that the content of Azerbaijani Wikipedia is dominated by these entity types. Another limitation is that due to the extraction method used to generate WikiAnn, there are many short segments that contain little more than a named entity. Our plan is to improve the dataset by adding content resulting in a more balanced representation of named entities.

Table 2. Performance of the models on the test set. Zero-shot models: DPO = Deep-Pavlov OntoNotes M-BERT model, FLO = Flair OntoNotes large XLM-RoBERTa model; models trained on the training set: XLMR = based on base-XLM-RoBERTa, mBERT = based on M-BERT (cased)

Target	Model	Acc	P	R	F1
Full	DPO	87.76	72.29	61.64	66.54
	FLO	88.47	71.88	66.83	69.26
	XLMR	**93.39**	80.21	**83.38**	**81.77**
	mBERT	93.36	**80.48**	83.09	**81.77**
Common	DPO	89.55	72.32	66.05	69.04
	FLO	90.26	71.93	71.61	71.77
	XLMR	**94.06**	81.30	**84.37**	82.81
	mBERT	94.05	**81.70**	84.10	**82.89**

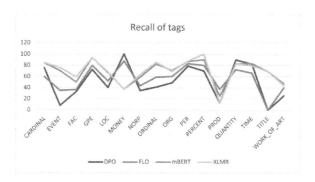

Fig. 5. Recall of tags

Table 3. Performance of the zero-shot models on the full corpus. DPO = DeepPavlov OntoNotes M-BERT model, FLO = Flair OntoNotes large XLM-RoBERTa model

Target	Model	Acc	P	R	F1
Full	DPO	87.67	**72.47**	60.82	66.13
	FLO	**87.97**	71.15	**64.77**	**67.81**
Common	DPO	89.44	**72.52**	64.99	68.55
	FLO	**89.74**	71.24	**69.22**	**70.21**

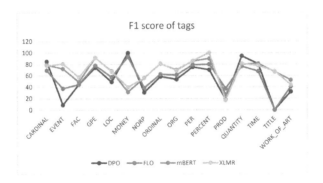

Fig. 6. F1 score of tags

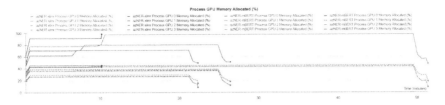

Fig. 7. Train GPU memory allocation

8   Conclusion

Of the zero-shot models, the Flair model, which is based on XLM-RoBERTa, has significantly better recall (Fig. 5) while the M-BERT-based DeepPavlov model has slightly higher precision (Fig. 6), but generally the Flair model is better. They perform better than the models that we trained on the final corpus on entity types which are underrepresented in the final corpus, especially on the numeric types of entities.

Of the models that we trained, the one based on XLM-RoBERTa performs slightly better than the BERT-based model (Table 2 and 3), but it is much more resource-hungry both at training and at inference time (see e.g. GPU memory usage at training time (Fig. 7)). The difference in performance does not seem to justify the extra cost. An interesting observation is that while of the English models, the one based on M-BERT has better precision while the one based on XLM-RoBERTa has higher recall, the models finetuned on our corpus show just the opposite pattern.

We release the corpus and the trained models to the public as there is a lack of Named Entity corpora and trained models for the Azerbaijani language.

References

1. Akbik, A., Bergmann, T., Vollgraf, R.: Pooled contextualized embeddings for named entity recognition. In: Burstein, J., Doran, C., Solorio, T. (eds.) Proceedings of the 2019 Conference of the North American Chapter of the Association for Computational Linguistics: Human Language Technologies, NAACL-HLT 2019, Minneapolis, MN, USA, 2–7 June 2019, Volume 1 (Long and Short Papers), pp. 724–728. Association for Computational Linguistics (2019). https://aclweb.org/anthology/papers/N/N19/N19-1078/
2. Akbik, A., Blythe, D., Vollgraf, R.: Contextual string embeddings for sequence labeling. In: Bender, E.M., Derczynski, L., Isabelle, P. (eds.) Proceedings of the 27th International Conference on Computational Linguistics, COLING 2018, Santa Fe, New Mexico, USA, 20–26 August 2018, pp. 1638–1649. Association for Computational Linguistics (2018). https://aclanthology.info/papers/C18-1139/c18-1139
3. Aliod, D.M., van Zaanen, M., Smith, D.: Named entity recognition for question answering. In: Cavedon, L., Zukerman, I. (eds.) Proceedings of the Australasian Language Technology Workshop, ALTA 2006, Sydney, Australia, 30 November–1 December 2006, pp. 51–58. Australasian Language Technology Association (2006). https://aclanthology.info/papers/U06-1009/u06-1009
4. Bowman, S.R., Angeli, G., Potts, C., Manning, C.D.: A large annotated corpus for learning natural language inference. In: Màrquez, L., Callison-Burch, C., Su, J., Pighin, D., Marton, Y. (eds.) Proceedings of the 2015 Conference on Empirical Methods in Natural Language Processing, EMNLP 2015, Lisbon, Portugal, 17–21 September 2015, pp. 632–642. The Association for Computational Linguistics (2015). http://aclweb.org/anthology/D/D15/D15-1075.pdf
5. Chiu, J.P.C., Nichols, E.: Named entity recognition with bidirectional LSTM-CNNs. TACL **4**, 357–370 (2016). https://transacl.org/ojs/index.php/tacl/article/view/792
6. Dai, A.M., Le, Q.V.: Semi-supervised sequence learning. In: Cortes, C., Lawrence, N.D., Lee, D.D., Sugiyama, M., Garnett, R. (eds.) Advances in Neural Information Processing Systems 28: Annual Conference on Neural Information Processing Systems 2015, 7–12 December 2015, Montreal, Quebec, Canada, pp. 3079–3087 (2015). http://papers.nips.cc/paper/5949-semi-supervised-sequence-learning
7. Devlin, J., Chang, M.W., Lee, K., Toutanova, K.: Bert: Pre-training of deep bidirectional transformers for language understanding. In: Burstein, J., Doran, C., Solorio, T. (eds.) Proceedings of the 2019 Conference of the North American Chapter of the Association for Computational Linguistics: Human Language Technologies, NAACL-HLT 2019, Minneapolis, MN, USA, 2–7 June 2019, Volume 1 (Long and Short Papers), pp. 4171–4186. Association for Computational Linguistics (2019). https://aclweb.org/anthology/papers/N/N19/N19-1423/
8. Dolan, W.B., Brockett, C.: Automatically constructing a corpus of sentential paraphrases. In: Proceedings of the Third International Workshop on Paraphrasing, IWP@IJCNLP 2005, Jeju Island, Korea, October 2005, 2005. Asian Federation of Natural Language Processing (2005). https://aclanthology.info/papers/I05-5002/i05-5002
9. Ghazvininejad, M., et al.: A knowledge-grounded neural conversation model. In: McIlraith, S.A., Weinberger, K.Q. (eds.) Proceedings of the Thirty-Second AAAI Conference on Artificial Intelligence, New Orleans, Louisiana, USA, 2–7 February 2018, pp. 5110–5117. AAAI Press (2018). https://www.aaai.org/ocs/index.php/AAAI/AAAI18/paper/view/16710

10. Grundkiewicz, R., Heafield, K.: Neural machine translation techniques for named entity transliteration. In: Chen, N.F., Banchs, R.E., Duan, X., 0005, M.Z., 0001, H.L. (eds.) Proceedings of the Seventh Named Entities Workshop, NEWS@ACL 2018, Melbourne, Australia, 20 July 2018, pp. 89–94. Association for Computational Linguistics (2018). https://aclanthology.info/papers/W18-2413/w18-2413

11. Heinzerling, B., 0001, M.S.: BPEMB: tokenization-free pre-trained subword embeddings in 275 languages. In: Calzolari, N., et al. (eds.) Proceedings of the Eleventh International Conference on Language Resources and Evaluation, LREC 2018, Miyazaki, Japan, 7–12 May 2018. European Language Resources Association (ELRA) (2018)

12. Hovy, E.H., Marcus, M.P., Palmer, M., Ramshaw, L.A., Weischedel, R.M.: OntoNotes: the 90 solution. In: Moore, R.C., Bilmes, J.A., Chu-Carroll, J., Sanderson, M. (eds.) Human Language Technology Conference of the North American Chapter of the Association of Computational Linguistics, Proceedings, New York, New York, USA, 4–9 June 2006. The Association for Computational Linguistics (2006). http://acl.ldc.upenn.edu/N/N06/N06-2015.pdf

13. Klie, J.C., Bugert, M., Boullosa, B., Eckart de Castilho, R., Gurevych, I.: The INCEpTION platform: machine-assisted and knowledge-oriented interactive annotation. In: Proceedings of the 27th International Conference on Computational Linguistics: System Demonstrations, Santa Fe, New Mexico, pp. 5–9. Association for Computational Linguistics (2018). https://www.aclweb.org/anthology/C18-2002

14. Lample, G., Ballesteros, M., Subramanian, S., Kawakami, K., Dyer, C.: Neural architectures for named entity recognition. In: Knight, K., Nenkova, A., Rambow, O. (eds.) NAACL HLT 2016, The 2016 Conference of the North American Chapter of the Association for Computational Linguistics: Human Language Technologies, San Diego California, USA, 12–17 June 2016, pp. 260–270. The Association for Computational Linguistics (2016). http://aclweb.org/anthology/N/N16/N16-1030.pdf

15. Pan, X., Zhang, B., May, J., Nothman, J., Knight, K., Ji, H.: Cross-lingual name tagging and linking for 282 languages. In: Barzilay, R., Kan, M.Y. (eds.) Proceedings of the 55th Annual Meeting of the Association for Computational Linguistics, ACL 2017, Vancouver, Canada, 30 July–4 August, Volume 1: Long Papers. pp. 1946–1958. Association for Computational Linguistics (2017). https://doi.org/10.18653/v1/P17-1178. https://doi.org/10.18653/v1/P17-1178

16. Paul, S.: Weights & Biases (2021). https://wandb.ai/site/. Accessed 18 Apr 2021

17. Peters, M.E., et al.: Deep contextualized word representations. In: Walker, M.A., Ji, H., Stent, A. (eds.) Proceedings of the 2018 Conference of the North American Chapter of the Association for Computational Linguistics: Human Language Technologies, NAACL-HLT 2018, New Orleans, Louisiana, USA, 1–6 June 2018, Volume 1 (Long Papers), pp. 2227–2237. Association for Computational Linguistics (2018). https://aclanthology.info/papers/N18-1202/n18-1202

18. Peters, M.E., Neumann, M., Zettlemoyer, L., tau Yih, W.: Dissecting contextual word embeddings: Architecture and representation. In: Riloff, E., 0001, D.C., Hockenmaier, J., Tsujii, J. (eds.) Proceedings of the 2018 Conference on Empirical Methods in Natural Language Processing, Brussels, Belgium, 31 October–4 November 2018. pp. 1499–1509. Association for Computational Linguistics (2018). https://aclanthology.info/papers/D18-1179/d18-1179

19. Quirk, C., Mooney, R.J., Galley, M.: Language to code: learning semantic parsers for if-this-then-that recipes. In: Proceedings of the 53rd Annual Meeting of the Association for Computational Linguistics and the 7th International Joint Conference on Natural Language Processing of the Asian Federation of Natural Language Processing, ACL 2015, Beijing, China, 26–31 July 2015, volume 1: Long Papers, pp. 878–888. The Association for Computer Linguistics (2015). http://aclweb.org/anthology/P/P15/P15-1085.pdf

20. Raiman, J., Raiman, O.: DeepType: multilingual entity linking by neural type system evolution. In: McIlraith, S.A., Weinberger, K.Q. (eds.) Proceedings of the Thirty-Second AAAI Conference on Artificial Intelligence, New Orleans, Louisiana, USA, 2–7 February 2018, pp. 5406–5413. AAAI Press (2018). https://www.aaai.org/ocs/index.php/AAAI/AAAI18/paper/view/17148

21. Rajpurkar, P., Zhang, J., Lopyrev, K., Liang, P.: Squad: 100, 000+ questions for machine comprehension of text. In: Su, J., Carreras, X., Duh, K. (eds.) Proceedings of the 2016 Conference on Empirical Methods in Natural Language Processing, EMNLP 2016, Austin, Texas, USA, 1–4 November 2016, pp. 2383–2392. The Association for Computational Linguistics (2016). http://aclweb.org/anthology/D/D16/D16-1264.pdf

22. Rodríguez, J.D., Caldwell, A., Liu, A.: Transfer learning for entity recognition of novel classes. In: Bender, E.M., Derczynski, L., Isabelle, P. (eds.) Proceedings of the 27th International Conference on Computational Linguistics, COLING 2018, Santa Fe, New Mexico, USA, 20–26 August 2018, pp. 1974–1985. Association for Computational Linguistics (2018). https://aclanthology.info/papers/C18-1168/c18-1168

23. Ruder, S., Howard, J.: Universal language model fine-tuning for text classification. In: Gurevych, I., Miyao, Y. (eds.) Proceedings of the 56th Annual Meeting of the Association for Computational Linguistics, ACL 2018, Melbourne, Australia, 15–20 July 2018, Volume 1: Long Papers, pp. 328–339. Association for Computational Linguistics (2018). https://aclanthology.info/papers/P18-1031/p18-1031

24. Sang, E.F.T.K., Meulder, F.D.: Introduction to the conll-2003 shared task: Language-independent named entity recognition. In: Daelemans, W., Osborne, M. (eds.) Proceedings of the Seventh Conference on Natural Language Learning, CoNLL 2003, Held in cooperation with HLT-NAACL 2003, Edmonton, Canada, 31 May–1 June 2003, pp. 142–147. ACL (2003). http://aclweb.org/anthology/W/W03/W03-0419.pdf

25. Stubbs, A., Kotfila, C., Uzuner, Ö.: Automated systems for the de-identification of longitudinal clinical narratives: overview of 2014 i2b2/uthealth shared task track 1. J. Biomed. Inf. **58** (2015). https://doi.org/10.1016/j.jbi.2015.06.007

26. Tjong Kim Sang, E.F.: Introduction to the CoNLL-2002 shared task: Language-independent named entity recognition. In: COLING-02: The 6th Conference on Natural Language Learning 2002 (CoNLL-2002) (2002). https://www.aclweb.org/anthology/W02-2024

27. Williams, A., Nangia, N., Bowman, S.R.: A broad-coverage challenge corpus for sentence understanding through inference. In: Walker, M.A., Ji, H., Stent, A. (eds.) Proceedings of the 2018 Conference of the North American Chapter of the Association for Computational Linguistics: Human Language Technologies, NAACL-HLT 2018, New Orleans, Louisiana, USA, 1–6 June 2018, volume 1 (Long Papers), pp. 1112–1122. Association for Computational Linguistics (2018). https://aclanthology.info/papers/N18-1101/n18-1101

28. Wolf, T., et al.: Transformers: state-of-the-art natural language processing. In: Proceedings of the 2020 Conference on Empirical Methods in Natural Language Processing: System Demonstrations, pp. 38–45. Association for Computational Linguistics, Online (2020). https://doi.org/10.18653/v1/2020.emnlp-demos.6. https://www.aclweb.org/anthology/2020.emnlp-demos.6

29. Wu, S., Dredze, M.: Beto, Bentz, Becas: the surprising cross-lingual effectiveness of Bert. In: Inui, K., Jiang, J., Ng, V., 0001, X.W. (eds.) Proceedings of the 2019 Conference on Empirical Methods in Natural Language Processing and the 9th International Joint Conference on Natural Language Processing, EMNLP-IJCNLP 2019, Hong Kong, China, 3–7 November 2019, pp. 833–844. Association for Computational Linguistics (2019). https://doi.org/10.18653/v1/D19-1077

30. Yadav, V., Bethard, S.: A survey on recent advances in named entity recognition from deep learning models. In: Bender, E.M., Derczynski, L., Isabelle, P. (eds.) Proceedings of the 27th International Conference on Computational Linguistics, COLING 2018, Santa Fe, New Mexico, USA, 20–26 August 2018, pp. 2145–2158. Association for Computational Linguistics (2018). https://aclanthology.info/papers/C18-1182/c18-1182

Using BERT Encoding and Sentence-Level Language Model for Sentence Ordering

Melika Golestani[1]([✉]), Seyedeh Zahra Razavi[2], Zeinab Borhanifard[1],
Farnaz Tahmasebian[3], and Hesham Faili[1]

[1] School of Electrical and Computer Engineering, College of Engineering,
University of Tehran, Tehran, Iran
{melika.golestani,borhanifardz,hfaili}@ut.ac.ir
[2] Department of Computer Science, University of Rochester, Rochester, USA
srazavi@cs.rochester.edu
[3] Department of Computer Science, Emory University, Atlanta, USA
ftahmas@emory.edu

Abstract. Discovering the logical sequence of events is one of the cornerstones in Natural Language Understanding. One approach to learn the sequence of events is to study the order of sentences in a coherent text. Sentence ordering can be applied in various tasks such as retrieval-based Question Answering, document summarization, storytelling, text generation, and dialogue systems. Furthermore, we can learn to model text coherence by learning how to order a set of shuffled sentences. Previous research has relied on RNN, LSTM, and BiLSTM architecture for learning text language models. However, these networks have performed poorly due to the lack of attention mechanisms. We propose an algorithm for sentence ordering in a corpus of short stories. Our proposed method uses a language model based on Universal Transformers (UT) that captures sentences' dependencies by employing an attention mechanism. Our method improves the previous state-of-the-art in terms of Perfect Match Ratio (PMR) score in the ROCStories dataset, a corpus of nearly 100K short human-made stories. The proposed model includes three components: Sentence Encoder, Language Model, and Sentence Arrangement with Brute Force Search. The first component generates sentence embeddings using SBERT-WK pre-trained model fine-tuned on the ROCStories data. Then a Universal Transformer network generates a sentence-level language model. For decoding, the network generates a candidate sentence as the following sentence of the current sentence. We use cosine similarity as a scoring function to assign scores to the candidate embedding and the embeddings of other sentences in the shuffled set. Then a Brute Force Search is employed to maximize the sum of similarities between pairs of consecutive sentences.

Keywords: Sentence ordering · Event sequencing · Story reordering · BERT pretrained model · Sentences-level language model

© Springer Nature Switzerland AG 2021
K. Ekštein et al. (Eds.): TSD 2021, LNAI 12848, pp. 318–330, 2021.
https://doi.org/10.1007/978-3-030-83527-9_27

1   Introduction

Modeling text coherence and logical sequences of events is a fundamental problem in natural language processing [25]. Coherence represents the logical connections between the words, sentences and events in a text. An event is generally considered to be the verb of a sentence along with its constellation of arguments, such as subject and object [10]. In a coherent narrative text, events follow a logical order, which makes it possible for a reader to make sense of the text. In NLP tasks, "Sentence Ordering" models are suggested to learn high-level structure that causes sentences to appear in a specific order in human-authored texts and by learning to order sentences we can model text coherence [25].

"Sentence ordering" refers to organizing a given shuffled set of sentences into a coherent order [25]. Sentence ordering assists in modeling coherence in text, which in turn can be applied in a variety of tasks such as multi-document summarization [2,21], story understanding [31], and retrieval based QA systems [25]. A key factor to solve the problem of sentence ordering is to find a coherent sequence of events appeared in the input sentences. In natural language processing, events are often meant to be the verbs of sentences and their dependencies, such as the subject and the object [29]. A number of studies have proposed methods to order events based on their temporal and causal relations [31], or the semantic roles [9]. The researchers developed a Skip-thought [18] encoder-decoder model utilizing an RNN. It takes a sentence and encodes it into a constant-length vector, followed by previous and subsequent sentences. Therefore, all input is first encrypted using a hidden network vector; then its output is decrypted from that vector. Pichotta & Mooney [34] replaced the RNN with an LSTM, and proposed a sentence-level language model to predict the next sentence for the script inference task. Nevertheless, skip-thought's architecture's simplicity results in a lower quality of creating sentences embeddings compared to many newer methods and networks like BERT [12]. The system uses an RNN-based encoder-decoder architecture, whereas SBERT-WK [39] uses a Transformer-based architecture and an attention mechanism to encode the sentences into vectors.

According to [9], a statistical script system model an event sequence as a probabilistic model and infer additional events from a document events. This system teaches the linguistic model of events; despite this, some critical information in the sentence can be ignored because only verbs and their dependents are used. Thus, the clue words (adverbs such as "then", "before", and "after") are omitted.

In this paper, we propose a sentence-level language model to solve the problem of sentence ordering. Language models have been popular for years at the word and letter levels [19,41]. LSTMs [16] and RNNs [26] have been vastly used for teaching language models at the word and letter levels is beneficial [5,17,17,28,38]. These models take a single word or character as input at time t, update the hidden mode vector, and predict the next word or character at time $t + 1$. Kiros used a sentence level language model based on the RNN [18]. Pichotta in [34] used LSTM-based sentence-level models for script inference due to the problem of RNNs, the vanishing gradients. RNNs and LSTMs encrypt information about one sentence and decode information about the following sentence. Despite this, these networks not use a self-attention mechanism [33] for encoding sentences, and some information is lost.

We use a sentence level language model based on the universal transformers (UT) [11]. A generalization of the Transformer model, the UT model is a parallel-in-time recurrent sequence model. The UT model combines two aspects of feed-forward models: parallelism and global receptive field. An additional feature is the position-based halting mechanism. Using a self-attention mechanism, the Universal Transformer refines its representations for all sentences in the sequence in parallel.

Our model involves three components: the first component encodes sentences; the second one uses a neural network to teach the language model at the sentence level by universal transformers (UT) and to predict the next sentence. The last component uses the cosine similarity and Brute Force search to order sentences. We aim to design a model that can capture the sequence of events by arranging a set of sentences.

The model we propose is designed to organize shuffled sentences of short stories. By using this method, we encode sentences by the SBERT-WK model, which causes us to pay attention to every word within a sentence equal to its importance and transform the sentence into a vector. Thus the embedding contains the clue words information. To capture the relationship between Sentences, We use a UT-based language model, which predicts the next sentence of the current sentence. Finally, we use a Brute Force search, using the scoring function based on cosine similarity, which is scored between the candidate sentence and other sentences, to maximize the sum of similarities between two consecutive sentences. As dataset, we use ROCStories [30], which includes around 100K short 5-sentence stories, written by human turkers. The gold data follows the order similar to the original order in the stories.

The main applications of sentence ordering can be mentioned as: extractive and multi-document text summarization [2], retrieval based QA systems [25], storytelling [30], text coherence modeling [25], discourse coherence [13], and text generation systems [7].

2   Related Work

Understanding relations between sentences has become increasingly important for various NLP tasks, such as multi-document summarization [2], text generation [7], and text coherence modeling [25]. Moreover, learning the order of sentences can help in modeling text coherence [25]. In sentence ordering, the goal is to arrange a set of unordered sentences in a cohesive order. Ordering models aim to identify patterns resulting sentences to appear in a specific order in a coherent text. Several previous studies have addressed the task of sentence ordering for a set of data such as news articles [2,6,21].

Previous methods suggested on the task of sentence ordering fall into two categories: traditional approaches, and deep learning-based approaches. Traditional approaches to coherence modeling and sentence ordering often apply probabilistic models [21]. Barzilay utilized content models to represent topics as HMM states [4], then employed hand-crafted linguistic features, including Entity Grid, to model the document structure [3]. [30] suggested using n-gram overlapping to pick a final sentence from two human-made options of the ROCStories stories. In [35], a similar method is used to arrange the set of unordered sentences of the stories. As the next sentence, they pick the sentence with the most n-gram overlaps with the current sentence. They measured an overlap up to 4-gram using Smoothed-BLEU [24].

In recent years, researchers used neural approaches to solve sentence ordering tasks. [1] proposed SkipThought + Pairwise model. The method involves combining two points identified from the unary embedding of sentences without considering context and a pairwise model of sentences based on their relative composition in context. However, as SkipThought model [18] was applied to map sentences into vector space, some information is missing. Another method proposed in [23] is a productive model that is called Seq2Seq + Pairwise. A Seq2Seq model based on an encoder-decoder architecture is used to predict the following sentence, having one. This way, the model learns a probabilities distributions over sentences.

Gong employed an end-to-end sentence ordering method, LSTM + PtrNet [14]. After getting encrypted and decoded by LSTM models, pointer networks are being used to arrange sentences. Another method proposed in [25], called LSTM + Set2Seq, uses LSTM and attention mechanism to encode sentences and learn a representation of context. Then a pointer network is applied to ranks sentences. [40] proposed Hierarchical attention networks (HAN). The idea is to capture the information of clue words to learn the dependency between sentences. The system uses a word encoder with a BiLSTM architecture, an attention layer that creates sentence embedding, and an attention mechanism to encode and decode a group of sentences together. Although LSTM and BiLSTM-based models show improvement, they are less efficient comparing to a BERT-based encoder model. This is mostly because of the fact that BiLSTM models do not look at both directions of a word simultaneously. In contrast, BERT is trained to learn both left and right positions at the same time.

[27] proposed a CBoW model that generate sentence embedding using the average of the word embedding vectors of the words that compose the sentence. This embedding is used in [35] to suggest a baseline, where cosine similarity between embeddings of pairs of sentences is used to order the pairs. This has two essential defects: it does not include many sentence information such as clue words and there is no way for modelling sentences' dependencies.

[35] presents sentence correlation measure (SCM) for sentence ordering. This measure has three main components:

1. A sentence encoding component based on the pretrained SBERT-WK [39];
2. A scoring component based on the cosine similarity;
3. A ranking component based on a Brute Force search.

None of the above components need access to training data which provides an advantage where limited data is available [35]. The method does not work as well as HAN or LSTM + Set2Seq when enough training data is available, since dependencies between sentences are not captured.

[20] proposed RankTxNet ListMLE, which is a pointer-based model. This method relies on a pre-trained BERT model for encoding sentences and a self-attention based transformer network for encoding paragraphs. To predict a relative score for each sentence, they use a feed-forward network as a decoder which determines each sentence's position in a paragraph.

Our proposed model has some similarity with the methods presented in [14] and [25] in using neural networks for predicting sentence ordering in a pairwise manner. However, we employ a BERT-based model for sentence encoding, in contrast to the LSTM-based model they used. Moreover, by applying universal transformers we encode a group of sentences and learn a language model.

3   Methodology

3.1   Task Formulation

The sentence ordering takes the story S as input, which its sentences are probably unsorted:

$$S : s_1, s_2, ..., s_n \tag{1}$$

where n is the length of the sequence or the number of sentences in each sequence. It outputs a permutation of the sentences like o so that o is equal to o^*:

$$s(o_1^*) > s(o_2^*) > ... > s(o_5^*), \tag{2}$$

where o^* is to the order of the sentences in the gold data.

3.2   Sentence-Level Language Model for Sentence Ordering (SLM)

We proposed Sentence-level Language Model (SLM) for Sentence Ordering compose of Sentence Encoder, Story Encoder, and Sentence Organizer. The architecture of the proposed model is shown in Fig. 1. Sentence encoder gets sentence as input and encoded it into a vector using a fine-tuned pre-trained SBERT-WK [39]. The embedding pays more attention to the sentence's crucial parts, such as the verbs and clue words. Furthermore, stop words are omitted. Then, Story Encoder takes the sentence encoder as an input and learns the sentence level language model using an encoder-decoder architecture based on universal transformers (UT) [11]. UT couples parallelism with the global receptive field in a feed-forward model. The UT model also includes position-based halting [11]. The UT-based encoder-decoder component corrects vector representations for each position (sentence) in parallel by combining information from different positions using self-attention and applying a repetitive transfer function [11]. Hence dependencies between the sentences are captured. The vector is learned from the hidden state and then decodes the vector and indicates the next sentence's candidate.

What matters at runtime is that during training, information are transferred to all nodes at time $t+1$ from all nodes at time t. Thus, parallelism is created, which allows all tokens processed at the same time [11].

In the Sentence Organizer, we can rate each sentence and the candidate based on their similarity. We use the cosine similarity as the scoring function. The arrangement is made using a Brute Force search in all state spaces to maximize the sum of the cosine similarity between two consecutive sentences like the sentence ordering component in [35], as follows:

$$\sum_{i=1,\dots,4} S\big(s(o_i), s(o_{i+1})\big) = \max \sum_{\substack{i,j=1,\dots,5 \\ i \neq j}} S(s_i', s_j), \qquad (3)$$

where $S(s_i', s_j)$ represents the cosine similarity between s_i' and s_j, and s_i' is the candidate for the next sentence of the i-th sentence, represented with s_i. $s(o_i)$ represents the i-th sentence in the order of output, and s_i is the i-th sentence in the non-ordered permutation of sentences or the input's order.

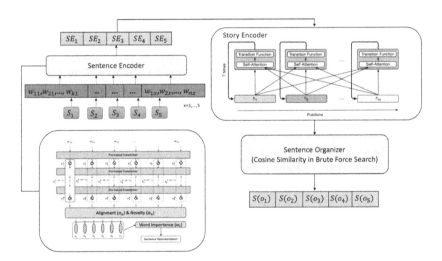

Fig. 1. Showing the SLM in the abstract. During model training, sentence ordering is given to the network correctly to learn and model the relationships and dependencies between the sentences. During testing, input sentences are shuffled. Where w_{j_i} is the jth word in the ith sentence and $s(o_i)$ is the i-th sentence in output order. The goal is to output an s(o) equal to $s(o^*)$ (this represents the gold data ordering).

Our model is trained again using the universal sentence encoder (USE) embeddings [8] to compare them to SBERT-WK embeddings, and additionally, we employ the BiLSTM [36] network to learn the LM. Also, we apply the nearest neighbor search, which is a greedy algorithm. The NN search calculations for sentence ordering are presented in [35]. Consequently, we train, evaluate, and test nine different models, including the following:

- Fine-tuned pretrained SBERT-WK + UT + BFS,
- Pretrained SBERT-WK + UT + BFS,
- Pretrained SBERT-WK + BiLSTM + BFS,
- Pretrained SBERT-WK + UT + NN,
- Pretrained SBERT-WK + BiLSTM + NN,
- USE + UT + BFS,
- USE + BiLSTM + BFS,
- USE + UT + NN,
- USE + BiLSTM + NN,

So we can assess the effect of change on each component.

4 Experiment

4.1 Dataset

We used ROCStories dataset (a commonsense story dataset) [30]. The dataset contains 98,162 five-sentence stories with an average word count of 50 words. 3,742 of stories have two choices as the fifth sentence or the final sentence. The corpus has been presented for a shared task called LSDSem [32] where models are supposed to choose the correct ending to a four-sentence story. All the stories and options are generated by human. This dataset has some essential characteristics that make it a fit for our task of learning sequences of events: ROCStories contains causal and temporal relationships among daily events. This makes it possible to learn the narrative structure of a wide range of events. The dataset contains a collection of daily non-fictional short stories suitable for the training of coherent text models.

4.2 Baselines and Competitors

The proposed method is compared with five baselines as follows: Sentence n-gram overlap [35], SkipThought + Pairwise [1], Seq2Seq + Pairwise [23], Continues Bag of Words (CBoW) [35], Sentence Correlation Measure (SCM) [35]. The competitors methods follow as: Hierarchical Attention Networks (HAN) [40], LSTM+PtrNet [14], LSTM+Set2Seq [25], and RankTxNet ListMLE [20].

4.3 Metrics

The metrics we use to evaluate story ordering outputs are "Kendal's Tau" and "PMR", introduced below.

1. Kendall's Tau *(tau)*
   Kendal's Tau measures the quality of arrangements by Equation (4),

   $$\tau = 1 - ((2 \cdot number\ of\ inversions))/(N \cdot (N-1)/2) \qquad (4)$$

   where N represents the sequence length, and *number of inversions* is equal to how many binaries' relative order is wrongly predicted. This measure for sentence ordering is correlated with human judgment, according to [22].
   The value of this criterion is in the range $[-1, 1]$; the lower limit indicates the worst case, and $\tau = 1$ when the predicted order equals to the order in the gold data are the same.
2. Perfect Match Ratio (PMR)
   PMR defined as following, calculates the ratio of exactly matching sentence orders without penalizing incorrect ones.

   $$PMR = ((\#\ of\ Correct\ Pairs))/(N \cdot (N-1)/2) \qquad (5)$$

   where N represents the sequence length. One can see that the PMR is always in the range of 0 and 1, where $PMR = 1$ indicates the predicted order is exactly the same as the gold order, and a $PMR = 0$ means that the predicted order is precisely the contrary of the gold order.

4.4 Results and Analysis

As mentioned in Sect. 3, SLM has three components. First, a sentence encoder, which is designed based on SBERT-WK. Second, a story encoder, which trains a sentence-level language model and learns the dependencies between the sentences. In this component, the UT network is used. The third component is sentences' organizer which calculates the cosine similarity between sentence embedding vectors and employs a Brute Force search to maximize the sum of similarities among consecutive sentences.

In addition to SLM, we trained and tested nine other models by replacing each component with other algorithms or architectures to select the best algorithm and compare SLM with them. These nine models were constructed by replacing SBERT-WK encoding with USE vectors, the UT network with a BiLSTM one, and the BFS with a nearest neighbor search.

The parameters of the SLM are given in Table 1. The BERT vectors have 768 dimensions, while the USE ones have 512 dimensions. Following previous works [25, 40], we randomly split the dataset into training (80%), test (10%), and validation (10%) sets, where they contain 392645, 49080, and 49080 sentences respectively.

Based on Table 2, SBERT-WK outperforms USE due to its better architecture for sentence encoding. In all cases, UT is superior to BiLSTM, which was expected as UT has an attention mechanism. Due to NN's greedy nature, NN may not always find the global optimal solution and may become stuck in the local optimal, whereas BFS never will. So BFS is better than NN. That is why the best results are happening where we use fine-tuned SBERT-WK embedding,

Table 1. Parameters of the SLM. SLM encodes sentences with SBERT-WK embeddings and learns a language model with the UT network. Also, the USE embeddings with d=512 instead of the SBERT-WK ones are used to allow for a better choice. So hidden layer size of that is 4× 512.

Method components	Tau
Initial learning rate (α)	0.5
Regularization (λ)	10^z-5
Size of embedding vectors (d)	768
Hidden layer size (h)	4×768

Table 2. SLM results by changing each component.

Method components	Tau	PMR
SLM (Fine tuned SBERT-WK + UT + Brute Force Search)	0.7547	0.4064
SBERT-WK + UT + Brute Force Search	0.7465	0.3893
USE + UT + Brute Force Search	0.7206	0.373
SBERT-WK + BiLSTM + Brute Force Search	0.7317	0.3762
USE + BiLSTM + Brute Force Search	0.7044	0.3545
SBERT-WK + UT + Nearest Neighbor Search	0.64	0.2755
USE + UT + Nearest Neighbor Search	0.6162	0.267
SBERT-WK + BiLSTM + Nearest Neighbor Search	0.6214	0.2576
USE + BiLSTM + Nearest Neighbor Search	0.5980	0.2511

UT to capture dependencies between sentences, cosine similarity as a scoring function, and searching the entire state space to maximize the total similarity of consecutive sentences.

Figure 2 shows the results of the proposed model, SLM, along with the baselines and competitors. SLM has improved by about 3.2% and 4.2% compared to LSTM + PtrNet, and more than 4.3% and 4.8% compared to LSTM + Set2seq in τ and PMR, respectively. This performance improvement, is due to the use of a SBERT-WK model sentence encoders and employing an attention mechanism at the story encoder utilizing universal transformers. Taking advantage of the mentioned components, SLM can capture the "intradependecy" and "interdependency" of sentences very well. Intradependency of a sentence refers to the relations among each sentence's words, while interdependency refers to each sentence's relations with other sentences of the story. Our method is also superior to the HAN network, increasing τ criterion by more than 2.2% and PMR criterion by 1%. This could be because of the fact that the sentences are encoded using the BERT-based model in the SLM. HAN, however, uses a BiLSM encoder and multi-head attention layer.

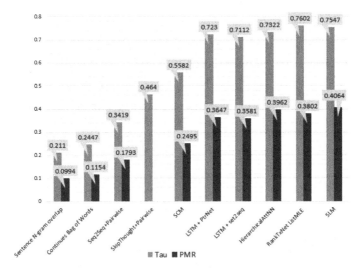

Fig. 2. Kendall's tau (τ) and perfect match ratio (PMR) on test set for ROCStories datasets. The results of the model, compared to the baselines and competitors.

Besides, SLM performed about 2.6% better than RankTxNet in PMR. However, the Kendall's τ score gives RankTxNet a slight superiority. The difference is not significant, and can happen as a result of random parameters of the network [15,37].

5   Conclusion

We presented a language-model-based framework to solve sentence ordering task. A sequence of shuffled sentences is inputted to our framework, where the output should be a coherent order of the given set. We achieved state-of-the-art performance in PMR scores on ROCStories dataset. We learned that SBERT-WK is a suitable choice for sentence encoding. We analyzed how the method is changed by using the USE to encode sentences. We also found that Universal Transformers perform better for story encoding and learning the sentence-level language model comparing to BiLSTM models. Moreover, we compared Brute Force Search with Nearest Neighbor Search to order sentences. As future work, we plan to develop more robust models to fulfill ordering of instances with longer input sequences.

References

1. Agrawal, H., Chandrasekaran, A., Batra, D., Parikh, D., Bansal, M.: Sort story: sorting jumbled images and captions into stories. In: Proceedings of the 2016 Conference on Empirical Methods in Natural Language Processing, Austin, Texas, pp. 925–931. Association for Computational Linguistics, November 2016. https://doi.org/10.18653/v1/D16-1091. https://www.aclweb.org/anthology/D16-1091

2. Barzilay, R., Elhadad, N.: Inferring strategies for sentence ordering in multidocument news summarization. J. Artif. Intell. Res. **17**, 35–55 (2002)
3. Barzilay, R., Lapata, M.: Modeling local coherence: an entity-based approach. Comput. Linguist. **34**(1), 1–34 (2008)
4. Barzilay, R., Lee, L.: Catching the drift: probabilistic content models, with applications to generation and summarization. In: Proceedings of the Human Language Technology Conference of the North American Chapter of the Association for Computational Linguistics: HLT-NAACL 2004, Boston, Massachusetts, USA, 2 May–7 May 2004, pp. 113–120. Association for Computational Linguistics (2004). https://www.aclweb.org/anthology/N04-1015
5. Bengio, Y., Ducharme, R., Vincent, P., Janvin, C.: A neural probabilistic language model. J. Mach. Learn. Res. **3**, 1137–1155 (2003)
6. Bollegala, D., Okazaki, N., Ishizuka, M.: A bottom-up approach to sentence ordering for multi-document summarization. Inf. Process. Manag. **46**(1), 89–109 (2010)
7. Bosselut, A., Celikyilmaz, A., He, X., Gao, J., Huang, P.S., Choi, Y.: Discourse-aware neural rewards for coherent text generation. In: Proceedings of the 2018 Conference of the North American Chapter of the Association for Computational Linguistics: Human Language Technologies, Volume 1 (Long Papers), New Orleans, Louisiana, pp. 173–184. Association for Computational Linguistics, June 2018. https://doi.org/10.18653/v1/N18-1016. https://www.aclweb.org/anthology/N18-1016
8. Cer, D., et al.: Universal sentence encoder for English. In: Proceedings of the 2018 Conference on Empirical Methods in Natural Language Processing: System Demonstrations, Brussels, Belgium, pp. 169–174. Association for Computational Linguistics, November 2018. https://doi.org/10.18653/v1/D18-2029. https://www.aclweb.org/anthology/D18-2029
9. Chambers, N., Jurafsky, D.: Unsupervised learning of narrative event chains. In: Proceedings of ACL-08: HLT, pp. 789–797 (2008)
10. Chambers, N., Jurafsky, D.: Unsupervised learning of narrative schemas and their participants. In: Proceedings of the Joint Conference of the 47th Annual Meeting of the ACL and the 4th International Joint Conference on Natural Language Processing of the AFNLP, pp. 602–610 (2009)
11. Dehghani, M., Gouws, S., Vinyals, O., Uszkoreit, J., Kaiser, Ł.: Universal transformers. arXiv preprint arXiv:1807.03819 (2018)
12. Devlin, J., Chang, M.W., Lee, K., Toutanova, K.: BERT: pre-training of deep bidirectional transformers for language understanding. In: Proceedings of the 2019 Conference of the North American Chapter of the Association for Computational Linguistics: Human Language Technologies, Volume 1 (Long and Short Papers), Minneapolis, Minnesota, pp. 4171–4186. Association for Computational Linguistics, June 2019. https://doi.org/10.18653/v1/N19-1423. https://www.aclweb.org/anthology/N19-1423
13. Elsner, M., Austerweil, J., Charniak, E.: A unified local and global model for discourse coherence. In: Human Language Technologies 2007: The Conference of the North American Chapter of the Association for Computational Linguistics; Proceedings of the Main Conference, pp. 436–443 (2007)
14. Gong, J., Chen, X., Qiu, X., Huang, X.: End-to-end neural sentence ordering using pointer network. arXiv preprint arXiv:1611.04953 (2016)
15. Haddad, H., Fadaei, H., Faili, H.: Handling OOV words in NMT using unsupervised bilingual embedding. In: 2018 9th International Symposium on Telecommunications (IST), pp. 569–574. IEEE (2018)
16. Hochreiter, S., Schmidhuber, J.: Long short-term memory. Neural Comput. **9**(8), 1735–1780 (1997)

17. Jozefowicz, R., Vinyals, O., Schuster, M., Shazeer, N., Wu, Y.: Exploring the limits of language modeling. arXiv preprint arXiv:1602.02410 (2016)
18. Kiros, R., et al.: Skip-thought vectors. In: Advances in Neural Information Processing Systems, pp. 3294–3302 (2015)
19. Kozielski, M., Rybach, D., Hahn, S., Schlüter, R., Ney, H.: Open vocabulary handwriting recognition using combined word-level and character-level language models. In: 2013 IEEE International Conference on Acoustics, Speech and Signal Processing, pp. 8257–8261. IEEE (2013)
20. Kumar, P., Brahma, D., Karnick, H., Rai, P.: Deep attentive ranking networks for learning to order sentences. In: AAAI, pp. 8115–8122 (2020)
21. Lapata, M.: Probabilistic text structuring: experiments with sentence ordering. In: Proceedings of the 41st Annual Meeting of the Association for Computational Linguistics, pp. 545–552 (2003)
22. Lapata, M.: Automatic evaluation of information ordering: Kendall's tau. Comput. Linguist. **32**(4), 471–484 (2006)
23. Li, J., Jurafsky, D.: Neural net models of open-domain discourse coherence. In: Proceedings of the 2017 Conference on Empirical Methods in Natural Language Processing, Copenhagen, Denmark, pp. 198–209. Association for Computational Linguistics, September 2017. https://doi.org/10.18653/v1/D17-1019. https://www.aclweb.org/anthology/D17-1019
24. Lin, C.Y., Och, F.J.: Automatic evaluation of machine translation quality using longest common subsequence and skip-bigram statistics. In: Proceedings of the 42nd Annual Meeting of the Association for Computational Linguistics (ACL-04), pp. 605–612 (2004)
25. Logeswaran, L., Lee, H., Radev, D.: Sentence ordering and coherence modeling using recurrent neural networks. In: Proceedings of the AAAI Conference on Artificial Intelligence, vol. 32 (2018)
26. Medsker, L.R., Jain, L.: Recurrent neural networks. Des. Appl. **5**, 64–67 (2001)
27. Mikolov, T., Chen, K., Corrado, G., Dean, J.: Efficient estimation of word representations in vector space. CoRR abs/1301.3781 (2013). http://dblp.uni-trier.de/db/journals/corr/corr1301.html#abs-1301-3781
28. Mikolov, T., Deoras, A., Kombrink, S., Burget, L., Černockỳ, J.: Empirical evaluation and combination of advanced language modeling techniques. In: Twelfth Annual Conference of the International Speech Communication Association (2011)
29. Mostafazadeh, N.: From Event to Story Understanding. University of Rochester (2017)
30. Mostafazadeh, N., et al.: A corpus and cloze evaluation for deeper understanding of commonsense stories. In: Proceedings of the 2016 Conference of the North American Chapter of the Association for Computational Linguistics: Human Language Technologies, pp. 839–849 (2016)
31. Mostafazadeh, N., Grealish, A., Chambers, N., Allen, J., Vanderwende, L.: Caters: causal and temporal relation scheme for semantic annotation of event structures. In: Proceedings of the Fourth Workshop on Events, pp. 51–61 (2016)
32. Mostafazadeh, N., Roth, M., Louis, A., Chambers, N., Allen, J.: LSDSEM 2017 shared task: the story cloze test. In: Proceedings of the 2nd Workshop on Linking Models of Lexical, Sentential and Discourse-level Semantics, pp. 46–51 (2017)
33. Parikh, A., Täckström, O., Das, D., Uszkoreit, J.: A decomposable attention model for natural language inference. In: Proceedings of the 2016 Conference on Empirical Methods in Natural Language Processing, Austin, Texas, pp. 2249–2255. Association for Computational Linguistics, November 2016. https://doi.org/10.18653/v1/D16-1244. https://www.aclweb.org/anthology/D16-1244

34. Pichotta, K., Mooney, R.J.: Using sentence-level LSTM language models for script inference. In: Proceedings of the 54th Annual Meeting of the Association for Computational Linguistics (Volume 1: Long Papers), Berlin, Germany, pp. 279–289. Association for Computational Linguistics, August 2016. https://doi.org/10.18653/v1/P16-1027. https://www.aclweb.org/anthology/P16-1027

35. Pour, M.G., Razavi, S.Z., Faili, H.: A new sentence ordering method using BERT pretrained model. In: 2020 11th International Conference on Information and Knowledge Technology (IKT), pp. 132–138. IEEE (2020)

36. Schuster, M., Paliwal, K.K.: Bidirectional recurrent neural networks. IEEE Trans. Signal Process. **45**(11), 2673–2681 (1997)

37. Sennrich, R., Haddow, B., Birch, A.: Neural machine translation of rare words with subword units. In: Proceedings of the 54th Annual Meeting of the Association for Computational Linguistics (Volume 1: Long Papers), Berlin, Germany, pp. 1715–1725. Association for Computational Linguistics, August 2016. https://doi.org/10.18653/v1/P16-1162. https://www.aclweb.org/anthology/P16-1162

38. Sutskever, I., Vinyals, O., Le, Q.V.: Sequence to sequence learning with neural networks. In: Proceedings of the 27th International Conference on Neural Information Processing Systems, NIPS 2014, Cambridge, MA, USA, vol. 2, pp. 3104–3112. MIT Press (2014)

39. Wang, B., Kuo, C.C.J.: SBERT-WK: a sentence embedding method by dissecting BERT-based word models. IEEE/ACM Trans. Audio Speech Lang. Process. **28**, 2146–2157 (2020)

40. Wang, T., Wan, X.: Hierarchical attention networks for sentence ordering. Proc. AAAI Conf. Artif. Intell. **33**, 7184–7191 (2019)

41. Woodland, P.C., Povey, D.: Large scale discriminative training of Hidden Markov models for speech recognition. Comput. Speech Lang. **16**(1), 25–47 (2002)

Using Presentation Slides and Adjacent Utterances for Post-editing of Speech Recognition Results for Meeting Recordings

Kentaro Kamiya$^{(\boxtimes)}$, Takuya Kawase, Ryuichiro Higashinaka, and Katashi Nagao

Graduate School of Informatics, Nagoya University, Nagoya, Japan
{kamiya,kawase,nagao}@nagao.nuie.nagoya-u.ac.jp,
higashinaka@i.nagoya-u.ac.jp
https://en.nagoya-u.ac.jp

Abstract. In recent years, the use of automatic speech recognition (ASR) systems in meetings has been increasing, such as for minutes generation and speaker diarization. The problem is that ASR systems often misrecognize words because there is domain-specific content in meetings. In this paper, we propose a novel method for automatically post-editing ASR results by using presentation slides that meeting participants use and utterances adjacent to a target utterance. We focus on automatic post-editing rather than domain adaptation because of the ease of incorporating external information, and the method can be used for arbitrary speech recognition engines. In experiments, we found that our method can significantly improve the recognition accuracy of domain-specific words (proper nouns). We also found an improvement in the word error rate (WER).

Keywords: Automatic speech recognition · Post-editing · Presentation slides in meetings

1   Introduction

For the task of speaker diarization and minutes generation for presentations in meetings, automatic speech recognition (ASR) systems are becoming increasingly used [7,15,17,21]. However, for meetings in specialized fields, ASR systems still cannot recognize speech correctly since such speech contains domain-specific words. Generally, off-the-shelf ASR systems are trained with a large amount of general speech data. As a result, the language and acoustic models are not suitable for recognizing speech in specific domains.

In this paper, we propose a post-editing method for automatically correcting ASR results in meeting recordings. In meetings, slides are commonly used to accompany the explanation of the speaker. Additionally, many people hold

© Springer Nature Switzerland AG 2021
K. Ekštein et al. (Eds.): TSD 2021, LNAI 12848, pp. 331–340, 2021.
https://doi.org/10.1007/978-3-030-83527-9_28

discussions with each other in meetings. Thus, slide information and utterances adjacent to the target utterance (i.e., the utterance to be recognized by the ASR engine) may be useful for correcting ASR results. We use a transformer-based machine translation model for implementing this post-editing model. We acknowledge that domain adaptation is a popular method for improving ASR results for speech in specific domains; however, we focus on post-editing in this work because it facilities the incorporation of external information such as slide information, and the method can be applied to the results of arbitrary speech recognition engines.

For evaluation, we prepared a dataset of meeting recordings, consisting of speaker utterances as well as the slides they used. Using the dataset, we evaluated our method in terms of how accurately we can recognize domain-specific words (we focus on proper nouns in this work). As a result, we found that the method can significantly improve the recognition accuracy of domain-specific words. We also found an improvement in the word error rate (WER).

2 Related Work

The demand for recognizing speech in specific domains has been growing more and more in recent years. There are two typical approaches to this problem: domain adaptation and post-editing.

In domain adaptation, which is an active area in speech recognition, domain-specific data are used to adapt acoustic/language models; various techniques, such as deep neural networks, unsupervised learning, and data augmentation, have been investigated [1,10,20]. Domain-specific data have also been used for the rescoring of ASR hypotheses and have shown promising results [4,11].

Post-editing makes corrections to ASR results. Using neural sequence-to-sequence models for post-editing is becoming a common approach to improving ASR performance. Guo et al. [8] proposed a sequence-to-sequence spelling correction model. To train the model, they used a corpus containing pairs of speech recognition results and transcriptions. D'Haro et al. [6] used a machine translation model for correcting ASR results; they verified the method with a robot command dataset and human-human recordings in a tourism queries dataset. Cucu et al. [5] also used a post-editing model for correcting ASR results for their weather forecast data and reported a significant improvement in WER.

Our approach also employs post-editing. The difference from the previous studies is that we utilize slide information and adjacent utterances as inputs for the model of post-editing. We use a transformer-based neural translation model for post-editing, which facilitates the incorporation of such information.

3 Proposed Method

In meetings, most presenters use slides (such as with Microsoft PowerPoint and Keynote) to convey their intent by leveraging illustrations, figures, animation, and so forth. Therefore, it is likely that their speech contains words and phrases

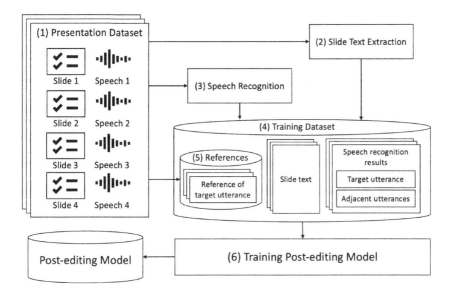

Fig. 1. Process of training post-editing model

found in the slides, providing useful clues for speech recognition. In addition, in a meeting, people hold discussions centering around a presentation topic. Our idea for improving ASR results is to post-edit them with the information that we can obtain from the slides in a presentation and utterances adjacent to a target utterance.

3.1 System Architecture

Figure 1 shows the system architecture for training our post-editing model. The process that is performed at each step is described below.

(1) We first prepare a presentation dataset. The dataset contains meeting recordings that include speech as well as the presentation slides appearing when the speech was made. The dataset contains timestamps regarding when a speech was made as well as when the slides were shown.

(2) To obtain the information of the slides, we extract text from the slides by using our slide text extraction module. For most presentation slides, the XML format is used. Therefore, the module parses the slides with an XML parser in order to obtain a document object model, which is then used to extract the textual content.

(3) We run an ASR engine on the speech data in the dataset in order to obtain ASR results. The ASR engine can be an arbitrary one because we post-edit the ASR results. In the following experiment, we use a cloud-based ASR

Fig. 2. Example of meeting

engine, but other locally-installed software such as Kaldi[1] and Julius[2] can also be used.

(4) By amassing the text of the slides and the ASR results obtained in the previous steps, we prepare a training dataset. The text and slides are aligned by their timestamps so that we can utilize the slide text for post-editing an utterance in question. In addition, by using the timestamp information, we can obtain utterances adjacent to the target utterance, which can also be used as information for post-editing.

(5) We make manual transcriptions of speech data, which are necessary as references for training the post-editing model.

(6) The final step is to train the post-editing model. In the training, we use a transformer-based machine translation model that has been found effective for automatic correction of ASR results [9,16]. We turn to recent encoder-decoder models, such as BART [14] and T5 [18], which can be used to perform conversion between pairs of text. The advantages of such models is the ease of incorporating external information. We can simply concatenate additional textual content to the input so that such information can be taken into account. When incorporating slide information and adjacent utterances, we use N adjacent slides and utterances.

After the post-editing model is trained, the ASR results, the slide text, and the text of adjacent utterances are input to the post-editing model, which outputs the corrected ASR results.

4   Experiments

We first describe how we created our dataset. Then, we show the methods for comparison, including a baseline and variants of our proposed method. We then describe our evaluation metrics followed by the experimental results.

4.1   Data Preparation

For creating the dataset, we collected slides and speech from actual presentations in meetings that we held in our laboratory every week (See Fig. 2). Table 1 shows

---

[1] https://github.com/kaldi-asr/kaldi.
[2] https://github.com/julius-speech/julius.

Table 1. Dataset statistics

No. of meetings	17
No. of presentations	52
No. of utterances	7,548
Average no. of participants per meeting	4.4
Average no. of presentations per meeting	3.1
Average no. of slides per presentation	7.3
Average no. of utterances per presentation	145.2
Average no. of utterances per slide	19.8
Average no. of words per text in slide	12.7
Average no. of words per utterance	16.8

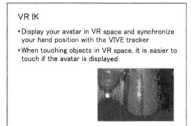

VR IK

• Display your avatar in VR space and synchronize your hand position with the VIVE tracker
• When touching objects in VR space, it is easier to touch if the avatar is displayed

Speaker	Utterance
A	I'm talking about VIRK, well, actually, it was easy to measure the distance to the wall because of the display.
B	So what does it look like?
A	Well, I can see my hands.
B	I thought you could already see them.
C	Ah, it's just that he saw it for the first time, and that we have been working with a robot, not a human.

Fig. 3. Slide being shown (left) and utterances (right) when slide was being presented. Text in slide and utterances were originally in Japanese and were translated by authors.

the dataset statistics. We had the data of 17 meetings, in each of which there were multiple presentations. The number of participants in a presentation was up to five. The topic of the presentations was virtual reality (VR), and each presentation had one presenter.

The meetings were recorded by separate microphones attached to each participant. We divided the speech data into utterances by using pauses lasting over 1000 ms. Then, the split speech data were recognized by the Microsoft Speech-to-Text API[3] to obtain speech recognition results. The number of utterances was 7,548 in total. For the utterances, we created manual transcriptions as references. Note that the utterances here contain those of the presenters as well as those of the other participants in the meetings.

In the meetings, we also recorded timestamps for each slide. These timestamps were synchronized to those of the utterances. Hence, we could align utterances with the slides. The text in the slides was extracted by our slide text extraction module. Figure 3 shows an example of a slide and the utterances made when the slide was being presented to the participants. Note that

---

[3] https://azure.microsoft.com/en-us/services/cognitive-services/speech-to-text/.

the utterances were made by multiple speakers because the participants actively made comments during the presentation of the speaker.

Before training our post-editing model, as pre-processing, we normalized the text (e.g., unifying numeric expressions and full-width/half-width Japanese characters) because text may have inconsistent spellings and may affect the training of a post-editing model.

4.2   Methods for Comparison

We prepared seven methods for comparison. One of the methods was the Simple model. The Simple model is a naive post-editing model, and it does not use slides nor the adjacent utterance information. The other six models were variants of the proposed method. The variants differed in the number of slides/utterances used as inputs to the post-editing model. We decided the maximum number of adjacent slides and utterances to be two ($N = 2$) because slides/utterances that are chronologically far from the current speech are unlikely to contain content related to the speech of the current speaker.

(a) **Simple (Baseline):** For implementing this model, we used a transformer-based encoder-decoder model, BART [14]. BART is a self-supervised denoising auto-encoder model for machine translation and other natural language generation tasks. We used a BART model pretrained with sentences from Japanese Wikipedia (18M sentences)[4]. The Japanese BART model had 12 layers with a hidden size of 1024 and vocabulary size of 32,000. We fine-tuned the model by using our dataset. The fine-tuning was done by using a GPU server (Quadro RTX 6000). The Adam optimizer [12] was used with hyperparameters $\beta_1 = 0.9, \beta_2 = 0.98$, and $\epsilon = 10^{-6}$. The batch size was 32. It took approximately one hour to conduct the training for each fold (we performed cross validation; see Sect. 4.4). This Simple model was trained with the ASR results as input and transcriptions as output. The model does not use adjacent slides and utterances as input.

(b) **Adjacent Slide 1 (AS1):** This is one variant of the proposed method. We used the same model as Simple. The difference is the use of external information in order to improve post-editing. In AS1, in addition to a target utterance, the text of adjacent slides is appended to the input. In this variant, in addition to the current slide, one previous and one subsequent slide are used as additional input to the post-editing model. The input format used to train the model is "target utterance" [SEP] S["text of slides"]. Here, "target utterance" indicates tokenized text of a target utterance. [SEP] indicates a special separator token. "Text of slides" indicates the tokenized text of a slide, and "S[]" is a marker for which the content within the square brackets is slide information.

(c) **Adjacent Slide 2 (AS2):** This variant is the same as (b) but uses two previous and subsequent slides as additional information.

---

[4] https://github.com/utanaka2000/fairseq/blob/japanese_bart_pretrained_model/
JAPANESE_BART_README.md.

(d) **Adjacent Utterance 1 (AU1):** This variant uses adjacent utterances as additional information instead of slide text. In AU1, in addition to a target utterance, the text of adjacent utterances is appended to the input. In addition to the current utterance, one previous and one subsequent utterance are used as additional input to the post-editing model. The input format used to train the model is "target utterance" [SEP] U["adjacent utterances"]. "Text of slides" indicates the tokenized text of a slide, and "S[]" is a marker that indicates that the content within the square brackets is utterance information.

(e) **Adjacent Utterance 2 (AU2):** This variant is the same as (d) but uses two previous and subsequent utterances as additional information.

(f) **Adjacent Slide and Utterance 1 (ASU1):** In addition to the target utterance, this variant uses both the slide text and adjacent utterances. We use one previous and subsequent slide and utterance as additional information. The input format for the model is "target utterance" [SEP] S["text of slides"] U["adjacent utterances"].

(g) **Adjacent Slide and Utterance 2 (ASU2):** This variant is the same as (f) but uses two previous and subsequent slides and utterances.

4.3   Evaluation Metrics

For evaluation, we used WER, which is a common metric for ASR evaluation. In addition to WER, we evaluated whether domain-specific words, especially proper nouns, were correctly recognized. We calculated precision, recall, and F1 score, which are defined as below.

- Precision

$$\frac{\# \text{ of correctly predicted proper nouns}}{\# \text{ of predicted proper nouns}}$$

- Recall

$$\frac{\# \text{ of correctly predicted proper nouns}}{\# \text{ of all proper nouns in the reference}}$$

- F1 score

$$\frac{2 \times \text{Precision} \times \text{Recall}}{\text{Precision} + \text{Recall}}$$

We used MeCab [13], a morphological analyzer for Japanese, together with a dictionary, NEologd [19], to extract proper nouns in the utterances. Out of all 7,548 utterances, the number of utterances that included proper nouns was 1,997. In these utterances, the total number of proper nouns was 2,821, and the average number of proper nouns per utterance was 1.41 with the standard deviation of 0.70. For each utterance containing proper nouns, we calculated the precision, recall, and F1 score. Then, we calculated the average of these values.

Table 2. Evaluation results. Original denotes results of ASR system. (a) is Simple model, which does not use adjacent slides nor adjacent utterances. (b)–(g) use adjacent slides and/or utterances. Asterisks indicate that proposed method's score was significantly better than Simple model ($p < 0.05$). Wilcoxon signed-rank test with Bonferroni's correction was used for statistical testing. All 7,548 utterances were used for evaluating WER, and utterances containing proper nouns (1,997 utterances) were used for calculating precision, recall, and F1 score.

	Post-editing model	WER	Precision	Recall	F1
Original	–	24.28	0.790	0.793	0.792
Baseline	(a) Simple	22.93	0.824	0.820	0.822
Proposed	(b) AS1	22.79*	0.838*	0.839*	0.839*
	(c) AS2	22.79*	0.838*	0.835*	0.837*
	(d) AU1	22.78*	0.829	0.823	0.826
	(e) AU2	22.87	0.829	0.824	0.826
	(f) ASU1	**22.65***	**0.843***	**0.840***	**0.841***
	(g) ASU2	22.72*	0.841*	0.839*	0.840*

Table 3. Example of outputs produced by ASR system and different models (translated from Japanese by authors). Proper nouns are shown in bold.

Model	Transcript
Original (ASR system)	First, I'll talk about **VRIK**; actually, I displayed an **awata** in **ARU** space and synchronized the position of my hand with the **BIKE Tracker**.
Simple	First, I'll talk about **VR**; actually, I displayed a **VR** in **ARU** space and synchronized the position of my hand with the **VR Tracker**.
ASU1	Well, first, I'll talk about **VR**; actually, I displayed an **avatar** in **VR** space and synchronized the position of my hand with the **VIVE Tracker**.
Reference	First, I'll talk about **VRIK**. I displayed an **avatar** in **VR** space and synchronized the position of my hand with the **VIVE Tracker**.

4.4   Results

Since our dataset contains 17 meetings, we performed 17-fold cross validation. In each fold, the test data was one meeting, and the rest of the meetings were used as the training and development data.

As shown in Table 2, we observed that all metrics of the ASU1 model achieved the highest score. Compared with the original ASR system, the ASU1 model achieved 4.9 points of absolute improvement in F1 score and a 6.7% relative improvement in WER. Moreover, it achieved 1.9 points of absolute improvement in F1 score and a 1.2% relative improvement in WER when compared with the

Simple model. The WER and F1 score of the ASU1 model were significantly better than the Simple model (baseline), verifying that utilizing adjacent slides and utterances was effective for post-editing, especially in correcting proper nouns.

The scores of the ASU2 model were lower than those of the ASU1 model. This indicates that it is better to focus on information related to the current point of a speech; the content of slides and utterances that are far from the current point of a speech probably contains irrelevant content, which may lead to erroneous edits. Since AU1, AU2, AS1, and AS2 made improvements and ASU1 and ASU2 performed better than such variants, it suggests that the slide information and the information of adjacent utterances are complementary to each other.

Table 3 shows an example of outputs produced by the ASR system and the Simple and ASU1 models. These utterances were translated from Japanese to English by the authors. The reference text contained some domain-specific words: "VRIK," "avatar," "VR," and "VIVE." We can see that the ASR model could not recognize some of these domain-specific words and produced "awata" (in reference to "avatar"), "ARU" (in reference to "VR"), and "BIKE" (in reference to "VIVE"). Our proposed ASU1 model corrected these misrecognized words accurately.

5 Summary and Future Work

In this study, we proposed a post-editing model for ASR results that utilizes adjacent slides and utterances in presentations. We prepared our own dataset composed of slides and utterances for experiments and evaluated our post-editing model to determine whether adjacent slides and utterances are effective for post-editing ASR results. As a result, our method can significantly improve the recognition accuracy of domain-specific words. We also found an improvement in the word error rate (WER). This leads to our conclusion that the use of adjacent slides and utterances is effective for post-editing of ASR results.

As future work, we would like to extend our use of slide data. In this research, we only used the text in slides, but slides have more information such as images, figures, and animation. We can take advantage of these slide features. We also plan to apply other post-editing models, such as the multi-channel transformer [2,3], in order to improve the post-editing performance.

References

1. Asami, T., Masumura, R., Yamaguchi, Y., Masataki, H., Aono, Y.: Domain adaptation of DNN acoustic models using knowledge distillation. In: Proceedings of ICASSP, pp. 5185–5189. IEEE (2017)
2. Camgoz, N.C., Koller, O., Hadfield, S., Bowden, R.: Multi-channel transformers for multi-articulatory sign language translation. In: Bartoli, A., Fusiello, A. (eds.) ECCV 2020. LNCS, vol. 12538, pp. 301–319. Springer, Cham (2020). https://doi.org/10.1007/978-3-030-66823-5_18
3. Chang, F.J., Radfar, M., Mouchtaris, A., King, B., Kunzmann, S.: End-to-end multi-channel transformer for speech recognition. In: Proceedings of ICASSP, pp. 5884–5888. IEEE (2021)

4. Corona, R., Thomason, J., Mooney, R.: Improving black-box speech recognition using semantic parsing. In: Proceedings of the 8th IJCNLP, pp. 122–127 (2017)

5. Cucu, H., Buzo, A., Besacier, L., Burileanu, C.: Statistical error correction methods for domain-specific ASR systems. In: Dediu, A.-H., Martín-Vide, C., Mitkov, R., Truthe, B. (eds.) SLSP 2013. LNCS (LNAI), vol. 7978, pp. 83–92. Springer, Heidelberg (2013). https://doi.org/10.1007/978-3-642-39593-2_7

6. D'Haro, L.F., Banchs, R.E.: Automatic correction of ASR outputs by using machine translation. In: Proceedings of Interspeech, pp. 3469–3473 (2016)

7. Doan, T.M., Jacquenet, F., Largeron, C., Bernard, M.: A study of text summarization techniques for generating meeting minutes. In: Dalpiaz, F., Zdravkovic, J., Loucopoulos, P. (eds.) RCIS 2020. LNBIP, vol. 385, pp. 522–528. Springer, Cham (2020). https://doi.org/10.1007/978-3-030-50316-1_33

8. Guo, J., Sainath, T.N., Weiss, R.J.: A spelling correction model for end-to-end speech recognition. In: Proceedings of ICASSP, pp. 5651–5655. IEEE (2019)

9. Hrinchuk, O., Popova, M., Ginsburg, B.: Correction of automatic speech recognition with transformer sequence-to-sequence model. In: Proceedings of ICASSP, pp. 7074–7078. IEEE (2020)

10. Iyer, R.M., Ostendorf, M.: Modeling long distance dependence in language: topic mixtures versus dynamic cache models. IEEE Trans. Speech Audio Process. $7(1)$, 30–39 (1999)

11. Jonson, R.: Dialogue context-based re-ranking of ASR hypotheses. In: Proceedings of IEEE 2006 Workshop on SLT, pp. 174–177 (2006)

12. Kingma, D.P., Ba, J.: Adam: a method for stochastic optimization. arXiv preprint arXiv:1412.6980 (2014)

13. Kudo, T.: MeCab: yet another part-of-speech and morphological analyzer (2006). http://mecab.sourceforge.jp

14. Lewis, M., et al.: Bart: denoising sequence-to-sequence pre-training for natural language generation, translation, and comprehension. arXiv preprint arXiv:1910.13461 (2019)

15. Li, M., Zhang, L., Ji, H., Radke, R.J.: Keep meeting summaries on topic: abstractive multi-modal meeting summarization. In: Proceedings of ACL, pp. 2190–2196 (2019)

16. Mani, A., Palaskar, S., Meripo, N.V., Konam, S., Metze, F.: ASR error correction and domain adaptation using machine translation. In: Proceedings of ICASSP, pp. 6344–6348. IEEE (2020)

17. Nagao, K.: Meeting analytics: creative activity support based on knowledge discovery from discussions. In: Proceedings of the 51st Hawaii International Conference on System Sciences (2018)

18. Raffel, C., et al.: Exploring the limits of transfer learning with a unified text-to-text transformer. arXiv preprint arXiv:1910.10683 (2019)

19. Sato, T., Hashimoto, T., Okumura, M.: Implementation of a word segmentation dictionary called mecab-ipadic-NEologd and study on how to use it effectively for information retrieval. In: Proceedings of the Twenty-Three Annual Meeting of the Association for Natural Language Processing, pp. NLP2017-B6. The Association for Natural Language Processing (2017)

20. Sun, S., Zhang, B., Xie, L., Zhang, Y.: An unsupervised deep domain adaptation approach for robust speech recognition. Neurocomputing **257**, 79–87 (2017)

21. Wang, Q., Downey, C., Wan, L., Mansfield, P.A., Moreno, I.L.: Speaker diarization with LSTM. In: Proceedings of ICASSP, pp. 5239–5243. IEEE (2018)

Leveraging Inter-step Dependencies for Information Extraction from Procedural Task Instructions

Nima Nabizadeh[1(✉)], Heiko Wersing[2], and Dorothea Kolossa[1]

[1] Cognitive Signal Processing Group, Ruhr University Bochum, Bochum, Germany
{nima.nabizadeh,dorothea.kolossa}@rub.de
[2] Honda Research Institute Europe GmbH, Offenbach, Germany
heiko.wersing@honda-ri.de

Abstract. Written instructions are among the most prevalent means of transferring procedural knowledge. Hence, enabling computers to obtain information from textual instructions is crucial for future AI agents. Extracting information from a step of a multi-part instruction is usually performed by solely considering the semantic and syntactic information of the step itself. In procedural task instructions, however, there is a sequential dependency across entities throughout the entire task, which would be of value for optimal information extraction. However, conventional language models such as transformers have difficulties processing long text, i.e., the entire instruction text from the first step to the last one, since their scope of attention is limited to a relatively short chunk of text. As a result, the dependencies among the steps of a longer procedure are often overlooked. This paper suggests a BERT-GRU model for leveraging sequential dependencies among all steps in a procedure. We present experiments on annotated datasets of text instructions in two different domains, i.e., repairing electronics and cooking, showing our model's advantage compared to standard transformer models. Moreover, we employ a sequence prediction model to show the correlation between the predictability of tags and the performance benefit achieved by leveraging inter-step dependencies.

Keywords: Information extraction · Procedural task · Instructional text · Long-term dependencies

1 Introduction

Procedural task instructions describe how to perform various tasks to accomplish the desired goals, usually by spelling out the procedure step by step. An instruction is comprised of a list of inter-related sub-tasks, i.e., steps, for achieving a goal that can be cooking a particular dish for dinner or repairing a broken device. Information Extraction (IE) from written instructions has gained more attention in recent years since the number of free instructions on the internet

© Springer Nature Switzerland AG 2021
K. Ekštein et al. (Eds.): TSD 2021, LNAI 12848, pp. 341–353, 2021.
https://doi.org/10.1007/978-3-030-83527-9_29

has increased remarkably, providing a wealth of knowledge in various domains. Moreover, AI systems advanced rapidly in their capabilities, tackling ever more challenging tasks. As a result, equipping ML systems with the ability to interpret instructions originally written for human recipients, and extracting their practical knowledge, would confer immense capabilities and benefits.

The optimal representation structure for this knowledge depends on the application and the intended purpose of the extracted information. In robotics, one popular type of knowledge is commonsense, which is often depicted as relation-entity triples. Commonsense knowledge might contain general facts about objects and actions (*e.g., knives are used for cutting*) [12], object models for grasping and recognition [13,29], or context knowledge about human environments, relating objects to their potential locations [11,26]. The task of commonsense knowledge extraction from text usually begins with tagging the words in particular sentences with corresponding labels for specifying the elements of relation-entity triples among the entities [9,18].

Apart from sentence-level information extraction, researchers also pursued the extraction of major workflow from procedures [1,19,20,36,37]. Extracting the workflow from instructions requires identifying specific entities in the text, for example by word labeling, and then capturing the temporal relationships among those entities, often utilizing graphical models. In both types of tasks, including sentence-level information extraction and extracting the workflows, labeling the words in the text, i.e., token classification, appears to be an inseparable part of the information extraction. Therefore in this paper, we frame our goal of information extraction from instructions as a token-classification task, where various elements, e.g., tools, actions, and objects, need to be mapped to their respective token labels.

The process of token classification regularly begins with generating a high-dimensional representation from the text at each timestep, e.g., each word token, and then classifying the produced embeddings over a set of labels. The transformer-based language models such as BERT [8] constitute a drastic leap forward in generating contextualized word embeddings. These models distinctly improved benchmarks in sequence tagging tasks, such as named entity recognition [34], part-of-speech tagging [31], semantic role labeling [40], and many more. Such massive transformer models are often pre-trained on a considerable amount of data in an unsupervised fashion and can be fine-tuned to various downstream tasks, requiring comparably few labeled examples for information extraction [39].

Still, transformer-based models have difficulties processing long sequences since the self-attention mechanism's computation and memory requirement scales quadratically with the sequence length. Consequently, the span of input text in such models is often truncated to different partitions with a limited number of tokens (e.g., 512 tokens for BERT). As a result, these models cannot capture dependencies among the various chunks of the input text corresponding to the different task steps, and the partitioning could potentially result in the loss of crucial cross-partition information. Such cross-partition dependencies, e.g., among the objects used in the task's various steps, inherently exist in many instructions. For instance, authors in [21] showed that in repair manuals, the next required tool at each step is predictable by only looking at the previously used tools without even processing the text. This is because the order of tools used in a repair task corresponds to the arrangement of partially shared components among different devices of related categories. Their work, utilizing a Variable-order Markov model, revealed that the dependency among the used tools in a repair task could go beyond ten previous steps; however, leveraging the information from ten previous steps often requires processing text with more than 512 tokens. Similar sequential dependencies exist in cooking tasks: special ingredients are usually used in specific orders and with particular kitchenwares that are sometimes predictable by looking at the temporal order of steps. For example, the authors in [32] utilized this property of cooking objects. By training *bi-* and *tri*-gram predictors on cooking recipes, they improved the model's performance in interpreting referring expressions to the kitchenware.

Towards this aim, we simply combine a pre-trained BERT model with a bidirectional recurrent neural network, allowing us to leverage the inter-step information for token classification and consequently, for information extraction. In the following sections, after reviewing the related work in Sect. 2, we introduce the model in Sect. 3. In Sect. 4 we present the details of the datasets, the experiments and the results. Finally, conclusions are drawn, both on our achieved results and on future work, in Sect. 5.

2   Related Work

For the task of information extraction from how-to instructions, one generation of the methods utilized various types of pattern-matching techniques, often by designing domain-specific rules [16,27]. For example, in [12] general dependency parsers were adopted to extract a structure from each sentence and then mapped these structures to the hand-crafted rules for inferring each token's role in the text. In light of recent advancements in deep neural networks for text processing, pattern-matching techniques were substituted by deep text processing models in later works.

Some researchers approached the interpretation of how-to procedures as a relation classification task. In [23] authors suggested a hierarchical bi-directional LSTM for predicting relations such as *is_next_of* or *is_subtask_of* between two steps in wikihow instructions. Their suggested two-level architecture, i.e., word- and step-level, outperformed comparable models based on convolutional neural networks. On similar data, [41] stacked three LSTM networks to encode task titles, step gist (a brief and concise summary of the step), and step explanations for predicting steps' relevance and ordering. Our method resembles these works in the sense that we also produce step-level representations along with the word-level ones. However, their work does not cover word labeling.

Since the introduction of the transformer-based language models, researchers have been fine-tuning pre-trained BERT or its offspring to information extraction tasks [28]. In procedural task instructions, researchers in [18] used BERT to extract commonsense triples from cooking recipes by labeling the words as tools, associated action, and object. Still, this work did not consider the long-term dependencies among different steps of their task and their corresponding entities. In [6,30] a BERT-BiLSTM-CRF model is presented for relation extraction and named entity recognition. The BiLSTM-CRF layer classifies BERT's embeddings over the word labels, leveraging information among different word tokens but not among the different steps of the task.

Another research track aims to reduce the quadratic memory and computational requirements of self-attention mechanism in transformers, using some form of sparse attention pattern [3,4,15]. Among these works, Longformer [3] improved the state-of-the-art in long-document processing and also allows fine-tuning a pre-trained model. Their approach employs attention patterns that combine local and global information, scaling linearly with the sequence length. The most advanced type of attention pattern of Longformer, i.e., global + sliding window, benefits from local attention on each word's immediate neighbors and the global attention on a few pre-selected tokens, e.g., the special classification token [CLS] in BERT. Although Longformer reduces the memory requirement and allows the model to process larger chunks of text, it still has a relatively high complexity of $O(n \times z)$, where n is the input sequence length, and z is the sliding window size. In our paper, we additionally compare our result with the Longformer's performance. One important characteristic of information extraction from instructions is that there are distinct boundaries in the text, i.e., the beginning and the end of each manual, inside which the information needs to be leveraged for the token classification task. However, in common language modeling, such boundaries do not exist in the text, and the long-document processing models attempt to capture as much context as possible.

3   Model

This section describes the proposed method for modeling long-term dependencies among the entities in various steps of procedural task instructions. Our proposed model comprises four general parts: 1 - Generating token-level representations, 2 - Obtaining step-level representations, 3 - Leveraging the obtained step-level information, and 4 - Classifying the final representations.

3.1   Token-Level Representation

The first step of the token classification task is to produce a contextualized embedding for each token by processing the chunk of text that the token exists in it. We used a pre-trained BERT base-cased model for this task. In our experiments, we also tried the Roberta base model [17]; however, it did not give a better result than BERT.

3.2   Step-Level Representation

Leveraging the inter-step dependencies becomes easier in a hierarchical setting by producing step-level representations for the chunks of the token-level representations processed by BERT. We tried multiple approaches for condensing a group of token-level information into a single embedding representing a step, including averaging and min- and max-pooling of the word embeddings. In another experiment, we also used BERT's special sentence classification token, [CLS], for the step-level representation. Since min-pooling yielded a slightly better result, we did not consider the other methods in the later evaluations. Formally, if $v_i = \text{emb}(w_{ij})$ is BERT's embedding of the ith word token in the jth step of the procedure, the pooled representation of the jth step (s_j) becomes

$$s_{j,d} = \min_{i \in [1,T]} v_{i,d}, \tag{1}$$

where minima are computed per dimension d and T is number of tokens in step j.

3.3   Leveraging Step-Level Information

After generating the step-level representations, we need to determine how much information from the past and future steps should be involved in the current step's token classification. To this aim, the step-level embeddings are passed through a bi-directional recurrent layer with Gated Recurrent cells (GRU) [5] that have 256 units in each direction. GRU cells store and filter the information from all steps using their update and reset gate, determining the amount of step-level information that is beneficial for the ultimate classification task.

$$\begin{aligned}
\overrightarrow{h_j} &= \overrightarrow{\text{GRU}}(s_j), j \in [1, L] \\
\overleftarrow{h_j} &= \overleftarrow{\text{GRU}}(s_j), j \in [L, 1]
\end{aligned} \tag{2}$$

In Eq. 2, $\overrightarrow{h_j}$ is the forward hidden state and $\overleftarrow{h_j}$ is the backward hidden state of the GRU at step j, and L is the index of last step in the procedure.

3.4   Classifying the Final Representations

In the last level, we concatenate the token-level representations with the hidden state of the GRU at each step. A fully connected (FC) layer of size 512 performs the final classification over a pre-defined set of labels. The probability distribution for all possible tags of the ith word token in the jth step (P_{ij}) would be derived by:

$$P_{ij} = \text{FC}(\text{emb}(w_{ij}) \oplus \overrightarrow{h_j} \oplus \overleftarrow{h_j}), \tag{3}$$

where $\oplus$ denotes concatenation.

Figure 1 shows the model architecture with two consecutive steps in a repair manual as examples.

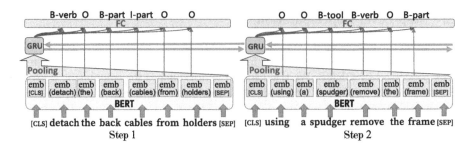

Fig. 1. The complete architecture of the proposed BERT-GRU model with two short, subsequent steps in a repair manual as examples

4   Experiments and Results

In this section, we describe the datasets we used for evaluating the performance of the proposed model and we assess our results in comparison to the baselines.

4.1   Datasets

We evaluate the model of Sect. 3 on two datasets of instructional text: the MyFixit dataset [22], a collection of repair manuals for electronics, and the "recipe named entities" (r_NEs) from the English Recipe Flow Graph Corpus [37], containing annotated cooking recipes.

MyFixit Dataset. The first part of the evaluation is on the human-annotated part of the MyFixit dataset; a semi-structured dataset scraped from the iFixit website. In the MyFixit data, all manuals have been divided into their constituent steps, where at each step, the user typically disassembles one particular device component. The steps of manuals in the "Mac Laptop" category are annotated with the step's required tools, detached component, and the removal verbs, i.e., the verbs that indicate the acts of detachment from the device. These entities are annotated in IOB (Inside–Outside–Beginning) format. In total, 1,497 manuals with 36,973 steps have human annotations. The MyFixit data instructions are often longer than 512 word tokens, with an average size of 944 words per manual and a maximum manual length of 3509 words.

Recipe Named Entities Dataset. The r_NEs dataset was initially introduced in [35], and later extended by [37]. It contains 300 cooking recipes from the Allrecipes UK/Ireland website, which are annotated for recipe named entities. The annotation tags of this dataset include Food (F), Tool (T), Duration (D), Quantity (Q), Action by chef (Ac), Action by food (Af), Action by tool (At), Food state (Sf), and Tool state (St). The instructions in r_NEs are often shorter than those in the MyFixit dataset, with an average size of 132 words per recipe and a maximum size of 444 words.

4.2   Experiments

We implemented the proposed model in PyTorch using the Hugging Face Transformers library [33]. The maximum sequence length per training example for BERT-GRU was chosen as 40 word tokens, which is close to the average number of words at each step for both datasets. Surprisingly, increasing the sequence length did not improve the performance of our model. In contrast, for the baseline BERT model, the maximum sequence length was kept at 512 tokens. As another baseline, we also compare with the performance of the BiLSTM-CRF model [10] previously introduced in [22]. The BiLSTM-CRF receives a stack of FLAIR [2], and GloVe [24] word embeddings as input. For the Longformer, we employed the pretrained model with default hyperparameters, including the maximum sequence length that is 4096 word tokens. We used sliding windows plus global attention on the [CLS] token for the attention pattern.

For the evaluation, we did 10-fold cross-validation, randomly splitting the data into 80% training, 10% hyperparameter tuning (development set), and 10% testing. During training, only the parameters of the GRU and the fully connected layer are learned using the Adam optimizer [14]. The batch size for the BERT and BERT-GRU models is set to 10 instructions, and for the Longformer, the batch size is one. We report the average F1 score of labeling each tag in the test set as the evaluation measure.

Table 1 shows the F1 scores for word labeling in the MyFixit dataset. It can be seen that our model improves the performance for every tag in the MyFixit dataset. Previously, the classification of tokens that represent disassembled objects had yielded the poorest performance among all other tags for both BERT and BiLSTM-CRF models. The reason for this could be the widest variety of word tokens that are tagged with this label in the dataset (for a detailed analysis of dataset labels, please refer to [22]). It can be seen that the BERT-GRU model shows the most F1 score improvement for the disassembled objects.

Table 1. Average F1 score of word labeling for the MyFixit dataset

Model	Tag			Average
	Tool	Removal verb	Disassembled object	
BiLSTM-CRF [10]	0.95	0.95	0.88	0.93
BERT [8]	0.95	0.97	0.90	0.94
Longformer [3]	0.96	0.97	0.96	0.96
BERT-GRU	**0.97**	**0.98**	**0.97**	**0.97**

Similarly, Table 2 shows the performance of BERT-GRU for labeling the r_NEs dataset. We did not include the Longformer in this evaluation, since the instructions' lengths in this dataset are less than BERT's maximum allowed length.

Table 2. The average F1 score of word labeling in recipe named entities (r_NEs) dataset

Model	Tag										Average
	F	T	D	Q	Ac	Ac2	Af	At	Sf	St	
BiLSTM-CRF	0.91	0.88	0.90	0.75	0.91	0.47	0.37	0.25	0.65	0.82	0.69
BERT	0.92	0.89	0.89	0.74	0.93	0.45	0.50	0.17	**0.68**	0.82	0.70
BERT-GRU	0.92	**0.90**	**0.92**	**0.76**	**0.95**	**0.56**	0.50	**0.29**	0.67	**0.86**	**0.73**

From Table 2, we can observe that the BERT-GRU model again improves the average F1 score. The F1 score of most tags except for F (food), Af (action by food) and Sf (food state) is improved. We hypothesize that the BERT-GRU model enhances word labeling performance more for the entities that have more substantial sequential dependencies. In other words, there are some entities with particular tags, e.g., tools, that are predictable better by looking at the previous and next steps. For examining this hypothesis, we developed a sequential model that reflects the predictability of various entities mentioned in the procedure, ignoring the words' semantics.

4.3   Analysis of Sequential Dependencies

The purpose of the model in this section is to illustrate the degree of predictability of different entities in a task, only by looking at the sequential dependencies among the entities in a procedure, but forgoing any additional text-processing. This work resembles event ordering [7], or script learning [25] tasks.

In this experiment, every word token within the entity spans, i.e., each token annotated with a tag except "O" is encoded as a one-hot vector in a vocabulary of entities. Let $\mathcal{V}$ denote the vocabulary of lemmatized entity names. A complete step is represented by a multi-hot vector that sums all entity vectors of the step. The model is trained to predict the probability of observing each entity from $\mathcal{V}$ in a step, based on the sequence of the entities seen in the preceding and following steps. Every instruction has a first step (Start) and a final step (End) that are added to all instructions.

Similar to the model in Sect. 3, the sequential model consists of a bidirectional GRU layer but with state size 128. The output layer has $|\mathcal{V}|$ neurons and a sigmoid activation function that estimates the probability of observing each entity in $\mathcal{V}$. The model takes the multi-hot vector of the next step as the ground truth during training, and its parameters are learned by minimizing the binary cross-entropy loss in Eq. 4 using the Adam optimizer [14] with a learning rate of 0.001.

$$H(y, \hat{y}) = -\frac{1}{|\mathcal{V}|} \sum_{i \in \mathcal{V}} y_i \cdot \log(\hat{y}_i) + (1 - y_i) \cdot \log(1 - \hat{y}_i) \qquad (4)$$

Here, $\hat{y}_i$ denotes the probability of the i-th entity in the model output and y_i is the corresponding target value. Figure 2 illustrates the unrolled graph of the sequential model used for analyzing the predictability of various entities.

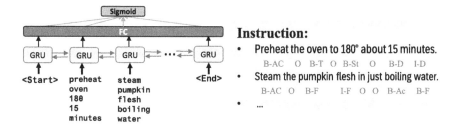

Fig. 2. Unrolled graph of the sequential model for analyzing the predictability of entities in procedural text

For the inference, we sampled entities from the output distribution that have the probability $(\hat{y}_i)$ above a certain threshold. For the evaluation, the datasets are split identical to Sect. 4.2, with the same portions and random seeds. The threshold value and the training stop criteria are determined using the development set. As in Sect. 4.2, we look at the average F1 score of returning correct entities of each step as the evaluation measure.

Table 3 shows the results of this evaluation. Here, the second row shows the F1 score of the predictor model, and the last row shows the difference between the performance of baseline BERT and the BERT-GRU extractor models. It can be seen that the greatest improvement of the BERT-GRU model is achieved for the tags with the highest predictability. There is a strong correlation between the sequential dependencies and the BERT-GRU extraction improvement in the r_NEs dataset (Spearman rank correlation $\rho = 0.81$) and a moderate correlation in the MyFixit dataset ($\rho = 0.5$). This experiment shows that if sequential

Table 3. Comparison between the predictability of different tags and the performance benefit achieved by BERT-GRU over BERT

A: Recipe named entities (r_NEs) dataset

Tags	F	T	D	Q	Ac	Ac2	Af	At	Sf	St
Predictability F1 score	0.55	0.63	0.66	0.33	0.63	0.74	0.43	0.80	0.44	0.65
Extraction Improvement	0.00	0.01	0.03	0.02	0.02	0.11	0.00	0.12	-0.01	0.04

B: MyFixit dataset

Tags	Tool	Removal verb	Disassembled object
Predictability F1 score	0.73	0.70	0.71
Extraction Improvement	0.02	0.01	0.07

dependencies exist among entities in a task, the BERT-GRU model can leverage it for the token classification task. The correlation is better observable in the r_NEs dataset due to the larger verity of labels, while in MyFixit, the low number of label types reduces the power of the test.

5 Conclusion

We propose the BERT-GRU architecture for information extraction from procedural task instructions. The model combines the power of BERT for text processing with the capabilities of recurrent neural networks in sequence prediction. As a result, the GRU layer allows for leveraging long-term dependencies among the entities in text from the beginning to the end of each instruction and vice versa. Our experiments show that limiting the span of the self-attention mechanism to smaller chunks of text and using a GRU layer for transferring long-span dependencies improves the model performance compared to a pure transformer architecture. Our design requires less memory when compared to the transformer-based models for long document processing and does not need a special CUDA kernel.

We additionally employ a sequence prediction model to predict the correct sequence of entities, e.g., the used tools, only by observing the entities mentioned in the surrounding steps and ignoring the full text. This experiment is used to verify our hypothesis that the extraction of entities with higher predictability benefits more from leveraging inter-step dependencies.

Our approach for constructing the step-level representation would be improved if the model could focus more on the specific tokens inside the entity spans that carry the essential information for the IE task. It is possible to partially filter out some words outside the entities and reduce the noise from steps' representations by part-of-speech tagging and syntactic parsing. Transformers with a random attention pattern, similar to a recently published work [38], may also provide the model the chance to attend more strongly to those specific tokens. We intend to incorporate these ideas in our model to make optimal use of any available contextual information while keeping the model efficient in size and computational effort.

References

1. Abend, O., Cohen, S.B., Steedman, M.: Lexical event ordering with an edge-factored model. In: Proceedings of the 2015 Conference of the North American Chapter of the Association for Computational Linguistics: Human Language Technologies, pp. 1161–1171 (2015)
2. Akbik, A., Bergmann, T., Vollgraf, R.: Pooled contextualized embeddings for named entity recognition. In: 2019 Annual Conference of the North American Chapter of the Association for Computational Linguistics, NAACL 2019, pp. 724–728 (2019)
3. Beltagy, I., Peters, M.E., Cohan, A.: Longformer: the long-document transformer. arXiv preprint arXiv:2004.05150 (2020)

4. Child, R., Gray, S., Radford, A., Sutskever, I.: Generating long sequences with sparse transformers. arXiv preprint arXiv:1904.10509 (2019)
5. Cho, K., et al.: Learning phrase representations using RNN encoder-decoder for statistical machine translation. In: Proceedings of the 2014 Conference on Empirical Methods in Natural Language Processing, pp. 1724–1734. ACL (2014)
6. Dai, Z., Wang, X., Ni, P., Li, Y., Li, G., Bai, X.: Named entity recognition using BERT BiLSTM CRF for Chinese electronic health records. In: 2019 12th International Congress on Image and Signal Processing, Biomedical Engineering and Informatics (CISP-BMEI), pp. 1–5. IEEE (2019)
7. Dalvi, B., Tandon, N., Bosselut, A., Yih, W.T., Clark, P.: Everything happens for a reason: discovering the purpose of actions in procedural text. In: Proceedings of the 2019 Conference on Empirical Methods in Natural Language Processing and the 9th International Joint Conference on Natural Language Processing (EMNLP-IJCNLP), pp. 4486–4495 (2019)
8. Devlin, J., Chang, M.W., Lee, K., Toutanova, K.: BERT: pre-training of deep bidirectional transformers for language understanding. arXiv preprint arXiv:1810.04805 (2018)
9. Diwan, N., Batra, D., Bagler, G.: A named entity based approach to model recipes. In: 2020 IEEE 36th International Conference on Data Engineering Workshops (ICDEW), pp. 88–93. IEEE (2020)
10. Huang, Z., Xu, W., Yu, K.: Bidirectional LSTM-CRF models for sequence tagging. CoRR abs/1508.01991 (2015). http://arxiv.org/abs/1508.01991
11. Jebbara, S., Basile, V., Cabrio, E., Cimiano, P.: Extracting common sense knowledge via triple ranking using supervised and unsupervised distributional models. Semant. Web **10**(1), 139–158 (2019)
12. Kaiser, P., Lewis, M., Petrick, R.P., Asfour, T., Steedman, M.: Extracting common sense knowledge from text for robot planning. In: 2014 IEEE International Conference on Robotics and Automation (ICRA), pp. 3749–3756. IEEE (2014)
13. Kehoe, B., Matsukawa, A., Candido, S., Kuffner, J., Goldberg, K.: Cloud-based robot grasping with the google object recognition engine. In: 2013 IEEE International Conference on Robotics and Automation, pp. 4263–4270. IEEE (2013)
14. Kingma, D.P., Ba, J.: Adam: a method for stochastic optimization. In: 3rd International Conference on Learning Representations, ICLR (2015)
15. Kitaev, N., Kaiser, L., Levskaya, A.: Reformer: the efficient transformer. arXiv preprint arXiv:2001.04451 (2020)
16. Lau, T.A., Drews, C., Nichols, J.: Interpreting written how-to instructions. In: IJCAI, pp. 1433–1438 (2009)
17. Liu, Y., et al.: Roberta: a robustly optimized bert pretraining approach. arXiv preprint arXiv:1907.11692 (2019)
18. Losing, V., Fischer, L., Deigmoeller, J.: Extraction of common-sense relations from procedural task instructions using bert. In: Proceedings of the 11th Global Wordnet Conference, pp. 81–90 (2021)
19. Maeta, H., Sasada, T., Mori, S.: A framework for procedural text understanding. In: Proceedings of the 14th International Conference on Parsing Technologies, pp. 50–60 (2015)
20. Malmaud, J., Wagner, E., Chang, N., Murphy, K.: Cooking with semantics. In: Proceedings of the ACL 2014 Workshop on Semantic Parsing, pp. 33–38 (2014)
21. Nabizadeh, N., Heckmann, M., Kolossa, D.: Target-aware prediction of tool usage in sequential repair tasks. In: Nicosia, G., et al. (eds.) LOD 2020. LNCS, vol. 12566, pp. 156–168. Springer, Cham (2020). https://doi.org/10.1007/978-3-030-64580-9_13

22. Nabizadeh, N., Kolossa, D., Heckmann, M.: Myfixit: an annotated dataset, annotation tool, and baseline methods for information extraction from repair manuals. In: Proceedings of Twelfth International Conference on Language Resources and Evaluation (2020)
23. Park, H., Motahari Nezhad, H.R.: Learning procedures from text: codifying how-to procedures in deep neural networks. In: Companion Proceedings of the The Web Conference 2018, pp. 351–358 (2018)
24. Pennington, J., Socher, R., Manning, C.D.: Glove: global vectors for word representation. In: Empirical Methods in Natural Language Processing (EMNLP), pp. 1532–1543 (2014)
25. Pichotta, K., Mooney, R.: Learning statistical scripts with LSTM recurrent neural networks. In: Proceedings of the AAAI Conference on Artificial Intelligence, vol. 30 (2016)
26. Samadi, M., Kollar, T., Veloso, M.: Using the web to interactively learn to find objects. In: Proceedings of the AAAI Conference on Artificial Intelligence, vol. 26 (2012)
27. Schumacher, P., Minor, M., Walter, K., Bergmann, R.: Extraction of procedural knowledge from the web: a comparison of two workflow extraction approaches. In: Proceedings of the 21st International Conference on World Wide Web, pp. 739–747 (2012)
28. Shi, P., Lin, J.: Simple bert models for relation extraction and semantic role labeling. arXiv preprint arXiv:1904.05255 (2019)
29. Tenorth, M., Klank, U., Pangercic, D., Beetz, M.: Web-enabled robots. IEEE Robot. Autom. Mag. 18(2), 58–68 (2011)
30. Tian, C., Zhao, Y., Ren, L.: A Chinese event relation extraction model based on bert. In: 2019 2nd International Conference on Artificial Intelligence and Big Data (ICAIBD), pp. 271–276. IEEE (2019)
31. Tsai, H., Riesa, J., Johnson, M., Arivazhagan, N., Li, X., Archer, A.: Small and practical bert models for sequence labeling. arXiv preprint arXiv:1909.00100 (2019)
32. Whitney, D., Eldon, M., Oberlin, J., Tellex, S.: Interpreting multimodal referring expressions in real time. In: 2016 IEEE International Conference on Robotics and Automation (ICRA), pp. 3331–3338. IEEE (2016)
33. Wolf, T., et al.: Transformers: state-of-the-art natural language processing. In: Proceedings of the 2020 Conference on Empirical Methods in Natural Language Processing: System Demonstrations, pp. 38–45 (2020)
34. Yamada, I., Asai, A., Shindo, H., Takeda, H., Matsumoto, Y.: Luke: deep contextualized entity representations with entity-aware self-attention. arXiv preprint arXiv:2010.01057 (2020)
35. Yamakata, Y., Carroll, J., Mori, S.: A comparison of cooking recipe named entities between Japanese and English. In: Proceedings of the 9th Workshop on Multimedia for Cooking and Eating Activities in conjunction with The 2017 International Joint Conference on Artificial Intelligence, pp. 7–12 (2017)
36. Yamakata, Y., Imahori, S., Maeta, H., Mori, S.: A method for extracting major workflow composed of ingredients, tools, and actions from cooking procedural text. In: 2016 IEEE International Conference on Multimedia & Expo Workshops (ICMEW), pp. 1–6. IEEE (2016)
37. Yamakata, Y., Mori, S., Carroll, J.A.: English recipe flow graph corpus. In: Proceedings of the 12th Language Resources and Evaluation Conference, pp. 5187–5194 (2020)
38. Zaheer, M., et al.: Big bird: transformers for longer sequences. arXiv preprint arXiv:2007.14062 (2020)

39. Zhang, R., et al.: Rapid adaptation of bert for information extraction on domain-specific business documents. arXiv preprint arXiv:2002.01861 (2020)
40. Zhang, Y., Wang, R., Si, L.: Syntax-enhanced self-attention-based semantic role labeling. arXiv preprint arXiv:1910.11204 (2019)
41. Zhou, Y., Shah, J.A., Schockaert, S.: Learning household task knowledge from wikihow descriptions. arXiv preprint arXiv:1909.06414 (2019)

Speech

DNN-Based Semantic Rescoring Models
for Speech Recognition

Irina Illina$^{(\boxtimes)}$ and Dominique Fohr

Université de Lorraine, CNRS, Inria, Loria, 54000 Nancy, France
{irina.illina,dominique.fohr}@loria.fr

Abstract. In this work, we address the problem of improving an automatic speech recognition (ASR) system. We want to efficiently model long-term semantic relations between words and introduce this information through a semantic model. We propose *neural network (NN) semantic models* for rescoring the N-best hypothesis list. These models use two types of representations as part of DNN input features: static word embeddings (from *word2vec*) and dynamic contextual embeddings (from *BERT*). Semantic information is computed thanks to these representations and used in the hypothesis pair comparison mode. We perform experiments on the publicly available dataset TED-LIUM. Clean speech and speech mixed with real noise are experimented, according to our industrial project context. The proposed BERT-based rescoring approach gives a significant improvement of the word error rate (WER) over the ASR system without rescoring semantic models under all experimented conditions and with n-gram and recurrent NN language model (Long Short-Term model, LSTM).

Keywords: Automatic speech recognition · Semantics · Embeddings · BERT

1 Introduction

The performance of ASR is determined by the precision with which spoken words are modeled. Using acoustic and linguistic knowledge, an ASR system generates the best hypothesis corresponding to the recognized sentence. Our work is performed in the context of an industrial project. Due to the constraints of this project, we chose to study only the *N-best list rescoring approaches* to improve recognition accuracy.

State of the art ASR systems only take into account acoustic (acoustic model), lexical, and syntactic information (local n-gram language models (LM)). It may be of interest to incorporate additional knowledge into the decoding process to help ASR tackle not only clean conditions but also mismatched conditions, noisy environments, conditions specific to a particular application, etc. Some studies have attempted to include such information in an ASR. In [5], recognizer score, linguistic analysis, grammar construction, semantic discrimination score are used to rescore the N-best list. [9] indicate that articulation

© Springer Nature Switzerland AG 2021
K. Ekštein et al. (Eds.): TSD 2021, LNAI 12848, pp. 357–370, 2021.
https://doi.org/10.1007/978-3-030-83527-9_30

can provide additional information in rescoring. The use of external knowledge sources such as knowledge graph is proposed in [10]. The authors proposed to utilize the *DBpedia* knowledge graph in form of a connected graph. An N-best rescoring based on a Statistical Language Model or Dynamic Semantic Model is designed in [21].

In this article, we want to introduce semantic information in the ASR system via the N-best rescoring. Previous studies have shown that this information can be useful for ASR rescoring. The integration of semantic frames and target words in the recurrent neural network LM [1], the use of an in-domain LM and a semantic parser [2], the introduction of the semantic grammars with ambiguous context information [6] improve the accuracy of the transcriptions. Several techniques including subword units, adaptive softmax, and knowledge distillation with a large-scale model to train Transformer LMs are proposed in [8]. The authors have shown that the combination of all these techniques can significantly reduce the size of the model and improve the ASR accuracy with N-best rescoring. [14] introduce a deep duel model composed of an LSTM-based encoder followed by fully-connected linear layer and binary classifier. In [15], this approach is improved by employing ensemble encoders, which have powerful encoding capability. [18] adapt BERT [3,23] to sentence scoring, and the left and right representations are mixed with a bidirectional language model.

In our work, we aim to add long-range semantic information to ASR by reevaluating the list of ASR N-best hypotheses. This research work has been carried out in the framework of an industrial project that aimed to perform the ASR in noisy conditions (fighter aircrafts). We are interested in two types of experimental conditions: clean conditions, and the context of noisy test data. These conditions are very common in real applications. We believe that some ASR errors can be corrected by taking into account distant contextual dependencies. In noisy conditions, the acoustic information is less reliable. We hope that in noisy parts of speech, the semantic model might help to remove acoustic ambiguities. The main points of the proposed rescoring approaches are: (a) rescoring the ASR N-best list using two types of continuous semantic models applied to each hypothesis: static word-based *word2vec* [12] and dynamic sentence-based BERT; (b) using a deep NN (DNN) framework on these semantic representations; (c) comparing hypotheses two per two; (d) combining semantic information with the ASR scores of each hypothesis (acoustic and linguistic).

Compared to [18], where only one sentence is taken at inference and masked word prediction is performed with BERT, we use hypothesis pairs and the sentence prediction capability of BERT. Compared to our previous work [11], we employ a more powerful model (BERT) and train a DNN network. Compared to [14], we use an efficient transformer model (BERT) to compare hypotheses.

2   Proposed Methodology

2.1   Introduction

For each of the hypothesized word w of the sentence to recognize, an ASR system provides an acoustic score $P_{ac}(w)$ and a linguistic score $P_{lm}(w)$. The best sentence hypothesis is the one that maximizes the likelihood of the word sequence:

$$\hat{W} = \arg\max_{h_i \in H} \prod_{w \in h_i} P_{ac}(w)^\alpha \cdot P_{lm}(w)^\beta \qquad (1)$$

$\hat{W}$ is the recognized sentence (the end result); w is a hypothesized word; H is the set of N-best hypotheses; h_i is the i-th sentence hypothesis; α and β represent the weights of the acoustic and the language models.

To take into account the semantic information, one powerful solution can be to re-evaluate (*rescore*) the best hypotheses of the ASR system. In [11] we proposed to introduce the semantic probability for each hypothesis $P_{sem}(h)$ to take into account the semantic context of the sentence. This was performed through a definition of context part and possibility zones. In this rescoring approach, $P_{ac}(h)$, $P_{lm}(h)$, and the semantic score $P_{sem}(h)$ are computed separately and *combined* using specific weights α, β and γ (for $P_{sem}(h)$) for each hypothesis:

$$\hat{W} = \arg\max_{h_i \in H} P_{ac}(h_i)^\alpha \cdot P_{lm}(h_i)^\beta \cdot P_{sem}(h_i)^\gamma \qquad (2)$$

In the current work, we propose a DNN-based rescoring models that rescore a pair of ASR hypotheses, one at a time. We use hypothesis pairs to get a tractable size of the DNN input vectors. Each of these pairs is represented by *acoustic, linguistic*, and *semantic* information. In our current approach, semantic information is introduced using two types of semantic representations: *word2vec* or BERT.

2.2   DNN-Based Rescoring Models

The main idea behind our rescoring approach is: (a) to train DNN-based rescoring models with input features extracted from the ASR N-best list of training data; (b) to apply these models to each hypothesis pair of N-best list of a sentence to be recognized and recompute the hypothesis scores; (c) to select as the recognized sentence the hypothesis with the best recomputed score.

As mentioned before, our DNN-based rescoring models rescore *pairs of ASR hypotheses*. For each pair of hypotheses (h_i, h_j), the expected *DNN output* is: 1, if WER of h_i is lower than WER of h_j; otherwise, 0.

The global algorithm of the N-best list rescoring is as follows. From the N-best list of a sentence to recognize, for each hypothesis hi we want to compute the cumulated score $score_{sem}(h_i)$. To perform this, for each hypothesis pair (h_i, h_j) in the N-best list of this sentence:

– We apply the DNN rescoring model and obtain the output value $v_{i,j}$ (between 0 and 1). A value $v_{i,j}$ greather than 0.5 means h_i is better than h_j.
– We update the scores of both hypotheses as:

$$score_{sem}(h_i) \mathrel{+}= v_{i,j}; \quad score_{sem}(h_j) \mathrel{+}= 1 - v_{i,j} \qquad (3)$$

After dealing with all the hypothesis pairs, for each hypothesis h_i, we obtain the cumulated score $score_{sem}(h_i)$ and employ it as a pseudo probability $P_{sem}(h_i)$, combined with the acoustic and linguistic likelihoods according to the Eq. (2).

word2vec-Based Rescoring Approach. For this method, we define the contextual part and the possibility zones of the N-best list [11]. A *context part* consists of the words common to all the N-best hypotheses generated by the ASR for one sentence. We assume that this part captures the semantic information of the topic context of the sentence. We represent the contextual part with the average of the *word2vec* embedding vectors of the words of the contextual part:

$$V_{context} = \sum_{w \in context} V_{word2vec}(w)/nbrw_{context} \qquad (4)$$

where $nbrw_{context}$ is the number of words in the context part, and $V_{word2vec}(w)$ corresponds to a *word2vec* embedding vector w of the contextual part.

The *possibility zones* of a hypothesis are the set of words that do not belong to the contextual part. Possibility zones correspond to the area where we want to find the words to be corrected. We represent the possibility zones of each hypothesis by the average of the *word2vec* embedding vectors of the words of the possibility zones:

$$V_{hi} = \sum_{w \in h_i, w \notin context} V_{word2vec}(w)/nbrw_{poss} \qquad (5)$$

where $nbrw_{poss}$ is the number of words in the possibility zones.

For a pair of hypotheses (h_i, h_j), the input vector for DNN network of the proposed *word2vec*-based rescoring model could contain the following features:

- context part vector $V_{context}$;
- possibility part vector V_{hi} for hypothesis h_i;
- possibility part vector V_{hj} for hypothesis h_j;
- cosine distance between $V_{context}$ and V_{hi};
- cosine distance between $V_{context}$ and V_{hj};
- acoustic score of h_i: $P_{ac}(h_i) = \prod_{w \in h_i} P_{ac}(w)$;
- acoustic score of h_j: $P_{ac}(h_j) = \prod_{w \in h_j} P_{ac}(w)$;
- linguistic score of h_i: $P_{lm}(h_i) = \prod_{w \in h_j} P_{lm}(w)$;
- linguistic score of h_j: $P_{lm}(h_j) = \prod_{w \in h_j} P_{lm}(w)$.

During training, the DNN output is set to 1 (or 0) if the first (or the second) hypothesis of the hypothesis pair achieved the lowest WER. The *main advantage* of the proposed approach is that acoustic, linguistic, and semantic information are trained together thanks to NN-based framework. Then, according to equation

(3), we obtain the cumulated score $score_{sem}(h_i)$. This cumulated score is used as $P_{sem}(h_i)$ with an appropriate weighting factor γ for combination according to Eq. (2). The hypothesis which obtains the greatest combined score is chosen as the recognized sentence. The proposed DNN configuration for the *word2vec*-based rescoring model is presented in the left side of Fig. 1, and corresponds to a neural network with 3 fully connected layers. Fully-connected layers are used to process the hypothesis pair-level representations, presented previously, and a sigmoid activation is used at the last layer to give $v_{i,j}$ in output. We call this rescoring model $word2vec_{sem}$.

BERT-Based Rescoring Approach. BERT is a multi-layer bidirectional transformer encoder that achieves state-of-the-art performance for multiples natural language tasks. The pre-trained BERT model can be fine-tuned using task-specific data [19].

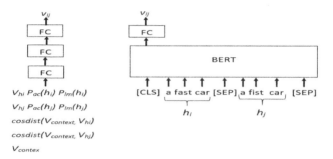

Fig. 1. Architecture of the proposed DNN networks (inference stage): (left) *word2vec*-based rescoring DNN network; (right) BERT-based rescoring DNN network.

As the cosine distance is not meaningful for BERT semantic model [24,25], we cannot use it to compare the hypotheses, as we did with the *word2vec* model. So, we only compute the semantic information at the sentence level, as described below.

In our approach, we propose to take a pre-trained BERT model and fine-tune it using application-specific data. Two methods can be used to fine-tune the BERT: masked LM and next sentence prediction. We are basing our BERT fine-tuning on a task similar to the last one. We fine-tune BERT using only embeddings of CLS tokens (see Fig. 1, right side). We enter a hypothesis pair (h_i, h_j), that we want to compare, to a BERT model. The output is set to 1 (or 0) if the first (or the second) hypothesis achieved the lowest WER. For each hypothesis h_i, we obtain the cumulated score $score_{sem}(h_i)$ (see Eq. (3)) and use it as a pseudo probability $P_{sem}(h_i)$. As for the *word2vec*-based rescoring model, this semantic probability is combined with the acoustic and linguistic likelihoods according to Eq. (2) with an appropriate weighting factor γ (to be optimized). In the end, the hypothesis that obtains the highest combined score is chosen as the recognized sentence. We call this rescoring model $BERT_{sem}$.

3   Experimental Conditions

3.1   Corpus Description

TED-LIUM corpus [4], containing recordings from TED conferences, is used. This corpus is publicly available. Each conference is focused on a particular subject, so the corpus is well suited to our study of exploring the semantic information. The train, development and test partitions provided within the corpus, are employed: 452 hours for training, 8 conferences for development, and 11 conferences for test (see Table 1).

This research work was carried out as *part of an industrial project*. The project concerns the recognition of speech in noisy conditions, more precisely in a *fighter aircraft*. To get closer to real aircraft conditions, we add noise to the development and test sets: noise added at 5 dB and 10 dB Signal-to-Noise Ratio (SNR) of an F-16 from the NOISEX-92 corpus [20]. F-16 Fighting Falcon is a single-engine multirole fighter aircraft. The noise is *not added to the training part*. In addition to that, the proposed approaches are evaluated in clean conditions (development and testing).

Table 1. The statistics of the TED-LIUM dataset.

Data	Nbr. of talks	Nbr. of words	Duration	Nbr. of segments
Train	2,351	4,778,000	452 h	268,000
Development	8	17,783	1 h 36	507
Test	11	27,500	2 h 37	1,155

3.2   Recognition System

The recognition system based on the Kaldi voice recognition toolbox [17] is employed. TDNN (Time Delay Neural Network) [16,22] triphone acoustic models are trained on the training part (without added noise) of TED-LIUM. We perform State-level Minimum Bayes Risk training. The lexicon and LM were provided in the TED-LIUM distribution. The lexicon contains 150k words. We perform recognition using the 4-grams and RNNLM (LSTM) models [11]. We want to explore if using more powerful LM, the proposed rescoring models can improve the ASR. In all experiments, during rescoring, the LM (4-grams or RNNLM) is not modified. The 4-grams LM has 2 million grams. 4-grams and RNNLM were estimated from a textual corpus of 250 million words.

As usual, we employ the development set to choose the best parameter configuration and the test set to evaluate the proposed methods with this best configuration. We compute the WER to measure the performance. It is not possible to calculate the perplexity of our models, because the proposed models only compare two hypotheses. Therefore, in this article, we will not be providing any results related to perplexity. According to our previous work on the semantic model [11], we chose to employ an N-best list of 20 hypotheses. This size of the N-best list is reasonable to generate the pairs of hypotheses and to have a tractable computational load during the training of rescoring models.

3.3   Rescoring Models

During DNN rescoring model training, the hypothesis pairs that get the same WER are not used. During evaluation (with development and test sets), all hypothesis pairs are considered. For all experiments, combination weights are: $\alpha = 1, \beta$ is between 8 and 10. γ is between 80 and 100.

word2vec-**Based Rescoring Model.** We train the *word2vec* model on a text corpus of one billion words extracted from the *OpenWebText* corpus. The size of the generated embedding vector is 300 and the embedding models 700k words. DNN configuration for *word2vec*-based rescoring model is a neural network with 3 fully connected layers (see Fig. 1, left part). The dropout is 30%.

BERT-Based Rescoring Model. We download the pre-trained BERT models provided by Google [19]. We perform the experiments using models with $4, 8$, or 12 transformer layers and the size of the hidden layers is 128, 256, or 512 neurons. In the figures, we note these models as *LxxHyyy*. For instance, *L8H256* means the BERT model with 8 transformer layers and 256 as the size of each hidden layer. Three epochs of fine-tuning are performed with mini-batch size of 32 samples.

4   Experimental Results

4.1   Impact of Hyperparameters

In this section, we investigate the different hyperparameters of the proposed models. As our task concerns noisy conditions, we decided to perform this study on speech in noisy conditions. The hyperparameters are studied on the development set of TED-LIUM and the best values were applied for the final evaluation on the test set. We use 4-grams LM for recognition. During rescoring the LM is not modified.

4.1.1   *word2vec*-Based Rescoring Model

Impact of Training Corpus Size. We utilize three different sizes of the training data: 1 million pairs of hypotheses (corresponding to 100 TED-LIUM talks of the training set), 6.6 million pairs of hypotheses (500 TED-LIUM talks of the training set), and 13.2 million pairs of hypotheses (1000 TED-LIUM talks of the training set). We observe the similar performance of the *word2vec*-based model for all data sizes. For lack of space, we do not give these results in the article and will use 500 training talks.

Impact of Different DNN Input Features. We evaluate three configurations (*config1, config2, config3* in Fig. 2): in *config1*, the DNN input contains only acoustic scores differences, linguistic scores differences and cosine differences for each hypothesis pair (3 features); in *config2*, we utilize the acoustic, linguistic scores, and cosine distances (6 features); *config3* implements all input features, presented in Sect. 2.2 (906 features). Figure 2 shows that *config1* achieves the best performance and *config3* is less efficient than *config1*. Then, embedding features provide no benefit. It is possible, that the relevant acoustic and linguistic data are diluted because the size of the embedding features (900) tends to dominate the size of the acoustic and linguistic features (4). In the following experiments, a *word2vec* rescoring model based on 500 training talks and *config1* will be used.

4.1.2 BERT-Based Rescoring Model

Acoustic and LM probabilities combination (see Eq. (2)) is not used in these experiments. They will be used in the overall evaluation.

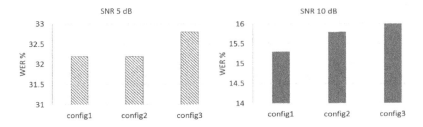

Fig. 2. ASR WER (%) on the TED-LIUM development set for different *word2vec* model configurations (different DNN input features). SNR of 5 and 10 dB. 4-grams LM, training using 100 talks.

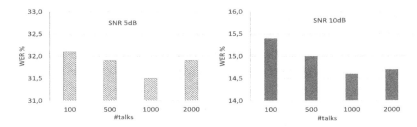

Fig. 3. ASR WER (%) on the TED-LIUM development corpus as function of the amount of BERT fine-tuning data. SNR of 5 dB and 10 dB, 4-grams LM, L8H128 $BERT_{sem}$ model.

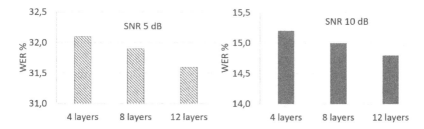

Fig. 4. ASR WER (%) on the TED-LIUM development corpus according to the number of layers for the BERT model. SNR of 5 dB and 10 dB, 4-grams LM, $LxH128\ BERT_{sem}$ model fine-tuned using 1000 training talks.

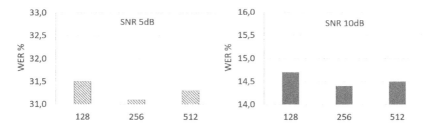

Fig. 5. ASR WER (%) on the TED-LIUM development corpus as function of the size of hidden layer of BERT. SNR of 5 and 10 dB, 4-grams LM, $L12Hyyy\ BERT_{sem}$ fine-tuned on 1000 talks.

Impact of the Training Corpus Size. Figure 3 presents the results on the development corpus using $L8H128\ BERT_{sem}$ rescoring model with different amounts of data, i.e. pairs of N-best hypotheses, for fine-tuning. These results show that increasing the size of the fine-tuning data has a significant effect on the WER: more fine-tuning data is profitable to obtain an efficient BERT-based semantic model up to 1000 talks, beyond a degradation is observed.

Impact of the Number of Hidden Layers. Figure 4 shows the recognition performances as a function of the number of layers of the $BERT_{sem}$ model. The size of the hidden layers is 128 and the size of the fine-tuning data is 1000 talks. Using 12 layers gives the best performance for the two SNR levels. We observe that this parameter plays an important role.

Impact of the Hidden Layers Size. Figure 5 reports the importance of the hidden layers size. We use the $L12Hyyy$ BERT model fine-tuned on 1000 training talks. We may observe a variation according to the size of the hidden layers. The best performance is obtained for a size of 256.

In conclusion, we can say that for the BERT-based rescoring model, it is important to utilize a large enough corpus for fine-tuning the model and to choose a model with many transformer layers. The size of 256 for hidden layers, 12 layers and 1000 talks for fine-tuning seems to be a good compromise. These values will be used in the following.

4.2   Global Results

To further analyze the impact of proposed rescoring models, Table 2 and 3 report the WER for the development and the test sets of TED-LIUM with noise conditions of 10 and 5 dB and with clean speech. In the tables, method *Random* corresponds to the random selection of the recognition result from the N-best list, without the proposed rescoring models. Method *Baseline* corresponds to not using the rescoring models (*standard ASR*). Method *Oracle* represents the maximum performance that can be obtained by searching in the N-best hypotheses: we select the hypothesis which minimizes the WER for each sentence. The other lines of the table display the performance of the proposed approaches. For all experiments, the N-best list of 20 is used.

For the proposed rescoring models, we study 3 configurations:

– Rescoring using only the scores $score_{sem}(h)$ computed with rescoring models as presented in Sect. 2.2 (denoted X_{sem} in Tables). In this case, in equation (2) $\alpha = 0$, $\beta = 0$, and $\gamma = 1$.
– Rescoring using a combination of the score $score_{sem}(h)$, and the acoustic score $P_{ac}(h)$ (denoted X_{sem} *comb. with ac. scores* in Tables). In this case, $score_{sem}(h)$ is used as a pseudo probability and multiplied to the acoustic likelihood with a proper weighting factor γ (to optimize). In this case, $P_{lm}(h)$ is not used, namely, in Eq. (2) $\beta = 0$.
– Rescoring using a combination of the score $score_{sem}(h)$, the acoustic $P_{ac}(h)$, and the linguistic score $P_{lm}(h)$ (X_{sem} *comb. with ac./ling. scores* in Tables).

We present the results only for the best BERT-based rescoring model $L12H256$ fine-tuned using 1000 training talks.

From Table 2, we can observe that $word2vec_{sem}$ rescoring model gives a small but *significant improvement* compared to the baseline system (confidence interval is computed according to the matched-pairs test [7], used for deciding whether the difference in error-rates between two algorithms tested on the same data set is statistically significant). Unsurprisingly, the proposed BERT-based rescoring model outperforms the *word2vec*-based model. It is important to note that in the *word2vec*, the word embeddings are static and a word with multiple meanings is conflated into a single representation. In the BERT model, the word embeddings are dynamic and more powerful, because one word can have several embeddings in the function of the context words.

Adding the acoustic score to the rescoring models (X_{sem} *comb. with ac. scores* in Tables) improves the performance. Indeed, the acoustic score is an important feature and should be taken into account. On the other hand, adding the linguistic score during rescoring gives no improvement compared to the X_{sem} model. We do not present this result in the tables. Using the linguistic and acoustic scores in the BERT rescoring model ($BERT_{sem}$ *comb. with ac./4-grams scores*) brings only small improvement compared to $BERT_{sem}$ *comb. with ac. score*: Google's BERT model, trained on billions of sentences, probably captures the linguistic structure of the language better than an n-gram LM trained on a much smaller corpus.

Table 2. ASR WER (%) on the TED-LIUM development and test sets, SNR of 10 and 5 dB, and no added noise. N-best hypotheses list of 20 hypotheses, **4-grams LM**. L12H256 $BERT_{sem}$ model fine-tuned on 1000 training talks.

Methods/Systems	SNR 5 dB		SNR 10 dB		No added noise	
	Dev	Test	Dev	Test	Dev	Test
Random system	33.5	41.3	16.9	22.9	10.6	12.1
Baseline system	32.7	40.3	15.7	21.1	8.7	8.9
$word2vec_{sem}$	32.1	39.2	15.3	20.6	8.5	8.8
$word2vec_{sem}$ comb with ac. scores	31.8	39.2	15.2	20.5	8.5	8.8
$word2vec_{sem}$ comb.with.ac./4 grams.sc	31.5	38.8	15.2	20.4	8.5	8.8
$BERT_{sem}$	31.1	38.7	14.4	19.8	8.0	8.7
$BERT_{sem}$ comb with ac. scores	**30.6**	**37.9**	14.2	**19.4**	7.9	8.6
$BERT_{sem}$ comb with ac./4 grams sc	**30.6**	**37.9**	**14.1**	**19.4**	**7.8**	**8.5**
Oracle	27.5	33.2	11.2	15.0	5.2	4.7

Table 3. ASR WER (%). N-best hypotheses list of 20 hypotheses. TED-LIUM development and test sets, SNR of 10 and 5 dB, and no added noise. **RNNLM (LSTM)**. L12H256 $BERT_{sem}$ model fine-tuned on 1000 talks.

Methods/Systems	SNR 5 dB		SNR 10 dB		No added noise	
	Dev	Test	Dev	Test	Dev	Test
Random system	29.2	38.4	13.9	20.2	8.9	10.8
Baseline system	28.2	37.1	12.3	17.7	6.6	7.2
$word2vec_{sem}$	27.4	36.3	12.0	17.5	6.6	7.2
$word2vec_{sem}$ comb with ac. scores	27.3	35.6	12.1	17.5	6.8	7.2
$word2vec_{sem}$ comb.with.ac./RNNLM sc	27.3	35.5	12.0	17.4	6.6	7.2
$BERT_{sem}$	27.0	35.9	12.0	17.4	7.1	8.1
$BERT_{sem}$ comb with ac. scores	26.6	**35.3**	11.6	17.1	6.9	7.1
$BERT_{sem}$ comb with ac./RNNLM sc	**26.5**	35.4	**11.5**	**16.9**	**6.0**	**6.6**
Oracle	23.1	30.2	8.3	12.1	3.8	3.5

For BERT-based rescoring results, all improvements are significant compared to the baseline system. On the test set, $BERT_{sem}$ comb. with ac./4-grams scores obtains an absolute improvement of 2.4% for 5 dB (37.9% versus 40.3%), 1.7% for 10 dB (19.4% WER versus 21.1% WER), and 0.4% for clean speech (8.5% versus 8.9%) compared to the baseline system. This corresponds to about of 6% (for 5 dB), 8% (for 10 dB), and 4% (for clean speech) of relative WER improvement.

To better model long-range dependencies of LM, we perform the ASR experiments using a more powerful RNNLM (LSTM). In this case, the RNNLM is used. RNNLM is applied on the ASR word lattices and employed to generate the

N-best list. Table 3 reports the results for the same set of experiments but using RNNLM. We can observe that the proposed rescoring methods give consistent and *significant* improvements, except for clean speech. In clean conditions, only $BERT_{sem}$ *comb. with ac./RNNLM scores* give an improvement compared to the baseline system. Finally, the best system ($BERT_{sem}$ *comb. with ac./RNNLM scores*) on the test set gives relative improvement of about 4.6% for 5 dB (35.4% versus 37.1%), 4.5% for 10 dB (16.9% versus 17.7%), and 8.3% for clean conditions (6.6% versus 7.2%) compared to the baseline system. These improvements are *significant*. We observe also, that in the case of RNNLM, for some cases, the improvements are smaller compared to the 4-grams case. It is possible that RNNLM may reduce the effect of semantic rescoring because RNNLM takes better into account the long-range context dependences.

5   Conclusion

The goal of this article is to improve the ASR using a rescoring of ASR N-best hypotheses. The main idea of the proposed approaches is to model the semantic characteristics of words and their contexts. Two approaches are proposed: *word2vec*-based and BERT-based rescoring models. The information, extracted thanks to these representations, is learned using DNN-based training. Acoustic and linguistic information is integrated too. To evaluate our methodology, the corpus of TED-LIUM conferences is used. The best rescoring system based on BERT, combined with acoustic and linguistic scores, brings between 4% and 8% of relative WER improvement compared to the baseline system. This is true for 4-grams or RNNLMs, and evaluated in clean and noisy conditions. These improvements are statistically significant.

Acknowledgments. The authors thank the DGA (*Direction Générale de l'Armement, part of the French Ministry of Defence*), Thales AVS and Dassault Aviation who are supporting the funding of this study and the "Man-Machine Teaming" scientific program.

References

1. Bayer, A., Riccardi, G.: Semantic language models for automatic speech recognition. In: Proceedings of the IEEE Spoken Language Technology Workshop (SLT) (2014)
2. Corona, R., Thomason, J., Mooney, R.: Improving black-box speech recognition using semantic parsing. In: Proceedings of the The 8th International Joint Conference on Natural Language Processing, pp. 122–127 (2017)
3. Devlin, J., Chang, M.-W., Toutanova, K.: BERT: Pre-training of deep bidirectional trans-formers for language understanding. In: NAACL-HLT (2019)
4. Fernandez, H., Nguyen, H., Ghannay, S., Tomashenko, N., Estève, Y.: TED-LIUM 3: twice as much data and corpus repartition for experiments on speaker adaptation. In: Proceedings of SPECOM, pp. 18–22 (2018)

5. Fuchun P., Roy S., Shahshahani B., Beaufays F.: Search results based N-best hypothesis rescoring with maximum entropy classification. In: ASRU, pp. 422–427 (2013)
6. Gaspers, J., Cimiano, P., Wrede, B.: Semantic parsing of speech using grammars learned with weak supervision. In: Proceedings of the HLT-NAACL, pp. 872–881 (2015)
7. Gillick, L., Cox, S.: Some statistical issues in the comparison of speech recognition algorithms. In: Proceedings of ICASSP, vol. 1, pp. 532–535 (1989)
8. Huang, H., Peng, F.: An empirical study of efficient ASR rescoring with transformers. In: arXiv:1910.11450v1 (2019)
9. Jinyu, L., Tsao, Y., Lee, C.-H.: A study on knowledge source integration for candidate rescoring in automatic speech recognition. In: ICASSP, vol. 1, pp. 837–840 (2005)
10. Kumar, A., Morales, C., Vidal, M.-E., Schmidt, C., Auer, S.: Use of knowledge graph in rescoring the N-best list in automatic speech recognition. arXiv:1705.08018v1 (2017)
11. Level, S., Illina, I., Fohr, D.: Introduction of semantic model to help speech recognition. In: Sojka, P., Kopeček, I., Pala, K., Horák, A. (eds.) TSD 2020. LNCS (LNAI), vol. 12284, pp. 377–385. Springer, Cham (2020). https://doi.org/10.1007/978-3-030-58323-1_41
12. Mikolov, T., Sutskever, I., Chen, K., Corrado, G.S., Dean, J.: Distributed representations of words and phrases and their compositionality. Adv. Neural. Inf. Process. Syst. **26**, 3111–3119 (2013)
13. Mikolov, T., Kombrink, S., Burget, L., Cernocky, J.-H., Khudanpur, S.: Extensions of recurrent neural network language model. In: Proceedings of the ICASSP, pp. 5528–5531 (2011)
14. Ogawa, A., Delcroix, M., Karita, S., Nakatani, T.: Rescoring N-best speech recognition list based on one-on-one hypothesis comparaison using encoder-classifier model. In: Proceedings of the ICASSP (2018)
15. Ogawa, A., Delcroix, M., Karita, S., Nakatani, T.: Improved deep duel model for rescoring N-best speech recognition list using backward LSTMLM and ensemble encoders. In: Proceedings of Interspeech (2019)
16. Peddinti, V., Povey, D., Khudanpur, S.: A time delay neural network architecture for efficient modeling of long temporal contexts. In: Interspeech (2015)
17. Povey D., et al.: The Kaldi speech recognition toolkit. In: Proceedings of IEEE Workshop on Automatic Speech Recognition and Understanding (2011)
18. Shin, J., Lee, Y., Jung, K.: Effective sentence scoring method using BERT for speech recognition. Proc. Mach. Learn. Res. **101**, 1081–1093 (2019)
19. Turc, I., Chang, M.-W., Lee, K., Toutanova, K.: Well-read students learn better: on the importance of pre-training compact models. arXiv:1908.08962v2 (2019)
20. Varga, A., Steeneken, H.: Assessment for automatic speech recognition: II. NOISEX-92: a database and an experiment to study the effect of additive noise on speech recognition systems. Speech Commun. **12**(3), 247–251 (1993)
21. Verhasselt, J., Dercks, H.: N-best list rescoring in speech recognition. J. Acoust. Soc. Am. **128**(6) (2010)
22. Waibel, A., Hanazawa, T., Hinton, G., Shikano, K., Lang, K.J.: Phoneme recognition using time-delay neural networks. IEEE Trans. Acoust. Speech Sig. Process. **37**(3), 328–339 (1989)

23. Wang, A., Cho, K.: BERT has a mouth, and it must speak: BERT as a Markov random field language model. In: Proceedings of the Workshop on Methods for Optimizing and Evaluating Neural Language Generation, pp. 30–36 (2019)
24. https://github.com/hanxiao/bert-as-service/
25. https://github.com/hanxiao/bert-as-service#q-thecosine-similarity-of-two-sentenc e-vectors-is-unreasonably-high-eg-always-08-whats-wrong

Identification of Scandinavian Languages from Speech Using Bottleneck Features and X-Vectors

Petr Cerva[✉], Lukas Mateju, Frantisek Kynych, Jindrich Zdansky, and Jan Nouza

Institute of Information Technologies and Electronics, Technical University of Liberec, Studentska 2, 46117 Liberec, Czech Republic
petr.cerva@tul.cz

Abstract. This work deals with identification of the three main Scandinavian languages (Swedish, Danish and Norwegian) from spoken data. For this purpose, various state-of-the-art approaches are adopted, compared and combined, including i-vectors, deep neural networks (DNNs), bottleneck features (BTNs) as well as x-vectors. The best resulting approaches take advantage of multilingual BTNs and allow us to identify the target languages in speech segments lasting 5 s with a very low error rate around 1%. Therefore, they have many practical applications, such as in systems for transcription of Scandinavian TV and radio programs, where different persons speaking any of the target languages may occur. Within identification of Norwegian, we also focus on an unexplored sub-task of distinguishing between Bokmål and Nynorsk. Our results show that this problem is much harder to solve since these two language variants are acoustically very similar to each other: the best error rate achieved in this case is around 20%.

Keywords: Spoken language identification · Scandinavian languages · x-vectors · Bottleneck features · Deep neural networks

1 Introduction

The Scandinavian category of languages is also referred to as North Germanic. It includes many related languages and dialects, from which the most widely spoken is, by a large margin, the triplet comprising Swedish, Danish and Norwegian. The first language, Swedish, is spoken by 9.2 mil. people and is written in a manner similar to Danish. However, Danish, a native language for 5.6 mil. people, sounds different from Swedish. The third language, Norwegian, spoken by 5.2 mil. people, shares many similarities with the first two languages so that a native Norwegian speaker is able to understand Danish as well as Swedish.

Interestingly, Norwegian has two standards, Bokmål ('Book Tongue') and Nynorsk ('New Norwegian'). The former standard is a Norwegianized variety of

© Springer Nature Switzerland AG 2021
K. Ekštein et al. (Eds.): TSD 2021, LNAI 12848, pp. 371–381, 2021.
https://doi.org/10.1007/978-3-030-83527-9_31

Danish and it is used by almost 85% of citizens in Norway. The latter variant is a language form based on Norwegian dialects (mostly from the west coast) and a puristic opposition to Danish. It is spoken by approximately 15% of the Norwegians.

There exist many differences between Bokmål and Nynorsk. For example, Bokmål has an optional feminine gender, favors noun-heavy expressions, heavily relies on prefixes like an-, be-, het- and the suffix -else, etc. On the contrary, Nynorsk has (more) Western diphthongs, and the feminine gender is compulsory for all feminine words; it favors verbal expressions over noun use, many abstract nouns are shorter, etc.

1.1   Motivation for This Work

In our long-term project we have been developing a multi-lingual broadcast transcription and monitoring platform. One of its modules is devoted for spoken language identification. In this contribution, we focus on the identification of the three main Scandinavian languages. As mentioned above, they are mutually understandable – at least to a certain extent – and it often happens that, e.g., in a Norwegian TV program, a speaker using Swedish or Danish may appear. Some TV stations add subtitles in such situations, some do not. In radio broadcasting, subtitling is not possible at all. For automatic speech transcription, it is necessary to identify those parts of spoken content and assign them the proper language-specific modules. The same must also be done in other automated speech processing services used, e.g., in call centers.

Since these three languages are rather similar on the phonetic level, the identification task is not as easy as in the cases of more distant languages. Its complexity can be compared to, e.g., distinguishing between Czech and Slovak or Spanish and Catalan.

In case of Norwegian, we also investigate the possibility of distinguishing between Bokmål and Nynorsk. The hypothesis for this part of our work is that acoustic differentiation between them is possible, albeit only to a limited extent, on the basis of their origin and other slight differences in spelling and pronunciation. We focus on this sub-tasks since the existence of these two variants significantly complicates ASR of Norwegian due to the above-described lexical differences. The phenomenon of their mixing occurs even more often than for individual Scandinavian languages: each time Norwegian is transcribed, one of the standards must be chosen based on the prevailing features in the spoken content, or sometimes also on the speaker's preference.

2   State-of-the-Art Approaches to LID

Over the years, different advanced modeling techniques have been successfully applied to the task of language identification (LID). One of the more popular approaches is based on the total variability factor analysis; it is known as the i-vector framework [5]. An i-vector maps an utterance to a fixed-length representation. It jointly contains information about the speaker, language, and more.

The computed i-vectors can be classified using, e.g., cosine scoring, multi-class logistic regression, or Gaussian models. The major drawback of the i-vectors is the degraded performance on shorter utterances [15].

Recently, deep learning has also been applied to LID in two major ways, indirect and direct. In the former case, BTNs have become the go-to state-of-the-art features widely used in many systems [9,21] due to their superior performance. These features are usually first extracted from a DNN trained to discriminate individual physical states of a tied-state triphone model, and later used as inputs to either i-vector- [6] or DNN-based systems [10]. The training data (monolingual/multilingual) and the architecture of the BTN extractors (e.g., the placement of the bottleneck layer) have thoroughly been studied [7].

In the latter case, numerous end-to-end DNN-based systems have been proposed. Initially, they were trained to make a frame-level decision based on a frame-level input. At first, a probability vector (with a size corresponding to the number of the target languages) is computed for each frame. After that, the probability vectors are averaged, and the class with the greatest value is chosen as the language spoken in the utterance. In [15], a feed-forward fully connected (FC) DNN outperformed the baseline i-vector system on short utterances. Since then, other complex architectures, including convolutional neural networks [16], time-delay neural networks (TDNNs) [10] or recurrent neural networks (RNNs) have been successfully adopted. The context modeling powers of RNNs have notably been exploited. Long short-term memory (LSTM) RNNs [14], gated recurrent unit RNNs [13] and bidirectional LSTM RNNs [8] have all yielded excellent results.

More recently, the focus of the DNNs has shifted from frame-level decisions to a single representation of the whole reference. In this case, the variable-length input utterance is mapped into a fixed-sized vector. After that, the vector can either be applied directly to produce the final decision or extracted and later used as an input to a classifier (analogically to the i-vectors). The mapping is usually done by integrating the statistics pooling layer [2] or learnable dictionary encoding [3]. Moreover, an attention mechanism has been proposed [12]. In [11], an angular proximity loss function was introduced.

Finally, the x-vector embeddings [23] yielded the best results in the 2017 NIST language recognition evaluation (LRE17) [22]. These embeddings, initially developed for speaker recognition [24], are able to encode various attributes of an input utterance including its length, channel information, speaker's gender, speaking rate or even spoken content [20]. They can be extracted using various DNN architectures with a temporal pooling layer and provide robust representations when a large amount of training data is used. The authors of [23] achieved the best results by using multilingual BTNs, data augmentation, and a discriminating Gaussian classifier.

3   Datasets and Metrics

The dataset of Scandinavian languages used in this work consists of two parts. The first part, the train sub-set, contains 7 h of speech utterances for every target language (i.e., for Bokmål, Nynorsk, Danish and Swedish). The second evaluation part consists of an additional 2,000 utterances (500 for every language) with an average length of 5 s. Note that all of the speakers represented in the training part of the data are different from those in the evaluation set. The acoustic channel is the same for all utterances and corresponds to broadcast news (the Norwegian data comes from the RUNDKAST database [1]).

For evaluation, the error rate (ER) and C_{avg} values are utilized. The first metric is defined as:

$$ER = \frac{F_{\text{utt}}}{N_{\text{utt}}}, \tag{1}$$

where F_{utt} is the number of falsely classified utterances, and N_{utt} is the total number of evaluated utterances. The latter metric is the official metric of the 2015 NIST Language Recognition Evaluation, C_{avg}. Detailed information about this closed set multi-language cost function and its definition can be found in the 2015 LRE Evaluation [26].

4   Baseline i-Vector System and Direct Methods

To set a baseline performance, a 600-dimensional i-vector system has been trained using a full covariance GMM-UBM based system and logistic regression model. Within this training, MFCCs filtered by voice activity detection are employed. Note that this baseline approach follows the lre07 recipe, presented in Kaldi ASR toolkit [19].

The following three DNN architectures represent direct methods and they process the input speech segment frame-by-frame. That means that during the classification phase, a probability vector is obtained for each frame of given utterance (i.e., by doing a forward pass). These vectors are then averaged, and the language with maximum average probability is selected as an output.

4.1   Feed-Forward FC DNN

The first architecture we adopt is a feed-forward FC DNN. This network was trained to directly distinguish between the target languages (i.e., direct method) by using a soft-max layer. During the training, the DNN hyper-parameters are set as follows: five hidden layers, 1,024 neurons per hidden layer, the rectified linear unit (ReLU) activation function, a learning rate of 0.08, and 20 training epochs. The network is trained over filter bank coefficients (FBCs) and the input feature vector is formed as a concatenation of 15 previous frames, current frame, and 15 following frames (i.e., 0.3-s context).

4.2   TDNN Architecture

The next utilized architecture is represented by TDNN, which allows for capturing longer context in the input signal in a non-recursive way. It operates on frames with a temporal context centered on the current frame. The TDNN layers are built on top of the context of the earlier layers, and the final context is thus a sum of the partial ones.

Table 1. Results of various LID approaches on a) the set of three Scandinavian languages and b) the extended set also distinguishing between Bokmål or Nynorsk (i.e., containing four languages).

	3 languages		4 languages	
	$ER[\%]$	$C_{avg}[\%]$	$ER[\%]$	$C_{avg}[\%]$
Logistic regression + i-vectors	15.5	13.3	31.1	20.7
NN-based classifiers over FBCs				
DNN	16.0	10.4	31.3	20.9
TDNN	14.6	12.1	30.3	20.2
FSMN	17.9	13.1	32.2	21.5
TDNN classifier over BTNs				
BTNs-DNN-1	5.9	3.9	20.3	13.5
BTNs-FSMN-17	**0.7**	**0.1**	10.9	7.2
BTNs-stacked-17 from [7]	5.2	2.5	15.9	10.6
FSMN-based x-vectors with width of 512 neurons + DNN classifier				
Over FBCs	3.7	2.7	22.9	15.2
Over BTNs-FSMN-17	1.2	0.2	**10.5**	**7.0**

Our trained TDNN also consists of five hidden layers, each with 1,024 neurons. The input context of each layer required to compute output at one time step includes three preceding inputs, the current input, and three following inputs (from the preceding layer). This setting matches the input context window size of the feed-forward DNN and the remaining hyper-parameters and input features are also unchanged.

4.3 FSMN Architecture

Finally, vectorized feed-forward sequential memory networks (FSMNs) [25] are employed. This topology allows us to eliminate the recursion by adding several memory blocks with trainable weight coefficients into each layer of a standard feed-forward FC DNN. The memory blocks use a tapped-delay line structure to encode the long context information into a fixed-size representation.

This means that, in fact, FSMNs represent a generalization of TDNNs – the delayed inputs to each FSMN layer are weighted by the above-mentioned trainable matrix rather than concatenated in a fixed order as in the case of TDNNs. The important difference is that FSMNs in fact employ the sum pooling over time in order to limit the number of trainable parameters, while TDNNs reduce the computation demands by using sub-sampling, which unfortunately limits the possibility of exploiting time dependencies in the input signal. To match the previous settings, the FSMN has 5 hidden layers, each with 1,024 neurons, and the context is the same as for the TDNN-based classifier.

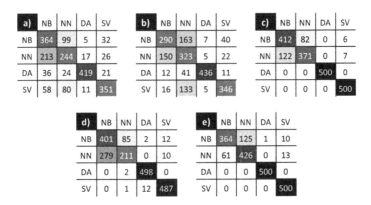

Fig. 1. Confusion matrices of different systems: a) i-vectors, b) TDNN-based classifier over FBCs, c) TDNN-based classifier over multilingual BTNs-FSMN-17, d) x-vectors over FBCs, and e) x-vectors over multilingual BTNs-FSMN-17. The abbreviations NB, NN, DA and SV stand for Bokmål, Nynorsk, Danish and Swedish, respectively.

4.4   Results

The results yielded by the i-vector system are presented in the first row of Table 1 and the results of three NN-based classifiers in its subsequent three rows. We can see that all these methods perform on a similar level and that the lowest ERs are yielded by the TDNN-based classifier. The results also show that the ERs calculated over the extended set including Bokmål or Nynorsk are approximately two times higher than for three languages (e.g., compare 30.3% ER with 14.6% ER for the TDNN classifier). This fact is also evident from the confusion matrices depicted in Fig. 1. Here, matrix a) corresponds to the i-vector system and matrix b) to the TDNN-based architecture, where most of the errors are caused by confusion between Bokmål and Nynorsk (and vice versa). The second most frequent source of errors for the TDNN classifier is Swedish, which is often incorrectly identified as Nynorsk. However, even the ER values achieved for the set of three languages are too high. In the next section, we try to reduce all these errors by employing BTN features.

5   BTN-Based Approaches

Two different types of bottleneck extractors are investigated. The first, monolingual DNN-based type, represents a baseline architecture. The second, advanced multilingual FSMN-based extractor, yielded the best results in an extensive study focused on LID of Slavic languages in [4]. It also corresponds (except the BTN layer) to the architecture that we use to train the multilingual acoustic model for our ASR system. Note that, in both these cases, the BTN features form an input to the TDNN classifier, which yielded the best results in the previous section.

5.1   Monolingual Feed-Forward FC BTNs

The first conventional type of BTN extractor corresponds to a feed-forward FC topology with five hidden layers, the third one being the bottleneck layer. This DNN utilizes 1,024 neurons per hidden layer (39 for the bottleneck layer) and ReLU activation functions (sigmoid for the bottleneck layer). Their input is formed by 39 FBCs computed from 25 ms long frames with frame-shifts of 10 ms each. The DNN operates in the context of 11 frames (five preceding and five following the current frame). Normalization of the input feature vectors is performed within a 1-s window. These BTN features are trained as monolingual to discriminate between physical states (senones) of the tied-state tri-phone acoustic model of 48 Czech phonemes (including models of noises). The speech database used for the training contains 270 h of Czech speech recordings. The resulting basic BTNs are further denoted as BTNs-DNN-1.

5.2   Multilingual FSMN-Based BTNs

The more advanced FSMN-based extractor produces features denotes as BTNs-FSMN-17. Its input is again formed by 39 FBCs computed from 25-ms-long frames, but this time with frame-shifts of 12.5 ms each (the frame-shift is increased to speed up the speech recognition process in our current ASR system, where we utilize this multilingual topology for acoustic modelling). In this case 11 hidden layers are utilized, out of which the tenth one is the BTN layer. The widths of common layers and of the BTN layer are 512 and 39 neurons, respectively. The context of each layer has nine elements, (four preceding and four following the current frame). The extractor is trained as multilingual for 17 languages (including, e.g., Swedish and Norwegian, English and 11 main Slavic languages) using block soft-max [7]. The training database contains 2,300 h of clean speech and 240 h of augmented speech data to improve the robustness to a) reverberation/noise [17] and b) telephone/speech codecs [18].

5.3   Results

Results of this experiment (see the third section in Table 1 show that even the basic monolingual BTNs significantly outperform the best TDNN-based classifier. For example, the ER for four languages is reduced from 31.3% to 20.3%. We can also see that the system with multilingual BTNs-FSMN-17 yields much better results than in the case of BTNs-DNN-1. At the same time, it allows us to distinguish between the triplet of languages with a very low ER of just 0.7% (see the confusion matrix c) in Fig. 1). We can also see that the identification of Bokmål and Nynorsk is also possible, but with a much higher ER of 20% (see the first two rows and columns of the confusion matrix).

For comparison, we also evaluated the extractor of stacked BTNs as presented in [7]. This extractor is trained by its authors for the same number of 17 languages as our FSMN-based extractor, but the representation of individual languages in its training set is different. The obtained results show that these

Table 2. The structure of FSMN-based x-vector extractor.

Layer	Layer context	Total context	Input × Output
FSMN 1	$\ell \pm 4$	9	40×256
FSMN 2	$\ell \pm 4$	17	256×256
FC 1	ℓ	17	$256 \times w$
Pooling	$\ell \pm 20$	57	$(41 \cdot w) \times w$
FC 2	ℓ	57	$w \times w$
Softmax	–	57	$w \times N_{languages}$

Table 3. Results for the FSMN-based x-vectors with cosine distance on the 4-language set for different width of the pooling layer.

Pooling layer's width	20	39	80	128	256	512	1024
$ER[\%]$		23.5	23.2	23.6	23.9	23.9	**22.9**	25.7

80-dimensional BTNs (denoted as BTNs-stacked-17 in Table 1) outperform the monolingual BTNs-DNN-1 but yield significantly worse results than our BTNs-FSMN-17.

6   The Use of X-Vectors

In this work, FSMN-based architecture is used for x-vector extraction. Its structure is described in Table 2, where the symbol ℓ denotes the current frame, on which the temporal context is centered. The pooling layer computes only the means of the frames (omitting the variances) in the context of 41 consecutive frames. In all neurons, the exponential linear unit (ELU) is used as the activation function.

On the input, each frame of the signal is represented by 39 FBCs computed from 25-ms-long frames with frame-shifts of 10 ms each. Table 2 shows that the extractor operates with a total context of 57 frames, which corresponds to 0.57 s. The parameter w stands for the dimensionality of the computed x-vectors. The x-vectors are extracted after the pooling layer. Note that, in training, we utilize a multiclass cross entropy objective function to classify $N_{languages}$.

6.1   Results

In the first experiment, cosine distance is used for classification and the x-vectors are extracted with a frame-shift of 41 frames (i.e., the context size of the pooling layer). The final x-vector representing the whole utterance is then obtained as an average of the shifted vectors. The results for different dimensionality of the x-vectors are presented in Table 3. Here, the lowest ER of 22.9% has been achieved for the size equal to 512 (the other ERs are just slightly worse). However, this ER value is much higher than in the case of the BTNs.

Table 4. Results of the FSMN-based x-vectors with width of 512 neurons on the 4-language set for different NN-based classifiers

Number of hidden layers	0	1	2	3	4	5
$ER[\%]$	22.7	20.5	**20.2**	20.3	21.3	21.7

To decrease it further, several different NN-based classifiers have been employed instead of cosine distance in the next experiment. These classifiers vary in the number of hidden layers used. The width of each layer is always 512 neurons. In this case, the x-vectors are extracted from the input utterance with shifts of one frame. The resulting sequence then forms the input to the classifier (i.e., the x-vectors are not averaged as for the use of the cosine distance). The results are presented in Table 4, where the lowest ER of 20.2% was achieved for 2 hidden layers. This value is by 2.7% lower than for the cosine distance.

The complete results for this setting (i.e., a width of 512 neurons and the DNN-based classier with two hidden layers) are shown on the penultimate row in Table 1 and correspond to the confusion matrix d) in Fig. 1. Here, we can see that the x-vectors over FBCs work well for three languages, but fail in the more difficult four-language task, where Nynorsk is in most cases misclassified as Bokmål.

The comparison of these results with the previous ones shows that x-vectors over FBCs outperform the i-vectors as well as the direct methods over the same features and achieve the ER value similar to basic monolingual BTNs. However, they are not able to outperform BTNs-FSMN-17, which benefits from a very large amount of the multilingual training data. Note that this data does not need to cover all target languages for identification (e.g., Danish is not included in our case).

In the last experiment, x-vectors are extracted using BTNs-FSMN-17 as input features. The results (see the last row in Table 1 and the matrix e) in Fig. 1) imply that this combination yields much better results than the extraction of x-vectors from FBCs. The results are also similar to the ones achieved by the TDNN-based classifier over the same features: the ER is slightly better for the 4-language set but slightly worse for the three languages (compare the sixth row with results in Table 1 with the last one).

7   Conclusions

In this paper, we have focused on the identification of four closely related Scandinavian languages, Swedish, Danish, and two Norwegian variants, Bokmål and Nynorsk. The experimental evaluation performed on short utterances (with an average length of 5 s) has shown that the direct NN-based classifiers trained on standard acoustic features (i.e., FBCs) perform comparably with the baseline i-vector-based system. A detailed analysis of the results in the form of confusion matrices has shown that all these systems generally make mistakes for all languages, with most errors occuring, as expected, between Bokmål and Nynorsk.

The x-vectors extracted using FBCs have improved the results (except the ones between the Norwegian variants) in both ER and C_{avg} by better representing the utterances. Finally, the best results by a large margin are yielded by using multilingual BTNs as input features for the TDNN-based classifier or FSMN-based x-vector extractor. In these cases, the overall achieved ER around 1.0% for Swedish, Danish and Norwegian makes these approaches fully suitable for all applications where multiple Scandinavian languages may occur.

However, the great acoustic similarity between Bokmål and Nynorsk still causes ER around 20% for these two variants of Norwegian and opens a space for further research. A possible solution is to use an ASR with a mixed Bokmål and Nynorsk lexicon (and a language model) and perform the identification of these two variants later, based on their lexical features.

Acknowledgement. This work was supported by the Technology Agency of the Czech Republic (Project No. TO01000027), and by the Student Grant Competition of the Technical University of Liberec under project No. SGS-2019-3017.

References

1. Amdal, I., Strand, O.M., Almberg, J., Svendsen, T.: RUNDKAST: an annotated Norwegian broadcast news speech corpus. In: LREC 2008, Marrakech, Morocco, pp. 1907–1913 (2008)
2. Cai, W., Cai, Z., Liu, W., Wang, X., Li, M.: Insights in-to-end learning scheme for language identification. In: ICASSP 2018, Calgary, AB, Canada, pp. 5209–5213 (2018)
3. Cai, W., Cai, Z., Zhang, X., Wang, X., Li, M.: A novel learnable dictionary encoding layer for end-to-end language identification. In: ICASSP 2018, Calgary, AB, Canada, pp. 5189–5193 (2018)
4. Cerva, P., Mateju, L., Zdansky, J., Safarik, R., Nouza, J.: Identification of related languages from spoken data: moving from off-line to on-line scenario. Comput. Speech Lang. **68**, 101180 (2021)
5. Dehak, N., Torres-Carrasquillo, P.A., Reynolds, D.A., Dehak, R.: Language recognition via i-vectors and dimensionality reduction. In: Interspeech 2011, Florence, Italy, pp. 857–860 (2011)
6. Fer, R., Matejka, P., Grezl, F., Plchot, O., Cernocky, J.: Multilingual bottleneck features for language recognition. In: Interspeech 2015, Dresden, Germany, pp. 389–393 (2015)
7. Fer, R., Matejka, P., Grezl, F., Plchot, O., Vesely, K., Cernocky, J.H.: Multilingually trained bottleneck features in spoken language recognition. Comput. Speech Lang. **46**, 252–267 (2017)
8. Fernando, S., Sethu, V., Ambikairajah, E., Epps, J.: Bidirectional modelling for short duration language identification. In: Interspeech 2017, Stockholm, Sweden, pp. 2809–2813 (2017)
9. Ferrer, L., Lei, Y., McLaren, M., Scheffer, N.: Study of senone-based deep neural network approaches for spoken language recognition. IEEE/ACM Trans. Audio Speech Lang. Process. **24**(1), 105–116 (2016)
10. Garcia-Romero, D., McCree, A.: Stacked long-term TDNN for spoken language recognition. In: Interspeech 2016, San Francisco, CA, USA, pp. 3226–3230 (2016)

11. Gelly, G., Gauvain, J.: Spoken language identification using LSTM-based angular proximity. In: Interspeech 2017, Stockholm, Sweden, pp. 2566–2570 (2017)
12. Geng, W., Wang, W., Zhao, Y., Cai, X., Xu, B.: End-to-end language identification using attention-based recurrent neural networks. In: Interspeech 2016, San Francisco, CA, USA, pp. 2944–2948 (2016)
13. Geng, W., Zhao, Y., Wang, W., Cai, X., Xu, B.: Gating recurrent enhanced memory neural networks on language identification. In: Interspeech 2016, San Francisco, CA, USA, pp. 3280–3284 (2016)
14. Gonzalez-Dominguez, J., Lopez-Moreno, I., Sak, H., Gonzalez-Rodriguez, J., Moreno, P.J.: Automatic language identification using long short-term memory recurrent neural networks. In: Interspeech 2014, Singapore, 14–18 September 2014, pp. 2155–2159 (2014)
15. Lopez-Moreno, I., Gonzalez-Dominguez, J., Plchot, O., Martinez, D., Gonzalez-Rodriguez, J., Moreno, P.J.: Automatic language identification using deep neural networks. In: ICASSP 2014, Florence, Italy, pp. 5337–5341 (2014)
16. Lozano-Diez, A., Zazo-Candil, R., Gonzalez-Dominguez, J., Toledano, D.T., Gonzalez-Rodriguez, J.: An end-to-end approach to language identification in short utterances using convolutional neural networks. In: Interspeech 2015, Dresden, Germany, pp. 403–407 (2015)
17. Malek, J., Zdansky, J.: On practical aspects of multi-condition training based on augmentation for reverberation-/noise-robust speech recognition. In: Ekštein, K. (ed.) TSD 2019. LNCS (LNAI), vol. 11697, pp. 251–263. Springer, Cham (2019). https://doi.org/10.1007/978-3-030-27947-9_21
18. Málek, J., Žďánský, J., Červa, P.: Robust recognition of conversational telephone speech via multi-condition training and data augmentation. In: Sojka, P., Horák, A., Kopeček, I., Pala, K. (eds.) TSD 2018. LNCS (LNAI), vol. 11107, pp. 324–333. Springer, Cham (2018). https://doi.org/10.1007/978-3-030-00794-2_35
19. Povey, D., et al.: The Kaldi speech recognition toolkit. In: ASRU 2011, Waikoloa, HI, USA (2011)
20. Raj, D., Snyder, D., Povey, D., Khudanpur, S.: Probing the information encoded in x-vectors. In: ASRU 2019, Singapore, pp. 726–733 (2019)
21. Richardson, F., Reynolds, D.A., Dehak, N.: Deep neural network approaches to speaker and language recognition. IEEE Sig. Process. Lett. **22**(10), 1671–1675 (2015)
22. Sadjadi, S.O., et al.: The 2017 NIST language recognition evaluation. In: Odyssey 2018, Les Sables d'Olonne, France, pp. 82–89 (2018)
23. Snyder, D., Garcia-Romero, D., McCree, A., Sell, G., Povey, D., Khudanpur, S.: Spoken language recognition using x-vectors. In: Odyssey 2018, Les Sables d'Olonne, France, pp. 105–111 (2018)
24. Snyder, D., Garcia-Romero, D., Sell, G., Povey, D., Khudanpur, S.: X-vectors: robust DNN embeddings for speaker recognition. In: ICASSP 2018, Calgary, AB, Canada, pp. 5329–5333 (2018)
25. Zhang, S., Liu, C., Jiang, H., Wei, S., Dai, L., Hu, Y.: Feedforward sequential memory networks: a new structure to learn long-term dependency. CoRR abs/1512.08301 (2015)
26. Zhao, H., et al.: Results of the 2015 NIST language recognition evaluation. In: Interspeech 2016, San Francisco, CA, USA, pp. 3206–3210 (2016)

LSTM-XL: Attention Enhanced Long-Term Memory for LSTM Cells

Tamás Grósz[(⊠)] and Mikko Kurimo

Department of Signal Processing and Acoustics, Aalto University, Espoo, Finland
{tamas.grosz,mikko.kurimo}@aalto.fi

Abstract. Long Short-Term Memory (LSTM) cells, frequently used in state-of-the-art language models, struggle with long sequences of inputs. One major problem in their design is that they try to summarize long-term information into a single vector, which is difficult. The attention mechanism aims to alleviate this problem by accumulating the relevant outputs more efficiently. One very successful attention-based model is the Transformer; but it also has issues with long sentences. As a solution, the latest version of Transformers incorporates recurrence into the model. The success of these recurrent attention-based models inspired us to revise the LSTM cells by incorporating the attention mechanism. Our goal is to improve their long-term memory by attending to past outputs. The main advantage of our proposed approach is that it directly accesses the stored preceding vectors, making it more effective for long sentences. Using this method, we can also avoid the undesired resetting of the long-term vector by the forget gate. We evaluated our new cells on two speech recognition tasks and found that it is more beneficial to use attention inside the cells than after them.

Keywords: Attention · LSTM · RNNLM · Speech recognition

1 Introduction

Long short-term memory cells (LSTM) [3] are standard solutions for language models (LM) [21]. The main issue with LSTM is that it tries to summarize all essential information of a sentence using a fixed-length long-term vector. This is a hard task; long sequences are especially problematic [1]. One way to address this problem is to compliment them with attention to capture long-range dependencies. Currently, many solutions use an attention layer right after the LSTM cell. This approach allows the LSTM to capture short-term information, and the attention can handle the long-term context. Some go even further by suggesting that the recurrent layers are obsolete, and attention can entirely replace them [20]. However, some recent empirical results show that using recurrent and attention layers together is still a viable solution in the language modeling domain [12]. These findings indicate that LSTMs are not obsolete, and with appropriate modifications, they could once again become state-of-the-art models.

We should mention that Transformers [20] have been proposed as an alternative to recurrent networks. The key idea behind Transformers is the usage of self-attention and the encoder-decoder network structure. Despite their immense success in natural language processing, they still suffer from a problem called context fragmentation. Context fragmentation refers to the fact that the standard Transformer processes separated

K. Ekštein et al. (Eds.): TSD 2021, LNAI 12848, pp. 382–393, 2021.
https://doi.org/10.1007/978-3-030-83527-9_32

fixed-length segments of the input. Consequently, it cannot capture information beyond its current input segment, limiting its effectiveness. As a solution to this problem, the new Transformer-XL introduces recurrence in the model, by reusing the hidden state of the previous segment [5].

Here, we propose a modification of the long-term memory part within an LSTM cell to effectively deal with long-term information. Our work is motivated by Transformer-XL, but instead of introducing recurrence into an attention-based model, we do the opposite. We hypothesize that using attention within the LSTM cell enables it to remember long-term information efficiently, without hindering its short-term memory. To achieve this, we extend the long-term memory part to store a few previous outputs and use attention to accumulate these vectors into a long-term memory vector. This adjustment allows the cell to directly remember a few preceding outputs and focus on the relevant ones. At the same time, these remembered outputs provide long-term information since they are influenced by past outputs, which might not be part of the stored memory anymore. As Transformer-XL inspired our approach, we name our proposed model LSTM-XL.

In our experiments, we compare this new LSTM-XL cell with the standard one. Furthermore, we also use global and local attention after the LSTM layer to see whether it is beneficial to incorporate attention into the cell or not. We show how our method performs as a LM on two speech recognition tasks (a Finnish and a Hungarian one).

Our findings confirm that integrating the attention into the LSTM is helpful when used inside the LM of an ASR system. The empirical results show that this new LSTM-XL cell consistently outperforms the standard one and the local attention-based system. Furthermore, LSTM-XL is on par with global attention (sometimes even better) while using far less memory and computations.

2 Methods

2.1 LSTM

The LSTM is a type of recurrent unit that introduced a memory cell beyond the short time recurrence. This cell gathers long-term information and the three gates (input, output and forget) regulates the flow of information within the unit. Formally, given the current input (x_t), the previous cell memory (c_{t-1}) and output (h_{t-1}) the gate values are calculated as

$$i_t = \sigma(W_i x_t + U_i h_{t-1} + b_i)$$
$$o_t = \sigma(W_o x_t + U_o h_{t-1} + b_o) \tag{1}$$
$$f_t = \sigma(W_f x_t + U_f h_{t-1} + b_f),$$

where σ is the Sigmoid function. Then the new cell memory is estimated by

$$c_t = f_t * c_{t-1} + i_t * tanh(W_c x_{t-1} + U_c h_{t-1} + b_c). \tag{2}$$

Lastly, the output of the LSTM cell for time t can be calculated as $h_t = o_t * tanh(c_t)$. As we can see, the problem with this model is that we are forcing it to summarize all past information into c_t. This process is not an efficient way to accumulate long-term information, especially if we consider that the forget gate could clear this vector, throwing away its content that might be needed in a further step.

2.2 Global and Local Attention

The attention mechanism was proposed to solve a major issue with LSTM, namely that their long-term cell memory is an information bottleneck. C_t is expected to compress all necessary information into a fixed-length vector at each time step, which in case of very long sentences a sub-optimal solution.

Attention deals with past context differently; it calculates importance values for the previous vectors and then produces their weighted average as the current output. This weighting of the past allows the network to recognize the relevant parts of the long-term information. There are many types of attention; here, we used the simple additive attention [1]. Commonly the attention mechanism is described as a three-step process as it consists of the computations of queries, keys, and values. In this terminology, the query is computed from the output of the RNN. The keys, calculated from the stored past outputs, are queried to find the relevant ones. Lastly, value computation produces the final output for the given timestep. When combined with an LSTM layer, global attention scans the past vectors produced by the LSTM cells (h_i) and queries them with the previously calculated vector (s_{t-1}) to get the new attention scores. Formally,

$$a_{t,i} = \text{Softmax}(V\text{score}(h_i, s_{t-1}))$$
$$\text{score}(h_i, s_{t-1}) = \tanh(W([h_i; s_{t-1}])),$$
(3)

where W and V are weight matrices that contain the trainable parameters. The final output can be calculated as $s_t = \sum_{i=0}^{t} a_{t,i} * h_i$. In our case, the query is the previous output (s_{t-1}), and we calculate the alignment between the query and the keys using the score function. Then, we apply V to transform the scores and a softmax function normalizes them. Lastly, the past vectors are multiplied with the attention scores ($a_{t,i}$) and summed to get the final output, hence the name additive attention.

Using all the past hidden vectors (sometimes even the future ones too) in the computation of $a_{t,i}$ is occasionally unrealistic. As can be expected, it is quite computationally heavy for long sentences, To alleviate this, we can restrict the past information, and use only a limited amount of previous outputs ($h_{t-N}, \ldots, h_{t-1}$) in Eq. 3. This constrained version is called local attention, and it is widely used as it speeds up the sequence processing. One risk of using only a limited context is that it might not contain the most relevant past information. Thus local attention is forced to work with less information, usually leading to worse results than the global one.

3   LSTM-XL

We can see that both LSTM and attention-based models have a problem dealing with long-term information. A recently proposed model, Transformer-XL, solves this issue by adding recurrence to the Transformer model and with that modification achieves superior results [5]. This modification inspired us to revise the structure of the LSTM cell.

The main issue is how long-term memory is handled (Eq. 2). Instead of forcing the cell to compress all past information into a single vector, we propose extending it to actually store a few previous (M) outputs and then apply attention to calculate the current c_t. The reason for using only M vectors is simple. Storing a limited amount of past outputs allows better memory usage and obtain speed ups for long utterances. Naturally, this also means that LSTM-XL has an extra hyperparameter (M), that we need to tune. First, we calculate the attention weights for the vectors stored in the long-term memory (indexed by $i \in [t - M - 1, \ldots, t - 2]$);

$$a_t = \text{Softmax}(V\text{score}(h_i, h_{t-1})). \tag{4}$$

An important thing to note here is that we use short-term memory (h_{t-1}) to query the stored keys. Then Eq. 2 is modified so that the new cell state is calculated by using the attention weights;

$$c_t = f_t * \sum_{j=t-M-1}^{t-2} a_j * h_j \\ + i_t * \tanh(W_c x_{t-1} + U_c h_{t-1} + b_c). \tag{5}$$

After this, we use c_t to calculate the output (h_t), then forward only h_t and the new memory to the cell for the next time-step. This process is depicted in Fig. 1.

Instead, we use c_t to calculate h_t, then send it along with the updated memory to the next timestep. Naturally, storing the previous outputs for the calculation of c_t increases the memory consumption of the cell. At the same time, it alleviates the information bottleneck issue. This new model recalculates c_t from the stored M outputs, and attention allows it to focus on the relevant parts. Creating a long-term information vector from the stored outputs is a better solution than just continuously updating it, as in the latter case, it might choose to forget some vital information in a preceding step. The attention-enhanced long-term memory has direct access to the previous M outputs, providing transitive knowledge about older outputs.

One further issue with attention, as noted in [6], is that attention is expected to perform too many tasks at once. In a memory augmented neural LM, the attention layer's output is primarily used to predict the next token. Simultaneously, the vectors are also used to compute the key for the attention mechanism and encode relevant content. The authors of [6] claim that using the attended vectors in such a multipurpose way complicates the training procedure. Their solution, the Key-Value-Predict attention, separates these functions and has outputs for each functionality. LSTM-XL does something similar, as it uses the attention mechanism mainly to extract long-term memory content. The next token's prediction is generated by the cell, which has access to other information (short-term memory and input embedding) besides the attended memory. This gives our proposed method an edge over the standard method. LSTM-XL is not forced to maintain a very constrained long-term memory vector but rather consider multiple previous outputs to construct one. Compared with the approach, which employs attention after the LSTM layer, we can see that LSTM-XL's advantage is that it can handle short- and long-term information separately. In contrast, the attention layer after the LSTM cells usually struggles with this separation, and it has to learn how to find these important pieces of information using a single mechanism.

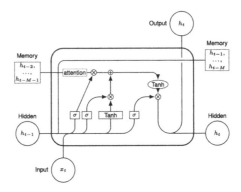

Fig. 1. The new LSTM cell workflow, modifications are highlighted with red color. Note that the long-term memory stores M outputs, while the short-term memory provides the query vector. (Color figure online)

4   Training Corpora

In our **Finnish** experiments, we used the combination of three acoustic corpora, namely the Speecon [9], Speechdat [14] and the Finnish parliamentary data [11]. The acoustic model was trained using this combined data, which contains approximately 1000 h of speech. To test our systems, the YLE broadcast news set was utilized, in the same way as in [16, 18]. The LMs were trained using the Finnish Text Collection [2], which contains 12M sentences and about 143M tokens. We selected 10000 random sentences as development data to tune the hyperparameters such as the learning rate and the number of training epochs.

To test our models in a low-resource setting, we utilized a **Hungarian** corpus. As acoustic data, we used the Szeged Broadcast News corpus [19], which has approximately 30 h of Hungarian speech. 22 h of speech was used for training, 2 h for tuning the hyperparameters and 4 h to test the recognizers. To train the Hungarian LMs the Origo corpus [19] was utilized. This dataset was automatically collected from a Hungarian online news portal and consists of 2.7M sentences, 54.2M tokens in total.

5   Experimental Setup

To build the acoustic models, we followed the chain recipe of Kaldi [13]. The final model was a time-delay neural network (TDNN) trained using the lattice-free maximum mutual information (lf-MMI) criterion. The only difference between the Finnish and Hungarian acoustic models is that the Finnish one is speaker-dependent (uses i-vectors), while the Hungarian model is speaker-independent.

On the LM part, we experimented with n-gram models and recurrent neural networks (RNN). To build the n-grams, the VariKN tool [15] was applied, while the RNNs were trained with TheanoLM [7][1]. In our experiments, we opted for a simple network

---

[1] Source code: https://github.com/GrosyT/theanolm.

structure, just like the one used in [16], which might also be usable as part of an online decoder. The first hidden layer is a linear embedding layer, which has 500 neurons, and it was not pre-trained. The embeddings were feed into the recurrent layer, containing 1500 LSTM or LSTM-XL cells. In the case of LSTM, we also experimented with using global and local attention to accumulate the outputs of the recurrent layer. After some preliminary experiments with LSTM-XL, we determined that the optimal context-size of the long-term memory is 10. Local attention had a context window of 10 vectors, the same as the memory size of LSTM-XL. Afterwards, three highway layers processed the information before the softmax output layer. As regularization, dropout was applied between the highway layers and before the output layer. To train the networks, we minimized the cross-entropy loss with an AdaGrad optimizer. These networks were used to rescore lattices in the second pass of the decoding, after a 3-gram model (VariKN).

5.1 Subword Language Models

Building an automatic speech recognition system for a morphologically rich language is not an easy task. In the case of an English system, we can expect that a large vocabulary would cover the language well. Using large dictionaries for agglutinative languages is not an optimal solution since new, out-of-vocabulary (OOV) words are frequently formed. Besides the high OOV-rate, the training of the LM is also problematic as a large number of words mean that we have a limited amount of training examples for each. Furthermore, it will also slow down the recognition process, especially in the case of a neural LM, as it requires huge input and output layers. As a solution to these problems, subwords have been proposed as new basic units of agglutinative LMs. Switching to them not just reduces the size of the vocabulary, but it also gives better coverage of the possible word forms.

To build a subword LM, first, words in the training text needs to be segmented into these subwords. One option to do this is by creating a rule-based system that is tailored to the specific language and its morphological rules. This approach requires extensive knowledge about the language in question and a lot of effort to create the rules, and a way to handle the OOVs. Alternatively, one can use a statistical method to generate statistical morphemes using a training text. The main advantage of this approach is that it can handle any morphologically rich language, without human interaction and knowledge. Morfessor Baseline [4] is an unsupervised algorithm that performs the segmentation and builds a lexicon of statistical morphs. It minimizes a loss function calculated from the current lexicon and the analyses of the training data, for more details see [4].

In our work, we utilized the Morfessor-2.0 toolkit [17] to perform the segmentation. The hyperparameter α was used to control the focus of the method and obtain different sized lexicons. After the segmentation, the +m+ boundary marking style was used to distinguish between the same morphs in different positions (pre- post-fix and inner morphs). For more information see [16].

388   T. Grósz and M. Kurimo

Table 1. Statistics of the different LM units.

LM unit	Finnish			Hungarian		
	Vocab. size	Unit/word	OOV	Vocab. size	Unit/word	OOV
Word	4110456	1	2.3%	420520	1	9.9%
$\alpha = 0.1$	606106	1.1	0.2%	183803	1.6	0.5%
$\alpha = 0.01$	170368	1.2	0.1%	53667	2.0	0.2%
$\alpha = 0.001$	34521	1.6	0.1%	11562	2.9	0.3%

6 Results

6.1 Cost Analysis

First, we investigate the extra costs of using attention inside or after an LSTM layer. Local attention after LSTM has the same cost as LSTM-XL if the attended context has the same length (M). On the other hand, employing global attention means that we must store all hidden vectors, and the memory cost depends on the length of the token sequence (S). If S is considerably bigger than M, then global attention's memory consumption becomes problematic. This problem is most pressing during the rescoring step when we need to store the past vectors for many paths in the lattice. The majority of the computational cost is spent on processing the keys while computing the queries, and the final value requires only a small amount of computations. It means that the processing time is determined by M for LSTM-XL and by S when global attention is used. This is especially problematic for subword systems, as splitting the words increases the S considerably. The Finnish subword vocabulary that gave the best WER, resulted in an average sequence length of 19.6, while for Hungarian, this was 66.4. So, in theory, to compute the probabilities of an average token sequence in the Finnish data, the global attention performed approximately 1.4-times more computation than LSTM-XL, which had a memory size of 10. This ration was even higher, 3.5 for the Hungarian corpus.

Using the global attention has some practical inconveniences. It took significantly longer to perform the training and the lattice-rescoring steps than with any other model. The fastest solution, of course, was the LSTM approach. Compared to the time that was needed to rescore with LSTM models, we observed only a slight increase when we switched to LSTM-XL or local attention, approximately 12% on average in case of the best Finnish subword units. On the other hand, the global attention was extremely slow, requiring almost twice as much time as simple LSTMs. This considerable gap between the runtimes highlights that global attention is not really a practical solution.

6.2 Finnish

Table 1 summarizes the vocabulary sizes and out-of-vocabulary (OOV) rates of LMs built on different units. As can be seen, even with an enormous word-based vocabulary, we still got a 2.3% OOV on the test set. In contrast, subword vocabularies reduced the percentage of words that cannot be constructed to a minimum. Looking at the morphemes, we can see that prioritizing the lexicon size reduced the number of units drastically. Consequently, words were split into more parts, resulting in longer sequences.

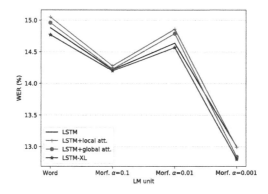

Fig. 2. WER of Finnish RNNLMs using different LM units.

Table 2. Perplexity (PPL), WER and CER values of Finnish RNNLMs using the best LM units. The development set consists of the 10.000 randomly selected sentences from the textual data.

LM unit	LM type	Dev. PPL	Test PPL	WER (%)	CER (%)
Morf. $\alpha = 0.001$	VariKN	229.9	306.7	15.73	4.55
	LSTM	70.6	87.7	13.00	4.23
	LSTM+local att.	86.9	96.4	12.99	4.08
	LSTM+global att.	**65.8**	91.0	**12.84**	4.05
	LSTM-XL	66.0	**83.4**	**12.80**	**3.92**
	Transformer-XL [10]	66.3	**83.2**	12.95	4.23

Figure 2 shows the WERs of the tested approaches for Finnish ASR. The first thing to notice is that using attention (global or local) after the LSTM layer is mostly harmful, except for $\alpha = 0.001$. These findings suggest that using attention-based LM for a morphologically rich language might not be useful as simple LSTM can function better. However, LSTM-XL contradicts this hypothesis and manages to outperform the standard LSTM models consistently. Next, looking at subword RNNLMs, we can see that the WER of all subword choices drops compared to the word units, confirming that morphs are better units for this task.

Comparing local and global attention, it is clear that the global one is far better. LSTM-XL, which uses local attention inside the cell, succeeded in outperforming the conventional LSTM and the LSTM+global att. version. Table 2 summarizes the best results, which were achieved by segmenting the text with $\alpha = 0.001$. In this case, it is crucial to use short-term information (where subwords are part of the current word), and long-term information (the previous words). LSTMs followed by the global attention, and the new LSTM-XL turned out to be better at this than LSTM cells alone. LSTM+global att. achieved 12.84% WER, while LSTM-XL yielded 12.80%, both of which were significantly better than the 13% error rate of the LSTM cell[2]. We also

---

[2] We used a Signed Paired Comparison test (p < 0.001).

compared the character error rates (CER) of the two best approaches, as it is also a meaningful metric for agglutinative languages. Global attention had a CER of 4.05%, while LSTM-XL produced 3.92%, meaning that LSTM-XL managed to reduce the CER by 7.2% relative compared to the simple LSTM. Although that difference between the WERs of two best models is insignificant, the CERs indicate that LSTM-XL managed to choose better subwords. This prompted us to investigate the produced outputs further.

Upon closer inspection, we noticed two common types of mistakes in the ASR output; one related to compound words and the other in the case of double letters. The first issue was basically caused by splitting compound words into separate parts, for example: recognizing "seitsemänkymmentäneljä" (seventy-four) as "seitsemänkymmentäneljä" or merging two words into one by mistake (e.g. "puolitoistavuotiaana" instead of "puolitoista vuotiaana"). The second common problem was caused by double letters, as the ASR system sometimes recognized them as a single letter: the word "tyynnyttää" (calm/soothe) was recognized as "tyynyttää" (with only one n). Out of these two issues, the first one (extra or missing space in the output) was the most severe. If we disregard it, the WER of the LSTM-XL model drops to 11.4% from 12.8%. Naturally, these compound errors plagued the other systems too, ignoring these types of mistakes, the LSTM model achieved 11.7% WER and the LSTM+global att. yielded 11.6%. The second error type (double letters) amounted for approximately 3.5% of the remaining errors. Once we disregarded this category too, the WERs sank even lower; 11.0% for the LSTM-XL, which is significantly better than the 11.2% achieved with global attention and the 11.3% got by using the baseline LSTM.

Lastly, we calculated the perplexities (PPL) of the best subword systems (see Table 2). Naturally, the simple n-gram built by VariKN gave the worst values, and standard LSTM-based RNNLM offered a considerable improvement. What is interesting is that adding attention after the LSTM layer resulted in increased PPL on the test set, although the global attention achieved excellent performance on the validation data. The cause for this might be overfitting, as the textual training and development sets are from a slightly different domain than the spoken test set. Also, it is possible that adding attention after the LSTM cells made it harder for the LM to predict high probabilities for the correct words. Still, it managed to give a lower WER than the network that did not use attention. Lastly, we can see that LSTM-XL reached the lowest PPL on the test set, outperforming all other alternatives.

Naturally, the question arises, how well these models fare compared to Transformers. Although the use of Transformer-based models is out of the scope of this study, a recent article explored their performance for Finnish ASR [10]. Jain et al. trained BERT and Transformer-XL LMs [10], using the same training data as in our experiment, allowing us to compare their results with ours. The best WER achieved by a second-pass rescoring with Transformer-XL on our test set is 12.95%, which is slightly worse than the LSTM-XL's 12.80%.

We should note here that the Transformer-XL model was used to rescore nbest lists instead of directly rescoring the lattices as in [10]. Furthermore, the Transformer-XL had far more parameters than LSTM-XL. Still, this finding reinforces our hope that LSTM-XL is a viable competitor for Transformers.

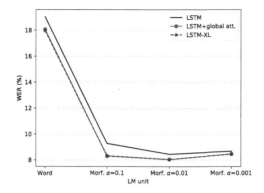

Fig. 3. WER of Hungarian RNNLMs using different LM units.

Table 3. WER of Hungarian RNNLMs using the best subword units.

LM unit	LM type	WER (%)	CER (%)
Morf. $\alpha = 0.01$	VariKN	11.75	2.80
	LSTM	8.44	2.22
	LSTM+global att.	**8.04**	**1.94**
	LSTM-XL	**8.04**	**1.93**

6.3 Hungarian

Next, we tested a low-resource scenario, where we had only limited amount of data to train our system. First, we examined the OOV rates of different Hungarian lexicons (see Table 1). For the word-based system, we restricted the vocabulary to have a reasonable size by using only the most frequent words that appeared at least three times in the training text. This vocabulary had a very high OOV rate, which in turn caused a high recognition error. Naturally, including more words in the dictionary could reduce the OOV rate, but it would also increase the computational cost, so we opted for subwords instead. As can be seen in Table 1, using morphemes as subword units decreased the vocabulary size considerably. The OOV rate of all subword systems was also extremely low compared to the word-based approach. Based on the considerably lower OOV rates, we could expect subword LMs to perform better than the word-based one. Compared to the Finnish data, we can see that we got more units/words and much longer sequences, thus long-term memory becomes more crucial for good results.

Figure 3 presents the results of the Hungarian recognition systems. Here, we did not use local attention as we already saw that it is inferior to the global one. As anticipated, the word-based systems yielded far worse WERs than the subword LMs. Interestingly, the gap between the word-based systems and the subword LMs is quite large, probably because of the limited training data. The optimal α value for this data was 0.01, and the RNNLMs achieved the best results in this case (Table 3). From the results, it is clear that attention enhanced models have a clear advantage over standard LSTM. We can also see that global attention and our proposed cell are on pair (the differences are smaller than 0.1%) and achieve almost the same WERs. Still, LSTM-XL proved to be much faster than the global attention mechanism.

The Hungarian models were also affected by the two typical errors identified in the Finnish ASR case. Assuming that we could entirely solve both issues (compounding words and double letters), the best WER of LSTM-XL would drop to 5.8% (from 8.04%), while LSTM with global attention would yield 5.9% and LSTM could achieve 6.1%. These large possible gains highlight the need for further studies. Our hypothesis is that a simple post-processing system like the one presented in [8] could correct a large portion of these errors, significantly improving the ASR systems. Unfortunately, investigating this theory is out of the scope of this work.

7   Conclusions

In this paper, we proposed the integration of attention into the long-term memory of LSTM cells. We achieved this by replacing the cell memory with a new mechanism. It stores some of the preceding hidden outputs and extracts the relevant information from those by employing attention. This new type of LSTM cell was evaluated as part of the LMs on two ASR tasks. The experimental results show that this modification is beneficial; the proposed LSTM-XL managed to reach the same performance as the composite of LSTM and global attention requiring considerably less memory and computation.

References

1. Bahdanau, D., Cho, K., Bengio, Y.: Neural machine translation by jointly learning to align and translate. In: 3rd International Conference on Learning Representations, ICLR, Conference Track Proceedings, San Diego, CA, USA, 7–9 May 2015 (2015)
2. Bartis, I.: The Helsinki Korp version of the Finnish text collection (1998). http://urn.fi/urn:nbn:fi:lb-2016050207
3. Cheng, J., Dong, L., Lapata, M.: Long short-term memory-networks for machine reading. In: Proceedings of the 2016 Conference on Empirical Methods in Natural Language Processing, pp. 551–561. Association for Computational Linguistics, Austin, Texas, November 2016. https://doi.org/10.18653/v1/D16-1053
4. Creutz, M., Lagus, K.: Unsupervised discovery of morphemes. In: Proceedings of the ACL-02 Workshop on Morphological and Phonological Learning, MPL 2002, vol. 6, pp. 21–30. Association for Computational Linguistics, Stroudsburg, PA, USA (2002). https://doi.org/10.3115/1118647.1118650
5. Dai, Z., Yang, Z., Yang, Y., Carbonell, J., Le, Q., Salakhutdinov, R.: Transformer-XL: attentive language models beyond a fixed-length context. In: Proceedings of the 57th Annual Meeting of the Association for Computational Linguistics, pp. 2978–2988. Association for Computational Linguistics, Florence, Italy, July 2019. https://doi.org/10.18653/v1/P19-1285
6. Daniluk, M., Rocktaschel, T., Welbl, J., Riedel, S.: Frustratingly short attention spans in neural language modeling. In: Proceedings of International Conference on Learning Representations (ICLR), November 2017
7. Enarvi, S., Kurimo, M.: TheanoLM - an extensible toolkit for neural network language modeling. In: Proceedings of Interspeech, Proceedings of the 17th Annual Conference of the International Speech Communication Association (INTERSPEECH), International Speech Communications Association (2016), pp. 3052–3056. https://doi.org/10.21437/Interspeech.2016-2618

8. Guo, J., Sainath, T.N., Weiss, R.J.: A spelling correction model for end-to-end speech recognition. In: ICASSP 2019–2019 IEEE International Conference on Acoustics, Speech and Signal Processing (ICASSP), pp. 5651–5655 (2019). https://doi.org/10.1109/ICASSP.2019.8683745

9. Iskra, D., Grosskopf, B., Marasek, K., van den Heuvel, H., Diehl, F., Kiessling, A.: SPEECON - speech databases for consumer devices: Database specification and validation. In: Proceedings of the Third International Conference on Language Resources and Evaluation (LREC 2002). European Language Resources Association (ELRA), Las Palmas, Canary Islands, Spain, May 2002

10. Jain, A., Rouhe, A., Grönroos, S.A., Kurimo, M.: Finnish ASR with deep transformer models. In: Proceedings of Interspeech (2020)

11. Mansikkaniemi, A., Smit, P., Kurimo, M.: Automatic construction of the Finnish parliament speech corpus. In: Proceedings of Interspeech, pp. 3762–3766 (2017). https://doi.org/10.21437/Interspeech.2017-1115

12. Merity, S.: Single headed attention RNN: stop thinking with your head. ArXiv abs/1911.11423 (2019)

13. Povey, D., et al.: The Kaldi speech recognition toolkit. In: IEEE 2011 Workshop on Automatic Speech Recognition and Understanding. IEEE Signal Processing Society, December 2011

14. Rosti, A., Rämö, A., Saarelainen, T., Yli-Hietanen, J.: SpeechDat Finnish database for the fixed telephone network. Technical report, Tampere University of Technology (1998)

15. Siivola, V., Creutz, M., Kurimo, M.: Morfessor and VariKN machine learning tools for speech and language technology. In: Proceedings of Interspeech, vol. 2007, pp. 185–188, August 2007

16. Smit, P.: Modern subword-based models for automatic speech recognition. Aalto University publication series DOCTORAL DISSERTATIONS; 97/2019, Aalto University (2019)

17. Smit, P., Virpioja, S., Grönroos, S.A., Kurimo, M.: Morfessor 2.0: toolkit for statistical morphological segmentation. In: Proceedings of the Demonstrations at the 14th Conference of the European Chapter of the Association for Computational Linguistics, pp. 21–24. Association for Computational Linguistics, April 2014

18. Smit, P., Virpioja, S., Kurimo, M.: Advances in subword-based HMM-DNN speech recognition across languages. Comput. Speech Lang. **66** (2021)

19. Tóth, L., Grósz, T.: A comparison of deep neural network training methods for large vocabulary speech recognition. In: Habernal, I., Matoušek, V. (eds.) TSD 2013. LNCS (LNAI), vol. 8082, pp. 36–43. Springer, Heidelberg (2013). https://doi.org/10.1007/978-3-642-40585-3_6

20. Vaswani, A.,et al.: Attention is all you need. In: Guyon, I., Luxburg, U.V., Bengio, S., Wallach, H., Fergus, R., Vishwanathan, S., Garnett, R. (eds.) Advances in Neural Information Processing Systems, vol. 30, pp. 5998–6008. Curran Associates, Inc. (2017)

21. Young, T., Hazarika, D., Poria, S., Cambria, E.: Recent trends in deep learning based natural language processing [review article]. IEEE Comput. Intell. Mag . **13**(3), 55–75 (2018). https://doi.org/10.1109/MCI.2018.2840738

Improving RNN-T ASR Performance with Date-Time and Location Awareness

Swayambhu Nath Ray[(⊠)], Soumyajit Mitra, Raghavendra Bilgi, and Sri Garimella

Alexa Speech, Amazon, Bangalore, India
{swayar,ssomit,rrbilgi,srigar}@amazon.com

Abstract. In this paper, we explore the benefits of incorporating context into a Recurrent Neural Network (RNN-T) based Automatic Speech Recognition (ASR) model to improve the speech recognition for virtual assistants. Specifically, we use meta information extracted from the time at which the utterance is spoken and the approximate location information to make ASR context aware. We show that these contextual information, when used individually, improves overall performance by as much as 3.48% relative to the baseline and when the contexts are combined, the model learns complementary features and the recognition improves by 4.62%. On specific domains, these contextual signals show improvements as high as 11.5%, without any significant degradation on others. We ran experiments with models trained on data of sizes 30K hours and 10K hours. We show that the scale of improvement with the 10K hours dataset is much higher than the one obtained with 30K hours dataset. Our results indicate that with limited data to train the ASR model, contextual signals can improve the performance significantly.

Keywords: End-to-end speech recognition · RNN-T · Contextual ASR · Contextual RNN-T

1 Introduction

Humans often use contextual information to disambiguate a particular utterance and understand incoming speech. The contextual information forms prior knowledge which can be the knowledge about a particular user or world knowledge acquired from many users. In use cases such as voice assistants, there is a lot of prior information about ASR queries. Since we train ASR on data collected from multiple users, which have been said at different contexts, some contextual information is implicitly captured and learned by the model. However, effective use of context may further improve ASR performance. For RNN-T based ASR, there is not much prior work in leveraging contextual information such as state of the device, dialog state, time at which the utterance was spoken, and state or country of origin etc.

In this paper, we focus on providing date-time and geographical information to RNN-T based ASR [1,4,5]. We hypothesize that date-time can be an useful signal for ASR as it carries information about type of utterances, e.g. Christmas related queries

---

S. N. Ray, S. Mitra and R. Bilgi—Equal contribution.

© Springer Nature Switzerland AG 2021
K. Ekštein et al. (Eds.): TSD 2021, LNAI 12848, pp. 394–404, 2021.
https://doi.org/10.1007/978-3-030-83527-9_33

will occur frequently in December. Similarly, geographical location may encapsulate user accent, and therefore benefits ASR. We demonstrate the efficacy of explicitly providing contextual information to RNN-T based ASR using up to 30K hours of de-identified queries from smart speakers.

The rest of the paper is organized as follows. We review prior work around the use of context in end-to-end (E2E) ASR in Sect. 2. Our context representation techniques and details of the models are outlined in Sect. 3. Section 4 contains the experimental details. Results and discussions are presented in Sect. 5. Finally, Sect. 6 concludes the paper.

2 Prior Work

In the literature, contextual information has been successfully used in the language modelling. In [11], location and spoken queries are used for on-the-fly adaptation of the n-gram language model. In neural models, context is often supplied either via embeddings or one-hot vectors. In [8], RNN language model is adapted based on input contextual information. Where as in [6], context embeddings are used to control a low-rank transformation of the recurrent layer weight matrix. For document classification task, temporal information has been shown to be useful [13]. Explicitly extracting contextual information also improved the results [10]. In Knowledge graphs, time information is used to learn relation between entities [3]. For RNN-T ASR, using contextual embeddings as input has been recently explored [14]. This work incorporated contextual meta data such as music playing state, and dialog state information to RNN-T encoder. Since dialog state information is available only at the end of first turn (or utterance), it can be applied to improve recognition of subsequent turns (or utterances). Where as, in our work presented here, we explore using context that is applicable to all utterances (Fig. 1).

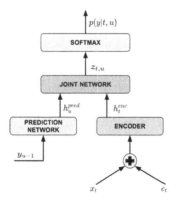

Fig. 1. Incorporating context embeddings into RNN-T ASR. Audio features at each frame are concatenated with e_t which is either per-frame context embeddings or one-hot vector

3   Context Representation with RNN-T

In order to use contextual information such as date-time and geo-location in RNN-T ASR, it first needs to be transformed from textual representation to continuous representation. RNN-T model consists of encoder network h^{enc}, prediction network h_u^{pred} and joint network $z_{t,u}$. A typical RNN-T network follows the following operations:

$$h_t^{enc} = f^{enc}(x_1, x_2, \cdots, x_t) \tag{1}$$

$$h_u^{pred} = f^{pred}(y_1^{pred}, \cdots, y_{u-1}^{pred}) \tag{2}$$

$$z_{t,u} = f^{join}(h_t^{enc}, h_u^{pred}) \tag{3}$$

$$P(y_u|x_1, \cdots, x_t, y_1, \cdots, y_{u-1}) = softmax(z_{t,u}) \tag{4}$$

where $x_1 \cdots x_t$ are the audio feature inputs to the RNN-T encoder and $y_1 \cdots y_u$ are the corresponding label sequence.

We extend this by adding contextual information to the encoder network by concatenating feature vector x with context vector e. Context vector e can be derived or presented to the network in multiple ways, such as:

1. one-hot representation of the context (o)
2. transforming context (c) using a contextual embedding matrix W
3. feature engineered constant sized vectors (f).

The advantage of representing context as embedding is that it provides the flexibility of combining multiple contextual signals in a lower dimensional space. In our experiments, we use 64 dimensional contextual embeddings.

$$h_{ctx_{one-hot}}^{enc} = f^{enc}(x; o) \tag{5}$$

$$h_{ctx_{embed}}^{enc} = f^{enc}(x; Wc) \tag{6}$$

$$h_{ctx_{feature-engg}}^{enc} = f^{enc}(x; f) \tag{7}$$

3.1   Date Time as Context

A typical date-time information in our dataset looks like - $2020 - 01 - 01T13 : 21$. We extract the following information from this datum:

Hour - 13, Weekday - Wednesday, Week No. - 1, Month - 1

In order to bias RNN-T recognition with temporal information, we consider two methods to convert the above information into a continuous vector representation.

Embedding Representation. In this method, we learn embedding matrices for hour (24), weekday (7), week number (53) and month (12), where the numbers in the bracket indicate the maximum number of embedding vectors we use for representing corresponding information. These contexts are passed through an embedding layer to generate contextual vectors which are then averaged to represent the complete date-time information. This averaged embedding is used as biasing signal within RNN-T, and is learnt along with RNN-T model training. Assuming embedding vectors of hour, weekday, week number, and month to be h_t, wd_t, wn_t and m_t respectively, then

$$e_t = (h_t + wd_t + wn_t + m_t)/4 \tag{8}$$

In the rest of the paper, this embedding method is addressed as TimeEmbeddingLookUp

Positional Encoding. The above embedding approach (Sect. 3.1) does not explicitly encode the temporal proximity and cyclical nature of time information. To capture this, we represent the date-time information using an 8-dimensional feature-engineered vector with the following entries:

$$\begin{bmatrix} sin(\dfrac{2\pi.hour}{24}), & cos(\dfrac{2\pi.hour}{24}) \\ sin(\dfrac{2\pi.weekday}{7}), & cos(\dfrac{2\pi.weekday}{7}) \\ sin(\dfrac{2\pi.weeknum}{53}), & cos(\dfrac{2\pi.weeknum}{53}) \\ sin(\dfrac{2\pi.month}{12}), & cos(\dfrac{2\pi.month}{12}) \end{bmatrix}$$

The above representation can clearly express the repetitive behaviour of temporal information. In the following sections, this embedding method is referred to as TimePositionalEncoding.

3.2 Location as Context

In this work, we used location information up to the state level in the US. The state information for utterances are collected from de-identified user specified information. Given that accent typically varies across the US states, location information is a strong signal to adapt the model to learn these variations. Instead of using all available location information, we clustered utterances with location information to form 20 clusters. The number of clusters are decided empirically with the objective of avoiding multiple centres getting mapped to the same state. Approximate geo-location information available from latlong[1] is used to obtain the state-level geo-location, and euclidean distance is used as the distance metric to learn the cluster centroids. With this we got 20 cluster centroids which are closer in distance. The clusters also include locations outside the US, which correspond to small percentage of users using the devices outside the main region. For some utterances, the location information is not available and we assign it to None cluster. We explored transforming geo-location using an embedding layer (GeoEmbeddingLookUp), and also encoding it as a one-hot vector (GeoOneHot) to bias the RNN-T model.

---

[1] https://www.latlong.net/category/states-236-14.html.

3.3   Combination of Context

We also ran experiments combining date-time and location information to bias the RNN-T search. We expect the date-time and location together to be a much stronger signal than either individual signals alone. We use embedding approach to combine the context (CombinedTimeGeo), where the embedding matrix is learned to map combined context into lower dimension contextual embedding vector.

4   Data and Experimental Setup

4.1   Datasets

For our experiments, we used de-identified human-labelled speech data collected from queries to voice controlled far-field devices. The dataset was randomly split into train, dev and eval. The training set comprised of 30K hours of de-identified human-labelled US English recordings. Each recording includes meta information such as time stamp and optional US state from which it originated. The eval set consists of approximately 100 hours of generic utterances. We also evaluate our models on a communication specific test set of 23 hours of utterances. Both the evaluation test sets are mutually exclusive. We refer to the former as Eval test set and the latter as Comms test set.

4.2   Experimental Setup

Full Resource RNN-T ASR. The baseline RNN-T model consists of 5 encoder layers of 1024 hidden units, with a final layer output dimension of 512. The prediction network has an embedding layer of 512 units, 2 LSTM layers of 1024 units, and a final output dimension 512. The joint network is a feed forward network of 512 hidden units and a final output dimension of 4001. The 4001 dimensional output, corresponds to the number of subword tokens, is passed through a final softmax layer. The subword vocabulary was generated using the byte pair encoding algorithm [12].

The contextual RNN-T ASR model has an additional embedding layer generating embedded representation of 64 dimensions which are appended to the input of the encoder at every time step. The two exceptions being:

1. the positional time encoding has an 8 dimensional context vector
2. one-hot geographical information has a 21 dimensional context vector

All the models are trained on 30K hours of training data.

Low Resource RNN-T ASR. We also trained both the baseline and contextual models on 10K hours of data. The main motivation for this study is to analyze the effect of context in the low training data regime. In order to prevent over-fitting, we scaled down the number of parameters of the models. Number of hidden units of both the encoder and decoder layers were reduced to 760. The feed-forward joint network is also removed. The encoder and decoder outputs are summed and provided as an input to the softmax layer. All other specifications are kept consistent with the full-resource models.

Both full-resource and low-resource models use a 64-dimensional log filter bank energy features computed over 25 ms window with 10 ms shift. Each feature vector is stacked with 2 frames to the left and down sampled to a 30 ms frame rate. We also augment the acoustic training data with SpecAugment [9] to improve the robustness. All models are trained using the Adam optimizer [7], with a learning rate schedule including an initial linear warm-up phase, a constant phase, and an exponential decay phase [2]. These hyper-parameters are not specifically tuned for this work.

5   Results and Discussion

5.1   Overall WER Comparison

Table 1 shows the overall Relative Word Error Rate Reduction (WERR) with respect to the baseline RNN-T model without context. Performance of our baseline system is below 10% WER absolute. The magnitude of improvement on Comms test set is more than that of Eval test set, which signifies that these contextual signals are more favourable for communication specific utterances. Overall, incorporating geo-location information as one-hot provides the maximum WERR of 3.48%. Based on the performance, we chose TimeEmbeddingLookUp and GeoOneHot models for further analyses.

Table 1. Relative WERRs of full resource contextual models w.r.t baseline

Model	Eval	Comms	#params
Baseline	–	–	58.4M
TimeEmbeddingLookUp	**1.73%**	**2.68%**	58.7M
TimePositionalEncoding	1.33%	2.39%	58.4M
GeoEmbeddingLookUp	1.47%	1.6%	58.6M
GeoOneHot	**2.27%**	**3.48%**	58.5M

5.2   Domain-Wise WER Comparison

We show the WER improvement of Eval set for various domains in Table 2. In general, we see gains on all top domains of interest with both approaches. Geo-location exhibits superior performance in domains like Music and CallingAndMessaging etc. These domains capture region specific preferences for music and video along with accent variations of proper nouns. On the other hand temporal context shows improvement on domains where queries come mostly at a certain point of time in a day, e.g. DailyBriefing, Weather etc.

Table 2. Per-domain relative WERR (%) breakdown on top 10 frequent domains selected from the test set. Analysis was done using the full resource model.

Domain	TimeEmbeddingLookUp	GeoOneHot
Music	1.72	**3.57**
Shopping	2.03	1.49
CallingAndMessaging	2.04	**5.68**
Global	0.86	2.58
DailyBriefing	**4.55**	0.91
Knowledge	2.14	1.97
Video	3.13	**6.26**
Weather	**5.92**	4.67
Information	1.44	1.96
ScienceAndTechnology	−0.49	−2.17

Table 3. Relative WERRs of combined contextual model w.r.t baseline. Both the models are trained on complete 30K hours of data

Model	Eval	Comms
Baseline	–	–
CombinedTimeGeo	**3.6%**	**4.62%**

5.3   Combined Context

The effect of combining the two contextual signals is captured in Table 3. Combining the contextual information shows superior performance compared to individual contextual models (Table 1). This establishes the additive effect of the location and date-time signals. In domain-wise study, we see a similar additive effect on several domains like CallingAndMessaging (6.05%), Knowledge (4.44%), Video (7.86%) and Weather (11.56%) etc. Moreover, in domains like ScienceAndTechnology, where neither of the individual contextual models showed any improvement, the combined model performed significantly better (6.61% WERR).

5.4   Low Resource Simulation

In practice we often face data scarcity while developing ASR for a new language or locale. In such cases, we can easily leverage contextual information as they are readily available to gain additional performance benefits. We simulated this situation by randomly selecting a 10K hours subset from the full training data, and trained both the baseline and the contextual models on this subset. The model sizes have also been reduced to avoid over-fitting as described in Sect. 4.2. Table 4 shows that the magnitude of gains have increased as compared to full resource, which demonstrates the efficacy of these contextual signals for low resource scenarios.

Table 4. Relative WERRs of Low Resource contextual models wrt baseline

Model	Eval test set	Comms test set	#params
Baseline	–	–	38M
TimeEmbeddingLookUp	4.03%	3.66%	38.2M
GeoOneHot	4.29%	3.76%	38.1M

Table 5. WERR (%) for top 3 and bottom 3 performing month and geographical state/country

Model	Top 3 (WERR)	Bottom 3 (WERR)
TimeEmbeddingLookUp	December (11.61)	November (0.25)
	February (10.49)	August (−0.64)
	January (5.24)	September (−4.86)
GeoOneHot	Germany (9.48)	Ohio (1.52)
	Hawaii (5.38)	Florida (1.02)
	Washington (4.77)	California (0.79)

5.5 Month and State-Wise WER Comparison

To further understand the effect of our proposed methods, we performed a month-wise and state-wise WERR analyses for date-time and geo-location based models respectively. We have captured the best and worst performing month/state for date-time/geo-location models in Table 5. The date-time information enhances the performance of RNN-T for some winter months considerably. On the other hand, geo-location signal significantly enhance the performance on utterances coming from low resource regions like Germany, Hawaii and its nearby locations. This can be mostly attributed to difference in acoustics of utterances coming from these regions as they are different from that of other regions captured by the geo-location clusters. Even for the worst performing region, we do not see any degradation of performance with geo-location as context.

Table 6. Comparison of contextual model output and baseline output

Reference	Baseline output	Contextual output	Context used
Good night and **happy hanukkah**	Good night and happy hobbiter	Good night and **happy hanukkah**	Time
What's the **christmas cat story**	What's the christmas car story	What's the **christmas cat story**	Time
Call **guillermo**	Call galermo	Call **guillermo**	Geo-location
Turn to my **kirk franklin** radio	Turn to my park franklin radio	Turn to my **kirk franklin** radio	Geo-location

5.6   Baseline and Contextual Model Outputs

In Table 6 we compare a few example predictions from baseline and contextual model. We see that, the time information helps in recognition of phrases like "hanukkah" and "christmas cat", which the baseline model fails to recognize. These phrases are seen in December which is implicitly captured by the contextual model.

Similar to time, when we use location information as context, it captures the accent variations and local preferences of music and videos. The contextual model was able to capture the local accent variation and correctly output "guillermo" while the baseline model outputs "galermo" which is somewhat phonetically similar to the correct phrase. Similarly "kirk franklin" was correctly recognized compared to incorrect baseline output of "park franklin" which shows that the model was able to capture local variation in music preferences without any external supervision.

Fig. 2. t-SNE plot for geo-embeddings

5.7   t-SNE Plot Analysis

Embeddings are meant to capture some implicit information about the context it represents. To understand the significance of the embedding vectors learnt by the models, we projected the 64 dimensional geo-location and month embedding vectors from GeoEmbeddingLookUp and TimeEmbeddingLookUp on 2-D space using t-SNE with default parameters of Embedding Projector[2].

In Fig. 2 we show the t-SNE plot for the learnt geo-embedding vectors. We can see that the geographically close states in the US have formed clusters in the embedding space (e.g. - California:Washington, Illinois:Ohio etc.) which seems to capture local

---

[2] https://projector.tensorflow.org/.

Fig. 3. t-SNE plot for month embeddings

variations like regional movies and song preference and also local accents. We can also see a clear demarcation between the US locations and the non-US locations like Brazil, Germany and India. Users across the US and the non-US will have different accents which are captured by the model. This proves that the geographical location distribution is important for the model and the model has learnt that without any external supervision.

Figure 3 shows the t-SNE plot for embedding vectors corresponding to month. We can observe a clear temporal ordering among the learnt month vectors which demonstrate the capacity of our models to implicitly learn the ordering among months from data. This phenomenon also proves that the temporal ordering of months is somewhat important for the task of ASR. Note that, we have not imposed any ordering constraint on any of our models.

6 Conclusions

In this paper, we explored the benefits of using contextual signals to improve the overall performance of end-to-end ASR based on RNN-T. We demonstrated the effectiveness of date-time and location as context by building ASR models on 30K and 10K hours of data. We provided empirical evidence that biasing ASR using contextual signals improves the overall accuracy. The use of individual contextual signals improved the ASR WER up to 3.48% relative, and where as their combination resulted in about 4.62% relative gain. Our analysis with t-SNE plot of embedding vectors for both geo-location and date-time context showed that the model was able to extract meaningful information from these signals and improving ASR, thereby possibly reducing the need for additional training data which is now critical for performance improvement. As a part of future work, we would like to add dynamic contextual signals along with these static ones to further enhance RNN-T ASR performance.

References

1. Chan, W., Jaitly, N., Le, Q., Vinyals, O.: Listen, attend and spell: a neural network for large vocabulary conversational speech recognition. In: 2016 IEEE International Conference on Acoustics, Speech and Signal Processing (ICASSP), pp. 4960–4964. IEEE (2016)
2. Chen, M.X., et al.: The best of both worlds: combining recent advances in neural machine translation. arXiv preprint arXiv:1804.09849 (2018)
3. Dasgupta, S.S., Ray, S.N., Talukdar, P.: HyTE: hyperplane-based temporally aware knowledge graph embedding. In: Proceedings of the 2018 Conference on Empirical Methods in Natural Language Processing, pp. 2001–2011. Association for Computational Linguistics, Brussels, Belgium, October–November 2018. https://doi.org/10.18653/v1/D18-1225. https://www.aclweb.org/anthology/D18-1225
4. Graves, A.: Sequence transduction with recurrent neural networks. arXiv preprint arXiv:1211.3711 (2012)
5. Graves, A., Fernández, S., Gomez, F., Schmidhuber, J.: Connectionist temporal classification: labelling unsegmented sequence data with recurrent neural networks. In: Proceedings of the 23rd International Conference on Machine Learning, pp. 369–376 (2006)
6. Jaech, A., Ostendorf, M.: Low-rank RNN adaptation for context-aware language modeling. CoRR abs/1710.02603 (2017). http://arxiv.org/abs/1710.02603
7. Kingma, D.P., Ba, J.: Adam: a method for stochastic optimization. arXiv preprint arXiv:1412.6980 (2014)
8. Mikolov, T., Zweig, G.: Context dependent recurrent neural network language model. In: 2012 IEEE Spoken Language Technology Workshop (SLT), pp. 234–239 (2012). https://doi.org/10.1109/SLT.2012.6424228
9. Park, D.S., et al.: SpecAugment: a simple data augmentation method for automatic speech recognition. arXiv preprint arXiv:1904.08779 (2019)
10. Ray, S.N., Dasgupta, S.S., Talukdar, P.: AD3: attentive deep document dater (2019)
11. Scheiner, J., Williams, I., Aleksic, P.: Voice search language model adaptation using contextual information. In: 2016 IEEE Spoken Language Technology Workshop (SLT), pp. 253–257 (2016). https://doi.org/10.1109/SLT.2016.7846273
12. Shibata, Y., et al.: Byte pair encoding: a text compression scheme that accelerates pattern matching. Technical Report DOI-TR-161, Department of Informatics, Kyushu University (1999)
13. Vashishth, S., Dasgupta, S.S., Ray, S.N., Talukdar, P.: Dating documents using graph convolution networks (2019)
14. Wu, Z., Li, B., Zhang, Y., Aleksic, P.S., Sainath, T.N.: Multistate encoding with end-to-end speech RNN transducer network. In: ICASSP 2020–2020 IEEE International Conference on Acoustics, Speech and Signal Processing (ICASSP), pp. 7819–7823. IEEE (2020)

BrAgriSpeech: A Corpus
of Brazilian-Portuguese Agricultural
Reported Speech

Brett Drury[1]([⊠]) [iD] and Samuel Morais Drury[2]

[1] LIAAD-INESC-TEC, Porto, Portugal
[2] Colégio Puríssimo, Rio Claro, SP, Brazil

Abstract. Agriculture is one of Brazil's largest industries. In Brazil, the price of crops such as sugarcane is driven not only by the production levels but also by speculation and rumour. Also, some crop derivatives such as ethanol have their prices regulated by the government. Reported comments from influential speakers such as government ministers and agricultural-business leaders can impact the prices and in some cases the level of production of food products. Currently, there are no corpora in Brazilian-Portuguese that contains agricultural-related speech, the speakers and their employer. BrAgriSpeech is a corpus that uses linguistic rules and pre-trained models to extract reported speech, the speaker and where available the speaker's employer as well as a discourse connector that connects the speaker with the quote. The resource has 6982 quotes which are in JSONL format. A sample of 50 quotes was manually evaluated and had an accuracy of 0.77 for quote identification, 0.82 for the identification of the speaker and 0.87 for the identification of the discourse connector. The resource is publicly available to encourage further research in the area.

1   Introduction

Agriculture is one of Brazil's largest industries, consequently, the fluctuation of price and quantity of agricultural produce is of national importance. Agricultural prices can fluctuate because of the quantity of produce as well as speculation and rumour. Economic and political actors can influence prices through comment and reported speech in the news media [7]. Brazil regulates the prices [5] of crop derivatives such as ethanol, also it controls the imports of competing agricultural goods[1]. Therefore it is arguable that comments and reported speech from influential economic and political actors can affect the price as well as the quantity of food produced in Brazil. There is currently no corpus of agriculturally related speech in Brazilian-Portuguese. BrAgriSpeech has therefore been developed to bridge this gap in the research literature. It has 6982 examples of reported speech from economic and political actors as well as business leaders. The speech examples have a quote, speaker, discourse connector and where available the speaker's employer. The corpus has been made publicly available so that researchers can use the corpus for further investigation on the effect of speech on agricultural production as well as the patterns of speech and use of language in the public commentary about agricultural policy and business.

---

[1] https://bit.ly/2PrDUtO.

© Springer Nature Switzerland AG 2021
K. Ekštein et al. (Eds.): TSD 2021, LNAI 12848, pp. 405–412, 2021.
https://doi.org/10.1007/978-3-030-83527-9_34

The remainder of the paper will cover the following 1. Related Work, 2. Extraction Methodology, 3. Evaluation, 4. BrAgriSpeechs Linguistic Characteristics, 5. Resource Overview and 6. Conclusion.

2 Related Work

The related work in this area is sparse because this domain is a niche area of research. The main corpus located in the area of Brazilian agricultural news is BrAgriNews [2]. BrAgriNews is a corpus of Brazilian-Portuguese agricultural news and is the source material for BrAgriSpeech. BrAgriNews spans the period 1996 to 2016 and has 96784 documents. It makes a simple attempt to mark quotations in the news by identifying quote delimiters such as quote marks (") which delimit quotes. It does not attempt to locate the speaker or quotes that are not delimited by quote markers. It does however have entities and sentiment tags for words within the quotes.

There were no directly comparable resources to BrAgriSpeech found in the literature review, however, [8] produced a vocabulary and corpus of what the authors called semi-popularization articles in the agricultural domain. The genre of publication is described by the authors as scientific articles aimed at the lay reader. The corpus however was quite small as consisted of only seven hundred documents and was in English.

The Fame speech corpus [4] is a corpus of audio speech recorded from the radio rather than written speech, however it does contain recorded material about agriculture. The final corpus located in the literature search is the Minho Quotation Resource [1] which is a business-related speech corpus that has direct speech from English Language news stories. It has a small number of quotes that are related to agriculture.

There are a small number of papers that extract quotes or reported speech from news articles. Several approaches use rules, for example, [11] used rules to extract quotes from European-Portuguese texts, and [1] used Open Calais[2] which in turn used rules to extract quotes. And [12] used rules to extract quotations from Indonesian online news. The final approach found in the literature review was [10] who used rules and a dependency parser to identify quotes. The rule-based approach seems to gain high precision at the cost of the recall.

There have been some attempts to use machine learning techniques to extract quotes from text. The unique approach that was found in the literature review was [9] who used a Conditional Random Field to predict if a token is part of a quote or not, and they compared it to a Maxent Classifier. They used features such as verbs and labels of words that are in the current span as the current token.

3 Extraction Methodology

The BrAgriSpeech corpus was extracted using a ruled based approach because it is relatively simple to implement, and has high precision. The rules detected two types of speech: 1. quotes delimited by quote marks ("), and 2. quotes which are not delimited

---

[2] Open Calais.

by quote marks. Each quote has quote attribution to a speaker and where possible the speaker's employer.

The rules that extracted the quotes are patterns that identify a sequence of particular linguistic features. The linguistic features are detected at the sentence level, and consequently, the source texts from BrAgriNews were split into sentences using a modified sentence splitter. The modified sentence splitter joined candidate sentences that had one quote mark with the previous sentence. This is because if the candidate quote had more than one sentence then the sentence splitter would split into more than one sentence.

The rules parse the sentence with a Part of Speech of Tagger (POS) and a Named Entity Tagger. Also, a further rule is applied which looks for pairs of quote delimiters such as ". For there to be a candidate quote one of the following sequence criteria must be met:

- Speaker, Verb, and Quote Marks (opening and closing)
- Quote Marks (opening and closing), Verb and Speaker

The named entity detector identifies the speaker by identifying the person class of a candidate phrase within a sentence. If there is no matching phrase then a pronoun would be identified, for example, ele/ela (he/she), by the POS tagger. The POS tagger identifies the verb, between the speaker and the quote, this verb will be referred to as the discourse connector. A further modification was made to the rules where the employer of the speaker is identified by looking for a connector between the speaker and a company entity, which also is detected with the entity tagger. The connectors are *do/da* which is the Portuguese equivalent of the word *of*. For example, "Gilvan Sampaio do Instituto Nacional de Pesquisas Espaciais" where the speaker Gilvan Sampaio is connected to the organisation Instituto Nacional de Pesquisas Espaciais by the connector *do*. A representative example of this rule-based approach is "Essa estimativa leva em conta a falta de chuvas durante o desenvolvimento fisiológico das plantas", destacou o presidente da consultoria, Plínio Nastari", which in English is: "This estimate takes into account the lack of rain during the physiological development of plants highlighted the president of consulting, Plínio Nastari.". A workbook with the code for this section of the corpus can be found here.

The second rule set uses similar rules but does not look for quote marks, but takes the discourse connectors from the previous step, and uses this set of verbs to connect to the speaker. For example, "A Cutrale, maior indústria de laranja do País, ja processou pouco mais de 30% das frutas desta safra, diz o diretor corporativo Carlos Viacava" which is in English is "Cutrale, the largest orange industry in the country, has already processed just over 30% of the fruits of this harvest, says the corporate director". There are no speech delimiters, however there is a discourse connector (diz) and a candidate speaker (Carlos Viacava). It is possible using the aforementioned sequences to infer the speech portion of the sentence.

The resource is a combination of the output of both sets of rules.

4 Evaluation

An evaluation of the information extraction methodology was made where a random sample of fifty quotes was selected and three domain experts evaluated if the quote, verb and speaker were correct. The employer was not evaluated because there were insufficient examples. The margin of error from this sample is 0.13, therefore there is a 95 per cent chance that the real evaluation value is within 13 per cent of the evaluation value that is presented here.

The evaluation metric used a discrete score where the results are either correct or not. The evaluation metric was accuracy which is simply $accuracy = \frac{correct\_instances}{total\_instances}$. The average accuracy of the evaluation is: Quote, 0.77 ($\pm$0.02), Verb, 0.87 ($\pm$0.02) and Speaker, 0.82 ($\pm$0.08).

In addition to average accuracy and standard deviation, a Fleiss Kappa Coefficient [3] was computed for Quote, Verb and Speaker, and the results were 0.85, 0.76 and 0.68, which indicates that there was strong agreement between the annotators. Although there was stronger disagreement between the annotators for speaker identification than for quote identification. In short, the results demonstrate that the quote was accurately found, however, the discourse connector (verb) and speaker identification were more accurately found than the remainder of the quote.

5   BrAgriSpeech's Linguistic Characteristics

To provide some illustration of the nature of the corpus some basic linguistic analysis was made. The first one was the breakdown of the percentage of Part of Speech Tags (POS) that make up the corpus. The results are in Fig. 1. The figures in Fig. 1 don't add up to one because of rounding errors, and POS tags that had a value of less than three per cent are excluded so that Fig. 1 is not crowded.

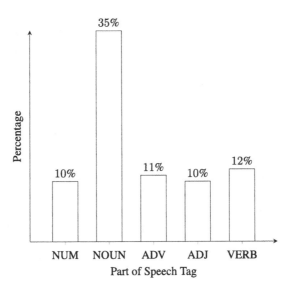

Fig. 1. Percentage of POS tags in BrAgriSpeech

The most frequent POS tag is a Noun, which is due to the speaker referring to "objects" such as the ethanol and markets. The verbs and adjectives often refer to actions of objects such as markets rising or falling, or state of objects such as poor harvest. The numeric tag has a quite high value because the speakers often quantified the verb, for example, "the sugar futures market moved down by five per cent today".

Nouns describe some of the topics that are being discussed in the resource, therefore a simple frequency analysis of Nouns is shown in Fig. 2.

Fig. 2. Most frequent nouns in BrAgriSpeech

The figure demonstrates that the most common nouns are related to markets (mercado), government (governo), money (dinheiro) and president (presidente). It is possible to assume that the majority of the reported speech in the source corpus, BriAgriNews, is mainly related to market news and conditions. Also, the most frequent nouns demonstrate the role of government in agriculture in Brazil. This is not a surprise because the Brazilian government does intervene in the agricultural market, such as paying subsidies to Brazilian farmers[3].

The main product and crop that is shown in the most frequent noun analysis is etanol (ethanol) and Cana-de-açúcar (sugarcane), and this frequency reflects the dependency of Brazil on ethanol which is produced from sugarcane as it is used as a gasoline substitute by low-income consumers.

A frequency analysis of the speakers was made, and it was found that the most frequent speakers in the corpus are the following:

- Fernando Henrique Cardoso
- Michel Temer
- Dilma Rousseff
- Vlamir Brandalizze
- Luiz Inacio Lula

---

[3] http://www.oecd.org/brazil/brazil-agriculturalpolicymonitoringandevaluation.htm.

Three of the most frequent speakers: Michel Temer, Dilma Rousseff and Luiz Inacio Lula are former presidents of Brazil. The remainder, Vlamir Brandalizze, is a director of Brandalizze Consulting, and Fernando Henrique Cardoso is an academic. The presence of three ex-presidents in the resource indicates the importance of the source material and agriculture in general to the Brazilian economy.

6   Resource Overview

The corpus is supplied in JSONL format[4] in a text file which is located here. Each line of the text file is a valid JSON statement and is a dictionary, which is a set of key-value pairs, where the key is a unique identifier. An overview of the resource is presented in Fig. 3. The Figure shows the keys of the dictionary and its position in the resource hierarchy.

The top level of the resource is "Quote ID", and "BrAgriNews File Name". The Quote ID is a unique numeric identifier for a quote. Quote ID starts at zero and also points to another dictionary. The BrAgriNews File Name key holds the value of the name of the source file in the BrAgriNews[2] corpus. The resource is organised in this manner because a single BriAgriNews file may have more than one quote.

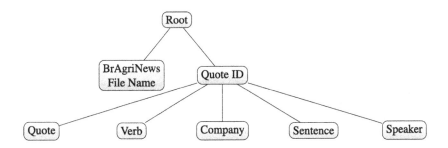

Fig. 3. Overview of BrAgriSpeech Corpus

The second level dictionary has the following keys:

- Sentence
- Quote
- Verb
- Company
- Speaker

The sentence key has a value of a string which is the sentence from which the associated quote is taken from. The sentence key always has a value. The keys: Quote, Verb, Company and Speaker have values which are one of the following: 1. Null/None when there is no information or 2. A Dictionary. The sub-dictionary has the following

---

[4] https://jsonlines.org.

keys: start position, end position and value. The value key has a value of a string that reflects the parent key, therefore the value key of the quote parent key will have the quote and the value key of the speaker parent key will have the speaker's name. The start position and end position keys hold the position information in the sentence for the value key pair.

An example of an entry in the resource is shown below. The example shows that the File Name: CIENCIA_2003_6476.txt, has one quote which has the ID "0". The speaker is Marcelo Lopes de Oliveira, and the discourse connector (verb) is "diz" (said). The quote is "Mas isso não é razão para pânico" (but this is no reason to panic).

- {"0": {"Quote": {"End Position": 33, "Value": "Mas isso não é razão para pânico", "Start Position": 1}, "Verb": {"End Position": 39, "Value": "diz", "Start Position": 36}, "Speaker": {"End Position": 65, "Value": "Marcelo Lopes de Oliveira", "Start Position": 40}, "Sentence": "Mas isso não é razão para pânico, diz Marcelo Lopes de Oliveira e Souza, do INPE (Instituto Nacional de Pesquisas Espaciais).", "Company": {}}, "BRAGRINEWS_FILE_NAME": "CIENCIA_2003_6476.txt"}

The entry is valid JSON, and although it was generated using Python, it should be readable using other languages.

7   Conclusion

BrAgriSpeech is a resource that has captured speech information from the BrAgriNews corpus. It is focused on reported speech in the Brazilian agricultural domain and has captured the agricultural speech record between the 1990s to 2016. It captures speech around the market and natural events such as price rises and droughts. Speech in this resource is directly reported in the media, and therefore it can be assumed that candid or truthful speech will not be present. The speech that is recorded is planned and uses various techniques to either manipulate audiences, downplay economically damaging events and overplay beneficial information. It is a resource that captures how public individuals communicate in the mass media to various audiences.

The resource has been freely available to stimulate research in the area of public discourse in Brazilian-Portuguese in an economically significant area.

Future work will be aimed at building an Ontology that contains an end-point for further information about the speaker, company and concepts such as ethanol and sugarcane. These entities will have a unique id so that these entities can be identified within the text. The Ontology will point to further resources such as DBPedia [6] so that further information can be gathered from these resources.

References

1. Drury, B., Almeida, J.J.: The Minho quotation resource. In: LREC, pp. 2280–2285 (2012)
2. Drury, B., Fernandes, R., de Andrade Lopes, A.: Bragrinews: Um corpus temporal-causal (português-brasileiro) para a agricultura. Linguamática 9(1), 41–54 (2017)
3. FLEISS, J.: The measurement of interrater agreement. In: Statistical Methods for Rates and Proportions (1981). https://ci.nii.ac.jp/naid/10016354243/en/

4. Heuvel, H., Yilmaz, E., van Leeuwen, D., Velde, H., Dijkstra, J.: FAME! Speech Corpus. Ph.D. thesis, Radboud University (2016)
5. Jales, M.d.Q.M., Costa, C.C.d.: Measurement of ethanol subsidies and associated economic distortions: an analysis of brazilian and us policies. Economia Aplicada **18**(3), 455–481 (2014)
6. Lehmann, J., et al.: DBpedia-a large-scale, multilingual knowledge base extracted from Wikipedia. Semant. Web **6**(2), 167–195 (2015)
7. Maligkris, A.: Political speeches and stock market outcomes. In: 30th Australasian Finance and Banking Conference (2017)
8. Muñoz, V.L.: The vocabulary of agriculture semi-popularization articles in English: a corpus-based study. Engl. Specif. Purp. **39**, 26–44 (2015)
9. Pareti, S., O'keefe, T., Konstas, I., Curran, J.R., Koprinska, I.: Automatically detecting and attributing indirect quotations. In: Proceedings of the 2013 Conference on Empirical Methods in Natural Language Processing, pp. 989–999 (2013)
10. Salway, A., Meurer, P., Hofland, K., Reigem, Ø.: Quote extraction and attribution from Norwegian newspapers. In: Proceedings of the 21st Nordic Conference on Computational Linguistics, pp. 293–297 (2017)
11. Sarmento, L., Nunes, S.: Automatic extraction of quotes and topics from news feeds. In: DSIE 2009-4th Doctoral Symposium on Informatics Engineering (2009)
12. Syaifudin, Y., Nurwidyantoro, A.: Quotations identification from Indonesian online news using rule-based method. In: 2016 International Seminar on Intelligent Technology and Its Applications (ISITIA), pp. 187–194. IEEE (2016)

Exploiting Large-Scale Teacher-Student Training for On-Device Acoustic Models

Jing Liu[1]([✉]), Rupak Vignesh Swaminathan[1],
Sree Hari Krishnan Parthasarathi[1], Chunchuan Lyu[2], Athanasios Mouchtaris[1],
and Siegfried Kunzmann[1]

[1] Alexa Machine Learning, Amazon, Seattle, USA
{jlmk,swarupak,sparta,mouchta,kunzman}@amazon.com
[2] School of Informatics, University of Edinburgh, Edinburgh, Scotland, UK

Abstract. We present results from Alexa speech teams on semi-supervised learning (SSL) of acoustic models (AM) with experiments spanning over 3000 h of GPU time, making our study one of the largest of its kind. We discuss SSL for AMs in a small footprint setting, showing that a smaller capacity model trained with 1 million hours of unsupervised data can outperform a baseline supervised system by 14.3% word error rate reduction (WERR). When increasing the supervised data to seven-fold, our gains diminish to 7.1% WERR; to improve SSL efficiency at larger supervised data regimes, we employ a step-wise distillation into a smaller model, obtaining a WERR of 14.4%. We then switch to SSL using larger student models in low data regimes; while learning efficiency with unsupervised data is higher, student models may outperform teacher models in such a setting. We develop a theoretical sketch to explain this behavior.

Keywords: Speech recognition · Acoustic models · Edge computing · Student-teacher learning · Semi-supervised learning

1 Introduction

Semi-supervised learning (SSL) has a rich history in automatic speech recognition (ASR) [1,11,14,17,21]. Self-training is a commonly used technique employing confidence measures [12,32]. Student-teacher distillation techniques [2,9], foregoing full decoders and confidence models, have been shown to be effective for SSL [19]. SSL methods for end-to-end ASR have been studied in [6,13,16,25,36]. Furthermore, investigations with SSL in combination with data augmentation, pretraining and iterative self-training are done in [41] and [38].

Recently, student-teacher distillation techniques for hybrid HMM-LSTM models have been shown to scale to very large data sets (1 million hours) for models with high capacity [27,28]. The efficacy of model compression using student-teacher distillation is well established [23,34,35]. In this context we study learning curves for AM for two tasks: (a) smaller footprint modeling, and (b) low training-data regimes.

K. Ekštein et al. (Eds.): TSD 2021, LNAI 12848, pp. 413–424, 2021.
https://doi.org/10.1007/978-3-030-83527-9_35

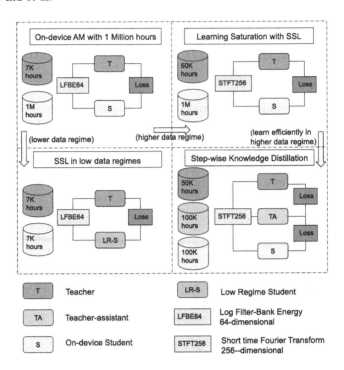

Fig. 1. Overview of our SSL approach progressing through 4 experiments. a) Top-left: Analysis of models using large unsupervised data. b) Top-right: Analysis of models in large supervised and unsupervised data regimes. c) Bottom-right: Improving learning efficiency in higher data regimes. d) Bottom-left: SSL studies in low data regimes.

Our motivation for low footprint AM comes from edge computing, where models are capacity restricted in terms of compute and memory [31,39,40]. We are interested in understanding if SSL, at very large data regimes for small models, can still yield gains in accuracy. In [24], mean squared errors between the teacher and the student hidden representations are explored as a regularization term in knowledge distillation. We demonstrate that a step-wise distillation approach, introduced in [23] can be effective, although this comes at the cost of more computation at training time. In low data regimes, SSL is an effective technique to reduce annotation costs [5,14,17,21]. For our second task, using knowledge distillation for SSL, we find that to achieve a performance comparable to that of a fully supervised system, the proportion of required supervised data decreases as the amount of total data increases. However, we find that in low data regimes, students can be better than teachers.

Our contributions in this work are as follows: (1) we establish the robustness of small capacity semi-supervised models trained on 1 million hours of data; (2) we show an effective way to mitigate the learning saturation problem at higher data regimes for an on-device acoustic model; (3) we report results of a model distilled from a teacher trained on transcribed low-resource data, and present an empirical risk analysis. Figure 1 describes the approach we follow in this paper.

We begin with a discussion on model configurations in Sect. 2. In Sect. 3, we present SSL for small footprint AMs. We show that such models can exploit a large amount of unsupervised data. However, when the amount of supervised data is increased from 7,000 h to 52,000 h the gains decrease. To mitigate this, we discuss a step-wise distillation into a smaller model. We then transition into experiments conducted in low resource settings in Sect. 4.

2 System Description

We now describe acoustic model configurations used in this work. It is a hybrid system, with an LSTM [10] estimating the senone posterior probabilities corresponding to clustered triphone HMM states. The HMMs are single state models using low-frame rate features [29], which are computed on speech signals every 10 ms, with a 25 ms analysis window. A running causal mean estimate is computed and subtracted from the features, and the resulting features are normalized by applying a global mean and variance normalization. The models are trained with the cross-entropy (CE) criterion, followed by sequence discriminative training using state-level minimum Bayes risk (sMBR) loss [15]. We follow an exponential learning rate decay for twelve epochs. More details on model configurations can be found in Table 1.

3 SSL for Small Footprint AM

In this section, we begin with an analysis of acoustic model complexity with supervised and unsupervised data for smaller and larger model footprints. We then investigate a method for efficient model distillation in larger supervised data regimes.

3.1 Learning Curves on Large Unsupervised Data

In Fig. 2, on TST1 test data, we analyze the learning curves for on-device and cloud student models, taught by the same teacher network. Accuracy is reported as relative word error rate reduction (WERR) [7,26]. Given model A's WER (WER_A) and a baseline B's WER (WER_B), the WERR of A over B is computed as $WERR = (WER_B - WER_A)/WER_B$.

The vertical axis is the relative WERR (%) against baseline LSTM AMs which are trained with CE criterion on the fully supervised 7,000 h training data. The horizontal axis corresponds to the amount of unsupervised data. Each sub-epoch in the axis corresponds to about 60,000 h of unsupervised data, totaling to 1 million hours. From Fig. 2, we see that the relative WERR improves steadily for both cloud and on-device student AMs as we use increasing amount of unsupervised data. When using 1 million hours unsupervised data, the relative WERR for on-device and cloud student AMs are 14.3% and 14.6% respectively in CE comparing with its fully supervised models.

Table 1. Model configurations

Common configurations for all experiments
• Features are stacked and subsampled 33 Hz
• 5 layers and 768 neurons/layer BLSTM teachers with 78 million parameters
• Teacher model is cross-entropy and sequence trained
• Teacher model trained with distributed trainer from [33]
• Output posterior distribution over 3183 senones
• Data selection for unsupervised data as in [28]
• Training/test data are sampled from de-identified speech data
• Student training strategy with compressed posteriors as in [28]
• TST1: Test data consists of 100 h of speech data
• TST2: Test data consists of 30 h of speech data
Section 3.1 Configurations for on-device AM
• 64-dimensional log filter-bank energies (LFBE)
• 5 layers and 428 neurons/layer Uni-LSTM on-device student AMs with 8 million parameters
• Cross entropy training of student models with distributed trainer from [4]
• sMBR training of student model with distributed trainer from [33]
• 7,000 h of supervised training data with TST1 test data
• 1 million hours of unsupervised speech data
Section 3.2 Configurations for studying learning saturation
• 256-dimensional STFT features [18,30]
• Teacher and student model architectures: same as above
• Distributed training strategy: same as above
• 52 K hours supervised training data with TST1 test data
• 1 million hours of unsupervised speech data
Section 3.3 Configurations for step-wise distillation
• 256-dimensional STFT features
• Teacher and student model architectures: same as above
• Distributed training strategy: same as above
• 50 K hours supervised training data with TST1 test data
• 100 K hours unsupervised data
Section 4 Configurations for low resource experiments
• 64-dimensional LFBE features
• 5 layers and 768 neurons/layer Uni-LSTM students with 24 million parameters
• Teacher and student models trained with distributed trainer from [33]
• Total training data is 7000 h with TST2 test data
• Supervised data ranges from 100 h up to 7000 h
• The rest of the data is treated as unsupervised data

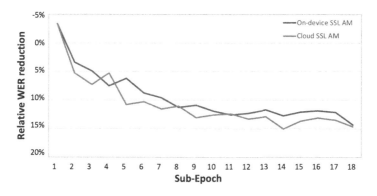

Fig. 2. On TST1: relative WERR (%) per sub-epoch of the 1 million hour SSL models against baseline LSTM AMs that are trained with CE criterion on the fully supervised 7,000 h training data.

Table 2. On TST1: relative WERR (%) for sequence training of SSL students. The baseline LSTM AMs are trained with CE criterion in a fully supervised setting with 7,000 h of data

WERR (%)		
System	On-device	Cloud
Baseline supervised CE	0	0
Baseline supervised CE + sMBR	18.2	9.7
SSL CE	14.3	14.6
SSL CE + sMBR	25.7	24.0

We perform sequence level discriminative training only on the 7,000 h supervised dataset, demonstrating that the gains at the CE stage also carry over to the sMBR stage. Table 2 shows WERR for on-device and cloud student AMs using the same 4-gram LM. The WERRs for SSL CE + sMBR and supervised CE + sMBR are 25.7% and 18.2% respectively for on-device AMs.

3.2   Learning Saturation for On-Device SSL System

In the following experiment, we increase the supervised data by about 7 times to 52,000 h. We then gradually increase the amount of unsupervised data set to 1 million hours, computing WERR against a supervised model trained with 52,000 h of supervised data. From Table 3, we get a relative WERR of 6.06% by adding up to 540 K hours of unsupervised data. If we further increase unsupervised data from 540 K hours to 1 million hours, the additional relative WERR is only 1%. We conclude that learning starts to saturate at 540 K hours. Adding additional unsupervised data helps little with accuracy improvement.

Table 3. On TST1: relative WERR (%) for SSL student AM with 8M parameters. Both the baseline and SSL AM are trained with 52k hours of fully supervised data.

WERR (%)	Unsupervised (hours)
6.05%	540 K
6.62%	720 K
6.86%	900 K
7.05%	1M

Table 4. On TST1: relative WERR (%) for teacher assisted knowledge distillation method. The baseline model is the cross-entropy trained model on supervised data (row 4). WERR values are computed against baseline model's WER.

Index	AM	Params (M)	Stage	WERR (%)
1	Teacher	78	sMBR	33.0
2	Cloud	28	sMBR	21.67
3	TA	28	sMBR	25.97
4	On-device	8	CE	0
			sMBR	17.7
5	KD	8	CE	9.2
			sMBR	15.7
6	TAKD	8	CE	14.4
			sMBR	19.0

3.3 Improving the Efficiency of Knowledge Distillation

In this section, we study a distillation method to improve the learning efficiency at higher data regimes. Specifically, we reduce the gap between the teacher and student models through an intermediate teacher assistant [23].

The supervised part of the training data consists of about 50K hours of supervised US English speech, and the unsupervised part consists of about 100K hours of unsupervised data. The unsupervised training data is used for training the teacher assistant. We perform step-wise teacher assisted knowledge distillation. The first-step knowledge distillation happens through a 78-million-parameter bidirectional LSTM teacher model and a 28-million-parameter teacher assistant model. The second-step knowledge distillation occurs between the 28-million-parameter teacher assistant model and an 8-million-parameter student network using only the soft-targets from the teacher assistant.

Table 4 shows relative WERR against a baseline cross-entropy student model (row 4) trained with 50,000 h of supervised data. Rows 1, 2 and 3 show WERR of the teacher, supervised cloud model, and SSL-trained teacher assistant models evaluated against baseline. Sequence training with sMBR (in row 4) shows 17.7% relative WERR in a fully supervised system. The distillation results are presented in rows 5 and 6. The improvement over direct Knowledge Distillation (KD) is 9.2% relative. For Teacher Assisted Knowledge Distillation (TAKD), there is a substantial improvement of 14.4% compared to baseline supervised system, thus showing that step-wise distillation with a teacher assistant indeed helps with the efficiency for smaller models in large data regimes.

4 SSL in Low Resource Settings

In this section, we present our results on low resource settings with SSL; specifically, now the student model is larger, but the overall amount of data is restricted to 7,000 h.

4.1 Accuracy Gains with Unsupervised Data

Figure 3 shows learning curves for student models at fixed amount of supervised data. The actual amounts of supervised data are: 100, 250, 500, 1000, 3500 and 7000 h. Triangular markers on each curve correspond to student models trained with increasing amounts of unsupervised data by fixing the amount of supervised data.

Relative WERR is computed against a baseline model trained only on the supervised data corresponding to that curve of the same color. The circular solid

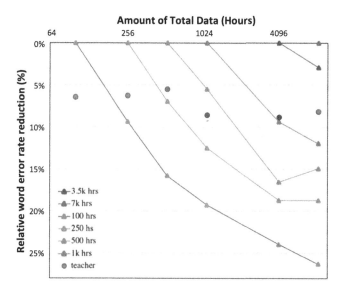

Fig. 3. On TST2: relative WERR (%) for different amounts of unsupervised data: each curve corresponds to a fixed amount of supervised data. Markers on each curve correspond to student models trained with increasing amounts of unsupervised data. Relative WERR is computed against the model trained only on the supervised data corresponding to that curve. The circular dots correspond to the BLSTM teacher models for the curves of the same color.

dots in this plot show the relative WERR for the teacher models. These dots line up vertically against the triangles corresponding to the baselines models.

For each curve, the slope of the curve becomes less steep as the amount of unsupervised data increases, meaning diminishing returns for additional data. Note that the student models can outperform the corresponding teacher model, once the student model observes unsupervised data.

4.2   An Analysis of Empirical Risk with Student-Teacher Learning

To simplify analysis, we restrict our setting to binary classification, and adopt notations from [3]. Let $Z = \{(x_i, y_i)\}_{i=1,\dots,N}$ be a supervised set drawn from a distribution D on $\mathcal{X} \times \{-1, 1\}$, where $\mathcal{X} = \{x_i\}_{i=1..N}$. Let $\mathbb{1}[A] : A \subset \mathcal{X} \to \{0, 1\}$ be an indicator function defined as $\mathbb{1}[A](x) = \begin{cases} 1 & \text{if } x \in A \\ 0 & \text{if } x \notin A \end{cases}$. Teacher and student network outputs are denoted $h^t(x)$ and $h^s(x)$ respectively, and are drawn from $\{-1, 1\}$. The empirical teacher-student training risk is

$$R_Z^{h^t}(h^s) := \frac{1}{N} \sum_{i=1,\dots,N} \mathbb{1}[h^t(x_i) \neq h^s(x_i)],$$

and the actual empirical risk of the student is

$$R_Z(h^s) := R_Z^y(h^s) = \frac{1}{N} \sum_{i=1,\dots,N} \mathbb{1}[y_i \neq h^s(x_i)].$$

Lemma 1 (Decomposition). *Given* $h^t, h^s, y \in \{-1, 1\}$, *we have*

$$R_Z(h^s) = R_Z(h^t)\big(1 - R_{acc(h^t)}^{h^t}(h^s) - R_{err(h^t)}^{h^t}(h^s)\big) + R_{acc(h^t)}^{h^t}(h^s)$$

where $acc(h^t) := \{x, y \in Z | h^t(x) = y\}$ *and* $err(h^t) := \{x, y \in Z | h^t(x) \neq y\}$.

Proof. Decomposing the student risk by partitioning Z on whether the teacher makes a mistake

$$
\begin{aligned}
R_Z(h^s) &= R_Z(h^t)\big(1 - R_{err(h^t)}^{h^t}(h^s)\big) + \big(1 - R_Z(h^t)\big) R_{acc(h^t)}^{h^t}(h^s) \\
&= R_Z(h^t)\big(1 - R_{acc(h^t)}^{h^t}(h^s) - R_{err(h^t)}^{h^t}(h^s)\big) + R_{acc(h^t)}^{h^t}(h^s)
\end{aligned}
$$

Theorem 1 (Truth Over Teacher).

$$R_Z(h^s) \leq R_Z(h^t) \iff \frac{R_{err(h^t)}^{h^t}(h^s)}{R_{acc(h^t)}^{h^t}(h^s)} \geq \frac{1}{R_Z(h^t)} - 1$$

Proof.

$$R_Z(h^s) \leq R_Z(h^t)$$

$$\Longleftrightarrow$$

$$R_Z(h^t)\big(1 - R^{h^t}_{acc(h^t)}(h^s) - R^{h^t}_{err(h^t)}(h^s)\big) + R^{h^t}_{acc(h^t)}(h^s) \leq R_Z(h^t)$$

$$\Longleftrightarrow$$

$$R^{h^t}_{acc(h^t)}(h^s) \leq R_Z(h^t)\big(R^{h^t}_{acc(h^t)}(h^s) + R^{h^t}_{err(h^t)}(h^s)\big)$$

$$\Longleftrightarrow$$

$$\frac{1}{R_Z(h^t)} \leq 1 + \frac{R^{h^t}_{err(h^t)}(h^s)}{R^{h^t}_{acc(h^t)}(h^s)}$$

$$\Longleftrightarrow$$

$$\frac{R^{h^t}_{err(h^t)}(h^s)}{R^{h^t}_{acc(h^t)}(h^s)} \geq \frac{1}{R_Z(h^t)} - 1$$

The better the teacher is, the easier a student model fits the true label compared to a false label. In particular, if the prediction error the teacher makes $R_Z(h^t)$ is better than random guess, namely $R_Z(h^t) < 0.5$, then it is necessary that $\frac{R^{h^t}_{err(h^t)}(h^s)}{R^{h^t}_{acc(h^t)}(h^s)} > 1$ so that $R_Z(h^s) \leq R_Z(h^t)$. From Theorem 1, for the student to be better than its teacher, the student's risk evaluated on the error set of the teacher (the erroneous teacher labels) has to be greater than the risk evaluated on the accuracy set of the teacher (the correct teacher labels) by a factor of $\frac{1}{R_z(h^t)} - 1$.

5 Discussion

In low data regimes, our experiments surprisingly showed that a student model's performance is not upper bounded by the teacher model used in learning. Our theoretical analysis indicates that this can happen, for example, when the student makes fewer errors on data with high teacher errors. We speculate this is because a capacity-restricted student model is able to generalize better than the teacher using the unsupervised data.

In high data regimes, we observed that the TAKD method facilitated efficient learning. We speculate that this could be due to step-wise distillation providing better calibrated posteriors for the eventual student to learn from. Indeed, it has been observed that in modern over-parameterized neural networks, posterior probabilities can become less calibrated [8]; using large amounts of supervised data could be making teacher models' estimates of posteriors less calibrated.

6 Conclusions and Future Work

Using BLSTM and LSTM as teacher and student models respectively, we studied SSL for AMs for two tasks: (a) for small footprint on-device models; and (b) a larger footprint, but lower training data regime. Despite smaller model capacity, on-device models were able to exploit 1 million hours of unsupervised data and achieve a 14.3% relative WER improvement after cross-entropy training and the gains could carry over to the sMBR stage. However, when we increased the supervised data from 7,000 h to 52,000 h, the learning efficiency decreased yielding only 7.1% relative improvements in WER. We utilized a step-wise distillation and recovered the WER gains. For SSL in low data regimes, using knowledge distillation, we found that to achieve a performance comparable to that of a fully supervised system, the proportion of required supervised data decreased as the amount of total data increased. However, we found that in low data regimes, students can be better than teachers. In future work, we would like to extend this large scale study to distill using sequence-based discriminative criterion [20, 22, 37] instead of the frame-level cross-entropy criterion. Finally, it would be informative to understand if the analyses carried out in this paper using hybrid models would carry over to end-to-end ASR systems.

Acknowledgements. We would like to thank Minhua Wu, Jangwon Kim, Srinivas Parthasarathy, Kishore Nandury and Brian King for their helpful discussions.

References

1. Amodei, D., Ananthanarayanan, S., et al.: Deep speech 2: end-to-end speech recognition in English and Mandarin. In: Procedings of ICML (2016)
2. Ba, J., Caruana, R.: Do deep nets really need to be deep? In: Advances in Neural Information Processing Systems, pp. 2654–2662 (2014)
3. Bégin, L., Germain, P., Laviolette, F., Roy, J.F.: PAC-Bayesian theory for transductive learning. In: Proceedings of of AISTATS (2014)
4. Chen, K., Huo, Q.: Scalable training of deep learning machines by incremental block training with intra-block parallel optimization and blockwise model-update filtering. In: Proceedings of ICASSP (2016)
5. Chen, L., Leutnant, V.: Acoustic model bootstrapping using semi-supervised learning. In: Proceedings Interspeech 2019, pp. 3198–3202 (2019). https://doi.org/10.21437/Interspeech.2019-2818. http://dx.doi.org/10.21437/Interspeech.2019-2818
6. Chen, Y., Wang, W., Wang, C.: Semi-supervised ASR by end-to-end self-training (2020)
7. Garimella, S., Mandal, A., Strom, N., Hoffmeister, B., Matsoukas, S., Parthasarathi, S.H.K.: Robust I-vector based adaptation of DNN acoustic model for speech recognition. In: Proceedings of Interspeech (2015)
8. Guo, C., Pleiss, G., Sun, Y., Weinberger, K.Q.: On calibration of modern neural networks. arXiv preprint arXiv:1706.04599 (2017)
9. Hinton, G., Vinyals, O., Dean, J.: Distilling the knowledge in a neural network. arXiv preprint arXiv:1503.02531 (2015)
10. Hochreiter, S., Schmidhuber, J.: Long short-term memory. Neural Comput. **9**(8), 1735–1780 (1997)
11. Huang, Y., Wang, Y., Gong, Y.: Semi-supervised training in deep learning acoustic model. In: Proceedings of Interspeech (2016)
12. Huang, Y., Yu, D., Gong, Y., Liu, C.: Semi-supervised GMM and DNN acoustic model training with multi-system combination and confidence re-calibration. In: Proceedings of Interspeech (2013)

13. Kahn, J., Lee, A., Hannun, A.: Self-training for end-to-end speech recognition. In: ICASSP 2020–2020 IEEE International Conference on Acoustics, Speech and Signal Processing (ICASSP), May 2020. https://doi.org/10.1109/icassp40776.2020. 9054295. http://dx.doi.org/10.1109/ICASSP40776.2020.9054295

14. Kemp, T., Waibel, A.: Unsupervised training of a speech recognizer: recent experiments. In: Proceedings of Eurospeech (1999)

15. Kingsbury, B.: Lattice-based optimization of sequence classification criteria for neural-network acoustic modeling. In: 2009 IEEE International Conference on Acoustics, Speech and Signal Processing, pp. 3761–3764 (2009). https://doi.org/ 10.1109/ICASSP.2009.4960445

16. Kurata, G., Audhkhasi, K.: Guiding CTC posterior spike timings for improved posterior fusion and knowledge distillation. CoRR abs/1904.08311 (2019). http:// arxiv.org/abs/1904.08311

17. Lamel, L., Gauvain, J.L., Adda, G.: Lightly supervised and unsupervised acoustic model training. Comput. Speech Lang. **16**, 115–129 (2002)

18. Li, J., Mohamed, A., Zweig, G., Gong, Y.: LSTM time and frequency recurrence for automatic speech recognition. In: 2015 IEEE Workshop on Automatic Speech Recognition and Understanding (ASRU), pp. 187–191 (2015). https://doi.org/10. 1109/ASRU.2015.7404793

19. Li, J., Zhao, R., Huang, J.T., Gong, Y.: Learning small-size DNN with output-distribution-based criteria. In: Proceedings of Interspeech (2014)

20. Li, J., et al.: High-accuracy and low-latency speech recognition with two-head contextual layer trajectory LSTM model. In: ICASSP 2020–2020 IEEE International Conference on Acoustics, Speech and Signal Processing (ICASSP), pp. 7699–7703 (2020). https://doi.org/10.1109/ICASSP40776.2020.9054387

21. Ma, J., Matsoukas, S., Kimball, O., Schwartz, R.: Unsupervised training on large amounts of broadcast news data. In: Proceedings of ICASSP (2006)

22. Manohar, V., Ghahremani, P., Povey, D., Khudanpur, S.: A teacher-student learning approach for unsupervised domain adaptation of sequence-trained ASR models. In: 2018 IEEE Spoken Language Technology Workshop (SLT), pp. 250–257 (2018). https://doi.org/10.1109/SLT.2018.8639635

23. Mirzadeh, S.I., Farajtabar, M., Li, A., Ghasemzadeh, H.: Improved knowledge distillation via teacher assistant: bridging the gap between student and teacher. arXiv preprint arXiv:1902.03393 (2019)

24. Moriya, T., et al.: Efficient building strategy with knowledge distillation for small-footprint acoustic models. In: 2018 IEEE Spoken Language Technology Workshop (SLT), pp. 21–28 (2018). https://doi.org/10.1109/SLT.2018.8639545

25. Munim, R.M., Inoue, N., Shinoda, K.: Sequence-level knowledge distillation for model compression of attention-based sequence-to-sequence speech recognition. In: ICASSP 2019–2019 IEEE International Conference on Acoustics, Speech and Signal Processing (ICASSP), pp. 6151–6155. IEEE (2019)

26. Parthasarathi, S.H.K., Hoffmeister, B., Matsoukas, S., Mandal, A., Strom, N., Garimella, S.: fMLLR based feature-space speaker adaptation of DNN acoustic models. In: Proceedings of Interspeech (2015)

27. Parthasarathi, S.H.K., Sivakrishnan, N., Ladkat, P., Strom, N.: Realizing petabyte scale acoustic modeling. IEEE J. Emerg. Sel. Top. Circuits Syst. **9**, 422-432 (2019)

28. Parthasarathi, S.H.K., Strom, N.: Lessons from building acoustic models from a million hours of speech. In: Proceedings of ICASSP (2019)

29. Pundak, G., Sainath, T.: Lower frame rate neural network acoustic models. In: Proceedings of Interspeech (2016)

30. Sak, H., Senior, A., Rao, K., Beaufays, F.: Fast and accurate recurrent neural network acoustic models for speech recognition. In: INTERSPEECH (2015)
31. Shi, W., Cao, J., Zhang, Q., Li, Y., Xu, L.: Edge computing: vision and challenges. IEEE Internet Things J. **3**, 637–646 (2016)
32. Siu, M.H., Gish, H., Richardson, F.: Improved estimation, evaluation and applications of confidence measures for speech recognition. In: Proceedings of European Conference on Speech Communication and Technology (1997)
33. Strom, N.: Scalable distributed DNN training using commodity GPU cloud computing. In: Proceedings of Interspeech (2015)
34. Watanabe, S., Hori, T., Le Roux, J., Hershey, J.R.: Student-teacher network learning with enhanced features. In: 2017 IEEE International Conference on Acoustics, Speech and Signal Processing (ICASSP), pp. 5275–5279 (2017). https://doi.org/10.1109/ICASSP.2017.7953163
35. Waters, A., Chebotar, Y.: Distilling knowledge from ensembles of neural networks for speech recognition. In: Interspeech (2016)
36. Weninger, F., Mana, F., Gemello, R., Andres-Ferrer, J., Zhan, P.: Semi-supervised learning with data augmentation for end-to-end ASR (2020)
37. Wong, J.H.M., Gales, M.: Sequence student-teacher training of deep neural networks. In: INTERSPEECH (2016)
38. Xie, Q., Dai, Z., Hovy, E., Luong, M.T., Le, Q.V.: Unsupervised data augmentation for consistency training (2020)
39. Yanzhang, H., et al.: Streaming end-to-end speech recognition for mobile devices. arXiv preprint arXiv:1811.06621 (2018)
40. Yu, W., Liang, F., He, X., Hatcher, W.G., Lu, C., Lin, J., Yang, X.: A survey on the edge computing for the Internet of Things. IEEE Access **6**, 6900–6919 (2017)
41. Zhang, Y., et al.: Pushing the limits of semi-supervised learning for automatic speech recognition (2020)

An AI-Based Detection System for Mudrabharati: A Novel Unified Fingerspelling System for Indic Scripts

F. Amal Jude Ashwin[1], V. Srinivasa Chakravarthy[1(✉)] (iD),
and Sunil Kumar Kopparapu[2] (iD)

[1] Bhupat and Jyoti Mehta School of Biosciences, Department of Biotechnology,
IIT Madras, Chennai, India
schakra@ee.iitm.ac.in
[2] TCS Research, Tata Consultancy Services Limited, Mumbai, India
sunilkumar.kopparapu@tcs.com

Abstract. Sign Language (SL) is a potential tool for communication in the hearing and speech-impaired community. As individual words cannot be communicated accurately using the SL gestures, fingerspelling is adopted to spell out names of people and places. Due to rich vocabulary and diversity in Indic scripts, and the abugida nature of Indic scripts that distinguish them from a prominent world script like the Roman script, it is cumbersome to use American Sign Language (ASL) convention for fingerspelling in Indian languages. Moreover, due to the existence of 10 major scripts in India, it is a futile task to develop a separate fingerspelling convention for each individual Indic script based on the geometry of the characters. In this paper, we propose a novel and unified fingerspelling system known as Mudrabharati for Indic scripts. The gestures of Mudrabharati are constructed based on the phonetics of Indian scripts and not the geometry of the glyphs that compose the individual characters. Unlike ASL that utilizes just one hand, Mudrabharati uses both the hands - one for consonants and the other for vowels; swarayukta aksharas (Consonant-Vowel combinations) are gestured by using both the hands. An Artificial Intelligence (AI) based recognition system for Mudrabharati that returns the character in Devanagari and Tamil scripts is developed.

Keywords: Fingerspelling · Sign Language · Indic scripts · Text entry software · Hand pose estimator · Finite state machine · Multilayer perceptron

1 Introduction

Sign language (SL) is a form of communication that uses gestures, facial expressions and body language and is predominantly used by the hearing and speech impaired people and also by healthy individuals in noisy places [1,12]. There are

© Springer Nature Switzerland AG 2021
K. Ekštein et al. (Eds.): TSD 2021, LNAI 12848, pp. 425–434, 2021.
https://doi.org/10.1007/978-3-030-83527-9_36

around 300 distinct SL's used across the world, each varying with the nation in which it is used [7,8]. Some of the examples of SLs are Indian Sign Language (ISL), American Sign Language (ASL) and German Sign Language (GSL) [2,4,16]. As of 2019, 70 million people across the world and 10 million people in India depend on SL for their core communication [9].

Sign language basically is appropriate for expressing language at conceptual level, and not adequate for communicating at alphabet level. Fingerspelling is a type of SL that uses hand gestures to represent alphabets of a written language. Fingerspelling is commonly used to spell names, places and other proper nouns that cannot be gestured precisely at word level. In ASL, Roman script is represented using 26 gestures corresponding to 26 distinct alphabets [2]. The gestures are inspired by the geometry of the alphabets and are easy to remember if the gesturer has prior knowledge of the written script. ASL can only serve English speaking population in India and is not relevant to those who primarily communicate in Indian languages. ASL adds another constraint of having knowledge of English language for its usage. Therefore, in India, ISL is used by the hearing and speech impaired people. Although, ISL has its own vocabulary for words, it lacks a vocabulary for fingerspelling of Indian scripts.

India is a land of a large number of languages. There are ten major scripts that are used to write most of the major languages of India. These scripts include: 1) Bengali (used for Bengali and Assamese), 2) Devanagari (used for Hindi and Marathi), 3) Gujarati, 4) Gurumukhi (used for Punjabi), 5) Kannada, 6) Malayalam, 7) Oriya, 8) Tamil, 9) Telugu and 10) Urdu. Most Indian writing systems are based on a peculiar feature known as the composite character or swarayukta akshara [3]. Linear writing systems like the Roman script used in English, and other Western European languages, consist of a set of characters written horizontally, left to right. Indian scripts consist of composite characters, which are combinations of smaller units, which have a vertical, multi-tier organization. Most major Indian languages are written from left to right, with the exception of Urdu that is written from right to left. A single composite character represents either a complete syllable, or the coda of one syllable and the onset of another [3,5]. Each of the major Indian scripts listed above (except Urdu) consists of about 16 vowels and about 37 consonants. Tamil has a much smaller number of consonants compared to other Indian languages. A novel and unified Indic script known as Bharati script was recently proposed, that incorporates the above common underlying phonetic organization of most Indic scripts [11].

Due to the complex construction of characters and rich variations in Indian scripts, it is an Himalayan endeavor to device a fingerspelling convention that is based on the geometry of the scripts. Moreover, such a convention can only be used in the part of the country that uses the script. In order to overcome this problem, we propose for the first time, a unified, novel fingerspelling convention for all the 10 major Indian scripts called Mudrabharati. The Mudrabharati fingerspelling convention was inspired by the recently proposed Bharati script [11]. Although there is a great diversity among the glyphs used in different Indic scripts, phonetically most major Indic scripts (other than Urdu) have a common organization. Mudrabharati exploits the phonetical homology among the Indian scripts and uses two hands to fingerspell a character in any Indian script.

The main contribution of this paper is (a) the proposal of a novel single fingerspelling convention that spans over a number of Indic languages called Mudrabarathi (Sect. 2), and (b) a machine learning based functional visual detection system for Mudrabharati by considering the example of Devanagari and Tamil scripts.

2 Fingerspelling Convention for Mudrabharati

Indic characters are not just vowels and consonants, but are also formed by the combination of these two. A single composite character in Indic scripts can have up to 3 consonants and a vowel. Therefore, the number of characters in a typical Indic script (with the exception of Tamil) is in the scale of over ten thousand and it is practically impossible to assign unique gesture to each of them based on their geometry. However, based on the phonetical nature of the alphabets, they can be broadly classified into three categories; (a) Consonant Akshara, (b) Vowel Akshara and (c) Swarayukta Akshara in addition to punctuation.

(A) **Consonant Akshara:** Phonetically, most consonants are plosives i.e. they are uttered as bursts [13]. In order to mimic the same, consonants are gestured as flashes. Nine positions and 5 different gestures are assigned to the consonant hand (see Fig. 1(B)). As is evident, 45 unique characters can be gestured using the consonant hand.

(B) **Vowel Akshara:** Vowels can be uttered continuously without any pauses. Since the number of vowels is much smaller than the consonants in Indic scripts, unique gestures are assigned to each vowel (see Fig. 1(C)). The time unit for which a letter is uttered is called Matra. Based on the temporal scale selected, a vowel can either be uttered for a shorter duration (one matra) known as hrasva, or for a longer duration (two matras) known as dheerga. Dheergas are represented using the same gesture as the corresponding shorter vowel, but are gestured for a longer duration.

(C) **Swarayukta Akshara:** These sounds are produced by the combination of a consonant and a vowel akshara. Since the right hand is used to gesture consonants and the left hand is used to gesture vowels, the convention permits the gesturer to represent the swarayukta akshara. Upon gesturing the consonant akshara (right hand) and the vowel akshara (left hand) simultaneously, a swarayukta akshara is rendered (see Fig. 1(E)).

(D) **Punctuation:** Along with characters, punctuation can also be gestured in Mudrabharati. The workspace of the vowel hand has two positions; the top workspace is used to gesture vowels while the bottom workspace is used to represent punctuation. The gesture and the corresponding punctuation is explained in Fig. 1(D).

As it can be observed, the complete alphabet set of Indic script can be gestured using both the left and the right hand with the duration of the gesture also playing a role in alphabet representation. The gestures are based on the articulation of the alphabets and not the shape/glyph of the alphabet making

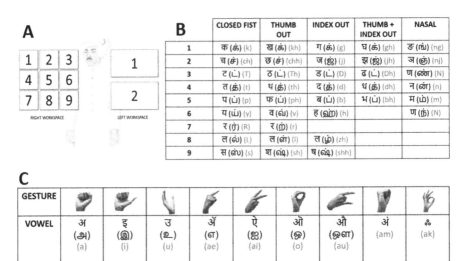

A

Right Workspace:

1	2	3
4	5	6
7	8	9

RIGHT WORKSPACE

Left Workspace:

1
2

LEFT WORKSPACE

B

	CLOSED FIST	THUMB OUT	INDEX OUT	THUMB + INDEX OUT	NASAL
1	क (க்) (k)	ख (க்) (kh)	ग (க்) (g)	घ (க்) (gh)	ङ (ங்) (ng)
2	च (ச்) (ch)	छ (ச்) (chh)	ज (ஜ்) (j)	झ (ஜ்) (jh)	ञ (ஞ்) (nj)
3	ट (ட்) (T)	ठ (ட்) (Th)	ड (ட்) (D)	ढ (ட்) (Dh)	ण (ண்) (N)
4	त (த்) (t)	थ (த்) (th)	द (த்) (d)	ध (த்) (dh)	न (ன்) (n)
5	प (ப்) (p)	फ (ப்) (ph)	ब (ப்) (b)	भ (ப்) (bh)	म (ம்) (m)
6	य (ய்) (y)	व (வ்) (v)	ह (ஹ்) (h)		ण (ந்) (N)
7	र (ற்) (R)	र (ர்) (r)			
8	ल (ல்) (L)	ल (ள்) (l)	ल (ழ்) (zh)		
9	स (ஸ்) (s)	श (ஶ்) (sh)	ष (ஷ்) (shh)		

C

GESTURE									
VOWEL	अ (அ) (a)	इ (இ) (i)	उ (உ) (u)	अॅ (எ) (ae)	ऐ (ஐ) (ai)	ओ (ஒ) (o)	औ (ஒள) (au)	अं (am)	◌ॐ (ak)

D

GESTURE									
PUNCTUATION	Period	Comma	Space	Next line	Question mark	Exclamation	Double quotes	Semi-colon	Delete word	Backspace character
	.	,	_	/n	?	!	"	;		

E

	अ (அ) (a)	इ (இ) (i)	उ (உ) (u)	अॅ (எ) (ae)	ऐ (ஐ) (ai)	ओ (ஒ) (o)	औ (ஒள) (au)	अं (am)	अः (aha)
क (க்) (k)	क (க) (ka)	कि (கி) (ki)	कु (கு) (ku)	कॅ (கெ) (kae)	कै (கை) (kai)	को (கொ) (ko)	कौ (கௌ) (kau)	कं (kam)	कः (kaha)

Fig. 1. (A) Positions used by the gesturer for the right and the left hand. Right workspace has 9 different positions for the consonants, while the left workspace has 2 positions – 1 for vowel, 2 for punctuation, (B) The position and gesture combination and corresponding alphabet for consonants, the gesture and the corresponding character for (C) vowels, (D) punctuation and (E) Formulation of swarayukta akshara by combining consonant and vowel akshara.

the proposed Mudrabharathi independent of the language (unified across most Indic languages). This formulation makes it easy for people to recall and gesture the potentially large number of alphabets in Indic scripts. Uniformity across several Indic languages is also a very important feature of this representation. This formulation is one of the contribution of this paper. In the next section we describe an automated system to machine recognize Mudrabarathi.

3   Detection System for Mudrabharati

The detection system is constructed by combining the following modules: (A) a face detector, (B) a hand-pose estimator, (C) self-organizing maps, (D) gesture predictor and (E) finite state machines for consonant and vowel recognition. Python programming language is used to develop the backend system. Please note that the emphasis is on constructing a functional system and not the type of algorithm used to achieve each functionality.

(A) **Face Detector:** The Haar cascade pre-trained face detection model from Open Source Computer Vision (OpenCV) Library is used with the default parameters for the face detector module [14].

(B) **Hand Pose Estimator:** Real-time hand pose estimation is performed using the pre-trained tensor graph developed based on convolutional pose machines (CPM). CPM consists of a sequence of convolutional neural networks that produces 2D belief maps at each stage for the 21 key points [15]. The input to stage 1 is the RGB frame (gesturer) captured by the webcam. For stages 2 and 3, the output from the previous stage along with the input image is fed to accurately locate the key point. Therefore, the output from stage 3 is the predicted output of the network. The workspace is split into right and left and the inputs are fed to the network separately to localize and estimate the pose of both the hands of the user. The 21 key points for each hand are returned as the output from the network. With the help of an adjacency matrix, the key points are linked to construct the predicted skeletal structure of the hand.

(C) **Self Organizing Maps:** Kohonen's self-organizing map (SOM) algorithm [6] is used to predict the position of the hands. A trained 3×3 SOM is used for the right hand, and a 1×2 map is used for the vowel hand. The pixel coordinate of the hand is fed as input to the SOM.

(D) **Gesture Predictor:** The 21 key points predicted by the hand pose estimator are normalized and fed as input to the pre-trained multi-layer perceptron with 20 hidden nodes and n output classes (n is the number of available gestures). The hidden nodes are modelled as sigmoid activation function and the output nodes are modeled using soft-max activation function. The class corresponding to the node that shows maximum activity for a given workspace of the frame is considered as the predicted gesture of the corresponding hand.

(E) **Finite State Machines:** The system can exist in two states; the relaxed state where the user is not gesturing any sign and gesture state, where the system is ready to process gestures. Relaxed state is similar to the 0 decibel state of a speaker where no sound is produced. The toggle between these two states is different for the consonant and the vowel hand. Figures 2 and 3 explain the switch between different states for consonant and vowel hands.

  (a) **Consonants:**

    i. **Relaxed state to gesture n states:** Once the user is in relaxed state with relaxed gesture, they can enter the gesture n ($= 1, 2, 3, \cdots$) state by representing gesture n using right hand.

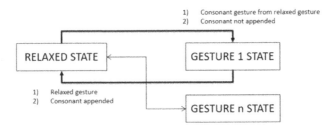

Fig. 2. Finite state machine for consonants.

   ii. **Gesture n state to relaxed state:** The system switches back to relaxed state from any other state when the user signs relaxed gesture using the right hand or when the user has successfully gestured a consonant and the system recognizes and appends the character. In the later scenario, the system enters relaxed state and the user cannot switch to any other gesture state unless they voluntarily sign the relaxed gesture and then the intended gesture. This ensures that the consonants are gestured as plosives and not continuously.

(b) **Vowels:**

   i. **Relaxed state to gesture n states:** Similar to consonants, the user can enter the gesture n state by signing the corresponding gesture.

   ii. **Gesture n state to relaxed state:** As vowels are continuous, the toggle from gesture state to relaxed state is performed only when the relaxed gesture is signed.

   iii. **Gesture n state to gesture m state:** The switch from one vowel gesture state to another vowel gesture state happens when the user signs the gesture m. Unlike consonants, the user does not have to sign relaxed gesture and then the intended gesture to toggle between two vowel gesture states.

   iv. **Gesture n state to and from gesture n dheerga state:** Once the gesture n has been recognized and appended by the system, if the user sustains the same gesture, then the system will toggle to the dheerga state. Upon successfully appending the dheerga vowel, the system goes back to the shorter version of gesture n state.

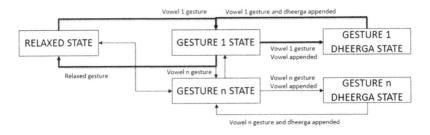

Fig. 3. Finite state machine for vowels.

4   Working of the System

4.1   Calibration Step

As the positions can vary based on the location of the camera, the gesturer has to calibrate the system before beginning to gesture. Initially, the gesturer has to go to position 1 using right hand and record the pixel coordinate. Then, the gesturer has to go to position 9 and record the pixel coordinate (see Fig. 1(A)). The other coordinates are calculated by the system using position 1 and position 9 (see Table 1). Since the left workspace is the mirror of the right workspace about the face, the left hand coordinates are calculated from the right hand positions.

Table 1. Calibrated hand position estimation (see Fig. 1(A))

SNo.	Position	Formula
1	x_1, y_1	Recorded during calibration
2	x_2, y_2	$(x_1 + x_9)/2, y_1$
3	x_3, y_3	x_9, y_1
4	x_4, y_4	$x_1, (y_1 + y_9)/2$
5	x_5, y_5	$(x_1 + x_9)/2, (y_1 + y_9)/2$
6	x_6, y_6	$x_9, (y_1 + y_9)/2$
7	x_7, y_7	x_1, y_9
8	x_8, y_8	$(x_1 + x_9)/2, y_9$
9	x_9, y_9	Recorded during calibration
1*	x_1^L, y_1^L	x_2, y_2
2*	x_2^L, y_2^L	x_7, y_7

The positions are egocentric to the face coordinates. Whenever the gesturer moves sideward, the SOM moves accordingly making the system user position dependent. While calibrating, the size of the face is also recorded by the system. Therefore, if the gesturer moves forward or backward post calibration, the spacing between the positions are automatically adjusted based on the size of the face. Final allocentric positions are calculated using (1).

$$\text{Position}_n = \left(\left(\frac{f}{f_0}\right) x_n - fc_x, \left(\frac{f}{f_0}\right) y_n - fc_y \right) \tag{1}$$

Face size in frame t is denoted as f, face size in calibrated frame is represented as f_0 and the coordinates of face in frame t is $fc_{x,y}$.

4.2   Character Prediction

Post calibration, the system captures the frame using the webcam and processes the global window (see Fig. 4) as follows,

1. The face is detected in the global window and the size and coordinate of the face are recorded.
2. Based on the coordinate of the face, the frame is split into right and left workspace.
3. The local window of the left workspace is fed to the hand pose estimator to localize and predict the 21 key points of the vowel hand.
4. Simultaneously, the 21 key points of the consonant hand is predicted using the local window of the right workspace.
5. The positions of the hands are estimated using the corresponding SOM and the egocentric hand coordinates.
6. The intended gesture is predicted by reshaping the 21 key points and feeding it to the gesture predictor. Thus, the position and gesture of both the hands are returned from the system.
7. The gesture and position are matched with the dictionary. If it is a hit, then the corresponding character is returned by the system for frame t.

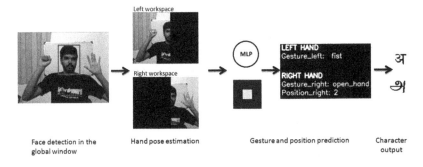

Fig. 4. Algorithm flow for global window processing captured using webcam and prediction of character in Devanagari and Tamil script.

4.3   Experimental Results

The video of the developer formulating sentences in Devanagari and Tamil scripts is published in the Mudrabharati YouTube channel [10]. The Hindi sentence is a patriotic phrase made up of 3 words (8 characters) and took ≈ 20 s to complete gesturing the sentence, while the Tamil sentence is a line from Thirukural that consists of 7 words (30 characters) and was gestured in 75 seconds using Mudrabharati and the detection system. With practice the gesturing speed can be improved. Nevertheless in the current scenario, where there is no option to fingerspell in Indic languages, it is probably the only functional and usable system for the hearing and the speech impaired.

5   Conclusion

Mudrabharati, unified across several Indic languages, can be used by the hearing and speech impaired people to communicate words written in Indic scripts. This removes the constraint on the user to be English language aware to spell Indic words in ASL. This novel convention cuts down the need to learn an additional language to gesture and permits the signers to convey words (particularly proper nouns) in their native tongue. Since the convention is unified for all Indian scripts, one can convey any formulated sentence in nearly any Indian language using Mudrabharati with no knowledge of the corresponding script.

The fully functional detection system can be integrated with technologies such as Augmented Reality and text-to-speech systems to develop assistive devices for communication by the deaf community. Upon discovering an efficient vibrotactile feedback method for sounds, the system can be recommended for initial stages of speech therapy as it encompasses all the possible phonics. Further, the proposed finite state machine algorithm can be utilised to develop a comprehensive and sequential detection system for other sign languages.

The detection system can also potentially be used as a base to develop a text-entry and manipulation software for all Indian languages without requiring any special keyboards or plug-ins. Currently, during the COVID-19 pandemic scenario, touchless text-entry software has a special relevance in order to minimize human contact with shared computer systems. The non-contact aspect of Mudrabharati can be used in order to increase sanitation and safety.

References

1. Berke, J.: Who uses sign language? Deaf and other non-verbal users of sign language (2018). https://www.verywellhealth.com/sign-language-nonverbal-users-1046848
2. Carmel, S.: International hand alphabet charts. National Association of the Deaf (United States) (1982)
3. Daniels, P.T., Bright, W.: The World's Writing Systems. Oxford University Press, Oxford and New York (1996)
4. Hammarström, H., Forkel, R., Haspelmath, M.: German Sign Language. Glottolog 3.0. Max Planck Institute for the Science of Human History, Jena (2017)
5. Ishida, R.: An introduction to Indic scripts. In: Proceedings of the 22nd International Unicode Conference (2002)
6. Kohonen, T.: Self-organized formation of topologically correct feature maps. Biol. Cybern. **43**(1), 59–69 (1982)
7. Kyle, J., Woll, B.: Sign Language: The Study of Deaf People and Their Language. Press Syndicate of the University of Cambridge, Cambridge (1985)
8. Lewis, M.P., Simons, G.F., Fennig, C.D.: Deaf Sign Language. Ethnologue: Languages of the World (2013)
9. Mininstry of Statistics: Disabled Persons in India: A statistical profile. Ministry of Statistics and Programme Implementation (2016)
10. Mudrabharati: Mudrabharati calibration and results video. https://youtu.be/iGKguuqGw6o

11. Naik, M., Chakravarthy, V.S.: A comparative study of complexity of handwritten Bharati characters with that of major Indian scripts. In: 2017 International Joint Conference on Neural Networks, pp. 3050–3057 (2017)

12. Perlmutter, D.M.: The Language of the Deaf. New York Review of Books, New York (1991)

13. Rao, P.B.: Salient phonetic features of Indian languages in speech technology. Sadhana **36**(5), 587–599 (2011)

14. Viola, P., Jones, M.: Rapid object detection using a boosted cascade of simple features. In: IEEE Conference on Computer Vision and Pattern Recognition, pp. 511–518 (2001)

15. Wei, S., Ramakrishna, V., Kanade, T., Sheikh, Y.: Convolutional Pose Machines. CoRR abs/1602.00134 (2016). http://arxiv.org/abs/1602.00134

16. Zeshan, U.: Sign Language of Indo-Pakistan: A Description of a Signed Language. John Benjamins Publishing Co., Philadelphia (2000)

Is There Any Additional Information in a Neural Network Trained for Pathological Speech Classification?

C. D. Rios-Urrego[1]($\boxtimes$)🄳, J. C. Vásquez-Correa[1,2]🄳,
J. R. Orozco-Arroyave[1,2]🄳, and E. Nöth[2]🄳

[1] Faculty of Engineering, University of Antioquia UdeA, Medellín, Colombia
cdavid.rios@udea.edu.co
[2] Pattern Recognition Lab, Friedrich-Alexander-Universität Erlangen-Nürnberg,
Erlangen, Germany

Abstract. Speech is a biomarker extensively explored by the scientific community for different health-care applications because its reduced cost and non-intrusiveness. Specifically, in Parkinson's disease, speech signals and deep learning methods have been explored for the automatic assessment and monitoring of patients. Related studies have shown to be very accurate to discriminate pathological vs. healthy speech. In spite of the high accuracies observed to detect the presence of diseases from speech, it is not clear which additional information about the speakers or the environment is implicitly learned by the deep learning systems. This study proposes a methodology to evaluate intermediate representations of a neural network in order to find out which other speaker traits and aspects are learned by the system during the training process. We trained models to detect the presence of Parkinson's disease from speech. Then, we used intermediate representations of the network to classify additional speaker traits such as gender, age, and the native language. It is important to detect which information is available inside the neural network that can lead to *open the black-box* and to detect possible algorithmic biases. The results indicate that the network, in addition to adjusting its parameters for disease classification, also acquires knowledge about gender of the speakers in the first layers, and about speech tasks and the native language in the last layers of the network.

Keywords: Pathological speech · Parkinson's disease · Speech processing · Deep learning · Neural networks

1 Introduction

Speech allows to evaluate and monitor different symptoms of patients suffering from neurodegenerative diseases. The main benefit of using this biomarker is that it is non-invasive, and it can be captured remotely at a very low cost. Different biomarkers of Parkinson's disease (PD) including speech have been

© Springer Nature Switzerland AG 2021
K. Ekštein et al. (Eds.): TSD 2021, LNAI 12848, pp. 435–447, 2021.
https://doi.org/10.1007/978-3-030-83527-9_37

studied for the development of computer aided tools to support the diagnosis and monitoring of patients [12]. PD is a neurological disorder caused by the progressive loss of dopaminergic neurons in the substantia nigra of the brain [7]. This disease is characterized by resting tremor, rigidity, bradykinesia, postural instability, among other symptoms [7,9]. Speech impairments observed in PD patients are typically grouped and called hypokinetic dysarthria. The main speech symptoms include reduced intensity, harsh and breathy voice quality, increased voice nasality, monopitch, monoludness, imprecise articulation of consonants, and involuntary introduction of pauses [16].

Deep learning has enabled advances in the automatic assessment of speech in PD patients. Different researchers have reported promising results in the classification of PD patients vs. Healthy Controls (HC) subjects. The researchers have used different deep learning architectures such as Convolutional Neural Networks (CNNs) [18,19,21], Recurrent Neural Networks (RNNs) with Long Short-Term Memory (LSTM) units [1,14], fully connected networks [3,5,14], and their combination [8]. However, obtaining a large number of samples for training these architectures is difficult and expensive. Therefore, the scientific community has explored transfer learning techniques for training these models. Several authors have explored the feature extraction or fine-tuning method where network weights trained with a base corpus are adjusted to a target database [8,13,20]. In most cases, it has been observed improvements in performance.

Although the advances in the study of Parkinson's speech using deep learning architectures, there are no studies about the interpretation and understanding of other speaker or environmental traits possibly learned during the training of the neural network. The detection of additional demographic information possible learned by the network could help in the process to *open the black-box* and to detect possible algorithmic biases. An approximation to this goal was presented in the field of automatic speech recognition in [17]. The authors evaluated the transferability of a neural network to be fine-tuned with utterances in different languages, in order to track the language-specificity of each layer. The results indicated that the first 2 layers are fully transferable among languages, layers 2–8 are highly transferable but they evidence some specific-language features. Finally, the last layers are language-dependent, but they can be fine-tuned to the target specific languages.

The main objective of this study is to perform preliminary experiments to help in discovering which are the layers of a CNN that are involved in the process of learning particular information potentially useful to characterize different speaker traits such as age, gender, native language, speech disorders, and others. To address the aforementioned objective, we trained a ResNet-based model with data from three corpora in different languages to discriminate between PD and HC speakers. Then, we used four intermediate representations or embedding vectors from the network in order to classify additional demographic data from the speakers. Based on the work described by J. A. Thompson in [17] for automatic speech recognition, we hypothesize that the level of abstraction in a deep neural network is distributed in the following order: simpler traits can be found in early stages of the network such as gender, while pathology and language detection are more complex characteristics that might be present in later stages of the architecture. With respect to age, we believe that it is not possible to identify it precisely in this work because the participants evaluated are all elderly; therefore, there is not enough variability in age. To the best of our knowledge, this is the first study in the field of pathological speech processing that attempts to identify speaker traits that are implicitly learned by a neural network in intermediate layers in addition to the labels used for the supervised training.

The rest of the paper is as follows: Sect. 2 describes the different corpora considered for this study. Section 3 explains the different stages of the methodology addressed to recognize which information is available in intermediate representations of a CNN. Section 4 shows the main results obtained in this study. Finally, Sect. 5 contains the conclusions and future trends derived from this study.

2   Data

We considered speech corpora in three different languages: Spanish, German, and Czech. Each database contains HC subjects and PD patients evaluated by specialized neurologists according to the Movement Disorder Society - Unified Parkinson's Disease Rating Scale (MDS-UPDRS-III) [4]. All recordings were captured in noise controlled conditions, and the speech signals were down-sampled to 16 kHz. Table 1 summarizes the information about the patients and healthy speakers from the three corpora.

Table 1. Demographic information from the speakers in each corpus. **G.**: gender (**M.** male or **F.** female). Values are reported in terms of mean $\pm$ standard deviation.

	G	PD-Spanish		PD-German		PD-Czech	
		PD	HC	PD	HC	PD	HC
# subjects	M	25	25	47	44	30	30
	F	25	25	41	44	20	19
Age [years]	M	61.3 ± 11	60.5 ± 12	66.7 ± 9	63.8 ± 13	65.3 ± 10	60.3 ± 12
	F	60.7 ± 7	61.4 ± 7	66.2 ± 10	62.6 ± 15	60.1 ± 9	63.5 ± 11
Range of Age [years]	M	33–81	31–86	47–82	44–83	43–82	41–77
	F	49–75	49–76	41–84	44–85	41–72	40–79
Years since diagnosis	M	8.7 ± 6	–	7.0 ± 6	–	6.7 ± 5	–
	F	12.6 ± 12	–	7.1 ± 6	–	6.8 ± 5	–
MDS-UPDRS-III	M	37.8 ± 22	–	22.1 ± 10	–	21.4 ± 12	–
	F	37.6 ± 14	–	23.3 ± 12	–	18.1 ± 10	–
MDS-UPDRS-III speech item	M	1.4 ± 0.9	–	1.4 ± 0.6	–	0.9 ± 0.5	–
	F	1.3 ± 0.8	–	1.2 ± 0.5	–	0.7 ± 0.6	–

Figure 1 shows the distribution of the MDS-UPDRS-III scores for each database. Note that PD-Spanish patients are in a more severe stage of the disease. Note also that PD-German patients are in an intermediate stage, while

PD-Czech patients have the lowest MDS-UPDRS-III score, which indicates that many of the Czech-PD patients are in an earlier stage of the disease.

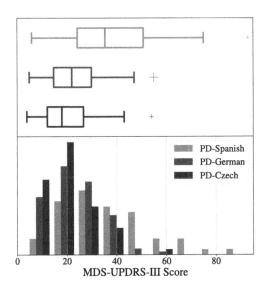

Fig. 1. Distribution of the MDS-UPDRS-III score for each database.

PD-Spanish: We considered the PC-GITA database [11], which contains recordings of 50 PD patients and 50 HC subjects. All participants are Colombian native speakers. The subjects produced a total of 21 speech tasks, including: 10 sentences, a monologue, a read text, isolated words, rapid repetition of 6 diadochokinetic (DDK) tasks, sustained vowels, and modulated vowels. All patients were in ON state at the time of the recording, i.e., under the effect of their daily medication.

PD-German: A total of 176 German native speakers (88 PD patients and 88 HC subjects) are considered for this study [2]. Each participant performed different speech tasks including: a monologue, a read text, reading of question-answer-pairs, 5 sentences, 7 isolated words, rapid repetition of 8 DDKs, and sustained vowels. The patients were recorded as well in ON state, i.e., under the effect of their daily medication.

PD-Czech: This corpus consisted of 50 PD patients and 49 HC subjects, Czech native speakers [15]. A total of 4 speech tasks are included: a monologue, a read text, a DDK (/pa-ta-ka/), and sustained vowels. All PD patients were recruited at their first visit to the clinic and were examined before symptomatic treatment to start. Disease duration was based upon patients' self-report [10].

3   Methods

The methodology addressed in this study consists of the following main stages: the corpora is pre-processed, then a CNN is trained using spectrograms, then embeddings are extracted at different layers of the network, and finally the classification of each trait is performed using a support vector machine. This methodology is summarized in Fig. 2.

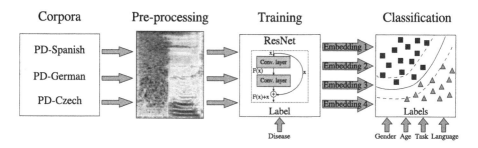

Fig. 2. General methodology.

3.1   Pre-processing

All signals are down-sampled to 16 kHz, then they are segmented into 500 ms chunks with 250 ms time-shift. From each chunk, a time-frequency representation is obtained using the Short-Time Fourier Transform (STFT) to feed the CNNs. Each spectrogram is obtained using Hanning windows of 32 ms and a step-size of 8 ms, forming 63 time frames per chunk. Each representation is transformed into a Mel-scale spectrogram with 128 Mel filters; therefore, the final representation to feed the CNN is 128×63.

3.2   Training

The training of each database is performed using a ResNet-based CNN. This topology has stood out in deep learning because it tries to solve the vanishing gradient problem [6]. A ResNet consists of a series of layers and an identity mapping that adds the input from the block to the output, that is, instead of trying to learn from a direct mapping of x and with a function $H(x)$, a residual function $H(x) = F(x) + x$ is defined. $F(x)$ represents the stacked layers of the neural network and x is the identity function, which is passed directly to the output of the residual block.

We are using a ResNet model with 6 residual blocks and 3 main blocks with 16, 32, and 64 feature maps, respectively. Table 2 shows details of the implemented architecture. The convolutional layers are represented as $(I \times O \times K, S)$, where I and O are the number of input and output channels, respectively, K is

Table 2. Architecture of the ResNet-based model implemented in this study. Conv.: Convolution, Avg. Pool.: Average pooling, FC: Fully connected. Emb.: embedding vector.

Stage	Type of layer	Output size	Emb. size	Emb. size after PCA
Conv. 1	Conv. $(1 \times 16 \times 3,1)$	$128 \times 63 \times 16$	258048	72
Block 1	Conv. $(16 \times 16 \times 3,1)$ Conv. $(16 \times 16 \times 3,1)$ } $\times 2$	$128 \times 63 \times 16$	258048	101
Block 2	Conv. $(16 \times 32 \times 3,2)$ Conv. $(32 \times 32 \times 3,1)$ } $\times 2$	$64 \times 32 \times 32$	131072	121
Block 3	Conv. $(32 \times 64 \times 3,2)$ Conv. $(64 \times 64 \times 3,1)$ } $\times 2$	$32 \times 16 \times 64$	65536	117
Pooling	Avg. Pool. $(32,16)$	$1 \times 1 \times 64$		
Output	FC $(64,2)$	$1 \times 1 \times 2$		

the kernel size, and S is the stride. ReLu activations are considered in the hidden layers, and a Softmax activation function is applied in the output to make the final decision.

3.3   Embedding Extraction

For the classification of the different speaker traits, we extract intermediate network representations or embedding vectors from the previously trained models. A total of 4 representations of the network are obtained. The first embedding corresponds to the output of the first convolutional layer shown in Table 2. The second, third, and fourth embedding vectors are obtained at the output of Blocks 1, 2, and 3 from the ResNet model, respectively. A flatten operation upon each representation is performed to convert the matrix into a vector. Then, we computed the mean and standard deviation of each representation obtained from all spectrograms of the same participant in order to create a fixed-length vector to represent each subject. Finally, the dimension of the embedding vectors is reduced using Principal Component Analysis (PCA) with 95% of the total variance. Table 2 also indicates the original dimension of the extracted embedding vectors, and the number of components after PCA, which are used for the later classification of the speaker traits.

3.4   Classification

The embedding representations extracted from the neural network in the different blocks are used to classify different aspects from the speakers such as age, gender, native language, and speech tasks. We used a support vector machine classifier with a radial basis function. Each experiment is trained and evaluated following a speaker independent 10-fold cross-validation strategy. The procedure is repeated 10 times for a better generalization of the results. The parameters of the classifier are optimized through a grid-search where

$C \in \{0.001, 0.005, \cdots, 50, 100\}$ and $\gamma \in \{0.0001, 0.001, \cdots, 100\}$. Finally, the performance of each classifier is evaluated in terms of the accuracy, the area under the ROC curve (AUC), the F1-score, and Cohen's kappa coefficient (κ) for the different problems.

4 Experiments and Results

4.1 Base Models

Different models are trained to classify PD patients vs. HC subjects by implementing the architecture shown in Table 2 and using PD-Spanish, PD-German, and PD-Czech corpora in order to train three language-dependent models. Finally, we consider the combination of the 3 corpora in order to train a language independent model. The models are trained using a cross-entropy loss function and a Stochastic Gradient Descent (SGD) optimizer in Pytorch. The results are obtained following a speaker independent 10-fold cross-validation strategy. Table 3 shows the results obtained for each model. Note that the best model is obtained with the PD-Spanish, followed by PD-German and finally PD-Czech. The results are consistent with the ones observed in Fig. 1, where it is shown that PD-Spanish patients are in the most advanced stage of the disease, thus their classification should be easier. PD-German patients are in an intermediate stage and PD-Czech patients are in an early stage. It is important to mention that the accuracies reported for the 3 databases are similar to those obtained in previous studies [2,10,18]. Finally, the resulting model when combining the 3 databases yields an accuracy of 70% and an AUC value of 0.75. The accuracies obtained for each language in the combined model are 76%, 71%, and 65%, for Spanish, German, and Czech, respectively.

Table 3. Classification of PD vs. HC subjects for the three language dependent and for the language independent models. AUC: Area under the ROC curve. Values are reported in terms of mean $\pm$ standard deviation.

Corpus	Accuracy (%)	F1-Score (%)	AUC
PD-Spanish	90.0 $\pm$ 3.5	89.9 $\pm$ 3.7	0.91 $\pm$ 0.06
PD-German	75.0 $\pm$ 6.3	74.8 $\pm$ 6.4	0.74 $\pm$ 0.10
PD-Czech	68.8 $\pm$ 2.2	68.8 $\pm$ 2.3	0.68 $\pm$ 0.04
3-Databases	69.9 $\pm$ 9.8	68.8 $\pm$ 9.4	0.75 $\pm$ 0.09

4.2   Classification of Age, Gender and Task

Four embedding vectors extracted from intermediate activations of the previously trained neural network are used to classify age, gender, and the speech tasks produced by each subject from the corpora. For age classification, we divided the ages of the participants from each database into 3 equally distributed classes to perform a multi-class classification. For the specific case of speech task classification we only considered 3 tasks that are common in the 3 databases: (1) DDKs, (2) monologue, and (3) read text. The accuracy obtained for each embedding on each corpus and for each classification problem is shown in Table 4.

Table 4. Classification of age, gender, and speech task for the PD-Spanish, PD-German and PD-Czech databases using intermediate embeddings (Emb.). Acc.: Accuracy. Values are reported in terms of mean ± standard deviation.

	Age			Gender			Task		
	PD-Spanish	PD-German	PD-Czech	PD-Spanish	PD-German	PD-Czech	PD-Spanish	PD-German	PD-Czech
	Acc. (%)	Acc. (%)	Acc. (%)	Acc. (%)	Acc. (%)	Acc. (%)	Acc. (%)	Acc. (%)	Acc. (%)
Emb. 1	35.1 ± 1.6	32.8 ± 0.0	36.2 ± 1.0	81.2 ± 1.4	49.4 ± 0.0	60.6 ± 0.0	59.1 ± 1.4	**48.9 ± 0.6**	63.4 ± 0.6
Emb. 2	36.5 ± 1.0	32.8 ± 0.0	35.6 ± 0.6	**84.6 ± 0.8**	49.4 ± 0.0	60.6 ± 0.0	58.8 ± 1.2	43.6 ± 1.1	66.5 ± 0.6
Emb. 3	37.0 ± 1.4	32.8 ± 0.0	33.7 ± 2.0	84.5 ± 1.6	49.4 ± 0.0	63.6 ± 0.8	55.2 ± 0.7	42.8 ± 1.2	72.0 ± 0.9
Emb. 4	36.0 ± 2.1	32.6 ± 0.4	30.9 ± 2.8	81.9 ± 1.9	**85.6 ± 0.8**	**78.9 ± 0.8**	**64.2 ± 1.5**	48.0 ± 0.6	**74.2 ± 0.7**

The results show that in general the network is not able to accurately identify the age of the participants in none of the intermediate embedding. However, note that the results for PD-Spanish are slightly better because the range of age in such corpus is higher than the observed one for PD-German and PD-Czech (see Table 1). This result can be explained having in mind that all speakers are elderly and are in a similar range of age. Conversely, gender and speech tasks are accurately recognized in intermediate layers of the neural network. This results indicate that our model implicitly learned information about the gender of the speakers and the speech tasks performed by the participants. Gender is identified for PD-Spanish from the first layers of the network, while for PD-German and PD-Czech, information about gender is only evidenced in the fourth embedding. Finally, information about speech tasks in PD-Spanish and PD-Czech appear in the last layers of the network. The model trained for PD-German does not find information about the speech task performed by the speakers.

Figure 3 shows a visual representation of the activations using PCA in the last embedding for PD-German and PD-Czech, and the second embedding for PD-Spanish. The aim is to observe how the gender information is present in intermediate parts of the network for each corpus. The figure shows how it is possible to identify the gender of the speakers in the three corpora, which confirms that the network implicitly learns the gender of the speakers. Specifically, for the PD-Spanish plot (left), there are 2 clusters where it is possible to identify male and female speakers. It is also possible to differentiate patients and controls, where patients (circles) are located in the bottom right part of the figure, while controls (triangles) are distributed in the left part of the figure. For the case of PD-German (center), the discrimination between male and female speakers is clearer. There is a trend for patients to be found in the bottom part of the figure, and controls in the upper part of the figure. Finally, for PD-Czech (right), it is observed that males are on the left side, while females are on the right side of the figure. For this case, it is not possible to observe clusters to differentiate controls and patients. This is why this model has the lowest accuracy in that classification problem (see Table 3).

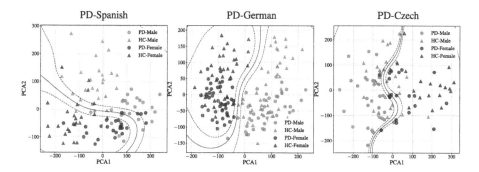

Fig. 3. Visualization of best embeddings for gender classification after applying PCA with 2 principal components.

Regarding the speech task classification, the scatter plots in Fig. 4 indicate that for the three corpora it is possible to differentiate the DDK tasks from continuous speech utterances like the monologue and the read text, which are highly overlapped. These differences are observed even for PD-German, in which the accuracy for speech-task classification is very small. This result is expected because the nature of the DDK tasks, which makes it totally different than spontaneous speech utterances like the monologue or the read text. In addition, note in the scatter plot on the left (PD-Spanish) that it is possible to differentiate PD patients and HC subjects. HCs (triangles) are observed in the upper part of the figure, while the patients are mainly found in the bottom part of the figure. This behavior is only observed for the PD-Spanish model because it is the most accurate one (90.0%) when discriminating PD patients from HC subjects.

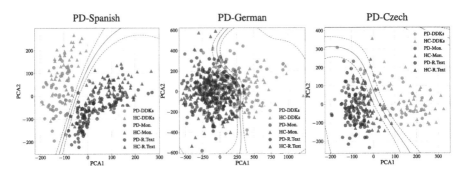

Fig. 4. Visualization of best embedding for speech task classification after applying PCA with 2 principal components.

4.3   Classification of Language

The previously trained model using the three corpora is considered for this experiment. The same four embedding activations are extracted to test whether there is information about the language of the participants in intermediate representations of the CNN. The results are shown in Table 5. Note that the native language of the participants can be identified only in the fourth embedding. This fact indicates that despite never using language information during the training process, later stages of the CNN are able to differentiate the language of each participant, which can be considered as a deeper and more complex information about the speaker, similar to the presence of the disease. Moreover, this result agrees with the one obtained in [17], where the authors conclude that the first layers of a CNN trained with several languages are fully transferable between languages, while the last layers are highly language dependent, as it was confirmed by our experiments.

Table 5. Language classification using embeddings (Emb) extracted from a model trained with the 3 databases. Acc.: Accuracy. Values are reported in terms of mean ± standard deviation

	Language		
	Acc. (%)	F1-Score (%)	κ
Emb. 1	35.6 ± 0.16	33.6 ± 0.2	0.040 ± 0.002
Emb. 2	33.8 ± 0.15	32.4 ± 1.3	0.007 ± 0.003
Emb. 3	41.5 ± 1.08	42.6 ± 0.1	0.141 ± 0.021
Emb. 4	**82.1 ± 0.23**	**84.3 ± 0.1**	**0.765 ± 0.002**

A visual representation using PCA of the activations obtained from the last embedding is shown in Fig. 5. Clusters of each language are observed. Particularly, speakers from the Czech corpus are very well separated, while some of the

Spanish and German speakers are overlapped. Additionally, it is possible to differentiate PD patients and HC subjects for the PD-Spanish corpus (gray), where the patients are clustered in the lower part of the figure, while the controls are in the central part the plot. For the Czech and German corpora, the distinction between patients and HCs is not that clear as in PD-Spanish. However, in some cases patients tend to group in the center of each language-cluster, while the controls tend to surround each of these subgroups.

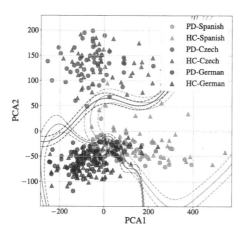

Fig. 5. Visualization of the 4th embedding for language classification after applying PCA with 2 principal components.

5   Conclusion

This paper proposes a methodology to analyze which aspects and speaker traits a CNN can learn when it is trained to classify pathological speech signals. Initially, we trained 4 different models using a CNN based on a ResNet topology. We considered 3 language dependent models trained with different PD databases in Spanish, German and Czech, as well as a language independent model combining the three corpora. We then extracted four intermediate activations of the trained CNNs to evaluate different aspects and traits such as age, gender, speech task and native language of the participants.

The results indicate that the network not only extracts information about the presence of the disease, but also acquires knowledge at different stages to recognize the gender of each participant, the speech tasks uttered by the subjects, and the native language of the speakers. The results showed that the gender can be detected from the first layers of the network for the case of PD-Spanish, and at intermediate and later stages for PD-German and PD-Czech. For the recognition of speech tasks, high accuracies were obtained in the last stage of the network for the Spanish and Czech corpora. Information about the age of the subjects was not observed in intermediate activation layers of the CNNs, probably because there is not enough variability of the age of the participants in the considered corpora, i.e., all of them are elderly speakers. Finally, the results showed that only the final stage of the CNN contains information about the native language of the participants. The gender of the speaker can be considered a simple trait because it is present in early, intermediate, and later stages of the network, while more complex information such as speech task, native language, and the presence of the disease can only be identified in the last layers of the network.

These results suggest that information obtained in all layers of the CNN are gender-dependent. The first layers shown to be independent from language and speech task. Deeper layers show to be dependent from the speech tasks and the native language of the speaker. The results obtained in this study will allow to perform a better oriented transfer learning process and to understand what the neural network learns during training. There are layers with information about certain speaker traits that can be highly transferable to different corpora without the need of fine-tuning the full neural network. This aspects can be explored in further research.

Acknowledgments. The work reported here was financed by CODI from University of Antioquia by grant Number 2017-15530. This project has received funding from the European Unions Horizon 2020 research and innovation programme under the Marie Sklodowska-Curie Grant Agreement No. 766287.

References

1. Arias-Vergara, T., et al.: Automatic detection of voice onset time in voiceless plosives using gated recurrent units. Digital Signal Process. **104**, 102779 (2020)
2. Bocklet, T., et al.: Automatic evaluation of parkinson's speech-acoustic, prosodic and voice related cues. In: Proceedings of INTERSPEECH, pp. 1149–1153 (2013)
3. Caliskan, A., et al.: Diagnosis of the parkinson disease by using deep neural network classifier. Istanbul University J. Electr. Electron. Eng. **17**(2), 3311–3318 (2017)
4. Goetz, C.G., et al.: Movement Disorder Society-sponsored revision of the Unified Parkinson's Disease Rating Scale (MDS-UPDRS): Scale presentation and clinimetric testing results. Mov. Disord. **23**(15), 2129–2170 (2008)
5. Grósz, T., et al.: Assessing the degree of nativeness and parkinson's condition using gaussian processes and deep rectifier neural networks. In: Proceedings of INTERSPEECH (2015)
6. He, K., Zhang, X., Ren, S., Sun, J.: Identity mappings in deep residual networks. In: Leibe, B., Matas, J., Sebe, N., Welling, M. (eds.) ECCV 2016. LNCS, vol. 9908, pp. 630–645. Springer, Cham (2016). https://doi.org/10.1007/978-3-319-46493-0_38
7. Jankovic, J.: Parkinson's disease: clinical features and diagnosis. J. Neurol. Neurosurge. Psychiatry **79**(4), 368–376 (2008)
8. Mallela, J., et al.: Voice based classification of patients with amyotrophic lateral sclerosis, parkinson's disease and healthy controls with CNN-LSTM using transfer learning. In: Proceedings of ICASSP, pp. 6784–6788. IEEE (2020)
9. McKinlay, A., et al.: A profile of neuropsychiatric problems and their relationship to quality of life for parkinson's disease patients without dementia. Parkinsonism Related Disorders **14**(1), 37–42 (2008)

10. Novotný, M., et al.: Glottal source analysis of voice deficits in newly diagnosed drug-naïve patients with parkinson's disease: Correlation between acoustic speech characteristics and non-speech motor performance. Biomed. Signal Process. Control **57**, 101818 (2020)
11. Orozco-Arroyave, J.R., et al.: New Spanish speech corpus database for the analysis of people suffering from parkinson's disease. In: Proceedings of LREC, pp. 342–347 (2014)
12. Orozco-Arroyave, J.R., et al.: Apkinson: the smartphone application for telemonitoring parkinson's patients through speech, gait and hands movement. Neurodegenerative Dis. Manage. **10**(3), 137–157 (2020)
13. Rios-Urrego, C.D., Vásquez-Correa, J.C., Orozco-Arroyave, J.R., Nöth, E.: Transfer learning to detect parkinson's disease from speech in different languages using convolutional neural networks with layer freezing. In: Sojka, P., Kopeček, I., Pala, K., Horák, A. (eds.) TSD 2020. LNCS (LNAI), vol. 12284, pp. 331–339. Springer, Cham (2020). https://doi.org/10.1007/978-3-030-58323-1_36
14. Rizvi, D.R., et al.: An LSTM based deep learning model for voice-based detection of parkinson's disease. Int. J. Adv. Sci. Technol. **29**(5), 8 (2020)
15. Rusz, J.: Detecting speech disorders in early Parkinson's disease by acoustic analysis. Habilitation thesis, Czech Technical University in Prague (2018)
16. Spencer, K.A., Rogers, M.A.: Speech motor programming in hypokinetic and ataxic dysarthria. Brain Lang. **94**(3), 347–366 (2005)
17. Thompson, J.A., et al.: How transferable are features in convolutional neural network acoustic models across languages? In: Proceedings of ICASSP, pp. 2827–2831. IEEE (2019)
18. Vásquez-Correa, J.C., Orozco-Arroyave, J.R., Nöth, E.: Convolutional neural network to model articulation impairments in patients with Parkinson's disease. In: Proceedings of INTERSPEECH, pp. 314–318 (2017)
19. Vavrek, L., et al.: Deep convolutional neural network for detection of pathological speech. In: Proceedings of SAMI, pp. 000245–000250. IEEE (2021)
20. Wodzinski, M., et al.: Deep learning approach to parkinson's disease detection using voice recordings and convolutional neural network dedicated to image classification. In: Proceedings of EMBC, pp. 717–720. IEEE (2019)
21. Wu, H., et al.: Convolutional neural networks for pathological voice detection. In: Proceedings of EMBC, pp. 1–4. IEEE (2018)

On Comparison of XGBoost and Convolutional Neural Networks for Glottal Closure Instant Detection

Michal Vraštil[(✉)] and Jindřich Matoušek[ⓘ]

Department of Cybernetics, New Technology for the Information Society (NTIS),
Faculty of Applied Sciences, University of West Bohemia, Plzeň, Czech Republic
{vrastilm,jmatouse}@kky.zcu.cz

Abstract. In this paper, we progress further in the development of an automatic GCI detection model. In previous papers, we compared XGBoost with other supervised learning models just as with a deep one-dimensional convolutional neural network. Here we aimed to compare a deep one-dimensional convolutional neural network, more precisely the InceptionV3 model, with XGBoost and context-aware XGBoost models trained on the same size datasets. Afterward, we wanted to reveal the influence of dataset consistency and size on the XGBoost performance. All newly created models are compared while tested on our custom test dataset. On the publicly available databases, the XGBoost and context-aware XGBoost with the context of length 7 shows similar and better performance than the InceptionV3 model. Also, the consistency of the training dataset shows significant performance improvement in comparison to the older models.

Keywords: Glottal closure instant (GCI) · Pitch mark · Detection · Classification · Extreme gradient boosting · Convolutional neural network

1 Introduction

Machine learning and especially deep learning are gaining more attraction in many areas of speech processing, replacing the established and refined speech processing techniques (such as auto-correlation, convolution, Gaussian mixture models, or hidden Markov models) [17].

Detection of glottal closure instants (GCIs) could be viewed as a task of determining peaks in the *voiced parts* of the speech signal that corresponds to

This research was supported by the Czech Science Foundation (GA CR), project No. GA19-19324S, and by the grant of the University of West Bohemia, project No. SGS-2019-027. Computational resources were supplied by the project "e-Infrastruktura CZ" (e-INFRA LM2018140) provided within the program Projects of Large Research, Development and Innovations Infrastructures.

© Springer Nature Switzerland AG 2021
K. Ekštein et al. (Eds.): TSD 2021, LNAI 12848, pp. 448–456, 2021.
https://doi.org/10.1007/978-3-030-83527-9_38

the moment of glottal closure, a significant excitation of the vocal tract during speaking. In previous papers [13,14], it was demonstrated that classical machine learning models, and especially the ones based on *extreme gradient boosting* (XGBoost), were capable of outperforming the traditionally used algorithms on several test datasets [14]. In [12] we further improved the XGBoost model and reveal a new context-aware XGBoost model which shows even better performance when compared to our previous work. Recently [15], the deep one-dimensional convolutional neural network, more precisely the InceptionV3 model, beats in performance XGBoost model from [14].

GCI detection task is a two-class classification problem. Models have to decide whether a peak in a speech waveform is a GCI or not [2]. In opposite to that, the traditionally used algorithms, which need the expertise of the user, manually defined rules and carefully selected thresholds to identify GCI candidates from local maxima of various speech representations (see, e.g. [6]). The advantage of a machine learning model is that if a training dataset is available and has relevant features identified from raw speech, classifier parameters are set up automatically without manual tuning. The drawback of this method could be that the identification of relevant features may be time-consuming and tricky, especially when done manually.

There are more less two main approaches in supervised machine learning, classical supervised learning, and deep supervised learning. In this paper, we used the XGBoost model as a member of the classical approach. The XGBoost model is built on top of the gradient boosting algorithm which uses ensembled decision trees as an underlying model. This algorithm trains the first decision tree on the input data. The length of the decision tree is considered before training as one of the hyperparameters. Afterward, another decision tree is trained on the residuals (difference between inputs and outputs of the first decision tree) and so forth until the specified level is reached (set as another hyperparameter) [4].

Convolutional neural networks (CNNs) as an example of the deep learning approach can be used for its ability to extract features automatically. Essentially, deep learning can help in finding the mapping between complex dependencies in raw speech and the corresponding GCIs. CNNs can be directly fed with the raw speech signal without any processing requirement, such as feature identification, extraction, selection, dimension reduction, etc. [5,8]. The ability to perform very well in GCI detection was already shown in [1,7,15,18,20].

In this paper, we focus on the comparison between XGBoost as an example of the classical supervised learning model and deep convolutional neural network as a case of deep supervised learning. Our first research question was if we could further improve XGBoost performance by training it on the same size dataset as CNN. Our second research question was about finding the influence of the data consistency on the XGBoost performance because in [12–14] the XGBoost was trained on the manually labeled data of smaller size and tested on the automatically labeled data. Finally, we compared all models used in this paper on our custom test dataset.

2   Experimental Data

For the training stage of both our XGBoost model and InceptionV3-1D CNN, we used clean 3200 utterances in wave format in the total amount of 338.28 min. All of them were sampled with a 16 kHz sampling rate. We will refer to this further as **n200**. Those data came from 16 diverse speakers and languages. For testing purposes, we chose 2 random records from each speaker. The XGBoost model was also trained on lower-sized datasets. Those datasets were chosen to contain balanced amount of records from each speaker and we will refer them as **n004** for 4 records from each speaker and simultaneously as **n008**, **n016**, **n032** and finally **n064**. The n004 dataset was specially chosen because we wanted to compare the XGBoost trained on this dataset with the model from [12] and so both of these datasets have more less same size. Ground truth GCIs were detected from contemporaneous EGG recordings by the Multi-Phase Algorithm (MPA) [11] and shifted towards the neighboring minimum negative sample in the speech signal.

Table 1. Training and testing datasets overview

Stage	Dataset description	Tag
Training	All 200 records from 16 speakers	n200
	Only 64 records from 16 speakers	n064
	Only 32 records from 16 speakers	n032
	Only 16 records from 16 speakers	n016
	Only 8 records from 16 speakers	n008
	Only 4 records from 16 speakers	n004
Testing	Yet unseen 2 records from 16 speakers	testDataset1
	Mix of the KED, BDL and SLT datasets	testDataset2

The first test dataset consists of two records from each speaker. In total it includes 32 records. We will refer to it as **testDataset1**. The second dataset which was used for testing and comparison with other algorithms consists of a US male (BDL) and a US female (SLT) from the CMU ARCTIC database [3,9]. Each voice consists of 1132 phonetically balanced utterances of total duration ≈54 min per voice. The KED TIMIT database [3], comprising 453 phonetically balanced utterances (≈20 min) of a US male speaker was also used. Further, we will refer to this to test dataset as **testDataset2**. All datasets are summarized in Table 1.

3   Feature Extraction

Convolutional neural network computes features automatically as was described in [15]. For the XGBoost model, we chose the same features as described in [12]. For a quick overview, the features used are shown in Table 2. Features followed by * were computed with the context of 6 surrounded peaks. On the Fig. 1 there are shown basic extracted features from filtered speech signal as described in [12]. The letter A stands for negative peak amplitude, the letter B for positive peak amplitude, the letter C stands for positive peak width, the letter D for negative peak width, and the letter E stands for the two successor peaks amplitudes ratio. For other features see [12].

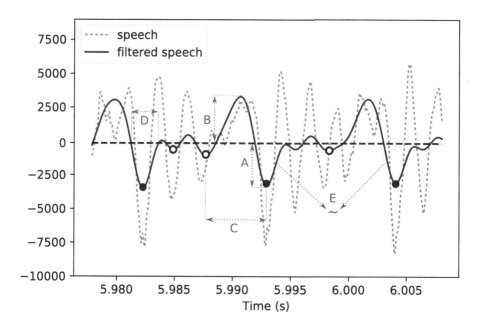

Fig. 1. Extracted features from filtered speech signal

The Context-aware XGBoost model consists of two XGBoost classifiers in tandem. The first of them takes the dataset and predicts the probability of each GCI. This information as well as all features used for its computation are then recorded to the internal context dataset. Afterward, the context of the 7 surrounding GCI, more precisely their probabilities, are assigned to each negative peak. Each peak is then classified again with the second XGBoost model. More detailed description is in [12].

4   Methods of Evaluation

As for the evaluation step of our trained models ones for we choose two kinds of measures. The standard classifier measures and specialized GCI methods. For standard classifier measures we used F1, Recall and Precision [19].

To compare the proposed Inception model with different GCI detection algorithms, specialized GCI detection measures that concern the *reliability* and *accuracy* of the GCI detection algorithms were used [16]. The former includes the percentage of glottal closures for which exactly one GCI is detected (*identification rate*, IDR), the percentage of glottal closures for which no GCI is detected (*miss rate*, MR), and the percentage of glottal closures for which more than one GCI is detected (*false alarm rate*, FAR). The latter includes the percentage of detection with the identification error $\zeta \leq 0.25$ ms (*accuracy to* ± 0.25 ms, A25) and the standard deviation of the identification error ζ (*identification accuracy*, IDA). In addition, we use a more *dynamic evaluation measure* [10] that combines the reliability and accuracy in a single score (E10) and reflects the local *pitch period* T_0 pattern (determined from the ground truth GCIs). A more detailed explanation of used comparison methods could be found in [15].

Table 2. XGBoost model features overview

Index	Feature name	Index	Feature name
1	Neg. peak amplitude*	11	Pos. peak amplitude*
2	Time difference*	12	Peak width*
3	Peak correlation*	13	Neg. peak ratio*
4	ZCR	14	HNR
5	Energy	15	Spectral centroid
6	Spec. band width	16	Spectral roll of
7	MFCC	17	F0 est.
8	Welch max. freq	18	Welch max. amp.
9	Spectral flux	19	Formant frequencies
10	Peak slope	20	

5 Experiments and Results

In our first research experiment we put together the InceptionV3-1D model from [15], the XGBoost models trained on all train datasets sizes from **n004** up to **n200** and context-aware XGBoost trained also on the **n200** train dataset. Hyperparameters for all XGBoost models used in this paper were chosen the same as in [12]. Results were evaluated on the F1, Precision (P), and Recall (R) scores. We trained the context-aware XGBoost model only for **n200** dataset because of the computational cost of the context-aware XGBoost. We also wanted to explore that if so far best resulting XGBoost n200 could be even further improved. As we can see on this test dataset the top-performing model is the InceptionV3-1D CNN. Another interesting fact is that non-context XGBoost n200 performed better than its context version. All results are summarized in the Table 3.

Our next research experiment was inspired by the fact that in [15] we compared the XGBoost and InceptionV3-1D CNN models while the XGBoost model was trained on a smaller dataset with manually labeled data and evaluated on the dataset with automatically labeled data. So here we decided to train XGBoost on

Table 3. Comparison of GCI detection of the proposed InceptionV3-1D CNN with XGBoost models.

Dataset	Model	F1 (%)	R (%)	P (%)
TestDataset1	InceptionV3-1D	**98.94**	**98.94**	**98.94**
	XGBoost ctx7 n200	98.26	98.68	97.84
	XGBoost n200	98.3	98.68	97.84
	XGBoost n064	98.13	98.44	97.83
	XGBoost n032	97.91	98.22	97.6
	XGBoost n016	97.90	98.14	97.65
	XGBoost n008	97.56	97.68	97.44
	XGBoost n004	97.45	97.69	97.23

n200 dataset which is exactly the same as for InceptionV3-1D CNN training and tested on the testDataset2, which is also identical as for InceptionV3-1D CNN. The results are summarized in Table 4. We also included the "old" XGBoost models [12,14] in the results in Table 4.

As we can see XGBoost model trained on **n200** dataset and the context-aware XGBoost model trained on the same dataset show similar and better performance than InceptionV3-1D CNN. Both of them show also better performance than XGBoost models [12,14] trained on manually labeled data.

Thus, we further investigated the influence of data consistency on the performance of the XGBoost model. In this experiment, the XGBoost model was trained iteratively on the dataset with variable size starting from **n004** up to **n200** and was evaluated on the **TestDataset2**. The summary of this experiment is given in Table 5 and it also includes the XGBoost model trained on the smaller dataset with hand-crafted ground-truth GCIs [14].

Here it is worthy of notice that even the XGBoost model trained on the consistent **n004** dataset shows better performance than XGBoost models from [12,14] and the best results were achieved with the context-aware XGBoost algorithm with a context of 7.

Table 4. Comparison of GCI detection of the proposed InceptionV3-1D CNN with XGBoost models.

Dataset	Model	IDR (%)	MR (%)	FAR (%)	IDA (ms)	A25 (%)	E10 (%)
TestDataset2	InceptionV3-1D	95.87	2.46	1.68	0.35	**99.41**	95.35
	XGBoost ctx7 n200	**96.22**	1.81	1.98	0.32	99.19	**95.48**
	XGBoost n200	96.16	1.80	2.04	0.32	99.18	95.40
	XGBoost ctx7 [12]	96.11	2.20	1.69	0.26	98.92	95.20
	XGBoost [12]	95.93	2.40	**1.67**	**0.25**	98.96	95.01
	XGBoost [14]	95.22	**1.30**	3.48	0.29	99.21	94.49

454   M. Vraštil and J. Matoušek

Table 5. Comparison of GCI detection of the proposed InceptionV3-1D CNN with XGBoost models.

Dataset	Model	IDR (%)	MR (%)	FAR (%)	IDA (ms)	A25 (%)	E10 (%)
TestDataset2	XGBoost ctx7 n200	**96.22**	1.81	1.98	0.32	99.19	**95.48**
	XGBoost n200	96.16	1.80	2.04	0.32	99.18	95.40
	XGBoost n064	96.15	1.83	2.02	0.37	99.16	95.38
	XGBoost n032	96.15	1.74	2.11	0.33	99.18	95.40
	XGBoost n016	96.08	1.83	2.09	0.32	99.18	95.33
	XGBoost n008	95.98	1.81	2.20	0.31	99.18	95.23
	XGBoost n004	95.97	1.75	2.28	0.33	99.18	95.22
	XGBoost ctx7 [12]	96.11	2.20	1.69	0.26	98.92	95.20
	XGBoost [12]	95.93	2.40	**1.67**	**0.25**	98.96	95.01
	XGBoost [14]	95.22	**1.30**	3.48	0.29	**99.21**	94.49

6 Conclusions

In the first part of this paper, we put together and test all proposed models on the **TestDataset1**. Results can be seen in Table 3. Here it is remarkable that InceptionV3-1D shows better performance than XGBoost ctx7. It is also worthy of notice that in the Table 3 non-context version of the XGBoost classifier shows slightly better performance than the context-aware model. This could be caused by different sizes and kinds of the two test datasets. Further work will address these findings. In our next experiment we verified that on the **TestDataset2** the context-aware XGBoost model with context of 7 shows better performance than non-context XGBoost model, old XGBoost [14] and even InceptionV3-1D [15] as can be seen in Table 4. Further, we verified that train and test data consistency improves the performance of the XGBoost classifier. As shown in Table 5, XGBoost trained on the **n004** dataset yields better performance than XGBoost models from [12,14].

References

1. Ardaillon, L., Roebel, A.: GCI detection from raw speech using a fully-convolutional network. In: IEEE International Conference on Acoustics Speech and Signal Processing, Barcelona, Spain, pp. 6739–6743 (2020). https://doi.org/10.1109/ICASSP40776.2020.9053089
2. Barnard, E., Cole, R.A., Vea, M.P., Alleva, F.A.: Pitch detection with a neural-net classifier. IEEE Trans. Signal Process. **39**(2), 298–307 (1991). https://doi.org/10.1109/78.80812
3. Black, A.W., Lenzo, K.A.: FestVox Speech Synthesis Databases. http://festvox.org/dbs/index.html
4. Chen, T., Guestrin, C.: XGBoost: a scalable tree boosting system. In: Proceedings of the 22nd ACM SIGKDD International Conference on Knowledge Discovery and Data Mining, KDD 16, New York, NY, USA, pp. 785–794 (2016). https://doi.org/10.1145/2939672.2939785

5. Dhillon, A., Verma, G.K.: Convolutional neural network: a review of models, methodologies and applications to object detection. Progr. Artif. Intell **9**, 85–112 (2020). https://doi.org/10.1007/s13748-019-00203-0

6. Drugman, T., Thomas, M., Gudnason, J., Naylor, P., Dutoit, T.: Detection of glottal closure instants from speech signals: a quantitative review. IEEE Trans. Audio Speech Lang. Process. **20**(3), 994–1006 (2012). https://doi.org/10.1109/TASL.2011.2170835

7. Goyal, M., Srivastava, V., Prathosh, A.P.: Detection of glottal closure instants from raw speech using convolutional neural networks. In: INTERSPEECH, Graz, Austria, pp. 1591–1595 (2019). https://doi.org/10.21437/Interspeech.2019-2587

8. Kiranyaz, S., Ince, T., Abdeljaber, O., Avci, O., Gabbouj, M.: 1-D convolutional neural networks for signal processing applications. In: IEEE International Conference on Acoustics Speech and Signal Processing, Brighton, United Kingdom, pp. 8360–8363 (2019). https://doi.org/10.1109/ICASSP.2019.8682194

9. Kominek, J., Black, A.W.: The CMU ARCTIC speech databases. In: Speech Synthesis Workshop, Pittsburgh, USA pp. 223–224 (2004)

10. Legát, M., Matoušek, J., Tihelka, D.: A robust multi-phase pitch-mark detection algorithm. In: INTERSPEECH, Antwerp, Belgium, vol. 1, pp. 1641–1644 (2007)

11. Legát, M., Matoušek, J., Tihelka, D.: On the detection of pitch marks using a robust multi-phase algorithm. Speech Commun. **53**(4), 552–566 (2011). https://doi.org/10.1016/j.specom.2011.01.008

12. Matoušek, J., Vraštil, M.: Context-aware XGBoost for glottal closure instant detection in speech signal. In: Sojka, P., Kopeček, I., Pala, K., Horák, A. (eds.) TSD 2020. LNCS (LNAI), vol. 12284, pp. 446–455. Springer, Cham (2020). https://doi.org/10.1007/978-3-030-58323-1_48

13. Matoušek, J., Tihelka, D.: Classification-based detection of glottal closure instants from speech signals. In: INTERSPEECH, Stockholm, Sweden, pp. 3053–3057 (2017). https://doi.org/10.21437/Interspeech.2017-213

14. Matoušek, J., Tihelka, D.: Using extreme gradient boosting to detect glottal closure instants in speech signal. In: IEEE International Conference on Acoustics Speech and Signal Processing, Brighton, United Kingdom, pp. 6515–6519 (2019). https://doi.org/10.1109/ICASSP.2019.8683889

15. Matoušek, J., Tihelka, D.: A comparison of convolutional neural networks for glottal closure instant detection from raw speech. In: IEEE International Conference on Acoustics Speech and Signal Processing. Toronto, Canada (2021)

16. Naylor, P.A., Kounoudes, A., Gudnason, J., Brookes, M.: Estimation of glottal closure instants in voiced speech using the DYPSA algorithm. IEEE Trans. Audio Speech Lang. Process. **15**(1), 34–43 (2007). https://doi.org/10.1109/TASL.2006.876878

17. Purwins, H., Li, B., Virtanen, T., Schl, J., Chang, S.Y., Sainath, T.: Deep learning for audio signal processing. IEEE J. Sel. Topics Signal Process. **13**(2), 206–219 (2019). https://doi.org/10.1109/JSTSP.2019.2908700

18. Reddy, G.M., Rao, K.S., Das, P.P.: Glottal closure instants detection from speech signal by deep features extracted from raw speech and linear prediction residual. In: INTERSPEECH, Graz, Austria pp. 156–160 (2019)

19. Stapor, K.: Evaluating and comparing classifiers: review, some recommendations and limitations. In: Kurzynski, M., Wozniak, M., Burduk, R. (eds.) Proceedings of the 10th International Conference on Computer Recognition Systems CORES 2017, Advances in Intelligent Systems and Computing, vol. 578, pp. 12–21. Springer, Cham (2018). https://doi.org/10.1007/978-3-319-59162-9_2

20. Yang, S., Wu, Z., Shen, B., Meng, H.: Detection of glottal closure instants from speech signals: a convolutional neural network based method. In: INTERSPEECH, Hyderabad, India, pp. 317–321 (2018). https://doi.org/10.21437/Interspeech.2018-1281

Emotional State Modeling
for the Assessment of Depression
in Parkinson's Disease

P. A. Pérez-Toro[1,2(✉)], J. C. Vasquez-Correa[1,2], T. Arias-Vergara[1,2,3], P. Klumpp[1], M. Schuster[3], E. Nöth[1], and J. R. Orozco-Arroyave[1,2]

[1] Pattern Recognition Lab, Friedrich-Alexander-Universität Erlangen-Nürnberg, Erlangen, Germany
paula.andrea.perez@fau.de
[2] Faculty of Engineering, Universidad de Antioquia UdeA, Calle 70 No. 52-21, Medellín, Colombia
[3] Department of Otorhinolaryngology, Head and Neck Surgery, Ludwig-Maximilians University, Munich, Germany

Abstract. Parkinson's disease (PD) results from the degeneration of dopamine in the substantia nigra, which plays a role in motor control, mood, and cognitive functions. Some processes in the brain of a PD patient can be overlapped with non-motor functions, where some of the same brain circuitry that is related to mood regulation is also affected. Commonly, most patients experience motor symptoms such as speech impairments, bradykinesia, or resting tremor; while non-motor symptoms such as sleep disorders or depression may also appear in PD. Depression is one of the most common non-motor symptoms developed by patients and is also associated with the rapid progression of motor impairments. This study proposes the use of the *"Pleasure, Arousal, and Dominance Emotional State Model"* (PAD) to capture similar aspects related to mood and affective states in PD patients. The PAD representation is commonly used to quantify and represent emotions in a multidimensional space. Acoustic information is used as input to feed a deep learning model based on convolutional and recurrent neural networks, which are trained to model the PAD representation. The proposed approach consists of performing transfer knowledge from the PAD model for the classification and the assessment of depression in PD. F1-scores of up to 0.69 are obtained for the classification of PD patients vs. healthy controls and of up to 0.85 for the discrimination between depressive PD vs. non-depressive PD patients, which confirms that there is information embedded in the PAD model that can be used to detect depression in PD.

Keywords: Depression · Parkinson's disease · PAD emotional state model · Speech analysis

1   Introduction

Parkinson's Disease (PD) is a neurological disorder characterized by the progressive loss of dopaminergic neurons in the mid brain [15], which is involved in the movement

ⓒ Springer Nature Switzerland AG 2021
K. Ekštein et al. (Eds.): TSD 2021, LNAI 12848, pp. 457–468, 2021.
https://doi.org/10.1007/978-3-030-83527-9_39

control, mood, and attention. The most common motor symptoms are rigidity, bradyki-nesia, resting tremor, among others, which also affect the muscles involved in the speech production. Some of the voice impairments include pitch instability, decreased loud-ness, and hypokinetic dysarthria [7]. Non-motor complications also affect the patients. The most common non-motor symptoms include sleep disorders, cognitive impair-ments, and depression [21]. Depressive symptoms in PD would fluctuate likewise as motor symptoms [26], where its prevalence is up to 50%. Moreover, depression in PD is frequently associated with rapid progression of motor symptoms and cognitive impair-ments [24]. As in depression, the reduction of serotonin levels is present in PD, which is directly involved in a patient's mood [16,31]. The standard scale to evaluate the neu-rological state of PD patients is the Movement Disorders Society – Unified Parkinson's Disease Rating Scale (MDS-UPDRS) [13], which contains four different sections, in which the first part contains one item to evaluate depression according to the patients' daily routines.

Most of the studies in the literature have focused on the assessment of motor symp-toms rather than in the evaluation of cognitive, mood, or language disturbances. There are several studies focused on modeling speech deficits of patients such as the effects on phonation and articulation [1], the prediction of the dysarthria levels in patients [4], or the classification of PD patients and Healthy Control (HC) subjects [20,30]. In [1,4,30], the assessment of PD was performed by using the PC-GITA [22] dataset. These studies reported accuracies of up to 84% to classify PD patients and correlations of up to 0.57 to predict dysarthria levels in PD. Other datasets have also been considered in other studies such as [20], where the assessment of PD in Czech native speakers with PD achieved accuracies of up to 88%. However, symptoms related to verbal fluency and semantic problems are also present in the patients [19,29]. For instance, there are some studies that consider the use of different Natural Language Processing (NLP) methods to evaluate PD patients [9,12,23], where accuracies of up to 82% have been reported to discriminate between PD patients and HC subjects.

The automatic assessment of depression using acoustic and linguistic information have also been studied. In [11], the authors reported significant differences in measures related to the second formant between depressive patients and HC subjects, which were similar to those results obtained from PD patients without any depressive symptom in [11]. The prediction of depression in PD according to the Geriatric Depression Scale (GDS) was addressed in [6]. Classical acoustic and prosodic descriptors such as Mel Frequency Cepstral Coefficients (MFCCs) and formant frequency based measures were considered. The authors reported a Spearman's correlation of -0.21 between the pre-dicted and real GDS evaluation. This indicates the difficulty of this kind of task related to pathological speech.

The contribution of this study includes: (1) Use of novel emotional posteriors based on the *"Pleasure, Arousal, and Dominance Emotional State Model"* (PAD) represen-tation [17], (2) analysis of different emotional components in PD, and (3) evaluation of low-dimensional feature vectors in the classification of PD/HC and the detection of depression in PD, where F1-score of up to 0.85 were achieved.

2 Datasets

2.1 Parkinson's Disease Assessment

This dataset considers spontaneous speech recordings from 70 PD patients and 70 HC subjects, all of them native Colombian Spanish speakers. The recordings are part of an extended version of the PC-GITA corpus [22]. The task consisted of asking the participants to describe their daily routines. The average duration of the monologues is 48 ± 29 s for the PD patients and 45 ± 24 for the HC subjects. The patients were evaluated by an expert neurologist and labeled according to the MDS-UPDRS-III score, which ranges from 0 to 132. Since only one neurologist was involved in the labeling process, there is no variation in the data due to disagreement among multiple labelers. Table 1 shows additional information of the participants.

Table 1. General demographic information of the subjects in the PC-GITA dataset

	PD patients F/M	HC subjects F/M
Number of subjects	36/34	34/36
Age [years]	59.8 (11.1)/62.6 (10.6)	59.4 (10.6)/62.8 (11.1)
Time since diagnosis [years]	11.8 (10.3)/8.7 (5.4)	
MDS-UPDRS-III	36.4 (18.7)/40.4 (19.7)	
Speech item of the MDS-UPDRS-III	1.3 (0.8)/1.5 (0.9)	

PD patients: Parkinson's patients. HC subjects: Healthy Controls. Values are expressed as mean (standard deviation). F: female. M: male. The MDS-UPDRS-III ranges from 0 to 132. The speech item ranges from 0 to 4.

Additionally, the influence of possible significant differences produced by demographic data were discarded by performing a Mann-Whitney U test for age ($p \gg 0.05$), and a Chi-Square test for gender ($p = 1.00$).

2.2 Assessment of Depression in Parkinson's Disease

The considered data include spontaneous speech recordings from 25 Depressive PD patients (D-PD) and 35 Non-Depressive PD patients (ND-PD). They were labeled according to the depression item of the first part of MDS-UPDRS, which ranges from 0 to 4. D-PD are the patients with the item higher than zero, while the ND-PD patients are those with this item equal to zero. The participants did the same task as in the PC-GITA dataset. The participants are native Spanish speakers from Colombia. The average duration of the recordings is 84 ± 34 s for the D-PD patients and 80 ± 37 for the ND-PD patients. Additional demographic information of the PD patients are included in Table 2. This dataset was recorded by the GITA research group[1] from the University of Antioquia (Medellín, Colombia). Unfortunately, it is not yet publicly available due to privacy reasons.

---

[1] Research group on applied telecommunications (GITA): https://gita.udea.edu.co/.

Table 2. General demographic information of the subjects in the Depression in Parkinson's Disease dataset

	D-PD patients F/M	ND-PD patients F/M
Number of subjects	15/10	17/18
Age [years]	66.1 (10.3)/68.8 (9.1)	60.3 (13.2)/66.3 (10.3)
Time since diagnosis [years]	6.4 (5.3)/8.1 (4.5)	13.7 (12.7)/7.3 (4.8)
MDS-UPDRS-III	33.3 (18.8)/35.3 (16.6)	26.5 (10.2)/36.3 (1.7)
Speech item of the MDS-UPDRS-III	1.0 (0.8)/1.5 (0.7)	1.3 (0.7)/1.6 (1.0)
Depression item of the MDS-UPDRS-I	1.4 (0.7)/1.3 (0.7)	0.0/0.0

D-PD patients: Depressive Parkinson's patients. ND-PD patients: Non-Depressive Parkinson's patients. Values are expressed as mean (standard deviation). F: female. M: male. The MDS-UPDRS-III ranges from 0 to 132. The speech and depression items range from 0 to 4.

Additionally, the influence of possible significant differences produced by demographic data were discarded by performing a Mann-Whitney U test for age, MDS-UPDRS-III, and Speech item of the MDS-UPDRS-III ($p \gg 0.05$), and a Chi-Square test for gender ($p = 0.99$).

2.3 Auxiliary Dataset: IEMOCAP

The Interactive Emotional Dyadic Motion Capture (IEMOCAP) [3] is an acted, multi-speaker and multimodal dataset collected by the University of Southern California. It consists of five sessions, which contain a total of 10039 utterances from ten different English native speakers. Each session is composed by a pair of speakers (male and female). This dataset contains dimensionally scaled attributes for valence, arousal, and dominance. Sessions 1 to 4 were used for training, while session 5 was used for validation. Additionally, speech signals with different SNR (20 and 30 dB) were produced by adding Gaussian noise to increase the robustness of the approach.

3   Methods

3.1   PAD Emotional Model

It aims to represent and quantify the emotions in a multidimensional space. In this representation, the emotions can be identified as calm-agitated (arousal), pleasant-unpleasant (valence), or dominant-submissive (dominance). According to the aforementioned, any emotion can be defined as a linear combination of valence, arousal, and dominance within a 3-dimensional circumflex model (see Fig. 1).

Our approach aims to capture similar aspects related to the mood and affective states in PD patients, since impairments in speech production together with depression may appear in PD, producing negative effects in the communication capabilities and social interaction of the patient [16].

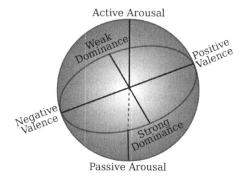

Fig. 1. PAD emotional model

3.2 Deep Learning Based Model

Three different models are trained in order to address three binary-classification problems using the IEMOCAP database [3]: (1) active vs. passive arousal (accuracy = 67%, F1-score = 0.64), (2) positive vs. negative valence (accuracy = 88%, F1-score = 0.88), and (3) strong vs. weak dominance (accuracy = 80%, F1-score = 0.82).

Figure 2 shows the proposed model, in which the input is defined as a 3D-multi-channel log-magnitude Mel spectrogram. Each dimension is formed by taking a sequence of 500 ms and 3 different resolution windows: 16 ms, 25 ms, and 45 ms. It aims to model different aspects related to articulation and prosody information by combining Convolutional Neural Networks (CNN) and Gated Recurrent Units (GRU) [2,10].

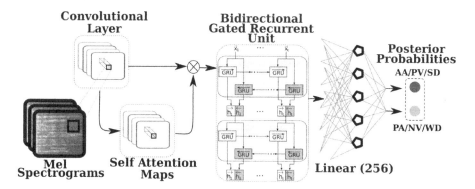

Fig. 2. General architecture of the pre-trained model based on the PAD emotional model. It consists of four parts: (1) an 8-filter convolutional layer with a max pooling layer, with batch normalization, and a leaky-ReLU activation, (2) a self-attention map layer, (3) a Bi-GRU of 2 stacked layers with 128 hidden units and batch normalization, (4) one linear layer with 256 units with dropout, and (5) a linear layer with two units for the posterior probabilities. AA: Active Arousal. PA: Passive Arousal. PV: Positive Valence. NV: Negative Valence. SD: Strong Dominance. WD: Weak Dominance.

A CNN with 8 filters with a kernel size of $(1, 3)$ followed by a max pooling layer $(1, 2)$, a batch normalization layer, and a leaky-Rectifier Linear Unit (leaky-ReLU) activation were considered in this approach. The CNN and max pooling were only performed in one dimension to keep the temporal context. A Self-attention map layer was also included to increase the capability of the system to focus on some specific parts in the spectral representation [5]. Later on a Bidirectional GRU (Bi-GRU) with 2 stacked layers with 128 hidden states and a batch normalization layer was used in order to model the temporal dynamics of the extracted features by the CNN weighted by the self-attention map. A linear layer of 256 units together with a dropout regularization (probability = 0.3) were considered before the classification layer. The final linear layer consisted of 2 units in order to obtain the posterior probabilities by using a Sigmoid activation function. This activation was considered to observe the contribution of each dimension (e.g. active vs. passive arousal) by taking independent outputs. Furthermore, four functionals were computed across the sequences (mean, standard deviation, minimum and maximum) to form a static vector. This output was used to perform a transfer knowledge for the classification of PD patients and HCs, and for the assessment of depression in PD. Our hypothesis is that depression will exhibit higher performance than the classification of PD/HC because this approach may provide more information about mood, emotion, or affective patterns.

3.3 Baseline Features

The proposed approach is compared w.r.t. a set of baseline features extracted using the "IS16_ComParE" [25] feature set from the openSMILE toolkit [8]. The extracted features comprise several acoustic measures based on spectral, cepstral, linear predictive coding, and perceptual linear prediction analysis, among others. It includes also articulation features based on formant frequencies, and prosody features based on pitch and loudness.

3.4 Optimization and Classification

The discrimination capability of the extracted posteriors is evaluated by using a Radial Basis Function-Support Vector Machine (RBF-SVM). The optimal parameters of the RBF-SVM are found through a grid search where $C \in \{10^{-5}, 10^{-4}, ..., 10^5\}$ and $\gamma \in \{10^{-5}, 10^{-4}, ..., 10^5\}$. The classification of PD/HC followed a nested Leave-One-Speaker-Out (LOSO) Cross-Validation (CV) strategy with an internal 10-fold to optimize the hyper-parameters. In the case of the assessment of depression a nested LOSO CV strategy with an internal 5-fold was considered because the dataset is smaller. Early and late fusion strategies were considered. The early fusion consists in merging the different sets of features before performing the classification and making the final decision. The late fusion is performed by applying the median rule of the normalized scores of the different RBF-SVM classifiers.

4   Experiments and Results

Two classification experiments are considered: (1) PD vs. HC and (2) D-PD vs. ND-PD. Early and late fusion strategies are considered to combine different extracted features.

We performed a Kruskal-Wallis test with Bonferroni correction for both experiments and for all features to evaluate whether there are significant differences between groups. The null hypothesis is rejected ($p \ll 0.05$) for all features sets and both classification problems.

4.1 Experiment 1: PD Vs. HC Subjects

In this case only the dataset described in Sect. 2.1 is considered. The box plots of the extracted descriptors for the classification of PD are shown in Fig. 3.

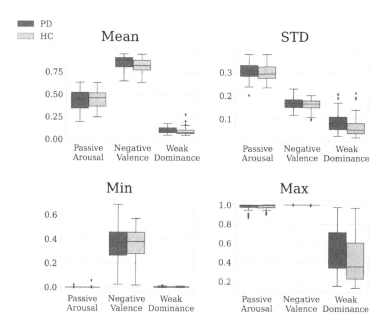

Fig. 3. Box plots of differences between PD patients and HC subjects according to the posterior probabilities from the proposed model for the passive arousal, negative valence, and weak dominance. STD: standard deviation. Min: minimum. Max: maximum

For visualization purposes, the passive arousal, negative valence, and weak dominance are only considered to analyze the distribution of the descriptors in the box plots, since those are the variables that can better being related to depression. However, the active arousal, positive valence, and strong dominance can contribute in information for the discrimination. Notice that according to the plots the valence and the dominance are the features that apparently provide more separability between the classes (PD and HC). PD patients tend to have higher weak dominance and negative valence in comparison with the HC.

Table 3. Results for the discrimination of PD patients and HC subjects

Experiments	Features	F1-Score	UAR	Sens	Spec	Number of features
Separate PAD models	Arousal	0.54	55	39	71	8
	Valence	0.62	62	67	57	8
	Dominance	**0.67**	**67**	**74**	**60**	**8**
Early fusion	**A+V**	**0.69**	**69**	**63**	**74**	**16**
	A+D	0.61	62	56	67	16
	V+D	0.58	58	59	57	16
	A+V+D	0.69	69	60	77	24
Late fusion	A+V	0.63	63	54	71	16
	A+D	0.63	63	53	73	16
	V+D	0.66	66	71	61	16
	A+V+D	**0.67**	**67**	**67**	**67**	**24**
Baseline	**openSMILE**	**0.69**	**70**	**73**	**66**	**6373**

UAR: Unweighted Average Recall. Sens: Sensitivity. Spec: Specificity. A: Arousal.

V: Valence. D: Dominance. UAR, Sens, and Spec are given in [%].

Table 3 shows the results using the proposed features for the classification of PD/HC. Consistent with what we observed in Fig. 3, dominance yields the highest results for each feature separately. The early fusion strategy provides the most accurate results (F1-score = 0.69), similar to the ones obtained for the baseline features (F1-score = 0.69). The late fusion strategy does not show improvements w.r.t. other features or fusion strategies. These results may indicate that there is emotional information that can discriminate PD patients and HC subjects. Unfortunately, a score related to mood, depression or anxiety is not available for the participants in this dataset.

4.2 Experiment: Depressive Vs. Non-Depressive PD Patients

This experiment is carried out by using the dataset previously described in Sect. 2.2. Note that a trend is shown in the boxplots for the detection of depression in PD (see Fig. 4).

Notice that for the D-PD patients the mean of the passive arousal, negative valence, and weak dominance are mostly higher than for the ND-DP patients. Additionally, something that deserves special attention is that the standard deviation for the passive arousal and negative valence tend to be smaller, which may indicates monotonicity in speech, a common symptom observed in depressive people [27,28].

Table 4 shows the results of the classification of depression in PD patients. This classification problem exhibits better results in comparison to the classification of PD vs. HC. Arousal (F1-score = 0.76) and dominance (F1-score = 0.76) are the features that provide more information for the classification of depression using each feature separately.

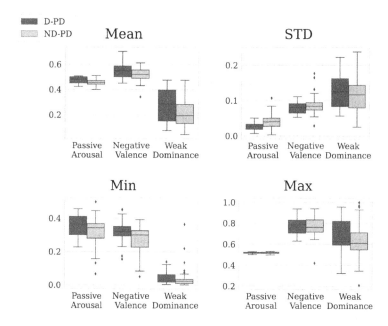

Fig. 4. Box plots of differences between ND-PD and D-PD patients subjects according to the posterior probabilities from the proposed model for the passive arousal, negative valence, and weak dominance. STD: standard deviation. Min: minimum. Max: maximum

Table 4. Results for the classification of depression in Parkinson's Disease

Experiments	Features	F1-Score	UAR	Sens	Spec	Number of features
Separate PAD models	**Arousal**	**0.76**	**79**	**88**	**69**	**8**
	Valence	0.65	64	56	71	8
	Dominance	0.76	77	80	74	8
Early fusion	A+V	0.73	74	76	71	16
	A+D	**0.79**	**77**	**68**	**86**	**16**
	V+D	0.60	60	60	60	16
	A+V+D	0.70	70	71	68	24
Late fusion	A+V	0.67	68	72	63	16
	A+D	0.79	79	84	74	16
	V+D	0.69	69	68	69	16
	A+V+D	**0.85**	**86**	**88**	**83**	**24**
Baseline	openSMILE	0.55	54	48	68	6373

UAR: Unweighted Average Recall. Sens: Sensitivity. Spec: Specificity. A: Arousal.
V: Valence. D: Dominance. UAR, Sens, and Spec are given in [%].

Although valence by itself does not achieve good results, using the different fusion strategies in some cases the performance increases, i.e., this feature is complementary to the others. The most accurate result is obtained using late fusion of the combination of the arousal, valence, and dominance with an F1-score of 0.85. Moreover, the baseline result is outperformed in all of the experiments. Additionally, the Spearman's correlations between each set of features and the different scores from the MDS-UPDRS are performed in order to discard the influence of the severity of the disease. None of the performed correlations w.r.t. the MDS-UPDRS-III and the speech item of the MDS-UPDRS-III achieve correlations higher than 0.17, while for the depression item of the MDS-UPDRS-I we obtained correlations of up to 0.45.

5 Discussion and Conclusions

A deep learning approach based on the discrimination of different zones of the PAD representation was proposed to extract acoustic and emotional information for the classification between PD vs. HC subjects and also between depressive vs. non-depressive PD patients. The depression label for the PD patients was obtained according to one of the items included in the first part of the MDS-UPDRS scale. A combination of several descriptors obtained from the transfer knowledge of the proposed model was used to address the different classification problems. The extracted features provide a compressed representation linked to each PAD zone, allowing possible clinical interpretation. Thus, these posteriors can be used in the clinical practice to evaluate specific affective and mood disorders in patients with PD. Besides, one additional advantage of this approach is that the representation leads to form a low-dimensional feature vector. The classification of PD vs. HC obtained similar results using the baseline and the proposed features (F1-score = 0.69). For the assessment of depression in PD the results using the baseline feature were not satisfactory, where the performance achieved with the proposed features indicate an improvement of up to 30% absolute using a late fusion strategy. We confirmed our hypothesis that using the proposed approach the classification of depression in PD was more accurate than the discrimination between PD vs. HC. It may suggest that there is embedded emotional information in speech linked to the depression state of PD patients. In addition, we observed that monopitch and monoloudness may be intensified in Parkinson's speech by the appearance of depressive symptoms. It can be explained because those are common characteristics in both diseases [14, 18]. Despite of languages in training and test models to be different (English and Spanish, respectively), the model was suitable to extract acoustic information for the classification tasks. Further works will consider other databases in Spanish to train the models, once they are available.

We are aware of the limitations of this study, where the clinical evaluation and the size of data need to be increased. Additionally, some precise clinical data on speech, cognition, and depression is not available. Although the results showed to be promising, further experiments with larger corpora are necessary in order to find more conclusive results. We are currently collecting more data for further research including tasks of spontaneous conversations and picture description. Finally, other approaches based on language processing will also be explored in the future.

Acknowledgements. This work was funded by the European Union's Horizon 2020 research and innovation programme under Marie Sklodowska-Curie grant agreement No. 766287 and the CODI PRG2020-34068 project from University of Antioquia. Tomás Arias-Vergara is under grants of Convocatoria Doctorado Nacional-785 financed by COLCIENCIAS.

References

1. Arias-Vergara, T., et al.: Parkinson's disease and aging: analysis of their effect in phonation and articulation of speech. Cogn. Comput. **9**(6), 731–748 (2017)
2. Badshah, A.M., et al.: Speech emotion recognition from spectrograms with deep convolutional neural network. In: Proceedings of PlatCon 2017, pp. 1–5. IEEE (2017)
3. Busso, C., Bulut, M., Lee, C.C., et al.: IEMOCAP: interactive emotional dyadic motion capture database. Lang. Resour. Eval. **42**(4), 335 (2008)
4. Cernak, M., et al.: Characterisation of voice quality of Parkinson's disease using differential phonological posterior features. Comput. Speech Lang. **46**, 196–208 (2017)
5. Chen, M., et al.: 3-D convolutional recurrent neural networks with attention model for speech emotion recognition. IEEE Signal Process. Lett. **25**(10), 1440–1444 (2018)
6. Cummins, N., et al.: Analysis of acoustic space variability in speech affected by depression. Speech Commun. **75**, 27–49 (2015)
7. Duffy, J.R.: Motor speech disorders: substrates, differential diagnosis, and management. Elsevier Health Sciences (2013)
8. Eyben, F., et al.: Opensmile: the Munich versatile and fast open-source audio feature extractor. In: Proceedings of the 18th ACM International Conference on Multimedia, pp. 1459–1462. ACM (2010)
9. Eyigoz, E., et al.: From discourse to pathology: automatic identification of Parkinson's disease patients via morphological measures across three languages. Cortex **132**, 191–205 (2020)
10. Fernandez, R., et al.: Using deep bidirectional recurrent neural networks for prosodic-target prediction in a unit-selection text-to-speech system. In: Proceedings of Interspeech (2015)
11. Flint, A.J., et al.: Abnormal speech articulation, psychomotor retardation, and subcortical dysfunction in major depression. J. Psychiatr. Res. **27**(3), 309–319 (1993)
12. García, A.M., et al.: How language flows when movements don't: an automated analysis of spontaneous discourse in Parkinson's disease. Brain Lang. **162**, 19–28 (2016)
13. Goetz, C.G., et al.: Movement disorder society-sponsored revision of the unified Parkinson's disease rating scale (MDS-UPDRS): scale presentation and clinimetric testing results. Mov. Disord. **23**(15), 2129–2170 (2008)
14. Holmes, R.J., et al.: Voice characteristics in the progression of Parkinson's disease. Int. J. Lang. Commun. Disorders **35**(3), 407–418 (2000)
15. Hornykiewicz, O.: Biochemical aspects of Parkinson's disease. Neurology **51**(2 Suppl 2), S2–S9 (1998)
16. Marin, H., et al.: Parkinson's symptoms or depression? Look for clinical signs: how to sort through overlapping symptoms using DSM-IV-TR diagnostic criteria. Curr. Psychiatry **6**(7), 78–84 (2007)
17. Mehrabian, A.: Pleasure-arousal-dominance: a general framework for describing and measuring individual differences in temperament. Curr. Psychol. **14**(4), 261–292 (1996)
18. Moore, E., II., et al.: Critical analysis of the impact of glottal features in the classification of clinical depression in speech. IEEE Trans. Biomed. Eng. **55**(1), 96–107 (2007)
19. Murray, L.L., et al.: Productive syntax abilities in Huntington's and Parkinson's diseases. Brain Cogn. **46**(1–2), 213–219 (2001)

20. Novotný, M., et al.: Automatic evaluation of articulatory disorders in Parkinson's disease. IEEE/ACM Trans. Audio Speech Lang. Process. **22**(9), 1366–1378 (2014)
21. Ojo, O.O., et al.: Frequency of cognitive impairment and depression in Parkinson's disease: a preliminary case-control study. Niger. Med. J. J. Niger. Med. Assoc. **53**(2), 65 (2012)
22. Orozco-Arroyave, J.R., et al.: New Spanish speech corpus database for the analysis of people suffering from Parkinson's disease. In: Proceedings of the LREC 2014, pp. 342–347 (2014)
23. Pérez-Toro, P.A., Vásquez-Correa, J.C., Strauss, M., Orozco-Arroyave, J.R., Nöth, E.: Natural language analysis to detect Parkinson's disease. In: Ekštein, K. (ed.) TSD 2019. LNCS (LNAI), vol. 11697, pp. 82–90. Springer, Cham (2019). https://doi.org/10.1007/978-3-030-27947-9_7
24. Schrag, A., et al.: Depression rating scales in Parkinson's disease: critique and recommendations. Mov. Disord. **22**(8), 1077–1092 (2007)
25. Schuller, B., et al.: The interspeech 2016 computational paralinguistics challenge: deception, sincerity & native language. In: Proceedings of the Interspeech, pp. 2001–2005 (2016)
26. Seki, M., et al.: Clinical features and varieties of non-motor fluctuations in Parkinson's disease: a Japanese multicenter study. Parkinsonism. Relat. Disord. **19**(1), 104–108 (2013)
27. Stasak, B., et al.: An investigation of emotional speech in depression classification. In: Proceedings of the Interspeech, pp. 485–489 (2016)
28. Stassen, H.H., et al.: Speech characteristics in depression. Psychopathology **24**(2), 88–105 (1991)
29. Vanhoutte, S., et al.: Quantitative analysis of language production in Parkinson's disease using a cued sentence generation task. Clin. Ling. Phonet. **26**(10), 863–881 (2012)
30. Vasquez-Correa, J.C., et al.: Parallel representation learning for the classification of pathological speech: studies on Parkinson's disease and cleft lip and palate. Speech Commun. **122**, 56–67 (2020)
31. Vriend, C., et al.: Depression and impulse control disorders in Parkinson's disease: two sides of the same coin? Neurosci. Biobehav. Rev. **38**, 60–71 (2014)

Attention-Based End-to-End Named Entity Recognition from Speech

Dejan Porjazovski[(✉)], Juho Leinonen, and Mikko Kurimo

Department of Signal Processing and Acoustics, Aalto University, Espoo, Finland
{dejan.porjazovski,juho.leinonen,mikko.kurimo}@aalto.fi

Abstract. Named entities are heavily used in the field of spoken language under-standing, which uses speech as an input. The standard way of doing named entity recognition from speech involves a pipeline of two systems, where first the auto-matic speech recognition system generates the transcripts, and then the named entity recognition system produces the named entity tags from the transcripts. In such cases, automatic speech recognition and named entity recognition systems are trained independently, resulting in the automatic speech recognition branch not being optimized for named entity recognition and vice versa. In this paper, we propose two attention-based approaches for extracting named entities from speech in an end-to-end manner, that show promising results. We compare both attention-based approaches on Finnish, Swedish, and English data sets, underlin-ing their strengths and weaknesses.

Keywords: Named entity recognition · Automatic speech recognition · End-to-end · Encoder-decoder

1 Introduction

Named entity recognition (NER) is one of the main natural language processing (NLP) tasks. The goal of this task is to find entities and classify them into predefined cate-gories. These categories can vary depending on the application area, but the most com-mon ones include person, location, organization, and date.

Named entities are heavily used in spoken language understanding (SLU) [4, 10, 16], where the goal is to understand what has been spoken. For example, SLU is an essential part of personal assistants in home automation and smartphone devices. These personal assistants usually take speech as input, in which case the named entities need to be recognized from spoken data.

Doing NER from speech imposes several challenges for the system. There are far fewer annotated training data for spoken language than for textual data. The speech can be informal, not following the conventional syntax of the language, which can cause difficulties in detecting the entities. The generated transcripts from an automatic speech recognition (ASR) system usually do not contain capitalization and punctuation, which can cause the system to miss the entities.

The most common approach for doing named entity recognition from speech is through a pipeline approach. In this approach, the ASR system generates transcripts,

© Springer Nature Switzerland AG 2021
K. Ekštein et al. (Eds.): TSD 2021, LNAI 12848, pp. 469–480, 2021.
https://doi.org/10.1007/978-3-030-83527-9_40

and the NER system detects the entities in those transcripts. The output of the ASR system is usually lower-cased and noisy, in the sense that the word order can be mixed, words might be missing or misspelled, etc. When developing a NER system for speech data, these factors need to be taken into account.

It is possible to try to restore the capitalization and the punctuation from the transcribed speech as explored in [7]. A maximum entropy model was used for NER on transcripts generated by a speech recognition system for Chinese, utilizing n-best lists [23]. These approaches improve the performance of the system on noisy speech data but they are still sensitive to the speech recognition output and error propagation. To deal with that, an end-to-end (E2E) approach was proposed that directly extracts named entities from French speech [6]. The authors used an architecture similar to the Deep Speech 2 [1], which was trained using the CTC algorithm [8]. A similar approach of E2E named entity recognition using the Deep Speech 2 architecture for the English language was explored in [22]. This is different from our proposed models, which use either attention-based encoder-decoder (AED) or a hybrid CTC/AED architecture.

In this paper, we propose two approaches for doing E2E NER from speech. To the best of our knowledge, this is the first attempt at NER using AED architecture in an E2E manner. The first approach is called augmented labels (AL) and it is either a standard AED or a hybrid CTC/AED architecture, where the transcripts are augmented with named entity tags during training. The second is a multi-task (MT) approach, where there are two decoder branches. One branch for doing automatic speech recognition and another one for doing named entity recognition.

2 Data

For the Finnish experiments, we used the Finnish parliament data set [15], consisting of about 1500 h of recordings from the Finnish parliament. Since we do not have true named entity labels for this data set, we used a separate NER system to annotate it. The NER system is a bidirectional LSTM (BLSTM) neural network [9] with a Conditional random field (CRF) [12] layer on top, that utilizes morph, character and word embeddings. The architecture is explained in more detail in [18]. The number of tokens and named entity tags in the data set are presented in Table 1.

Table 1. Data distribution for the Finnish parliament data set.

Parameters	Count
Audio length	1500 h
Total tokens	7.3 M
Unique tokens	337423
PER tags	44984
LOC tags	73860
ORG tags	65463

For the Swedish experiments, we used the Sprakbanken corpus, which is a public domain corpus hosted by the National Library of Norway. It consists of 259 h of recordings. Since the corpus does not contain ground truth named entities, we used the Swedish BERT model [14] to obtain the annotations. The number of tokens and named entity tags are presented in Table 2.

Table 2. Data distribution for the Swedish data set.

Parameters	Count
Audio length	259 h
Total tokens	1.4 M
Unique tokens	69310
PER tags	23258
LOC tags	7585
ORG tags	2231

Even though the goal of this paper is mainly focused on low-resource languages like Finnish and Swedish, we additionally wanted to verify the performance of the models on a well-known language, like English.

For the English experiments, we used the whole LibriSpeech data set [17], consisting of about 1000 h of recordings. The named entities for this data set were obtained using the large uncased BERT model [5], fine-tuned on the CoNLL 2003 data set [19], which we lower-cased before training. For testing the model with gold-standard named entity tags, we used a data set which is a subset of a combination of multiple speech recognition data sets, such as CommonVoice, LibriSpeech, and Voxforge. We will call this data set English-Gold. The data set is annotated and provided by [22]. The number of tokens and named entity tags in the English data sets are presented in Table 3.

Table 3. Data distribution for the English LibriSpeech and English-Gold data sets.

Parameters	LibriSpeech	English-Gold
Audio length	1000 h	148 h
Total tokens	9.6 M	1.3 M
Unique tokens	87600	41379
PER tags	194172	50552
LOC tags	66618	23976
ORG tags	11415	5025

3   Methods

To do E2E named entity recognition from spoken data, we will explore two approaches. In the first approach, we will build an attention-based encoder-decoder model for ASR by augmenting the labels with NER tags. In the second approach, we will explore multi-task learning where the model simultaneously learns to transcribe speech and annotate it with named entity tags. Additionally, for the English and Swedish experiments, we utilize the CTC loss, as explored in [21].

Generally, the E2E ASR models can benefit from an external language model [20] but in our experiments we exclude it. The reason for that is because the augmented labels approach produces an output where each word is followed by a named entity tag. In such a case, adding an external language model trained on text will not benefit us. On the other hand, the baseline ASR models can benefit from an external language model but the goal of this paper is to explore an alternative way of doing named entity recognition from speech, as opposed to the standard pipeline approach.

3.1   Pipeline NER Systems

To see how our proposed models perform in comparison to the pipeline approach, where an ASR system generates the transcripts and then a NER system annotates them, we trained BLSTM-CRF models for each of the data sets. The architecture of these models is identical to the NER branch in the multi-task approach, described later in the paper. The models are trained on the original transcripts for each of the data sets. Since the English-Gold data set is small, we used the LibriSpeech model to initialize the weights and then fine-tune it on that particular data.

3.2   Baseline ASR System

The baseline ASR architecture is the same as the augmented labels approach, which is explained later in the paper. The only difference is that for the training of the baseline models, we used the original transcripts, whereas for the augmented labels approach we used the original transcripts augmented with named entity tags. We choose the architectures to be identical so that we can give a fair comparison between them.

3.3   Augmented Labels Approach

For this approach, we developed an attention-based encoder-decoder architecture that takes audio features as input and produces transcripts with named entity tags. Let $X = (x_1, x_2, ..., x_T)$ be the audio features, where each feature is represented as x_i and i is the order of the feature. Additionally, we define the output character set $Y = (y_1, y_2, ..., y_T)$, where y consists of all the characters plus the special tokens: <UNK>, <sos>, <eos>, O, PER, LOC, and ORG. The goal is to model the conditional probability:

$$P(Y|X) = \prod_i P(y_i|Y_{<i}, X) \tag{1}$$

In simpler terms, it predicts the i-th output character, given the previous characters and the input features X. It does this using an encoder and a decoder.

The encoder is a BLSTM neural network, that uses audio features as input and compresses them in a single hidden representation. This hidden representation is used to initialize the decoder.

The decoder is an LSTM neural network that takes the hidden vector, produced by the encoder and generates the transcripts using an attention mechanism. As an attention mechanism, we used Luong attention [13]. The scoring function for the attention is hybrid + location-aware, as described in [3]. It is defined as:

$$
\begin{aligned}
\text{score}(h_{\text{enc}}, h_{\text{dec}}) = v * \tanh(W^e * h_{\text{enc}} \\
+ W^d * h_{\text{dec}} + W^c * \text{conv} + b)
\end{aligned}
\tag{2}
$$

where, h_{enc} and h_{dec} are the hidden states of the encoder and the decoder, $tanh$ is a hyperbolic tangent non-linearity, v and b are learnable weights, together with the W matrices. The location-aware element $conv$ is a convolution defined as:

$$
\text{conv} = F * \alpha_t
\tag{3}
$$

where, F is a learnable matrix and α_t is the alignment vector.

For the experiments where we additionally used the CTC loss, the final ASR loss is calculated as:

$$
L_{asr} = \lambda L_{ctc} + (1 - \lambda)L_{aed}
\tag{4}
$$

where, L_{ctc} is the CTC loss, L_{aed} is the decoder loss and λ is the weighting factor that determines the contribution of the separate loss functions to the final loss.

As true labels, we used the transcripts, augmented with named entity tags, in a way that each word is followed by its tag. This way, the model will jointly produce ASR transcripts and NER tags.

3.4 Multi-task Approach

The multi-task approach is an attention-based encoder-decoder architecture, similar to the augmented labels approach. The difference between them is that this approach has two separate decoder branches. The first branch does the automatic speech recognition and is like the one in the augmented labels. The second one does the named entity tagging and it consists of BLSTM with a CRF layer on top. This approach uses hard parameter sharing, where the encoder is shared between both branches. Since it is a multi-task learning approach, we have two separate loss functions that need to be jointly optimized. The final loss function is calculated as:

$$
L = \beta L_{asr} + (1 - \beta)L_{ner}
\tag{5}
$$

where L_{asr} is the loss from the ASR decoder, L_{ner} is the loss from the NER decoder, and β is a weighting factor that determines the contribution of both loss functions.

Similar to the augmented labels approach, in the experiments where we utilized the CTC loss, the ASR loss L_{asr} is calculated as in Eq. 4.

4   Experiments

In all the experiments, we used logarithmic filter banks with 40 filters and Adam optimizer [11]. For the multi-task approach, after the models converged, we additionally froze the encoder and the ASR decoder and trained only the NER branch, which improved the multi-task NER results on most of the data sets. We will refer to this model as MT*. The code was developed using Pytorch and is publicly available.[1]

Speech features consist of a large number of timesteps, so processing them using a standard BLSTM network is computationally expensive. To deal with that we used a pyramidal BLSTM network. The pyramidal structure reduces the computational time by concatenating every two consecutive timesteps in each layer.

In the Finnish and English experiments, the encoder consists of 5 pyramidal BLSTM layers, whereas in the Swedish experiments we used 3 normal and 2 pyramidal BLSTM layers. The reason for that is because the Swedish data set consists of short utterances, so there are not many timesteps to be processed. The hidden size of the BLSTM networks is 450 in all the experiments, except for the Finnish, where we used a hidden size of 300. After the last BLSTM layer, a dropout of 0.1 is applied.

In the augmented labels approach, the decoder consists of a character embedding layer with a size of 150 and a single layer LSTM network. For the English and Swedish experiments, the LSTM has a size of 450, whereas for the Finnish experiments, it has a size of 300. The location-aware element in the attention has 150 filters for the English and Swedish, and 100 filters for the Finnish experiments. A dropout of 0.1 is applied after the attention mechanism.

In the multi-task approach, the ASR decoder is identical to the one in the augmented labels, for all the experiments. The NER decoder uses pre-trained 300 dimensional fastText word embeddings [2] as an input to the one-layer BLSTM. The size of the BLSTM layer is 450 for the English and Swedish experiments, and 300 for the Finnish ones. The BLSTM is followed by a fully connected layer with the same size and a dropout layer with a probability of 0.1. In the end, the output is passed through a CRF layer that produces the tag probabilities.

Since the English-Gold data is relatively small with only 148 h, we used the LibriSpeech data to pre-train the model and then fine-tune it on the English-Gold data set.

In all the experiments, we allocated data for testing, which was not used during training. As a loss function, we used the negative log-likelihood. For combining the ASR and NER losses, as in Eq. 5, we used β weighting factor of 0.8. For the Swedish and English experiments, we additionally utilized the CTC loss, together with negative log-likelihood, like in the Eq. 4, with a λ weighting factor of 0.2.

5   Results

In this section we present the results obtained on Finnish, Swedish, and English data sets, comparing both the augmented labels and multi-task approaches. For the evaluation of the ASR results, we used the word error rate (WER) metric, and for the evaluation of the named entity recognition results, we used the micro average F1 score.

---

[1] https://github.com/Tetrix/E2E-NER-for-spoken-Finnish.

5.1 Finnish Results

In Table 4, we can see how both the augmented labels and multi-task approaches compare against the baseline ASR model in terms of WER when evaluated on the Finnish parliament data. From the results, we can notice that both approaches perform in pair with the baseline ASR model, falling slightly behind. We can also see that the multi-task approach performs slightly better than the augmented labels approach in terms of WER. In Table 5, we can see how both approaches perform in terms of precision, recall, and F1 score. Additionally, we evaluated our models on the original transcripts and on the transcripts that were generated by the models. We used the multi-task and the fine-tuned multi-task models to do the evaluation on the original transcripts. From the results, we can see that the fine-tuned multi-task model performs slightly better than the standard multi-task model. On the transcripts generated by the model, which is a harder task, we compared both multi-task approaches, along with the augmented labels and the pipeline approach. The ASR transcripts for the pipeline approach were generated using the multi-task model, for all the data sets. From the results, we can see that the fine-tuned multi-task approach achieved the best F1 score. We can also notice that both multi-task approaches perform better than the pipeline approach, whereas the augmented labels approach falls behind.

Table 4. WER on the Finnish test set.

Model	WER
Baseline ASR	**34.95**
AL	36.06
MT	35.80

Table 5. Precision, recall and F1 score for the Finnish test set.

Transcripts	Model	Prec	Rec	F1
Original	MT	93.70	92.88	93.29
	MT*	93.75	93.69	**93.72**
Generated	Pipeline	93.63	85.64	89.46
	AL	92.65	81.61	86.78
	MT	93.35	87.80	90.49
	MT*	93.17	88.80	**90.93**

5.2 Swedish Results

Next, we present the Swedish results. In Table 6, we can see how both approaches perform in terms of WER, in comparison to the baseline model. Similar to the Finnish experiments, we can see that both models fall slightly behind the baseline ASR model.

Additionally, we can observe that the augmented labels approach performs better than the multi-task approach. From Table 7, we can see how our models perform on the NER task when evaluated on the original and the generated transcripts. When evaluated on the original transcripts, the fine-tuned multi-task model performs better than the standard multi-task model, similar to the Finnish experiments. On the transcripts generated by the models, we can observe that the augmented labels approach achieves the highest F1 score. We can also observe that both the augmented labels and the fine-tuned multi-task approaches outperform the pipeline approach.

Table 6. WER on the Swedish test set.

Model	WER
Baseline ASR	**33.44**
AL	33.82
MT	34.58

Table 7. Precision, recall and F1 score for the Swedish test set.

Transcripts	Model	Prec	Rec	F1
Original	MT	97.76	91.27	94.40
	MT*	98.32	93.48	**95.84**
Generated	Pipeline	69.35	79.37	74.02
	AL	74.96	78.13	**76.51**
	MT	70.14	77.94	73.83
	MT*	74.19	76.67	75.41

5.3 English Results

Next, we present the results obtained on the English data sets. In Table 8, we can see how our models perform in terms of WER when evaluated on the LibriSpeech and the English-Gold test sets. From the table, we can see that both approaches perform slightly better than the baseline ASR model trained on the LibriSpeech data. On the English-Gold, on the other hand, the multi-task model performs slightly better than the baseline, whereas the augmented labels yields worse results. On the Libri clean test set, both approaches perform really close, whereas on the Libri other test set, the multi-task approach performs slightly better. Additionally, the multi-task approach performs better than the augmented labels on the English-Gold test set as well.

On the NER task, presented in Table 9, when evaluated on the original transcripts, the fine-tuned multi-task approach outperforms the normal multi-task approach on all the English data sets. On the transcripts generated by the models, we can see that the pipeline approach is better than our proposed E2E models on the LibriSpeech test sets. On the manually annotated English Gold test set, on the other hand, the multi-task approach achieves the best F1 score. Additionally, both the multi-task and the augmented labels approaches perform better than the pipeline approach.

Table 8. WER on the LibriSpeech and English-Gold test sets.

Model	Libri clean	Libri other	English-Gold
Baseline ASR	12.74	31.61	23.26
AL	**12.34**	30.88	23.51
MT	12.35	**30.56**	**23.07**

Table 9. Precision, recall and F1 score for the English test sets.

		Libri clean			Libri other			English Gold		
Transcripts	Model	Prec	Rec	F1	Prec	Rec	F1	Prec	Rec	F1
Original	MT	87.82	86.01	86.90	86.95	86.23	86.59	64.44	77.09	70.20
	MT*	88.41	86.46	**87.43**	87.55	86.13	**86.83**	81.86	68.02	**74.30**
Generated	Pipeline	76.43	79.09	**77.74**	64.07	74.40	**68.85**	79.24	71.28	75.05
	AL	79.77	63.47	70.69	70.21	52.15	59.85	82.60	69.30	75.21
	MT	74.63	76.77	75.68	60.90	73.44	66.59	77.04	84.89	**80.78**
	MT*	76.33	77.10	76.72	63.33	71.75	67.29	81.86	68.02	74.30

6 Analysis of the Results

To further investigate the NER performance of the models, we plotted confusion matrices. In Fig. 1, we can see how the augmented labels and fine-tuned multi-task approaches perform on individual named entity classes on the Finnish data set. We can notice from the confusion matrices that both approaches are doing a pretty good job at detecting the entities, especially the location. On the other hand, they sometimes confuse non-entities with entities. This is especially visible in the person and organization classes, where some non-entities are tagged with either of them.

Similar to the Finnish results, in Fig. 2, we can observe that on the Swedish data set, the models do not have difficulties recognizing the entities. Furthermore, we can see that in a small number of cases, the models confuse the person entity with a location. Additionally, we can see that most of the mistakes that the models make are by confusing non-entities with entities, just like in the Finnish results.

On the English-Gold test set, as shown in Fig. 3, we can observe that the models make more mistakes than on the other data sets. That is especially the case with the

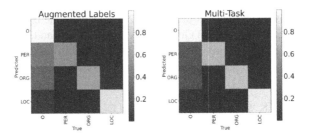

Fig. 1. Confusion matrices for the AL and MT* models, evaluated on the transcripts generated by the models, using the Finnish parliament test set.

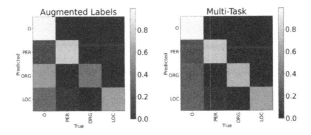

Fig. 2. Confusion matrices for the AL and MT* models, evaluated on the transcripts generated by the models, using the Swedish test set.

organization entity. The reason for that could be because there are far fewer organization entities in the LibriSpeech and English-Gold data sets, in comparison to the other entities. To ensure that the bad recognition score for the organization entity is expected, we additionally compared the score to the one obtained by the pipeline model. When evaluated on the test data, the pipeline approach also got a low score for the organization entity. Generally, since the English-Gold data set is a combination of many different data sets, it is expected that the domain mismatch negatively impacts the NER.

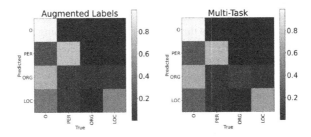

Fig. 3. Confusion matrices for the AL and MT* models, evaluated on the transcripts generated by the models, using the English-Gold test set.

7 Conclusion

In this paper, we presented two approaches for end-to-end named entity recognition and evaluated them on Finnish, Swedish, and English data sets. We showed that both approaches perform similarly in terms of WER, against the baseline models. Even though the WER results are not in pair with the current state of the art, the goal of this paper is to show that named entities can be learned in an E2E manner, without sacrificing too much of the ASR performance. This allows the ASR part to be optimized for the NER task and vice versa. In terms of the F1 score, both approaches achieve promising results. When comparing both systems, the multi-task approach outperforms the augmented labels approach on the NER task by a significant margin, in all the experiments, except the Swedish, when evaluated on the transcripts generated by the models. When compared against the standard pipeline approach, our proposed models achieve better results on most of the experiments. Generally, we can say that the multi-task approach is more flexible, allowing us to additionally fine-tune the NER branch, which gives an improvement in almost all the experiments. In the future, we plan to replace the models with a Transformer architecture and see how it performs in comparison to the BLSTMs.

Acknowledgment. This work was supported by the Kone Foundation. This work was supported by the Academy of Finland (grant 329267) and EU's Horizon 2020 research and innovation programme via the project MeMAD (GA 780069). The computational resources were provided by Aalto ScienceIT.

References

1. Amodei, D., et al.: Deep speech 2: end-to-end speech recognition in English and mandarin. In: International Conference on Machine Learning, pp. 173–182 (2016)
2. Bojanowski, P., Grave, E., Joulin, A., Mikolov, T.: Enriching word vectors with subword information. Trans. Assoc. Comput. Ling. **5**, 135–146 (2017)
3. Chorowski, J.K., Bahdanau, D., Serdyuk, D., Cho, K., Bengio, Y.: Attention-based models for speech recognition. In: Advances in Neural Information Processing Systems, pp. 577–585 (2015)
4. Deoras, A., Sarikaya, R.: Deep belief network based semantic taggers for spoken language understanding. In: Interspeech, pp. 2713–2717 (2013)
5. Devlin, J., Chang, M.W., Lee, K., Toutanova, K.: BERT: pre-training of deep bidirectional transformers for language understanding. arXiv preprint arXiv:1810.04805 (2018)
6. Ghannay, S., et al.: End-to-end named entity and semantic concept extraction from speech. In: 2018 IEEE Spoken Language Technology Workshop (SLT), pp. 692–699. IEEE (2018)
7. Gravano, A., Jansche, M., Bacchiani, M.: Restoring punctuation and capitalization in transcribed speech. In: 2009 IEEE International Conference on Acoustics, Speech and Signal Processing, pp. 4741–4744. IEEE (2009)
8. Graves, A., Fernández, S., Gomez, F., Schmidhuber, J.: Connectionist temporal classification: labelling unsegmented sequence data with recurrent neural networks. In: Proceedings of the 23rd International Conference on Machine Learning, pp. 369–376 (2006)
9. Hochreiter, S., Schmidhuber, J.: Long short-term memory. Neural Comput. **9**(8), 1735–1780 (1997)

10. Jeong, M., Lee, G.G.: Jointly predicting dialog act and named entity for spoken language understanding. In: 2006 IEEE Spoken Language Technology Workshop, pp. 66–69. IEEE (2006)

11. Kingma, D.P., Ba, J.: Adam: a method for stochastic optimization. arXiv preprint arXiv:1412.6980 (2014)

12. Lafferty, J., McCallum, A., Pereira, F.C.: Conditional random fields: probabilistic models for segmenting and labeling sequence data. In: Proceedings of the 18th International Conference on Machine Learning 2001 (ICML 2001), pp. 282–289 (2001)

13. Luong, M.T., Pham, H., Manning, C.D.: Effective approaches to attention-based neural machine translation. arXiv preprint arXiv:1508.04025 (2015)

14. Malmsten, M., Börjeson, L., Haffenden, C.: Playing with words at the national library of Sweden - making a Swedish BERT (2020)

15. Mansikkaniemi, A., Smit, P., Kurimo, M., et al.: Automatic construction of the Finnish parliament speech corpus. In: INTERSPEECH, vol. 8, pp. 3762–3766 (2017)

16. Mesnil, G., He, X., Deng, L., Bengio, Y.: Investigation of recurrent-neural-network architectures and learning methods for spoken language understanding. In: Interspeech, pp. 3771–3775 (2013)

17. Panayotov, V., Chen, G., Povey, D., Khudanpur, S.: Librispeech: an ASR corpus based on public domain audio books. In: 2015 IEEE International Conference on Acoustics, Speech and Signal Processing (ICASSP), pp. 5206–5210. IEEE (2015)

18. Porjazovski, D., Leinonen, J., Kurimo, M.: Named entity recognition for spoken Finnish. In: Proceedings of the 2nd International Workshop on AI for Smart TV Content Production, Access and Delivery, pp. 25–29 (2020)

19. Sang, E.F., De Meulder, F.: Introduction to the CoNLL-2003 shared task: language-independent named entity recognition. arXiv preprint cs/0306050 (2003)

20. Toshniwal, S., Kannan, A., Chiu, C.C., Wu, Y., Sainath, T.N., Livescu, K.: A comparison of techniques for language model integration in encoder-decoder speech recognition. In: 2018 IEEE Spoken Language Technology Workshop (SLT), pp. 369–375. IEEE (2018)

21. Watanabe, S., Hori, T., Kim, S., Hershey, J.R., Hayashi, T.: Hybrid CTC/attention architecture for end-to-end speech recognition. IEEE J. Sel. Topics Sig. Process. **11**(8), 1240–1253 (2017)

22. Yadav, H., Ghosh, S., Yu, Y., Shah, R.R.: End-to-end named entity recognition from English speech. arXiv preprint arXiv:2005.11184 (2020)

23. Zhai, L., Fung, P., Schwartz, R., Carpuat, M., Wu, D.: Using N-best lists for named entity recognition from Chinese speech. In: Proceedings of HLT-NAACL 2004: Short Papers, pp. 37–40 (2004)

Incorporation of Iterative Self-supervised Pre-training in the Creation of the ASR System for the Tatar Language

Aidar Khusainov[✉], Dzhavdet Suleymanov, and Ilnur Muhametzyanov

Tatarstan Academy of Sciences, Kazan, Russia
http://antat.ru/ips

Abstract. In this paper, we study the iterative self-supervised pretraining procedure for the Tatar language speech recognition system. The complete recipe includes the use of base pre-trained model (the multilingual XLSR model or the Librispeech (English) Wav2Vec 2.0 Base model), the next step was a "source" self-supervised pre-training on collected Tatar unlabeled data (mostly broadcast audio), then the resulting model was used for additional "target" self-supervised pretraining on the annotated corpus (target domain, without using labels), and the final step was to fine-tune the model on the annotated corpus with labels. To conduct the experiments we prepared a 328-h unlabeled and a 129-h annotated audio corpora. Experiments on three datasets (two proprietary and publicly available Common Voice as the third one) showed that the first "source" pretraining step allows ASR models to show on average 24.3% lower WER, and both source and target pretraining - 33.3% lower WER than a simple finetunes base model. The resulting accuracy for the Common Voice (read speech) test dataset is WER 5.37%, on the private TatarCorpus (read clean speech) is 4.65%, and for the spontaneous speech dataset collected from the TV shows is 22.6%, all of the results are the best-published results on these datasets. Additionally, we show that using a multilingual base model can be beneficial for the case of fine-tuning (10.5% less WER for this case), but applying self-supervised pretraining steps eliminates this difference.

Keywords: Iterative pretraining · Self-supervised learning · Speech recognition · The Tatar language

1 Introduction

Recent results in many domains like NLP and Computer Vision benefited from the use of self-supervised pretraining method, which can be described as a process of learning robust universal representations based on unlabeled datasets. In the field of speech analysis, this approach was implemented within the wav2vec2 model, which made it possible to obtain high-quality results for the English language with a minimum amount (from 10 min of records) of labeled data [5]. The idea of the technology is to use a large amount of unlabeled data to construct an acoustic representation of the speech

© Springer Nature Switzerland AG 2021
K. Ekštein et al. (Eds.): TSD 2021, LNAI 12848, pp. 481–488, 2021.
https://doi.org/10.1007/978-3-030-83527-9_41

signal samples. Wav2Vec2 model solves a problem that does not require manual anno-tation of the corpus. It uses the CPC (Contrastive Predictive Coding) criterion, and the model needs to distinguish the true speech representation from distractors that are uni-formly sampled from other masked time steps of the same utterance [6,9,14]. In [10], it is shown that features, revealed by the model in the process of solving this problem, demonstrate robustness to changes in the domain and the language. An illustration of the model from the original article wav2vec2 [5] is shown in Fig. 1.

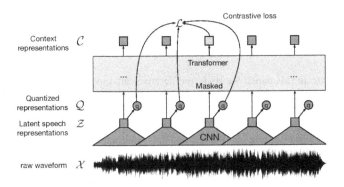

Fig. 1. An illustration of the work of the wav2vec2 model, which learns the contextual represen-tation of audio fragments based on unlabeled data [5]

And if a few years ago the vast majority of recognition systems were based on the "classical" ASR systems that consist of separate acoustic models, a pronunciation model, and a language model, recently end-to-end systems (E2E) have come to the fore. E2E ASR systems allow obtaining a better result, however, they require a large amount of training data, which is not available for low-resource languages. One way to over-come the lack of training data is to pre-train the system on data for related languages or to use a model that has been trained for high-resources language with a lot of labeled data. The possible benefits of using the wav2vec2 E2E approach are as follows: sys-tems are becoming more robust to various background noises, dialects, pronunciation features; moreover, for low-resource languages, it's much easier to find a significant amount of unlabeled data.

In this paper, we describe the results of experiments on the creation of Tatar speech recognition systems. We compare different training scenarios, the full scenario consists of 4 training steps:

1. Base self-supervised pretraining (BaseSS).
2. Source self-supervised pretraining (SourceSS).
3. Target self-supervised pretraining (TargetSS).
4. Target fine-tuning (TargetFT).

All scenarios are shown in Fig. 2. In the following sections, we give a training procedure description, provide details of data collection, and present the comparative analysis of the experiments' results.

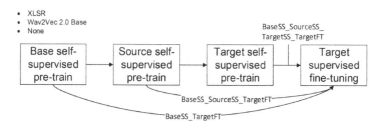

Fig. 2. Model training options

2 System Description

This article uses an approach with iterative self-supervised pretraining steps on audio data that is increasingly closer to the target domain. We implement 4 main training stages: base self-supervised pretraining (BaseSS), source self-supervised pretraining (SourceSS), target self-supervised pretraining (TargetSS), and target supervised fine-tuning (TargetFT), and analyze the effect of each pretraining step on the resulting recognition quality of ASR systems. The first stage is the BaseSS pretraining step. This step is the initial training where a (very) large dataset is used. The resulting model learned acoustic representation for a wide variety of noise conditions and speakers' variability. For our experiments we have chosen three possible alternatives to use as the base pre-trained model:

1. No pre-trained model.
2. Base Wav2Vec 2.0 Librispeech model (language: English, total duration: 1000 h).
3. Multilingual XLSR model (53 languages, total duration: 56k h).

For the second training step, we use source datasets consisting of heterogeneous Tatar audio data. This data allows the model to start learning language-specific acoustic features with a diverse set of speakers, noise conditions, etc. Data for the SourceSS stage were collected from TV shows, radio transmissions, audiobooks, and YouTube videos. More on data collection procedure can be found in the Data Collection section.

The TargetSS stage performs additional self-supervised training with the target Tatar datasets that have annotations, but they are not used here. We haven't set any hard restrictions on the style of speech for Target datasets due to the small number of available annotated Tatar speech corpora. Therefore, we use all of the existing data including both close-distance microphones read speech and broadcast spontaneous speech.

And at the last stage, the Tatar annotated speech corpus is used to fine-tune the model obtained at the previous stages. Additional training is based on the CTC (Connectionist Temporal Classification) algorithm [6,7]. A randomly initialized layer with a dimension equal to the number of elements in the dictionary is added to the model. For the case of the Tatar language, the dictionary consists of 39 elements: 38 letters and an additional character '—' as a words' separator.

3   Data Collection

The multistage approach that we chose for the training of ASR systems dictates the training data requirements. We need an unlabeled dataset for self-supervised pretraining steps and annotated dataset for supervised fine-tuning. To the moment there are two available datasets for the Tatar language: one from the CommonVoice project [1], and another from the TatarCorpus dataset [11]. Both datasets contain read speech with good SNR, all audios are manually annotated. To collect unlabeled datasets we obtained audios from several sources: a private dataset of audiobooks from Tatar book publishing company, records of TV and radio broadcasting, YouTube videos.

The resulting unlabeled corpus consists of 4 subcorpora:

1. Subcorpus of audiobooks: read speech recorded in studio conditions, 520 files with a total duration of 114 h.
2. Subcorpus of television broadcasting: spontaneous speech, variety of external noises and background music, 62 files - 733 h.
3. Subcorpus of two radio stations' recordings: read and spontaneous speech, background music, 398 files - 215 h.
4. Subcorpus of scientific video lectures from the YouTube platform: mostly read speech, good recording quality, 100 files - 87 h.

We carried out some basic preprocessing of the obtained video and audio files, which included audio track extraction from video files and audio file conversion to 16 bits per sample, 16 kHz mono PCM format. Taking into account the specifics of the initial data (long audiobooks, 12-h fragments of TV snippets, 40-min YouTube clips), the next task was to divide audio files into shorter fragments containing speech. The goal was to convert all data into 5–30 s fragments, where each fragment contains the speech of only one speaker. To solve this problem, we used the Silero-VAD tool [4]. Selective analysis of resulting fragments showed that the model coped with filtering music content that was present in radio and TV air while retaining speech segments with background music. But the duration of split fragments varied markedly. Based on the recommendations of the developers of the wav2vec2 model [3], short (less than 4.5 s) and long (longer than 30 s) audio files were filtered. The summary statistics on the number of files and their duration for each subcorpus are presented in Table 1.

The annotated corpus of Tatar speech, which was used for target self-supervised pretraining and target fine-tuning steps, consists of 3 parts:

1. Tatar speech corpus "TatarCorpus" [11]: close-microphone recordings, read speech - 99 h and 9 min, 500 speakers.
2. Subcorpus of television broadcasting: crowdsource annotation using the web-service [12] - 1 h and 33 min.
3. The Tatar part of the CommonVoice corpus [1] - 28 h and 47 min, 15 speakers.

Table 1. The characteristics of unlabeled speech corpus for the Tatar language

Subcorpus	Initial duration	After splitting	After filtering
Audiobooks	114 h	105 h	58 h
Television broadcasting	733 h	472 h	202 h
Radio stations' recordings	215 h	146 h	29 h
YouTube clips	87 h	81 h	39 h
Total	1 151 h	804 h	328 h

To construct a test subcorpus we chose recordings of 10 random speakers (5 male, 5 female) from the "TatarCorpus" (1 h and 37 min); for the Common Voice part, we used the original division into training and test samples, proposed by the creators of the corpus (3 h and 33 min); for the subcorpus of TV broadcasts we don't have speaker-level annotation, so the selection of 110 test fragments was carried out randomly throughout the corpus (5 min). In total it gave us 5 h 15 min test subcorpus.

As a language model for the speech recognition system, a 4-gram statistical model was built using the KenLM tool [8]. The total amount of training data was 8,760,330 sentences containing 116 million words. We downloaded and processed Tatar texts from the Internet (archives of leading news agencies, newspapers, magazines, websites of state institutions and departments, forums) and used some parts of the Tatar national corpus "Tugan Tel" [15].

4   Experiments

In total, we trained 8 different models. Taking into account the existence and type of the base model and self-supervised training steps used we will name our models in None, Base, XLSR_[SourceSS]_[TargetSS]_TargetFT format. The experiments were carried out on the fairseq platform [3]. Pretraining was carried out on 8 V100 32 GB video cards.

The recognition quality values were calculated separately for all test subcorpora. Word error rates (WER) for all built systems are presented in Table 2.

The best recognition quality on the test corpus achieved by the Base_SourceSS _TargetSS_TargetFT model: 5.67 WER even though using XLSR as the base model looked promising because of the amount of training data (56k h) and variety of languages (53, including Tatar) used during training. However, it is worth noting that on two of three test subcorpus (CommonVoice and TV) XLSR-based models show better performance than Base ones. Better quality on these subcorpora can be partially explained by the fact that CommonVoice data and Babel (telephone conversational speech) were included in the XLSR training corpus, therefore the model learned essential features right from the initial stage of training.

Table 2. Recognition quality of all trained models, WER

Model	CommonVoice	TatarCorpus	TV	Overall
None_SourceSS_TargetFT	9.54	6.98	31.42	9.30
None_SourceSS_TargetSS_TargetFT	8.17	5.99	30.78	8.04
Base_TargetFT	7.55	6.35	30.80	7.58
Base_SourceSS_TargetFT	5.80	5.08	25.08	5.98
Base_SourceSS_TargetSS_TargetFT	5.57	**4.65**	26.00	**5.67**
XLSR_TargetFT	5.73	6,52	30,03	6.39
XLSR_SourceSS_TargetFT	6.49	6.47	22.76	6.80
XLSR_SourceSS_TargetSS_TargetFT	**5.37**	5.62	**22.60**	5.77
Previous best published results	26.76 [2]	12.89 [13]	–	–

The previous best value showed by the "canonical" ASR system, built on separate acoustic models, a pronunciation model, and a language model, on the "TatarCorpus" test dataset is equal to 12.89 WER [13]. The best model proposed in this work on the same test subcorpus showed a value of 4.65 WER (Base_SourceSS_TargetSS_TargetFT). The WER values showed by the system [2] were taken as the base values for comparing the quality on the CommonVoice test dataset. The best value presented there is 26.76 WER, while our proposed system showed a value of 5.37 WER (XLSR_SourceSS_TargetSS_TargetFT).

Much higher error rates for TV test subcorpus can be explained by the complexity of spontaneous speech and partially by the fact that annotations were collected through crowdsourcing and contain mistakes. Some analysis of test TV audio fragments showed that there are several aspects that we will keep in mind in our future work:

1. Poorly distinguishable words at the beginning or end of the fragment that were not manually annotated, but were recognized by the ASR system. For instance, reference phrase 'isemendage', hypothesis 'manova isemendage' where 'manova' is an ending of a surname, where the starting part of it is not audible due to background noise);
2. Short interjections, often borrowed from the Russian language. For instance, reference phrase 'nu anda hal itep beterese', hypothesis 'anda hal itep beterese', where word 'nu' is a Russian interjection meaning 'well');
3. Other inaccuracies in annotations. For example, reference phrase 'president rostem minnehanov ta', hypothesis 'president rostam min'nehanov ta' with difference in nn' (Tatar n letter) letters; annotator made a mistake in spelling the surname in Russian and Tatar.

The second type of mistake can be influenced by the language model and not directly related to the training procedure of acoustic models. So we calculated WERs for the systems without the use of LM. The results are presented in Table 3.

With these "raw" acoustic WER values, we still see the same correlation: both SourceSS and TargetSS pretraining steps allow models to perform better on test datasets. The only two exceptions of this fact can be seen in comparison between Base_SourceSS_TargetFT and Base_SourceSS_TargetSS_TargetFT, XLSR_SourceSS_

Table 3. Recognition quality of all trained models without language model, WER

Model	CommonVoice	TatarCorpus	TV	Overall
None_SourceSS_TargetFT	16.81	14.50	36.53	16.61
None_SourceSS_TargetSS_TargetFT	14.06	13.12	35.58	14.22
Base_TargetFT	13.50	13.05	38.54	13.75
Base_SourceSS_TargetFT	8.83	10.08	28.17	9.47
Base_SourceSS_TargetSS_TargetFT	8.15	**9.13**	27.71	8.70
XLSR_TargetFT	11.76	12.35	32.97	12.31
XLSR_SourceSS_TargetFT	9.57	10.97	**22.91**	10.16
XLSR_SourceSS_TargetSS_TargetFT	**7.94**	9.57	24.15	**8.63**

TargetFT and XLSR_SourceSS_TargetSS_TargetFT for TV test subcorpus. For these two cases, the additional TargetSS step leads to an increase of WER for 3% and 5%, respectively. The increase in the quality of speech recognition for each type of model is presented in Table 4.

Table 4. Influence of self-supervised pre-training steps on recognition quality, % WER

Base model	SourceSS	TargetSS	Both SourceSS and TargetSS
None	N/A	−14.37%	N/A
Base	−31.16%	−8.09%	−36.73%
XLSR	−17.45%	−15.02%	−29.85%

5 Conclusion

This paper presents the results of experiments on building a Tatar speech recognition system using an iterative self-supervised pretraining procedure. We prepared 128-h annotated and 340-h unlabeled speech corpora. We propose two additional pretraining steps between the base pre-trained system and target fine-tuning. The first step that we called SourceSS uses unlabeled data from various sources (TV and radio broadcasting, YouTube clips, audiobooks) while the second TargetSS uses only an audio part from annotated target dataset. The testing of the proposed speech recognition systems confirmed good (SOTA) performance for different types of speech (read and spontaneous) and noise conditions. SourceSS step gave on average 24.3% WER improvement, TargetSS - 12.5%; both pretraining - 33.3%. These values were calculated for models that haven't used language models. As for absolute numbers, the best model in our experiments showed 5.37% WER for the Common Voice test dataset and 4.65% WER for TatarCorpus, which are 79.9% and 63.9% better than the previously published best result on these datasets.

References

1. Commonvoice (2021). https://commonvoice.mozilla.org/
2. Commonvoice tatar benchmark (2021). https://paperswithcode.com/sota/speech-recognition-on-common-voice-tatar
3. Fair-seq, wav2vec 2.0 pytorch example (2021). https://github.com/pytorch/fairseq/tree/master/examples/wav2vec
4. Silero vad: pre-trained enterprise-grade voice activity detector (vad), number detector and language classifier (2021). https://github.com/snakers4/silero-vad/
5. Baevski, A., Zhou, H., Mohamed, A., Auli, M.: Wav2vec 2.0: a framework for self-supervised learning of speech representations. In: Proceedings of NeurIPS (2020)
6. Baevski, A., Auli, M., Mohamed, A.: Effectiveness of self-supervised pre-training for speech recognition. CoRR abs/1911.03912 (2019). http://arxiv.org/abs/1911.03912
7. Graves, A., Fernandez, S., Gomez, G.: Connectionist temporal classification: labelling unsegmented sequence data with recurrent neural networks. In: Proceedings of the 23rd International Conference on Machine Learning, Pittsburgh, PA, USA (2006)
8. Heafield, K.: KenLM: faster and smaller language model queries. In: Proceedings of the Sixth Workshop on Statistical Machine Translation, pp. 187–197. Association for Computational Linguistics, Edinburgh, July 2011. https://www.aclweb.org/anthology/W11-2123
9. Kahn, J., et al.: Libri-light: a benchmark for ASR with limited or no supervision. CoRR abs/1912.07875 (2019). http://arxiv.org/abs/1912.07875
10. Kawakami, K., Wang, L., Dyer, C., Blunsom, P., van den Oord, A.: Learning robust and multilingual speech representations (2020)
11. Khusainov, A.: Design and creation of speech corpora for the Tatar speech recognition and synthesis tasks. In: Proceedings of the 3rd International Conference on Turkic Languages Processing, Kazan, Russia, pp. 475–484 (2015)
12. Khusainov, A.: Instrument dlya rasrpredelennogo sozdaniya annotirovannyh korpusov. In: Proceedings of the 8th International Conference on Turkic Languages Processin, Ufa, Russia (2020)
13. Khusainov, A.: Recent results in speech recognition for the Tatar language. In: Ekštein, K., Matoušek, V. (eds.) TSD 2017. LNCS (LNAI), vol. 10415, pp. 183–191. Springer, Cham (2017). https://doi.org/10.1007/978-3-319-64206-2_21
14. Schneider, S., Baevski, A., Collobert, R., Auli, M.: wav2vec: unsupervised pre-training for speech recognition. CoRR abs/1904.05862 (2019). http://arxiv.org/abs/1904.05862
15. Suleymanov, D., Khakimov, B., Gilmullin, R.: Korpus tatarskogo yazyka: konceptualnye i lingvisticheskiy aspekty. Vestnik TGGPU, pp. 211–216 (2011)

Speakers Talking Foreign Languages in a Multi-lingual TTS System

Zdeněk Hanzlíček[✉], Jakub Vít, and Markéta Řezáčková

NTIS – New Technology for the Information Society, Faculty of Applied Sciences,
University of West Bohemia, Univerzitní 22, 306 14 Plzeň, Czech Republic
{zhanzlic,jvit,juzova}@ntis.zcu.cz
http://www.ntis.zcu.cz/en

Abstract. This paper presents experiments with a multi-lingual multi-speaker TTS synthesis system jointly trained on English, German, Russian, and Czech speech data. The experimental LSTM-based TTS system with a trainable neural vocoder utilizes the International Phonetic Alphabet (IPA) which allows a straight combination of different languages. We analyzed whether the joint model is capable to generalize and mix the information contained in the training data and whether particular voices can be used for the synthesis of different languages, including the language-specific phonemes. The intelligibility of generated speech was assessed by an SUS (Semantically Unpredictable Sentences) listening tests containing Czech sentences spoken by non-Czech speakers. The performance of the joint multi-lingual model was also compared with independent single-voice models where the missing non-native phonemes were mapped to the most similar native phonemes. Besides the Czech sentences, the preference test also contained the English sentences spoken by Czech voices. The multi-lingual model was preferred for all evaluated voices. Although the generated speech did not sound like a native speaker, the phonetic and prosodic features were definitely better.

Keywords: Speech synthesis · Multi-lingual TTS

1 Introduction

When building a TTS voice model, each voice usually gets its individually trained model [13]. Another approach is to train all voices together to form a multi-speaker model [3,8]. A more complex task is combining various languages by using multi-lingual models [7,15].

In this paper, we present our initial experiments on multi-lingual modeling in LSTM-based speech synthesis. We used a typical parametric TTS system which is formed by several LSTM recurrent neural networks [4]. The resulting speech signal is built by a neural vocoder based on WaveRNN [6] architecture. For our experiments, we used English, German, Russian, and Czech speech data to train one joint speech model. To be able to work jointly with unequal phonetic sets of particular languages, we used the IPA phonetic alphabet [5].

K. Ekštein et al. (Eds.): TSD 2021, LNAI 12848, pp. 489–498, 2021.
https://doi.org/10.1007/978-3-030-83527-9_42

In our initial experiment described in this paper, we analyze how intelligible are the non-Czech voices when forced into the Czech language which is generally considered as a very difficult language. Besides, we also analyzed the Czech voices speaking English. To evaluate the intelligibility of produced speech, we conducted an SUS listening test. The performance of the joint multi-lingual model was also compared with independent single-voice models utilizing phonetic mapping. In the preference test, the multi-lingual model was preferred for all evaluated voices. The results suggest good phonetic knowledge generalization and transfer between different languages by the multi-lingual LSTM models.

This paper is structured as follows: Sect. 2 describes our experimental multi-lingual system. Section 3 introduces a single-voice model with phonetic mapping that is used for comparison. Listening tests and evaluation are presented in Sect. 4.

2   TTS Implementation

Our TTS system implementation is a modification of a standard LSTM parametric speech synthesis architecture [14]. The system is depicted in Fig. 1; it consists of two main parts: a model for the mapping of the input linguistic information to speech parameters (MFCCs, F0, and duration) and a trainable WaveRNN [6] neural vocoder for building the resulting speech signal. In our previous work [11], we showed that WaveRNN outperforms the traditional vocoders such as WORLD [9].

The statistical parametric speech synthesis uses linguistic features as input. These features are extracted from input text representation. We used common features such as current, previous and following phoneme identity, phoneme-in-word position, word-in-phrase position and frame-in-phoneme position (for frame-aligned versions). The linguistic-to-acoustic mapping is realized with the use of multi-layer bi-directional LSTM neural networks.

Based on our previous experiments [11], we used the following system setting:

- duration model: 2 hidden layers with 128 LSTM cells
- lf0 model: 2 hidden layers with 128 LSTM cells
- MFCC model: 3 hidden layers with 512 LSTM cells
- vocoder model: WaveRNN with 768 GRU cells

Since we employed the multi-speaker approach, i.e. one model trained for many voices, a speaker identification code was also added to the network input to distinguish the particular voices. Although the system is multi-lingual, the language information was not used as a network input. We assume that the input linguistic features contain the most relevant information for both training and synthesis. However, we did not verify this supposition.

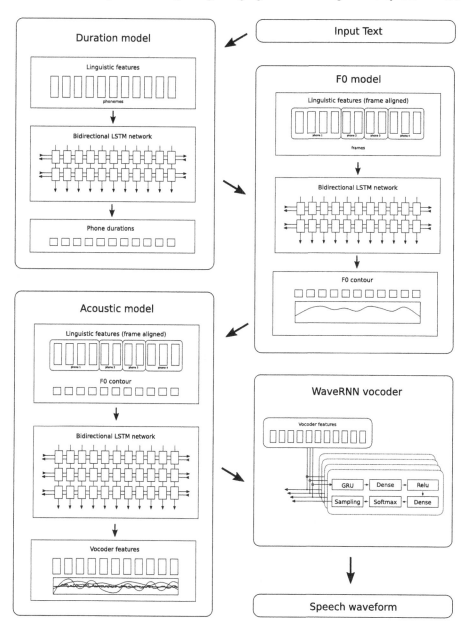

Fig. 1. An overall scheme of the TTS implementation.

2.1 Phonetic Alphabet

A common phonetic alphabet used for computer applications is SAMPA [12] which is defined for individual languages and is not directly applicable for multi-language tasks since different language-specific phonemes can be assigned to the same symbol.

We decided to use directly the International Phonetic Alphabet (IPA) [5] that is defined universally for all languages and allows a straight and natural combination of different languages. The complete list of phonemes[1] included in our data, including diacritic combinations, is presented in Table 1.

During model training, each used phoneme was transformed into unique phone embedding. Depending on the language of a particular voice, the training set covered various parts of the complete set. One embedding table was shared for all languages, therefore the model should share and transfer the knowledge between the particular voices and languages.

3   Single-Voice System with Phonetic Mapping

To demonstrate and evaluate the effect of sharing and generalizing the phonetic knowledge by a multi-lingual system, the system was compared with a simple single-voice system. Such a system trained on one voice could be also forced to generate a foreign language when missing phonemes in the foreign phonetic alphabet are appropriately substituted by available ones. Such a phonetic mapping can be defined for any language combinations, however, the substitution of some language-specific phonemes can be ambiguous or very approximative.

Phonetic mappings employed in our experiments are defined in Table 2. Only phonemes missing in the target language are listed, i.e. the other phonemes remain unchanged. Although automatic methods for mapping between different languages exist [1], mapping tables for our baseline system were created manually. The selection of assigned phonemes took account of the linguistic features of particular languages and the final tuning was done experimentally by using the training data.

We had to cope with several language-specific issues, e.g. presence/absence of the glottal stop [ʔ]. It is habitually transcribed and used in Czech[2], but is not ordinarily included in the English or Russian phonetic alphabet (is not transcribed). A similar speech sound could be also detected in both English and Russian, however, it is not taken as an individual phoneme, it is considered as an inherent part of the following vowel. Therefore, the glottal stop is removed when converting from the Czech to English or Russian alphabet.

Some phonemes are very difficult to substitute, since no similar phone is available in the target alphabet. A good example are the Czech voiced alveolar fricative trill [r̝] and voiceless alveolar fricative trill [r̝̊]; they appear e.g. in words *moře* [mor̝ɛ] and *keř* [kɛr̝̊]. Our proposed substitutions voiced [ʒ/z] and unvoiced [ʃ/s] correspond rather to a distorted pronunciation of foreigners starting with a Czech language study, and therefore, these substitutions sound relatively naturally in a voice with a foreign accent.

---

[1] We realize that IPA is describing primarily phones, not phonemes, nevertheless it can be used for phonemic transcription, too.

[2] Though the glottal stop [ʔ] is rather a phone than a phoneme in the Czech language, too.

Table 1. The complete list of phonemes sorted by the IPA number in a line-wise manner. Composed phonemes (e.g. diphthongs and affricates) or phonemes with diacritical marks are usually described by a corresponding sequence of IPA numbers.

IPA	Languages	IPA	Languages	IPA	Languages
p (101)	cz, de, en, ru	pf	de	pʲ	ru
b (102)	cz, de, en, ru	bʲ	ru	t (103)	cz, de, en, ru
ts	cz, de, ru	tʃ	cz, de, en	tʲ	ru
d (104)	cz, de, en, ru	dz	cz	dʒ	cz, de, en
dʲ	ru	c (107)	cz	ɟ (108)	cz
k (109)	cz, de, en, ru	kʲ	ru	g (110)	cz, de, en, ru
gʲ	ru	ʔ (113)	cz, de	m (114)	cz, de, en, ru
mʲ	ru	m̩	cz	ŋ (115)	cz, de, en
n (116)	cz, de, en, ru	nʲ	ru	ɲ (118)	cz
ŋ (119)	cz, de, en	ɲ:	de	r (122)	cz, de, ru
r̥	cz	rʲ	ru	ɾ	cz
ɽ	cz	f (128)	cz, de, en, ru	fʲ	ru
v (129)	cz, de, en, ru	vʲ	ru	θ (130)	en
ð (131)	en	s (132)	cz, de, en, ru	sʲ	ru
z (133)	cz, de, en, ru	zʲ	ru	ʃ (134)	cz, de, en
ʒ (135)	cz, de, en	ʂ (136)	ru	ʐ (137)	ru
ç (138)	de	x (140)	cz, de, ru	xʲ	ru
ɣ (141)	cz	ʁ (143)	de	h (146)	de, en
ɦ (147)	cz	ɹ	en	j (153)	cz, de, en, ru
l (155)	cz, de, en	lʲ	ru	ɫ	cz
w (170)	en	ç:	ru	z:	ru
ɫ (209)	ru	tɕ (215)	ru	i (301)	de, ru
i:	cz, de, en	ɪ̆	ru	e (302)	de, ru
eɪ	en	e:	de	ĕ	ru
ɛ (303)	cz, de, en, ru	ɛʊ	cz	ɛə	en
ɛ̃	de	ɛ̃:	de	ɛ:	cz, de
a (304)	cz, de, ru	aɪ	de, en	aʊ	cz, de, en
ã	de	ã:	de	a:	cz, de
ɑ:	en	ɔ (306)	de	ɔɪ	en
ɔɣ	de	ɔ:	en	o (307)	cz, de, ru
oʊ	cz	õ:	de	o:	cz, de
u (308)	de, ru	u:	cz, de, en	y (309)	de
y:	de	ø (310)	de	ø:	de
œ (311)	de	œ:	de	ɒ (313)	en
ʌ (314)	en	ɨ (317)	ru	ʉ (318)	ru
ɪ (319)	cz, de, en, ru	ɪə	en	ʏ (320)	de
ʊ (321)	cz, de, en, ru	ʊə	en	ə (322)	de, en, ru
əʊ	en	ɵ (323)	ru	ɐ (324)	de, ru
æ (325)	de, en, ru	ɜ:	en		

Table 2. Phonetic maps between particular languages.

Czech to English

Default	Mapped	Default	Mapped	Default	Mapped	Default	Mapped
ts	t + s	dz	d + z	c	t + j	ɟ	d + j
ʔ	–	m̩	m	ɲ	n + j	r	ɹ
r̝̊	ʒ	r̩	ʃ	r̝	ɹ	x	h
ɣ	h	fi	h	l̩	l	ɛʊ	ɛ + ʊ
ɛː	ɛ	a	ʌ	aː	ɑː	o	ɒ
oʊ	ɒ + ʊ	oː	ɔː				

Czech to German

Default	Mapped	Default	Mapped	Default	Mapped	Default	Mapped
c	t + j	ɟ	d + j	m̩	m	ŋ̍	m
ɲ	n + j	r̝̊	ʒ	r̝	ʃ	r̩	r
ɣ	h	fi	h	l̩	l	ɛʊ	ɛ + ʊ
oʊ	ɔ + ʊ						

Czech to Russian

Default	Mapped	Default	Mapped	Default	Mapped	Default	Mapped
tʃ	tɕ	dz	d + z	dʒ	d + z̢	c	tʲ
ɟ	dʲ	ʔ	–	m̩	m	ŋ̍	m
ɲ	nʲ	ŋ	n	r̝̊	z̢	r̝	ʂ
r̩	r	ʃ	ʂ	ʒ	z̢	ɣ	x
fi	x	l	ɬ	l̩	ɬ	iː	i
ɛʊ	e + ʊ	ɛː	e	aʊ	a + ʊ	aː	a
oʊ	o + ʊ	oː	o	uː	u		

English to Czech

Default	Mapped	Default	Mapped	Default	Mapped	Default	Mapped
θ	s	ð	z	h	fi	ɹ	r
w	v	eɪ	ɛ + j	ɛə	ɛ + r	aɪ	a + j
ɑː	aː	ɔɪ	o + j	ɔː	oː	ɒ	o
ʌ	a	ɪə	ɪ + a	ʊə	ʊ + r	ə	ɛ
əʊ	ɛ + ʊ	æ	a	ɜː	ɛ		

4   Experiments and Results

4.1   Experimental Speech Data

For our experiments, we utilized 16 voices of very good speech quality. The composition of training data is shown in Table 3. The training data were used to train one shared TTS model. The quality of the speakers was on a professional level. The size of the particular data sets was on average 20 h of recorded speech.

Table 3. Training data for neural network used in this experiment.

Language	Speakers	Duration [hours]
Czech	7	169
English	5	97
German	2	44
Russian	2	39

4.2 SUS Listening Test

To evaluate the intelligibility of produced speech, we conducted a listening test with sentences generated using the SUS (Semantically Unpredictable Sentences) methodology [2, 10], i.e. particular words cannot be determined from the sentence context and must be recognized individually.

Ten voices were selected covering all languages present in the corpora. For each speaker, two unique Czech sentences 5–6 words long were generated; several examples are listed in Table 4. The test participants were instructed to listen to the sentence and write down all words which they recognized. Ten native Czech listeners participated in the test. Each utterance could be played only once. For the assessment of word accuracy, the recognized word was considered correct only if it exactly matches the original text; the partial word similarity was not taken into account.

As expected, the best accuracy was achieved for Czech voices (98 and 100%). The remaining results differed for particular voices and were probably influenced by the unexpected strangeness of some sentences and the phonetic complexity of some words. No language-specific order was evident. The average word accuracy was 89% for all voices, ranging between 84 and 94%.

Table 4. Examples of sentences used in the SUS listening test with an illustrative English translation.

Czech SUS	Ignorujte neúčinné jesle anebo zobrazení
English translation	Ignore the ineffective nursery or display
Czech SUS	Vlakmistr vadne se schodišťovým opeřencem
English translation	The train driver fades with a staircase bird.
Czech SUS	Vertikála leze mezi klobásovým papírem
English translation	A vertical crawls within a sausage paper.
Czech SUS	Úbor slábne s kozím arbitrem
English translation	The dress weakens with a goat-like arbitrator
Czech SUS	Houževnatý výtisk byl civilizovaný senior
English translation	The tenacious printout was a civilized senior.
Czech SUS	Vyzvi pochybné pravoúhelníky i vniknutí
English translation	Challenge the suspicious rectangles and entry

4.3   Preference Listening Test

Another preference listening test was conducted for a direct comparison of the cross-language performance of the single-voice and multi-lingual models[3]. Again, we focused primarily on the Czech utterances spoken by foreign voices because Czech was the native language of all test participants. Besides, the test also included English sentences produced by the Czech voices. All the listeners can speak English sufficiently to assess these English sentences adequately.

The test contained 10 sentences for each voice, 80 sentences in total. The Czech sentences were synthesized by 2 English, 2 German and 2 Russian voices; the same sentences were used for all voices. The other 2 Czech voices were used to synthesize the English sentences. All sentences (10 English and 10 Czech) were selected from internet news and were about 6-10 words long.

15 listeners participated in the test. They were instructed to focus on the correct pronunciation, however, they could also take account of other relevant features. The results are presented in Table 5. Multi-lingual models were preferred for all individual voices; the average preference rate was 57.5% for multi-lingual models, 14.9% for single-voice models and the remaining 27.6% without preference.

Table 5. Results of preference listening test for individual voices.

Voice	Sentence	Preference [%]		
		single-model	none	multi-model
English 1	Czech	5.3	19.3	75.3
English 2		24.0	32.0	44.0
German 1		14.0	35.3	50.7
German 2		34.0	21.3	44.7
Russian 1		8.7	21.3	70.0
Russian 2		17.3	31.3	51.3
Czech 1	English	5.3	31.3	62.0
Czech 2		10.7	28.7	60.7
average		14.9	27.6	57.5

The participants of the test could also add a summarizing comment on their evaluation. All listeners agreed that no sentence sounded like a fully native speaker, both sounded rather like a foreigner trying to speak another language with his/her specific phonetic and intonation patterns. The default language could be mostly recognized. However, one sentence usually sounded more phonetically precise and also its overall prosody appeared more natural.

---

[3] Audio samples available at https://bit.ly/2Ryog0I.

5   Conclusion

In this paper, we presented our initial experiments with a multi-language multi-speaker TTS system jointly trained on English, German, Russian, and Czech speech data. Our experimental LSTM-based TTS system uses directly the International Phonetic Alphabet (IPA) that allows to join several less-or-more different phonetic alphabets naturally.

To assess how good the model can generalize and join the phonetic knowledge across different speakers and languages, we synthesized Czech sentences by various foreign non-Czech voices and English sentences by 2 Czech voices. In an SUS listening test, the participants were able to understand most of the words even with 1 playback limitation. In a preference test, the joint multi-lingual model was preferred to independently trained single-voice models. It suggests a good phonetic knowledge generalization and transfer between different languages by the joint models.

In our future work, we plan to add other foreign languages, e.g. Spanish and French. We also intend to optimize the representation of particular phones for the network input, e.g. by splitting the IPA transcription to core phone and its diacritical marks, or by a representation of phones with their articulatory features, that are also included in the IPA standard.

Acknowledgment. This research was supported by the Czech Science Foundation (GA CR), project No. GA19-19324S, and by the grant of the University of West Bohemia, project No. SGS-2019-027. Computational resources were supplied by the project "e-Infrastruktura CZ" (e-INFRA LM2018140) provided within the program Projects of Large Research, Development and Innovations Infrastructures.

References

1. Badino, L., Barolo, C., Quazza, S.: A general approach to TTS reading of mixed-language texts. In: Proceedings of ISCA Speech Synthesis Workshop (2004)
2. Benoît, C., Grice, M., Hazan, V.: The SUS test: a method for the assessment of text-to-speech synthesis intelligibility using semantically unpredictable sentences. Speech Commun. **18**(4), 381–392 (1996)
3. Fan, Y., Qian, Y., Soong, F.K., He, L.: Multi-speaker modeling and speaker adaptation for DNN-based TTS synthesis. In: Proceedings of IEEE International Conference on Acoustics, Speech and Signal Processing, ICASSP pp. 4475–4479 (2015)
4. Hochreiter, S., Schmidhuber, J.: Long short-term memory. Neural Comput. **9**, 1735–1780 (1997)
5. International Phonetic Association: Handbook of the International Phonetic Association: A Guide to the Use of the International Phonetic Alphabet. Cambridge University Press (1999)
6. Kalchbrenner, N., Elsen, E., Simonyan, K., Noury, S., Casagrande, N., Lockhart, E., Stimberg, F., van den Oord, A., Dieleman, S., Kavukcuoglu, K.: Efficient neural audio synthesis. Proc. Mach. Learn. Res. **80**, 2410–2419 (2018)
7. Li, B., Zen, H.: Multi-language multi-speaker acoustic modeling for LSTM-RNN based statistical parametric speech synthesis. In: Proceedings of Interspeech 2016, pp. 2468–2472 (2016)
8. Luong, H.T., Wang, X., Yamagishi, J., Nishizawa, N.: Training multi-speaker neural text-to-speech systems using speaker-imbalanced speech corpora. In: Proceedings of Interspeech 2019, pp. 1303–1307 (2019)

9. Morise, M.: D4C, a band-aperiodicity estimator for high-quality speech synthesis. Speech Commun. **84**, 57–65 (2016)
10. Tihelka, D., Matoušek, J.: The design of Czech language formal listening tests for the evaluation of TTS systems. In: Proceedings of International Conference on Language Resources and Evaluation, LREC 2004, pp. 2099–2102 (2004)
11. Vít, J., Hanzlíček, Z., Matoušek, J.: Czech speech synthesis with generative neural vocoder. In: Ekštein, K. (ed.) TSD 2019. LNCS (LNAI), vol. 11697, pp. 307–315. Springer, Cham (2019). https://doi.org/10.1007/978-3-030-27947-9_26
12. Wells, J.: Handbook of Standards and Resources for Spoken Language Systems, chap. SAMPA computer readable phonetic alphabet, pp. 684–732. Mouton de Gruyter, Berlin and New York (1997)
13. Ze, H., Senior, A., Schuster, M.: Statistical parametric speech synthesis using deep neural networks. In: Proceedings of IEEE International Conference on Acoustics, Speech and Signal Processing, ICASSP 2013, pp. 7962–7966 (2013)
14. Zen, H.: Acoustic modeling in statistical parametric speech synthesis - from HMM to LSTM-RNN. In: Proceedings of MLSLP (2015)
15. Zhang, Y., et al.: Learning to speak fluently in a foreign language: Multilingual speech synthesis and cross-language voice cloning. In: Proceedings of Interspeech 2019, pp. 2080–2084 (2019)

Voice Activity Detection for Ultrasound-Based Silent Speech Interfaces Using Convolutional Neural Networks

Amin Honarmandi Shandiz[(✉)] and László Tóth

Institute of Informatics, University of Szeged, Szeged, Hungary
{shandiz,tothl}@inf.u-szeged.hu

Abstract. Voice Activity Detection (VAD) is not easy task when the input audio signal is noisy, and it is even more complicated when the input is not even an audio recording. This is the case with Silent Speech Interfaces (SSI) where we record the movement of the articulatory organs during speech, and we aim to reconstruct the speech signal from this recording. Our SSI system synthesizes speech from ultrasonic videos of the tongue movement, and the quality of the resulting speech signals are evaluated by metrics such as the mean squared error loss function of the underlying neural network and the Mel-Cepstral Distortion (MCD) of the reconstructed speech compared to the original. Here, we first demonstrate that the amount of silence in the training data can have an influence both on the MCD evaluation metric and on the performance of the neural network model. Then, we train a convolutional neural network classifier to separate silent and speech-containing ultrasound tongue images, using a conventional VAD algorithm to create the training labels from the corresponding speech signal. In the experiments our ultrasound-based speech/silence separator achieved a classification accuracy of about 85% and an AUC score around 86%.

Keywords: Silent Speech Interface · Speech/silence classification · Voice Activity Detection · Convolutional neural network

1 Introduction

Voice Activity Detection (VAD) is an important component in many speech processing applications, for example automatic speech recognition (ASR) [2,13] and speech enhancement [26]. Its main role is to detect the presence or absence of speech [26], but sometimes it also involves a voiced/unvoiced decision [16]. Its application can not only significantly reduce the computational costs, but it may also influence the speech recognition accuracy [3]. In speech enhancement, VAD is used to identify frames which contain only noise to remove them from the signal [26]. In machine learning-based speech synthesis, removing noisy segments and pauses may help generate more accurate models.

In this paper we work with silent speech interfaces (SSI), which aim to convert articulatory signals to acoustic signals. In our case, the articulatory input corresponds to a sequences of ultrasound images that record the movement of the tongue during

© Springer Nature Switzerland AG 2021
K. Ekštein et al. (Eds.): TSD 2021, LNAI 12848, pp. 499–510, 2021.
https://doi.org/10.1007/978-3-030-83527-9_43

speaking. The goal is to convert this recording of the articulatory movement into a speech signal. Many possible approaches exist for this, but the most recent studies all apply deep neural networks (DNNs) for this task [5,8,22,24,27], and here we also apply neural structures that combine convolutional neural network (CNN) layers and recurrent layers such as the long short-term memory (LSTM) layer.

Similar to speech applications, voice activity detection may also be useful in SSI systems, for example for sparing with the energy consumption in wearable SSI devices. However, in this case creating VAD algorithms is much more difficult, as the lack of speech does not correspond to a lack of high-amplitude input signal. The tongue position is continuously being recorded and presented by the ultrasound imaging tool, even when the subject is not speaking.

In this paper we first demonstrate that the application of VAD may impact the accuracy of our SSI neural model, the speech synthesis network we apply, and even the evaluation metric we use. Then we implement a CNN to separate silence and speech frames based on the ultrasound tongue images, so we basically create a VAD algorithm that works with ultrasound images. Finally, we evaluate the performance of this algorithm experimentally, and we also compare the performance of our SSI framework with and without using the VAD algorithm.

The paper is organized as follows. In Sect. 2, we briefly present our SSI approach, the we talk about the problem of voice activity detection in Sect. 3. Then the experimental setup is described in Sect. 4 and the experiments are presented and discussed in Sect. 5. We close the paper with conclusions in Sect. 6.

2   The Ultrasound-Based SSI Framework

Our SSI system follows the structure recommended by Csapó et al. [5]. The input of the system is a sequence of ultrasound tongue images (UTI) that were recorded at a rate of 82 frames per second. The goal of the SSI system is to estimate the speech signal that belongs to the articulatory movement recorded in the ultrasound images, so the SSI system has to create a model for the articulatory-to-acoustic mapping. We estimate this mapping using deep neural networks (DNNs). For the training procedure, we assume that the speech signal was also recorded in parallel with the ultrasound video, as this speech signal serves as the training target. Also, to reduce the amount of training data required, we estimate a dense spectral representation instead of the speech signal itself. In practice it means that our SSI network converts the ultrasound video into a mel-spectrogram, and the output speech signal is generated from the mel-spectrogram using the WaveGlow neural vocoder [17]. It was shown by Csapó et al. that this approach is feasible, and it can generate intelligible speech from a sequence of ultrasound images [5].

Here, we evaluate the accuracy of spectral regression by two simple metrics. One of them is simply the Mean Squared Error (MSE) loss for the training of the neural network. The other one is the Mel-Cepstral Distortion (MCD) between the original speech signal and the speech signal reconstructed from the ultrasound input [12], which is a popular metric of speech quality in speech synthesis [10].

3   Voice Activity Detection from Speech and from Ultrasound

The main role of Voice Activity Detection is to estimate the presence or absence of speech [26]. In the simplest case, that is, in a quiet environment the lack of speech activity corresponds to silent parts in the input signal. Hence, the simplest VAD algorithms compare conventional acoustic features such as the signal's energy to a threshold [20]. Exceeding the threshold signs the presence of speech (VAD = 1), otherwise the signal is identified as silence (VAD = 0). However, the task becomes much more difficult under noisy conditions. The speech phones can be voiced and unvoiced, and the most difficult is to separate unvoiced parts from background noise. Thus many VAD algorithms extend the two-class classification to 3 classes, corresponding voiced, unvoiced and silent (V/UV/S) parts [16,26]. Moreover, under noisy conditions simple acoustic features such as the signal's energy may be insufficient, so several more sophisticated features have been proposed. For example, the classic paper by Atal et al. performs the prediction based on five different measurements including zero-crossing rate, speech energy, correlation features, 12-pole linear predictive coding (LPC), and the energy of the prediction error [2]. Other authors used features such as the zero-crossing rate, spectral or cepstral features, empirical mode decomposition (EMD), and so on [2,7,16]. More recent studies apply machine learning methods to perform the voiced/unvoiced decision [6,14,18,19]. Mondal et al. applied clustering over temporal and spectral parameters to implement their VAD [15].

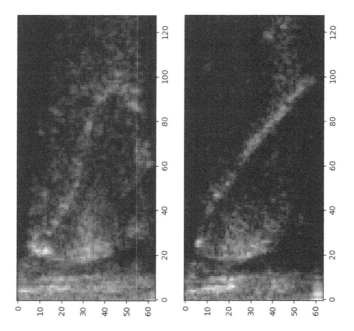

Fig. 1. Two UTI examples from the database, one for a speech (vowel) frame (left) and one for a silent frame (right).

While there are a lot of studies on voice activity detection from speech, the input of our SSI system consists of ultrasound tongue images (UTIs). Figure 1 shows two examples of the tongue position recorded by the device, when the subject is speaking (producing a vowel) and when he is not – the diagonal light stripes in the images correspond to the tongue of the speaker. After examining several samples, we got the impression that speaking versus remaining silent typically results in more drastic changes in the speech signal than in the corresponding ultrasound tongue images, so voice activity detection based on the latter is presumably much harder. In the following we train a CNN to perform the voiced/invoiced classification using such ultrasound images. As the structure of this VAD-CNN and the network that we apply for the SSI task are very similar, we describe them together in the next Section.

4 Experimental Setup

4.1 The Ultrasound Dataset

For the experiments we used the English TAL corpus [21]. It contains parallel ultrasound, speech and lip video recordings from 81 native English speakers, and we used just the TaL1 subset which contains recordings from one male native speaker. We partitioned his files into training, testing and validation sets using 1015, 24 and 50 files, respectively. To preprocess the ultrasound images we applied minmax normalization to the $[-1, 1]$ range, and resized the images to 64 * 128 pixels using bicubic interpolation. As regards the normalization of the speech mel-spectrogram features, we tried different normalization techniques, but we got the best results with the standard mean-deviance normalization (standardization). These 80 mel-spectrogram coefficients served as the training target values for the SSI network.

4.2 CNNs for the SSI and for the VAD Task

Convolutional Neural Networks are currently the most popular tool in image recognition, as they proved very powerful in extracting complex features from images by creating very deep network architectures [11]. Standard CNNs convolve 2D filters with the images, but when the input is a video or a time series, CNNs can be extended to 3D by considering time as the third dimension [9,28]. Recurrent neural networks such as the LSTM can also be very effective in extracting and combining temporal information from a sequential input [23]. However, these networks are known to be slow, so variants such as the quasi-recurrent neural network have been proposed [4]. This is why several authors apply 3D-CNNs to substitute recurrent layers when applying CNNs to a sequence of images [28]. Here, we experiment with two neural network configurations in our SSI framework, that is, to estimate a speech mel-spectrogram from a sequence of ultrasound images. The first network is a 3D-CNN, following the proposal of Tóth et al. [25]. The second configuration combines the 3D-CNN layers with and additional BiLSTM layer, as it may be more effective in aggregating the information along the time axis. The structure of the two networks is compared in Table 1. The input for both networks is the same, a short sequence of adjacent UTI frames. The output corresponds to the 80 mel-spectral coefficients that has to be estimated for the WaveGlow speech synthesis step, and the network is trained to minimize the MSE between the target and the output spectral vectors.

We also trained a CNN to perform VAD from the ultrasound images. In this case we applied simple frame-by-frame training, so the input consisted of a single image, and we applied a 2D-CNN to classify the actual frame as silence or speech (Si/Sp). The architecture of this network is shown in Table 2. The network has just a single output that estimates the probability of the actual frame containing silence. This network was trained with the binary cross-entropy loss function.

Table 1. The structure of the 3D-CNN and the 3D-CNN + BiLSTM networks in Keras for the SSI task. The differences are shown in bold.

Conv3D	Conv3D + BiLSTM
Conv3D(30,(5,13,13),strides=(5,2,2))	Conv3D(30,(5,13,13),strides=(5,2,2))
Dropout(0.2)	Dropout(0.2)
Conv3D(60,(1,13,13),strides=(1,2,2))	Conv3D(60,(1,13,13),strides=(1,2,2))
Dropout(0.2)	Dropout (0.2)
MaxPooling3D(poolsize=(1,2,2))	MaxPooling3D(poolsize=(1,2,2))
Conv3D(90,(1,13,13),strides=(1,2,1))	Conv3D(90,(1,13,13),strides=(1,2,1))
Dropout(0.2)	Dropout(0.2)
Conv3D(85,(1,13,13),strides=(1,2,2))	Conv3D(85,(1,13,13),strides=(1,2,2))
Dropout(0.2)	Dropout(0.2)
MaxPooling3D(poolsize=(1,2,2))	MaxPooling3D(poolsize=(1,2,2))
Flatten()	**Reshape((5, 340))**
Dense(500)	**Bidirectional(LSTM(320,**
Dropout(0.2)	**return_sequences=False))**
Dense(80,activation='linear')	Dense(80,activation='linear')

Table 2. The structure of the 2D-CNN used for classification of speech/silent ultrasound images.

Conv2D
Conv2D(32, (3, 3), padding='same', Activation='relu')
MaxPooling2D((2,2))
Conv2D(64, (3, 3), padding='same', activation='relu')
MaxPooling2D((2,2))
Conv2D(128, (3, 3), padding='same', Activation='relu')
MaxPooling2D((2,2))
Flatten()
Dense(128, activation='relu'))
Dense(1, activation='sigmoid')

5   Results and Discussion

5.1   The Impact of VAD on the MCD Metric and on Speech Synthesis

In the first experiment our goal was to demonstrate how the application of VAD may influence our results. Notice that this first experiment did not involve SSI: we simply converted the speech signals to mel-spectrograms, and then reconstructed them using WaveGlow (see Fig. 2). We applied the Mel-Cepstral Distortion (MCD) metric to quantify the difference between the original and the reconstructed speech signals. For voice activity detection and silence removal we used the VAD implementation available from WebRTC [1]. As shown in the first two rows of Table 3, retaining longer silent parts before and after the speech signal does influence the MCD. We performed more experiments with preserving longer silent parts, and Fig. 3 shows that we obtained consistently increasing MCD values. This result indicates that MCD (at least, the implementation we used) is sensitive to the amount of silence in the input. We should mention that some authors explicitly exclude the non-speech frames from the calculation of MCD [10], but most papers do not clearly describe this step.

In the third row of Table 3 we present one more experiment where we performed two analysis-synthesis steps. Theoretically, the analysis and synthesis steps should be the perfect inverse of each other, so experiment c) should give the same result as experiment a). However, we obtained a slightly different MCD value. The probable explanation is that the WaveGlow speech synthesis network does not give a prefect reconstruction, and it is sensitive to certain parameters such as the duration of the silent parts or the positioning of the input windows.

Table 3. MCD values of the speech analysis-synthesis process when applying silence removal with three different VAD configurations.

Configuration	MCD
A: VAD (window length = 10 ms)	1.55
B: VAD (window length = 10 ms), plus keeping 180 ms silence at both ends	2.03
C: applying A after B	1.34

5.2   The Impact of VAD on the SSI

In the second experiment we evaluated how the application of VAD on the training corpus influences the performance of our SSI system. In these UTI-to-speech conversion experiments we used the ultrasound data set presented in Sect. 4.1, and the two network configurations we described in Table 4. Both models were trained using the Adam optimizer with a initial learning rate of 0.0002. We repeated the experiment with using the original training data and with removing most of the silent parts from the speech signals using the WebRTC VAD implementation.

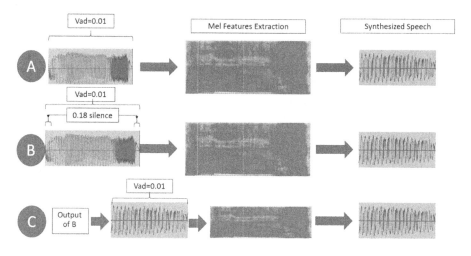

Fig. 2. Illustration of the experimental configurations applied in Table 3.

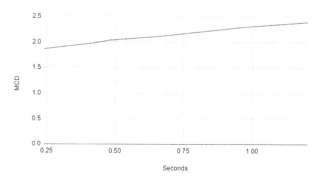

Fig. 3. Retaining more silence increases the MCD.

In Table 4 we report the MSE of the training process and the MCD values obtained from comparing the originals speech signals with those synthesized from the UTI input. The first thing we may notice is that the 3D-CNN+BiLSTM network produced much lower MSE rates and also slightly lower MCD errors. This shows the clear advantage of using a BiLSTM layer instead of a simple Dense layer. Second, the MCD scores are much higher in this case than in the previous experiment. This is because there we worked with the original spectrograms, so the reported MCD values of 1.3–2.0 were caused by the inaccuracy of the WaveGlow neural vocoder. Here, the spectrograms were estimated from the UTI images, so the errors of our spectral estimation network and the WaveGlow network add up. Our best MCD score of 3.08 corresponds to a low-quality but intelligible speech [5]. In comparison, Ribeiro et al. obtained an MCD score of 2.99 on the same corpus using more sophisticated encoder-decoder networks [21].

As the last observation, we can see that retaining more silence in the corpus results in significantly lower MSE rates during training. The trivial explanation is that estimating silence is much easier for the network than estimating the spectrum of various speech sounds. However, the reduction of the MSE is misleading, as the MCD values on the test set have increased. Although this increase is not significant, it warns us that adding more training samples from a single class – especially, from a trivial class – may have a detrimental effect on the performance of a DNN, as it might shift the focus of training.

Table 4. Evaluation metrics of the SSI system after training the models with removing or retaining silence in the speech data.

	Removing silence by VAD			VAD + keeping 180 ms silence		
	MSE (dev)	MSE (test)	MCD	MSE (dev)	MSE (test)	MCD
Conv3d	0.46	0.45	3.20	0.30	0.33	3.29
Conv3d+BiLSTM	0.39	0.42	3.08	0.259	0.29	3.13

5.3   Classification of Speech and Silence from Ultrasound

In the previous experiment the VAD algorithm was executed with the speech signal. However, in practical SSI applications the speech signal might not be available, so we should be able to perform the voice activity detection from the ultrasound input. With this aim, we performed experiments to separate speech and silence frames of the ultrasound video using the 2D-CNN presented earlier in Table 2. The training labels for this 2-class classification process were obtained as follows (see also Fig. 4). As we have the synchronized speech signals for the ultrasound videos, we first identified the speech frames that belong to each ultrasound image based on the ultrasound frame rate. We split the speech signal into frames and fed it to the speech VAD function to decide about the speech/silence label of each image. We used these target labels with the ultrasound images as input to train the 2D-CNN for ultrasound-based voice activity detection. We used the ReLU activation function for all layers except the last layer which applies a sigmoid activation function to produce an output value between 0 and 1. For training we used SGD optimization with an initial learning rate of 0.001. We extracted the speech/silence training labels from the same train, development and test files as earlier, and the amount of speech labels was approximately 2–3 times more than the number of frames labelled as silence.

The evaluation metrics for this 2-class task are shown in Table 5. Besides the usual classification accuracy, we also report the precision and recall values which show that the two classes were slightly imbalanced. This is also reflected by the confusion matrices which can be seen in Table 6. Thus, we also evaluated the AUC score based on the ROC of the classifier, which gave 0.89 for the development and 0.86 for the test set, respectively. Finally, we also mention that the F1 measure of 0.9 is also very good, and it could even be slightly improved by fine-tuning the decision threshold (which we did not adjust here). We also display the Cohen's Kappa values, which is a preferred metric in the case of imbalanced classes.

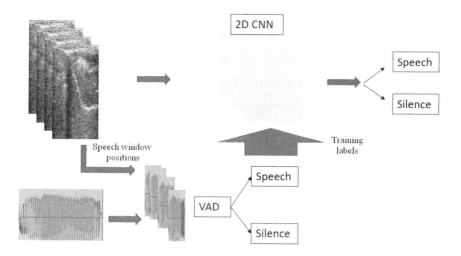

Fig. 4. Illustration of obtaining the VAD training labels and training the 2D-CNN for silence/speech classification.

Table 5. Evaluation metrics for the silence/speech classification task.

	Dev set	Test set
Accuracy	0.87	0.852
Recall	0.94	0.95
Precision	0.877	0.864
F1	0.91	0.9
ROC AUC	0.894	0.859
Cohen's Kappa	0.672	0.57

5.4   Replacing Speech-VAD by UTI-VAD

Finally, we repeated the experiment of Table 4, but this time using the UTI-based VAD algorithm instead of the speech VAD. As the results in Table 7 show, in this case we obtained even slightly better MSE rates than earlier with the standard VAD function. The MCD values are basically equivalent with those obtained earlier, and the slight advantage of training the system with the removal of the long silent parts remained. In summary, we can say that our ultrasound-based VAD algorithm performed similarly to the standard, speech-based VAD algorithm in this experiment.

Table 6. Confusion Matrices for the silence/speech classification task for the development and test sets.

Dev data				Test data			
	Predicted				Predicted		
Actual		Negative	Positive	Actual		Negative	Positive
	Negative	2850	1302		Negative	1671	1268
	Positive	502	9295		Positive	418	8096

Table 7. Training the SSI system with removing or retaining silence from the data using the ultrasound-based VAD algorithm.

	Removing silence by VAD			VAD + keeping 180 ms silence		
	MSE (dev)	MSE (test)	MCD	MSE (dev)	MSE (test)	MCD
conv3D	0.436	0.428	3.15	0.38	0.27	3.28
Conv3D+BiLSTM	0.393	0.41	3.05	0.35	0.26	3.12

6 Conclusion

Here we showed that – similar to voice activity detection for speech – ultrasound images can also be used to discriminate between Si/Sp segments. We estimated our training labels based on the parallel speech recording using a public VAD implementation. Our classifier attained a promising accuracy of 86% in discriminating frames of silence and speech. We also showed that preserving too much silence in the training set can influence both the training of the model and the quality of the generated speech. In the future, we plan to apply our VAD technique as a method of silence removal as an initial step before feature extraction. That it, we window the speech signal in synchrony with the ultrasound frames and feed them to the VAD, and perform the subsequent feature extraction steps for synthesizing speech or other related tasks by using only the frames retained by VAD.

Acknowledgements. This study was supported by grant NKFIH-1279-2/2020 of the Ministry for Innovation and Technology, Hungary, and by the Ministry of Innovation and the National Research, Development and Innovation Office within the framework of the Artificial Intelligence National Laboratory Programme and through project FK 124584. The GPU card used was donated by the NVIDIA Corporation.

References

1. WebRtc voice activity detection (1999). https://webrtc.org
2. Atal, B., Rabiner, L.: A pattern recognition approach to voiced-unvoiced-silence classification with applications to speech recognition. IEEE Trans. Acoust. Speech Signal Process. **24**(3), 201–212 (1976)

3. Benyassine, A., Shlomot, E., Su, H., Massaloux, D., Lamblin, C., Petit, J.: A silence compression scheme for use with G. 729 optimized for V. 70 digital simultaneous voice and data applications (recommendation G. 729 annex B). IEEE Commun. Mag. **35**(9), 64–73 (1997)
4. Bradbury, J., Merity, S., Xiong, C., Socher, R.: Quasi-recurrent neural networks. arXiv preprint arXiv:1611.01576 (2016)
5. Csapó, T.G., Zainkó, C., Tóth, L., Gosztolya, G., Markó, A.: Ultrasound-based articulatory-to-acoustic mapping with WaveGlow speech synthesis. In: Proceedings of the Interspeech 2020, pp. 2727–2731 (2020)
6. Deng, H., O'Shaughnessy, D.: Voiced-unvoiced-silence speech sound classification based on unsupervised learning. In: 2007 IEEE International Conference on Multimedia and Expo, pp. 176–179. IEEE (2007)
7. Haigh, J., Mason, J.: Robust voice activity detection using cepstral features. In: Proceedings of TENCon 1993. IEEE Region 10 International Conference on Computers, Communications and Automation, vol. 3, pp. 321–324. IEEE (1993)
8. Honarmandi Shandiz, A., Tóth, L., Gosztolya, G., Markó, A., Gábor Csapó, T.: Improving neural silent speech interface models by adversarial training. arXiv e-prints pp. arXiv-2104 (2021)
9. Ji, S., Xu, W., Yang, M., Yu, K.: 3d convolutional neural networks for human action recognition. IEEE Trans. Pattern Anal. Mach. Intell. **35**(1), 221–231 (2012)
10. Kominek, J., Schultz, T., Black, A.: Synthesizer voice quality of new languages calibrated with mean cepstral distortion. In: Proceedings of the SLT, pp. 63–68 (2008)
11. Krizhevsky, A., Sutskever, I., Hinton, G.E.: ImageNet classification with deep convolutional neural networks. Adv. Neural. Inf. Process. Syst. **25**, 1097–1105 (2012)
12. Kubichek, R.: Mel-cepstral distance measure for objective speech quality assessment. In: Proceedings of the Pacific Rim Conference, pp. 125–128 (1993)
13. Lokhande, N.N., Nehe, N.S., Vikhe, P.S.: Voice activity detection algorithm for speech recognition applications. In: IJCA Proceedings on International Conference in Computational Intelligence (ICCIA 2012), pp. 1–4, no. 6 (2012)
14. Moattar, M.H., Homayounpour, M.M., Kalantari, N.K.: A new approach for robust realtime voice activity detection using spectral pattern. In: 2010 IEEE International Conference on Acoustics, Speech and Signal Processing, pp. 4478–4481. IEEE (2010)
15. Mondal, S., Barman, A.D.: Clustering based voiced-unvoiced-silence detection in speech using temporal and spectral parameters. In: 2015 IEEE International Conference on Research in Computational Intelligence and Communication Networks (ICRCICN), pp. 390–394. IEEE (2015)
16. Nirmalkar, B., Kumar, S.: Voiced/unvoiced classification by hybrid method based on cepstrum and EMD (2016)
17. Prenger, R., Valle, R., Catanzaro, B.: WaveGlow: a flow-based generative network for speech synthesis. In: Proceedings of the ICASSP, pp. 3617–3621 (2019)
18. Qi, F., Bao, C., Liu, Y.: A novel two-step SVM classifier for voiced/unvoiced/silence classification of speech. In: 2004 International Symposium on Chinese Spoken Language Processing, pp. 77–80. IEEE (2004)
19. Qi, Y., Hunt, B.R.: Voiced-unvoiced-silence classifications of speech using hybrid features and a network classifier. IEEE Trans. Speech Audio Process. **1**(2), 250–255 (1993)
20. Rabiner, L.R., Schafer, R.W., et al.: Digital Processing of Speech Signals. Prentice-Hall, Englewood Cliffs (1978)
21. Ribeiro, M.S., et al.: TaL: a synchronised multi-speaker corpus of ultrasound tongue imaging, audio, and lip videos. arXiv preprint arXiv:2011.09804 (2020)

22. Saha, P., Liu, Y., Gick, B., Fels, S.: Ultra2Speech - a deep learning framework for formant frequency estimation and tracking from ultrasound tongue images. In: Martel, A.L., et al. (eds.) MICCAI 2020. LNCS, vol. 12263, pp. 473–482. Springer, Cham (2020). https://doi.org/10.1007/978-3-030-59716-0_45
23. Schmidhuber, J., Hochreiter, S.: Long short-term memory. Neural Comput. **9**(8), 1735–1780 (1997)
24. Tatulli, E., Hueber, T.: Feature extraction using multimodal convolutional neural networks for visual speech recognition. In: Proceedings of ICASSP, pp. 2971–2975 (2017)
25. Tóth, L., Shandiz, A.H.: 3D convolutional neural networks for ultrasound-based silent speech interfaces. In: Rutkowski, L., Scherer, R., Korytkowski, M., Pedrycz, W., Tadeusiewicz, R., Zurada, J.M. (eds.) ICAISC 2020. LNCS (LNAI), vol. 12415, pp. 159–169. Springer, Cham (2020). https://doi.org/10.1007/978-3-030-61401-0_16
26. Verteletskaya, E., Sakhnov, K.: Voice activity detection for speech enhancement applications. Acta Polytechnica **50**(4) (2010)
27. Yu, Y., Shandiz, A.H., Tóth, L.: Reconstructing speech from real-time articulatory MRI using neural vocoders. arXiv preprint arXiv:2104.11598 (2021)
28. Zhao, S., Liu, Y., Han, Y., Hong, R., Hu, Q., Tian, Q.: Pooling the convolutional layers in deep convnets for video action recognition. IEEE Trans. Circuits Syst. Video Technol. **28**(8), 1839–1849 (2017)

How Much End-to-End is Tacotron 2 End-to-End TTS System

Daniel Tihelka[1(✉)], Jindřich Matoušek[1], and Alice Tihelková[2]

[1] New Technologies for the Information Society, Pilsen, Czech Republic
{dtihelka,jmatouse}@ntis.zcu.cz
[2] Department of English Language an Literature, Faculty of Arts,
University of West Bohemia, Pilsen, Czech Republic
atihelko@kaj.zcu.cz

Abstract. In recent years, the concept of end-to-end text-to-speech synthesis has begun to attract the attention of researchers. The motivation is simple – replacing the individual modules that TTS traditionally built on with a powerful deep neural network simplifies the architecture of the entire system. However, how capable are such end-to-end systems of dealing with classic tasks such as G2P, text normalisation, homograph disambiguation and other issues inseparably linked to text-to-speech systems?

In the present paper, we explore three free implementations of the Tacotron 2-based speech synthesizers, focusing on their abilities to transform the input text into correct pronunciation, not only in terms of G2P conversion but also in handling issues related to text analysis and the prosody patterns used.

Keywords: End-to-end speech synthesis · Tacotron 2 · WaveRNN · MelGan · Text processing · Homograph disambiguation · Prosody patterns

1 Introduction

There has been a marked increase in the research on end-to-end TTS systems in recent years [1,9,11,20,24], because when connected to a deep-neural/network (DNN), it appears to be an elegant and powerful solution to various tasks in a TTS unified under an AI framework.

When an end-to-end TTS system is mentioned, its usual concept involves the replacement of the individual (and to some extent independent) internal modules, such as text normalisation, homograph disambiguation (or NLP in general), phonetic transcription (G2P) and/or prosody estimation, by a sequence of consecutive neural networks, where these cannot be clearly mapped to the individual tasks that the text passes through in the classic TTS system structure [21].

One of the most widely known end-to-end TTS frameworks is *Tacotron* [24], recently enhanced to *Tacotron 2* [20], providing higher-quality output due to the use of a DNN-based WaveNet [16] speech vocoder. The whole system can be viewed as a single DNN taking a raw text input, converting it into speech, while, due to practical reasons, there is still a clear split-point building an interface between a *front-end*

© Springer Nature Switzerland AG 2021
K. Ekštein et al. (Eds.): TSD 2021, LNAI 12848, pp. 511–522, 2021.
https://doi.org/10.1007/978-3-030-83527-9_44

(encoder-decoder) that transforms the input text into mel-spectral representation, and *back-end* (vocoder) converting the mel-spectra into the output waveform.

Considering the lack of specialised modules which can be developed, tested and evaluated independently of each other, the question of how the whole DNN is capable of dealing with standard TTS tasks arises. In the present paper, we have, therefore, examined the capabilities of three open-source Tacotron 2 implementations, namely TensorFlowTTS [22], NVidia Tacotron-2 [14] and Tacotron2-WaveRNN [13], in the various TTS tasks.

We have set several assumptions in regard to the examined systems, however. First, we used the implementation "as they are", without any further modifications, except for the minimum of those required for the systems to work for Czech. Second, we focused on the "special" cases where we expect some additional knowledge of the structure and/or content of the synthesized text while not providing any such information in order to examine whether the DNN framework is able to learn it. Third, we did not compare the quality of the output speech, since it is mostly affected by the particular speech decoder used in the individual systems.

2 Tacotron 2 Details

The Tacotron 2 structure was first introduced in [20]. It replaced, and simplified, to some extent, the original Tacotron [24], where the Griffin-Lim vocoder [4] was used to convert the mel-spectrum into speech. For example, the new model uses simpler building blocks, such as vanilla LSTM and convolutional layers in the encoder-decoder, instead of "CBHG" stacks and GRU recurrent layers in the original Tacotron. Also, each decoder step corresponds to a single spectrogram frame, avoiding the use of "output layer reduction factor".

The input text is passed through embeddings, convolution and biLSTM networks, which represent the encoder part of the encoder-decoder structure of the Tacotron 2. The output of the encoder is then consumed by an attention network that summarises the full encoded sequence for each decoder output step. The decoder part is an auto-regressive recurrent neural network, predicting a mel-spectrogram from the encoded input sequence, one frame at a time.

The whole encoder-(attention)-decoder structure is trained independently on a vocoder, where text (orthographic) transcriptions of the speech corpus recordings are at the input and mel-spectra computed from the corresponding speech [20] are at the output of it. Similarly, the vocoder is trained on the combination of the computed mel-spectra and speech from which these were obtained. There is a possibility to fine-tune the vocoder by re-training it on mel-spectra estimated by the (trained) front-end, but we did not explore this possibility as we expect that it would mostly affect the quality of speech rather than the correctness of the output.

While the vocoder in the original Tacotron 2 was realised by the WaveNet [20] DNN structure (conditioned by mel-spectra instead of linguistic features as in [16]), the independence of the front-end (encoder-decoder) and back-end (vocoder) allows us to use any other neural network structure able to convert the spectrum into speech. In the tested incarnations of the Tacotron 2, we have the following combinations:

- *WaveRNN* vocoder [8] in Tacotron 2-WaveRNN
- *WaveGlow* vocoder [15] in NVidia
- *MelGan* vocoder [10] in TensorFlow-TTS (TFT+MGan)
- *Multiband MelGan* vocoder [26] in TensorFlow-TTS (TFT+mbMGan)
- *Parallel WaveGan* vocoder [25] in TensorFlow-TTS (TFT+pWGan); for English only since it generated a noise only for Czech.

all of them, naturally, use their own implementation to obtain the mel-spetrum from the speech signal. The number of training epochs and other settings was left on the defaults for each of the systems; only the batch size was adjusted to effectively use the GPU resources used during training.

However, when looking inside all of the implementations, there is a set of utilities called "text cleaners", containing hard-coded rule- and dictionary-based algorithms through which the input test is passed before going to the Tacotron 2 DNN. Among others, the most important task of the module is to expand abbreviations and numbers into their orthographic form (see the description of *Numbers and abbreviations* on Sect. 3), and it is thus highly language-dependent. Except for a few minor differences without any significant impact on the behaviour, all of the tested implementations share the same code.

To be able to test the Tacotron 2 on the Czech language, we first had to implement the Czech version of the cleaners module. However, we created only a minimum version of the module, able to carry out not much more than text lower casing, since the other tasks are much more complex due to language inflection, and, furthermore, they violate the notion of how the end-to-end system is viewed.

3   Tests Design

The absence of explicit modularisation in the Tacotron 2 system, as mentioned in Sect. 1, makes the testing more difficult. Since the output of the Tacotron 2 itself is a mel-spectrum, unsuitable for the planned evaluation, we have to use the output speech – thus, the full end-to-end system was evaluated.

To prove the capabilities of the given Tacotron 2 incarnations, the tested sentences can split into the sets described below, each focusing on a single task which is supposed to be handled by the TTS system. Thus, the tests were designed to "stress" the abilities of end-to-end systems which are traditionally handled by dedicated modules, such as phonetic transcription, text normalisation, linguistic analysis or prosody contour estimation [21]. Let us also emphasize that all the sets were synthesised as one batch passed through the systems, with no other information than the input text shown here provided to the systems.

Generic TTS

This is the test of the very fundamental capability of converting the text into meaningful speech. For English, given its irregular pronunciation, we used the default phrases provided with the TensorFlow TTS, as it contains the uncommon word "boatswain"/boːsn/ as well as an out-of-dictionary word "bo-sun" for which an appropriate pronunciation must be estimated by the system.

> Unless you work on a ship, it's unlikely that you use the word boatswain in everyday conversation, so it's understandably a tricky one.
> The word - which refers to a petty officer in charge of hull maintenance - is not pronounced boats-wain.
> Rather, it's bo-sun to reflect the salty pronunciation of sailors, as The Free Dictionary explains.

For Czech, with rather regular G2P conversion, we used 5 pangrams to ensure that all the accented characters in various contexts occur in the text:

> *Příliš žluťoučký kůň úpěl ďábelské ódy.*
> *Hleď, toť čarovný je loužek, kde hedvábné štěstíčka září.*
> *Vodní žíňky běží kolem lesní tůně a kadeřemi svými čeří stříbrosvit měsíce.*
> *Qvído, kouzelníkův učeň s ďolíčky utírá prach z vílích křídel.*
> *Ó, náhlý úsvit oblažil zemětvář prolínajícím hřejivým dotekem svým.*

The correctness of the phonetic transcription has also been checked for homographs in English and for loanwords for Czech, as described further.

Prosody Patterns in Questions

As the end-to-end systems do not have any explicit prosody generator, we were curious how the prosody patterns specific to the individual question types would be realised. In the English language, yes-no questions, alternative questions and wh-questions are distinguished, with some nuances depending on their semantic function. Yes-no questions usually have rising intonation, although falling intonation is also possible, such as in rhetorical questions, question tags or negative questions expressing an exclamation (e.g. *Isn't she clever!*), but these need some kind of speaker intention understanding. Alternative questions have rising intonation where two alternatives are present and falling intonation where more than two alternatives are involved (e.g. *Will you have cheese, ham or yoghurt?*). Finally, wh-questions have falling intonation. For the purpose of the test, the following set of basic yes-no and wh-questions types was built:

> Son, what are you saying?
> What's wrong with that?
> What shall I do?
> You don't remember him?
> Any new pain on your eye?
> Haven't we just been through this?

For Czech, there are similar prosody patterns for yes-no question (rising) and wh-questions (falling) [6] as in English; thus in the test we used the following questions:

Pozná systém doplňovací větu?
Není to chyba vstupních dat?
Kdy se to podaří dokončit?
Proč stále váháte?
Bude to fungovat?
Půjdeš dnes do kina?
Dá se na to odpovědět jen ano či ne?
Máš hlad?
Dáš si něco ostřejšího?

Homograph Disambiguation

This test was specific to the English language, where homograph words were placed within meaningful phrases. The question to answer was whether the DNN structure is able to learn that the words have differing pronunciation based on their meaning. We used 17 words *record, read, live, minute, tear, wind, conflict, progress, row, import, insult, advocate, research, bow. lead, sow* and *wound*, and put both variants into 17 phrases such as:

Did you record/rɪˈkɔːd/ this record/ˈrekərd/?
Have you read/red/ that book that all the people read/riːd/?
In the age of universe, a minute/ˈmɪnɪt/ is only a minute/maɪˈnjuːt/ time tick.
You can't tear/teər/ this picture with my tear/tɪər/ on it.
You should lead/liːd/ the debate about the importance of lead/led/ as a material.
. . .

Loan Words

In contrast to the previous, this set was used solely for Czech. There were 21 phrases designed to prove the capability to handle the irregular pronunciation of loanwords in Czech; the 4 phrases out of the 21 were these:

Kybernetický mikroorganismus motivoval detailní trénink exotických serotoninových studií.
Aktivní frekvence.
I laik rozpozná ischias.
Kognitivní disonance.
. . .

Numbers and Abbreviations

In all the three Tacotron 2 implementations (and even in others, such as e.g. Deep-Minds's version [12]), there is a rather primitive module with hard-coded rule-based text normalisation, through which the input text is processed before it is passed to the Tacotron's DNN. As already noted, the implementations either share the same code or have only minimal differences in it.

For English, the module carries out the following actions (in the given ordering):

lowercase, replacing multiple white space occurrences by one

numbers normalizer, where the numbers are transcribed to strings with the help of `inflect.py` module [2]; it also handles the expansion of [$] sign (but not [£] or others).

abbreviations normalizer, with a list of 18 abbreviations, such as *mrs, mr, dr*, etc., replaced by a simple string match

whitespace unifier, replacing multiple white character occurrences by a single space

character filter, removes all the non-supported characters, such as numerals; for Czech, all the accented characters were added.

This text normalisation is extremely simplified. For example, numbers larger than $3,000$ are read in groups of two numerals. Having enough representative data, the encoder-decoder on which the Tacotron 2 front-end is based should be capable of learning at least simple replacement rules. The main reason for the existence of the cleaners, we believe, is that in the speech corpora available, there are not enough samples on which to train. And since the entities to be normalised are removed from the input by the hard-coded rules, the DNN does not even have a chance to train on them.

The situation is considerably more difficult for Czech, where the task of the normalisation of numbers, abbreviations and others is significantly more complex due to language inflection. Therefore, we did not attempt to provide even basic implementation of the text normalisation modules for Czech, and there is no default distributed within the tested systems. Instead, we focus on the use of text-to-text transfer transformer (T5) model [3] to handle this level of normalisation in a language-independent way, not ready to be integrated yet, however.

According to the presumptions stated in Sect. 1, the numbers and abbreviations were excluded from the tests, since for English they will be handled by rules anyway, while for Czech they would simply be ignored by the cleaners.

Spelling

The reading of abbreviations not translated into words, such as HMM, TTS and so on, is not handled by the cleaner codes at all, so we tried to test if the Tacotron 2 itself is able to learn them. The analysis of the JLS speech corpus showed that there are several abbreviations such as FBI (168 occurrences), PRS (51 occs.), CIA (15 occs.), USSR (5 occs.) and few others with fewer than 10 occurrences, giving over 250 occurrences to train spelling on. Moreover, there are 16 occurrences of "etc." and 4 of "e.g.", not handled by cleaners as well.

In theory, the Tacotron 2 may be able to learn some of the spellings, so we prepared three phrases with the abbreviation occurring in the training data and three with the abbreviation not being there:

> The FBI discovered them among PRS employees.
> Situation in USSR was influenced by CIA.
> Let's buy some fruit like apples, oranges, etc.
> The TTS was also tested on LJS speech corpus.
> A BBC documentary.
> It accepted the recommendations from the AAIB.

In the Czech corpus, there are 22 phrases designed to handle the spelt abbreviations (for the unit selection synthesizer), plus several more sentences where such abbreviations occur spontaneously, giving a total of 41 occurrences of them. This is significantly less than for English, yet we decided to test them as well on two phrases, the first containing abbreviations among the training data, the second being the opposite:

> Zkratky JZD, univerzita ZČU, řízení SLP i velká VŇ byly v korpusu.
> Ale OPBH ani CHKO tam nebyly.

4   Evaluation

All the systems were evaluated on the same datasets, with the parameters set to default values as provided by the implementations. For English, the LJ Speech Dataset [5] was used, as it is currently the de-facto standard in evaluation. For the Czech language, however, we had to use used our own proprietary voice, Jan [23].

All the texts synthesised by the tested Tacotron 2 implementations were analysed by the authors. A phrase was considered correct if the evaluated phenomenon was rendered correctly, i.e. the correct pronunciations were used in the case of *homographs*, or all the accented characters were read correctly in the case of Czech. The overall results are shown in Table 1, where the first is the number of correct reads followed by the number of evaluated phrases.

Table 1. The number of correct reads from all the prompts in the given set

		NVidia	WaveRNN	TFT+MGan	TFT+mbMGan	TFT+pWGan
English	Generic texts	1/3	3/3	1/3	1/3	1/3
	Questions	2/5	2/5	4/5	2/5	4/5
	Homographs	7/17	6/17	5/17	5/17	3/17
	Spelling	1/7	0/7	1/7	2/7	1/7
Czech	Generic texts	0/5	0/5	3/5	2/5	N/A
	Questions	7/9	5/9	4/9	3/9	N/A
	Loan words	7/21	7/21	6/21	2/21	N/A
	Spelling	0/2	0/2	0/2	0/2	N/A

It can be seen that none of the systems did particularly well for their default settings. Only the NVidia version was able to read all the three generic sentences as expected, including the OOV "bo-sun"; the others had a problem with the reading of "boatswain". In Czech, the systems were able to read some of the pangrams correctly, while in the others there were mistakes in the words "Hled'", "Ó" and "učeň". The exception were NVidia and WaveRNN which was not ale to read any pangram correctly, with multiple mispronunciations in each (NVidia also tended to lisp).

Regarding the prosody, the correct pattern was mostly used in less that 50% of samples. It cannot be clearly said, however, that there is a one type of mismatch. There were even cases in Czech where the rising pattern was used correctly, but not rising enough, making the phrase sound unfinished (pattern used as a phrase delimiter [7, 19]).

The correct homograph was mostly missed and similar results were for loanwords in Czech, but these are a hard task, to be fair.

As for the cases with correct spelling, it was in the BBS and PCR abbreviations which were in the corpus. The only other success was for *multiband melgan* vocoder in TensorFlowTTS, where "etc." was read correctly as "et cetera". For Czech, none of the abbreviations was spelled, as expected.

It was also observed in TensorFlowTTS that different mel-spectra were obtained by the Tacotron frontend for the same input text, resulting in different speech generated from these spectra. As being caused the nature of the DNN model the Tacotron is built on, it also occurs in other tested implementations. Unfortunately, further analysis showed that the difference is significant enough to change the correct rendering of the phrase, as related to the phenomena we focus on here; some of the samples are shown in Table 2.

Table 2. The samples of correct/incorrect pronunciation variance for the individual systems after the base evaluation

		NVidia	WaveRNN	TFT+ MGan	TFT+ mbMGan	TFT+ pWGan
English	...record ...	✓	✗	✓	✓	✓
	...minute ...	✓	✗	✓	✗	✗
	...tear ...	✗	✗	✗	✓	✓
	...wind ...	✗	✓	✗	✗	✗
	What's wrong with that?	✗	✗	✓	✓	✓
	What shall I do?	✓	✗	✓	✗	✓
	You don't remember him?	✗	✗	✗	✗	✓
Czech	Kybernetický ...	✓	✓	✓	✗	
	Poník v Palestině	✗	✓	✓	✓	
	Exministrova deviza	✓	✓	✓	✗	
	Exhalace působí bronchitidu	✓	✗	✓	✗	
	Kognitivní disonance	✗	✓	✗	✗	
	Proč stále váháte?	✓	✓	✗	✗	
	Bude to fungovat?	✓	✗	✓	✗	
	Máš hlad?	✓	✓	✗	✗	

Therefore, to ensure that the correct results were not obtained by chance, for English we re-generated and re-evaluated three more runs for these outputs. The Table 3 shows the number of correct reads on the re-evaluated data (first number) related to the number of correct reads in the original data in Table 1. As an incorrectly read phrase is now treated any phrase for which at least one incorrect reading was evaluated among the additional three variants.

Table 3. The number of correct re-evaluations of the prompts which were correct before

		NVidia	WaveRNN	TFT+MGan	TFT+mbMGan	TFT+pWGan
English	Questions	2/2	2/2	2/4	0/2	3/4
	Homographs	3/7	4/6	0/5	0/5	0/3
	Spelling	1/1	0/0	1/1	2/2	1/1

It can be seen that the questions are read correctly in a majority of cases, except for the MelGan-based vocoders; the main drop is in reading homographs. The most consistent behaviour was observed for WaveRNN, where only one out of four readings was evaluated as incorrect (still counts as incorrect variant in Table 3) in two of the homographs. Even though this was not evaluated, just as the correct reads were rendered incorrectly, the opposite case could occur as well. And similar results would also be likely to be obtained for Czech.

In the end, let us remember that the evaluation was focused on the correct rendering of speech; the overall quality or naturalness were not taken into account. The very informal evaluation could be that the worst quality was obtained by TFT+MGan version, while the clearest and most natural speech was obtained by NVidia, followed by TFT+mbMGan (and TFT+pWGan for English). Especially for the TensorFlowTTS implementation, however, there were sometimes problems with the ending of the synthesis, where the speech continued in murmuring after the given text was read. This is, nevertheless, a known problem of the Tacotron attention mechanism, which is mitigated by, e.g. FastSpeech model [17, 18].

5   Conclusion

While the end-to-end system attracts increasing attention, it is definitely not a "silver bullet" to the TTS. In the current state-of-the-art, the end-to-end rather means the replacement of the dedicated G2P, prosody generator and speech generation modules. The remaining tasks, mostly connected with NLP are beyond the capabilities of the current systems – the hard-coded rule-based text normalisation is one of the weakest points of the current end-to-end systems. Of course, there are multiple ways of tuning the system parameters to obtain slightly better results, but due to the combinatoric explosion of the parameters, it is far beyond the scope of this paper.

We also see a disadvantage of the Tacotron 2 in the unification under the unified encoder-decoder + vocoder networks. It can be seen from the paper that the evaluation of such a system requires the evaluation of output speech, which is impossible to automate nowadays. Splitting the whole systems into independent modules, as traditionally carried out, enables developing and evaluating each of the modules independently of the others (even using different datasets). In this way, all the tasks which were shown to fail, namely spelling, homographs and loanwords, could be solved independently – for example we are working on the use of transformer-based models [3], with very promising results in the G2P task, and our intention is to use the transformers for the task of text normalisation as well. Subsequently, we plan to to integrate such a module with the Tacotron 2 (or any other end-to-end system), with the connection realised on the level of DNN layers. This will allow us to transfer a rich representation of the information learned by a particular DNN into the following one, avoiding the need for "serialising" it through a text. In this way, we can build a "real" end-to-end TTS system.

Acknowledgement. This research was supported by the Czech Science Foundation (GA CR), project No. GA19-19324S. Computational resources were supplied by the project "e-Infrastruktura CZ" (e-INFRA LM2018140) provided within the program Projects of Large Research, Development and Innovations Infrastructures.

References

1. Donahue, J., Dieleman, S., Bińkowski, M., Elsen, E., Simonyan, K.: End-to-end adversarial text-to-speech (2021)
2. Dyson, P., Coombs, J.R.: inflect 5.3.0 (2021). https://pypi.org/project/inflect/
3. Řezáčková, M., Tihelka, D., Švec, J.: T5g2p: Using text-to-text transfer transformer for grapheme-to-phoneme conversion. In: Interspeech 2021, Brno, Czech Republic (2021)
4. Griffin, D.W., Lim, J.S.: Signal estimation from modified short-time fourier transform. IEEE Trans. Acoust. Speech Signal Process. **32**, 236–243 (1984)
5. Ito, K., Johnson, L.: The lj speech dataset (2017). https://keithito.com/LJ-Speech-Dataset/
6. Jůzová, M., Tihelka, D.: Difficulties with wh-questions in czech tts system. In: Text, Speech, and Dialogue. Lecture Notes in Computer Science, vol. 9924, pp. 359–366. Springer, Heidelberg (2016). https://doi.org/10.1007/978-3-319-45510-5_41
7. Jůzová, M., Tihelka, D., Volín, J.: On the extension of the formal prosody model for TTS. In: Text, Speech, and Dialogue, Lecture Notes in Computer Science, vol. 11107, pp. 351–359. Springer, Heidelberg (2018). https://doi.org/10.1007/978-3-030-00794-2_38
8. Kalchbrenner, N., et al.: Efficient neural audio synthesis. In: Dy, J., Krause, A. (eds.) Proceedings of the 35th International Conference on Machine Learning. Proceedings of Machine Learning Research, vol. 80, pp. 2410–2419. PMLR (2018)
9. Kulkarni, A., Colotte, V., Jouvet, D.: Improving transfer of expressivity for end-to-end multispeaker text-to-speech synthesis (2021). https://hal.archives-ouvertes.fr/hal-02978485, working paper or preprint
10. Kumar, K., et al.: Melgan: generative adversarial networks for conditional waveform synthesis (2019)
11. Lu, Y., Dong, M., Chen, Y.: Implementing prosodic phrasing in Chinese end-to-end speech synthesis. In: ICASSP 2019–2019 IEEE International Conference on Acoustics, Speech and Signal Processing (ICASSP), pp. 7050–7054 (2019). https://doi.org/10.1109/ICASSP.2019.8682368
12. Mama, R.: Tacotron-2 (2021). https://github.com/Rayhane-mamah/Tacotron-2
13. McCarthy, O.: Wavernn (2021). https://github.com/fatchord/WaveRNN
14. NVIDIA: Tacotron 2 (without wavenet) (2021). https://github.com/NVIDIA/tacotron2
15. NVIDIA: Waveglow: a flow-based generative network for speech synthesis (2021). https://github.com/NVIDIA/WaveGlow
16. van den Oord, A., et al.: WaveNet: a generative model for raw audio. CoRR abs/1609.03499 (2016). https://arxiv.org/abs/1609.03499
17. Ren, Y., et al.: Fastspeech 2: fast and high-quality end-to-end text to speech (2021)
18. Ren, Y., et al.: Fastspeech: fast, robust and controllable text to speech (2019)
19. Romportl, J., Matoušek, J.: Formal prosodic structures and their application in NLP. In: Matoušek, V., Mautner, P., Pavelka, T. (eds.) TSD 2005. LNCS (LNAI), vol. 3658, pp. 371–378. Springer, Heidelberg (2005). https://doi.org/10.1007/11551874_48
20. Shen, J., et al.: Natural TTS synthesis by conditioning wavenet on mel spectrogram predictions. In: 2018 IEEE International Conference on Acoustics, Speech and Signal Processing (ICASSP), pp. 4779–4783 (2018). https://doi.org/10.1109/ICASSP.2018.8461368
21. Taylor, P.: Text-to-Speech Synthesis, 1st edn. Cambridge University Press, New York (2009)
22. Tensorflowtts: Real-time state-of-the-art speech synthesis for tensorflow 2 (2021). https://github.com/TensorSpeech/TensorFlowTTS
23. Tihelka, D., Hanzlíček, Z., Jůzová, M., Vít, J., Matoušek, J., Grůber, M.: Current state of text-to-speech system ARTIC: a decade of research on the field of speech technologies. In: Sojka, P., Horák, A., Kopeček, I., Pala, K. (eds.) TSD 2018. LNCS (LNAI), vol. 11107, pp. 369–378. Springer, Cham (2018). https://doi.org/10.1007/978-3-030-00794-2_40

24. Wang, Y., et al.: Tacotron: towards end-to-end speech synthesis. In: Proceedings of Interspeech 2017, pp. 4006–4010 (2017). https://doi.org/10.21437/Interspeech.2017-1452
25. Yamamoto, R., Song, E., Kim, J.M.: Parallel wavegan: a fast waveform generation model based on generative adversarial networks with multi-resolution spectrogram. In: ICASSP 2020–2020 IEEE International Conference on Acoustics, Speech and Signal Processing (ICASSP), pp. 6199–6203 (2020). https://doi.org/10.1109/ICASSP40776.2020.9053795
26. Yang, G., Yang, S., Liu, K., Fang, P., Chen, W., Xie, L.: Multi-band melgan: faster waveform generation for high-quality text-to-speech. In: 2021 IEEE Spoken Language Technology Workshop (SLT), pp. 492–498 (2021). https://doi.org/10.1109/SLT48900.2021.9383551

CNN-TDNN-Based Architecture for Speech Recognition Using Grapheme Models in Bilingual Czech-Slovak Task

Josef V. Psutka[1,2](✉)📷, Jan Švec[1,2]📷, and Aleš Pražák[2]📷

[1] Department of Cybernetics, University of West Bohemia, Pilsen, Czech Republic
`psutka_j@kky.zcu.cz, honzas@kky.zcu.cz`
[2] NTIS - New Technologies for the Information Society, UWB, Pilsen,
Czech Republic
`aprazak@ntis.zcu.cz`

Abstract. Czech and Slovak languages are very similar, not only in writing but also in phonetic form. This work aims to find a suitable combination of these two languages concerning better recognition results. We would like to show such a contribution on the Malach project. The Malach speech of Holocaust survivors is highly emotional, filled with many disfluencies, heavy accents, age-related coarticulation, and many non-speech events. Due to the nature of the corpus, it is very difficult to find other appropriate data for acoustic modeling, so such a combination can significantly improve the amount of training data. We will discuss the differences between the phoneme and grapheme way of combining Czech with Slovak. We will also compare different architectures of deep neural networks (TDNN, TDNNF, CNN-TDNNF) and tune the optimal topology. The proposed bilingual ASR approach provides a slight improvement over monolingual ASR systems, not only at the phoneme level but also at the grapheme.

Keywords: Speech recognition · Multilingual training · Robustness · Acoustic modeling

1 Introduction

This work aims to find a suitable combination of two languages (Czech and Slovak) in terms of acoustic modeling. The Czech and Slovak languages are very similar, not only in writing but also phonetically. In low-resource tasks, the possibility of such a combination is undoubtedly a great benefit. We would like to show such a contribution on the Malach project [8]. The Malach speech is highly emotional, filled with many disfluencies, heavy accents, age-related coarticulation, and many non-speech events (see more details in [3,14,18]). Due to the nature of the corpus, it is very difficult to find other appropriate data for acoustic modeling, so such a combination can significantly improve the amount of training data.

© Springer Nature Switzerland AG 2021
K. Ekštein et al. (Eds.): TSD 2021, LNAI 12848, pp. 523–533, 2021.
https://doi.org/10.1007/978-3-030-83527-9_45

In recent years, grapheme-based models have been widely used in many speech recognition applications [5,6,23,24]. Experiments in various languages have shown that the quality of the resulting recognizer significantly depends on the grapheme-to-phoneme relation of the underlying language. Most Slavic languages have a relatively close relationship between graphemes and phonemes. Thus both languages, Czech and Slovak, should be well suited for a grapheme-based approach to acoustic modeling [7,9,11]. It has been shown that ASR using just grapheme as a sub-word unit yields acceptable WER.

The use of graphemes instead of phonemes simplifies the development of an automatic speech recognition (ASR) because a relatively complicated phonetic transcription step can be skipped. This is still the case even when grapheme-to-phoneme (G2P) methods are used (e.g. Phonetisaurus [12]). The limitation of G2P is mainly because it is a machine learning method with limited accuracy, especially for OOV words. Such words are often words with unsystematic pronunciation (e.g. derived from foreign languages).

The article [23] showed the benefits of using grapheme-based acoustic for searching in large spoken archives (Malach archives). Unlike other papers that tend to migrate from one language to another [5] or [10] or [7], our efforts aim to create a bilingual (Czech-Slovak) acoustic model (AM). We will also discuss the optimal architecture of deep neural networks (TDNN, TDNNF, CNN-TDNNF) and tune the optimal topology to obtain the best recognition results.

The following section briefly describes the differences and the similarities between Czech and Slovak languages from a phonetic and graphemic point of view. The training and test datasets are presented in Sect. 3. In Sect. 4 we describe typical acoustic modeling setups. The experiments and results are described in Sect. 5. The conclusions are presented in Sect. 6.

2   Differences and Similarities Between Czech and Slovak

As mentioned in the introduction, the Czech and Slovak languages are very similar, not only in writing but also phonetically. Czech orthography is considered a model of many other Balto-Slavic languages using the Latin alphabet. From this point of view, we can understand Slovak as its direct descendant. Both orthographies use similar diacritics and also have a similar, usually interchangeable relationship between the letters and the sounds they are supposed to represent. The fact that both languages were in the past the official languages used in one state (in Czechoslovakia for more than 40 years) also has a significant share in the great similarity. In this article, we will not deal with all linguistic subdisciplines. We will focus only on the phonetic and graphemic form of languages. You can find a more detailed comparison (for the purposes of acoustic modeling) of Czech and Slovak in [9,11,20].

2.1   Graphemes

The **Czech** language uses 42 letters, i.e. 26 letters of basic Latin alphabet supplemented by 15 letters with diacritical marks. These marks are slash [ˇ], comma

[´] and a circle [°]. Special treatment has a digraph [*ch*], which is also included among the letters of the Czech alphabet and represents phoneme /x/ (SAMPA is used in all cases of phonetic notation [4,22]). There are two ways to write long /u:/ in Czech: [*ú*] and [*ů*]. The difference is that [*ů*] cannot occur in the initial position, while [*ú*] occurs almost exclusively in the initial position or at the beginning of the root of the word in the compound. These two letters have the same pronunciation.

The **Slovak** alphabet has 46 letters which makes it the longest Slavic and European alphabet. It contains 26 letters of basic Latin alphabet (same letters as in Czech). Together with 17 letters with diacritical marks. Slovak, unlike Czech, also contains two more diacritical marks: two dots [¨] and a canopy [ˆ] and does not contain a circle [°]. But only 5 of the 17 diacritical letters differ from Czech ([*ä*] [*ľ*] [*ĺ*] [*ô*] [*ŕ*]). We can also find two more digraphs in Slovak, i.e. [*dz*] and [*dž*]. These letters represents phonemes /dz/ and /dZ/.

In addition to the letters of Czech and Slovak alphabets, non-original names (especially persons and geographical elements) often retain Latin letters with diacritical marks in their original form, i.e. from other alphabets, most often German umlauts. All letters and differences between the Czech and the Slovak alphabet can be seen in the Table 1.

Table 1. Czech and Slovak alphabet

	basic Latin letters				digraphs	
		with diacritical marks				
Cz	a b c d e f g h i j k l m	á č ď é í ň	ě ů ř	ch		
Sk	n o p q r s t u v w x y z	ó š ť ú ý ž	ä ĺ ľ ô ŕ		dz dž	

2.2 Phonemes

The basic **Czech** phonetic alphabet consists of 10 vowels, 30 consonants and 3 dipthongs. Most of the vowels have not only a short but also a long variant, e.g. /a/ and /a:/. There is one "domestic" dipthong /o_u/ (*pouto*) and two dipthongs that appear mostly in foreign words /a_u/ (*auto*) and /e_u/ (*euro*). Consonants may be divided into 8 plosives (/p/, /b/, /t/, /d/, /c/, /J\/, /k/ and /g/), 4 affricates (/t_s/, /d_z/, /t_S/ and /d_Z/), 11 fricatives (/f/, /v/, /s/, /z/, /Q\/ (*tři*), /P\/ (*řád*), /S/, /Z/, /j/, /x/ and /h\/), 2 liquids (/r/ and /l/) and 5 nasals (/m/, /n/, /N/, /J/ and /F/). 11 consonants come in pairs, having the same manner and place of articulation and differing just by the unvoiced/voiced characteristic, e.g. /p/ and /b/. The other consonants (i.e. liquids, nasals, and glide /j/) are always voiced. More details can be found in [18].

A phonetic inventory of **Slovak** contains 52 phonemes. It comprises 11 vowels, 37 consonants, and 4 dipthongs. There are 6 short (/a/, /e/, /i/, /o/, /u/ /{/) and 5 long (/a:/, /e:/, /i:/, /o:/ and /u:/) vowels. The only difference from

Czech is short vowel /{/ (*mäso*). Slovak has 4 diphthongs /i_ˆa/ (*piatok*), /i_ˆe/ (*mier*), /i_ˆu/ (*paniu*) and /u_ˆo/ (*kôň*), none of them appear in Czech. Of the consonants, there are 8 plosives (/p/, /b/, /t/, /d/, /c/, /J\/, /k/ and /g/), 4 affricates (/ts/, /dz/, /tS/ and /dZ/), 8 fricatives (/f/, /w/ (*vdova*), /s/, /z/, /S/, /Z/, /x/ and /h\/), and 17 sonorants (/r/, /r=/ (*vrch*), /r=:/ (*vŕba*), /l/, /l=/ (*vlk*), /l=:/ (*vĺča*), /L/ (*ľad*), /m/, /F/, /n/, /N\/ (*Slovensko*), /N/, /J/, /v/, /u_ˆ/ (*kov*), /i_ˆ/ (*kraj*), /j/). There are 10 unvoiced/voiced conso- nantal pairs in Slovak, e.g. /p/ and /b/. Other consonants (i.e. sonorants) are always voiced. Important information on the overlap between Czech and Slovak phonemes is summarized in Table 2 and further details can be found in [9,10,18].

Table 2. Czech and Slovak phonemes

	Vowels	Diftongs	Consonants	
Cz	a e i o u	e_u a_u o_u	p b t d c J\ k g t_s d_z t_S d_Z	Q\ P\
Sk	a: e: i: o: u: {	i_ˆa i_ˆe i_ˆu u_ˆo	f v s z S Z x h\ l r j m n J N F	r= r=: l= l=: L w u_ˆ N\ i_ˆ

3 Training and Test Data

Malach is an audiovisual archive originally collected in the 1990s to preserve the memories of Holocaust survivors. Today, these interviews are stored at the Shoah Foundation Institute at the University of Southern California (USC-SFI) along with other interviews with witnesses to the history of the entire 20th century (more than 54k of interviews). The Malach part of the archive contains testimonies in 32 languages of the personal memories of people who survived the World War II Holocaust. Most of them are in English (approximately half of the entire archive). More than 570 testimonies are in Czech (almost 1,000 h of video). Similar numbers (550 testimonies) are in Slovak. Interviews (in all languages) collected in the archive contain natural speech, full of disfluencies, emotional excitements, heavy accents, and often influenced by the high age of speakers (problems with keeping ideas). The average age of all speakers at the time of recording was about 75 years.

Czech: In 2014, the LDC released the Czech part of the Malach data [21]. The edi- tion contains 400 randomly selected testimonies for the purpose of training acous- tic models. Because only 15-minute segments were manually transcribed for each testimony, the acoustic modeling process has only 100 h of speech available. This amount of data theoretically contains up to 800 speakers (interviewer and inter- viewee for each testimony). In practice, the number of speakers is smaller because not all 15-min segments contain interviewers. Segments (segments roughly corre- spond to sentences) in which several speakers speak at the same time were omitted from the training process. Thus, less than 100 h of training data were available.

The rest of the Czech Malach corpus consists of 20 testimonies, which have been transcribed in full and are intended for development (10) and testing (10) purposes. These 20 testimonies (10 men and 10 women) have a total length of more than 20 h of speech (see Table 3 for details)

Slovak: The Slovak part of the Malach corpus was transcribed in the same way as the Czech one. Thus, 15 min of 400 different testimonies were transcribed for training purposes. And another 20 testimonies were fully transcribed to create the development and test part of the Slovak corpus (10 men and 10 women).

4   Experimental Setup

4.1   Acoustic Feature Extraction

Mel-frequency cepstral coefficients (MFCCs) were used as input not only to the HMM-GMM but also to the HMM-DNN. The window size was 32 ms. 40 MFCC bandpass filters were applied. These 40-dimensional MFCC feature vectors were computed every 10 milliseconds (100 frames per second). For HMM-GMM training only, the original 40 cepstral coefficients were extended by delta and delta-delta sub-features, and cepstral and variance normalizations were also applied.

Table 3. Statistics of training and test data-sets.

	Czech		Slovak	
	Train	Test	Train	Test
# of speakers	776	20	783	20
# of words	49k	10.3k	48k	10.5k
# of tokens	715k	63k	690k	68k
dataset length [hours]	87.5	8.9	87.2	8.8
# of phonemes	40		50	
# of graphemes	40		43	

4.2   Acoustic Modeling

The structure and parameters of the acoustic models in the LVCSR system were tuned using KALDI toolkit [16]. A set of phonetic production rules (different for Czech and Slovak) was used to obtain a phonetic basic form for each phrase used for both training and recognition. Special consideration was given to the phonetic transcription of foreign (e.g. German) words, details can be found in [18].

GMM: A monophone AM is trained from the flat start using the MFCCs features (static + delta + delta delta). Secondly, we trained the triphone AM.

Because the number of triphones is usually too large, decision trees are used to tie their states. Linear discriminant analysis (LDA) and Maximum Likelihood Linear Transform (MLLT) was also applied. LDA+MLLT projects five concatenated frames into 40 dimensions space. We used the feature-space Maximum Likelihood Linear Regression (fMLLR) and Speaker-adaptive training procedure (SAT) to adapt GMM models. The optimal number of states has been optimized on the development data. The whole training data were forced aligned using the resulting HMM-GMM model. This alignment is necessary as an input for DNN training [13,17].

TDNN_CE: Time Delay Neural Networks with Cross-Entropy have shown to be effective in modeling long-range temporal dependencies [26]. The first splicing was the Linear Discriminant Analysis (LDA) transform layer $(-2, -1, 0, 1, 2)$. Subsequent layers then had contexts $(-1, 0, 1)$, $(-1, 0, 1)$, $(-3, 0, 3)$ and $(-6, -3, 0)$. The $(-1, 0, 1)$ means that the first layer sees 3 consecutive frames of input thus the $(-3, 0, 3)$ means that the hidden layer sees 3 frames of the previous layer, separated by 3 frames. In total, we have five hidden layers with the ReLu activation functions containing 650 nodes each. The softmax output layer computes posteriors for clustered GMM based triphone states. The overall context is therefore 13 frames to the past and 7 to the future.

TDNNF_LF-MMI: Maximum mutual information (MMI) [2] is a discriminative objective function that aims to maximize the probability of the reference transcription while minimizing the probability of all other transcriptions. Povey et al. [17] applied MMI training with HMM-DNN models using a full denominator graph (hence the name lattice-free) by using a phone language model (instead of a word language model). Instead of a frame-level objective, the log-probability of the correct phone sequence as the objective function is used. The LF-MMI (Lattice-Free Maximum Mutual Information) training procedure has a sequence discriminative training criterion without the need for frame-level cross-entropy pre-training. In regular LF-MMI, all utterances are split into fixed-size chunks (usually 150 frames) to make GPU computations efficient. **Standard setup:** 12 TDNNF layers; dimension in the hidden layers is 1024, bottleneck dimension is 128; context is ±28 i.e. context per layer (1 1 1 0 3 3 3 3 3 3 3 3).

CNN-TDNNF_LF-MMI: It has been shown [1] that the locality, weight sharing and pooling properties of the convolutional layers have the potential to improve the recognition accuracy of ASR. The typical Kaldi CNN-TDNN models consist of 6 CNN layers followed by 10 TDNNF (factorized TDNN [15]) layers and two output layers: chain based (LF-MMI criterion) and cross-entropy criterion (xent). The first convolutional layer receives at input three matrices of speech features (the current, previous and next acoustic frames). It uses 64 filters of size 3×3 to perform time and feature space convolutions and outputs a $64 \times 40 \times 1$ volume. The following convolutional layers apply more filters (128 and finally 256), but preserve the size of the feature volume by decreasing the height from 40 to 20 and finally to 10.

4.3 Language Modeling

Czech: Spontaneous spoken Czech is often colloquial in nature, and colloquial Czech differs significantly from the standard Czech language. The presence of colloquial language poses major problems in obtaining additional data for language modeling. To be able to use suitable text sources (books, newspapers, etc.) for language modeling together with transcripts of Malach's testimonies, we approached colloquial words as pronunciation (phonetic) variants (see [19] for more details). The resulting trigram language model with modified Kneser-Ney smoothing contains 237k words (280k phonetical variants). Let us note, that for acoustic modeling, we used the non-standardized transcripts with the original colloquial variants.

Slovak: The Slovak language model was primarily based on training set transcriptions. We decided to create the same type of standardized lexicon as we did for Czech ASR. From these transcripts, we found that the number of typical colloquial words in Slovak is much lower than in the Czech language. However, the real data showed, that many pronunciation problems encountered in the speech of Slovak survivors, were caused by a long term mutual influence of Czech and Slovak languages due to the common state of both nations (e.g. Czech endings in Slovak words, Czech pronunciation of a part of Slovak words, etc.). See [20] for more details. We interpolated obtained language models with additional suitable text sources, thus the resulting trigram language model with modified Kneser-Ney smoothing contains 247k words (296k phonetical variants). All characteristics are summarized in Table 4.

Table 4. LVCSR setup.

	Czech	Slovak
#vocabulary	237k	247k
#phonetical variants	280k	296k
OOV rate	2.6%	2.2%
#OOV terms	1624	1532

4.4 Decoding

All recognition experiments were performed using our in-house real-time ASR system. We speeded up decoding using a parallel approach (Viterbi search on CPU and DNN segments scores on GPU [25]). The optimal weight/tradeoff between the acoustic model and the language model was set on the development data for each recognition experiment.

5   Experiments and Results

The analysis of the frequencies of the occurrence of phonemes in the Czech and Slovak training data revealed that the phonemes /N/ (*banka*), /F/ (*tramvaj*) and /e_u/ (*euro*) practically do not appear in the training data. Hence there is the difference between the theoretical number of phonemes (see Table 2) and the real number of phonemes (see Table 3). Therefore the Czech phonetic set contains 40 phonemes and the Slovak 50 phonemes, of which 36 phonemes occur in both languages. These 36 pairs of Slovak and Czech phonemes are similar and can be well mapped on each other. By combining these two phonetic sets, we obtain 54 different phonemes that cover both languages simultaneously. The common phonemes /a, e, i, o, u, a:, e:, i:, o:, u:, p, b, t, d, c, J\, k, g, t_s, d_z, t_S, d_Z, r, l, f, v, s, z, S, Z, x, j, h\, m, n, J/ plus special Czech phonemes /o_u, a_u, Q\, P\/ plus special Slovak phonemes /{, i_ˆa, i_ˆe, i_ˆu, u_ˆo, r=, r=:, l=, l=:, L, w, u_ˆ, N\, i_ˆ/ form the phonetics of the Czech-Slovak bilingual acoustics.

Several possible approaches to reduce this bilingual phonetic set have been tried. For example, merging long and short syllable-forming consonants together (e.g. /l=/ /l=:/), or merging long and short syllable-forming consonants with their non-syllable counterparts (e.g. /l/ /l=/ /l=:/), have unfortunately yielded insignificant or no improvement. Also, the combination of /{/ and /e/ into one model, which is a widely accepted practice in the Slovak ASR due to the massive tendency to pronounce /e/ instead of /{/ by the nowadays Slovak speakers, did not bring any significant improvement.

In the Table 5 can be seen the recognition results of phoneme-based LVCSR depending on different acoustic models. All DNNs topologies were optimized with respect to the number of layers, bottleneck dimensions, dimensions in the hidden layers and overall contexts on the development parts of the corpora. The best recognition results were obtained for **CNN-TDNN_LF-MMI**. The CNN-TDNN employed 8 layers of 2-dimensional convolutional layers (3×3). The input-output sizes of these convolutional layers (in the form of filter $\times$ height) were 64×40, 64×40, 128×20, 128×20, 256×10, 256×10, 512×5, 512×5. The optimal settings for sequential TDNNs are 15 TDNNFs, dimension in the hidden layer 2048, bottleneck dimension 512 in the first layer 256 elsewhere, context per TDNNF layer (0 1 1 1 3 3 3 3 5 5 5 7 7 7 9) i.e. overall context is ±68.

For practical reasons, we did not use digraphs ([*ch*], [*dz*] and [*dž*]) when designing the ASR system. In addition, for Czech we combined [*ú*] and [*ů*] together to one grapheme. As was mentioned in Sect. 2.1, these two letters have the same pronunciation and differ only in the position in a word. Thus the Czech graphemes contained 40 and the Slovak 43 graphemes, while 38 graphemes were the same. The combination of Czech and Slovak graphemes led to a set of 45 graphemes (i.e. [*a, b, c, d, e, f, g, h, i, j, k, l, m, n, o, p, q, r, s, t, u, v, w, x, y, z, á, č, ď, é, í, ň, ó, š, ť, ú, ý, ž*] plus special Czech graphemes [*ě, ř*] plus special Slovak graphemes [*ä, ĺ, ľ, ô, ŕ*]).

We tried several variants of graphemes reduction. For example, we tested whether it is possible to map the letter [w] on a grapheme [v], or to combine

Table 5. Recognition results of phoneme-based LVCSR

train data test data	Cz	Sk	Cz + Sk	
			Cz	Sk
GMM	26.00	28.22	27.13	27.57
TDNN_CE	23.27	25.22	24.20	24.80
TDNNF_LF-MMI	16.66	18.60	16.48	18.50
CNN-TDNNF_LF-MMI	16.49	18.74	16.23	18.43

the letters [ĭ] and [í] into one grapheme. None of these adjustments brought improvements. This is probably due to the fact that, for example, although the letter [w] is assumed to be pronounced the same as [v], this is not the case in all contexts (this can happen in foreign words, for example).

The Table 6 shows the recognition of grapheme-based LVCSR results depending on different acoustic models. The best recognition results were obtained also for **CNN-TDNN_LF-MMI**. But the overall context is slightly higher ±70.

Table 6. Recognition results of grapheme-based LVCSR

train data test data	Cz	Sk	Cz + Sk	
			Cz	Sk
GMM	29.89	30.66	30.45	29.56
TDNN_CE	26.44	26.42	26.91	27.06
TDNNF_LF-MMI	19.89	20.41	19.26	19.19
CNN-TDNNF_LF-MMI	19.40	19.53	18.64	19.34

6   Conclusion

The proposed Czech-Slovak bilingual ASR approach provides a slight improvement over monolingual ASR systems (Czech and Slovak), not only at the level of phonemes combination but also at the level of graphemes combination. The decrease in word error rate between bilingual and monolingual acoustic models based on phonemes was 1,6% relatively for Czech and 1,7% relatively for Slovak and for the grapheme-based 4% relatively for Czech and by 1% relatively for Slovak.

A direct comparison of both approaches is also very interesting, i.e. AM based on phonemes and graphemes. Bilingual phoneme-based AM provides better recognition results than the grapheme-based AM, as expected (2.41% for Czech and 0.91% for Slovak). However, the deterioration in recognition accuracy for grapheme-based AM is often compensated by a substantial simplification of the functionality of the proposed LVCSR system, as it is not necessary to address the phonetic transcription block.

The best recognition results were obtained for the optimized **CNN-TDNN**. The optimal overall context was ±70 for grapheme-based AM and ±68 for phoneme-based AM. When optimizing the network topology, it was found that as the context increases, the word error rate decreases, especially for a grapheme task. This is probably because the context partially replaces the function of phonetic transcription. In the future, we would like to analyze whether it is possible to combine other Slavic languages in the same way (such as Polish or Russian).

Acknowledgments. This paper was supported by the Technology Agency of the Czech Republic, project No. TN01000024.

References

1. Abdel-Hamid, O., Mohamed, A., Jiang, H., Deng, L., Penn, G., Yu, D.: Convolutional neural networks for speech recognition. IEEE/ACM Trans. Audio Speech Lang. Process. **22**(10), 1533–1545 (2014). https://doi.org/10.1109/TASLP.2014.2339736
2. Bahl, L., Brown, P., de Souza, P., Mercer, R.: Maximum mutual information estimation of hidden Markov model parameters for speech recognition. In: ICASSP 1986, pp. 49–52 (1986). https://doi.org/10.1109/ICASSP.1986.1169179
3. Byrne, W., et al.: Automatic recognition of spontaneous speech for access to multilingual oral history archives. IEEE Trans. Speech Audio Process. **12**(4), 420–435 (2004). https://doi.org/10.1109/TSA.2004.828702
4. Czech SAMPA. https://www.phon.ucl.ac.uk/home/sampa/czech-uni.htm
5. Kanthak, S., Ney, H.: Multilingual acoustic modeling using graphemes. In: Eurospeech 2003, pp. 1145–1148 (2003)
6. Killer, M., Stüker, S., Schultz, T.: Grapheme based speech recognition. In: Eurospeech 2003, pp. 3141–3144 (2003)
7. Lihan, S., Juhár, J., Čižmár, A.: Comparison of Slovak and Czech speech recognition based on grapheme and phoneme acoustic models. In: Interspeech 2006, pp. 149–152 (2006)
8. MALACH project (2006). https://malach.umiacs.umd.edu/
9. Mirilovič, M., Juhár, J., Čižmár, A.: Comparison of grapheme and phoneme based acoustic modeling in LVCSR task in Slovak. In: Esposito, A., Hussain, A., Marinaro, M., Martone, R. (eds.) Multimodal Signals: Cognitive and Algorithmic Issues. LNCS (LNAI), vol. 5398, pp. 242–247. Springer, Heidelberg (2009). https://doi.org/10.1007/978-3-642-00525-1_24
10. Nouza, J., Silovský, J., Zdánský, J., Cerva, P., Kroul, M., Chaloupka, J.: Czech-to-Slovak adapted broadcast news transcription system. In: Interspeech 2008, pp. 2683–2686. ISCA (2008)
11. Nouza, J., Zdansky, J., Cerva, P., Silovsky, J.: Challenges in speech processing of Slavic languages (case studies in speech recognition of Czech and Slovak). In: Esposito, A., Campbell, N., Vogel, C., Hussain, A., Nijholt, A. (eds.) Development of Multimodal Interfaces: Active Listening and Synchrony. LNCS, vol. 5967, pp. 225–241. Springer, Heidelberg (2010). https://doi.org/10.1007/978-3-642-12397-9_19

12. Novak, J.R., Nobuaki, M., Keikichi, H.: Phonetisaurus: exploring grapheme-to-phoneme conversion with joint n-gram models in the WFST framework. Nat. Lang. Eng. **22**(6), 907–938 (2016). https://doi.org/10.1017/S1351324915000315
13. Peddinti, V., Povey, D., Khudanpur, S.: A time delay neural network architecture for efficient modeling of long temporal contexts. In: Interspeech 2015, pp. 3214–3218 (2015)
14. Picheny, M., Tüske, Z., Kingsbury, B., Audhkhasi, K., Cui, X., Saon, G.: Challenging the boundaries of speech recognition: the MALACH corpus. In: Interspeech 2019, pp. 326–330 (2019). https://doi.org/10.21437/Interspeech.2019-1907
15. Povey, D., et al.: Semi-orthogonal low-rank matrix factorization for deep neural networks. In: Interspeech 2018, pp. 3743–3747 (2018). https://doi.org/10.21437/Interspeech.2018-1417
16. Povey, D., et al.: The Kaldi speech recognition toolkit. In: IEEE 2011 Workshop on Automatic Speech Recognition and Understanding (2011)
17. Povey, D., et al.: Purely sequence-trained neural networks for ASR based on lattice-free MMI. In: Interspeech 2016, pp. 2751–2755 (2016). https://doi.org/10.21437/Interspeech.2016-595
18. Psutka, J., Hajič, J., Byrne, W.: The development of ASR for Slavic languages in the MALACH project. In: ICASSP 2004, pp. iii–749 (2004). https://doi.org/10.1109/ICASSP.2004.1326653
19. Psutka, J., Hoidekr, J., Ircing, P., Psutka, J.V.: Recognition of spontaneous speech - some problems and their solutions. In: CITSA 2006, pp. 169–172. IIIS (2006)
20. Psutka, J., Ircing, P., Psutka, J.V., Hajič, J., Byrne, W., Mírovský, J.: Automatic transcription of Czech, Russian and Slovak spontaneous speech in the MALACH project. In: Eurospeech 2005, pp. 1349–1352. ISCA (2005)
21. Psutka, J.V., Psutka, J., Radová, V., Ircing, P., Matoušek, J., Müller, L.: USC-SFI MALACH interviews and transcripts Czech (2014). https://catalog.ldc.upenn.edu/LDC2014S04
22. Slovak SAMPA. http://www.ui.sav.sk/pp/speech/sampa_sk.htm
23. Švec, J., Psutka, J., Trmal, J., Šmídl, L., Ircing, P., Sedmidubský, J.: On the use of grapheme models for searching in large spoken archives. In: ICASSP 2018, pp. 6259–6263 (2018). https://doi.org/10.1109/ICASSP.2018.8461774
24. Trmal, J., et al.: The Kaldi OpenKWS system: improving low resource keyword search. In: Interspeech 2017, pp. 3597–3601 (2017). https://doi.org/10.21437/Interspeech.2017-601
25. Vaněk, J., Trmal, J., Psutka, J.V., Psutka, J.: Optimized acoustic likelihoods computation for NVIDIA and ATI/AMD graphics processors. IEEE Trans. Audio Speech Lang. Process. **20**(6), 1818–1828 (2012). https://doi.org/10.1109/TASL.2012.2190928
26. Waibel, A., Hanazawa, T., Hinton, G., Shikano, K., Lang, K.J.: Phoneme recognition using time-delay neural networks. IEEE Trans. Acoust. Speech Sig. Process. **37**(3), 328–339 (1989). https://doi.org/10.1109/29.21701

Dialogue

A Multimodal Model for Predicting Conversational Feedbacks

Auriane Boudin[1], Roxane Bertrand[1], Stéphane Rauzy[1], Magalie Ochs[2],
and Philippe Blache[1(✉)]

[1] LPL-CNRS and Aix-Marseille University, Marseille, France
{Auriane.Boudin,Roxane.Bertrand,Stephane.Rauzy,
Philippe.Blache}@univ-amu.fr
[2] LIS-CNRS and Aix-Marseille University, Marseille, France
Magalie.Ochs@univ-amu.fr

Abstract. We propose in this paper a statistical model in the perspective of predicting listener's feedbacks in a conversation. The first contribution of the paper is a study of the prediction of all feedbacks, including those in overlap with the speaker with a good accuracy. Existing model are good at predicting feedbacks during a pause, but reach a very low success level for all feedbacks. We give in this paper a first step towards this complex problem. The second contribution is a model predicting precisely the type of the feedback (generic vs. specific) as well as other specific features (valence expectation) useful in particular for generating feedbacks in dialogue systems. This work relies on an original corpus.

Keywords: Feedback · Linguistic interaction · Statistical model · Corpus study

1 Introduction

Conversational interactions are characterized by different phenomena showing participant's engagement. Among them, the most important are undoubtedly conversational feedbacks [33] which usually consist in brief signals produced by the interlocutor during the main speaker's speech and can be verbal (e.g. *yes*), vocal (e.g. *mhm*), and/or gestural (head movements, smiles). All linguistic interaction theories underline their crucial role during an interaction [16, 19]. We know in particular that they are mandatory to update the shared knowledge (*common ground*) and promote the alignment between participants which is necessary for mutual comprehension and success of the interaction [4, 24]. Understanding their behaviors and the conditions of their realization in a natural context is then of deep importance both for theoretical reasons, but also for applications in the perspective of human-machine interaction.

Feedbacks predictive cues have been studied in different modalities: prosodic [18, 25, 38], syntactic [9], gestural [17] semantic and pragmatic [2]. However, to date, no global model proposing a multimodal account of feedback realization and a prediction of feedback types exists. One of the reasons is that there exist only few corpora providing such information. The vast majority of existing resources focus on audio only, which explains the fact that most of the works rely on prosody, taking other modalities

© Springer Nature Switzerland AG 2021
K. Ekštein et al. (Eds.): TSD 2021, LNAI 12848, pp. 537–549, 2021.
https://doi.org/10.1007/978-3-030-83527-9_46

into account only to a certain extent. Corpora providing both video and audio are limited and generally do not bear annotation of the gestures involved in the description of these phenomena. Moreover, the processing of these multimodal data is still an open question. Overall, a multimodal model of feedbacks in natural interaction, describing and predicting their realization, has yet to be established.

We present in this paper an overview of the different feedback models and propose a new model involving a large set of multimodal features. Moreover, we propose to join time and type prediction, making it possible to explore the prediction of feedback occurrences concerning not only the site of realization for the feedbacks, but also their type. This work is based on an original corpus annotated at different levels. We propose a modeling approach rendering possible a clear interpretation of the model. The model and its evaluation are finally discussed.

2   Related Works

In this section, we propose an overview of the main feedback modeling works by focusing on three main information: the features they rely on, the time span of the observation window (in other words the segmentation) and the results.

Most of the works study feedbacks as a specific case of turn-taking. Among them, a seminal study has been proposed in [18] for predicting three different situations: turn changes (smooth switches) vs. turn retentions (holds) and backchannels (a feedback subtype). The signal is segmented into inter-pausal units (IPU) and at each pause longer than 50 ms, a set of features is extracted from the preceding IPU. Seven features are used in turn-yielding prediction: a falling or high-rising intonation at the end of the IPU; a reduced lengthening of IPU-final words; a lower intensity level; a lower pitch level; a point of textual completion; a higher value of three voice quality features: jitter, shimmer, and NHR; and a longer IPU duration. Six features are identified more precisely for backchannels: a rising intonation at the end of the IPU; a higher intensity level; a higher pitch level; a final POS bigram (Det-N, Adj-N, N-N); a lower value of noise-to-harmonics ratio (NHR); and a longer IPU duration. They fit multiple logistic regression to assess the relative importance of the different cues. This study show that the likelihood of the occurrence of a feedback is 30% when all 6 cues are present (the percentage of turn-taking being 65% with the 7 relevant cues). A cross-lingual study based on 3 languages has been proposed in [12].

This approach is adapted by [21] for detecting *"response relevant places"* (a response being feedbacks, short answers, clarification questions, etc. organized into 8 classes). The task called Response Location Detection consists in classifying into 3 main classes: hold (a response would be inappropriate), expected response, optional response. They completed the model of [18] by taking into account three different types of features: prosodic (pitch, intensity), contextual (turn and IPU length, last system dialogue act, pause duration) and lexico-syntactic (word form, POS, semantic classes). The observations are also based on an IPU segmentation (2,272 IPUs). Different learning algorithms and feature combinations have been applied. The model based on lexico-syntactic features obtains a 84.42% score of accuracy for the voted perceptron model, only slightly improved when adding prosodic features (84.64% accuracy with naive bayes).

In his work, [34] proposes a continuous model of turn-taking, predicting turn-shifts and their types (short backchannel or a longer utterance). It uses a set acoustic features (voice activity, pitch, intensity,spectral stability), completed by POS. Feature vectors are extracted from the signal each 50 ms. The model learned by a RNN reaches an F-Score of 0.762, using all features for the turn-shift prediction.

When focusing on feedback prediction independently from turn-taking, we find several rule-based approaches. In their reference work, [38] propose a famous rule based on prosodic cues (pitch region, its level, duration and localization and previous feedback realization). This rule has been completed by other algorithms in [25] aiming at determining the placement of feedbacks. These rules are based on prosodic and gaze features. They are implemented in a virtual listener. Note that this work also provide interesting information about human listener behavior and has been refined by a corpus study in [37]. In their work, [23] also propose to use several lexical and prosodic cues as well as the indication of speaker's gaze. Speaker features are sampled at a rate 30 Hz. Different probabilistic sequential model are trained for different encoding templates. The results show an F-score of 0.2562 (outperforming the Ward & Tsukahara method). On their side, [13] present an approach for predicting a specific type of feedbacks (backchannel continuers) on the basis of pause duration and POS. Their results show an F-measure of 35%.

To summarize, the different works usually focus on a subset of predictive cues, usually coming from a unique modality. None of them tries to give a global picture involving a multimodal set of features. Second, these works aim at predicting the site or the time for the feedback realization, but not the feedback type. Finally, as for the modeling aspects, no clear indication are usually given on the relative importance of the cues and more generally on the model's interpretation. The great variability and the scores obtained by the different techniques show the difficulty of the task.

3 Feedbacks: Typology, Cues

We distinguish between two feedback types: *generic* (displaying attention to the speaker) and *specific* (expressing responses to the content of the speaker's production) [4, 6, 36]. Generic feedbacks are often vocal item such as *mh* or gestural signals like nods. They express interest and understanding while specific feedbacks (e.g. brief verbal utterances, a particular tone of voice, etc.) correspond to an evaluation or comment. Some feedbacks are prototypical of one type (e.g. *mhm* is typically generic whereas *oh no* is specific), some others not. Feedbacks can be expressed in different modalities: verbal, visual or multimodal. Besides verbal feedbacks, which are in most of the cases brief lexical expressions, visual feedbacks can be realized in different ways: head movement (*nod, jerk, shake, tilt, turn, waggle*), facial expressions (*smile, laugh*) or eyebrow (*frowning, raising*). Bimodal feedbacks (involving both visual and verbal productions) are also very frequent and play an important role [17]. In some cases, bimodality can reinforce the function: for example, bimodal BCs show a stronger agreement than unimodal ones. Table 1 give some examples of the main feedback types and their modalities associated to different possible subtypes (note that our work focuses on French, but can be directly generalized to other languages).

Table 1. Feedback types

Type	Modality	Feedback
Generic	Verbal	oui, mh
	Visual	nod, smile
	Bimodal	nod+yeah, smile+ok
Specific /Agreement	Verbal	oui, d'accord, ok
	Visual	nod, smile
	Bimodal	nod+yeah, nod+ooh
Specific /Disagreement	Verbal	non
	Visual	shake
	Bimodal	shake+no, shake+mh
Specific surprise	Verbal	ah bon
	Visual	Raising, frowning, tilt
	Bimodal	raising+no
Specific /Fear	Verbal	non, oh non
	Visual	frowning, raising, shake
	Bimodal	shake+no, frowning+non

Typology: As shown in the table, specific feedbacks are described according to two levels of analysis: polarity (positive or negative) [1,15] and their expected/unexpected character [27]. This question of feedback subtype is crucial [4,33] and could explain the various and sometimes controversial cues found in the literature (*yes* for example can be either generic or specific).

Feedback Cues: Based on the literature as well as our experience, we propose to explore the role of a large set of features, from three modalities: speech (prosodic features, [5, 12,18,20,22,34,38]), verbal (lexico-syntactic features [10,18,21]) and visual (gestures, expressions, attitudes, [1,17,22,25]). Besides widely used features (e.g. POS, pauses, etc.), we also propose to involve less studied features.

Before entering into feature description, it is necessary to specify the frame unit into which the predictive features will be analyzed. In most of the cases, inter-pausal units (IPUs) are chosen, the features of the end of the main speaker's IPU are the input variable of the model. The problem in this case is that we miss many feedback produced in overlap with the speaker (representing 40% of feedbacks in our corpus). It is then necessary to chose another segmentation. One solution consists in segmenting the input by means of a rolling window. In some works, an arbitrary frame size of 30–50 is chosen [23,34]. However, this type of segmentation entails a huge problem of imbalanced classes when trying to predict feedback vs. no-feedback, including during speakers speech. We propose instead to segment on the basis of *events*, at each word, or during no-speech segments at nod or laugh. Such events form the right boundary of a predicting window of 2 s. This duration is arbitrary, but usually correspond to segments

Table 2. Predictive features

Speech	Short silent pause lasting at least 200 ms and maximum 1200 ms
	Long silent pause lasting at least 1200 ms
	Bigrams and trigrams of tones
Verbal	POS bigrams and trigams
	Discourse markers
	Positive, Negative, Concrete words
Visual	Laughs, Smiles
	Nods

larger enough to contain complete units (in terms of syntax and pragmatic contents). Table 2 present the complete set of features involved in our model.

At the prosodic level, besides pauses, we examine the intonation pattern given by a sequence of tone. Some specific tone n-grams before a pause followed by a feedback could correspond to a final intonation pattern which is often correlated with the introduction of a new information [14] and carries an important part of the interactional meaning [26]. Several studies have shown that the final intonation contour could be a good predict or for feedback occurrence. Tones also represent an intermediate level between low-level acoustic features such as pitch and phonological interpretations. Taking into account tone n-grams makes it possible to compare the influence of tones taken separately or by sequence.

Concerning lexico-syntactic features, we propose to include POS and semantic information about word polarity (positive, negative) and aspect (concreteness). These information can be associated to specific listener's reaction concerning a certain level of emotion, but also the use of a discourse referent associated to concrete words. On their side, discourse markers are the sign of discourse organization, often associated to transition between discourse units, that can be associated to reactions.

Finally, introducing visual features complete the multimodal description. Nods, laughs and smiles, that can by themselves constituting feedbacks, are also to be taken into account in the prediction, not only because of mimicry (a laugh can trigger a laugh feedback) , but also due to the importance of their communicative function [7].

4 The Dataset

This work focuses on French. Our dataset is built upon an existing corpus of natural conversations that we have completed with the different annotations. The corpus, called Cheese-Paco [3,28], contains 7 h of audio-video recording. The participants, in dyads, were installed face-to-face. They first had to read a short story before having a free conversation. Cheese-Paco is composed of 27 interactions, each lasting an average of 17 min. A manual transcription has been done, including different information such as noise, laugh, pause, elision, unexpected events. This transcription has been automatically aligned onto the signal thanks to the SPPAS system [8] that returns the list of

542 A. Boudin et al.

phonemes, syllables and IPUS. The MarsaTag analyzer [31] has been applied to extract the lemmas and POS. Moreover, smiles and nods were annotated semi-automatically using the HMAD toolkit [29,30]. In this work, we used a subset of data composed of 4 dyads for a total of about one hour. The corpus contains 769 feedbacks, 2,739 IPUs and 15,215 words.

Feedback Annotation: Feedbacks have been manually annotated by 3 annotators. The annotation guide considers the distinction between specific and generic feedbacks to which we added the two subtypes (valence +/- positive and +/- expected). In order to facilitate the annotation, a pre-processing has been done for identifying automatically the possible feedbacks on the basis of different signals: laughs, smiles shorter than 200 ms, repetitions, interjections. Annotators had to check whether these suggestions was correct and when necessary add feedbacks non identified during pre-processing. The second annotation step consists in identifying the feedback type. Five categories are possible: one for generic feedbacks and four for specific feedback sub-types (+/- positive, +/- expected). Finally, annotators were asked to determine the feedback boundaries.

Lexico-Syntactic Features: Besides POS, we annotated lexical-semantic information (concreteness, valence) on the basis of word lists given in [11]. We also identified discourse markers. Concerning POS, we kept only bigrams and trigrams with a frequency higher than 40.

Prosodic Features: We used the automatic pitch modeling tool MOMEL-INTSINT [32] which consists in two steps. The first consists in modeling the f0 based on a sequence of transitions between successive points on the curve (anchor points). The procedure of calculation of MOMEL is based on the relationship between the median, minimum and maximum values of each speaker's pitch range. The Octave-Median Scale used by the authors allows to compare speakers with different pitch ranges (typically males versus females) In a second step, the anchor points obtained from MOMEL are automatically coded by an alphabet of tonal symbols T(op), B(ottom), M(id) referring to absolute values and *Higher, Lower, Same, Upstepped, Downstepped* (referring relative values) and give rise to an intonation pattern represented by the key/midpoint and the span of the speaker's pitch range. We also encode, as it is the case in different studies, the length of the pause (with a threshold of 1,2 s between short and long pauses).

Gestures, Expressions: Nods has been annotated semi-automatically. The automatic step relies on the HMAD system [30] which returns the time interval of the nod. A manual correction is then done, identifying when necessary missing nods and correcting time boundaries. The annotation of smiles follow the same procedure, and distinguishes 2 levels of smile (noted S3 and S4 in the following) [29].

5   Data Analysis

We give in this section a brief overview of the main statistical characteristics of our dataset. These statistics are in line with the literature [25]: feedback are frequent and

Table 3. Feedback frequency per minute and per type

Feedback type		Frequency per minute
Specific	Positive-expected	1.62
	Positive-unexpected	2.06
	Negative-expected	0.84
	Negative-unexpected	0.34
	Total specific	**4.85**
Generic		**4.44**
Total feedback		**9.3**

their production is a consistent phenomenon. Our data revealed a frequency of 9.3 feedback per minute (see Table 3). Specific feedback are slightly more frequent than generic. Regarding the sub-type of specific feedbacks, there is more often positive than negative feedback. The most frequent is the positive-unexpected feedback, the less is negative-unexpected.

The most frequent feedback realizations are verbalization, laughs [6] and nods [1,35]. We find interesting to see how nods, laughs, verbalization and smiles are used according to the generic/specific function of the feedback. Figure 1 reveal the sum of feedback produced with at least one of these items (for a total of 769 feedbacks). Even if all feedbacks are mainly produced with verbal items (interjections, repetitions and other short lexical elements), this tendency is stronger for specific feedbacks. This can be explained by the fact that specific feedbacks need more details and context-dependent interventions. Verbal items for generic feedbacks are mostly interjections and plays the role of continuers. As expected, nods are significantly more used for generic than specific feedback [4]. Conversely, laughs and smiles are widely used as specific feedbacks (and are very rare for generic ones). Finally, generic feedbacks are mainly produced with nods and/or verbalization, whereas specific feedbacks are primarily produced with verbalization/laugh and/or smile. We also noticed that generic feedbacks are produced in overlapping 34% of the time and specific feedback are produced in overlapping 41% of the time.

6 The Model

We applied a statistical processing, logistic regression, that fits with our dataset specificities. At the difference with most of other predicting models, our goal is to predict both the position and the type of feedback to be produced during a conversation. We use for that a two-stage approach based on two models: one predicting the realization of a feedback, the second predicting its type (generic vs. specific). In this approach, *logit* is then used as a hierarchical classification technique. One interest of using *logit* also lies in the fact that it returns a probability for the classification. This is interesting in the perspective of implementing the model in a human-machine communication system, offering the possibility to introduce a fine variability in the feedback production.

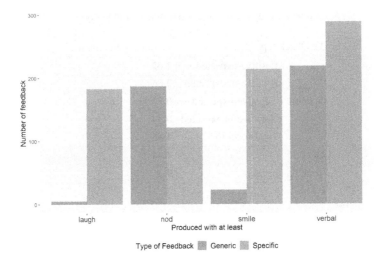

Fig. 1. Description of feedback production

We also chose logistic regression in order to take into consideration different questions about the dataset (the size is rather small and learning techniques are prone to overfitting) as well as dimensionality and interpretability of the model.

The probability to produce a given type of feedback (or the probability that the feedback is produced at a given time location) is modeled by the *logit* equation:

$$\text{logit}(p) = \ln\left(\frac{p}{1-p}\right) = a_0 + a_1 x_1(t) + ... + a_j x_j(t) + ... \tag{1}$$

where $x_j(t)$ are the predictors which depend on the time location t and which can adopt binary, categorical or continuous types. In a first step, the parameters of the *logit* model (i.e. the a_i coefficients) are estimated on the training sample. An inspection of the result allows to decide which predictor contributes significantly to the prediction. The model is finally formed with the subset of relevant predictors. A probability p is thus attributed to any combined values of the predictors. To convert this probability into a binary response, we apply the following classifier equation:

$$\text{if } (p > p_{\text{threshold}}) \{\text{response} = 1\} \text{ else } \{\text{response} = 0\} \tag{2}$$

where $p_{\text{threshold}}$ is for example the averaged probability to produce a feedback. This threshold value is estimated on the training sample. The model thus provides us with a binary prediction which depends on the predictor values in input.

The performance of the model is afterwards evaluated by using standard metrics based on the confusion matrix of the predictions versus the observations. A cross-validation strategy is applied in order to quantify the potential presence of overfitting problems. This evaluation procedure will be also applied in order to measure the relative contribution of a given subset of predictors (e.g. grouped by modalities).

Predicting the Occurrence of a Feedback: The problem of predicting the time location of the feedbacks is difficult since it requires to include in the training table events where feedback does not occur. In our strategy, we considered all time locations corresponding to the end of an event (e.g. end of a word, of a pause, of a laugh or smile, etc.) as an entry of the table and we encoded the value of the binary dependent variable as 0 (i.e. absence of feedback). In addition we inserted in the table the list of observed feedbacks (i.e. with the binary dependent variable at 1). This strategy comes to the standard binary classifier model. In our case, the difficulty lies in the imbalanced character of the binary distribution (i.e. the no feedback events are massively dominant).

Note that dynamical models based on HMM, CRF, LSTM RNN have been proposed for predicting occurrences of feedbacks or related situations (see for example [23, 34]). These models integrate the information produced by the main speaker as well as information on the current state of the listener. However, they reach very low F-score results unless they restrict the prediction of feedbacks during pauses only.

Predicting the Type of Feedback: For the task of predicting the type of feedback the training sample is a table containing for each observed feedback:

- The binary dependent variable (encoded as 1 if the feedback has the desired type an 0 otherwise)
- The predictors of binary type (e.g. absence or presence of a given POS trigram, absence of presence of a pause, ...) or continuous type (e.g. number of tokens).

The *logit* model takes this training table as input, the relevant predictors are identified and the final model is adopted which allows to compute for any combination of predictor values the predicted type of feedback in output through Eq. 2.

7 Results

We propose in the following to discuss the results obtained for different feature combinations and clustered by modality. For each combination of coefficients, the accuracy and the Cohen's kappa scores have been obtained by running a Monte Carlo cross-validation (on 100 trials with a ratio 80%-20% for the training versus the evaluation sample). Quoted errors are the 1σ standard deviation on the estimates of these parameters.

Feedback Occurrence: Concerning the prediction of feedback occurrence, let's note first that our modeling leads to a good accuracy whatever the feature combination. Also note that in their work, [18] mention that the likelihood of occurrence of a feedback is 30% when involving all their predicting cues. As underlined previously, the main difficulty in this task is that classes are imbalanced and most of the input samples concern no-feedbacks, explaining the rather low kappa value. But also note that this value is significantly higher than random.

Table 4 shows the emergence of 12 features: pauses, laughs, smiles (S3 and S4), 4 tone bigrams, 3 POS bigrams and number of tokens. Interestingly, each modality contribute to the prediction. Expression and visual features (laughs and smile) are

Table 4. Prediction of feedback occurrences

Feat. combination	Formula	Accuracy	Kappa
All	S4 + S3 + Pause + Laugh + S4 + N-Det + S3 + Det-N + DH + SS + Dem-V + SD + MD + TokenNb	0.78 ± 0.008	0.099 ± 0.01
Visual	Laugh + S4 + S3	0.81 ± 0.005	0.039 ± 0.012
Prosody	Pause DH + SS + SD + MD	0.82 ± 0.013	0.114 ± 0.019
Lexico-synt	TokenNb + N-Det + Det-N + Dem-V	0.64 ± 0.109	0.007 ± 0.009

unsurprisingly correlated with feedback realization, confirming the literature. In terms of prosody, the presence of pauses also confirm existing results. More precisely, we observe 4 tonal bigrams: *DH, SS, SD* and *MD*. The DH pattern could correspond to a rise intonation contour (to be compared with the L-H% contour in [18]). On its side, the MD bigram corresponds to a fall. This pattern can be find in several works, even though with different consequences: [18] indicate that this intonation contour is likely to result in turn change or a continuation by the same speaker (with no feedback) where [38] indicate that a region of low pitch lasting at least 110 milliseconds is considered as a feedback-inviting cue. The *SD* and *SS* bigrams could also refer to such feedback-inviting-cues. In terms of lexico-syntactic cues, the most important feature is the number of tokens. This information is in fact complex: it can be related to speech rate, but also to the syntactic structure (grammatical words are small, their number increase when the syntactic structure is more complex). In both cases, this information could be in relation with "completude": more tokens could be associated to a more complete unit.

Generic/Specific Prediction: Table 5 shows the accuracy for predicting the different feedback subtypes. In this case, the classes are more balanced, leading to a better kappa. We obtain, in spite of the task difficulty, interesting results.

In this table, we present the different models for each subtype : generic vs. specific, and for the specific feedbacks positive vs. negative and expected vs. unexpected. In the +/- generic classification, the main features are visual (laughs, smiles and nods), which is in line with the literature. As for prosody, three patterns occur: *DHL, DH, TL*. The T tone refers to a maximum in the speaker's pitch range and DH refers to a rise. We know that high values of f0 are often considered more salient (focus, emphatic style) which could be more associated with specific feedbacks (conveying for example stance, emotion, etc.). When comparing the different combinations, the all features gives the best results. The POS bigrams tend to show the opening of a new structure, which could play in favor of generic feedbacks (continuers).

Concerning the prosody, a short pause just before the feedback is the most salient cue for positive feedbacks. It is difficult to interpret this result, unless considering that positive responses are preferred and preferentially occur in a short delay. Note that surprisingly, the feature *PositiveToken* does not play a role in this task. Results concerning +/- expected information are less reliable. Prosody features show two tonal bigrams, *LH*

Table 5. Prediction of feedbacks subtypes

Feat. combination	Type	Formula	Accuracy	Kappa
All	Generic	Laugh + Smile + Nod + DHL + Adv-Clit + Det-N + N-Prep + DH + TL + Dem-V	0.62 ± 0.0369	0.255 ± 0.067
	Positive	Clit-V-Det + Pause($<$1s2) + Smile + Pd.Vm. + Disc.Mark + SD + MS + Aux-V	0.61 ± 0.046	0.093 ± 0.081
	expected	V-Adv + LH + LU + N-Adj + Det-N + LUD + PositiveToken	0.51 ± 0.048	0.037 ± 0.098
Visual	Generic	Laugh + Smile + Nod	0.59 ± 0.035	0.229 ± 0.054
	Positive	Laugh	0.41 ± 0.046	0.007 ± 0.053
	Expected	x	x	x
Prosody	Generic	DHL + DH + TL	0.50 ± 0.034	0.069 ± 0.049
	Positive	Pause($<$1s2) + SD + MS	0.67 ± 0.16	0.054 ± 0.1
	Expected	LH + LU + LUD	0.48 ± 0.048	0.048 ± 0.073
Lexico-synt	Generic	Adv-Clit + Det-N + N-Prep + Dem-V	0.57 ± 0.036	0.134 ± 0.073
	Positive	Clit-V-Det + Dem-V + Disc.Mark + Aux-V	0.57 ± 0.068	0.047 ± 0.087
	Expected	V-Adv + N-Adj + Det-N + PositiveToken	0.51 ± 0.05	0.045 ± 0.094

and *LU*, corresponding to a rise that could be associated with a new information (that could be for example associated with a surprise feedback).

8 Conclusion

We have presented in this paper different models addressing for the first time both the prediction of feedbacks and of their types. Our approach shows that a multimodal combination of predictive features can lead to a good accuracy level and represent, to the best of our knowledge, a state of the art for this double classification task. This statistical modeling constitutes the first step for future systematic studies based on different machine learning techniques. In terms of application, this model has been implemented in an automatic dialogue system and is currently under evaluation.

References

1. Allwood, J., Cerrato, L.: A study of gestural feedback expressions. In: First Nordic Symposium on Multimodal Communication, pp. 7–22. Copenhagen (2003)
2. Allwood, J., Cerrato, L., Jokinen, K., Navarretta, C., Paggio, P.: The MUMIN coding scheme for the annotation of feedback, turn management and sequencing phenomena. Lang. Resour. Eval. **41**(3), 273–287 (2007)
3. Amoyal, M., Priego-Valverde, B., Rauzy, S.: PACO : a corpus to analyze the impact of common ground in spontaneous face-to-face interaction. In: LREC procs (2020)

4. Bavelas, J., Cates, L., Johnson, T.: Listeners as co-narrators. J. Pers. Soc. Psychol. **79**(6), 941 (2000)
5. Beňuš, Š, Gravano, A., Hirschberg, J.: Pragmatic aspects of temporal accommodation in turn-taking. J. Pragmatics **43**(12), 3001–3027 (2011)
6. Bertrand, R., Espesser, R.: Co-narration in French conversation storytelling: a quantitative insight. J. Pragmatics **111**, 33–53 (2017)
7. Bertrand, R., Ferré, G., Blache, P., Espesser, R., Rauzy, S.: Backchannels revisited from a multimodal perspective. In: Auditory-Visual Speech Processing (2017)
8. Bigi, B.: SPPAS: a tool for the phonetic segmentations of speech. In: The Eighth International conference on Language Resources and Evaluation, pp. 1748–1755 (2012)
9. Blache, P., Abderrahmane, M., Rauzy, S., Ochs, M., Oufaida, H.: Two-level classification for dialogue act recognition in task-oriented dialogues. In: COLING 2020 (2020)
10. Blache, P., Abderrahmane, M., Rauzy, S., Bertrand, R.: An integrated model for predicting backchannel feedbacks. In: IVA Procs, pp. 1–3 (2020)
11. Bonin, P., Méot, A., Bugaiska, A.: Concreteness norms for 1,659 French words: relationships with other psycholinguistic variables and word recognition times. Behav. Res. Meth. **50**(6), 2366–2387 (2018)
12. Brusco, P., Vidal, J., Beňuš, Š, Gravano, A.: A cross-linguistic analysis of the temporal dynamics of turn-taking cues using machine learning as a descriptive tool. Speech Commun. **125**, 24–40 (2020)
13. Cathcart, N., Carletta, J., Klein, E.: A shallow model of backchannel continuers in spoken dialogue. In: European ACL, pp. 51–58. Citeseer (2003)
14. Chafe, W.: Discourse, Consciousness and Time. University of Chicago Press, Chicago (1994)
15. Chovil, N.: Discourse-oriented facial displays in conversation. Res. Lang. Soc. Interact. **25**(1–4), 163–194 (1991)
16. Clark, H.: Using Language. Cambridge University Press, Cambridge (1996)
17. Ferré, G., Renaudier, S.: Unimodal and bimodal backchannels in conversational English. In: SEMDIAL Procs, pp. 20–30 (2017)
18. Gravano, A., Hirschberg, J.: Turn-taking cues in task-oriented dialogue. Comput. Speech Lang. **25**(3), 601–634 (2011)
19. Horton, W.: Theories and Approaches to the Study of Conversation and Interactive Discourse (2017)
20. Koiso, H., Horiuchi, Y., Tutiya, S., Ichikawa, A., Den, Y.: An analysis of turn-taking and backchannels based on prosodic and syntactic features in Japanese map task dialogs. Lang. Speech **41**(3–4), 295–321 (1998)
21. Meena, R., Skantze, G., Gustafson, J.: Data-driven models for timing feedback responses in a map task dialogue system. Comput. Speech Lang. textbf28(4), 903–922 (2014)
22. Morency, L.-P., de Kok, I., Gratch, J.: Predicting listener backchannels: a probabilistic multi-modal approach. In: Prendinger, H., Lester, J., Ishizuka, M. (eds.) IVA 2008. LNCS (LNAI), vol. 5208, pp. 176–190. Springer, Heidelberg (2008). https://doi.org/10.1007/978-3-540-85483-8_18
23. Morency, L.P., de Kok, I., Gratch, J.: A probabilistic multimodal approach for predicting listener backchannels. Auton. Agents Multi-Agent Syst. **20**(1), 70–84 (2010)
24. Pickering, M.J., Garrod, S.: Understanding dialogue: language use and social interaction. Cambridge University Press, Cambridge (2021)
25. Poppe, R., Truong, K.P., Reidsma, D., Heylen, D.: Backchannel strategies for artificial listeners. In: Allbeck, J., Badler, N., Bickmore, T., Pelachaud, C., Safonova, A. (eds.) IVA 2010. LNCS (LNAI), vol. 6356, pp. 146–158. Springer, Heidelberg (2010). https://doi.org/10.1007/978-3-642-15892-6_16
26. Portes, C., Bertrand, R.: Some cues about the interactional value of the ≪continuation≫ contour in French. In: IDP05 Procs, pp. 1–14 (2005)

27. Prévot, L., Gorisch, J., Bertrand, R.: A CUP of CoFee - a large collection of feedback utterances provided with communicative function annotations. In: LREC-2016 (2016)
28. Priego-Valverde, B., Bigi, B., Amoyal, M.: "Cheese!": a corpus of Face-to-face French interactions. a case study for analyzing smiling and conversational humor. In: LREC, pp. 467–475 (2020)
29. Rauzy, S., Amoyal, M.: SMAD: a tool for automatically annotating the smile intensity along a video record. In: HRC2020 (2020)
30. Rauzy, S., Goujon, A.: Automatic annotation of facial actions from a video record: the case of eyebrows raising and frowning. In: WACAI 2018. Porquerolles, France (2018)
31. Rauzy, S., Montcheuil, G., Blache, P.: MarsaTag, a tagger for French written texts and speech transcriptions. In: Second Asia Pacific Corpus Linguistics Conference (2014)
32. Rossi, M., Di Cristo, A., Hirst, D., Martin, P., Nishinuma, Y.: L'intonation: de l'acoustique à la sémantique (1981)
33. Schegloff, E.: Discourse as an interactional achievement: some uses of "uh huh" and other things that come between sentences. In: Tannen, D. (ed.) Analyzing Discourse: Text and Talk. Georgetown University Press (1982)
34. Skantze, G.: Towards a general, continuous model of turn-taking in spoken dialogue using LSTM recurrent neural networks. In: SIGdial, pp. 220–230 (2017)
35. Stivers, T.: Stance, alignment, and affiliation during storytelling: when nodding is a token of affiliation. Rese. Lang. Soc. Interact. 41(1), 31–57 (2008)
36. Tolins, J., Tree, J.F.: Addressee backchannels steer narrative development. J. Pragmatics 70, 152–164 (2014)
37. Truong, K.P., Poppe, R., Kok, I.D., Heylen, D.: A multimodal analysis of vocal and visual backchannels in spontaneous dialogs. In: Interspeech (2011)
38. Ward, N., Tsukahara, W.: Prosodic features which cue back-channel responses in English and Japanese. J. Pragmatics 32(8), 1177–1207 (2000)

Estimating Social Distance Between Interlocutors with MFCC-Based Acoustic Models for Vowels

Pavel Kholiavin$^{(\boxtimes)}$ [ID], Alla Menshikova [ID], Tatiana Kachkovskaia [ID], and Daniil Kocharov [ID]

Saint Petersburg State University, Saint Petersburg, Russia

Abstract. The present study is devoted to measuring speech entrainment between interlocutors of varying social distance based on their vowels' characteristics. 5 degrees of social distance were taken into consideration: siblings, friends, strangers of same and opposite gender, and strangers of significantly different age and social status. Speaker-dependent acoustic models of cardinal Russian vowels /i/, /a/, and /u/ were constructed and compared. We hypothesized that entrainment would be the strongest between siblings and decrease with increasing social distance. However, it was found that while entrainment is indeed strong for siblings, friends actually show less entrainment than strangers. Same-gender pairs showed stronger entrainment than opposite-gender pairs. Entrainment was also found to be vowel-dependent, with /a/ exhibiting the most variation.

Keywords: Phonetic entrainment · Vowels · Sociophonetics · MFCC · GMM

1 Introduction

It has been shown in many works that a person's speech can change considerably depending on whom he or she is talking to [3,14,17,20]. This phenomenon, known as "speech entrainment", has been studied extensively in recent years. Research has shown that there are numerous social, individual and situational factors that impact the degree of speech entrainment. Most importantly for the present study, it has been pointed out that the degree of entrainment can vary depending on social distance [6]. Speech entrainment can manifest itself at all levels of linguistic analysis: phonetic [14], lexical [9], and syntactic [19]. This paper deals with phonetic entrainment.

A number of studies considered measuring phonetic entrainment acoustically. Several studies explored measuring entrainment with vowel formants. [16], for example, analyzed vowel spaces (i.e. the first and second formants). The authors showed that the interlocutors' vowel spaces may converge for certain vowels and diverge for others, with the exact convergence pattern depending on the interlocutors themselves and their role in the conversation. In [1] it was shown that speakers of different dialects of English can accommodate their vowels to one another, with the degree of change depending

The research is supported by Russian Science Foundation (Project 19-78-10046 "Phonetic manifestations of communication accommodation in dialogue").

© Springer Nature Switzerland AG 2021
K. Ekštein et al. (Eds.): TSD 2021, LNAI 12848, pp. 550–557, 2021.
https://doi.org/10.1007/978-3-030-83527-9_47

on whether the interlocutors are aware that their dialects differ in this particular vowel and how much this particular vowel differs in these two dialects. In a study that analyzed phonetic accommodation in an imitation task [2], it was found that convergence is stronger for low vowels than it is for high ones. [7] dealt with native speakers of different regiolects of French. Sounds in key words were compared by means of a number of features, including vowel formant values and Mel-frequency cepstral coefficients, and it was shown that the imitated features can vary due to sociological reasons.

Acoustic modelling has been used to detect similarities in speech. [13] used non-sound-specific MFCC-based acoustic models commonly used for speaker recognition to evaluate differences between speakers. In [15], HMM acoustic models based on a read text are used for accent clustering.

The interlocutor factor is also frequently explored. In [12], an experiment based on a game of speech dominoes in French shows that phonetic convergence depends both on the interlocutors and the vowels analyzed. Stronger convergence was found for same-sex pairs of speakers and also for old friends. A paper on European Portuguese [5] also shows greater entrainment for same-sex pairs. In [4], it was similarly found that pairs that exhibit the strongest convergence are same-sex pairs with well-established social relationships. It was also observed that interlocutors who were related to each other showed stronger convergence than friends or strangers.

In this paper, we will use MFCC-based acoustic models for vowels to detect speech entrainment in dialogues between speakers of varying social distance. We expect this distance to be a factor influencing the degree of entrainment.

2 Material

The experiments described in the paper were based on the SibLing Corpus of Russian Dialogue Speech [10]. The corpus consists of studio recordings of task-oriented dialogues between Russian native speakers. The subjects completed two collaborative speaking tasks—a card matching game and a map task. Only the map task recordings were used for this study. In this task, the speakers were instructed to walk each other through four schematic maps (completion time—15 to 60 min). The recordings took place in a soundproof studio; the speakers were separated by a non-transparent screen.

The corpus contains 90 dialogues produced by 10 pairs of siblings of the same gender and similar age (23 to 40 years old). 5 pairs were male and 5 were female. Each sibling (core speaker) took part in 5 dialogues: with the other sibling, with a close friend of the same gender and close in age, with a stranger of the same gender and close in age (termed *stranger1*), with a stranger of the opposite gender and close in age (*stranger2*), and a stranger of the same gender, greater age, and a higher job position (*boss*).

The corpus contains $1,415,770$ sound occurrences in total, with each recording containing 7865 sounds on average (standard deviation = 4347) and the shortest recording containing 2777 sounds.

The Russian language is commonly described as having 6 vowel phonemes: /i/, /e/, /a/, /o/, /u/, and /ɨ/ [21]. Of these, the cardinal vowels /a/, /i/, and /u/ are the most frequent, which is why they were selected for analysis. Only stressed allophones of these vowels were chosen due to greater phonetic stability, since unstressed vowels are subject to varying degrees of reduction. The material contained 80,178 instances of /a/, 29,741 instances of /i/, and 20,219 instances of /u/ in stressed position.

3 Method

3.1 Acoustic Modelling

The manually created orthographic transcriptions of the recordings were used to create phonetic transcriptions with a rule-based grapheme-to-phoneme converter [8]. The recordings were converted to Mel-frequency cepstral coefficients (MFCC) feature vectors, and those features together with the transcriptions were used to build Gaussian mixture models (GMMs) for each sound.

The Kaldi speech recognition toolkit [18] was used for acoustic modelling. First, equally spaced forced alignment of sounds was performed, and for each sound a three-state Hidden Markov model was created. The output of the model's states were Gaussian mixture models—i.e. sums of Gaussian distributions which describe the MFCC features for the sound. After this, based on these models, speech sound boundaries were adjusted iteratively for a predefined number of iterations, and so were the models themselves based on the new boundaries. When the building was completed, the second state of each model was taken for analysis since the middle part of a sound is usually the most stable.

The speech of each interlocutor in each dialogue was used as building data separately, i.e. there were $72 \times 2 = 144$ building sets. This resulted in 144 sets of speaker-dependent acoustic models, each characterized by their means and covariance matrices.

It must be noted that since the transcriptions were created automatically and underwent forced alignment, neither the boundaries nor the actual transcriptions are perfect, especially considering that spontaneous speech is known to differ significantly from "ideal" realizations. This fact might impact the overall quality of the acoustic models but cannot be remedied without creating manual phonetic transcriptions of the recordings.

3.2 Distance Calculation

The acoustic models were then used to create distance matrices for each group of recordings. The symmetrized Kullback–Leibler divergence (D_{KL}) [11] was chosen as a distance metric between the GMMs:

$$D_{KL}(N_1||N_2) = \frac{1}{2}(tr(\Sigma_2^{-1}\Sigma_1) + (\mu_2 - \mu_1)^T \Sigma_2^{-1}(\mu_2 - \mu_1)$$
$$- k + ln\left(\frac{det\Sigma_2}{det\Sigma_1}\right)); \tag{1}$$

$$D_{KLsymmetrized}(N_1, N_2) = D_{KL}(N_1||N_2) + D_{KL}(N_2||N_1), \tag{2}$$

where N is a Gaussian distribution, k is its dimensionality, μ is its means vector, and Σ is its covariance matrix.

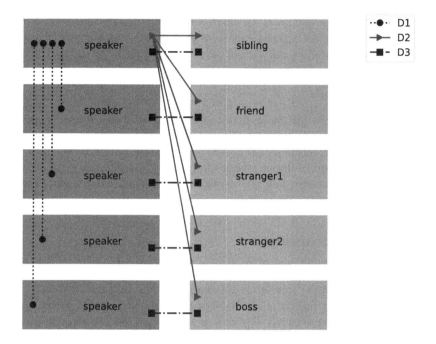

Fig. 1. Measures D1–D3 illustrated. Each pair of rectangles represents a single dialogue, dotted lines represent D1 values, solid gray lines represent D2 values, and dash-dotted lines represent D3 values.

There are several distance measures that can be used to estimate within-speaker vari-ability and speech entrainment, each based on comparing different types of recordings. Here we describe three different measures of distance: D1, D2, and D3. The three mea-sures are illustrated in Fig. 1.

The first measure, D1 (intra-speaker variability), is designed to show how a person's speech changes in all of the dialogues in which he or she took part. This measure is calculated as the distances between the core speaker in the sibling-sibling dialogue and the same speaker in the other four dialogues, which results in 4 values. The hypothesis is that the manner of communication for one speaker will change depending on his or her interlocutor as the result of increasing number of extralinguistic differences between the two (age, gender, degree of familiarity).

The second measure, D2 (speaker difference), is designed to show the difference between the speaker and his or her interlocutors. Here, the changes in the speech of the core speaker are disregarded, and only the variability in the interlocutors' speech is considered. The measure is calculated as the distances between the core speaker in the sibling-sibling dialogue and his or her interlocutors in all dialogues, which results in 5 values. Again, we hypothesize that this distance would grow with increasing social distance.

The third measure, D3 (interlocutor difference), is designed to show the degree of entrainment between interlocutors. It is calculated as the distance between the core speaker in each dialogue and his or her interlocutor in the same dialogue, which results in 5 values. Here we do not expect the measure to grow with increasing social distance, since the speaker might show entrainment despite or even due to the social distance.

3.3 Statistical Analysis

We tested the hypothesis that these distance measures vary systematically depending on the social distance between the interlocutors. For each of the measures D1–D3, we performed one-factor repeated-measures ANOVAs to test if there were significant differences between groups of distance values for dialogues of different types. Post-hoc paired Student's t-tests were run for those cases where a significant difference between the groups was found.

4   Results and Discussion

ANOVA tests indicate that intra-speaker variability is not present in the data. Table 1 shows that for D2 and D3 significant differences are observed for all sounds, while D1 does not show significance at all. Post-hoc t-tests (Table 2) reveal which types of dialogues show this significance. The lack of significance for D1 measure could be due to great variability within an acoustic model: it is quite possible that this general variability is too great for subtle changes between dialogues to be detected. The data shows that in sibling-sibling dialogues the distance values are smaller than in other types of dialogues, both with D2 and D3. This means that siblings speak in a similar way, which is in accordance with previous publications [4], where it was shown that related speakers show greater entrainment, though the fact can also be explained by physiological similarity.

Table 1. ANOVA results representing the influence of the interlocutor factor on phonetic entrainment using 3 distance measures. Double asterisks correspond to $p < 0.01$; empty cells stand for no significance ($p \geq 0.05$).

	Sound		
Distance measure	/i/	/a/	/u/
D1			
D2	**	**	**
D3	**	**	**

The rest of the data is less conclusive. Most cases with statistical significance are observed with the sound /a/, while /i/ had less, and /u/ had none except for dialogues with siblings. This proves that acoustic entrainment is a vowel-dependent process. Similar results were obtained in previous publications in [12] and [16] for French and English respectively.

Table 2. Statistically significant differences among dialogues between different interlocutors measured as paired t-tests for different sounds and 3 distance measures. Symbols < and > reflect the difference of the group means (smaller vs. greater). Single symbols correspond to $p < 0.05$, double—to $p < 0.01$; empty cells stand for no significance.

Measure	1st group	2nd group	Sound /i/	/a/	/u/
D2	Sibling	Friend	<<	<<	<<
	Sibling	Stranger1	<<	<<	<<
	Sibling	Stranger2	<<	<<	<<
	Sibling	Boss	<<	<	<<
	Friend	Stranger1		>	
	Friend	Stranger2	<		
	Stranger1	Stranger2	<<	<	
	Stranger2	Boss	>	>	
D3	Sibling	Friend	<<	<<	<<
	Sibling	Stranger1	<<	<	<<
	Sibling	Stranger2	<<	<<	<<
	Sibling	Boss	<<	<<	<<
	Friend	Stranger1		>>	
	Friend	Boss		>	
	Stranger1	Stranger2		<	

It can also be seen that *friend* dialogues frequently show greater distance than other dialogues, even than dialogues with strangers, which further contradicts our initial hypothesis about the order in which distance should increase. The finding appears to contradict earlier research [12], where close friends exhibited greater entrainment. We speculate that siblings and old friends actually do not converge in the dialogue as much as strangers, as their speech interaction was set up a long time ago. While siblings' voices are very similar to each other, friends' voices may differ significantly.

Stranger1 dialogues seem to be closer in terms of distance measures than *stranger2* dialogues, as demonstrated by measure D2 for the vowels /i/ and /a/ and measure D3 for the vowel /a/. This seems consistent with previous research [5,12], where stronger entrainment was observed in same-gender pairs of interlocutors.

No significant difference was found between *friend* and *stranger2* dialogues, which may mean that *stranger1* and *boss* dialogues induce more entrainment than *stranger2* dialogues. This can be explained by greater strength of gender as a factor than that of age and/or hierarchy.

It must be noted that MFCC represent the spectrum in its entirety, including the fundamental frequency and the spectral envelope, which are known to be gender-dependent. This might affect the results, i.e., same-gender pairs might appear to entrain more than opposite-gender pairs when it might not actually be the case.

It should also be pointed out that the material on which the study was based is quite limited. For example, it is possible that *boss* speakers behave differently depending on their interlocutor, and the current method would not be able to track that since each *boss* speaker participated only in 2 dialogues.

Another point concerns the interpretation of the results. GMM-based acoustic models provide a condensed normalized probabilistic representation of speech properties that cannot always be interpreted in terms of actual acoustic features, such as formant values. Therefore the current method cannot answer whether the significant differences that were found are perceptible by humans and what exactly their nature is from the phonetic point of view.

Given that speech entrainment within a dialogue manifests itself in various prosodic features, it should be noted here that acoustic models for vowels carry prosodic information as well. For example, if the interlocutors entrain in fundamental frequency, it is possible that acoustic models for vowels could show entrainment wholly or partly because of this. This presents an additional difficulty in interpreting the results from a phonetic standpoint.

5 Conclusions

This study has shown that a person's speech can vary depending on the interlocutor. By comparing acoustic models for three vowels, we have shown that there are great similarities between siblings. Dialogues with strangers (of the same or different age or gender) exhibit less similarity, and the least entrainment is observed in dialogues with friends. This is explained by the fact that phonetic closeness can be attributed either to physical relation or to actual phonetic entrainment, which seems to be more prevalent in dialogues with strangers. The open vowel /a/ was found to carry the most significance in detecting entrainment.

References

1. Babel, M.: Dialect divergence and convergence in New Zealand English. Lang. Soc. **39**(4), 437–456 (2010)
2. Babel, M.: Evidence for phonetic and social selectivity in spontaneous phonetic imitation. J. Phon. **40**(1), 177–189 (2012)
3. Babel, M., Bulatov, D.: The role of fundamental frequency in phonetic accommodation. Lang. Speech **55**, 231–248 (2012)
4. Bailly, G., Martin, A.: Assessing objective characterizations of phonetic convergence. In: 15th Annual Conference of the International Speech Communication Association (Interspeech 2014), pp. P–19 (2014)
5. Cabarrão, V., Trancoso, I., Mata, A.I., Moniz, H., Batista, F.: Global analysis of entrainment in dialogues. In: IberSPEECH, pp. 215–223 (2016)
6. Danescu-Niculescu-Mizil, C., Lee, L.J., Pang, B., Kleinberg, J.M.: Echoes of power: language effects and power differences in social interaction. In: Proceedings of the 21st International Conference on World Wide Web, pp. 699–708 (2012)
7. Delvaux, V., Soquet, A.: The influence of ambient speech on adult speech productions through unintentional imitation. Phonetica **64**(2–3), 145–173 (2007)

8. Evdokimova, V., Skrelin, P., Chukaeva, T.: Automatic phonetic transcription for Russian: speech variability modeling. In: Karpov, A., Potapova, R., Mporas, I. (eds.) SPECOM 2017. LNCS (LNAI), vol. 10458, pp. 192–199. Springer, Cham (2017). https://doi.org/10.1007/978-3-319-66429-3_18

9. Ireland, M.E., Slatcher, R.B., Eastwick, P.W., Scissors, L.E., Finkel, E.J., Pennebaker, J.W.: Language style matching predicts relationship initiation and stability. Psychol. Sci. **22**(1), 39–44 (2011)

10. Kachkovskaia, T., et al.: SibLing corpus of Russian dialogue speech designed for research on speech entrainment. In: Proceedings of the 12th Language Resources and Evaluation Conference, pp. 6556–6561. European Language Resources Association, Marseille, May 2020

11. Kullback, S., Leibler, R.A.: On information and sufficiency. Ann. Math. Stat. **22**(1), 79–86 (1951)

12. Lelong, A., Bailly, G.: Study of the phenomenon of phonetic convergence thanks to speech dominoes. In: Esposito, A., Vinciarelli, A., Vicsi, K., Pelachaud, C., Nijholt, A. (eds.) Analysis of Verbal and Nonverbal Communication and Enactment. The Processing Issues. LNCS, vol. 6800, pp. 273–286. Springer, Heidelberg (2011). https://doi.org/10.1007/978-3-642-25775-9_26

13. Lelong, A., Bailly, G.: Characterising phonetic convergence with speaker recognition techniques. In: The Listening Talker Workshop, pp. 28–31, May 2012

14. Levitan, R., Hirschberg, J.: Measuring acoustic-prosodic entrainment with respect to multiple levels and dimensions. In: Proceedings of Interspeech, pp. 3081–3084 (2011)

15. Minematsu, N., Kasahara, S., Makino, T., Saito, D., Hirose, K.: Speaker-basis accent clustering using invariant structure analysis and the speech accent archive. In: Odyssey. Citeseer (2014)

16. Pardo, J.: Expressing Oneself in Conversational Interaction, pp. 183–196. Psychology Press/Taylor & Francis, New York (2010)

17. Pardo, J.S.: On phonetic convergence during conversational interaction. J. Acoust. Soc. Am. **119**(4), 2382–2393 (2006)

18. Povey, D., et al.: The Kaldi speech recognition toolkit. In: IEEE 2011 Workshop on Automatic Speech Recognition and Understanding. IEEE Signal Processing Society, December 2011. IEEE Catalog No.: CFP11SRW-USB

19. Reitter, D., Moore, J.D., Keller, F.: Priming of syntactic rules in task-oriented dialogue and spontaneous conversation. In: Proceedings of the 28th Annual Conference of the Cognitive Science Society, pp. 685–690 (2006)

20. Weise, A., Levitan, S.I., Hirschberg, J., Levitan, R.: Individual differences in acoustic-prosodic entrainment in spoken dialogue. Speech Commun. **115**, 78–87 (2019)

21. Yanushevskaya, I., Bunčić, D.: Russian. J. Int. Phon. Assoc. **45**(2), 221–228 (2015)

Remote Learning of Speaking in Syntactic Forms with Robot-Avatar-Assisted Language Learning System

Taisei Najima[✉], Tsuneo Kato, Akihiro Tamura, and Seiichi Yamamoto

Graduate School of Science and Engineering, Doshisha University, 1-3 Tatara-miyakodani,
Kyotanabe-shi, Kyoto 6100394, Japan
ctwf0126@mail4.doshisha.ac.jp,
{tsukato,aktamura,seyamamo}@mail.doshisha.ac.jp

Abstract. To help second language (L2) learners acquire oral communication skills, dialogue-based computer-assisted language learning (DB-CALL) systems are attracting more interest than ever. When robot-assisted language learning (RALL) is used for realizing such systems, L2 learners are provided with a sense of reality and tension similar to that in a real L2 conversation. At the same time, there are increasing demands for remote learning, accelerated in part by the spread of the novel coronavirus. We have therefore developed a robot-avatar-assisted language learning system that simulates a trialogue in English with two robot avatars and a learner for remote learning. The conversation scenarios deal with various daily topics to keep the learner's interest and the system prompts the learner to acquire oral skills by using specific syntactic forms in conversation. We conducted a six-day remote learning experiment with ten Japanese university students to evaluate the learning effect, using eye gaze as an index of the learners' degree of concentration. Our findings demonstrated the effectiveness of our system for remote learning and showed that the learners' eye gaze activities changed between question answering and repeating tasks.

Keywords: Computer-assisted language learning · Remote learning · Learning effect · Eye gaze information

1 Introduction

With the increase in globalization, opportunities to communicate in English are becoming more prevalent and more important. It is said that one-on-one training with a skilled instructor is the best way to learn a second language [1]. However, in practice, most L2 learners take language classes for just a few hours a week and seldom have sufficient opportunities for oral training or communication with the teacher. In addition, teachers usually cannot tailor speaking exercises to individual learner's needs [2]. One way to address these issues is to use dialogue-based computer-assisted language learning (DB-CALL) systems for self-learning. DB-CALL systems are attractive because they offer opportunities for input, output, and interaction all of which are essential for L2 development [3]. Speaking out loud provides learners with opportunities to notice gaps in their

© Springer Nature Switzerland AG 2021
K. Ekštein et al. (Eds.): TSD 2021, LNAI 12848, pp. 558–566, 2021.
https://doi.org/10.1007/978-3-030-83527-9_48

L2 knowledge [4] and helps promote the proceduralization of existing linguistic knowledge that leads to automatization [6]. Although automatic speech recognition (ASR) and natural language processing (NLP) of L2 learners' speech have their challenges, DB-CALL systems provide L2 learners with opportunities for practicing conversations in contextualized scenes with explicit and implicit feedback on the learners' answers [13]. Moreover, DB-CALL systems have several advantages over human interlocutors, such as providing unlimited opportunities to speak, reducing anxiety about making mistakes [7,8] and potentially controlling all variables that impact the learning effect (e.g. learning items, level of vocabulary, feedback). [9].

While some DB-CALL systems (e.g., DEAL [10], POMY [11], and GREET [12]) provide virtual agents in 3D virtual worlds, conventional CALL systems do not always use realistic agents, so nonverbal information such as gestures and eye gaze activities is missing. This makes it difficult for learners to feel the same sense of reality and tension as real conversation in L2.

The implementation of social robots in language learning has provided nonverbal information and a greater sense of reality and tension, which consequently enhances the motivation and engagement of learners [14]. Khalifa et al. proposed a robot-assisted language learning system where two humanoid robots have a conversation and encouraged the learner to participate [15]. The system enables explicit and implicit learning while the physical embodiment enhances the learners' sense of reality and tension.

At the same time, there have been increasing demands for remote learning, accelerated in part by the spread of the novel coronavirus. This trend has produced a conflict between physical robots and virtual characters. There have been reports that physical embodiment enhances performance and the impression of social interactions [16]. Chang et al. conducted a comparative experiment of learning new English words through authentic learning in a mixed-reality environment with junior high school students. They integrated either real robots or virtual characters in a mixed-reality environment and found there was no significant difference in learning performance while interacting with real robots increased the students' sense of authenticity, their engagement and their learning motivation [17].

In this study, we created two robot avatars in a virtual space so that English conversation training can be conducted remotely. We carried out a remote learning experiment in which we connected this system to learners' homes with Zoom software and collected learner data including eye gaze information to analyze the learning effect of speaking in focused syntactic forms and the degree of concentration on the conversation.

2   Robot-Avatar-Assisted Language Learning System

In the proposed system, an L2 learner joins in a conversation with two robot avatars and practices his/her oral communication skill in L2. Figure 1 shows a screenshot of the system. A trialogue is simulated with a teacher avatar (A1), a student avatar (A2), and an L2 learner. The avatars' faces and hands are directed to the listener while speaking to clarify whom they are addressing. The robot avatars were modeled using Blender, and their movements and voices were controlled using Unity. Recorded voices of two native English speakers were used for the avatars.

The two avatars interact with each other by following a predefined conversation scenario. We created multiple scenarios on a variety of topics to keep the learner interested. While the scenarios have natural dialogue flows, they focus on specific syntactic forms and prompt the learner to use these forms in conversation. Specifically, a focused syntactic form is presented to the learner in a conversation between the avatars, and then a similar question is asked to the learner. We designed the scenarios in collaboration with a native English speaker who was teaching English at a junior high school to make the scenarios pedagogically appropriate for L2 learners.

The learning proceeds mainly through a question-and-answer task, where the teacher avatar (A1) first asks a question to the student avatar (A2), then A2 returns an example answer, and A1 asks a similar question to the learner. The learner can answer the question by referencing A2's previous answer. The series of the question and answer are embedded five times in each scenario, and the learner is given five opportunities to respond. Table 1 shows a part of the dialogue between the avatars and the learner.

The system is able to branch the next action depending on the response from the learner. When the learner asks for a repeat, A1 will repeat the same question up to three times. When the learner cannot come up with an answer, he or she is instructed to say, "I don't know," and the conversation moves on to the next question. When the learner makes a response, the teacher avatar asks the learner to repeat his/her answer to consolidate learning how to answer the question with the focused syntactic form.

In second language teaching, it is important to set appropriate learning items in accordance with the learners' linguistic ability. We therefore selected two syntactic forms for different proficiency levels: 1) causative verbs and inanimate subjects and 2) the past and present perfect tenses. These syntactic forms are linguistically important as they build the structure of a sentence. However, they are generally difficult for Japanese learners to use orally because their mother tongue does not have common syntactic forms that correspond exactly to the English forms. As the past and present perfect tenses are basic and the causative verbs and inanimate subjects are advanced, we focused on the usage of causative verbs and inanimate subjects for the higher proficiency class and the past and present perfect tenses for the lower proficiency class. We split the learners into one of the two classes on the basis of whether they could understand sentences with causative verbs and inanimate subjects correctly.

To evaluate the learners' listening comprehension, we set up repeating tasks in which the learners had to recite the example answers that A2 made. The repeating tasks have a slightly different protocol between the avatars and the learner from the question-and-answer tasks. The learner recites A2's example answer just after A2 presents it, while the learner responds to a question made by A1 in the question-and-answer task. Two scenarios are prepared for the repeating tasks, and five example responses are presented in each scenario. If a participant recites more than 60 percent of the words in an example sentence, it is considered a pass. If a participant gets more than six passes out of ten trials, the learner is assigned to the higher proficiency class. Otherwise, the learner is assigned to the lower proficiency class.

To enable remote learning, images are projected onto the learner's PC using the Zoom screen-sharing function. The system is controlled by the Wizard-of-Oz method to prevent unforeseen dialogue breakdown due to errors in automatic speech recognition

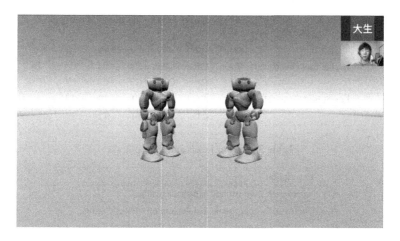

Fig. 1. Screenshot of robot-avatar-assisted language learning system

Table 1. Example of scenario focusing on causative verbs and inanimate subjects

Speaker	Utterance
A1	There are many attractive places in Japan
	What places make you happy in Japan?
A2	Kinkakuji Temple makes me happy in Japan
A1	I see
	What places make you happy in Japan?
Learner	...

(ASR). Empirically, the most frequent error was those of end point detection of learners' speech due to long pauses in the middle. Speech and movements of the learner, A1, and A2 were recorded using Zoom software.

3 Collection of Gaze Data

Eye gaze data of the learners were collected using Tobii Pro Nano, a screen-based eye tracker that is attached to a PC and acquires the position of viewpoints on the screen at a sampling frequency 60 Hz. It places no burden on the user as no glasses need to be worn.

We recorded the eye gaze data from the start to the end of each scenario. We then measured the gaze ratio to the robot avatars as an index of the learner's degree of concentration on the learning. For each sample point of the acquired gaze, if it overlapped with the robot avatar, we judged that the learner was gazing, and if not, we judged that the learner was not gazing. The gaze ratio was calculated by the time spent gazing at the avatars divided by the total time for each scenario.

Table 2. Scenario schedule of six-day remote learning experiment

	Day 1	Day 2	Day 3	Day 4	Day 5	Day 6
Higher proficiency class	T1	C1r	C2r	C3	C4	C5
	C1	C1	C2	C3v	C4v	C1
Lower proficiency class	T1	C1r	C2r	T1	T2	T3
	C1	C1	C2	T1v	T2v	T1

Table 3. Answer levels and their criteria

Level		Description
A	A-1	Appropriate contextually and syntactically
	A-2	Contextually appropriate, but containing syntactic errors.
B	B	Contextually appropriate, but not in the presented syntactic form.
C	C-1	Irrelevant to the question
	C-2	No answering or stating "I don't know."

4   Experiment

4.1   Experimental Methods

We conducted a six-day experiment of remote learning with the robot-avatar-assisted language learning system to collect L2 learners' responses and their eye gaze data during learning.

Ten Japanese university students aged 20 to 23 participated in the experiment. All were undergraduate or graduate students in the engineering and biomedical departments. They acquired Japanese as their L1 and learned English as L2.

Each participant completed two scenarios a day, which took 20 min in total. Table 2 shows the schedule of the six-day experiment. The symbols in the table represent identifiers of the scenarios. The initial letters 'T' and 'C' denote tenses and "causative verbs and inanimate subjects", respectively. The number following the initial letter is the scenario index. The final letter 'r' denotes repeating a task and 'v' denotes a variant of a scenario that has mostly the same dialogue flow but slightly different questions. Since the learners needed to comprehend the dialogue between the avatars, we assigned each learner to either the higher or lower proficiency class according to their listening ability. We set two sessions of repeating tasks (C1r and C2r) in which the learners recite example answers given by A2 on the second and third days to evaluate the learners' listening ability. Each learner was assigned to either of the classes on the fourth day. Five participants were assigned to the higher proficiency class and the other five to the lower proficiency class. On the first day and the final day, the same scenarios (T1 and C1) were conducted as the pre-test and post-test to evaluate the learning effect quantitatively.

4.2   Evaluation of Learning Effect

The participants' second responses in the pre- and post-tests were subjectively rated using the discrete answer levels shown in Table 3. Comprehensible answers with the

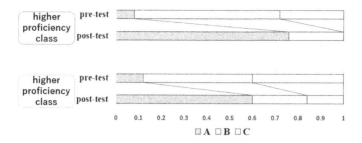

Fig. 2. Relative frequency distributions of answer levels in pre- and post-tests for each proficiency class

Table 4. Gaze ratios on teacher avatar (A1) and student avatar (A2) for each proficiency class

	A1 (%)	A2 (%)	Total (%)
Higher proficiency class	34.9	20.1	55.0
Lower proficiency class	32.1	17.1	49.2

focused syntactic form were rated as Level A. Contextually appropriate answers but not in the focused syntactic form were rated as Level B. No answer, answering with "I don't know" and irrelevant answers were rated as Level C.

Figure 2 shows the relative frequency distributions of the answer levels. The percentage of Level A answers increased by 68.0 point from 8.0% in the pre-test to 76.0% in the post-test for the higher proficiency class, and by 48.0 point from 12.0% in the pre-test to 60.0% in the post-test for the lower proficiency class. The percentage of Level C utterances decreased by 28.0 point from 28.0% in the pre-test to 0.0% in the post-test for the higher proficiency class, and by 24.0 point from 40.0% in the pre-test to 16.0% in the post-test for the lower proficiency class.

4.3 Analysis of Gaze Data

Using the collected eye gaze data, we measured the gaze ratios to A1 and A2 for each scenario and learner as indices of the degree of concentration. First, we calculated the average gaze ratios on A1 and A2 for each proficiency class to measure the difference in the degree of concentration between the classes. Table 4 lists the results. The percentages of the learners' gaze on A1 and A2 were 2.8% and 3.0% higher in the higher proficiency class than in the lower proficiency class, respectively.

Next, we examined the learners' gaze in each scenario. Figure 3 and Fig. 4 show the percentages of the learners' gaze on A1 (blue solid line) and A2 (orange dashed line) in each of the 12 scenarios for the higher and lower proficiency classes, respectively. In each figure, C1r and C2r (red font) represent repeating tasks, and we can see that the gaze ratios on A1 and A2 reversed only for these two tasks. The averages of the gaze ratios on A1 and A2 for each task are shown in Table 5. For the higher proficiency class, the percentage of gaze on A1 was 22.1% higher than that on A2 in the question-and-answer task, while that on A2 was 21.4% higher than that on A1 in the repeating task.

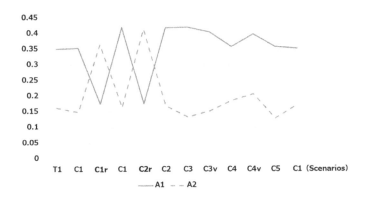

Fig. 3. Gaze ratios on two robot avatars in each scenario for higher proficiency class

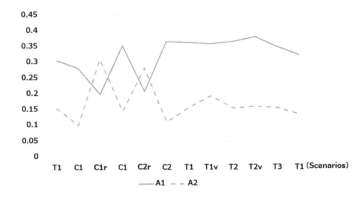

Fig. 4. Gaze ratios on two robot avatars in each scenario for lower proficiency class

The same was true for the lower proficiency class: in the question-and-answer task, the percentage of gaze on A1 was 19.9% higher than that on A2, while in the repeating task, the percentage of gaze on A2 was 9.2% higher than that on A1.

5   Discussion

The significant increases of Level A answers in both the higher and lower proficiency classes indicate that the participants became able to operate the focused syntactic forms in conversation through the six-day remote learning. Further, the significant decreases of Level C answers in both classes indicate that the participants became able to catch what was said in English.

The fact that the gaze ratio on A1 was higher than that on A2 in the question-and-answer tasks and that on A2 was higher than that on A1 conversely in the repeating tasks suggests that the gaze ratio can be an indicator of the learner's degree of concentration. This reversal of the gaze ratios was mainly due to the different protocol between the avatars and the learner: the learners tended to gaze more at the last utterer.

Table 5. Gaze ratios on two robot avatars in question-and-answer and repeating tasks

	Task	Average (%)		SD (%)	
		A1	A2	A1	A2
Higher proficiency class	Question-and-answer	38.4	16.3	13.2	4.6
(12 scenarios)	Repeating	17.6	39.0	9.4	11.7
Lower proficiency class	Question-and-answer	34.5	14.6	15.2	4.7
(12 scenarios)	Repeating	20.3	29.5	8.7	7.8

It also suggests the participants paid more attention to the questions made by A1 in the question-and-answer tasks and to the example answers made by A2 in the repeating tasks, which directly affect their answers rather than the dialogue between the robot avatars. On the other hand, the lower gaze ratio on A2 in the question-and-answer tasks suggest that the participants' attention on example answers was not always high in the question-and-answer tasks.

6 Conclusion

We developed a remote learning environment for communicating in L2 by creating robot avatars in a virtual space and connecting them to the learner's PC by using the screen-sharing function of Zoom software. A six-day remote learning experiment with ten participants revealed a significant increase of appropriate answers in focused syntactic forms.

The analysis of eye gaze data collected by a screen-based eye tracker suggested that the gaze ratio can be an indicator of the learner's degree of concentration. The gaze ratio on the teacher avatar(A1) was higher than that on the student avatar(A2) in the question-and-answer tasks, and that on A2 was higher than that on A1 in the repeating tasks. Further, the gaze ratio was generally higher in the higher proficiency class than in the lower proficiency class.

For future work, we will compare the learning effect and the learners' eye gaze with more participants in three settings,—this robot-avatar-assisted language learning system in remote operation, a real robot-assisted language learning system in remote operation, and a real robot-assisted language learning system in face-to-face operation—as we have not verified the statistical difference in terms of real robots vs robot avatars and remote learning vs face-to-face learning.

Acknowledgement. This work was supported by JSPS KAKENHI Grant Number 19K00927.

References

1. Bloom, B, S.: The 2 sigma problem: the search for methods of group instruction as effective as one-to-one tutoring. Educ. Res. **13**(6), 4–16 (1984)
2. Truscott, J.: What's wrong with oral grammar correction. Can. Mod. Lang. Rev. **55**, 437–456 (1999)

3. Long, M.H.: The role of the linguistic environment in second language acquisition. In: Handbook of Second Language Acquisition, pp. 413–468 (1996)
4. Swain, M.: Communicative competence: some roles of comprehensible input and comprehensible output in its development. In: Input in Second Language Acquisition, pp. 235–253 (1985)
5. Swain, M.: The output hypothesis: theory and research. In: Handbook of Research in Second Language Learning, pp. 471–483 (2005)
6. DeKeyser, R.M.: Practice in a Second Language: Perspective from Applied Linguistics And Cognitive Psychology. Cambridge University Press, Cambridge (2007)
7. Warschauer, M.: Computing face-to-face and electronic discussion in the second language classroom. CALICO J. **13**(2), 7–26 (1996)
8. Chang, S., Lee, J., Chao, P., Wang, C., Chen, G.: Exploring the possibility of using humanoid robots as instructional tools for teaching a second language in primary school. Educ. Technol. Soc. **13**(2), 13–24 (2010)
9. Hegelheimer, V., Chapelle, C.A.: Methodological issues in research on learner-computer interaction in CALL. Lang. Learn. Technol. **4**(1), 41–59 (2000)
10. Hjalmarsson, A., Wik, P., Brusk, J.: Dealing with DEAL: A dialogue system for conversation training. In: Proceedings of the 8th SIGdial Workshop on Discourse and Dialogue, pp. 132–135 (2007)
11. Lee, K., Kweon, S., Lee, S., Noh, H., Lee, G. G.: POSTECH immersive English study (POMY): dialog-based language learning game. IEICE Trans. Inf. Syst. **E97-D**(7), 1830–1841 (2014)
12. Vries, B.P., Cucchiarini, C., Bodnar, S., Strik, H., Hout, R.: Spoken grammar practice and feedback in an ASR-based CALL system. Comput. Assist. Lang. Learn. **28**(6), 550–576 (2015)
13. Bibauw, S., Francois, T., Desmet, P.: Discussing with a computer to practice a foreign language: research synthesis and conceptual framework of dialogue-based CALL. Comput. Assist. Lang. Learn. **32**(8), 827–877 (2019)
14. Randall, N.: A survey of robot-assisted language learning (RALL). ACM Trans. Hum. Robot Interact. **9**(1), 7:1–35 (2019)
15. Khalifa, A., Kato, T., Yamamoto, S.: Joining-in-type humanoid robot assisted language learning system. In: Proceedings of the Language Resources and Evaluation Conference(LREC 2016), pp. 245–249 (2016)
16. Wainer, J., Feil-Seifer, D., Mataric, M.,: Embodiment and human-robot interaction: a task-based perspective. In: The 16th IEEE International Symposium on Robot and Human Interactive Communication, pp. 872–877 (2007)
17. Chang, C., Lee, J., Wang, C., Chen, G.: Improving the authentic learning experience by integrating robots into the mixed-reality environment. Comput. Educ. **55**, 1572–1578 (2010)

Author Index

Printed in the United States
by Baker & Taylor Publisher Services